TACITUS

TACITUS

BY

RONALD SYME

CAMDEN PROFESSOR OF ANCIENT HISTORY

VOLUME II

OXFORD

AT THE CLARENDON PRESS

1958

Oxford University Press, Amen House, London E.C.4

GLASGOW NEW YORK TORONTO MELBOURNE WELLINGTON
BOMBAY CALCUTTA MADRAS KARACHI KUALA LUMPUR
CAPE TOWN IBADAN NAIROBI ACCRA

PRINTED IN GREAT BRITAIN
AT THE UNIVERSITY PRESS, OXFORD
BY CHARLES BATEY, PRINTER TO THE UNIVERSITY

CONTENTS

VOLUME II

PART VII

THE TIME OF WRITING

XXXV. THE DATE OF THE *ANNALES*

TACITUS' career as a senator, between the quaestorship and the consulate, coincided almost exactly with the fifteen years of Domitian's rule. Consul under Nerva in the brief interlude that brought Trajan to the power, Tacitus, when that emperor had terminated the conquest of Dacia and entered upon the tenth year of a prosperous reign, was writing the Domitianic books of the *Historiae*.

Nothing stands attested about his life after Pliny's letters fail, except one fact, the proconsulate of Asia—and not much before. Tacitus had broken with senatorial eloquence after the prosecution of Marius Priscus—so little gained for all the expense of time and talent. Historical studies drew him away. Tacitus never reverted. He finished the *Historiae*, and after a short interval (about three years) chose to go out as proconsul in 112.[1] Duty, curiosity, or discontent with what men said (or suppressed) when the *Historiae* were made public?

Life and writings hitherto permit no guess that Tacitus had been in any of the countries east of the Adriatic. The western provinces engage him, with a firm knowledge about Gaul and the Rhine, a sympathetic understanding of the native peoples. Digressions on the god Serapis or the Paphian cult of Venus do no more than certify the holder of a Roman priesthood, expert in sacerdotal learning and foreign worships.[2] Tacitus insists with due pride that he is the first Roman to write about Serapis. Perhaps there was more than erudition as the years passed—a response to the fascination of the exotic and ancient East.[3] But the author of the *Annales* was not destined to visit the land of Egypt, 'cognoscendae antiquitatis'. Nor is there any sign that he had been to Syria.[4]

---

[1] App. 23.

[2] *Hist.* II. 3; IV. 83 f.

[3] Tacitus may have felt a πόθος for the Orient. Luck or favour could have brought his parent, procurator of Belgica, within reach of the Egyptian prefecture.

[4] Observe the error about Antioch (II. 83. 2). See App. 61.

B

Thirty years as a senator could not leave a man in total ignorance about the province of Asia. Certain items kept recurring—the status of a city or a temple, disputes about boundaries or revenue.[1] Embassies came thick and fast, with petitions or honorary decrees, led by celebrities whose eloquence sounded over all the world. When Domitian towards the end of his reign ordained that half of the vineyards in the provinces should be destroyed, the interests of Asia were defended by the famous Scopelianus.[2]

An historian needed senatorial business (which he got from the *acta*) to fill out the chronicle of years that lacked colour and action. He did not have to know Asia. None the less, there is enough in the second historical work of Tacitus to reveal the man who had held the *fasces* in that province. Several crowded chapters are taken up with the affairs of Asia. There was a great earthquake in the reign of Tiberius: twelve cities which suffered damage are registered by name.[3] When rights of asylum come under scrutiny, the orators of Asia in emulation make appeal to all the resources of history and legend;[4] and eleven cities compete eagerly for a new privilege, to possess the temple dedicated to the worship of Tiberius Caesar, Livia, and the Senate.[5]

The author has a keen eye for anything that happened to earlier proconsuls—a prosecution just or unjust, and even a murder. He chronicles with careful detail the manner in which M. Silanus was done to death;[6] and he explains the unhappy plight of a proconsul, no speaker, confronted in the Senate with the most eloquent of all Asia.[7] Further, he notes with subdued satisfaction how in the older days Caesar's agent in Asia might be compelled to stand trial before senators.[8]

A proconsul on his first acquaintance with Asia would discover much to occupy and divert him. He found what he expected, the memorials of a long past and many rulers. He saw with astonishment (and perhaps with envy) the massive constructions that attested the present glory and opulence of the dynastic families at Pergamum and Ephesus.[9]

[1] Thus Rhodes, deprived of its status as a free city, but recovering it from Domitian, *SIG*[3], 819. Cf. XII. 58. 2: 'reddita Rhodiis libertas, adempta saepe aut firmata.'

[2] A pupil of Nicetes (Philostratus, *Vit. soph.* I. 21. 6).

[3] II. 47.   [4] III. 60–63.   [5] IV. 55 f.

[6] XIII. I. The historian could recall the fate of the proconsul Civica Cerialis (*Agr.* 42. I, cf. *ILS* 1374).

[7] III. 66. 2 (C. Junius Silanus). Note also L. Antistius Vetus and Barea Soranus, who had been proconsuls of Asia (XVI. 10; 30 ff.).

[8] IV. 15. 2.

[9] At Pergamum the great *Traianeum* on the acropolis (*Altertümer von Pergamon* v, 2 (1908), 1 ff.), and sundry benefactions of the emperor's friend Julius Quadratus (*suff.* 94),

If the first days were radiant and hospitable, vexations soon intervened—the turbulence of the mob, corruption and intrigue rampant among the local worthies. Magnates in the eastern cities had a bad name for pride and oppression.[1] Faction or various delinquencies got them into trouble with the Roman government;[2] and men of station had to be sent into exile.[3] In the professors and sophists prevailed levity, ostentation, and arrogance. Such men could also be dangerous. Philosophers before now had been known to requite the friendship of a Roman senator with espionage and delation.[4]

Religion was kept under proper control at Rome and in the towns of the western lands: the priest and magistrate tended to be the same person. The Greek divinities had been approved and domiciled long since, and the Roman government did not worry about extraneous beliefs or personal fancies. Certain creeds, however, denoted hostility towards the imperial authority, or criminal practices. They had invaded the cities of Asia, importing a new cause of social unrest.

Jews in conflict with Greeks were troublesome enough—crime, riot, and mutual denunciations. And the Jews had doctrinal schisms arising in their own communities, which a proconsul might prefer to despise and ignore, not least if he happened to be adept in questions of words and names.[5] But the Jews, though tolerated by the Roman government outside their country of origin, could not evade the consequences of their rebellion in the days of Nero. Hostility grew. When Tacitus was writing the *Annales*, the eastern lands from Mesopotamia round to Cyrene experienced massacre and atrocities.[6] Cause and blame may not have been easy to assess. That question no longer mattered when the insurrections detained or destroyed Roman armies

who came to be regarded as the second founder of the city. At Ephesus his peer Julius Celsus (*suff.* 92) was to be commemorated by a magnificent library (*Forschungen in Ephesos* v (1944)): it was completed by his son's heirs (*ILS* 8971).

[1] Thus the Cretan Claudius Timarchus, 'ut solent praevalidi provincialium et opibus nimiis ad iniurias minorum elati' (xv. 20. 1). By contrast, an eminent and wealthy Bithynian is well spoken of (xvi. 33. 1).

[2] Observe Claudius Aristion (*PIR²*, C 788), 'princeps Ephesiorum, homo munificus et innoxie popularis', so Pliny asserts (*Epp.* vi. 31. 3). He was absolved.

[3] Menemachus of Sardes was banished (Plutarch, *De exilio* 3. 600a): the dedicant of the *Praec. ger. r.p.* That treatise mentions (Julius) Pardalas of the same city, unpopular with the Roman authorities (17. 813f) and at variance with another magnate, Tyrrhenus (32. 825d). Not in *PIR¹*: which, however, notes (as J 298a) a Julius Pardalas, *idiologus* at Alexandria in 122/3 (*BGU* I, 250).

[4] It was, however, a man from the Roman *colonia* Berytus, P. Egnatius Celer the Stoic (*PIR²*, E 19), who denounced his patron Barea Soranus (xvi. 32. 3). The Greek Cassius Asclepiodotus of Nicaea (*PIR²*, C 486) proved a loyal friend (33. 1).

[5] *Acta apostolorum* 18. 17: καὶ οὐδὲν τούτων τῷ Γαλλίωνι ἔμελεν. This is L. Junius Annaeus Gallio, Seneca's brother, adopted by Junius Gallio (*PIR¹*, J 493), and proconsul of Achaia in 52 (*SIG³* 801: Delphi).

[6] p. 239.

in the rear of the Parthian War.[1] The anger must have been ferocious, though hardly a trace subsists, unless it be perhaps in the *Annales* of Tacitus.

The Senate under Tiberius banished Egyptian and Jewish rites from the capital. The cause was a pair of scandals involving Roman ladies of senatorial families.[2] Tacitus does not bother about that story. He leaves out the reason for what was done. Nor is he concerned to put on record the sharp repression of the cult of Isis—the temple demolished, the statue thrown into the Tiber. A paradoxical omission, the last to be expected of a Roman senator writing annals. He goes on to chronicle a deportation of four thousand Jews to Sardinia with savage satisfaction: if they perished in that insalubrious island, 'vile damnum'.[3]

There was a fresh source of disturbance. No governor of any eastern province with large and populous cities could now fail to take cognizance of the activities, whether condoned or punished, of a new religious sect emanating from Judaea. Pliny came across that sect when governor of Bithynia–Pontus. He acted (no sign of hesitation) and put to death several persons who, avowing the name and faith, could not be brought to recant, obdurate against threats or admonition. Then a doubt arose in Pliny's mind. He applied to the Emperor for guidance, professing now to be ignorant about the established and legal procedure: ought there not to be some charge or proof of criminal behaviour? Trajan made a brief reply. He approved the governor's action and refused to go into his perplexities.[4]

The testimony of Pliny is supplemented by the imperial rescript to Minicius Fundanus the proconsul of Asia, a decade later:[5] Minicius, a person of cultivated tastes, had been a friend of Pliny.[6] The historian

---

[1] Even if the Jews in Mesopotamia, as Groag assumed (P–W XIII, 1881) did not participate in the rising there, Trajan ordered Lusius Quietus to wipe them out (Arrian, *Parthica* fr. 79 Roos). Nor does it matter that there is no clear proof of an insurrection in Judaea itself. For the role played by apocalyptic prophecies see below, p. 518.

[2] Josephus, *AJ* XVIII. 65 ff.

[3] II. 85. 4. Such is the writer's preoccupation with Jews that, although he begins with both religions ('de sacris Aegyptiis Iudaicisque pellendis'), he reduces them abruptly to one ('ea superstitione'), the votaries of which were deported. The four thousand deportees were in fact Jews, cf. Josephus (l.c. 84).

[4] *Epp.* X. 96, with Trajan's answer (97). The governor had asked whether he should punish the 'nomen ipsum' or the 'flagitia cohaerentia nomini'. The Emperor brushed that aside—'si deferantur et arguantur, puniendi sunt.'

[5] Hadrian's rescript to Minicius (*suff.* 107, proconsul in 122/3) is attended with various problems (Eusebius, *Hist. eccl.* IV. 9, cf., briefly, E. Groag, P–W XV, 1821 f.). If the Emperor allowed only regular indictments for precise offences, that would be a notable and humane innovation. But it appears that apologists have 'interpreted' the rescript for their own purposes, cf. W. Schmid, *Maia* VII (1955), 1 ff.

[6] The recipient of *Epp.* I. 9; IV. 15; VI. 6; VII. 12. The death of his young daughter is related in V. 16 (cf. *ILS* 1030). For his opinions about oratory, p. 114. Minicius figures

Tacitus, carefully noting an incident at Rome in the sequel of the great conflagration under Nero, registers the origin of the name 'Christiani' with documentary precision.[1] When he made reference earlier (in Book VII) to recent events in Syria and in Palestine, he will not have omitted the procurator Pontius Pilatus—and some of his vicissitudes.[2]

Tacitus (it is a fair surmise) had conducted investigations into the behaviour and beliefs of those malcontents, discovering perhaps no deeds of crime or vice but only an invincible spirit that denied allegiance to Rome when allegiance meant worship of Caesar. Yet it was an 'exitiabilis superstitio'.[3]

For the rest, Tacitus has precise knowledge of cults and worship, exempt from all credulity. History and legend were the appeal. The proconsul on his tours of duty or recreation may have gone to inspect the residence of Tiberius Caesar at Rhodes. He notes a detail—the house is on the cliffs.[4] The scene (and the circumstantial narrations about the science of Thrasyllus) might encourage a man to mark astrological predictions with sharper vigilance than hitherto.[5]

Strange things could befall a Roman official in the eastern lands, and a change of conduct or beliefs. Some came empty and avid, easy prey to a magician or a bearded sage of abnormal sanctity.[6] The sceptical were not always immune. A governor of Cilicia had recently been converted at one of the shrines, renouncing his Epicurean impieties.[7]

The proconsul, a *quindecimvir* these many years, had a good reason for visiting the sacred places in Asia, notably such as concerned Apollo and the Sibyl—and a professional malice that penetrated the credentials of priests and prophets, perhaps not omitting to make trial of their performance. At Apollo's renowned sanctuary of Claros near Colophon, it was not a woman that held the office but a man, selected from certain families in Miletus. Tacitus knew about the reputable men

prominently in Plutarch's treatise *De cohibenda ira*. For an assessment of his personality, Groag, P-W xv, 1824 ff.

[1] xv. 44. 3: 'auctor nominis eius Christus Tiberio imperitante per procuratorem Pontium Pilatum supplicio affectus erat.'

[2] p. 449. Furthermore, xv. 44 is not only relevant to Nero and the fire at Rome—it has a place in the economy of the whole work as one of a series of spaced incidents, the culmination being the Jewish insurrection of 66.

[3] cf. Pliny, *Epp.* x. 96. 8: 'nihil aliud inveni quam superstitionem pravam, immodicam.' None the less Pliny had no doubts that they could and should be punished—'pertinaciam certe et inflexibilem obstinationem debere puniri' (ib. 3). For punishment of 'contumacia' cf. A. N. Sherwin-White, *Journ. Theol. Stud.*, N.S. III (1952), 199 ff.

[4] vi. 21. 1: 'per avia ac derupta (nam saxis domus imminet).'

[5] pp. 524 f.

[6] For the sage Euphrates cf. Pliny, *Epp.* I. 10 (p. 75).

[7] Plutarch, *De defectu oraculorum* 45. 434d–f.

of the province of Asia, and Tacitus furnishes exact annotation about the oracle. Claros had a visit from Germanicus Caesar, who (it was rumoured) received an ambiguous answer from the god.[1] When Trajan, departing from Rome in the autumn of 113, came to Asia, he may not have neglected to consult this famous oracle. In Syria the Imperator put the god of Heliopolis to the test, and, finding him reliable, asked and obtained a prediction about the Parthian War. The outcome duly vindicated the oracle.[2]

Another passage about the travels of Germanicus has a comment appended that bears upon the date of the *Annales*. The prince in his procession through Egypt came to Thebes and contemplated the mighty ruins of ancient splendour. A priest interpreted the inscribed memorials of the Kings. The sum and catalogue of tribute rendered by the nations of Asia was impressive—and comparable (the historian adds) to what is now exacted by two empires, by the 'vis Parthorum' or by the 'potentia Romana'.[3] After inspection of other monuments and marvels, the prince journeyed to the southern border of the country, to Elephantine and Syene—'once the extreme bounds of Rome's empire, which now reaches to the Indian Ocean'.

'Nunc rubrum ad mare patescit.'[4] The phrase is unmistakable, implying not merely a wide extension of conquest but the Orient subdued and dominion over the known world, with no rival empire left. The words stand for Alexander's glory, cheaply emulated by the magniloquence of the Roman generals who paraded in the eastern lands, Pompeius Magnus and Marcus Antonius;[5] and the notion recurs in the Augustan writers who extol Caesar's heir holding in his homage all the lands from the one shore of Ocean to the other.[6]

On the western edge of the world lay Gades, near the point from which the ancient geographers drew a line that ran by Taurus and Caucasus to India eastwards. Hercules had his renowned temple at

---

[1] II. 54. 4: 'et ferebatur Germanico per ambigua, ut mos oraculis, maturum exitum cecinisse.' Tacitus also registered an alleged consultation by Lollia Paullina (XII. 22. 1, with Andresen's emendation). Cichorius assumes that the proconsul must have visited Claros, *Römische Studien* (1922), 386 f. For its growing importance at this time, L. Robert, *Les Fouilles de Claros* (Conférence à Ankara, 1954), 20; G. Klaffenbach, *Das Altertum* I (1955), 214 ff. It is perhaps significant of Tacitus' opinions that he should omit the unfavourable omen in Egypt, namely, the sacred bull refusing to take food from Germanicus (Ammianus XXII. 14. 8).

[2] Macrobius I. 22. 14 ff.

[3] II. 60. 4.　　　　　　　　　　　　　[4] 61. 2. See further App. 71.

[5] Pliny, *NH* VII. 97: 'terris a Maeotis ad rubrum mare subactis' (Pompeius' dedication in the temple of Minerva), cf. Cicero, *In Cat.* III. 26. Also Virgil, *Aen.* VIII. 686: 'victor ab Aurorae populis et litore rubro' (Antonius).

[6] cf. the prophecy of Juppiter to Venus (*Aen.* I. 286 f.): 'nascetur pulchra Troianus origine Caesar | imperium Oceano famam qui terminet astris.' Also Ovid, *Met.* XV. 829 ff.

Gades, with legends, notable visitors, and anecdotes to match. In the temple was a statue, the image of Alexander. Julius Caesar, quaestor in Spain, wept when he beheld it (so little achieved), and there may have been stories about Pompeius Magnus.[1] Trajan in his dispatches to the Roman Senate affirmed that he had gone further than Alexander.[2] The assertion is ludicrous—but palliated if the Imperator cast a reckoning from far Gades in his own country, not from Rome.

The historian echoes the Emperor's sanguine claim, 'rubrum ad mare'. The words were not written before the year 116. The next year saw the conquests of Trajan lost or surrendered. Hence a most welcome precision of dating: the phrase could not have been employed after 117.

The conclusion is not wholly valid. Trajan's new province of Mesopotamia did not embrace Babylonia and the whole tract down to the Persian gulf. Tacitus' generous definition (if applied literally, and that is a question) would reckon the dependent kingdom of Mesene as lying within the limits of the enlarged empire. Though the Roman armies retired to the western bank of the Euphrates, the next ruler for reasons of prestige could not, and did not, resign the claim to suzerainty, however slightly it might correspond with the reality.[3] Trajan had conferred the diadem upon Parthamaspates at Ctesiphon as a royal vassal, and Rome kept the golden throne of the Arsacids.[4] If the retreat was a fact, not to be covered up, it did not mean that renunciation was irrevocable. Hadrian, his present emergencies mastered, might revert, if he chose, to the policy of conquest. Tacitus' phraseology is not invalidated by what happened in 117. If nothing else, Roman pride or resentment counselled him to let the words stand. The reader might divine a patriot's feelings—and an emperor's duty.

The passage permits a deduction. A book of the *Annales*, or a group of books, was composed (or published) in 116—or subsequently. Powerful arguments commend the theory that the whole work was designed as three sections of six books each.[5] Books I–VI, or rather books I–III (for the first hexad splits into two halves) will thus belong not earlier than 116.[6] They cannot be tied down to 117 as the forward date—and they might be several years later.

A further sign has been detected, the phoenix in Book VI. Hadrian in due and prompt tribute to the memory of 'Divus Traianus' issued

---

[1] J. Gagé, *Rev. ét. anc.* XLII (1940), 425 ff.; *Rev. hist.* CCV (1951), 189 ff.
[2] Dio LXVIII. 29. 1.
[3] P. L. Strack, *Untersuchungen zur r. Reichsprägung des zweiten Jahrhunderts* II (1933), 52.
[4] *HA, Hadr.* 13. 8; *Pius* 9. 7.
[5] Ch. XXI.
[6] For I–III as a unit see the end of App. 37.

coins bearing that emblem.[1] The phoenix symbolizes renewal and perpetuity, appropriate to the Empire in its 'aeternitas', to the imperial succession—and to a son's 'pietas' towards his parent. Had the bird been reported in 117? Tacitus devotes a whole chapter to an alleged appearance of the year 34, which occasioned much discourse and debate among the learned men of the Egyptians and the Greeks.[2]

The historian with deferential gravity registers the diverse computations of the sacred cycle—and, taking five hundred years as standard reckoning, with the latest officially certified specimen of a phoenix in the time of the third Ptolemy, avows that he cannot help sharing the doubts of those who impugned the authenticity of the manifestation in the days of Tiberius Caesar. It exhibited none of the signs or behaviour as prescribed by an ancient tradition. A phoenix was unique among all birds, by form and feather. There were pictures of it. Tacitus goes on to recount in poetic language the demise of the phoenix: the bird renewed, rising from the nest and dutifully transporting the remains of his parent to the temple of the Sun, a long journey, laden with fragrant fuel. Plain prose follows: 'it is not disputed that the bird in question is seen in Egypt, from time to time.'[3]

Such is the solitary digression of an exotic nature in all the *Annales*— and it stands in wilful prominence as the initial item in the solemn chronicle of a Roman year. Anybody might know about governmental exploitation of the Arabian bird, and the dawn of a new age at Rome soon became a familiar topic of jest and parody. When Claudius Caesar used the eight hundredth anniversary of Rome as a pretext for *Ludi Saeculares* only sixty-three years since the Augustan ceremony, ridicule was easy enough. Claudius did no good by exhibiting a phoenix, as symbol and document of a new 'saeculum'. The phenomenon was duly registered in the *acta diurna* of the City. Nobody was taken in.[4]

Tacitus, as is his wont, mocks the pretensions of sacerdotal lore. He may also be alluding to the erudite tastes of an emperor, and official deceits. 'Omnium curiositatum explorator', such is the notorious label of Hadrian.[5] If Hadrian's accession had evoked the fabulous creature, there is a touch of political satire in the Tacitean notice.

Caution is prescribed. Several traces of revision or insertion can be suspected in the first hexad of the *Annales*.[6] Tacitus might therefore

---

[1] P. L. Strack, o.c. II (1933), 52; H. Mattingly, *BMC, R. Emp.* III (1936), cxxvii.

[2] VI. 28. It was P. L. Strack who first pointed out the possible relevance to the year 117.

[3] ib. 6: 'ceterum aspici aliquando in Aegypto eam volucrem non ambigitur.'

[4] Pliny, *NH* x. 5. Pliny (citing a certain Cornelius Valerianus) and Dio (LVIII. 27. 1) give 36 as the year of the bird's appearance in Egypt.

[5] Tertullian, *Apol.* 5. 7.

[6] App. 37.

have added the brief reference to Trajan's conquests.[1] Perhaps (though not at all likely), the digression about the phoenix.[2]

Should the phoenix be accepted as a firm allusion to a dated event, some gain would accrue either way. If an insertion, it puts the termination of Book VI (but not indeed of the whole work) in the year 117. If not, Book VI can be even later than 117. Theories that make Tacitus finish the *Annales* as early as 117 or 118 begin to look unplausible.[3]

It is still not clear when the author set about his task, how long he took, and when he terminated. Style might be invoked. The *Annales* show a marked change from the *Historiae*. Not, however, such as is safely to be accounted for by lapse of time or assessed in terms of years. The length of the interval since the *Historiae* (about 109) remains unverifiable.

And there is the further change in Tacitus' manner, manifest between the first hexad and the third. Various explanations emerge, and some not unattractive.[4] Again, no sure criterion for the rhythm of composition—but perhaps an argument to support a date in Hadrian's reign. Omitting style and language, certain phenomena suggest that the third hexad failed to receive the final touches.[5] Death or collapse may be the reason.

Nothing forbids the assumption that Tacitus was writing as late as 120, or even 123.[6] The effort of style proves that he was not a ready composer; and great industry was needed where the history had to be constructed anew from documentary material, as in much of the first hexad.

Beginning, it might be surmised, about 115, or even, for all that can be known, as late as 117, Tacitus conceived a design of three hexads. An important inquiry emerges, concerning the *Annales* as a whole. If, as seems highly probable, Tacitus composed the great bulk under Hadrian, not perhaps completing the eighteen books before the sixth year of that emperor,[7] how far was he influenced by present events? He had chosen not to write of Trajan. But Trajan and the eastern wars might be illuminated by the *Annales*, indirectly yet powerfully—and so might Hadrian.

The search for allusions is liable to be deprecated as a mere exercise

---

[1] If so, it could be argued that I–III, possibly I–VI, were completed by 116. But see App. 71.

[2] Strack, assuming that Tacitus completed the *Annales* in 117 (o.c. 55) must also be assuming that the phoenix is a late insertion. Yet it is clear that the digression has a structural function—relief in the middle of a chronicle of murders. A precise parallel is the story of the hunt for fabulous treasure in Africa (XVI. 1 f.).

[3] App. 71. [4] p. 360 f. [5] App. 59 f.

[6] The assumption is relevant to the chronology of Juvenal, and of Suetonius, App. 75 and 77. [7] Or, on the other hypothesis, getting as far as XVI. 35.

of ingenuity. They can seldom be caught and fixed with certitude; and it is open to anybody to argue that Tacitus would have written much as he did if Trajan had never invaded Mesopotamia, if Hadrian had never inherited the imperial power. With this proviso, it entails no damage or deception to single out those items in the *Annales* that must have struck the reader with a sharp sense of relevance, or recognition.[1]

The reader could find not a few—and he might have a question to ask. One great work—was that not enough to exhaust what a man had to say, to satisfy ambition and renown?

Historians are often impelled to go on—or go backwards. While they write, the deeper past draws them, some before the task is done, thus modifying the original plan and point of departure. Others take up a second subject later on. Sallust perhaps altered his design, putting the exordium of his *Historiae* at 78 B.C. instead of 62, when Pompeius Magnus came back in glory from the East, or 60, the year of the three dynasts' fateful alliance.[2] Asinius Pollio, however, who elected the latter date, carried out his purpose, took up oratory again, and lived thereafter for thirty years at least, active, robust, and confident—and not under any call to turn back and narrate the rebellion of the Italians against Rome (it concerned his people and his family) or the civil wars of Marius and Sulla.

Tacitus' first thoughts about a subject went to the reign of Domitian. He soon saw that a Flavian history must lead off with January of the year 69. The annals of the earlier Caesars were now the given theme, discerned the more sharply by the very lapse of ages, and powerful in appeal. Tacitus responded.

The theme was fierce and sombre—the growth of despotism, the decline and fall of the aristocracy, the ruin of free speech and of human dignity. Tacitus utters a complaint. Happier were the historians who wrote about the Republic. They could tell of great wars, cities stormed, kings defeated and captured; or, turning to internal history, consuls against tribunes, land laws and corn laws, the strife between plebs and Senate. They, in truth, had free scope, but Tacitus was cramped: 'nobis in arto et inglorius labor.'[3]

---

[1] Tacitus devotes enormous care to the choice of small facts, of proper names, or of single words.

[2] Since he had already written a monograph on Catilina, the return of Pompeius Magnus in 62 or the compact of 60 would have been highly suitable. Observe also his sketch of Sulla, introduced by the words 'neque enim alio loco de Sullae rebus dicturi sumus' (*Jug.* 95. 2). The *Historiae*, beginning in 78, could hardly omit 'natura cultusque eius'.

[3] IV. 32. 2. He was thinking of Livy, with 'amère jalousie' according to Boissier, *Tacite* (1903), 130.

What were his reasons, open or unavowed? Livy in the preface to one of the later instalments of his history confessed that he had to go on, though glory enough had accrued.[1] Personal motive in Tacitus cannot be grasped—curiosity or fresh energy, strong conviction or anger.

There had been much to vex him while he brought the *Historiae* to completion—pageantry and official eloquence, gladiators and all the victory monuments. The Senate's value and honour diminished steadily. When Trajan went away to the eastern lands and stayed there, he left power in the hands of personal confidants or mere secretaries. Bulletins poured in from the Imperator, rapid and exultant, retailing the long sequence of kings and nations conquered at the end of the world. The Senate voted that Trajan should celebrate as many triumphs as he liked;[2] and the Senate was compelled to admit and to elect as consul a native chieftain, Lusius Quietus.[3]

Then the sudden collapse, with silence or laborious and deceitful excuses—and sheer perplexity for loyal senators. Trajan's failure, the accession of Hadrian, and sundry events in the sequel served only to sharpen the distrust of Tacitus. He was an old man now, in the sad years, and perhaps very bitter. While Trajan lived, he saw no prospect of honours like a second consulate or the city prefecture. It was vain to regret that the office fell to Glitius Agricola, general in the first war against the Dacians (Glitius had been consul in the same year as Tacitus). But who was Baebius Macer, and with what claims or credit, holding civil authority in Rome when Trajan died?[4] A new ruler sometimes brought a new *praefectus urbi*. Tacitus, it appears, had nothing to expect from Trajan's heir.[5]

And there was a general cause for despondency. Liberty and energy faded, fashions changed, and a younger generation (the men twenty years his junior) stood now in the ascendant. Tacitus may have endured malady, bereavement, and many vexations, with a gloomy foreboding of the end. It was time for a man to recede gracefully, acquiring merit from renunciation when his use or powers lapsed.[6]

---

[1] Pliny, *NH praef.* 16: 'satis iam sibi gloriae quaesitum, et potuisse se desidere, ni animus inquies pasceretur opere.' Perhaps from the *exordium* of Book CXXXIV.

[2] Dio LXVIII. 29. 2. Compare the protest of Cassius Longinus against excessive celebrations for victories in the East (XIII. 41. 4).

[3] p. 242.

[4] *HA, Hadr.* 5. 5. Baebius (*PIR²*, B 20), suffect consul in 103, was a friend and correspondent of Pliny (App. 25). The reasons for his high promotion cannot be divined.

[5] M. Annius Verus, suffect consul in Tacitus' year, became *praefectus urbi*, perhaps as the immediate successor of Baebius Macer (App. 13). Tacitus inserted an excursus on the office (VI. 11, attached to the obituary of L. Piso): that does not in itself prove a morbid or jealous interest.

[6] That is, becoming a 'pulcherrimae quietis exemplum', cf. Pliny (*Epp.* IV. 23. 4), on T. Pomponius Bassus (*suff.* 94).

The age of sixty excused attendance in the Senate, and the sixty-third year was widely believed to be dangerous.

Signs of age or disillusion have been sought in Tacitus' choice of subject, in the tone and fashion of the writing. With less success than might be fancied.[1] Compared with the *Historiae*, the *Annales* show the writer's manner pushed to the extreme limit. The vocabulary has become rigorously selective, with notable aversions. It is significant that Tacitus visits his disapprobation on the terms that had been annexed and degraded by governmental phraseology, that he also turns aside from benevolent and hopeful words.[2] But it is not a surprise. The phenomenon need not denote any change in fundamental views on men and government. Rather is it the result in Tacitus of a growing awareness of what he was about—of his powerful talent for the grim and the subversive. The author of the *Annales* is ruthless and ironical. At the same time gaiety and tolerance are disclosed in the speeches; and in the course of the work his sense of humour appears to grow deeper and wider.[3]

Nothing is known. What can be inferred is a firm defiance of extinction, a resolve to triumph through style and the effort of style. The seventh decade of life found him keen and vigorous. While engaged upon the Tiberian books Cornelius Tacitus was ready (against his normal reticence) to publish a clear announcement about future projects. If he lived, he would go back once again and deal with Caesar Augustus.[4]

The historian occupied a high eminence, and there was a solitude about him. He felt time passing swift and pitiless. The friends of his youth were dead, long ago, who had guided his steps in the days of Vespasian.[5] The nearest of them in age was Vipstanus Messalla: Tacitus had recently witnessed the induction of Vipstanus' son (consul in 115).[6]

Most of his seniors had perished, and many younger men also, resplendent in the arts of peace or war but extinguished in their prime. Licinius Sura and Sosius Senecio were sadly missed. Fabius Justus, the historian's close (or closest) friend, may not have had a long survival after his governorship of Syria.[7] And Pliny died in Bithynia.

Of Pliny's own senatorial circle, the dull Cornutus lived on, and

---

[1] p. 219. Some assert that Tacitus was prematurely aged, e.g. E. Kornemann, *Tacitus* (Wiesbaden, 1947), 45; or desperate, E. Paratore, *Tacito* (1951), 807.

[2] App. 66.   [3] Ch. XL.   [4] III. 24. 3 (p. 371).

[5] viz. the four speakers in the *Dialogus* (p. 63 f.).

[6] L. Vipstanus Messalla (*PIR*[1], V 469): only a name and a date.

[7] p. 74.

the elegant Minicius Fundanus.[1] Baebius Macer had reached an unpredicted summit as *praefectus urbi*. Catilius Severus and Pompeius Falco were now in charge of military provinces, safe adherents of the new ruler. Catilius, Falco (and others) had been shut out (it appears) from consular commands until a late season in Trajan's reign.[2] Each enjoyed a long life thereafter.[3] A greater surprise, Bruttius Praesens and Erucius Clarus came to the fore, winning renown in the Parthian War—and destined many years later for the highest of civil distinctions.[4]

The especial intimates of Tacitus among his equals in age or standing cannot be identified.[5] They were a variegated collection, including a number of aristocrats—some perhaps well known to Tacitus, or furnishing precious fragments of tradition, like the descendants of Asinius Pollio, or the Volusii, safe amiable men, to whose family the *Annales* carry an untainted testimony,[6] others no doubt whom he contemplated with disfavour—idle, pompous, and inept. Several men of birth and fashion were still extant from Domitian's reign.[7] The first for pedigree (and perhaps for nothing else) had been Calpurnius Crassus, perpetuating names historic and fatal: the victims of Claudius and Nero, the brief unhappy heir of Sulpicius Galba.[8]

Among the newer stocks the two Neratii (Marcellus and Priscus) earned fame for their accomplishments.[9] Annius Verus, also coeval with Tacitus, now became a personage—a steady tranquil man whom Hadrian held in affection;[10] and Julius Servianus refused to die.[11]

Elderly survivors with a long glance backwards measured present

[1] Cornutus Tertullus became proconsul of either Asia or Africa (*ILS* 1034); for Minicius in Asia, p. 468.

[2] p. 243.

[3] Catilius (*II ord.* 120) was holding the *praefectura urbis* in 138 (*HA, Hadr.* 24. 6 f.). Falco was still alive in 140, apparently interested in arboriculture (Fronto, p. 35 N = Haines I, p. 141).

[4] For the Parthian War, Ch. XX. Bruttius Praesens after his consulate (c. 118) governed Cappadocia and Moesia Inferior, and was proconsul of Africa (*AE* 1950, 66; *IRT* 545); further, he was governor of Syria late in Hadrian's reign (*AE* 1938, 137: Palmyra), and as *cos. II* opened the year 139, colleague of Antoninus Pius. Erucius Clarus (*suff.* 117), absent from the record of Hadrian's reign, dies early in 146 while holding a second consulate and the Prefecture of the City (*FO* XXVII).

[5] For the consuls of 97, p. 72, with App. 10; for some of Tacitus' coevals, App. 24.

[6] p. 302.

[7] e.g. the polyonymous M. Lollius Paullinus D. Valerius Asiaticus Saturninus (*suff.* 94), *praefectus urbi* and *ordinarius* in 125.

[8] pp. 9, 241. This man (*PIR*[2], C 259) is presumably the nephew of Piso Licinianus. For the stemma of the family cf. p. 385.

[9] Marcellus was to have a second consulate in 129.

[10] App. 86.

[11] It would be worth while knowing how Tacitus stood with the relatives of Hadrian (App. 87)—and with the friends of the four consulars executed in 118.

and past, not always with equity or bland indulgence, but pouncing upon scandal and paradox. Their scrutiny bore fiercely on names and families. The senatorial historian had to be a senatorial repertory in his own person, without lapse or error about rank, extraction, or nomenclature—and he wrote for a subtle and malicious audience.

While the *Historiae* depicted people whom Tacitus had known, the matter of the *Annales* brought fresh incitement—a submerged epoch waiting to be explored. The appeal was double. Tacitus now came upon names redolent of Rome's remotest antiquity, still extant under the Caesars, illustrious and doomed. At the same time he discerned the earliest traces of sundry recent families, grown faint already or carefully covered up for good reasons. Entering into possession of the fifty-four years from Tiberius to Nero's end, he became coeval therewith, like a senator who could recapture the whole age as one man's memory.

Tacitus prolonged his own experience into the past with a new point of vantage and a sharper insight into the social comedy. That earlier epoch showed the same setting and behaviour (though enhanced)—ostentation and folly, the appetite for rank and money, the sudden alternations in human affairs. And there no less, time in its passage made a mock of all pretensions and unmasked each man's secret nature before the end.

The *Historiae* could not fail to carry much that alarmed or angered the living.[1] In the *Annales* they saw damage to ancestors. Even when families became extinct, men might discover in some ancient misdemeanour the shape and model of their own, and take it for intentional, or conceive resentment at the implied contrast, if virtue and glory earned commemoration.[2]

Tacitus was not sorry to disinter the infamous or ridiculous. No historian familiar with the annals of Roman eloquence could miss the first action of the great Domitius Afer, a ferocious prosecutor in the days of Tiberius Caesar.[3] Nor would Tacitus fail to damn Afer at the end with a brief obituary.[4] The decease and testament of Afer's son by adoption (Domitius Tullus) stood out as a memorable event in Roman society towards the middle epoch of Trajan's reign. The fortune went to Domitia Lucilla, who belonged to a family group with powerful alliances.[5]

Ummidius Quadratus, legate of Syria for nine years, typifies a whole system: easy-going, elderly governors, and an ignoble policy in

---

[1] p. 229.

[2] IV. 33. 4: 'at multorum qui Tiberio regente poenam vel infamias subiere posteri manent', &c.   [3] IV. 52.   [4] XIV. 19.

[5] Pliny, *Epp.* VIII. 8. See further p. 605 and App. 87.

the eastern lands.[1] Tacitus brings out the contrast to the fame and energy of Corbulo, whom the envious Ummidius could not bear to meet and confront in Syria.[2] The Ummidii were a family of local repute and some opulence.[3] The governor's daughter, that robust old lady Ummidia Quadratilla, transmitted the inheritance to her grandson, a youth of exemplary conduct and (so it is proclaimed) resplendent with promise as an orator.[4] He acceded to the *fasces* in 118.[5]

Obscure or minor names are another matter. Some are there because they will recur in the narrative; but odd individuals by their casual entrances may have had for Tacitus a personal value no longer to be detected. Artful transition or a bare juxtaposition, apparently innocent, can sometimes furnish a clue. Deliberate choice by Tacitus has quietly brought in the forebears of persons excellent in station and renown. The narrative shows what they were like—informers and adherents of Seianus, fools, rogues, or reprobates.[6]

Two incidents exemplify, linked in sequence by the historian. Two crimes, he relates, made notable a single year under Nero. The one was a forged will. Tacitus gives the names.[7] Two of the culprits were worth it—Antonius Primus, bold and unscrupulous, and an aristocrat, Asinius Marcellus, the great-grandson of Pollio. Not so the other three, on first sight; and Tacitus adds two others, who were involved and punished in the judicial sequel. Scrupulous documentation—but perhaps the names evoked persons of rank and dignity in the society of his own day.[8]

The second crime follows. It was an event in itself, and welcome to Tacitus, enabling him to produce an oration. A slave had killed the city prefect. Tacitus puts the motive on clear record. It is highly discreditable to the victim.[9] So much for L. Pedanius Secundus,[10] the

---

[1] XII. 48. Ummidius was quaestor in 14 (*ILS* 972), *suffectus* c. 40.

[2] XIII. 8. 3. There followed a conflict about who was to receive the Parthian hostages.

[3] Varro, *RR* III. 3. 9. Casinum is their home.

[4] Pliny, *Epp.* VII. 24. He and Pedanius Fuscus (*cos.* 118) formed an 'egregium par' (VI. 11. 1), cf. App. 27; they may have been related. The history of the Ummidii after the legate of Syria presents several gaps and problems.

[5] *PIR¹*, V 603. A friend of Hadrian (*HA, Hadr.* 15. 7).

[6] p. 302 (Junius Rusticus, Caepio Crispinus, Julius Marinus, Q. Servaeus—all to be presumed ancestors of consulars known to Tacitus).

[7] XIV. 40.

[8] 41. 1 (Pompeius Aelianus, from Spain, and Valerius Ponticus). The will was that of Domitius Balbus, and the chief agent was a relative of his called Valerius Fabianus (40. 1). The nomenclature of these four persons suggests Romans from Spain or Narbonensis (cf. App. 78)—one or other might be connected with P. Aelius Hadrianus Afer, the Emperor's father, who married Domitia Paullina from Gades (*HA, Hadr.* 1. 2).

[9] XIV. 42. 1: 'haud multo post praefectum urbis Pedanium Secundum servus ipsius interfecit, seu negata libertate cui pretium pepigerat sive amore exoleti incensus et dominum aemulum non tolerans.'

[10] *PIR¹*, P 146 (*suff.* 43).

first consul from one of the new families in the group that Tacitus saw rise high and yet higher through the alliance and kinship of the dynasty. Hadrian's niece Julia was married to Cn. Pedanius Fuscus, consul in 118 as colleague of the Emperor.[1]

[1] *PIR*[1], P 144—Cn. Pedanius Fuscus Salinator, son-in-law of Julius Servianus. Perhaps related to his coeval, C. Ummidius Quadratus, *suffectus* in the same year. The Pedanii come from Barcino, in Tarraconensis (App. 87).

XXXVI. THE ACCESSION OF HADRIAN

THE historian did not survive to witness the sombre close of
Hadrian's principate. Yet he might divine the way that ruler
seemed destined to go. Tastes and tendencies in the new emperor,
and acts already—there was enough for any historian, from the first
days of the reign, even were he not by nature disposed to augur the
worst.

Tacitus had seen the power conferred upon various rulers before
Hadrian by the 'auctoritas patrum' and the 'consensus militum'—
to state the phraseology in its official type and order, generally inverted
by the facts;[1] and he knew what form of words an emperor uses when
he protests his own unworthiness or modestly craves legitimation,
being already in possession of authority. The early chapters of Book
I depict political behaviour, pitilessly—the fraudulent protestations
of loyal subjects, discreetly modulated between mourning and re-
joicing, and the eager rush to voluntary enslavement.[2] State ceremonial, public professions, and secret conflicts—the whole thing may
seem to hint and foreshadow the accession of Hadrian.

Tiberius Caesar put out an edict convoking the Senate. He had
already issued commands to the troops at Rome and abroad, so
Tacitus notes. Tiberius showed hesitations only when he had to speak
in the Senate.[3] He was afraid lest Germanicus, at the head of a large
army, be tempted to make a proclamation; and he wished to rule at
the call and summons of the 'res publica', not as one ensconced in the
power through a woman's intrigue and an old man's act of adoption.[4]
Moreover, hesitating, he dissembled; he wished to discover what was
in the thoughts of the leading senators. He marked down their looks
and words for subsequent rancour—as was subsequently discovered.[5]

---

[1] Nero duly spoke 'de auctoritate patrum et consensu militum' (XIII. 3. 1). But in fact
'sententiam militum secuta patrum consilia' (XII. 69. 2).

[2] I. 7. 1: 'at Romae ruere in servitium consules patres eques. quanto quis inlustrior,
tanto magis falsi et festinantes, vultuque composito ne laeti excessu principis neu tristiores
primordio, lacrimas gaudium, questus adulationem miscebant.'

[3] ib. 5: 'nusquam cunctabundus nisi cum in senatu loqueretur.'

[4] ib. 7: 'per uxorium ambitum et senili adoptione.' The sinister relevance of the phrase
was detected by P. L. Strack, *Untersuchungen zur r. Reichsprägung des zweiten Jahrhunderts*
II (1933), 52. That scholar did not, however, search the early chapters of Book I for further
indications.

[5] ib.: 'postea cognitum est ad introspiciendas etiam procerum voluntates inductam
dubitationem: nam verba vultus in crimen detorquens recondebat.'

These are ugly comments, and ill-founded. Occurring where they do in the narration they engender a doubt whether the historian has not another emperor in mind. The problem is very complicated. Several items seem to go back to a source which is also the source of Cassius Dio.[1] Tacitus has added point and venom. None the less, the remark about adoption, even if not written in innocence, cannot be explained and exploited as something that would not have been there unless to support an insinuation against Hadrian and Plotina Augusta.[2]

The Senate met, but only to hear the testament of Caesar Augustus (and to make arrangements for the funeral ceremony). Various discomforts awaited any new ruler. Curiosity or malice would ask how he stood with his predecessor, and with other members of the family. The testament of Augustus told more than the will of any Caesar afterwards. It opened with the complaint that 'atrox fortuna' had spoiled his plans for the dynasty,[3] and (most anomalous) the dead man took his widow into the name and family of the Julii, to be styled Julia Augusta.

Tacitus weighs the scales against Livia, with a suggestion of crime (that is, poison), linked to the story that Augustus had recently paid a visit to Agrippa Postumus on the island Planasia.[4] He further notes it as dubious whether Augustus was still alive when Tiberius returned on Livia's prompt summons;[5] and he asserts that Livia kept the death of the Princeps secret for a time, adding a corroborative detail—guards about the house and on the roads, and comforting bulletins.[6] He also insists on dragging Livia into the narration about the execution of Agrippa.[7]

Not all rumours were empty when a Caesar died. The news about Claudius was held back for a time, in order that the necessary dispositions should be made.[8] What was done by Agrippina could have

[1] p. 306 f. It can, however, be suggested, because of the formula with which Dio (LVII. 3. 3 f.) introduces the comments about adoption and dissimulation (cf. *Ann.* I. 7. 7), that he took them from a subsidiary source: perhaps Tacitus, cf. App. 36.

[2] If Tacitus made one insertion when revising Book I, there could be others. One insertion comes close to proof—Rhodes and secret vice (I. 4. 4), for Tacitus also grafted that theme on a passage in Book IV (57. 2, cf. App. 37).

[3] Cited by Suetonius, *Tib.* 23: not exploited by Tacitus.

[4] I. 5. 1 f. (p. 306).

[5] ib. 3, cf. Dio LVI. 31. 1 (alluding to 'most historians, and the best'). Suetonius reveals no doubt (*Tib.* 21. 1).

[6] ib. 4: 'acribus namque custodiis domum et vias saepserat Livia, laetique interdum nuntii vulgabantur.'

[7] 6. 2. He will have found her responsibility mooted in the sources, cf. Suetonius, *Tib.* 22; Dio LVII. 6. 3.

[8] XII. 68. 3: 'cunctos aditus custodiis clauserat, crebroque vulgabat ire in melius valetudinem principis, quo miles bona in spe ageret tempusque prosperum ex monitis Chaldaeorum adventaret.' Cf., briefly, and with a trivial detail, Suetonius, *Divus Claudius* 45. 1.

suggested what is said about Livia.[1] On the other hand, it is not likely that stories about Livia did not emerge before 54. The historian is not inventing. Yet one of the passages that he grafted on his main narrative is inartistic, namely the anecdote about Augustus' journey to Planasia.[2]

The consort of Caesar Augustus could not fail to be incriminated for the advancement of her son. Whether as wife or mother, she was a proud and powerful woman. Any sign of imperfect harmony would be gladly marked. When senators, loyal or insidious, came forward with sundry proposals for the honouring of Julia Augusta, Tiberius repulsed them. The historian implies envy.[3] He was not yet ready to allege discord between mother and son. It comes out later, and without due warrant.[4]

Augustus was another matter. If Tacitus had properly investigated the earlier career of Tiberius, there was a full bill—constraint, resentment, and secret antagonism.[5] What he contributes in Book I is negligible and flimsy. The men of understanding at the obsequies of Caesar Augustus suggest that the Princeps, choosing Tiberius to succeed, thought of his own renown, enhanced by the comparison.[6]

Though the Principate was dynastic from the outset, blood and family could not confer legitimate authority in the Roman State. Nor, indeed, had all the testaments of the Caesars been respected, and some were held back. Hence scandal and various conjectures. Tacitus himself may have heard an emperor's asseverations—for Domitian always said that his father's will had been tampered with.[7] When Tacitus came to terminate the second hexad of the *Annales*, he chose a suitable phrase for epilogue, noting how Claudius' will was suppressed, lest it provoke popular unrest, the stepson ousting the son.[8] The exordium of Book XIII follows, the first murder in Nero's reign.

There should have been a testament of Trajan, deposited for custody with the sacred virgins of Vesta.[9] It could only have appointed his personal heirs, but it was in effect a state document, and might

---

[1] cf. H. Willrich, *Hermes* LXII (1927), 76 f.; R. H. Martin, *CQ* XLVIII (1955), 123 ff.

[2] It interrupts the sequence, and it introduces two names (Fabius Maximus and his wife Marcia) that will not be mentioned again in the *Annales*. Cf. App. 37.

[3] 14. 2: 'muliebre fastigium in deminutionem sui accipiens.'

[4] e.g. I. 72. 4. It is a notion that came fairly late to Tacitus (App. 37). The imputations against Livia are not quite in harmony with the obituary (v. 1). Some may have been put in after that passage was written: which could have happened without Tacitus' having Plotina Augusta in mind.

[5] Ch. XXXII.

[6] 10. 7: 'sed quoniam adrogantiam saevitiamque eius introspexerit, comparatione deterrima sibi gloriam quaesivisse.' Cf. Dio LVI. 45. 3.

[7] Suetonius, *Dom.* 2. 3.

[8] XII. 69. 3: 'ne antepositus filio privignus iniuria et invidia animos vulgi turbaret.'

[9] Presumably, cf. Suetonius, *Divus Aug.* 101. 1.

have contained unfortunate items for preface or codicil. No trace survives—only idle fancies about names and intentions.[1]

No juridical embarrassment could arise. The document was invalid, having been revoked by the Imperator on his death-bed when he adopted a son. For that the senators had the word and signature of Plotina Augusta—and their own confidence or suspicions. Rumour spread, reviving or creating stories about Plotina's undue partiality for the kinsman of her consort.[2]

There was time (and cause) for worse than rumour to empoison the situation. The reign opened without the new emperor, whom the army in Syria and the needs of the 'res publica' proclaimed. Eleven months elapsed before his arrival.

When Tiberius Caesar confronted the Senate, he was ill at ease. His words betrayed his plight, with explanations that grew more and more involved.[3] The senators for their part dissembled—but some of the leading men, under cover of earnest or helpful advice, would not be sorry to make trouble.

Hadrian faced a like ordeal, but much worse, with senators interpreting every word, and every reticence. To accept honours or refuse them made an emperor vulnerable either way. For himself Hadrian had been guarded and discreet.[4] That was no shield—it could be dismissed as 'adrogans moderatio'.[5] Any mention of Plotina Augusta was a delicate matter; and the spectacle of Trajan's Parthian triumph, with the effigy of the dead Imperator on parade,[6] no doubt evoked a savage commentary from the 'prudentes'.

The state papers of his predecessor might help or hinder a ruler when he expounded the resources and emergencies of the Empire. Tiberius cited the counsel of Augustus, deprecating any further imperial expansion (and Tacitus adds a motive—fear or envy).[7] Hadrian can hardly have had any document to quote in support of his own policy—and when he appealed to secret instructions, deceit was imputed.[8]

For one act, not divulged to the Senate, Tiberius Caesar sought dishonest cover from his parent's mandate, according to Tacitus.[9] It was the execution of Agrippa Postumus. Hadrian, before he confronted the Senate, had much more to cover up or explain away.

---

[1] HA, Hadr. 4. 8 f. (p. 233 f.).　　　　　　　　　　　　　　　　　[2] Ch. XX.

[3] 11. 2: 'tunc vero nitenti ut sensus suos penitus abderet, in incertum et ambiguum magis implicabantur.'

[4] Dio LXIX. 2. 3; HA, Hadr. 6. 2 ff.　　　[5] cf. I. 8. 5.　　　[6] HA, Hadr. 6. 3.

[7] 11. 4: 'addideratque consilium coercendi intra terminos imperii, incertum metu an per invidiam.'

[8] HA, Hadr. 9. 2: 'quod omnia quae displicere vidisset Hadrianus mandata sibi ut faceret secreto a Traiano esse simulabat.'

[9] 6. 1: 'patris iussa simulabat'.

First of all, senators in peril of their lives, and one of the exiles, Calpurnius Crassus, killed when escaping from his penal island (so it was reported); then Avidius Nigrinus and his three accomplices in treason.[1] On what proof or document, and by whose command? Who among the agents and ministers of Hadrian deserved the credit— or the blame, should it all turn out to have been a mistake?

The episode of Agrippa Postumus, as narrated by Tacitus (with no plain answer), conveys the various embarrassments of sudden and secret deeds. When the officer of the Guard made his report, Tiberius was at a loss: not his order, and the Senate would have to be apprised. Hence crisis and perplexity in the Palace. Sallustius Crispus had issued the command. If anything became public, the minister was in equal danger from truth or falsehood. Sallustius passed a warning to Livia—absolute secrecy and no word to the Senate: there is only one source of authority.[2]

A Princeps was fortunate if he did not have to remove rival claimants. Caesar Augustus named a number of the leading consulars in his will, as heirs by default. That was ostentation, to impress posterity, so Tacitus insists, for Augustus hated most of them.[3] Tacitus had already put in a sinister comment about Tiberius and the 'principes', prematurely, before the Senate had even met.[4] The theme expands at the second session, when several senators by what they said incurred the suspicion and hostility of Tiberius. The historian here brings in an anecdote about Caesar Augustus. When near to his end the Princeps held discourse about the ambitions and capacities of three important consulars. Tacitus adds a fourth name, on a variant version—and, not content with that, asserts most unjustly that all except one were to perish in the sequel, through the machinations of Tiberius.[5]

The anecdote is more than peculiar. Not only the general discrepancy with the story of Tiberius' principate—it is interpolated into the account of a senatorial debate, and it disturbs the presentation. Perhaps an insertion, when Tacitus was revising Book I.[6] Suetonius and Cassius Dio, who can report many curious particulars about the accession of Tiberius, have missed this attractive and damaging disclosure. Whatever the source and authentication, Tacitus could not resist it.

When an emperor discusses who is 'capax imperii', he announces

[1] p. 244.

[2] 6. 3: 'eam condicionem esse imperandi ut non aliter ratio constet quam si uni reddatur.' Tacitus gives prominence to Sallustius Crispus: he had good reasons, even if Acilius Attianus, Hadrian's agent, had never existed.

[3] 8. 1: 'plerosque invisos sibi, sed iactantia gloriaque ad posteros.'

[4] 7. 7. (p. 481).   [5] 13. 2 f. (p. 380).   [6] App. 37.

the doom of any man he names. The implication is plain. It would be worth knowing how soon the topic or legend arose in imperial Rome. The next trace in the *Annales* is a remark made by Nero.[1] No record happens to survive of any speculations uttered by Nerva, or of any rival whom Trajan suppressed when he seized the power.[2] Trajan himself weighed the qualities of certain consulars, naming Neratius Priscus (so it is alleged).[3] There is another anecdote. Trajan brought up in familiar discourse the topic of 'capax imperii', challenging his guests to name ten men, but not waiting for their response. He exclaimed forthwith that he knew one for certain, Julius Servianus.[4]

The Tacitean notice is not casual or innocent. Apart from the providential parallel of the accession scene, a man of the time would discover without effort suggestive items (person or deed or motive) in the early years of the reign—friction between the Emperor and his friends, dynastic intrigues and ambitions, the Prefect of the Guard, the vicissitudes of influence and disgrace.

From strain or discord at Rome an emperor could seek relief in a journey to the provinces. A valid excuse offered—the armies had to be seen to. And the project could easily be announced, more than once. The Emperor did not always go.[5] Noble pretexts were to hand —Caesar was consumed with zeal for Rome and the 'res publica', he could not bear to inflict sorrow on loyal and loving subjects.[6] The plebs for their part knew no doubts. They wanted the food and games that his presence vouchsafed.[7] The upper orders at Rome were in two minds: was the ruler worse at home or away?[8]

A year after his arrival there were signs or a belief that Hadrian might be going abroad.[9] He left the city. Although, as it turned out,

---

[1] If he perished, 'habere subsidium rem publicam', namely, Memmius Regulus (XIV. 47. 1). Tacitus adds 'vixit tamen post haec Regulus quiete defensus'. Regulus, consul precisely thirty years earlier (in 31), must have been very old. Not a good anecdote. See further App. 60.

[2] p. 16 (the legate of Syria in 97).

[3] *HA, Hadr.* 4. 8—not very good (cf. p. 233 f.).

[4] Dio in the version of Zonaras (LXIX. 17. 3 Boissevain) attributes the remark to Hadrian —τὸν δὲ Σερουιανὸν τοῦτον Ἀδριανὸς καὶ τῆς αὐταρχίας ἄξιον ἐνόμισεν. Xiphilinus, however, has ὁ Τραϊανός (cf. Boissevain's edition of Dio, III, 656). Preferred by E. Groag, P–W x, 885—and a conversation ἐν συμποσίῳ fits Trajan better than Hadrian.

[5] III. 47. 2; IV. 4. 2.

[6] Thus Nero in 64, postponing a visit to the eastern lands—'deseruit inceptum, cunctas sibi curas amore patriae leviores dictitans. vidisse maestos civium vultus, audire secretas querimonias', &c. (XV. 36. 2 f.).

[7] XV. 36. 4: 'haec atque talia plebi volentia fuere, voluptatum cupidine et, quae praecipua cura est, rei frumentariae angustias, si abesset, metuenti.'

[8] ib.: 'in incerto erant, procul an coram atrocior haberetur.'

[9] Coins of 119 have FORT(VNA) RED(VX), H. Mattingly, *BMC, R. Emp.* III (1936), 410; for other types, including the Hercules of Gades, and the suggestion that a visit to the western provinces was envisaged, cf. ib. cxxix.

he intended nothing more than a 'peregrinatio suburbana' in Campania, it was perhaps enough to make men speculate whether Hadrian would come back to Rome, soon or ever.[1]

As it happened, Hadrian did not undertake a tour in the provinces until 121. The first years witnessed shows and pageantry and acts of benevolence.[2] Also legislation and reforms. It could be conveyed (and it was perhaps true) that Trajan had been unduly neglectful. The new Princeps was assiduous in the Senate.[3] About law and justice he had views of his own, and the impulse to intervene.[4] His enactments tended to be mild and humane.[5] He protected slaves from cruel treatment;[6] he declined to give the rich the benefit of the doubt;[7] and, making concessions to the soldiers, he deprecated the harshness of previous rulers.[8] Both his words and his behaviour let it be known that he did not set a high value on class and rank.[9]

Few senators would feel happy with a Princeps eagerly interfering everywhere, or welcome an outbreak of social legislation in favour of the lower orders.[10] With many enemies already (and creating more) Hadrian turned to senators who had been in scant esteem with Trajan, and to men without ancestors: from necessity, but also in revulsion from Trajan and Trajan's friends. Of his own agents in the first emergencies, Acilius Attianus, the Prefect of the Guard, was

---

[1] Tiberius in 21 announced a journey to Gaul—and was angry when an adulatory consular senator proposed an 'ovatio' on the occasion of his return from Campania (III. 47. 3 f.). For the possible relevance of 'Caesar in Campaniam' (IV. 57. 1), see below, p. 524. Tacitus carefully reported the predictions of the astrologers (which misled many), 'ferebant periti caelestium iis motibus siderum excessisse Roma Tiberium ut reditus illi negaretur' (IV. 58. 2.)

[2] HA, Hadr. 7 f.

[3] ib. 8. 6. Not, perhaps, very good evidence. For the importance of Hadrian's consilium, Dio LXIX. 7. 1.

[4] Dig. XXII. 5. 5: 'nam ipsos interrogare soleo' (from a rescript on the value of testimony).

[5] For a useful collection and comment, P. J. Alexander, Harvard Studies XLIX (1938), 141 ff. It is not unreasonable to assume that Hadrian was very active in the years 118–21.

[6] HA, Hadr. 18. 7 ff.; Dig. I. 6. 2 (the matron Umbricia, relegated because she had treated slave girls 'atrocissime'); XLVIII. 8. 6 (against castration, reinforcing the penalties of the senatus consultum passed under the consulate of Annius Verus and Neratius Priscus, i.e. in 97, cf. Dio LXVIII. 2. 4). It is unfortunate that Hadrian's decision about what was to be done with the household when a master was murdered (HA, Hadr. 18. 11, cf. the rescript in Dig. XXIX. 5. 1. 28) cannot be dated. Tacitus, Ann. XIV. 42 ff. may be relevant, cf. p. 448.

[7] Thus when boundary stones have been shifted, 'si splendidiores personae sunt quae convincuntur, non dubie occupandorum alienorum finium causa id admiserunt' (Dig. XLVII. 21. 2—in 119, to Terentius Gentianus the governor of Macedonia).

[8] BGU I, 140 = Mitteis–Wilcken, Grundzüge u. Chrestomathie II, 2 (1912), 373: τὸ αὐστηρότερον ὑπὸ τῶν πρὸ ἐμοῦ αὐτοκρατόρων σταθέν (in 119, to Rammius Martialis, Prefect of Egypt). [9] p. 249.

[10] Dio LXIX. 5. 1: ᾐτιῶντο μὲν δὴ ταῦτά τε αὐτοῦ καὶ τὸ πάνυ ἀκριβὲς τό τε περίεργον καὶ τὸ πολύπραγμον. Tiberius Caesar, by contrast, was hostile to governmental action for moral or social improvement.

dismissed, taking with him the blame for the execution of the four consulars. He was given a seat in the Senate, but not a consulship.[1] Marcius Turbo stood high. He had captured the confidence of a suspicious emperor: how long was the 'potentia' of Caesar's equestrian minister likely to endure?[2]

Discord of long date permeated the family circle. Several imperial ladies by their pretensions might be a cause of discomfort; old Servianus, whom the power had passed by, was a visible embarrassment; and the Princeps was confronted by his own presumed successor in the person of Pedanius Fuscus, only ten years his junior. Men of the time, reflecting upon the annals of an earlier dynasty, may have reckoned Pedanius among the ill-starred heirs, doomed to perish while an odious despot survived—'breves et infaustos populi Romani amores'.[3]

Hadrian, so various in his nature, seemed an epitome of all the Caesars from Tiberius to Nero; and not only various, but enigmatic, estranged, and forbidding.[4] His power of dissembling, and the hidden animosities, inevitably evoked the man whom Caesar Augustus in the end had been compelled to designate for empire.[5] No senator could fail to discern (and most would enjoy) the predicament of a ruler coming to the power after delay or frustrations, blighted and resentful under the shadow of his mighty predecessor.

The renown of the Imperator was secure, defended of necessity by Hadrian, and augmented by Hadrian's enemies: if Trajan seemed anywhere at fault, it was through love of fame, a noble infirmity.[6] Hadrian, however, was vulnerable on multiple counts. The surrender of the eastern conquests evoked grief, anger, and calumny. Soon Hadrian's whole foreign policy came in for damaging review—resentment against his predecessor was alleged, and distrust of the marshals. And there was oblique attack, deviating into a variety of themes and colouring men's appraisal of history ever since the days of Augustus.

Warfare in the East or renunciation, that was not the only point of

---

[1] HA, Hadr. 9. 3 (with the allegation that Hadrian wanted to kill him).

[2] cf. III. 30 (on the 'potentia' of Maecenas and Sallustius Crispus).

[3] II. 41. 3. He may have died soon after his consulate (118). His wife Julia, the daughter of Servianus, likewise finds no place in the written record of Hadrian's reign. There was a son, born in 118 (Dio LXIX. 17. 1).

[4] Compare the testimony of Fronto—'ut Martem Gradivum, ut Ditem patrem, propitium et placatum magis volui quam amavi' (p. 25 N = Haines I, p. 110).

[5] For Hadrian's 'dissimulatio', HA, Hadr. 14. 11; Victor, Epit. 14. 6.

[6] For δόξης ἐπιθυμία (Dio LXVIII. 17. 1) cf. F. A. Lepper, Trajan's Parthian War (1948), 191 ff.; M. I. Henderson, JRS XXXIX (1949), 129 f. Dio's defence of Trajan from the reproach of aggressiveness (ib. 7. 5) is flat and conventional.

argument. Dacia offered. Hadrian, so the rumour ran, wished to give up the new province beyond the Danube (envy being the motive). Only the admonition of his counsellors brought him to reason.[1] The story is idle malice: Dacia with its colonists and towns and forts had now existed for a decade, built as a bastion into the system of the Danubian defences. At first a consular command, Dacia was now made praetorian, with a single legion. That act may have impressed the ignorant, who gave no thought to the auxiliary regiments along the frontier. There is no sign that Hadrian cut down the total establishment.[2]

Not all imperial acquisitions were valuable. Some never paid for the cost or hazards of their retention. The notion is typical of the Hadrianic time and heavily emphasized in the peace of the Antonines.[3] Not that it was altogether a novelty. A stray fragment from the *Historiae* of Tacitus alludes to countries annexed at the ends of the world, often to Rome's advantage but sometimes detrimental.[4] Tacitus was writing in the season of Trajan's Dacian conquest. The allusion was equivocal and disquieting—had it not been readily applicable to an earlier dynasty and another region, to the island which Claudius Caesar incorporated in the Empire.[5]

Britain was a dubious asset. That could soon be seen, perhaps without Boudicca's rebellion. And later, despite the conquests achieved by three Flavian generals, the island still needed a large garrison.[6] When the biographer of Julius Agricola wrote history, he had a retreat to chronicle before the end of Domitian's reign.[7]

The stages in the withdrawal towards a short and satisfactory frontier baffle inquiry: it is not clear how much territory was surrendered by Domitian, how much by Trajan. Domitian took away a

---

[1] Eutropius VIII. 6. 2. Dio has a strange story about the removal of the superstructure of the Danube bridge (LXVIII. 13. 6). Some take the proposal to evacuate Dacia very seriously, thus A. v. Premerstein, *Bayerische S-B* (1934), Heft 3, 45. And there can be conjecture about Hadrian's counsellors, invoking the name of Julius Quadratus Bassus, cf. E. Kornemann, *Gestalten u. Reiche* (1943), 317; A. Stein, *Die Reichsbeamten von Dazien* (1944), 17.

[2] cf. R. Syme, *JRS* XLVI (1946), 164.

[3] Florus I. 33. 7: 'plus est provinciam retinere quam facere.' Cf. Appian, *proem*. 6.

[4] Orosius VII. 3. 7: 'ut verbis Corneli Taciti loquar, sene Augusto Ianus patefactus, dum apud extremos terrarum terminos novae gentes saepe ex usu et aliquando cum damno quaeruntur, usque ad Vespasiani duravit imperium.' It is not necessary, but it may be useful, to adduce Florus I. 47. 4: 'Armenios etiam et Britannos, ut non in usum, ita ad imperii speciem magna nomina adquisisse pulchrum ac decorum' (in reference to Augustus).

[5] Compare Appian on Britain, *proem*. 5: τὸ κράτιστον αὐτῆς ἔχουσιν ὑπὲρ ἥμισυ, οὐδὲν τῆς ἄλλης δεόμενοι· οὐ γὰρ εὔφορος αὐτοῖς ἐστιν οὐδ' ἣν ἔχουσι.

[6] Three legions and numerous *auxilia*. For a perhaps too favourable verdict see M. P. Charlesworth, *The Lost Province, or the Worth of Britain* (Gregynog Lectures, 1948: Cardiff, 1949), 41 ff.

[7] *Hist*. I. 2. 1: 'perdomita Britannia et statim missa' (above, p. 124).

legion, and both emperors had their wars to think about.[1] Neglect or over-confidence, a problem subsisted. Trouble might already have broken out before Trajan died.[2] The first years of Hadrian saw warfare, the wastage of troops, and the need for reinforcements.[3]

In 119 the legends of the Roman coinage assert a victory in Britain.[4] However that may be, at some time between 117 and 122 a grave disaster supervened, to join Armenia or Dacia among the topics of talk and speculation (not all of it judicious): a whole legion, IX Hispana, met its end.[5] A faint echo of debates about Britain is perceptible in a contemporary writer, who comes out with a peculiar version of past history: Nero thought of withdrawing the Roman legions from Britain but desisted lest he be thought hostile to the memory of his parent.[6]

Tacitus insists on judging the earlier rulers from the vantage point of Trajanic energy and Trajanic conquest. Reviewing provinces and armies under Tiberius, he must interpose the contrast with his own day: 'quanto sit angustius imperitatum'.[7] There pride speaks, elsewhere a melancholy engendered by what came after the wars of Trajan—unbroken peace and a ruler without any care for extending the Empire.[8]

An affront to Rome's honour might go unpunished because the Emperor feared the generals or grudged them renown; and the Senate did not care.[9] Domitius Corbulo, eager and active beyond the Rhine, was recalled by Claudius Caesar: the general's success would have

---

[1] No clear indications are furnished by the rebuilding in stone of the legionary camps at Isca in 100 (*AE* 1930, 110), Eboracum in 108 (*CIL* VII, 241).

[2] Not much can be based on *HA, Hadr.* 5. 2: 'Britanni teneri sub Romana ditione non poterant.'

[3] Fronto, p. 217 f. N = Haines II, p. 27: 'avo vestro Hadriano imperium obtinente quantum militum ab Iudaeis, quantum ab Britannis caesum.' For the reinforcements, above, p. 247. Note also the concentration of *auxilia*, fifty regiments attested on a diploma of 122 (*CIL* XVI, 69).

[4] BRITANNIA and other martial types in 119 have been taken to prove not only warfare but victory, or even a cessation of hostilities, cf. P. L. Strack, o.c. II (1933), 70; H. Mattingly, o.c. III (1936), clxiii; W. Weber, *CAH* XI (1936), 313 (with errors). Caution is prescribed: and there may have been more campaigns (or disasters) than one before Hadrian's arrival in 122.

[5] p. 247. Replaced by VI Victrix. Readers of the *Annales* would note how IX Hispana was cut to pieces in Boudicca's rebellion (XIV. 32. 3).

[6] Suetonius, *Nero* 18: 'etiam ex Britannia deducere exercitum cogitavit, nec nisi verecundia, ne obtrectare parentis gloriae videretur, destitit.' Some attach value to this passage. It has been argued that Nero formed the design precisely in 58 (and not after Boudicca's revolt), that he dropped it when he read the boastful promises of conquest contained in the testament of the legate Q. Veranius (XIV. 29. 1), cf. C. E. Stevens, *CR* LXV (1951), 4 ff. Against, E. Birley, *Roman Britain and the Roman Army* (1953), 1 ff. It should seem, however, that the passage has more relevance for Hadrian than for Nero.

[7] IV. 4. 3.

[8] IV. 32. 2: 'princeps proferendi imperi incuriosus erat.'

[9] IV. 74. 1: 'clarum inde inter Germanos Frisium nomen, dissimulante Tiberio damna, ne cui bellum permitteret. neque senatus in eo cura an imperii extrema dehonestarentur.'

been no less prejudicial than failure.[1] Cassius Longinus in Syria knew that the times had nothing to offer to military excellence. Peace holds sloth and energy in equal estimation.[2]

At Trajan's call Rome had shaken off its lethargy.[3] After a momentary invigoration, it lapsed again into the old ways, achieving what must, on a long perspective, have seemed foreordained. When Caesar Augustus laid firm and deep the foundations of ordered government, he may have divined, but could not proclaim, the purpose of it all— simply to abolish war and politics. With Hadrianus Augustus the thing was manifest, the evolution at its end.

---

[1] XI. 19. 3: 'sin prospere egisset, formidolosum paci virum insignem et ignavo principi praegravem.'

[2] XII. 12. 1: 'industriosque aut ignavos pax in aequo tenet.' The aphorism, like its context, is strongly Sallustian (p. 355).

[3] Florus, *praef.* 7 (quoted above, p. 218).

XXXVII. TACITUS AND HADRIAN

ROMAN conquest is exalted in the *Annales*. As depicted by Tacitus, Germanicus Caesar foreshadows in splendour and energy a martial emperor. The prince is also the victim of a jealous and suspicious ruler. Tiberius ordered him to desist from his enterprises in Germany (ostensibly so near to the crowning achievement). The Emperor was glad of a pretext to take his rival away from the command of devoted legions.[1] Alleging that he was needed in the eastern lands, Tiberius did his best to impede the legitimate ambitions of the young prince by appointing as governor of Syria Cn. Piso, a a man of intractable temper with a family tradition of hostility to the Caesars.[2] Germanicus and Piso first bickered and then quarrelled fiercely; and the death of Germanicus, with allegations of poison, receives heavy emphasis from the historian in his incrimination of the Emperor.

Otherwise Tacitus had only travel to record, and the peaceful investiture of a vassal king in Armenia. There is tragedy and pathos at the end. Germanicus died suddenly at Antioch, to the great grief of the province and the peoples thereabout. Foreign nations lamented, and kings—such was the clemency and nobility of the young Caesar. And some there were who noted the resemblance to Alexander, in his grace of form, his age, the manner of his end, and even the region in which he met his fate. They went on with the parallel, much to the advantage of Germanicus in the domestic virtues. Nor, as a man of war, was Germanicus inferior—he was not rash, and he was prevented from making an end of the Germans. Had he been sole arbiter of events, with the name and power of a monarch, he would no doubt have gained the military glory consonant with his superiority in virtue to the Macedonian.[3]

The artifice is patent, the laudation grotesque in its disproportion —and the historian evades responsibility. Would he have deprecated a comparison between Alexander and the Imperator who fell ill in Syria and died at Selinus?[4]

Another hero is Domitius Corbulo. When he arrived in the East, he drew all eyes, tall of stature and majestic in language, and he quickly imposed his prestige.[5] Corbulo also possessed that 'auctoritas' which enables a military man to dispense with mere eloquence.[6]

[1] II. 5. I. [2] 43. [3] 73.
[4] For Alexander and Trajan see App. 72. [5] XIII. 8. 3. [6] XV. 26. 3.

Yet the great general did not embark on active warfare for several years. The Parthian monarch immediately sent hostages; and the legions of Syria, lazy and corrupt from long inertia, needed training and discipline. More important, the policy of the Roman government. Tacitus implies all the time that Corbulo was very much a free agent. The inception of hostilities seems put down largely to his credit, and their scope is magnified: nothing less than the reconquest of all that Lucullus and Pompeius had won (so Corbulo thought) was demanded by the power and honour of the Empire.[1]

Roman pride is magnificently evoked when a general announces that he will impose the law of Rome upon the vanquished in place of a phantom monarch.[2] The phrase recalls, and perhaps parodies, Trajan's proclamation when he annexed Armenia.[3] The general was not Domitius Corbulo but his successor, Caesennius Paetus, going forth not to victory but to a careless foray that collapsed in a shameful capitulation.[4]

When Corbulo, to repair the damage with a show of force that should facilitate a political compromise, himself once more entered Armenia the next year, he trod in the steps of Lucullus—so Tacitus avers.[5] It may be observed that Caesennius Paetus had already chosen the identical route, over the river from Melitene.[6]

The enemy fell in with Corbulo's design. Tiridates, the prince who was asserting a claim to Armenia, opened negotiations, and, coming to a conference, removed the diadem from his head and dutifully deposited it beneath an image of Nero. Then the general put on a display of military ritual for the benefit of Tiridates, enhancing the majesty of the spectacle so as to fill him with admiration for the traditional observances of the Romans.[7] Empty pomp and ceremony, however, as the reader is reminded a little further on, belong to the vain predilections of orientals. The Parthian monarch was anxious lest Tiridates his brother suffer any humiliation when he journeyed to Rome for his investiture. The king did not know the Romans—with them all that matters is 'vis imperii'.[8]

Tacitus has made too much of Corbulo, and consequently of the

---

[1] XIII. 34. 2: 'dignum magnitudine populi Romani rebatur parta olim a Lucullo Pompeioque recipere.'

[2] XV. 6. 4: 'se tributa ac leges et pro umbra regis Romanum ius victis impositurum.'

[3] Dio LXVIII. 20. 3: Ῥωμαίων τε γὰρ εἶναι καὶ ἄρχοντα Ῥωμαῖον ἕξειν.

[4] XV. 13 ff. Trajan's armies encountered disasters (in one of which a consular legate perished): there is no record of a capitulation.

[5] XV. 27. 1.

[6] Not stated, but deducible from XV. 8. 1; 10. 3.

[7] XV. 30. 1: 'cuncta in maius attollens admiratione prisci moris affecit.'

[8] 31: 'scilicet externae superbiae sueto non inerat notitia nostri apud quos vis imperii valet, inania tramittuntur.'

Parthians, accepting for his own purposes the conventional estimate of their power as of equivalent imperial rank with the Romans.[1] If he wished, he could have demolished that estimate contemptuously, for he knew the provinces of the West and the northern barbarians.[2]

Tacitus (so it appears) accords undue space and importance to the eastern realms, with no little harm ensuing to the historical estimation of those matters ever after. The broad scene and the energetic general —colour, movement, and the distant peoples—it was irresistible. The regions beyond the Euphrates also engross a generous treatment in the last years of Tiberius and under Claudius. For the author a welcome relief—and lively appeal to the contemporary reader. For example, Seleucia, that renowned and powerful city, ancient Nineveh with the site of Alexander's victory not far away, or an Arsacid prince with Roman support installed at Ctesiphon;[3] and brief annotation touched upon attractive topics like the fabled Hellenic origin of Iberi and Albani, the tactics and equipment of the Sarmatae, and the mountain sanctuary of Hercules in the land of Adiabene.[4]

There is something else—and highly relevant not only to the structure of the *Annales* but to the understanding of the whole eastern question. As the diplomatic strategy of Tiberius Caesar demonstrated, the Parthian could be coerced or intimidated without undue effort. L. Vitellius, his legate in Syria, knew what to do.[5] He stirred up the Iberi or even enticed tribes to come over the Caucasus; a rival candidate took the field; and it was an easy device to disrupt the allegiance of the satraps and vassals. A vigilant reader of the *Annales* would not have to be dazzled and utterly deceived by Domitius Corbulo—or by Trajan the conqueror.

When the general sent by Tiberius Caesar made ready to pass the Euphrates, the natives reported a marvel, the sure sign of a safe crossing: the stream had risen, from no natural causes, and foaming eddies showed the shapes of diadems. The historian insidiously cites another interpretation: portents from rivers are known to be delusive, the enterprise would begin well and come to nothing.[6]

[1] e.g. Strabo XI. 515 (the Parthians as ἀντίπαλοι of the Romans). Tacitus, it is true, has 'vi Parthorum aut potentia Romana' (II. 60. 4); but the phrase 'Romani imperii aemulis' is used by the troops of Caesennius Paetus, alleging justification for a surrender (xv. 13. 2).

[2] *Germ.* 37. 4: 'quid enim aliud nobis quam caedem Crassi, amisso et ipse Pacoro, infra Ventidium deiectus Oriens obiecerit?'

[3] VI. 42. 1 f.; XII. 13. 2; VI. 42. 4.

[4] VI. 34. 2; 35. 1; XII. 13. 3. For Tacitus some of these items would evoke Sallust in the *Historiae*, describing or adorning the campaigns of Lucullus.

[5] VI. 32 ff.

[6] 37. 2: 'quidam callidius interpretabantur, initia conatus secunda neque diuturna,' &c. The normal portent for a conqueror was a sudden ebb in the river Euphrates (Xenophon, *Anabasis* I. 4. 18; Plutarch, *Lucullus* 24, cf. Sallust, *Hist.* IV. 60).

So indeed it befell when Trajan took the field against the Parthians. Glory and victory, effort and hazard, all was in vain.[1] Corbulo too had been a magnificent commander, yet his expeditions were hardly necessary; and the historian allows it to be inferred that Corbulo was pompous and not invariably truthful.[2]

Domitius Corbulo came down like a hurricane.[3] He swept through Armenia, taking Artaxata and taking Tigranocerta, with little opposition from the Armenians, and none from the Parthians. When the incompetence of Caesennius Paetus surrendered a Roman army, the Parthians knew better than to exploit their success to the full: they allowed the army to depart. It was an open secret since Lucullus, Pompeius, and Antonius (and not contradicted by the disaster of Crassus) that a Roman *imperator* could take the legions anywhere. Trajan came like Corbulo. A feeble empire, torn between rival claimants for the throne, succumbed ludicrously before the impact. The Roman invader went on. He could occupy Armenia and Mesopotamia, he might march to Ctesiphon. Could he return in safety?[4]

Defeat found Trajan at a loss. The military emperor who had been used to having his own way everywhere grew angry and intractable. Baffled before Hatra, he threw cavalry against the fortress and exposed his own person ostentatiously.[5] Other errors may be surmised.[6] The shock to Trajan's conceit produced or accelerated a grievous malady (Trajan himself could only put it down to poison).[7] A total collapse ensued. Death overtook the Imperator, mercifully, in his escape from the scene of his failure. He was returning to Rome for the ceremony of a Parthian triumph.

None of the Caesars hitherto had incurred a disaster of that magnitude.[8] Trajan left others to take the blame. That was not all. Obstinacy, the grudge against his kinsman, and a refusal to designate a successor imperilled the fabric of the Empire, and might easily have provoked a civil war.

A man of sombre judgement who could not refuse admiration to Trajan but discerned (perhaps well in advance) certain failings in the autocrat, had a plain duty as an historian. He would have to put on

[1] Dio LXVIII. 33. 1: μάτην ἐπόνησαν καὶ μάτην ἐκινδύνευσαν.
[2] xv. 16. 3.
[3] Lydus, *De mag.* III. 33, citing Celsus (i.e. presumably Marius Celsus, cf. App. 32).
[4] Compare the predicament of later invaders like Gordian III and Julian.
[5] Dio LXVIII. 31.
[6] Trajan seems to have been able to antagonize Greeks, Jews, and Arabs.
[7] Dio LXVIII. 33. 2. For an elaborate diagnosis of Trajan's illness see F. A. Lepper, *Trajan's Parthian War* (1948), 198 ff. The psychological factor tends to be overlooked.
[8] It had been common to speak of Domitian's false triumphs (cf. *Agr.* 39. 2; *Germ.* 37. 6); and Pliny's censure would now have fitted Trajan—'imperator is cuius pulsi fugatique non aliud maius habebatur indicium quam quod triumpharet' (*Pan.* 11. 4).

record somewhere the adequate technique (it had long been known, and was now vindicated) for dealing with the Parthians. Hence the full exposition of Tiberius' measures;[1] and the Claudian books were to reinforce the truth about Parthia.

Similarly, the Roman conquests in Germany. Tacitus is impelled to play up the exploits of Germanicus Caesar—but not without a corrective. The narrative discloses the difficulties, the hazards, and the cost, the little that was achieved even after a victory in the field. Further, the reasons of policy that Tacitus expounds as the gist of Tiberius' letters to Germanicus bear the imprint of sagacity and an incontrovertible moral.[2]

The event soon justified. When the invasions ceased, the German tribes gaily reverted to their normal quarrels. Arminius at once turned on Maroboduus, whose empire collapsed.[3] Arminius, however, could not keep his confederacy together, or even retain primacy among the Cherusci: after four years the hero of the Roman wars was assassinated by his own kinsfolk.[4]

Germanicus Caesar or Domitius Corbulo, the surface of the Tacitean narrations is deceptive. The historian duly adds his contribution to the great contemporary debate on Roman foreign policy. It might have been partisan, and easily predictable. It turns out to be something different—equitable and elusive. For all the pride of empire and the magnificent asseverations, there are unobtrusive signs or hints in the *Annales* that convey the arguments for diplomacy instead of war and battle beyond Rhine or Euphrates. If Tiberius Caesar showed good sense, was it right to condemn out of hand the successor of Trajan?

Hadrian reverted to the procedure that a long tradition commended. Taking Caesar Augustus as his model, he could circumvent the panegyrists of Trajan. The title 'Hadrianus Augustus', upon which he put emphasis after his understanding with the Parthian monarch in 123, was a powerful manifesto;[5] and he boasted that he had achieved much more through peace than had others by arms.[6]

Rome (it could be argued) had nothing to lose by conciliation towards the Arsacids, nothing to fear even from stability in the Parthian dominions. The system of vassal princes, however, exhibited various shortcomings. Rulers appointed by Rome often failed with

---

[1] VI. 32 ff. Further, Vitellius' meeting with the Parthian king at the Euphrates (p. 237) will have been narrated in Book VII.

[2] II. 26. 2 ff.: 'satis iam eventuum, satis casuum', &c. (presumably based upon an oration of Tiberius).

[3] II. 45 f. He was soon a fugitive and an exile (II. 62 f.). Tacitus cites (and does not impugn) Tiberius' estimate of his earlier great power.

[4] II. 88. [5] p. 248.

[6] Victor, *Epit.* 14. 10: 'iactabat palam plus se otio adeptum quam armis ceteros.'

their own people; and some proved untrustworthy.[1] In consequence the imperial power might have to stoop to ignoble devices, sowing discord or benefiting from a murder. That was not a calamity: the disgrace could be lightly borne by men of understanding.[2]

Trajan's irruption disturbed the equilibrium. He deposed some princes; others will have found the Imperator's manner intolerable. Hadrian was at great pains to heal the damage: he was patient and forbearing in all personal dealings with the vassals.[3]

The *Annales* convey the Hadrianic argument—through the mouth of Claudius Caesar. That emperor was clement towards foreign dynasties.[4] Though greatly incensed against Mithridates the ruler of Bosporus, he decided on mercy, for such was the tradition of Rome, and triumphs from broken adversaries are not worth having.[5]

Claudius was able to send out an Arsacid to rule over the Parthians, a certain Meherdates, who had lived for long years as a hostage at Rome. In his oration the Emperor rebuked the pretensions of the Parthians and put himself by act and policy on a level with Augustus (but omitted Tiberius).[6] After sage precepts to the address of the prince, and likewise to the Parthian envoys, Claudius Caesar ended with a firm pronouncement: Rome, having now the fullness of glory, desires only that the nations may abide in peace.[7]

No Tacitean condonation of an inglorious policy could be plain and open. Irony dominates. Tacitus is careful to report what happened to Meherdates, the 'urbis alumnus' (as Claudius styled him), not long after. Defeated by his rival and captured, Meherdates was mutilated—and kept alive for the opprobrium of Rome.[8]

Of Trajan not even the name stands anywhere in the *Annales*.[9]

---

[1] XII. 14. 1: 'levitate gentili et quia experimentis cognitum est barbaros malle Roma petere reges quam habere.'

[2] XII. 48. 2: 'omne scelus externum cum laetitia habendum; semina etiam odiorum iacienda, ut saepe principes Romani eandem Armeniam specie largitionis turbandis barbarorum animis praebuerint.' Such was the conclusion reached by Ummidius Quadratus, the legate of Syria, and his counsellors.

[3] Even towards the ruler of the Iberi who refused to come to meet him (*HA, Hadr.* 13. 9 —not early in the reign).   [4] XII. 20. 1: 'nobilitatibus externis mitis.'

[5] ib. 2: 'verum ita maioribus placitum, quanta pervicacia in hostem, tanta beneficentia adversus supplices utendum; nam triumphos de populis regnisque integris adquiri.' For the source and style of this chapter, App. 40.

[6] 11. 1: 'incipit orationem Caesar de fastigio Romano Parthorumque obsequiis, seque divo Augusto adaequabat, petitum ab eo regem referens, omissa Tiberii memoria.'

[7] ib. 3: 'rem Romanam huc satietate gloriae provectam ut externis quoque gentibus quietem velit.'

[8] 14. 3: 'ostentui clementiae suae et in nos dehonestamento.'

[9] Naturally enough. Some, however, deduce a disappointment with Trajan. For exaggerated notions about Tacitus' political credo and consequent disillusionment see p. 219. The débâcle in the East is another matter.

Tacitus pays homage to the Imperator after his own fashion—and not without ambiguity. Allusion to Hadrian is also covert, but not perhaps always discreet.

Hadrian impinges variously upon the author's thoughts. The treatment of Tiberius at his first presentation betrays disquieting symptoms. Not merely the hints and rumours inserted to the ruler's detriment—Tacitus overloads the narrative and impairs its proportions.[1] Perhaps there is something more—a pervasive influence. In so far as any later emperor coloured his whole portrayal of Tiberius, it might be Hadrian rather than Domitian.[2] Convinced (and with some excuse) of rancour and dissimulation in Hadrian (and unwilling to blame Trajan), Tacitus eagerly embraced a presumption about the heir and successor of Caesar Augustus, and cherished it to excess, despite the reasons that disposed him to approbation of Tiberius —and his avowals (weighty though intermittent) of doubt and perplexity.

At the same time, and conversely, Tacitus from a distant point of vantage should have been able to assess the arduous tasks and unhappy dilemmas that confronted the earlier rulers. Empire, as one of them told his friends, was a monster that had to be faced and mastered.[3] Tacitus might have admitted (could it be known) various palliations for Hadrian. The indulgence, it seems, was slight or muted. Anger and despair silenced charity. Soon or late, each of the Caesars went wrong before the end. Hadrian's reign had not even begun well. It opened with a suspicious adoption, the killing of a *nobilis*, and the execution of four consular marshals. An historian's studies confirmed a senator's insight into men and governments. What had been before would come again, and nothing stood certain except fate or chance and the 'ludibria rerum mortalium cunctis in negotiis'.[4]

An emperor who was also a philosopher meditated upon the eternal recurrence of things. As history is, so it was and shall be. Out of a man's experience or from the chronicle of old times it unfolds before his eyes in a sequence of stage plays. The theatre is the same, only the actors are different.[5]

The writing of history was esteemed a benefit when it abated discord, embellished the past, and strengthened the present age in

---

[1] App. 37.
[2] His conception of Hadrian's character can have taken shape before Trajan's death.
[3] Suetonius, *Tib.* 24. 1: 'ignaros, quanta belua esset imperium.'
[4] III. 18. 4.
[5] M. Aurelius, *Ad se ipsum* x. 27: συνεχῶς ἐπινοεῖν πῶς πάντα τοιαῦτα, ὁποῖα νῦν γίνεται, καὶ πρόσθεν ἐγένετο· καὶ ἐπινοεῖν γενησόμενα. καὶ ὅλα δράματα καὶ σκηνὰς ὁμοειδεῖς, ὅσα ἐκ πείρας τῆς σῆς ἢ τῆς πρεσβυτέρας ἱστορίας ἔγνως, πρὸ ὀμμάτων τίθεσθαι, οἷον αὐλὴν ὅλην Ἁδριανοῦ, κτλ.

felicity and contentment.[1] The epoch of the Julian and Claudian Caesars, however, was something better forgotten: only a chronicle of crime and tyranny, without any valid lesson. No emperor could approve a work like the *Annales* of Cornelius Tacitus. An evil past had come to life again. The evocation was vivid, insidious, and subversive. There are many talents in Tacitus, and one is for satire.

The living were immune. Junius Juvenalis proclaims that his attacks will be confined to those whose ashes are entombed beside the Latin or the Flaminian Way.[2] Of necessity. The poems confirm. Juvenal cannot visit scorn and derision on the men who have wealth and place and power. He anxiously avoids the new aristocracy now dominant, that issued largely from Spain or Narbonensis, and the dynastic houses from the eastern lands.[3] Nor can he touch the themes of imperial policy. Literature or fiction furnish most of his requirements, with an especial debt to the reigns of Nero and Domitian.[4]

Juvenal belonged to a family of equestrian fortune (not much by the standards of the metropolis). He was coeval with Suetonius Tranquillus, and a dozen years junior to Tacitus.[5] The scholarly Suetonius benefited from the patronage of Pliny, but Pliny gives no hint of Juvenal's existence. Suetonius sought, acquired, and then surrendered a post as military tribune—Pliny had solicited the legate of Britain in his favour.[6] Juvenal may (or may not) have served a stage in the 'militia equestris'.[7] He could not resist the call of the metropolis. Martial knew him, and sympathized with his early struggles for advancement.[8] Juvenal frequented the law courts and the schools of rhetoric. Whatever the nature and compass of his ambitions— success, money, a name as an advocate, or an advantageous employment in the imperial secretariat—he suffered some disappointment, with teaching perhaps as the last resort, and the writing of satire as his revenge.[9] No senatorial patrons are honoured in his poems, or even any of the

[1] To have rendered Republican history politically innocuous was one of Livy's principal achievements, cf. H. Dessau, *Gesch. der r. Kaiserzeit* I (1924), 545.

[2] Juvenal I. 170 f.

[3] cf. R. Syme, *Rom. Rev.* (1939), 490. Negative evidence of this kind impairs the view that Juvenal was a sincere and vigorous satirist of contemporary Roman society.

[4] As in the eighth satire, and in the fourth (p. 5).

[5] For his age, App. 74.　　　　　　　　　　　　　　　　　　[6] *Epp.* III. 8. 1.

[7] For the inscr. from the vicinity of Aquinum (*ILS* 2926, not seen since the eighteenth century) see App. 74.

[8] Martial VII. 24 and 91 (in 91 or 92); XII. 18 (100 or 101).

[9] It has been argued that he was banished by Domitian (with lasting effects on his character), see especially G. Highet, *TAPA* LXVIII (1937), 480 ff.; *Juvenal the Satirist* (1954), 23 ff. That view derives (with necessary modifications) from *Scholia* or *Vitae* of late antiquity. The principal *Vita* (in the *Codex Pithoeanus*) cites VII. 90 ff. and asserts that the poet incurred an emperor's resentment through attacks on an actor: 'ac statim per honorem militiae quamquam octogenarius urbe summotus est missusque ad praefecturam cohortis in extrema parte tendentis Aegypti'. A fictitious construction.

high equestrian dignitaries and heads of departments.[1] In the first
line of the seventh of his satires Juvenal appeals to Caesar as the sole
support of polite letters—'et spes et ratio studiorum in Caesare
tantum'. Hadrian gave no encouragement.

The chronology of Juvenal's writings has an importance transcend-
ing the mere biography of a poet. In the first satire he alludes to the
enormities of Marius Priscus, the proconsul of Africa, and the lenience
of exile as a penalty.[2] A recent event (it has been urged), and a clue
for dating. Not at all.[3] The case was notorious—and probably the
latest prosecution of a proconsul of consular rank. Juvenal mentions
Priscus again.[4] Marius Priscus need only be an allusion to a modern
work of classic rank, the letters of Pliny—or to that eminent orator
who was still alive and writing history. There is no proof that Juvenal
published anything before the death of Trajan. Nor is the term of his
literary activity precise. In the penultimate satire he refers to one of
the consuls of 127 as not long ago.[5] If the period of the satires be put
roughly at 115–30, a conclusion of some interest emerges. For a part at
least of the way the satires of Juvenal run parallel with the *Annales*: a
name, a theme, or an incident here and there might derive from Tacitus.[6]

Not that the satirist need be supposed deeply in the debt of the
historian, or catching from him the notion that a savage indignation
might profitably glut itself upon the dead. Tacitus and Juvenal could
be regarded as parallel and coeval phenomena. Style, tone, and sentiments are comparable. Juvenal has point and concentration, command of rapid narrative and of pictorial evocation—and a dramatic
power supremely manifested in scenes like the fall of Seianus or the
demoniac energy of a debauch.[7]

Remorseless preaching of the ancestral morality, denunciation of
vice, and sloth, and foreigners—the national Roman spirit speaks with
a fervour and a fury never known to the conquering Republic or to
the pride of the Augustan Empire. It was now on the defensive,
passionately insistent on ancient virtue and ancient heroism. Loud
and perhaps over-loud in their protestations, Juvenal and Tacitus
betray symptoms of defeat or insecurity. They are the last great names
in the literature of the Romans.[8]

Political oratory had been perpetuated for a season, as it were, in
the shape of political history. That ended now. Erudite compilation

---

[1] At least so far as can be established. The persons addressed in the last five poems look
like real persons, viz. Corvinus, Calvinus, Fuscinus, Volusius Bithynicus, and Gallius.

[2] I. 49 f.   [3] App. 75.   [4] VIII. 120.

[5] xv. 27, cf. XIII. 17 (discussed in App. 74).

[6] App. 75.   [7] x. 54 ff.; VI. 314 ff.

[8] cf. C. Merivale, *History of the Romans under the Empire* VIII (1876), 132 f.

held the field, gossip writing, or ethical tracts. Suetonius conceived
the notion of an encyclopedia to embrace the whole of Latin literature
arranged biographically (and not omitting the grammarians and professors).[1] The device, which was congenial to his talents, may have
suggested another enterprise. Suetonius went on to describe the lives
and habits of the Caesars, with a predilection for odd and scandalous
detail.[2]

The documentation was formidable—even extracts which Suetonius
culled from the private correspondence of the Julio–Claudian dynasty.
His occupation helped, with access to the archives—for Suetonius
after the tentative or thwarted aspirations of a scholar's existence,
wavering between books and a career, in the end slipped into the
secretariat after the accession of Hadrian.[3] He became Hadrian's
adviser 'a studiis'. Then he was put in charge of the imperial libraries
at Rome. Before long he acquired the important office 'ab epistulis'.
Suetonius' patron was a friend of the deceased Pliny, namely
Septicius Clarus, who became commander of the Guard in 119;
and along with Septicius he lost favour and employ in 122, when the
Emperor was in Britain.[4]

The work *De vita Caesarum* bore a dedication to Septicius, apparently with the title of his prefecture.[5] Six books, one for each
ruler, embraced the Caesars in their dynastic sequence from the
Dictator to Nero: a fitting term and climax, rounded off with a
brief epilogue about a spurious Nero.[6] Suetonius furnished two more
books, one for the three emperors of the year 69, the other for the
three Flavians, concluding an epoch and announcing a happier
season.[7] The sequel of emperors after Nero might be a later addition.[8]

The *Vitae* vary greatly in value, the furthest from his own lifetime
being the best, for they demanded less original work. Though precise
with detail concerning the emperors after Augustus, Suetonius is
chary in citation of authorities. Of the Roman annalists subsequent
to Livy, he names only one, precisely Cremutius Cordus.[9] For his

[1] It is here assumed that *De viris illustribus* is prior to the imperial biographies. It need
not be the work that Pliny incited Suetonius to publish (*Epp.* v. 10).

[2] Objectivity could cover prurience as well as detraction. But it would prove nothing
that this polymath also wrote περὶ ἐπισήμων πορνῶν (Lydus, *De mag.* III. 64).

[3] See now the details provided by the honorific inscription set up by the people of Hippo
Regius (*AE* 1953, 73).

[4] For sundry problems of chronology, App. 76.   [5] Lydus, *De mensibus* II. 6.

[6] *Nero* 57. 2. The continuation begins with 'progenies Caesarum in Nerone defecit'
(*Galba* 1).

[7] *Dom.* 23. 2: 'sicut sane brevi evenit, abstinentia et moderatione insequentium principum.'

[8] This could only be conjecture—but would be helpful if *Divus Titus* 4. 1 depends on
autopsy, cf. App. 76.

[9] *Divus Aug.* 35. 2 (for a fact); *Tib.* 61. 3 (without the name); *Cal.* 16. 1.

information, Suetonius had recourse to a great variety of sources. Method and design separated him from the historians—and the master of erudite technique may not have been reluctant to enhance the divergence, to parade a familiarity with abstruse documents, and sometimes to read them a lesson in the art of verification.[1]

Common sources were employed by Suetonius and by Tacitus, notably for the year of Tiberius' accession and for the year 69. The biographer may, or may not, have drawn upon the senatorial historian. He has been discreet—perhaps of set purpose. No single instance can be certified: at the most, perhaps veiled allusions expressing disagreement with the eminent consular.[2]

Suetonius estimated correctly the taste and market of the times. Readers were drawn to the personal items that formal history disdained.[3] There was room for a rival or supplement to the *Annales*—and the chronicle of ancient folly and depravity, compiled by a government official, carried no political danger.

Another feature of the age was a reaction against all writers of the Empire, not merely the most recent. Men were already conducting a retreat a long way into the past. A taste for Sallust was respectable and laudable. Hadrian preferred Coelius Antipater.[4] Hadrian was only twenty years younger than Tacitus. Yet Hadrian and others were going back beyond Cicero to Cato for oratory; they neglected Virgil, they extolled Ennius. Before long, archaistic predilections in vocabulary and style were matched by a discreet enthusiasm for suburban archaeology, sentimentally effusive about the quaint relics or ruins in the towns of early Latium.[5] Such pursuits could inspire no joy or vigour. There was nothing worth doing, and nothing worth writing about.[6]

The especial glory of the times was Cornelius Fronto (an orator and the tutor of an emperor) whom the virtues of the plain style cannot redeem from a feeble aridity.[7] Fronto pronounced upon

[1] *Divus Aug.* 7. 1 (the 'imaguncula' of the young Octavius, with the inscription attesting the *cognomen* 'Thurinus', which Suetonius gave to Hadrian); *Cal.* 8 (epigraphic evidence about the place and date of a Caesar's birth); *Nero* 52 (autographs of poems). The last item is relevant to *Ann.* XIV. 16. 1. For Suetonius' deliberate opposition to the historians, observe the sagacious remarks of Boissier, *Tacite* (1903), 96 f. [2] App. 77.

[3] For the growing interest in physical appearance and physiognomy cf. E. C. Evans, *Harvard Studies* XLVI (1935), 43 ff.; J. Cousin, *Rev. ét. lat.* XXXI (1953), 234 ff.

[4] *HA, Hadr.* 16. 6.

[5] M. Aurelius writes about an archaic religious inscription at Anagnia (Fronto, p. 66 N = Haines I, p. 174). Antoninus Pius was born at Lanuvium (*HA, Pius* I. 8), and other rulers liked living there. For Roman and Italian antiquities on the coins of Pius (in contrast to Hadrian's cosmopolitanism) see J. M. C. Toynbee, *CR* XXXIX (1925), 170 ff.

[6] E. Norden, *Die antike Kunstprosa* I (1898), 344.

[7] For his style, E. Norden, o.c. 362 ff. Fronto is overvalued on most counts by E. K. Rand in *CAH* XII (1939), 572 ff.

history as upon other topics, and he conceded that it ought to be written with splendour.[1] He even composed a stylized and laudatory history.[2] Fronto discusses Sallust very frequently, and comments with approbation upon the early annalists.[3] But no mention of Tacitus.[4] A long oblivion covered his name and writings.[5]

Nor did any Roman annalist or political historian take up the inheritance of Tacitus. When, in the age of turmoil after the peace of the Antonines, one of the marshals of Septimius Severus, a certain Marius Maximus, turned to authorship, he evaded the true subject and confined himself to the biographies of emperors, continuing Suetonius.[6] Contemporary events ought to have pulled a man back to the theme and manner of the consular historian. The past had returned, bringing the fate of a dynasty that had lasted for a century, the brief interlude before emperors were proclaimed by the armies, the sequence of wars.[7]

The type and model of Suetonius Tranquillus prevailed for centuries in the literature of the Latins, with late exponents in the line of Marius Maximus.[8] If biography is cheap and easy, so is edification. The age of Hadrian set the tone. An epitome or school manual provided a vehicle for conveying history without exertion or genuine enlightenment. A person called Florus set down the record of all the wars of the Romans from Romulus to Caesar Augustus.[9] The tone is pious and ecstatic, condensed Livy.

[1] p. 126 N = Haines II, p. 142: 'historia tamen potius splendide perscribenda.'

[2] On the exploits of L. Verus in the Parthian War.

[3] p. 113 f. N = Haines II, p. 48.

[4] It may afford entertainment to compare the feeble and imperfect remarks of Fronto on the eloquence of the Caesars (p. 123 N = Haines I, pp. 136 f.) with *Ann.* XIII. 3. 2.

[5] F. Haverfield, *JRS* VI (1916), 196 ff. See also App. 88. The letters of Pliny fare much worse in late antiquity, cf. S. E. Stout, *TAPA* LXXXVI (1955), 250 ff.

[6] For this person (*PIR*[1], M 233), consul suffect c. 198, and his writings, cf. G. Barbieri, *Riv. di fil.* LXXXI (1953), 36 ff.; 262 ff.

[7] A Latin historian of the Severan age, comparable to Tacitus, and in some respects superior, was invented by E. Kornemann, *Kaiser Hadrian und der letze große Historiker von Rom* (1905), 119. There was only the Greek senator Cassius Dio, almost the exact coeval of Marius Maximus.

[8] viz. the *Historia Augusta*. The heir of Tacitus, in every sense, is Ammianus Marcellinus, 'a principatu Caesaris Nervae exorsus' (XXXI. 16. 9).

[9] Annius Florus, or Annaeus Florus (*PIR*[2], A 650).

XXXVIII. TACITUS AND THE GREEKS

IF Latin letters declined, Greek civilization now rose again and flourished exuberantly. Its notable heralds were Dio Cocceianus and the amiable Plutarch—the sophist of Prusa and the sage of Chaeronea. Dio came to Rome and prospered, being taken up by a person of high rank. His patron—a cousin of Domitian—was condemned to death, and Dio was banished.[1] He travelled widely, and, returning under Nerva, soon earned the esteem of Trajan. The talents of Dio were variously exemplified—mythology and moral homily for the guidance of an emperor, exhortation of rival cities to peace and concord, and a firm deprecation of unrest among the poor.

The fame and wealth of Dio did not escape the envy and hatred of his fellow citizens.[2] The life of Plutarch passed without disturbance. A young student at Athens when Nero visited Greece, he lived on into the reign of Hadrian.[3] The governing class at Rome approved his doctrines, and the friend of the proconsuls proclaimed the harmony and parity of the two peoples in a sequence of historical biographies, Roman worthies paralleled with Greek.

Other scholars were not so usefully employed. This was not a renascence of science and of learning, of history or poetry: only eloquence, though it might carry the mask of philosophy.[4] Perceptible under the Flavian dynasty, the movement gains strength in the time of Trajan. Pliny happens nowhere to mention the teachings of Dio or of Plutarch; but Nicetes of Smyrna had been his instructor in rhetoric, and he chronicles with applause the advent of Isaeus at the beginning of Trajan's reign.[5] Tacitus was immune and hostile—the *Dialogus* has a cutting reference to the Asiatic declaimers.[6] Other senators were attracted, both the Italian and the provincial.

The Romans from the western provinces not only strengthened the governmental order—they were now in control. Yet by paradox they might seem (some of them at least) to be agents for the furtherance of Greek civilization rather than Roman. Their addiction to the higher

---

[1] For the essential facts, *PIR²*, D 93. His patron was T. Flavius Sabinus, the consul of 82 (cf. *PIR²*, F 355).

[2] Dio, *Or.* XLVI. 6 f. (rioting at Prusa); cf. also Pliny, *Epp.* X. 81 (his rivals and enemies). For his wealth, *Or.* XLVI. 5 ff.; his family, XLIV. 3 f.

[3] K. Ziegler, P-W XXI, 639 ff. His full name is (L.) Mestrius Plutarchus (*SIG³* 829, cf. 844), patently derived from L. Mestrius Florus (*suff.* c. 72).

[4] For the shady side of the 'Greek Renaissance' see Wilamowitz, *Der Glaube der Hellenen* II (1932), 458 ff.

[5] *Epp.* VI. 6. 3 (Nicetes); II. 3. 1 (Isaeus).   [6] *Dial.* 15. 3 (p. 115).

education was largely the cause. Plutarch had eminent Romans for friends and patrons, among them members of Pliny's circle, such as Sosius Senecio and Minicius Fundanus.¹ The Greek influence grew stronger and deeper. It was strikingly manifested in the generation of men some twenty years junior to Tacitus. Hadrian was passionately devoted to everything that was Greek.

The professors soon came to dominate the age. They paraded before their worshippers at international festivals, and famous cities might compete for the honour of a sophist's birthplace, the advantage of his lectures and his residence. They guided governments by persuasion and counsel, led embassies, and rose to be friends and favourites of the Caesars. Trajan had not disdained them; and, whatever his personal tastes, he saw their utility for advertising contentment with the Roman government.² Hadrian stood out as their patron, their accomplice—and even their rival. Rewards and renown were exorbitant. A single fact will symbolize a whole period—in 143 Herodes Atticus *consul ordinarius*, with Cornelius Fronto among the *suffecti* of the year.³

Fronto, the pride of Latin eloquence, came from the colony of Cirta in Numidia. Herodes was the great Athenian sophist, a millionaire, and a very nasty fellow.⁴ If the productions of the Greek publicists, to judge by survivals or surmise, were generally feeble or bombastic (and the nullity of Favorinus, for example, is convincingly attested),⁵ their conceit and arrogance knew no bounds. A Roman magistrate might have to give way. Polemo, returning to Smyrna, found that his mansion had been occupied by Aurelius Fulvus, proconsul of Asia. He evicted the intruder. The mild Aurelius bore no malice.⁶

The pretensions of the sophists were often inflated by pedigree as well as by worldly success. Polemo belonged to that family of Laodicea —it displayed wealth and eloquence even then—which had supplied

¹ K. Ziegler, P-W xxi, 687 ff. (the full list). Along with Sosius and Minicius, T. Avidius Quietus (*suff.* 93) and his brother (the parent of C. Avidius Nigrinus) deserve special mention (*PIR*², A 1410; 1407). Plutarch's consular friends cover a wide span, from Mestrius Florus, with whom he visited the battlefield of Bedriacum (*Otho* 14), to Minicius Fundanus (proconsul of Asia, 122/3).

² For Trajan and Dio, p. 40. Plutarch in his *Praec. ger. r.p.* (17. 813 ff.) insisted that the Greeks should always remember that they were subject to the authority of Rome, and be careful not to provoke government encroachment through the πλεονεξία καὶ φιλοτιμία τῶν πρώτων.

³ Less spectacular, perhaps, but no less significant are the *ordinarii* of the previous year, L. Cuspius Pactumeius Rufinus from Pergamum (*PIR*², C 1637) and L. Statius Quadratus, an Athenian (cf. *IG* ii², 2044; 3704, &c.).

⁴ P. Graindor, *Un milliardaire antique. Hérode Atticus et sa famille* (Cairo, 1930). For the bare facts about Ti. Claudius Atticus Herodes, *PIR*², C 802.

⁵ See the tract Περὶ φυγῆς (P. *Vat. gr.* 11).

⁶ Philostratus, *Vit. soph.* i. 25. 3. This proconsul is the future emperor Antoninus Pius (*cos.* 120).

Antonius and Augustus with a capable ruler over vassal kingdoms.[1] Though a few among the sophists (and especially the earlier) made their mark by talent alone, most of them derived from old dynastic or sacerdotal families, claiming descent from the founders of cities. While the Roman peace revived the prosperity of the world, and of the eastern lands in particular, the benefits went to a minority, and the rich grew richer.[2]

Rome in the past controlled the Empire through oligarchies in the cities, chieftains and dynasts in the country districts. Socially equal though local magnates might then be with the Roman governing order, and acceptable through birth, wealth, and education, they were not political equals. Their descendants, first through the patronage of the Caesars, and then by their own mass and importance, invade the Senate and help to rule the Empire. The new imperial aristocracy, in its Antonine development, embodies the alliance of the propertied classes, east and west, in concord under the monarchy.

The arms of Rome and the arts of Hellas, such, in the world empire, was the correct and predictable partnership. It worked out otherwise. Orientals of Greek speech and habit as consuls and proconsuls— that was more than had been expected. Whose the praise or blame? An easy indictment would lie against Hadrian, that 'Graeculus'. Justice and a few facts disclose a paradoxical revelation about the military emperor, his predecessor.[3]

The emergence of the Greeks in the governing class at Rome marks the culmination of the many triumphs of Hellenic civilization. The process is long and intricate, with many factors operating. It concerns literature and education as well as money, power, and government; and it is best conveyed not by abstractions but by persons and by social classes.

The Principate exhibits a dual origin. On the one hand, Pompeius and Antonius with the vassal princes and imperial resources of the eastern lands. On the other, Caesar victorious with the legions of Gaul, and Caesar's heir prevailing, not only through the arms of the West but with patriotic Roman sentiment behind him, in part genuine, in part mustered, enforced, and advertised.

[1] Polemo, son of the orator Zeno, and King of Pontus, *PIR*[1], P 405; Antonius Polemo the Sophist, *PIR*[2], A 862.

[2] For the wealth of the eastern provinces in the Flavio–Antonine period, as shown especially by buildings and donations, D. Magie, *Roman Rule in Asia Minor* I (1950), 582 ff.; for στάσις, ib. 599 ff.; on the role and behaviour of the πρῶτοι, J. H. Oliver, *Transactions of the American Philosophical Society*, N.S. XLIII, 4 (1953), 953 ff.; for magnates who got into trouble, above, p. 467.

[3] P. Lambrechts, *L'Antiquité classique* v (1936), 105 ff.; for the whole process, down to Marcus Aurelius, C. S. Walton, *JRS* XIX (1929), 38 ff.

Antonius had surrendered the dominions of the Roman People to foreign princes. The system survived, and most of the personnel. Caesar's heir, reconquering the East for Rome, became ruler of Egypt in his own person. Elsewhere the principal creatures of Antonius were kept and used—Polemo of Pontus, Archelaus the monarch of Cappadocia, the Galatian Amyntas, and Herod the Idumaean. When the victor of Actium completed his ordering of the eastern lands, the Roman provincial territory in Asia covered a smaller area than at any time since Pompeius.

If the Caesars, duly inheriting the *clientelae* of Pompeius Magnus and Antonius, attached the kings and dynasts to their following, they did not neglect the educated classes in the cities. The great exemplar was Theophanes of Mytilene whom Magnus took up, to be the chronicler of his military exploits and counsellor in politics.[1]

Here as elsewhere the Principate of Caesar Augustus is double-faced. It stands as the firm champion of Italy against the East, yet it is a monarchy in the East. Nor can Rome even pretend to be hostile to everything that is Greek. In arts and letters the age is all for classical Hellas against contemporary Hellenism. In fact Caesar Augustus disdains old Hellas, now weak and impoverished, and extends his favour to the chief men among the Greeks in Asia. The one exception is noteworthy, Eurycles the dynast of Sparta.[2]

Italian and Greek for ages past had met and mingled in Campania, Magna Graecia, and Sicily. There was another factor. Italians, self-exiled for profit in the eastern lands and long domiciled in the prosperous cities of Ionia and Phrygia during the great dispersal in the last age of the Republic, might return to display their talents in the rhetorical schools of the capital or seek employment from the central government in posts where local knowledge helped.[3]

The astute and opulent natives are more prominent. Augustus knew how to employ certain philosophers or men of letters—for their skilled advice, for the education of young princes, to manage his finances in Sicily, or to superintend the turbulent city of Tarsus.[4] The next emperor was accessible to the claims of scholarship and integrity,

---

[1] R. Laqueur, P–W v A, 2090 ff.

[2] Strabo VIII. 363: ὁ καθ' ἡμᾶς τῶν Λακεδαιμονίων ἡγεμών. Cf. further 366 (though this is no place to discuss the text of that passage, the position of C. Julius Eurycles, or the vicissitudes of the family).

[3] Also, in due course, Romans from the colonies founded in the East by Caesar, Antonius, and Augustus.

[4] See especially the evidence about Areus of Alexandria and Athenodorus, son of Sandon, of Tarsus (*PIR*², A 1035; 1288). Nestor, the tutor of Augustus' nephew Marcellus, went back to his native Tarsus, there to hold a primacy like that of Athenodorus (Strabo XIV. 675).

both of which qualities he found embodied in Thrasyllus the great astrologer, his companion at Rhodes and at Capreae.[1] Otherwise he disliked Greeks for their pretensions, their intrigues, and their adulation. Tiberius had not forgotten the ingratitude of old Archelaus the king of Cappadocia—who was summoned to Rome, arraigned before the Senate, and deprived of his kingdom.[2] And the descendants both of Theophanes and of Eurycles came to grief later in the reign.[3]

With Caligula the cause of Antonius revives, in a premature fashion and mainly ridiculous. Himself in the descent of the Triumvir, Caligula was proud of his ancestry on that side, scornful of the other.[4] Greek influences on his habits and policy derive from two sources. First of all, to abet him in extravagance, were the oriental princes (one of them his cousin) in whose company he grew up at the house of his grandmother Antonia.[5] Next, the freedmen of the imperial household, curbed and unobtrusive under Tiberius, but asserting their mastery over a young and inexperienced ruler. The arrogant Pallas was a descendant of kings in Arcadia, so he alleged.[6]

Neither topic lost relevance with the accession of Claudius. He, too, was under the control of the freedmen, his ministers, and he owed a great debt to one of the princes: Julius Agrippa managed the negotiations with the Senate when it made a vain bid for freedom—or rather for some candidate not of the dynasty—after the assassination of Caligula.[7]

When Claudius went to Britain, he took with him the faithful Xenophon of Cos to watch over his health.[8] The astrologer Balbillus was also of the company.[9] Those men, and others, held posts in the 'militia equestris'.[10] Furthermore, and suitably, members of the

[1] C. Cichorius, *Römische Studien* (1922), 390 ff.; W. Gundel, P–W VI A, 581 ff. Cichorius argues that Ennia Thrasylla (*PIR²*, E 65) is his grand-daughter, the wife of (Q. Naevius) Macro, Prefect of the Guard after Seianus. Thrasyllus wrote on Platonism, and may have edited Plato's works (Gundel, o.c. 583).

[2] II. 42. 2 f.   [3] VI. 18. 2 (cf. App. 62).   [4] Suetonius, *Cal.* 23. 1.

[5] Ptolemaeus the king of Mauretania (*PIR¹*, P 764) was a grandson of Antonius and Cleopatra.   [6] XII. 53. 2.

[7] Josephus, *AJ* XIX. 236 ff. The role of M. Julius Agrippa has perhaps been exaggerated, cf. V. Scramuzza, *The Emperor Claudius* (1940), 58.

[8] *SIG³* 804 (C. Stertinius Xenophon).

[9] *AE* 1924, 78 (Ephesus). It is here asssumed, despite the objections of Stein, that this man, the Prefect of Egypt in 55 (*PIR²*, C 813) is the same person as Balbillus the astrologer (B 38). For a summary of controversial views about identities see now D. Magie, *Roman Rule in Asia Minor* II (1950), 1398 ff. For a link with the royal line of Commagene see *PIR²*, C 1086, with stemma. Cichorius argued that Balbillus is the son of the astrologer Thrasyllus (*Römische Studien* (1922), 393 ff.). The poetess Julia Balbilla, who visited Egypt in Hadrian's retinue, was descended from the royal line of Commagene and from Βάλβιλλος ὁ σοφός (*CIG* 4730: Thebes).

[10] Thus Xenophon's brother, and his uncle (*SIG³* 805 f.); C. Julius Spartiaticus, grandson of Eurycles (*AE* 1927, 1); Ti. Claudius Dinippus (*AE* 1917/18, 1 f.).

aristocratic and dynastic families can now expect governmental employment in the eastern lands.[1]

The current gains force under Nero. In 55 Balbillus is appointed to the prefecture of Egypt.[2] Greeks are high in favour at court;[3] and a man from the Greek East enters the Roman Senate.[4] When Nero fell, Julius Alexander, a renegade Jew, was governing Egypt.[5]

Julius Alexander managed the proclamation of Vespasian at the right moment; and he acted as deputy in command to Titus at the siege of Jerusalem.[6] Orientals were now serving as tribunes in the legions. They benefited, like other adherents. At least one of them was at once given senatorial rank by the new emperor: Julius Celsus (from Ephesus or Sardes).[7] An opulent man from Pergamum, Julius Quadratus, also entered the Senate.[8]

Flavian policy towards the eastern lands could not be all of one piece. Vespasian had ready support from vassal princes and Greek cities; but Vespasian revoked Nero's benefaction to the province of Achaia and abolished local liberties elsewhere. His taxes were hated, and his person despised.

Happier prospects offered from his sons, educated in the full Hellenic stream of Neronian Rome. The elder was fluent in the language (prose or verse), and he had a talent for song and music. For which reasons—and for others—men opined that he would turn out a second Nero.[9] And, if that were not enough, there was the foreign woman, Berenice. The younger had not been long on the throne when he ordained the Capitoline Games: most items of that festival were patently Hellenic.[10] This at Rome; and by an honour accepted from

[1] The origin of the Prefect of Egypt Cn. Vergilius Capito is disputed, cf. A. Stein, *Die Präfekten von Ägypten* (1950), 31. L. Robert argues that he is from Miletus, *Hellenica* VII (1949), 209: he is probably Italian ultimately. One might well wonder about his predecessor, C. Julius Postumus; and, for that matter, there is C. Julius Aquila, in the time of Augustus, cf. *Rom. Rev.* (1939), 367: perhaps of a Pontic family, cf. the C. Julius Aquila of *ILS* 5883 (nr. Amastris), procurator of Bithynia–Pontus in 57/8 (*IGR* III, 15).

[2] XIII. 22. 1.

[3] G. Schumann, *Hellenistische und griechische Elemente in der Regierung Neros* (Diss. Leipzig, 1930); A. Momigliano, *CAH* x (1934), 727. C. Caecina Tuscus (*PIR²*, C 109) should not be included without proof.

[4] L. Servenius Cornutus from Acmonia in Phrygia (*MAMA* VI, 254; 262 = *ILS* 8817): his mother is Julia Severa, probably belonging to a dynastic family of Ancyra. Also perhaps M. Plancius Varus (*PIR¹*, P 334), cf. inscriptions from Perge in Pamphylia (e.g. *BSA Papers* XVII (1911), 246), and others from the city gate (A. Müfid Mansel, *Anadolu* II (1955), 61).

[5] For this remarkable man see A. Stein, P–W x, 153 ff.; E. G. Turner, *JRS* XLIV (1954), 54 ff.

[6] Josephus, *BJ* v. 45, &c. *P. Hibeh* 215 describes him as γενομένου καὶ ἐπάρχου πραι[τωρίου], which, so E. G. Turner argues (o.c. 61 ff.), indicates, not the command under Titus at Jerusalem, but the Guard Prefecture at Rome, shortly afterwards. That does not have to be.

[7] *ILS* 8971.

[8] *ILS* 8819.

[9] Suetonius, *Divus Titus* 3, cf. 7. 1.

[10] Suetonius, *Dom.* 4.

the Athenians (it was a startling novelty) the emperor graciously advertised a general benevolence towards the arts and letters of Hellas.[1]

Furthermore, Domitian's reign exhibits a decisive turn in the fortunes of oriental senators. Not only was an earlier group, the descendants of Theophanes, coming to the fore again.[2] Recent entrants rose to the consulship. For all their already proved utility to the imperial government, these men might have missed the supreme reward but for chance, Domitian's emergencies, and certain perils revealed in the year 89. The emperor saw a way to conciliate sentiment in the eastern aristocracies and counteract the popularity that Nero's memory continued to enjoy.[3]

The first of the oriental consuls was Julius Celsus who, passing through the official hierarchy, commanded a legion and governed provinces.[4] In 92 he reached the consulate. Two years later comes the turn of Julius Quadratus.[5] Before long the descendants of kings and tetrarchs, deriving from the Galatian lords, from Attalus the King, from the dynasties of Judaea, Cappadocia, Armenia, Commagene, and Cilicia, will sit in the Senate of Rome and command the armies of the Roman People.[6]

Trajan went much further than Domitian, and rapidly. To his friend Julius Quadratus he gave the governorship of Syria and a second consulate; and he admitted a number of men from the Greek East to the career of honours or promoted them by adlection. Not many, perhaps, in a Senate of six hundred or more, but of high distinction. Most of the eastern senators before Hadrian belong to dynastic or regal houses. Thus Julius Quadratus Bassus, who led Roman armies to the conquest of Dacia and governed the provinces of Cappadocia and Syria.[7] This man is linked with a powerful nexus of

---

[1] *IG* II², 1996 (the Athenian archonship): the only other reigning emperor to accept the honour was Gallienus. Domitian also rebuilt the Temple of Apollo at Delphi (*ILS* 8905).

[2] In the person of M. Pompeius Macrinus Theophanes (*suff.* 100 or 101). For his career, *IG* v, 1, 151. See also App. 62. The Euryclids come a little later, with C. Julius Eurycles Herculanus (P–W x, 580 ff.). And Q. Pompeius Falco (*suff.* 108) adds Euryclid items to his nomenclature (*ILS* 1035—not in 1035a). Why, it is far from clear.

[3] There was a false Nero about this time (Suetonius, *Nero* 57. 2).   [4] *ILS* 8971.

[5] *ILS* 8819. Quadratus had been legate of Lycia–Pamphylia, Celsus of Cilicia. Those appointments (which carried a promise of consulships) will have been made c. 89.

[6] Compare the genealogy of C. Julius Severus of Ancyra (*OGIS* 544)—Attalid, and from three Galatian princes. The Trajanic consular 'King Alexander' (ib. and *ILS* 8823) derives from a small dynasty in Cilicia Aspera, cf. Josephus, *AJ* XVIII. 140 (with the emendation of A. Wilhelm): for his ancestry (Cappadocian, Armenian, and Jewish), Groag in P–W x, 151. C. Julius Philopappus (*suff.* 109) is descended from the royal line of Commagene, which had Seleucid and Armenian blood (cf. *OGIS* 405); for the pedigree of Ti. Julius Alexander Berenicianus (*suff.* 116), who is related to King Alexander, see A. Stein, P–W x, 157.

[7] pp. 54, 243 f., cf. App. 14. The precise relationship of this man (*suff.* 105) to A. Julius Quadratus (*suff.* 94, *II ord.* 105) cannot be established.

families.[1] Like Vespasian's proclamation by the eastern armies, Trajan's war would accelerate the process. The Julius Alexander who fought the Parthians and captured Seleucia is either of royal stock or a grandson of the Jewish renegade.[2]

Trajan's father commanded a legion under Vespasian in Judaea and governed provinces in the East; and Trajan, defrauded of his Parthian War when a military tribune, had it at the end when he ruled the world. That war carried a splendid pretext to inspire and exalt the eastern half of the dual empire—the age-old quarrel taken up, Rome no longer the oppressor of the Greeks but a friend and a champion, revenge upon the Persian and the Mede, and a new Alexander.

The customary and normal scorn of a Roman for any contemporary Greeks must now undergo some abatement or disguise. Juvenal derides the needy adventurer—smooth, versatile, and corrupt—outwitting by low devices the ethical and dignified Roman.[3] Superior material was waiting for a genuine satirist, namely the great sophists in their greed and vanity—the voluble Favorinus who was a eunuch (or rather perhaps a hermaphrodite);[4] the intolerable Polemo, in perambulation from country to country with a princely household, with horses and hunting dogs;[5] the virtuous Dio rebuking the indigent at Prusa with the assertion that poverty is the mother of orderly behaviour.[6] Juvenal did not dare to use it. Nor could he touch the descendants of kings and tetrarchs.

The pride of nationalism found its most passionate adepts among Romans of municipal or provincial extraction, with many to echo Cato in aversion from a people of talkers, triflers, and technicians. 'Vitiorum omnium genitores', thus did the elder Pliny stigmatize the Greeks, because they used olive oil at their gymnastics.[7] But it is for Greek doctors that he reserves, like Cato, his fiercest tirades.[8]

The sentiments of Tacitus do not evade forecast.[9] No educated Roman could deny the intellectual primacy of Hellas, the magnitude

---

[1] Julius Severus (who entered the Senate under Hadrian) describes himself, among other things, as ἀνέψιον ὑπατικῶν Ἰουλίου τε Κοδράτου καὶ βασιλέως Ἀλεξάνδρου καὶ Ἰουλίου Ἀκύλου καὶ Κλ. Σεουήρου καὶ συγγενῆ συγκλητικῶν πλείστων (OGIS 544).

[2] p. 239. Perhaps Ti. Julius Alexander Julianus (suff. 117), rather than C. Julius Alexander Berenicianus (suff. 116), who is preferred by A. Stein, P–W x, 158.

[3] Juvenal III. 60 ff.

[4] Philostratus, Vit. soph. I. 8. 1; 25. 9, cf. the robust retort of a Cynic philosopher (Lucian, Demonax 12).

[5] Philostratus, Vit. soph. I. 25. [6] Or. XLVI. 11: ἡ γὰρ ἔνδεια σωφροσύνην ποιεῖ.

[7] NH xv. 19, cf. Silius, Punica xiv. 136 ff.

[8] NH xxiv. 4; xxix. 14. The hostility of Cato to all things Greek has been uncritically exaggerated: see D. Kienast, Cato der Zensor (1954), 115 f.

[9] For this theme see B. Hardinghaus, Tacitus und das Griechentum (Diss. Münster, 1932).

of the debt owed by the Romans to their instructors in all the arts of peace. The great writers of the Greek past defied criticism or dispraise: Tacitus quotes with approbation Plato's diagnosis of the souls of tyrants.[1] Honour rendered to the classics, however, might absolve a man from recognizing anything that had subsequently been done by Greeks in the kingdoms founded by the successors of Alexander.[2] He was free to draw the contrast between the inhabitants of Asia, who were a pack of luxurious and degenerate orientals, and the genuine sons of ancient Hellas.[3] At the worst, if Athens and Sparta were called up to bear witness, then those republics had indubitably failed. Failure resulted from a narrow and unenlightened policy. Diverse but equally culpable, neither Athens nor Sparta could establish an empire and bring the vanquished into concord and partnership with the victors.[4]

The Roman proconsul distrusted the Greeks for various reasons: cleverness and mendacity, subservience and volubility, and a cynical frankness about discreditable conduct. The Roman annalist, insistent on facts, nursed a double grievance against them—one Greek vice was fable and fiction about the remote past, the other was the magnification of historic glories. Sallust became sceptical: did the exploits of the Athenian People correspond with the report? Athens produced writers of genius: the Athenian authors enlarged the fame of the city.[5] Livy for his part succumbs to a prolonged bout of patriotic indignation. Greeks when they extolled Alexander pushed their effrontery to the limit.[6] They asserted that the Macedonian conqueror could easily have disposed of the Roman Republic in the age of its wars against the Samnites. Not only ignorance but criminal frivolity—some of them glorified the Parthians against Rome.[7]

The *Historiae*, so far as preserved, show a Tacitus uncommonly lenient towards the Greeks. No denunciation—he gently chides their propensity to antiquarian fabrications.[8] Hostility seems to grow as the

---

[1] VI. 6. 2: 'neque frustra praestantissimus sapientiae firmare solitus est', &c.

[2] The voluminous works of Cicero show few traces of any interest. For a typical Roman view, Lucan VIII. 696 f.: 'cum Ptolomaeorum manes seriemque pudendam | pyramides claudant indignaque Mausolea.' On Tacitus and Hellenistic history see now P. Treves, *Il mito di Alessandro e la Roma di Augusto* (1953), 159 ff. (not everywhere convincing).

[3] Cicero, *Pro Flacco* 61; *Ad Q. fratrem* I. 1. 16. Compare Pliny to Maximus (*Epp.* VIII. 24. 2).

[4] XI. 24. 4: 'quid aliud exitio Lacedaemoniis et Atheniensibus fuit, quamquam armis pollerent, nisi quod victos pro alienigenis arcebant?' Not in the surviving parts of Claudius' oration—but not novel, cf. Dionysius, *Ant. Rom.* II. 17; XIV. 6.

[5] *Cat.* 8. 2 ff. [6] IX. 17 ff.

[7] 18. 6: 'levissimi ex Graecis, qui Parthorum quoque contra nomen Romanum gloriae favent.' Presumably the historian Timagenes is meant, cf. P. Treves, o.c. 39 ff.

[8] *Hist.* II. 4. 1: 'quaeque alia laetum antiquitatibus Graecorum genus incertae vetustati adfingit.'

years pass. Distasteful experiences may have supervened when Tacitus was proconsul of Asia;[1] and a general resentment angered the Roman as he contemplated the tide of Hellenism resurgent all around. Athens lay on the way to the province of Asia. Going or returning, Tacitus may have seen a Roman senator in the robes and office of a Greek magistrate—for the young consular Aelius Hadrianus was archon in this year.[2]

The travels of Germanicus enable Tacitus to strike not once but twice. He tells how Athens welcomed the prince with the choicest attentions, with boasting about past glories in history and literature to confer dignity and importance on flattery.[3] Shortly afterwards Cn. Piso, the secret enemy of Germanicus, descended upon the city with angry fulminations: they were the dregs of all the nations, he exclaimed, the authentic Athenians had perished long ago.[4] And he recapitulated the errors and transgressions of the Athenians in their dealings with the Romans, or previously with the Macedonians.

Even the obituary notice of Arminius invited exploitation. From the Romans, says Tacitus, the champion of German liberties did not get the honour he deserved. The exaggerated prestige of Republican history is at fault—'dum vetera extollimus recentium incuriosi'. But that is not all. The Greeks reverence only what is Greek—'sua tantum mirantur'. Their historians do not even mention Arminius.[5]

Such was the pride and conceit of the Greeks. It did not inhibit them from bowing to superior force. They paid homage to their masters with the greater alacrity in that they knew it undeserved—and the deceit appealed to their cleverness. Nor would the proconsuls of the imperial Republic, bearing an authority that was regal, disdain the honours which the eastern lands so freely accorded to their saviours and benefactors. When, however, the worship of power, along with other prerogatives, became a monopoly for the advantage of the Caesars, the Roman and the senator promptly discovered that such practices jarred upon the tradition of the race, the dignity of the governing aristocracy.

To label a Princeps as good or bad, his attitude towards divine honours furnished the easiest of criteria. Malice might find scope

---

[1] Ch. XXXV.

[2] It is pure conjecture that Hadrian may have gone to Athens to assume the office in person: for the year, presumably 112/13, cf. *PIR*², A 184.

[3] II. 53. 3.

[4] 55. 1: 'non Athenienses tot cladibus exstinctos sed conluvionem illam nationum.'

[5] 88. 3. For Tacitus' extreme xenophobia in this passage see the comments of E. Norden, *Die germanische Urgeschichte in Tacitus Germania*³ (1923), 143 f.; *Neue Jahrbücher* I (1925), 44. For 'sua tantum mirantur', cf. Pliny, *NH* IV. 4: 'omnia sua mirantibus.' It is difficult to conceive which 'Graecorum annales' Tacitus could have in mind. Dessau called his complaint 'ein fast sinnloser Ausfall' (*Gesch. der. r. Kaiserzeit* II (1926), 101).

almost anywhere. Against the descendants of Theophanes was assigned among counts to their detriment the deification of their ancestor. 'Graeca adulatio', that is Tacitus' term for the cult of Theophanes.[1] It did not always suit his purpose to be contemptuous. When Tiberius Caesar declined a temple, the historian produces comment, including censure of the Emperor for his indifference to renown.[2] Subsequent developments in the cult of the Caesars could have provided genuine material for deriding both Greeks and emperors. There was also Greek erudition.

When Tiberius withdrew to Capreae, he took a small company with him: only one senator, but a number of scholars, especially Greeks, to entertain him with their converse.[3] No allusion to the quality of the entertainment. It could have been elucidated and mocked somewhere in Book V. The diversions on Capreae were learned and pedantic—the mother of Hecuba, what name Achilles assumed among the maidens, and what song the Sirens sang. They could also be dangerous. The Emperor would read up subjects and vex the experts over dinner.[4]

With Claudius, erudition again. Seneca saw its value for mockery, and for oblique allusion. Men complain (he says) that life is short. They are too busy. Yet most of their occupations are vain and futile —official business and the social round, vice, gaming, or athletic recreation.[5] Much that passes for scholarship is pure frivolity, and noxious. It was a malady of the Greeks—'Graecorum iste morbus fuit'—to compute the total of Ulixes' crew or discuss the authorship of the Homeric poems.[6] Rome has now become infected. A man will discourse learnedly on antiquities and origins, whence came the *cognomen* of a Claudius or a Valerius.[7]

Seneca winds up with a reference, pointed and contemporary, to the sacred precinct of the city of Rome. Sulla had been the last to extend the *pomerium*. The Mons Aventinus was not included. Of what profit can it be to weigh the reasons that antiquarians adduce? Or a myriad other things, fiction or the like—'quae aut paria sunt mendaciis aut similia.'[8]

The historian Tacitus duly makes fun of pedantry or fraud under the grave show of deference—his delight in the phoenix gives more than a hint of his technique.[9] The antiquarian emperor, when censor,

---

[1] VI. 18. 2.
[2] IV. 38. 4 f. Tacitus, however, seems to be satirizing the critics of Tiberius (cf. p. 315).
[3] IV. 58. 1.
[4] Suetonius, *Tib*. 70 (not in reference to Capreae).
[5] *De brevitate vitae* 12.   [6] 13. 2. Cf. *Epp*. 88. 6 ff.; 37 ff.   [7] 13. 4 f.
[8] 13. 9. For Claudius' extension of the *pomerium* see App. 40.
[9] VI. 28 (p. 472).

added three letters to the Roman alphabet: hence excuse for a learned digression, going back to the Trojan War, to Cadmus, to Cecrops.[1] In the year 53 the city of Ilium asked for privileges. Its cause was urged before the Senate by the boy Nero, recently adopted into the family of his great-uncle, Claudius. The youthful orator expatiated upon the Trojan origin of the Romans, upon Aeneas the ancestor of the Julian line—and, the historian is careful to add, other ancient matters not far removed from fable.[2] The understatement reveals what Tacitus thought of sacred and legendary history.

In the same year Claudius Caesar proposed that the island of Cos should be exempted from all taxation. He orated at great length about the antiquities of Cos, about Aesculapius the founder of medicine; and he retailed the catalogue of his descendants, famous practitioners, down to Xenophon the court doctor. For Xenophon's sake Claudius Caesar made the plea for Cos.[3] The occasion was welcome to Tacitus—ridicule of Hellenic science and of a Roman emperor, and irony. A year later the historian comes to the ultimate service that Xenophon rendered. When the poisoned mushroom seemed to fail its effect, Agrippina used the doctor to finish Claudius.[4]

For the prejudices of Tacitus full scope came with Nero, as the monarch's aspirations unfolded in a graduated assault upon publicity. So far the historian's adversions upon the Greeks and their habits might be put down largely to literary tradition, or the spirit of mockery. With Nero the addiction to all things Greek is exposed by Tacitus, not only as a scandal. It was a menace.

Nero had long been possessed of a yearning to drive chariots and sing to the harp.[5] His mother's murder removed the last restraints. After some experimentation, he began with 'ludi iuvenales' in the gardens beyond the Tiber. Audience and performers were select. Men and women of the aristocracy acted in stage plays, and the Emperor himself displayed his talent for song. A cohort of the Guard was in attendance with officers, and even the Prefect; and a company of Roman knights was enrolled, the 'Augustiani', to second and applaud their ruler's efforts.[6] He also took up the composition of poetry with great seriousness and a group of experts to help him.[7]

In the next year Rome witnessed the regular institution of a

[1] XI. 14.

[2] XII. 58. 1: 'Romanum Troia demissum et Iuliae stirpis auctorem Aeneam aliaque haud procul fabulis vetera.' Observe the verbal felicity of the poetic 'demissum' (Virgil, *Georg.* III. 35; *Aen.* I. 288; Horace, *Sat.* II. 5. 63).

[3] XII. 61.

[4] 67. 2: 'provisam iam sibi Xenophontis medici conscientiam adhibet.' Claudius had testified to Xenophon's 'scientia' (XII. 61. 2).

[5] XIV. 14. 1.   [6] 15.   [7] 16. 1.

quinquennial festival, the *Neronia*, on the Greek model: it included song and speech, athletics, and horse-racing. Like other innovations, the *Neronia* had a mixed welcome. Tacitus, in digression on the history of public spectacles at Rome, reproduces the arguments.[1] On the one side, the historian eloquently invokes (and strains) the resources of conservative indignation—Greek *gymnasia* with their adherent immorality, Roman senators degraded by stage performances. The next thing would be knights neglecting military service for athletics; and, becoming judges of voice production and musical connoisseurs, they would cease to be of use in the courts of law. And finally, with performances at night, anything might happen.[2]

Tacitus cannot resist the opportunity for declamation and satire. It is double-edged.[3] He goes on to furnish sober arguments in favour;[4] and he admits that the festival passed off quietly and decently, with no scandal at all.[5]

Nero persisted. He favoured the city of Neapolis (in 64), and, emboldened by his reception there, made his first exhibition as a singer before the Roman People at the second *Neronia* in the next year.[6] The imperial actor, however, was thinking of a larger stage, of Hellas and the sole audience worthy to adjudicate upon his virtuosity.

The first attempt had been abortive. From Neapolis Nero went on as far as Beneventum, but turned back.[7] And Hellas soon yielded to more potent visions of desire—the lands of the Orient, and especially Egypt.[8] That also came to nothing. In the end Nero did not leave Rome until late in the year 66.

The Hellenic tour was no doubt narrated with lavish detail for the ludicrous pageantry, exposing the vanity of the Greeks, the retribution

[1] XIV. 20. 1: 'varia fama, ut cuncta ferme nova.' Cf. the discussion in Livy provoked by a modification in the *ludi Romani*: it is introduced by the phrase 'sicut omnis novitas solet' (XXXIV. 54. 4).

[2] ib. 5: 'an iustitiam auctum iri et decurias equitum egregium iudicandi munus expleturos si fractos sonos et dulcedinem vocum perite audissent? noctes quoque dedecori adiectas', &c.

[3] For the deliberate (and damaging) exaggeration compare the words Tacitus puts into the mouth of Cossutianus Capito (XVI. 22, above, p. 332 f.).

[4] 21. 3: 'oratorum ac vatum victorias incitamentum ingeniis allaturas; nec cuiquam iudici grave aures studiis honestis et voluptatibus concessis impertire.'

[5] ib. 4: 'sane nullo insigni dehonestamento id spectaculum transiit.'

[6] XIV. 4. The historian may (or may not) have known a shocking fact—Nero as Apollo Citharoedus on the coinage of Rome (*BMC, R. Emp.* 1 (1923), clxxx; 245).

[7] XV. 34.

[8] XV. 30. 1: 'provincias Orientis, maxime Aegyptum, secretis imaginationibus agitans.' The word 'imaginatio' is uncommon and powerful, cf. Pliny, *NH* xx. 68: 'libidinum imaginationes in somno.' Hadrian, that curious and peregrinatory emperor, might have been expected to visit the land of marvels before long: observe that in 122 he was 'Alexandrina seditione turbatus, quae nata est ob Apidem' (*HA, Hadr.* 12. 1).

that now befell them, and the criminal folly of their Roman patron. Hitherto in the *Annales* Tacitus had not reproduced any public discourse of this emperor. He might now, with gaiety and with malice, undertake to stylize Nero's proclamation at the Isthmus of Corinth.[1] The language was pompous and condescending. Unexpected might be the gift, said the imperial orator, though no manifestation of Nero's noble generosity should come as a surprise. Not even in the days of their prosperity had the Hellenes all enjoyed freedom, being then enslaved either by men of their own race or by foreigners. The Emperor would have preferred to benefit Hellas in the epoch of her strength. What he now grants, however, issues not from compassion but from good will, and to requite the gods of Hellas for watching over him in their providence.[2]

The *Annales* convey several warnings to the address of the Emperor Hadrian. With Tiberius Caesar the author presents a ruler's devious and suspicious nature, resentful from disappointments, further distorted and darkened by the exercise of the supreme power. Indictments for high treason were the indelible blot upon that reign. Embracing not only acts but words and opinions, they subverted all freedom of speech. The historian Cremutius Cordus was threatened with a prosecution on various counts, not his writings only or principally.[3] Tacitus renders, or rather invents, this man's eloquent vindication of an historian's rights. He appends his own comment— how can one not deride the brute stupidity of those who hold the power! Let them punish opinion, they can never destroy it. Foreign tyrants or their imitators at Rome only perpetuate their own ignominy.[4]

Tacitus was writing about the time of Tiberius, he recalled Domitian—and he was not oblivious of the present.[5] Nor would his treatment of Claudius lack point and relevance—an omniscient emperor interfering everywhere, with a strong trend towards bureaucratic government. Above all, Nero. Here the peril lay in aesthetic tastes, Hellenic habits, and intellectual megalomania. Hadrian shared Nero's aptitude for certain of the arts, even painting and sculpture. Tacitus labels Nero in a striking phrase of his own creation as 'incredibilium cupitor'.[6] It suits Hadrian very well.

[1] *SIG*³ 814.

[2] For Nero's 'magnitudo animi' (XIII. 50. 2) see above, p. 416.

[3] G. M. Columba, *Atene e Roma* IV (1901), 361 ff.

[4] IV. 35. 5: 'quo magis socordiam eorum inridere libet qui praesenti potentia credunt extingui posse etiam sequentis aevi memoriam. nam contra punitis ingeniis gliscit auctoritas, neque aliud externi reges aut qui eadem saevitia usi sunt nisi dedecus sibi atque illis gloriam peperere.'

[5] Even a taste for the 'contiones' in Livy could be incriminated under a bad emperor (Suetonius, *Dom.* 10. 3).   [6] XV. 42. 2.

Nero might come again. So the world hoped, or feared. The age of Tacitus witnessed a sequence of false Neros. The sudden disappearance of Nero, the terror or the admiration his name evoked, and the prevalence of apocalyptic delusions won support for these impostors—and some were a nuisance to the Roman government.[1]

Nero (it was fancied) had fled over the Euphrates to find succour among the Parthians, and, although the Parthians surrendered a Nero to Domitian, faith held firm under Trajan. Most men believe that Nero still lives, so Dio of Prusa confessed.[2] When the Roman war failed in Mesopotamia and the Jews rose everywhere, a season arrived most propitious for his emergence.

Rome could not endure for ever. Destiny had ordained a term, and it was foretold in oracles that the East would have the power again.[3] The cycle of ages might be variously computed, and various portents would announce the end.[4] One such prediction (a ruler of the world arising in Judaea) had incited the Jews to rebel fifty years earlier.[5] That prophecy was indeed fulfilled, so the Romans argued—by the proclamation of Vespasian. The Jews refused to be convinced; and Jewish composers of Sibylline verses soon annexed the theme of Nero's return and wove it into their imprecations of revenge and deliverance.[6]

Nor had Nero yet passed wholly into the realm of the supernatural. The last Caesar of Augustus' line was only sixteen years older than Trajan. When Hadrian came to the power, Nero would be completing his eightieth year.

So far the delusions of rebels and fanatics. Cornelius Tacitus was well trained in the science of oracles, he knew the frivolous or fraudulent reckoning of numerical cycles.[7] Eager to refute vain fancies about kings coming out of the East and the doom of Rome, he would be no less alert to the true relevance of Nero.

---

[1] From what Tacitus says of the first (*Hist.* II. 8. 1) it follows that there were two more (at least) before 96: one under Titus (Dio LXVI. 19. 3 b–c, cf. *Or. Sib.* IV. 130 ff.), one in 88/89, much more formidable (*Hist.* I. 2. 1; Suetonius, *Nero* 57. 2), who was surrendered by the Parthians (cf. Statius, *Silvae* IV. 3. 110).

[2] *Or.* XXI. 10.

[3] Lactantius, *Div. Inst.* VII. 15. 11: 'Romanum nomen quo nunc regitur orbis—horret animus dicere, sed dicam quia futurum est—tolletur e terra et imperium in Asiam revertetur ac rursus Oriens dominabitur atque Occidens serviet.' Cf. H. Windisch, 'Die Orakel des Hystaspes', *Verhandelingen der kon. Ak. van Wetenschappen*, Afd. Letterkunde, N.R. XXVIII, 3 (1929); H. Fuchs, *Der geistige Widerstand gegen Rom in der antiken Welt* (1938), 31 ff.; A. Peretti, *La Sibilla babilonese* (1943), 303 ff.

[4] App. 73.

[5] *Hist.* V. 13. 2; Suetonius, *Divus Vesp.* 4. 5; Josephus, *BJ* VI. 312. See esp. E. Norden, *Neue Jahrbücher* XXXI (1913), 637 ff.

[6] *Or. Sib.* IV. 130 ff., &c. Nor will *Apocalypsis Ioannis* (especially c. 17) be neglected: the problems of that document are too complex to be discussed here.

[7] App. 73.

On a sober reflection much of Nero had already returned with
Hadrian. That could be known or forecast from the first days of the
reign, though none could have divined the full measure of his later
extravagances—Hadrian as second founder of Athens, displacing
Theseus, the title 'Olympius', or his infatuation for the beautiful
Antinous. To Tacitus and to some of his friends it was no consolation
to know that what in Nero's philhellenism had been ridiculous, premature, or calamitous now corresponded with the rational policy of
whoever ruled a Graeco-Roman world.[1]

The Empire had various 'arcana', some known long ago in the
revolutionary age but covered up in the Augustan peace, to be
abruptly disclosed later on, or emerging through a progressive revelation. Thus the military and provincial origins of the new form of
government, its hostility to the Roman *nobilitas*, its congenital preference for knights against senators. One of those potent secrets was
the dual nature of the Empire—Roman and Greek. With Antonius it
threatened to split the imperial dominions or subjugate the West to
the East. With Hadrian it was manifest and acknowledged, barely five
generations from the defeat of Antonius and the victory of the West.

[1] For the philhellenism of Hadrian see J. Beaujeu, *La Religion romaine à l'apogée de
l'empire* I (1955), 164 ff.

PART VIII

THE AUTHOR

―――――――

XXXIX. TACITEAN OPINIONS

THERE are 'arcana' everywhere in the behaviour of men and governments. The duty of the historian is not merely to register facts but to penetrate the recesses. Tacitus performs it, sharp and ruthless. The historian, too, has his secrets. What are the true sentiments behind the narrative, the eloquence, and the drama?

The first step is to mark his own declarations. It will not take one very far. The author in the prologue announces his design—he will tell the truth (and, it is implied, will benefit the community). What else was a man to say? The formula was inescapable. So closely do the Roman historians adhere to the shape and traditions of their art that it is not wholly vain to reconstruct the lost prologue of a lost annalist.[1]

Sallust in lengthy preliminaries allows something to be perceived of his ambitions and his discontents. More has to be divined. Livy, a franker writer, confesses honest yearning for the past, a patriot's anxiety about the present, admiration for the Roman power, and loyalty to the ideals of an older Rome. Tacitus gives very little away. His prefaces are splendid and formal. What assures their value is brevity, point, and impersonality.

A passage in the *Annales* declares a moral purpose. History will commemorate virtue and condemn iniquity for ever—'praecipuum munus annalium reor ne virtutes sileantur utque pravis dictis factisque ex posteritate et infamia metus sit'.[2] If such was the proper and principal function of history, other reasons lay behind the writing of it, as the historian might admit from his understanding of human behaviour and of his own character. Ambition was an avowable motive in a Roman. There was also curiosity, artistic sense, and the revolt from the inertia or mediocrity of the age—and perhaps other things, deeper still.[3]

――――

[1] p. 146.　　　　　　　　　　　　　　　　　　　　　　[2] III. 65. 1.

[3] Such as the guilty defence of a senator who owed station and success to Rome of the Caesars: to 'obsequium', not to 'libertas'.

When Roman politicians appeal to ancestral custom or the spirit of the constitution, a suspicion arises that their plea cannot be supported by exact legal precedents; and when Roman writers parade ethical claims, they do not always impose a conviction of authenticity. Sometimes the man's conduct stands in flagrant contrast. With others it is style and talent that engenders a doubt: their gifts of declamation and satire are too patent. Sallust has all the Catonian language and postures: his choice of subject and his treatment reveal him not at all archaic but very much a man of the revolutionary age, delighting in violence and discord.[1] Sallust brings into question the total sincerity of Cornelius Tacitus.

Some may accept Tacitus as primarily a moralist in his aspirations, reading into his words much more than the author intended.[2] Others will confess their perplexity. The lessons that Tacitus is supposed to inculcate are by no means unequivocal. Liberty and dignity—but also the precepts of a statecraft that a time-server, a politician, or a tyrant might be happy to annex and exploit. His writings (it can be argued) are morally subversive, not safely to be recommended for the instruction of the young.[3]

How much in Tacitus is the garb of fashion and convention? And what is left when the integument is stripped? The attempt to extricate the true opinions of the historian and fathom his personality is more than hazardous.

Like Sallust, Tacitus is not much concerned with the supernatural. The mysteries that matter lie in the hearts and behaviour of men. On the face of things the divine regiment of the universe is admitted, but seldom for any desired or happy end.[4] It suits the purpose of Tacitus to affirm that Heaven may intervene to punish mankind.[5] Further, he invokes the anger of the gods against the Roman People.[6] A striking and ominous phrase, but no confession of a creed. Elsewhere he concedes that the supernal powers remain indifferent to good and evil equally.[7]

---

[1] K. Latte, 'Sallust' (*Neue Wege zur Antike* II, 4, 1935), 56 ff.

[2] Thus F. Klingner takes traditional Roman 'virtus' to be the historian's chief preoccupation (*Die Antike* VIII (1932), 151 ff. = R. *Geisteswelt* (1943), 310 ff.); E. Kornemann alleges that edification assumes precedence over truth in the *Annales* (*Tacitus* (Wiesbaden, 1947), 40); and E. Paratore discovers a reversion to a narrow and moralistic outlook (*Tacito* (1951), 692).

[3] C. Merivale, *History of the Romans under the Empire* VIII (1876), 130.

[4] For Livy 'benignitas deum' (sixteen times) seems to mean something. In the *Annales* (four times) it is a conventional phrase, e.g., 'magna deum benignitate et modestia hiemis' (XII. 43. 2).

[5] *Hist.* I. 3. 2: 'non esse curae deis securitatem nostram, esse ultionem.'

[6] *Ann.* IV. 1. 2, cf. XVI. 16. 2.

[7] XVI. 33. 1: 'aequitate deum erga bona malaque documenta.'

When Agrippina is to be murdered, the gods furnish a fine night, as though to show up the crime.[1] Many portents followed close upon the deed: they meant nothing.[2] Tacitus does not have to worry about consistency. Nero bathed in the sacred springs from which an aqueduct took its rise: the Emperor fell ill, which proved divine resentment.[3]

In the *Historiae* Tacitus is openly sceptical about signs and wonders: common enough in unsophisticated ages, they now occur only in a season of crisis or panic.[4] The secret ordinances of fate, the voice of the oracles, and all the omens—these found credit, but after the event. Such is Tacitus' cool verdict upon the elevation of Vespasian and the fortune of the Flavian House.[5] Of Trajan's imperial destiny convincing evidence was no doubt produced in due course, though little has survived—only a hint of portents when he was consul, and the prophetic acclamation of the bystanders when he made sacrifice on the Capitol before setting out for Germany.[6]

A history of the Flavian period might have contained remarkable annunciations—a prophetic dream in Hercules' temple at Gades, a Messianic prediction in the land of Judaea, a wonder wrought on Mount Casius in Syria, or the river Euphrates preternaturally abating its flood. Opportunities abounded for a conventional and adulatory historian. When Tacitus, however, wrote of these matters, it will be conjectured that his choice went to a subtle procedure.

The recording of omens was a traditional feature in the annals of the Romans, and the effect of premonitory signs on the minds and actions of men provided a suitable commentary to great events.[7] Idle fables were to be deprecated, but a serious author had no right to omit a well-authenticated manifestation.[8]

Livy lamented that in his own day faith had evaporated, with no *prodigia* any more on official record or in the pages of historians.[9] When Livy came to narrate that epoch he will have ascertained that his regrets were premature. There was an adequate supply.[10] And in due course the end of Augustus furnished a whole crop.[11] Tacitus

---

[1] XIV. 5. 1: 'noctem sideribus inlustrem et placido mari quietam quasi convincendum ad scelus di praebuere.'

[2] 12. 2: 'crebra et inrita.'

[3] 22. 4: 'secutaque anceps valetudo iram deum adfirmavit.'

[4] I. 86. 1: 'et plura alia rudibus saeculis etiam in pace observata, quae nunc tantum in metu audiuntur.' Cf. IV. 26. 2: 'quod in pace fors seu natura, tunc fatum et ira dei vocabatur.'

[5] 10. 3: 'post fortunam credidimus.'   [6] Dio LXVII. 12. 1; Pliny, *Pan.* 5. 3 f.

[7] II. 78. 2 (their effect upon Vespasian and upon others).

[8] II. 50. 2 (comments on the strange bird at Regium Lepidum).

[9] XLIII. 13. 1.

[10] cf. Julius Obsequens (under 17 B.C.), presumably deriving from Livy, Book CXXXVII. Dio's sources for the reign of Augustus also had *prodigia*.

[11] Dio LVI. 29. 2 ff.; 45. 2.

eschews them. Not until the later books do the *prodigia* become a regular entry. It would be fanciful to discover a sceptical historian's relapse into antiquated credulities. The reason is plain: a stock device in the old annalistic tradition which Tacitus needed all the more because his subject now defied the fabric and canons of the 'res publica'.[1]

The religion of the Roman State, being a system of ritual performances, was easy to keep in repair. Most emperors knew their duty. Belief or behaviour hardly came in. The men whom birth or favour selected for the sacerdotal colleges, while absorbing various doses of antique tradition, seldom underwent any change, unless it be a keener flair for official impostures. It was clear profit for an historian to have held one of the priesthoods.[2]

Not every senator, however, was able to preserve the scepticism appropriate to that governing order which in past ages exploited religion so skilfully. In Rome of the Caesars high and low were riddled with all manner of superstitions. Curious particulars are disclosed about Tiberius Caesar, who denied belief in the gods and was negligent about religious observances.[3] Such items attract a biographer. The historian will have none of them. Trivial oddities conflicted with the majesty of history—and with his picture of a sombre, sagacious, and powerful ruler.[4]

Tiberius in a public edict brushed aside the notion of sacrilege, contemptuously.[5] One system of belief neither historian nor emperor could disparage. It was the science of the stars. Astrology offered a solution to the vexatious problem of fate and free will, and its credit was supported by the weighty authority of the Stoics. Tiberius Caesar was a convinced believer. Strange stories were told about his foreknowledge of events, and artful prosecutors saw the chance to exploit his creed and his suspicions by adding magic or astrology to an indictment. The theme turns up early in the *Annales*, with full detail. A silly nobleman of dynastic blood and hopes came to grief, perverted by the promises of the Chaldaeans.[6]

The principate, like all things, was assigned by destiny. Anecdotes bear witness to the firm and unshakeable faith of certain monarchs.

[1] p. 312. Some, however, opine that Tacitus was veering towards religious belief in the later books. Thus Ph. Fabia, *Journal des Savants*, 1914, 250 ff.; N. Eriksson, *Religiösitet och Irreligiösitet hos Tacitus* (Lund, 1935), 72.

[2] On Tacitus as a *quindecimvir*, pp. 65 f., 280, 465, 469, 518. His science comes out in small things as in large. For example, his feeling for the mysterious word 'caerimonia', cf. K. H. Roloff, *Glotta* XXXII (1952), 101 ff.

[3] Suetonius, *Tib.* 69; Pliny, *NH* XV. 135; XVI. 194; XXVIII. 23. But Tiberius was a pedant about the niceties of the state cult (p. 280 f.).

[4] Similarly, nothing about drink (Suetonius, *Tib.* 42. 1).

[5] I. 73. 4.   [6] II. 27 ff. (M. Scribonius Libo).

So confident was Vespasian in the horoscope of the Flavian House that he exclaimed in the Senate: 'my sons shall follow in my place, or no man shall.'[1] And Titus in his turn: when two nobles of high pedigree were discovered conspiring to seize power, all that he did was to tell them to stop it, for it was of no use—'principatum fato dari'. If there was anything else they wanted, they could have it.[2] Domitian studied the art. He discovered (it was said) the day on which a deed of blood would fall, he feared the fifth hour—and he could not escape.[3]

There were also stories about the imperial horoscope of Cocceius Nerva.[4] What Tacitus may have thought of them need not detain conjecture. In the *Historiae*, when discussing Otho's astrologer, he is hostile to the entire class and profession; omens, portents, and predictions about the destiny of the Flavian House excite his irony; and Vespasian's belief and practice is designated as a 'superstitio'.[5] The *Annales* seem to sound a different note. Was it some personal experience of the ageing consular when he was governor in Asia, or something that happened at Rome—or not rather the spell that Tiberius Caesar cast upon his historian during that long and pervasive frequentation?

When Tiberius in the year 26 went away to Campania, the astrologers announced that he would never come back. Hence the persuasion, which to many proved fatal, that the Emperor's end was near: for who could have conjectured a voluntary absence of eleven years? Time in its course showed how dark is the veil that hides the truth, how narrow the margin between science and its opposite.[6]

That Tiberius would never see Rome again turned out a true prediction ('haud forte dictum'). That was all. The experts had not been able to foretell anything else. Tacitus is suitably cautious and incomplete in his verdict.

The whole episode is introduced by Tacitus with strong emphasis, the sentence lacking a verb—'tandem Caesar in Campaniam'.[7] That phrase carried, or soon acquired, sharp relevance. Hadrian's first exit from Rome was a journey to Campania in 119. The occasion might have tempted the Chaldaeans, and the enemies of Hadrian.[8]

The new ruler himself was expert in horoscopes, it is alleged.[9]

---

[1] Suetonius, *Divus Vesp.* 25, cf. Dio LXVI. 12. 1 (not related to horoscopes).

[2] *Divus Titus* 9. 1.   [3] *Dom.* 16. 2.

[4] Dio LXVII. 15. 6.   [5] *Hist.* I. 22. 1; 10. 3; II. 78. 1.

[6] *Ann.* IV. 58. 2: 'mox patuit breve confinium artis et falsi, veraque quam obscuris tegerentur.'   [7] IV. 57. 1.

[8] p. 487. There is at least one sign of the historian's second thoughts in IV. 57 f. (App. 37); but there is nothing in the structure to suggest that the remarks about astrologers' predictions represent a subsequent insertion, and it would not be safe to use the passage for argument about the date of composition.

[9] *HA, Hadr.* 16. 7. Also an astrologer in the family, his great-uncle (ib. 2. 4). Hadrian's

So was Tiberius Caesar, though the historian keeps silent about his proficiency almost to the end. In the year 33 Tiberius summoned to Capreae the consul Sulpicius Galba, and, after a searching talk, disclosed his imperial destiny.[1]

Tiberius learned the art from Thrasyllus long ago at Rhodes, who was not only an astrologer, but a scholar of superior rank and unimpeachable science. Tiberius took him along the cliffs to try his skill, and to destroy him like others if found fraudulent. Thrasyllus alertly predicted that the exile would return to Rome and have the power. Then, invited to cast his own horoscope, he submitted to the test, thence ascertaining with wonder and terror that his life was in peril. That proof established his ascendancy.[2] Many other stories circulated. Thrasyllus lived with Tiberius on the island of Capreae and died only a few months before the Emperor, to whom he promised ten more years of rule.[3] The son of Thrasyllus, also an adept, discovered from the stars that the power must go to Nero. Tacitus affirms that he will note that prophecy in due course.[4]

Tacitus, avowing his own uncertainty, adds a digression on fate and chance.[5] The diverse tenets of the philosophers, Epicurean and Stoic, are summarily noted.[6] After which, Tacitus concludes by stating the almost universal belief of human kind—the future is determined at the hour of a man's birth; if some things fall out otherwise than predicted, that is due to the ignorance or the dishonesty of the astrologers, who thus ruin the credit of a science that has been corroborated in the past and in the present by notable testimonies.[7]

The structure of the universe and the spectacle of events might

horoscope, compiled by Antigonus of Nicaea, will be found in *Cat. codd. astr. gr.* VI, 67 ff. Cf. F. H. Cramer, *Astrology in Roman Law and Politics* (1954), 164 ff.

[1] VI. 20. 2: 'et tu, Galba, quandoque degustabis imperium.'

[2] 21. For the origin and family of Thrasyllus, p. 508. Also F. H. Cramer, o.c. 92 ff., and, for his political influence, 99 ff.

[3] Dio LVIII. 27. 3.

[4] VI. 22. 4. Cf. XIV. 9. 3 (no name, only the 'Chaldaei'). Dio (LXI. 2. 1 f.) also omits the name. That Nero's astrologer Balbillus (*PIR²*, B 38) is the son of Thrasyllus has been argued by C. Cichorius, *Römische Studien* (1922), 393 ff. Cf. p. 508.

[5] 22. 1: 'sed mihi haec ac talia audienti in incerto iudicium est, fatone res mortalium et necessitate immutabili an forte volvantur.'

[6] The second school referred to might not be Stoic but incipient Neo-Platonist, cf. (at some length) W. Theiler, *Phyllobolia für Peter von der Mühll zum 60. Geburtstag* (1945), 35 ff. It is argued that the proconsul of Asia might have come across the teaching (or the person) of the mysterious Gaius (on whom see *SIG³* 868 B and C; Praechter, P–W Supp. III, 535 ff.), the predecessor of Albinus. So much being not known about the historian, it hardly matters. E. Fraenkel dismisses the digression as 'halbgelehrtes Beiwerk' (*Neue Jahrbücher* VIII (1932), 230).

[7] 22. 3: 'ceterum plurimis mortalium non eximitur quin primo cuiusque ortu ventura destinentur', &c. Some have deduced Tacitus' conversion to astrology, e.g. R. Reitzenstein, *Neue Wege zur Antike* IV (1926), 28. That is quite unwarranted. For Tacitus' objectivity and positivism cf. P. Beguin, *L'Antiquité classique* XX (1951), 325; 334; XXIV (1955), 352 ff.

condemn a man to fatalism. Who could remain wholly a sceptic about astrology when Tiberius Caesar was a believer?[1] Yet some of the things that happened could shake any fatalism. Tacitus was deeply impressed by the character and the conduct of Marcus Lepidus, the most distinguished senator in the reign of Tiberius. By his prudence and his dignity Lepidus won the esteem of the Emperor, and great authority with him. Tacitus is moved to doubt whether the favour of princes is determined, like all things, by fate and the lot assigned at birth. A man's judgement counts—despite all, he might not be the prisoner of destiny.[2]

Tacitus writes history with the accent upon personality, penetrating to the deepest recesses in his search for motive.[3] So did Sallust. Fatalism or pessimism is no bar. Sallust puts the individual at the centre of affairs—Catilina for energy, ambition, and crime; Caesar and Cato because they excelled in 'virtus', while contrary in principle and behaviour. 'Virtus', though watered down by some moralists, retained for the Roman its primary meaning of courage and energy.[4] It might occur and be admired in bad men. Thus Lucan, on the elemental vigour of Caesar;[5] and another epic poet, Silius Italicus, singled out the 'improba virtus' of Hannibal.[6] In the past achievement of Rome Sallust assigns the credit to a few men only;[7] and, speaking for himself in the prologues to the monographs, Sallust insistently preaches a gospel of energy and action.[8]

The beliefs of Cornelius Tacitus have been a subject of disparagement among the learned, with a grave indictment levelled against him, a crushing verdict pronounced. As a thinker, he was an impostor—no philosophy, no system in his head, but confusion and a jumble of vague and half-baked ideas.[9] Others may suspect that it is by no means

[1] Mere contemporary belief, like that of Hadrian (*HA, Hadr.* 16. 7), would not have convinced him; and there is no trace of predictions about the destiny of Claudius, that patent παράδοξον (cf. III. 18. 4). Nor, emphasizing the year 23, does he bother to note that Tiberius had just passed the climacteric sixty-third of his life.

[2] IV. 20. 3: 'unde dubitare cogor fato et sorte nascendi, ut cetera, ita principum inclinatio in hos, offensio in illos, an sit aliquid in nostris consiliis', &c.

[3] That is clear. See, if necessary, J. Cousin, *Rev. ét. lat.* XXIX (1951), 228 ff.; J. Beguin, *L'Antiquité classique* XXII (1953), 322 ff.

[4] H. Haas, *Gymnasium* XLIX (1938), 163.   [5] I. 144 f.: 'sed nescia virtus stare loco.'

[6] *Punica* I. 58. See also Manilius v. 495 ff., describing the man of action who 'ipse sibi lex est', but with whom, in a good cause, 'improbitas fiet virtus'.

[7] *Cat.* 53. 4: 'paucorum civium egregiam virtutem cuncta patravisse.'

[8] M. Rambaud, *Rev. ét. lat.* XXIV (1946), 115 ff. That scholar alludes appropriately to Stendhal (129 f.). As for 'virtus' in Tacitus as a 'kräftiges Lebensgefühl', cf. R. Feger, *Würzburger Jahrbücher* III (1948), 303.

[9] R. v. Pöhlmann, *Bayerische S–B, phil.-hist. Kl.* 1910, Abh. 1, 63. M. L. W. Laistner, who blames Pöhlmann for adopting the yardstick of nineteenth-century rationalism (*The Greater Roman Historians* (1947), 115), fails to see that the inconsistencies of Tacitus are a merit.

an advantage for an historian to be shut up in the armour of an invulnerable doctrine.[1] Certitude is not given to mortals, and Tacitus is redeemed by his respect for the eternal ambiguities.[2]

One of those ambiguities is fundamental in the nature of man. The love of liberty and the love of domination spring from a single root, with good or evil ensuing. That was the diagnosis of Sallust.[3] History showed it valid for states as well as for individuals. The 'virtus' of the Roman People prevailed everywhere, subduing the kings and the nations. There was another side to conquest and dominion. The Romans themselves avow it.

The vanquished have left a most imperfect record of their hatred and resentment. In the first epoch of the Roman supremacy the philosopher Carneades, exhibiting his versatile talent at a public lecture, demonstrated to the imperial people that their much-vaunted justice was nothing but the right of the stronger.[4] Though a sceptic (he was head of the Academic School), Carneades alarmed his audience. Carneades was an exception—for the most part the upper classes in the Greek lands kept silent, for they owed security and status to Roman protection. Apart from some acrid pamphleteer in the paid service of the Pontic monarchy or a malignant historian who exalted the Parthians at the expense of Rome,[5] subversive criticism came from much lower down, in the shape of apocalyptic literature.[6]

Instead, faction strife at Rome and political prosecutions erupted with dangerous arguments. Cato was notable for his attacks upon corrupt and oppressive governors; and he freely conceded that the people of Rhodes had every right to aspire to freedom or pray for

---

[1] If many features in the make-up of Tacitus (as of other educated Romans) be described as 'Stoic', that does not take one very far, or very deep. For Tacitus' hostility to philosophers, Ch. XLI.

[2] The notions of 'fatum' and 'fortuna' in Tacitus continue to be discussed, e.g. P. Beguin, L'Antiquité classique xx (1951), 315 ff.; J. Kroymann, Satura (Festschrift O. Weinreich, 1952), 71 ff. Not much emerges. The words belong to literature rather than to dogma: 'fatum' is often that which is inexplicable, but not mysterious. Thus 'fato et vi Arminii' (I. 55. 3); and, most revealing, Nero's aversion from Octavia 'fato quodam an quia praevalent inlicita' (XIII. 12. 2). Compare the elder Seneca on the decline of oratory, 'fato quodam' (Controv. I, praef. 7). For sensible remarks see B. Walker, The Annals of Tacitus (1952), 248 f.

[3] Hist. I. 6: 'nobis primae dissensiones vitio humani ingenii evenere, quod inquies atque indomitum semper inter certamina libertatis aut gloriae aut dominationis agit.'

[4] Cicero, De re publica III. 8 ff., esp. 20 f. (mainly recovered from Tertullian and Lactantius).

[5] Metrodorus of Scepsis, 'cui cognomen a Romani nominis odio inditum est' (Pliny, NH xxxiv. 34); the anonymus of Livy IX. 18. 6, presumably Timagenes, 'felicitati urbis inimicus' (Seneca, Epp. 91. 13), who became hostile when he quarrelled with Augustus.

[6] H. Fuchs, Der geistige Widerstand gegen Rom (1938).

the defeat of the Romans.[1] Cicero, a century later, when an advocate for the prosecution or extolling Pompeius Magnus, declares how bitterly and how justly the empire of the Romans is detested in all the lands: the provinces make lamentation, free peoples complain, and kings are indignant.[2]

It was otherwise in the past. Nations would sooner be ruled by Rome than exercise dominion over others.[3] The Republic made war only for just and honourable reasons, such as self-defence or the protection of allies.[4] The world dominion that accrued might therefore be designated not as 'imperium' but as 'patrocinium orbis terrarum'. If in the sequel Roman behaviour confuted the engaging notion of a trusteeship over the nations, the declension could be assigned to a recent date, with most of the blame conveniently laid upon Sulla.[5]

Such was the explanation published by Cicero in one of his ethical treatises. To incriminate Sulla appealed to Sallust, but Sallust knew and affirmed that the evil change began much earlier.[6] Sallust, and certain other Roman historians, are not concerned to publish an apologia for empire. They tend to be angry, critical, and censorious; and their technique of dramatic composition, with resort to speeches or letters, facilitates a vivid (and sometimes sympathetic) portrayal of Rome's enemies, well equipped with powerful or insidious argumentation.

Sallust composes for Mithridates of Pontus a letter that methodically analyses the habits of Roman foreign policy—crafty, tenacious, and dishonest.[7] Another historian, Pompeius Trogus, furnished for the same monarch a lengthy oration charged with vigorous invective.[8] Trogus, writing under Augustus, compiled a survey, not of Rome but of the kingdoms of the world. Rome was subordinate to his design— and some discover in the author hostility or depreciation.[9]

Trogus was a new Roman of native stock from the province of Gallia Narbonensis.[10] The consular Cornelius Tacitus in his first monograph speaks eloquently for the vanquished in the harangue of the Caledonian chieftain, with fervid denunciation of imperial conquest—'the Romans call it empire, it is in fact murder and rapine and

---

[1] Quoted extensively in Gellius VI. 3. 16.
[2] *In Verrem* II. 3. 207; *De imp. Cn. Pompei* 65.
[3] *De imp. Cn. Pompei* 41.
[4] *De re publica* III. 35: 'noster autem populus sociis defendendis terrarum iam omnium potitus est.' Livy exemplifies the necessary conviction of 'iusta bella'. Modern investigation into the causes of the wars against Carthage and Macedon reveals a different story.
[5] *De officiis* II. 27.   [6] *Cat.* 10.
[7] *Hist.* IV. 69. 20: 'audendo et fallendo et bella ex bellis serendo.'
[8] Justin XXXVIII. 4-7 (in *oratio obliqua*).
[9] Perhaps wrongly, cf. H. Fuchs, o.c. 42 f.   [10] Justin XLIII. 5. 11 f.

profit; they make a desolation and they call it peace'.[1] The charge is echoed in shorter and more sober discourse by the heroic Caratacus in the presence of Claudius Caesar.[2] Boudicca was also brief.[3] The facts were there—what happened when the Romans annexed her father's kingdom (violence, rape, and robbery), and how the veterans behaved in their colony of Camulodunum.[4]

Elsewhere Tacitus, eschewing rhetoric, is plain and frank. The 'pax Romana' is a thing to be feared.[5] No disguise or palliation of imperialism—he speaks of 'vis Romana'.[6] The general Petillius Cerialis in an address to the Gallic deputies, while expounding a liberal theory, is adamant upon the rights of conquest.[7] Another general in his dealings with a German tribe lays down an iron law, with appeal to Heaven for its sanction: the weak have no rights.[8]

The loyal and ingenuous Livy could not fail to infuse an ethical colouration into the Roman claim to hold dominion over the nations.[9] And, not so ingenuous, he was ready to purge or suppress certain facts of discredit concerning Roman conduct towards foreign peoples.[10] Tacitus had no wish to spare the senatorial class or the imperial system. He knew how promotion and patronage operated: birth and wealth, mutual connivance or traffic, and posts of high command consigned to greed or to indolent seniority. Significant examples of cruelty or extortion are duly registered.[11]

There was a conventional theme—Rome's mission of peace in the world, with concord, prosperity, and ordered life. That could be assumed, or disregarded.[12] No other writer reveals so sharply the double face of Roman rule.[13] At the same time, he keeps a sense of proportion. He knew that the Roman power was something more than a product of craft and violence.

[1] *Agr.* 30. 7. The whole passage has Sallustian echoes. For the τόπος cf. Pliny, *NH* vi. 182 (on Ethiopia): 'nec tamen arma Romana ibi solitudinem fecerunt.'
[2] XII. 37. 1–4.   [3] XIV. 35.
[4] XIV. 31. For attempts to play down the Tacitean account see App. 69.
[5] XII. 33: 'qui pacem nostram metuebant.'
[6] III. 60. 3: 'regum etiam, qui ante vim Romanam valuerant.' Cf. 'vis imperii' in xv. 31 (quoted above, p. 493).
[7] *Hist.* IV. 73 f.
[8] XIII. 56. 1: 'patienda meliorum imperia: id dis, quos inplorarent, placitum ut arbitrium penes Romanos maneret, quid darent quid adimerent, neque alios iudices quam se ipsos paterentur.' For the deep pathos in the historian's account of the fate of this tribe see B. Walker, o.c. 33 f.
[9] Livy XXII. 13. 11: 'iusto et moderato regebantur imperio nec abnuebant, quod unum vinculum fidei est, melioribus parere.'
[10] For telling examples, H. Nissen, *Kritische Untersuchungen über die Quellen der 4. und 5. Dekade des Livius* (1863), 29 ff. Also P. G. Walsh, *AJP* LXXVI (1955), 369 ff.
[11] e.g. IV. 45 (L. Piso in Spain).
[12] One could perhaps manage without the panegyric of Aelius Aristides, Εἰς Ῥώμην.
[13] I. A. Richmond, *JRS* XXXIV (1944), 43.

It is cheap and easy to arraign great empires. And all too conventional.[1] Tacitus was responsive to the majesty of power. He looks back with longing to the martial Republic, and he extols the more recent conquerors. Did he desire and argue that Rome should revert to a policy of aggrandisement? No unequivocal answer can be given. If warfare (some might hope) dispelled the torpor and inertia of the times, conquest could disturb the equilibrium of the Empire, especially if it went beyond Euphrates and Tigris.[2] Dominion produced evil and paradoxical consequences. The victors in war were vanquished by peace.[3] Empire abroad engendered despotism at home. Marcus Brutus saw that dilemma long ago. Better forfeit empire than forfeit liberty—such was the answer of the Republican.[4]

As for the conquered peoples, being spared they were despised. Tacitus appears to nourish in hypertrophy all the prejudices of an imperial race. His anger bears most heavily upon the Greeks and the Jews. Hellas yielded to force or fate, conscious all through that her civilization was superior. The Jews asserted another kind of superiority and held aloof from the comity of nations, deaf to persuasion and recalcitrant even against armed compulsion. Their 'odium humani generis' put them beyond the pale.[5] To the Greeks Tacitus never attempts to deny the ancient renown of arts and letters, despite his prejudices; and he might easily divine or express what the Greeks thought about Roman philhellenes.

The Parthians ruled an empire, matched against Rome with historic claims: a strange empire—dispersed, elusive, and therefore not easily vulnerable. Tacitus is careful not to concede full parity.[6] If he shows up the failings in their dynasty and in their national habits, there is no animosity, but almost respect,[7] tempered perhaps with a tone of patronage.

Nor is there bitterness in Tacitus' narration of the German wars. Romans loudly praise the northern barbarians. It is for valour and the love of liberty—and some by imagination perceived how close these natives were to their own rude and heroic ancestors. Tacitus' admira-

---

[1] *Hist.* IV. 68. 5: 'is meditata oratione cuncta magnis imperiis obiectari solita contumeliasque et invidiam in populum Romanum effudit' (a Gallic rebel and demagogue).

[2] Cf. Ch. XXXVII.

[3] For the formula, cf. Pliny, *NH* XXIV. 5 (on Greek doctors): 'vincendoque victi sumus: paremus externis.'

[4] Quoted by Quintilian IX. 3. 95: 'praestat enim nemini imperare quam alicui servire: sine illo enim vivere honeste dicet, cum hoc vivendi nulla condicio est.'

[5] XV. 44. 4, used about a Jewish sect; cf. *Hist.* V. 5. 1 and Diodorus XXXIV. 1. 2. The phrase 'odium generis humani' elsewhere means misanthropy, cf. Seneca, *De tranquillitate animi* 15. 1; Pliny, *NH* VII. 80.

[6] p. 494.

[7] P. Treves, *Il mito di Alessandro e la Roma d'Augusto* (1953), 173.

tion is not confined to the *Germania* with its idealized, conventional, and nostalgic portrayal of virtue and integrity among the strong and untainted. He writes of Arminius as 'liberator haud dubie Germaniae', and accords him a title of renown that belonged of old to the Roman People itself, 'proeliis ambiguus, bello non victus'.[1] Similarly, warfare against Rome ennobles the Dacians by the defeats they inflict or suffer:[2] the phrase evokes the Cimbri and Teutones two centuries earlier.[3] Gaul had lapsed from her ancient martial glory, but Julius Vindex and the Gallic insurgents would deserve a proper commemoration.[4]

Courageous adversaries enhance the renown of their rivals or victors.[5] Even the untutored barbarian might add a testimony of admiration to the grandeur of Rome. Velleius Paterculus reports an engaging incident. An elderly German of venerable appearance, crossing the river Elbe in a small boat, is admitted to the sight and presence of the *imperator*; and he reverently retires, avowing in joy the happiest day of his life.[6]

Tacitus would have been pained if an honest native behaved like a courtier or a client. He insists upon dignity. The chieftain Segestes, who deserts to the Romans, is not rebuked as a traitor. The historian allows him to assert honourable motives—the common interest of the two peoples, and peace instead of war.[7] Another incident reveals a humorous sympathy. Envoys on a visit to the capital would not put up with inferior seats at the theatre. They went and sat among the senators. No nation, they exclaimed, excelled the Germans in sense of honour and in arms. Their demeanour won approbation.[8]

So much for the better and honourable sort of foreigner—potential Romans, as it were. Myriads of undesirable aliens now shared the Roman citizenship. Tacitus detests all mobs, civil or military, and most of all the populace of the capital. A word of approval can be spared for retainers of the old families:[9] the rest were the clients of the

[1] II. 88. 2. The τόπος can be traced from Livy IX. 18. 9 back to Lucilius, fr. 613 f. Marx (cf. F. Münzer, *Hermes* XLVIII (1913), 617).

[2] *Hist.* I. 2. 1: 'nobilitatus cladibus mutuis Dacus.'

[3] Velleius II. 8. 3: 'multis mox nostris suisque cladibus nobiles.'

[4] p. 463.

[5] The Romans exploited Porsenna and Pyrrhus to their own credit (the poet Ennius being influential for Pyrrhus). Later enemies were not treated with comparable generosity.

[6] Velleius II. 107. 2. A little later he describes the Germans as 'natum mendacio genus' (118. 1).

[7] I. 58. Compare the envoy Hasdrubal (Livy xxx. 42. 12 ff.).

[8] XIII. 54. 4: 'quod comiter a visentibus exceptum, quasi impetus antiqui et bona aemulatione.'

[9] *Hist.* I. 4. 3: 'pars populi integra et magnis domibus adnexa.' Cf. Livy IX. 46. 13: 'integer populus, fautor et cultor bonorum.'

dynasty. Rome became the common receptacle of all that everywhere was vile—'quo cuncta undique atrocia aut pudenda confluunt concelebranturque'.[1]

The precise abomination the historian has in mind was a new religion that promised the worst, having come from Judaea.[2] He elsewhere asserts that foreign cults permeate the households of the Roman magnates.[3] The invasion might not stop short at slaves and the urban poor. Claudius Caesar (according to Tacitus) denounced the prevalence of 'externae superstitiones' as one reason for the desuetude of the 'haruspices', that ancient institution of the Roman State.[4] It was more disturbing if dubious beliefs found a haven in families of the governing order. The Senate under Nero was apprised of allegations against a Roman matron, Pomponia Graecina, 'superstitionis externae rea'. It instructed her husband, A. Plautius, to go into the matter privately; and she was acquitted of any guilt.[5] Tacitus (it is clear) was alert for the earliest premonitions of what his own time feared and discovered.[6] Alien religions presented a double danger—the aristocracy weakened, the lower classes a prey to fanatics and false prophets.

In the mass the plebs was corrupt and superstitious and servile. Though no man of station and independence could help despising the slave in bondage or emancipated, aristocratic families acknowledged the loyal devotion of slaves and dependants in evil days; foreigners of respectable birth, and even Italians, had suffered disaster and the loss of personal liberty; while the authority of philosophic doctrines, affirming that only the wise man is truly free, implied that the slave ought to be treated with humanity. Class prejudice could not stand unshaken in the face of fact. Tacitus will not omit to celebrate the courage of slaves or humble clients;[7] and in Piso's conspiracy the freedwoman Epicharis was firm and resolute

---

[1] XV. 44. 3.

[2] He may have known it when proconsul of Asia (Ch. XXXV), if not earlier. Further, the Jewish rebellion cannot have failed to intensify Roman hostility—and few cared to discriminate. But observe Hadrian's rescript to Minicius Fundanus, in 122/3 (p. 468).

[3] At least through the mouth of Cassius Longinus (XIV. 44. 3).

[4] XI. 15. 1. Presumably deriving from a speech, cf. App. 40.

[5] XIII. 32. 2. Tacitus may have known her—'longa huic Pomponiae aetas et continua tristitia fuit.' She lived until about 83.

[6] Namely, the allegations against Flavius Clemens (cos. 95) and his wife Flavia Domitilla—ἐπηνέχθη δὲ ἀμφοῖν ἔγκλημα ἀθεότητος, ὑφ' ἧς καὶ ἄλλοι ἐς τὰ τῶν Ἰουδαίων ἤθη ἐξοκέλλοντες πολλοὶ κατεδικάσθησαν (Dio LXVII. 14. 2). It cannot be taken as certain that they were converts to Christianity: see now E. M. Smallwood, Class. Phil. LI (1956), 1 ff. It can be added that Groag's negative inference (PIR², F 240) from Ann. XV. 44 is not valid.

[7] II. 39 (Clemens, the slave of Agrippa Postumus); XIII. 44. 4 (the libertus of Octavius Sagitta); XIV. 60. 3 (the ancillae of Octavia).

under torture when knights and senators turned coward, denouncing friends and kinsfolk.[1]

When the penalty of death hung over four hundred slaves because one of their number had murdered their master, Tacitus furnishes through the oration of Cassius Longinus the arguments for severity, but none for mercy.[2] There is no statement of his own feelings. Yet he is careful to register the cause of the crime, which is to the discredit of the victim.[3] It would be premature to conclude that Tacitus shared the harsh sentiments that enforced the cruel verdict.[4] Nor, for all his hostility towards the followers of the 'exitiabilis superstitio' of Jewish origin, is it evident from his language that he admired and approved the spectacle of torments that Nero organized, punishing scapegoats for the pleasure of the mob and to avert suspicion from himself.[5]

---

[1] XV. 57.   [2] XIV. 43 f.

[3] 42. 1 (p. 479). For the relevance to certain incidents in Tacitus' own time, and perhaps to Hadrianic legislation, above, p. 448.

[4] Presumably he did not. On the other hand, not all senators will have approved the humanitarian tastes (and policy) of Hadrian, still less his hostility to class distinctions. For his legislation touching slaves and the lower orders, F. Pringsheim, *JRS* XXIV (1934), 143 f. Also above, p. 487.

[5] XV. 44. 5: 'unde quamquam adversus sontis et novissima exempla meritos miseratio oriebatur.' Are these Tacitus' sentiments, or those of the spectators? The former has been assumed, e.g. by A. Momigliano, *CAH* X (1934), 887. The latter appears more probable, cf. H. Fuchs, *Vigiliae Christianae* IV (1950), 65 ff.

This famous chapter has provoked an enormous literature (see a selection, thirty items, in *CAH* X, 982 f.), and more perplexity than is warranted. Nor has the knowledge and accuracy of the former proconsul often been conceded. Momigliano (o.c.) argues that Tacitus is confused, that he combines two separate versions. That does not have to be believed. Tacitus reproduces the mixed character of the situation itself—false charges of incendiarism and the genuine dislike incurred by the Christians ('per flagitia invisos').

XL. THE PERSONALITY OF TACITUS

RETICENCE was enjoined by the dignity of history. *Historiae* and *Annales* grudgingly concede two brief notes about the author's career as a senator, nothing about his origin, nothing about family or friends.[1] People known to Cornelius Tacitus must have been involved in the Pisonian conspiracy and its aftermath, suffering death or banishment—and some perhaps close to his family.[2] Nothing is said. The civil war of 69 touched persons of his acquaintance in the Rhineland, in the province of Narbonensis, and in northern Italy.[3] Again no sign. The mother of Julius Agricola was killed by soldiers at Albintimilium.[4] What the historian relates, when that town is sacked, is the heroic behaviour of an ordinary Ligurian woman.[5]

Some argue that Tacitus despised women.[6] The documents fall a long way short of proof. A consular in the Senate under Tiberius uses strong language. Women, he says, are not merely the weaker sex—they can be cruel, ambitious, and avid for power.[7] The speaker is deprecating their interference in military and civil affairs, he refers to the wives of functionaries, and he is fortified by a recent example: how the wife of Cn. Piso behaved in Syria.[8] Nor is there much weight in other allusions to the detriment of women.[9]

The daughters and wives of the *nobiles* asserted a proper claim to the prerogatives of birth and station; and indeed, aristocratic descent on the female side enjoyed recognition and validity.[10] Women emulated men in arrogance and licence. The last age of the Free State knew its political ladies—avid, unscrupulous, and unbridled.[11] The type was

---

[1] *Hist.* I. 1. 3; *Ann.* XI. 11. 1.

[2] The catalogue (XV. 71) is very lengthy.

[3] Thus his friend Vipstanus Messalla (*Hist.* III. 9. 3, &c.); and he has exact information about an earlier post held by Valerius Paullinus, procurator of Narbonensis and a friend of Vespasian (III. 43. 1).

[4] *Agr.* 7. 1 f.

[5] *Hist.* II. 13. Also, he refrains from mentioning the adhesion of Agricola to the Flavian cause—which was not perhaps as rapid as suggested in *Agr.* 7. 3: 'statim in partis transgressus est.'

[6] e.g. P. Wuilleumier, *Tacite, l'homme et l'œuvre* (1949), 80.

[7] *Ann.* III. 33. 3: 'non inbecillum tantam et imparem laboribus sexum sed, si licentia adsit, saevum ambitiosum potestatis avidum.'

[8] Note the verbal echo from III. 33. 3 to II. 55. 6. The allusion also touches Agrippina, though the speaker (Caecina Severus) had been a legate under Germanicus on the Rhine.

[9] e.g. XIV. 4. 1: 'facili feminarum credulitate ad gaudia.'

[10] Thus Rubellius Plautus, 'cui nobilitas per matrem ex Iulia familia' (XIV. 22. 1).

[11] The Sempronia of Sallust (*Cat.* 25)—or, better, Servilia and Fulvia.

perpetuated and enhanced in the women of the dynasty. Tacitus' portrayal is terrible and truthful. Julia Agrippina, the mother of Nero, is wholly authentic.[1]

Pride and insolence had its good side, in women as in men. Sharing the ambition of the husband (and by no means unconcerned in the making of his career), the wife shared the hazards also, going with him into exile or constant in the face of death. Such women did not fail to be commemorated in senatorial history for their 'fides' and their 'constantia'.[2]

The Romans were not tender-hearted. Least of all the governing order. There was no such word in the language. Cornelius Fronto affirms it.[3] However, a man cannot be a Roman, a senator, or a philosopher all the time.[4] As often, the biography of Julius Agricola supplies tone or facts as a corrective. Tacitus extols the wisdom and the chastity of Agricola's mother. She was firm but discreet in control of dangerous tendencies in the young man's education;[5] and Agricola's wife enables Tacitus to combine good sense with a delicate perception.[6] Which side had the historian's favour when the Senate held debate about proconsuls' wives may surely be divined: undue deference to grim archaic standards (the 'duritia veterum') is out of place, the age has become humane and civilized, and the men deserve the greater share of censure if their consorts misbehave.[7]

Catonian attitudes or conventions persisted. They might sometimes be eluded. The mother of Annaeus Seneca acquired a liberal education, despite her husband's 'antiquus rigor' which forbade her all but the rudiments of philosophy.[8] There were not many avowed champions of women's rights at Rome. Musonius Rufus, it is true, argued that boys and girls should go through the same course of education. But Musonius, who insisted on philosophy for women,

---

[1] p. 437.

[2] *Hist.* I. 3. 1: 'comitatae profugos liberos matres, secutae maritos in exilia coniuges.' Of the women in the famous group persecuted by Nero and by Domitian, Arria (widow of Thrasea Paetus), Fannia (her daughter), and Anteia were alive in 97 (Pliny, *Epp.* IX. 13. 5). For Tacitus virtue in women consists not merely in 'pudicitia' but in 'constantia' and 'fides', cf. R. Feger, *Würzburger Jahrbücher* III (1948), 315.

[3] Fronto, p. 176 N = Haines I, p. 280: 'philostorgus cuius rei nomen apud Romanos nullum est.' M. Aurelius learned from Fronto ὅτι ὡς ἐπίπαν οἱ καλούμενοι οὗτοι παρ' ἡμῖν εὐπατρίδαι ἀστοργότεροι πως εἰσίν (*Ad se ipsum* I. 11).

[4] Glimpses of private life show deep affection and sympathy: above all, Pliny on the death of Minicius Fundanus' daughter (*Epp.* V. 16).

[5] *Agr.* 4. 2 ff.

[6] 6. 1: 'idque matrimonium ad maiora nitenti decus ac robur fuit. vixeruntque mira concordia, per mutuam caritatem et in vicem se anteponendo.'

[7] III. 34 (the oration of Valerius Messallinus). Tacitus took his wife with him abroad (*Agr.* 45. 4). His father may have done the same. For the 'vie familiale' of officials, H. G. Pflaum, *Les Procurateurs équestres sous le Haut-Empire romain* (1950), 297 ff.

[8] *Ad Helviam matrem* 17. 3.

marriage for philosophers, and rigorous continence in both sexes, was an oddity.[1]

Anything can be discredited if it is turned into a doctrine, and men will concede to practice what they deny as theory. Seneca himself owed much to women. He is warmly grateful to Helvia, his mother's sister, for the affectionate care she devoted to him in infancy.[2] Helvia was a modest woman, shunning publicity. Egypt and the city of Alexandria, where her husband was Prefect, could invent no evil against her.[3] The name of Seneca's first wife is not known.[4] To his second, Pompeia Paullina, he was deeply attached, as the historian Tacitus with sympathy attests.[5]

Seneca's knowledge was not confined to home and family. Wit and words could take a man anywhere. Seneca won entrance to a circle where feminine influences were dominant—the lively sisters of Caligula, two aunts of Nero, and other ladies unrestrained.[6] If he is alleged the lover of a princess, the charge may be false, but it is not idle.[7] Seneca gained in poise and guile, in diplomacy and insight.[8] Tacitus may also have benefited from elegant frequentations.[9] The grave historian is sometimes a prisoner of his profession. If Tacitus makes imputations against the fair sex that are not always borne out in the experience of a liberal society, it is far from certain that he was a grim puritan.[10] He depicts gracefully the charms of Poppaea Sabina;[11] there is point and comedy in the reproaches with which she assails a

---

[1] For a text and translation of the fragments, C. E. Lutz, *Yale Classical Studies* x (1947), 3 ff.; for a sympathetic appreciation, M. P. Charlesworth, *Five Men* (1936), 33 ff. Seneca in youth became addicted to unworldly doctrines. His father was able to redeem him from vegetarianism (*Epp.* 108. 22).

[2] *Ad Helviam matrem* 19. 2.

[3] ib. 6. Her husband was C. Galerius (*PIR*[2], G 25).

[4] cf. *PIR*[2], A 617. She shared his exile, and it was presumably to her that he dedicated *De matrimonio*.

[5] xv. 63. 2: 'sibi unice dilectam.' She survived for a few years 'laudabili in maritum memoria'. Tacitus records, but does not support, the cheap imputation ('ut est vulgus ad deteriora promptum') about her rescue from the joint suicide (64. 2). Paullina happens to be mentioned only once by her husband (*Epp.* 104. 2).

[6] p. 258.

[7] Dio lx. 8. 5 (Julia Livilla, the daughter of Germanicus), cf. *Ann.* xiii. 42. 3 (in the invective of Suillius Rufus).

[8] His writings, however, tend to reproduce conventional or predictable opinions about the female sex, cf. Ch. Favez, *Rev. ét. lat.* xvi (1938), 335 ff.

[9] cf. G. Boissier, *Tacite* (1903), 27—a writer himself not unfamiliar with 'les salons'.

[10] Commenting on the seduction of Livia Julia by Seianus he says 'neque femina amissa pudicitia alia abnuerit' (iv. 3. 3). It elsewhere suits his purpose to affirm that Augustus transgressed against the 'clementia maiorum' when he punished 'culpam inter viros ac feminas vulgatam' (iii. 24. 2). Tacitus, like Tiberius, disapproved of moral regimentation.

[11] xiii. 45. 3: 'sermo comis nec absurdum ingenium. modestiam praeferre et lascivia uti', &c. Tacitus can report that Poppaea's mother had been the beauty of her day. He also notices that the lovely Livia Julia was ugly as a girl (iv. 3. 3).

dilatory bridegroom;[1] and a gentle malice shows up the society ladies who come to visit Agrippina after her fall from power.[2]

When a man looked back upon court life under the aristocratic monarchy, he might surrender to a strange fascination. There was luxury and vice and vulgarity. Yet the epoch exhibited a gaiety and a ruthless wit that had since departed from the world. The standards that now prevailed were sober and salubrious, without exhilaration. Society knew no entertainers as good as Passienus Crispus or Domitius Afer.[3] For a season there survived relics of the Neronian days and nights: not the best, and not all of them attractive. They might be discovered in the cabinet of the Emperor Domitian—Vibius Crispus, Fabricius Veiento, and lesser notorieties.[4] There had also been dashing and elegant females like Statilia Messallina, whose fourth husband was Julius Vestinus, and the fifth, Nero.[5]

Solid worth now occupied solidly the front ranks, and mediocrity that avoided without undue effort the reproach of cleverness. Sedate Transpadani or parsimonious provincials were matched with safe and suitable consorts. Pliny, who discovered in his friends an abundance of charm as well as of genius, is not able to produce a literary lady of any consequence.[6]

The upper classes were turning to philosophy with zeal or quiet reverence. It was edification that drew them, or the old myths newly interpreted for comfort and a brighter hope. Even the traditional pieties revived, since archaism was now in fashion. Beliefs of every sort converged or fused; and sublime speculations about the soul and its destiny found support in occult science or ascetic practices. Pythagoreanism kept and strengthened its complex appeal.[7] Darker arts and sundry foreign cults also had their devotees. Under Claudius and Nero allegations of sorcery figured among the treasonable charges brought against persons of rank.[8] The next epoch saw no diminution in the credit of magicians and theosophists.[9] Only the

---

[1] XIV. I. 2: 'cur enim differri nuptias suas?' &c.

[2] XIII. 19. I: 'nemo solari, nemo adire praeter paucas feminas, amore an odio incertas.' There is much more about women in the third hexad than in the first: the history had changed, not the views of the historian. Absent from I–VI, 'blanditiae' and 'blandimentum' occur in XIII–XVI twice and four times respectively.   [3] p. 328.

[4] p. 5. Among them Montanus (identity not certain): 'noverat ille | luxuriam imperii veterem noctesque Neronis' (Juvenal IV. 136 f.).

[5] PIR¹, S 625. According to the scholiast on Juvenal VI. 434, Messallina 'opibus et forma et ingenio plurimum valuit'. Cf. Ph. Fabia, Rev. phil. XIX (1895), 218 ff.

[6] One would wish to know about Pompeia Plotina, who is only mentioned incidentally (Epp. IX. 28. I).

[7] Not that much can be ascertained.

[8] XII. 22. I; 59. I; XVI. 8. 2; 31. I. Also earlier, in the case of Scribonius Libo (II. 27 ff.).

[9] Apollonius of Tyana will not be forgotten, that mysterious (and largely fictitious) character: on whom, E. Meyer, Hermes LII (1917), 371 ff. = Kl. Schr. II (1924), 133 ff.

disciples of Epicurus stood firm, not numerous or ever obtrusive, but a quiet force for good sense. The dearth of evidence may be deceptive. Trajan's consort avowed her adherence to that sect.[1] Many things in Hadrian must have disposed him to approval and sympathy.

At the same time problems of personal conduct acquired a sober emphasis from instructors lacking allegiance to rigid dogma. Honest Epictetus (who had been a slave) impressed those who made light of birth and wealth. Although Epictetus alarmed Silius Italicus (the opulent consular passed for a Stoic),[2] he earned the friendship of Hadrian.[3] A devout but sensible man like Plutarch (his religious beliefs are a strange farrago) was an amiable pattern of moral amelioration. Roman senators examined their souls and curbed their impulses to pride and anger.[4] The age had been gaining in humanity and toleration.

A certain dreariness ensued. The political situation had changed; and the men of birth or courage who for a time made doctrines appear dangerous existed no more. Tacitus, contemplating the past, utters a despairing call for energy and for heroism. He also admires a stylish refinement in conduct as in language. Various senators of the old days earn commendation for their 'elegantia vitae'. Conspicuous are Servilius Nonianus and Pomponius Secundus, an historian and a poet, as noble models of 'bonae artes'.[5]

The palm seems to go to a perfect voluptuary, whom he styles 'elegantiae arbiter'. Petronius was the fashionable pattern of all the social graces.[6] Yet Petronius both when governor of a province and as consul showed capacity for affairs. The studied elegance of his end, in harmony with the manner of his life, exhibited contempt for the essential vulgarity of his friend, the Emperor Nero. It also conveyed a gentle rebuke to the men of conscious rectitude. Petronius in his last hours drew solace and strength from song and verse, not from the doctrines of the wise or discourse about the immortality of the soul.[7]

Petronius is a pendant and contrast to the equally stylized exit of Seneca. Not that the historian is hostile to Seneca. He knew that the author of sermons possessed wit as well as sagacity and fortitude

---

[1] Only accident reveals it (*ILS* 7784+*SIG*³ 834: Athens).

[2] Arrian, *Diss. Epicteti* III. 8. 7.   [3] *HA, Hadr.* 16. 10.

[4] As Minicius Fundanus (*suff.* 107) testifies in Plutarch's *De cohibenda ira*. Cf. E. Groag, P–W xv, 1824 f.

[5] p. 328. Pomponius' 'dignitas vitae' had been extolled in *Dial.* 13. 3.

[6] xvi. 18 f. The character sketch has Sallustian features and an echo of III. 30. 2 (Sallustius Crispus and Maecenas), cf. App. 53. The *praenomen* 'C.' (18. 1, and, emended from 'ac', in 17. 1) was doubted by Nipperdey; and there is now (since 1946) T. Petronius Niger to be reckoned with (*suff.* c. 62).

[7] xvi. 19. 2: 'non per seria aut quibus gloriam constantiae peteret', &c.

—and he cannot have failed to enjoy the *Ludus de morte Claudi Caesaris*.[1]

The irony of Tacitus pervades whole episodes, such as the interchange of letters between Seianus and Tiberius, or is compressed into a curt phrase. His sarcasm took from Tiberius a sharper edge.[2] Another emperor deepened and widened his sense of humour— Claudius Caesar, erudite, pompous, or silly. There was rich material in the public pronouncements.[3] Tacitus exploits it, but not unduly. For example, the Roman Emperor, in sage admonishment, equips an Arsacid prince with the conventional precepts of civil government: the ruler will not be a despot, he must remember to treat the Parthians as citizens, not as slaves.[4] And, gratefully accepting the Senate's homage to Pallas, Claudius affirms that his freedman prefers to waive the grant of a sum of money, being modestly content to abide within the limits of his 'prior paupertas'.[5]

There is gaiety in Tacitus, and parody.[6] When Claudius Caesar, 'caelibis vitae intolerans', has been left a widower and wavers between the advertised attractions of three ladies, he summons the freedmen of the household, commanding a debate in proper form—for such is the setting contrived by the historian, in mockery of a cabinet council.[7] To convince the Senate that the Emperor must be united in matrimony to his niece, that was a task that called for the diplomatic talents of L. Vitellius, who duly produced an oration—in the manner of his master. Again, Seneca, ornate and subtle, outdoes his own performances in a private discourse to Nero; and Cossutianus Capito is made to parody the eloquence of the prosecutors, grotesque in exaggeration if it were not sinister and murderous.[8]

The humour is often cruel. An ominous cloud hangs over the light and frivolous at the garden party of Valeria Messallina.[9] The predicament of Roman knights at a compulsory entertainment under Nero is rendered in excruciating detail: they were crushed in the crowd, they fell mortally ill sitting there day and night, they were persecuted and terrorized all the time.[10]

---

[1] Or, for that matter, the *Satiricon*, though he mentions neither. See further p. 336.

[2] pp. 284, 319 f., 428 f.   [3] App. 40.

[4] XII. 11. 2: 'ut non dominationem et servos sed rectorem et cives cogitaret.'

[5] XII. 53. 3, cf. Pliny, *Epp.* VIII. 6. 8 ff. The setting is instructive—senators expelled 'qui remanendo impudentiam paupertati adicerent' (52. 3), and Pallas author of penalties against women who had relations with slaves (53. 1).

[6] Many have failed to see it, and have damaged their vocation. Thus V. Scramuzza— 'Tacitus would have been a better historian if he too had had a sense of humour' (*The Emperor Claudius* (1940), 21).

[7] XII. 1 f. For the placing of this scene, after tragic events and at the beginning of a book, cf. the treasure hunt in Africa (XVI. 1 ff.).

[8] Ch. XXV.   [9] XI. 31.   [10] XVI. 5. 2.

Tacitus wears a grim impersonal mask. He will not relent even for the innocent Britannicus, in whom some incautiously discovered the promise of future virtues.[1] A proud reserve was congenial to his nature—or had become so.

The fifteen years of Domitian might leave their mark on a man. Those who emerged from the ordeal were maimed in spirit, dazed and blunted, so Tacitus asserts.[2] Tacitus himself had not been condemned to silence all the time, and he made a good career.[3] Other senators were in a like case. Not all (and perhaps not Tacitus) deserve commiseration. Pliny in the last years of the reign benefited by a more conspicuous advancement. If Pliny conceived anger and remorse, the *Letters* betray no sign of lasting effects on his character.

The biography of Agricola offers a temperate defence of political opportunism. It is interrupted by a violent and personal outburst, challenging those who praise to excess the defiant enemies of despotism.[4] Courage and integrity perished, but the time-servers came through. Guilt and compunction (it can be argued) dwelt with Tacitus ever after, and revenge impelled him to write about the Caesars. Despotism was the subject. The author's contribution to the struggle for liberty and honour came late, it was equivocal, it was conveyed in words only. The writing mirrors the discord in his own soul.[5]

Exile or a setback can be the making of an historian. Even the enhancement of a grievance will help. Sallust would have been nowhere but for the vicissitudes in his career. Turning to authorship for consolation, he almost acknowledges the benefit.[6] Tacitus may have become uncomfortably aware of his own good fortune, oppression being a useful school for historians, if it does not extinguish them.

None the less, public life at Rome was enough, even without experience of the tyranny. Deceit and pretence held sway, with many hazards for a man who strove to rise by talent, and fierce competition everywhere among the orators. Success (and Tacitus had been very successful) brought on envy and detraction—from decayed speakers who could not bear to be condemned to silence, and from the acrid emulation of the young. Tacitus, who loathed subservience and had every reason for pride in what he had achieved, expresses an almost morbid fear of ostentation and 'iactantia'.[7] He may have encountered

---

[1] XII. 26. 2: 'neque enim segnem ei fuisse indolem ferunt, sive verum, seu periculis commendatus retinuit famam sine experimento.' See also XIII. 17. 1.

[2] *Agr.* 3. 1 f.

[3] The early priesthood must again be emphasized (Ch. VI).

[4] *Agr.* 42. 5 (p. 24).

[5] B. Walker, *The Annals of Tacitus* (1952), 198 f.; 202; 234 f.

[6] *Cat.* 4. 1: 'igitur ubi animus ex multis miseriis atque periculis requievit', &c.

[7] XI. 11. 1 (cf. p. 113). Observe his fancy for the depreciatory 'histrionalis' (*Dial.* 26. 2; 29. 3; *Ann.* I. 16. 3). A unique word, cf. *TLL*.

trouble and discomfort from the rancorous, from the pretentious—
and from the men who put earnestness before truth, secure under the
cover of an approved sanctity.

The senatorial life predisposed an historian to universal suspicion
about human motives.[1] His experience made him eager to go beneath
the surface, to show up hypocrisy and demolish every comforting
belief.[2] Yet it does not follow that Tacitus was harsh and gloomy as a
person.[3]

From the writings something may be inferred about his nature—
pride and intensity, the admiration of grandeur, a feeling for colour
and movement.[4] The imagery is vivid and violent. Disharmony
appears to dominate, yet the structural quality of the author's intelligence stands out clearly, in the perfectly turned episode, and no
less in the far-reaching design. An acute sense for words is paired
with an unerring memory. Hence echo and allusion everywhere,
favouring the play of wit and malice. Tacitus selects words or discards them, imperiously, the choice reflecting antipathies not merely
verbal, and even obsessions.[5] Wilful, contemptuous, and ever-con-
scious of the effort of style, a writer who could summon the unfailing
resources of wide reading, who had formed the habit of documentary
inquiry, and who was ferociously accurate in small details, may easily
in his personal dealings have become censorious and intractable.

What could be known about those matters? There is tact and poise
and tolerance in the *Dialogus*, which was composed (it may well be)
when the historian was already immersed in the turbulent theme
of civil war. Various passages in the *Annales* show a gift for rendering
contrary opinions in a spirit of equity.[6] Moreover, his personal in-
clination towards the humane solution can often be divined.[7] Tacitus
was an old man now. Age hardens and embitters. Tacitus is careful not
to appear querulous about innovation, or hostile to youth.[8]

Nothing forbids the guess that he was robust, at least intermittently
cheerful, and not unhappy as a husband. If his portrayal of angry and
domineering women is lively enough to excite a suspicion, on the

[1] e.g. *Agr.* 42. 4: 'odisse quem laeseris.'

[2] cf. Dionysius of Halicarnassus (discussing Theopompus): πάντα ἐκκαλύπτειν τὰ μυστή-
ρια τῆς τε δοκούσης ἀρετῆς καὶ τῆς ἀγνοουμένης κακίας (*Ad Pompeium* 6. 7). For the psychological penetration of Tacitus, which is sometimes doubted, it being argued that his
characters are stock types, see J. Cousin, *Rev. ét. lat.* XXIX (1951), 228 ff. For the value
of his pessimistic insight, G. Boissier, o.c. 131.

[3] E. Howald, *Vom Geist der antiken Geschichtsschreibung* (1944), 225.

[4] Cf. A. Salvatore, *Stile e ritmo in Tacito* (1950), 200 ff. For a comparison with Lucretius,
B. Walker, o.c. 5.

[5] App. 42; 51 f.

[6] XI. 6 f. (advocates' fees); XIII. 26 f. (freedmen); XIV. 20 f. (Greek games at Rome).

[7] pp. 533, 535.

[8] The elder Seneca was not so cautious (*Controv.* I. 8).

other side will be set the compassion and the pathos that go out to Octavia and to Pompeia Paullina. Conjecture is vain about the historian's manner of living.[1] What nothing else could disclose, a casual item reveals—Tacitus was a keen huntsman.[2]

Writing to Pliny, Tacitus urbanely describes himself as one who could learn as well as teach.[3] He also related how he once fell into conversation with a stranger whose spontaneous remarks likewise conveyed a parity of renown between the two orators.[4] Nothing was lost by courtesy—and not much is revealed. Friends of Pliny cannot always have felt at ease with this aloof man who detested exuberance and complacency. Tacitus and Pliny shared the prosecution of a proconsul, and they exchange letters. Otherwise they are not discovered in the same company. There are hardly any references to mutual friends.[5] Some of Pliny's advances may have been gently brushed aside. He once wrote a letter to Tacitus deprecating brevity in orators (for the best speeches are the longest), and craving a reasoned reply.[6]

Pliny exhibits most of the virtues that earn approbation, notably a disinclination to look beneath the surface. Unlike Tacitus, he admires all votaries of literature and the higher thought; and he is zealous to show respect towards the Greeks and their culture, in a conventional fashion. Pliny appears well equipped for the role he elected, to be a benevolent chronicler of Roman life. Not that artifice or pretence is absent. On the contrary, the letters are carefully contrived.[7] Parading candour, and not loath to be thought guileless, the author plays down that alert ambition which brought success swift and replendent. He is matched, unequal but not inept, against the majesty and the subtlety of Cornelius Tacitus.

The ironical manner of Tacitus derives its strength from a keen and malicious insight, which he scarcely troubles to disguise. It was not the act of a friend to compose a treatise on the decay of oratory so soon after Pliny's cherished *Panegyricus*; and there are passages that might allude to Pliny or to Pliny's instructor, the unimpeachable

---

[1] He might have lost his wife (death in childbirth was common), or divorced her. Baseless speculation about discord in another marriage, that of Agricola, deemed slow in his official career and hence blamed by his spouse, has been produced by E. Paratore, *Tacito* (1951), 90.

[2] Pliny, *Epp.* I. 6; IX. 10.

[3] Tacitus used the words 'ut magistro magister, ut discipulo discipulus' (*Epp.* VIII. 7. 1). Cf. p. 113.

[4] For this anecdote (*Epp.* IX. 23. 2 f.) see further below, p. 619.

[5] For Asinius Rufus and Julius Naso, App. 92. The *Letters* nowhere reveal Tacitus in any personal relation to men of rank and consequence (i.e. to contemporary orators or consulars).

[6] I. 20. There is no trace of an answer.

[7] p. 96.

Quintilian.[1] In the *Annales* the historical performance of Pliny's uncle comes in for criticism, once by name and at least once indirectly.[2] Furthermore, in choice of episode or in the manner of comment, the historian often has his eye upon persons living in his own age.[3]

Not all provinces of human behaviour interest him equally. Crimes arising from sexual desire, jealousy, or repulsion receive due attention. Thus the praetor who threw his wife out the window. The incident had a political significance as well—it illustrated Tiberius' exact care for justice, and the influence of Livia's friends.[4] Tacitus reports a shocking case of incest in a senatorial home:[5] some of his readers knew that the family was not some degenerate aristocratic stock but a new consular family from Patavium, that exemplary city in the northern zone of Italy.[6] The case of Octavius Sagitta, the magistrate who killed his mistress, created a stir at the time—and it fitted the dramatic structure admirably, for the next item brings on the fatal beauty of Poppaea Sabina.[7]

Sex is not among the main preoccupations of Tacitus—the senator knew that ambition or vanity is stronger. Nor is greed and rapacity, to which Sallust reverts repeatedly, with an obsession that may well excite grave doubts about the author.[8] But Tacitus has a keen eye for money and inheritance.[9] He notes how Agrippina in the last emergency was alert about a friend's possessions, Seneca about his own testament.[10]

Tacitus, as befits one who concentrates upon power in the political field, seizes and emphasizes ambition in the individual and the effort for social advancement, with the accompaniments of envy, hypocrisy, or conceit. No class or person is exempt. The results come out in the character and demeanour of the soldier who becomes an officer, the parvenu who rises to the consulate.[11] Rancour or secret aspirations are involuntarily revealed by some word or act; and the historian is not averse from chronicling the unedifying origins of a fortune and the moral lapses of good men.[12]

---

[1] p. 114 f.   [2] p. 292.

[3] pp. 302 f., 478 ff. Observe, as perhaps touching relatives of Pliny, Romanius Hispo (I. 74. 1), p. 336.

[4] IV. 22. Tacitus had already taken note of Urgulania, the praetor's mother, in another connexion (II. 34, cf. IV. 21. 1).

[5] VI. 49.

[6] The offender was the wife (her family name is not furnished) of Sex. Papinius Allenius (*cos.* 36), a Patavine (*ILS* 945). The fate of her younger son was presumably to be narrated in the Caligulan books (cf. Seneca, *De ira* III. 18. 3).

[7] XIII. 45.   [8] E. Howald, o.c. 162.   [9] p. 448.

[10] XIV. 6. 3; XV. 62. 1: 'ille interritus poscit testamenti tabulas.'

[11] I. 20. 2 (the *praefectus castrorum* Aufidienus Rufus): 'eo immitior quia toleraverat'; XI. 21. 3 (Curtius Rufus).

[12] Tacitus in the obituaries is able to add precise detail about the antecedents of *novi*

The father of Domitius Corbulo complained that he had been insulted by a young *nobilis*; and he made a great clamour about the roads in Italy, loudly denouncing corruption and neglect. He was ready and eager when invited to rectify the abuses. His zeal had deleterious results.[1] Corbulo himself does not go unscathed: Tacitus brings charges of pomposity, incomplete veracity, and prejudice.[2] The first introduction of the virtuous Barea Soranus shows him prime mover of the Senate's notorious decree in honour of the imperial freedman Pallas;[3] and Helvidius Priscus comes on view, exploiting public business to satisfy a private quarrel.[4] Other characters destined for prominence in the later narrative are likewise brought on the scene for a brief moment, insidiously.[5]

Tacitus, who had heard much declamation on the subject of Roman virtue (and who, in his writing, was impelled to honour the past), takes a quiet revenge, allowing it to be seen that the ancients were not always right—or their modern imitators genuine and useful. The old *nobilitas* had asserted a proud intransigence of speech and demeanour: it could be carried too far, degenerating into 'ferocia', a savage defiance both futile and histrionic.[6] 'Fides' and 'constantia' stood invulnerable together as an ideal of aristocratic conduct;[7] but 'constantia' was liable to harden into inhumanity, or cruel acts—'pro constantia rigor'.[8] Tiberius Caesar liked to be grim, he was enamoured of austerity.[9] Tiberius and others were rigorous to excess. In the army commanders stern discipline earned praise.[10] It was not so easy for them to show energy or judgement. The 'severitas' which commended (and shielded) the generals might prove negative—and deceptive.[11] Sulpicius Galba failed the test. Curtius Rufus was obsequious as well as harsh.[12] Q. Veranius, the legate of Britain, had a great reputation, but in the end he was found out: vanity and adulation of Nero.[13]

homines, e.g. III. 48. 1 (Sulpicius Quirinius); 75. 1 (Ateius Capito). Or he can be deliberately silent, XI. 21. 1 (Curtius Rufus).

[1] III. 31. 3 ff.   [2] pp. 297, 407, 493, 495.   [3] XII. 53. 2.
[4] XIII. 28. 3.   [5] p. 301.
[6] For 'ferocia', H. W. Traub, *TAPA* LXXXIV (1953), 250 ff. But there is hardly dispraise in 'de Calpurnio Pisone, nobili ac feroci viro' (IV. 21. 1).

[7] For 'constantia' as an upper-class and Stoic virtue, M. Grant, *Num. Chron.*[6] x (1950), 23 ff. The word has a column and a half in Gerber–Greef, 'fides' four columns.

[8] Seneca, *De ira* I. 18. 3, who narrates the savage execution of a soldier and a centurion by Cn. Piso (*cos.* 7 B.C.), Tiberius' friend. Galba had 'antiquus rigor' (*Hist.* I. 18. 3).

[9] I. 75. 4: 'cupidine severitatis in iis etiam quae recte faceret acerbus.'

[10] XII. 12. 1 (Cassius Longinus).

[11] And Tacitus may have come to conceive doubts about the impressive military façade of Trajan (p. 495).

[12] XI. 21. 3.

[13] XIV. 29. 1: 'magna, dum vixit, severitatis fama, supremis testamenti verbis ambitionis manifestus: quippe multa in Neronem adulatione addidit subiecturum ei provinciam fuisse si biennio proximo vixisset.'

Conversely but similarly, Tacitus points to the good side of bad men. Sometimes the indulgence is illusory. A man is permitted to make a speech of ostensible force and conviction, only to discredit himself by the contrast with the facts.[1] Yet there are unequivocal testimonials for redemption. The old Republic knew that vice and energy are not incompatible. That was not forgotten under the Empire. In the selection of proconsuls Tiberius Caesar deprecated any moral bar or inquisition.[2] Tacitus is glad to produce mixed characters or variegated careers.[3] So long as L. Vitellius governed provinces abroad, he conducted himself admirably, with 'prisca virtus'. Rome, the court, and his friendship with Claudius Caesar debased him.[4] Salvius Otho, sent away to Lusitania as a virtual banishment, proved a competent governor.[5] Likewise Petronius in Bithynia.[6]

Tacitus metes out a subversive justice, an equity without benevolence. He thus imparts a uniform and gloomy colouring to the whole picture of human life under the Caesars. For style he owes much to Sallust, and he has also assimilated the sentiments of that writer. Sallust put his own shortcomings to the utmost profit. Poverty of vocabulary and resources engendered monotony; but monotony is somehow overcome by rapidity and concentration. Tacitus is incomparably more subtle and more varied: yet all of one piece and colouring.

The *Annales* convey the traveller through a bleak land, without light or hope. 'Humanitas' and 'integritas', obsolete equipment, have long been discarded;[7] while 'veritas' and 'prudentia' now cease to have any value.[8] Fear holds domination, or fraud.[9] What abides for ever is discord and tyranny.[10]

The Revolution at Rome worked itself out in two stages, the one sudden, the other slow. The first act destroyed the Republic in civil war, the second wore down liberty and the aristocracy in the years of peace. Sallust is the child of the one epoch, Tacitus of the other.

---

[1] *Hist.* IV. 8 (Eprius Marcellus).   [2] III. 69.

[3] As was also Sallust (e.g. his Sulla, *Jug.* 95). See F. Krohn, *Personendarstellungen bei Tacitus* (Diss. Leipzig, 1934), 96 ff.

[4] VI. 32. 4.

[5] XIII. 46. 3: 'integre sancteque egit.' In *Hist.* I. 13. 4 it was only 'comiter administrata provincia'.   [6] XVI. 18. 2.

[7] 'Humanitas' only in *Germ.* 21. 3, and in *Agr.* 21. 3: 'idque apud imperitos humanitas vocabatur, cum pars servitutis esset.' And 'integritas' only in *Agr.* 9. 4.

[8] 'Veritas' is not found after the first hexad, nor is 'prudentia'. The latter word had been employed three times in the *Agr.*, then twice in the *Hist.*, and in *Ann.* IV. 11. 1 and 33. 2.

[9] The word 'metus' occupies eight and a half columns in Gerber–Greef.

[10] The emphatic adverbial form 'aeternum' occurs twice, attached to those themes (III. 26. 2; XII. 28. 2). It is no surprise to discover that 'felicitas' is admitted only in speeches in the *Annales* (XIII. 42. 4; XIV. 53. 2), that 'felix' occurs once there (XIII. 46. 1), 'beatus' twice (VI. 22. 2; XI. 20. 1), 'tranquillus' once (I. 3. 7). Cf. also App. 66.

Tacitus looks at history much as Sallust does. Yet it will not be fair to say that he simply imposes his own conceptions upon the history of Rome under the Caesars. The history was like that. The events colour, infect, and dominate the historian. Livy, when he relates the venerable past, confesses that his thoughts take on an antique hue.[1] Tacitus has withheld his avowal, but cannot evade scrutiny. The Tacitean Tiberius is a familiar and fatiguing subject. Another inquiry was relevant: how far has the historian been influenced by the Emperor, by the sombre, reticent, and sagacious figure of Tiberius Caesar?[2]

Tacitus is a poet and a dramatist, not different in that from other historians (such as deserve the name), but better. Of his personality and aspirations something may perhaps be gleaned on a negative count from characters he selects for censure, especially in the obituary notices. Thus a fluent and voluble speaker who earned easy success without lasting fame; a lawyer who debased his learning through subservience to the government; a prosecutor of genius who had no grace or dignity in the manner of his living.[3] More significant are the persons with whom he appears to identify himself—Cremutius Cordus, the historian, in magnificent argument for liberty of speech, Pomponius Secundus the consular dramatist, or even Annaeus Seneca, the imperial minister and man of letters.

[1] Livy XLIII. 13. 2: 'mihi vetustas res scribenti nescio quo pacto antiquus fit animus.'
[2] pp. 319 f., 428 f. (style and sarcasm); 523 ff. (astrology). Tiberius is the most impressive orator in the *Annales*.
[3] IV. 61 (Q. Haterius); III. 75 (Ateius Capito); XIV. 19 (Domitius Afer).

XLI. DOCTRINES AND GOVERNMENT

IT is not easy to nail down this elusive and complex character. How shall his political opinions be discovered and defined? Were they ever constant? Does a single doctrine obtain, from the first writings to the last? May not the author have changed with the passage of time, overcome by disillusion with the new era of enlightened autocracy or yielding to sombre thoughts as he studied the struggle between liberty and tyranny under the Caesars?[1]

At first sight and on the surface he is hostile to the monarchy. Not only bitter against the Caesars, but mocking the Principate for its inner falsity and perpetual contrast between promise and performance. One layer deeper, and something different is disclosed. For peace and stability, the rule of one man cannot be avoided. Hence acceptance of the monarchy, from pessimism or despair, from the lessons of experience and the logic of events. The argument is set forth with eloquence and power, and (as is typical of Tacitus) by a bad man trying to pass for plain and honest, none other than the orator Eprius Marcellus: he knew about the Republic, and he also knew the times one lived in; he rendered proper homage to the past while keeping in step with the present; one prays for a good emperor, and puts up with what comes along.[2]

That plea had no doubt been heard again in the high assembly, and too often—and it perhaps became painful for Tacitus to recall in the sequel. Obedience to authority ('obsequium'), once fervently extolled as duty to the Commonwealth whoever the ruler might be, began to wear thin and look shabby, not least if the despot were benevolent: that kind of despotism enfeebles the will and blunts intelligence. Ideal or tradition (Livy, Sallust, and the writing of senatorial history), a man might turn in the contrary sense, inclining his sentiments towards the Republic.

It would be advisable to ascertain what meaning the term had. If the Principate was equivocal, so were its enemies or its critics. Political language tends to be highly ambiguous; and the Romans, whose religion lacked dogma, found comfort and compensation in devout zeal for the 'res publica'. A pretender, insurgent against one of the Caesars, will assert the rights of Senate and People and stand as a champion of 'Libertas'. If he succeeds, he has vindicated constitutional principles and established legitimate government. Which is proper

---

[1] p. 219.   [2] *Hist.* IV. 8.

and comprehensible.[1] The imperial power, in so far as its source is legal, derives from delegated authority. That is irrefragable. How legitimation is in fact induced or enforced is another matter.

Tacitus may concede Republican aspirations, or rather (for he is very careful), report beliefs and rumours. Hence a reason for the popularity of Germanicus Caesar;[2] and that senator of admirable spirit Julius Vestinus, who hated and despised Nero, was believed to be a Republican, and therefore not liked by those who had C. Piso for their candidate.[3]

To bring back the Republic meant free competition for the consulate, government of every province by proconsuls, and the Senate in control of finance and armies and imperial policy. In short all that the Free State found impracticable, all that Caesar Augustus abolished. Nobody faced (and few confessed) the full implication.

Tacitus is devoid of illusions about the old order. In his own day (or rather in the times of which he wrote) some nobleman might express in word or attitude (less often by actions) a Republican allegiance, some novus homo, detesting subservience, might emulate the aristocratic traditions of pride and freedom. In the best of men it was not always convincing; and Tacitus had before his eyes the repugnant evidence of contemporary affectations when a Roman knight, the steady servant of the government, set up his statues of Republican heroes or eminent victims of imperial despotism.[4]

It early became evident that one man held all the power and authority. And it was not long before a theory developed, to save appearances and permit the senator to maintain his dignity: precisely the ideal of the middle path, liberty but not licence, discipline but not enslavement.[5] It suited Senate and senator. Like the claim or pretext of 'res publica', that ideal might be equivocal or fraudulent. The honest name of compromise lent itself to deceit or abasement. It was captured and paraded by bland intriguers, subtle careerists, or avowed agents of autocracy.

Yet Tacitus does not abandon all hope. Some aristocrats honourably avoided the extremes of abrupt contumacy and degrading servility. The prime model is Marcus Lepidus, deemed capable of empire.[6] His character and conduct made a powerful impression on the historian. When Lepidus intervened in the Senate, he spoke for good sense and moderation: his quality is commended by Tacitus in solemn

---

[1] For this type of political language, R. Syme, Rom. Rev. (1939), 155.
[2] I. 33. 2.
[3] XV. 52. 3.
[4] Pliny, Epp. I. 17 (Titinius Capito).
[5] Hist. I. 16. 4: 'imperaturus es hominibus qui nec totam servitutem pati possunt nec totam libertatem.' Cf. Dio LVI. 43. 4: βασιλευομένους τε ἄνευ δουλείας καὶ δημοκρατουμένους ἄνευ διχοστασίας.
[6] p. 380 f.

language.[1] There is also praise for L. Piso, the Prefect of the City.[2] L. Arruntius, uniting in his person vigour and graceful talents, preserved honour to the end, and showed dignity in the manner of his exit.[3] Again, L. Volusius Saturninus, who reached the age of ninety-three: the friendship of the Caesars had not impaired his safety or his reputation.[4] Nor were the newer consular families devoid of encouraging examples.[5]

Monarchy or Republic, that was not the real antithesis. Phrases, professions, and doctrines obscure the truth. The Romans themselves enjoyed a robust advantage: they had long been almost immune against political speculation. It was foreign—and it looked feeble when set against their own achievement in law and government.[6] Reputable thinkers, it is true, discovered at Rome the lineaments and substance of the mixed constitution, with three kinds of power operating in an even balance. Tacitus briefly registers the notion, only to brush it aside.[7] When the Republic went down, the system that emerged is the product of known and assessable forces. There had been doctrines about—but no sign of their domination in the field of history.[8]

The Principate (as was natural) quickly mustered support on various pleas, the words following the facts: Roman tradition and ethical claims were duly advertised. Tacitus knew the phraseology.[9] Before long the dynasty by its duration engendered a habit of mind, and a loyalty; and, when the power came to Nero, the argument could be published at Rome that rule by a king is the best dispensation, since the king is the guardian of the Commonwealth.[10] Sober men saw the apparent ridicule and solid advantages of hereditary succession.[11]

---

[1] IV. 20. 3: 'unde dubitare cogor fato et sorte nascendi, ut cetera, ita principum inclinatio in hos, offensio in illos, an sit aliquid in nostris consiliis liceatque inter abruptam contumaciam et deforme obsequium pergere iter ambitione ac periculis vacuum.' For Sallustian language here, and in the context, and in a speech of Lepidus (III. 50), above, p. 354.

[2] VI. 10. 3: 'nullius servilis sententiae sponte auctor et, quotiens necessitas ingrueret, sapienter moderans.' Only one instance appears to be recorded (III. 68. 2).

[3] VI. 48 (with a solemn and Sallustian comment, cf. p. 356).

[4] XIII. 30. 2 (the cos. suff. of A.D. 3).

[5] XIV. 47. I: 'Memmius Regulus, auctoritate constantia fama, in quantum praeumbrante imperatoris fastigio datur, clarus.'

[6] Cicero, De re publica I. 36 (the opinion of Scipio Aemilianus); II. I f. (that of Cato).

[7] IV. 33. I. An indication of the author's anti-Ciceronianism.

[8] R. Syme, o.c. 318 ff. The notion (widely entertained in recent times) that the political theorizing of Cicero exercised a powerful influence on the form of government established after the Civil Wars would have staggered a Roman and a consular.

[9] Ch. XXXI.

[10] Seneca, De clem. I. 4. 3: 'principes regesque et quocumque alio nomine sunt tutores status publici'; De ben. II. 20. 2: 'cum optimus civitatis status sub rege iusto sit.'

[11] cf. Gibbon, Decline and Fall, ch. vii, init.

They could profit from it without inner belief and without ceasing to profess a normal or deceitful devotion to the ideals of the 'res publica'. The monarchy now being so deeply rooted, a chance offered for the Palace and the Senate to live in amity and collaborate usefully, if the young prince gave heed to his counsellors. The first pronouncement from the throne, after alluding to the abuses of the previous reign (with promise of redress), went on to delimit the respective spheres of Caesar and the 'res publica'.[1]

It was too simple, it had all been heard before and would surely recur. Yet something might be gained by skill and patience—and by Seneca.[2] Tacitus gives careful attention to that minister of state. Not that Tacitus' preoccupations are wholly or narrowly political. He is perhaps more deeply concerned with moral and social matters. More important that the name or fabric of the Commonwealth, than the system of its laws and institutions, are 'mores virique'.

Domitius Corbulo is with the armies, Seneca and Thrasea Paetus occupy and share the domestic annals of Rome under Nero. Men who knew Seneca questioned his career and his principles; and in later days neither enemies nor friends (the latter in a minority) have found it easy to do him justice.

The historian Cassius Dio draws up a damaging indictment. It was not enough for Seneca to debauch a princess. He was exiled, but exile had not made him a better man. He now turned his attentions to Nero's mother. All his actions ran counter to the principles he advertised. Declaiming against tyranny, Seneca instructed a despot, and he abased himself in copious flattery of the freedmen of the court. A declared enemy of wealth, he acquired great riches and lived in luxury. Ethical preaching was no bar to unnatural vice—and the philosopher encouraged Nero in such practices.[3]

Cassius Dio, as a convinced advocate of absolute power in the State, is hostile to philosophers. In a discourse on high politics he puts firm counsel into the mouth of Maecenas. Not only are all innovators in religion a menace to the stability of society. The ruler

---

[1] XIII. 4. 2: 'discretam domum et rem publicam. teneret antiqua munia senatus, consulum tribunalibus Italia et publicae provinciae adsisterent: illi patrum aditum praeberent, se mandatis exercitibus consulturum.'

[2] Who, it is relevant, was proclaiming about this time that Caesar and Commonwealth were indissolubly (and beneficently) intertwined—'olim enim ita se induit rei publicae Caesar ut seduci alterum non possit sine utriusque pernicie' (*De clem.* I. 4. 3). Further, Seneca is present at no senatorial debate reported by Tacitus.

[3] Dio LXI. 10 (at some length). He also asserts that Seneca instigated Nero to murder his mother (12. 1); that he conspired against Nero (24. 1); that he insisted that the unwilling Pompeia Paullina should die with him (25. 1). That being so, it is incautious, at the least, to accept Seneca's responsibility for the rebellion in Britain (LXII. 1. 1 ,see App. 69).

will be on his guard against the purveyors of ideas: they have caused unnumbered woes to men and commonwealths.[1]

Dio's prejudices involve him in sorry misconceptions.[2] He regards Seneca primarily as a philosopher; and his aversion may be heightened by a double prejudice, literary and political—against one of the foremost names in Latin letters, and against a colonial Roman from the the western lands.[3] Tacitus at once shows discrimination. It is Seneca the statesman that matters. Men of books and theory tend to be too rigid: Seneca is a diplomat and a man of the world. Some writers (but not Tacitus) would extol also the practical genius of the banker and manager of property.[4] The historian, when introducing Seneca in the first transactions of Nero's reign, commends his union of moral strength with social tact—'honesta comitas'.[5]

He would not be Tacitus if he omitted to throw off a passing allusion not altogether complimentary to the prose style of Seneca or to the Neronian orations in which the imperial tutor paraded a sovereign's clemency and his own talent.[6] Some of the charges against Seneca were obvious—money, power, and the traffic in honours. They are conceded—or robbed of their full force by being lumped together with false allegations in the calumnies of a discredited advocate, Suillius Rufus, or retailed to Nero by anonymous detractors (among whom the alert reader would divine Ofonius Tigellinus).[7]

There was worse. For the security of the dynasty Seneca had to condone crime more than once. His conduct after the death of Britannicus came in for criticism, which Tacitus duly puts on record.[8] Again, Nero's dispatch to the Senate, retailing all the incriminations against Agrippina, with the whole clumsy story about the shipwreck. It was generally believed that Seneca had lent his talents to the composition of that damaging avowal, and he incurred severe blame.[9] It is not clear, however, that Tacitus shared that belief.[10]

[1] LII. 36. 4: μυρία γὰρ κακὰ καὶ δήμους καὶ ἰδιώτας τὸ πρόσχημά τινες τοῦτο προβαλλόμενοι δρῶσι. Compare the zest with which he retails Mucianus' denunciation of the Stoics (LXVI. 13. 1a).

[2] e.g. on Helvidius Priscus—ταραχώδης τε ἦν καὶ τῷ ὄχλῳ προσέκειτο (LXVI. 12. 2).

[3] Compare his dispraisal of Trajan's origin (LXVIII. 4. 1, discussed in App. 81).

[4] Pliny, discussing his vineyards, styles him 'minime utique mirator inanium' (*NH* XIV. 51).   [5] XIII. 2. 1.   [6] 3. 1; 11. 2.

[7] 42; XIV. 52—Tigellinus is introduced in the preceding chapter. Tacitus' indirect technique shows him a defender of Seneca, cf. R. Waltz, *Vie de Sénèque* (1909), 15; I. S. Ryberg, *TAPA* LXXIII (1942), 400.

[8] 18. 1: 'nec defuere qui arguerent viros gravitatem adseverantis quod domos villas id temporis quasi praedam divisissent', &c. Seneca's own defence emerges in *De ben.* II. 18. 6: 'dat tyrannus crudelis et iracundus qui munus suum fastidire te iniuriam iudicaturus est.'

[9] XIV. 11. 3: 'ergo non iam Nero, cuius inmanitas omnium questus antibat, sed Seneca adverso rumore erat quod oratione tali confessionem scripsisset.' Quintilian cited the words 'salvum me esse adhuc nec credo nec gaudeo', assigning them to Seneca (VIII. 5. 18).

[10] cf. W. H. Alexander, *Class. Phil.* XLIX (1954), 94 ff.

Shielding Seneca, Tacitus for once puts to benevolent employ his own sharp insight into human ambiguities and dilemmas.[1] Insight into government rendered another and necessary service. How great was Seneca's influence on affairs? It is not easy to reach a just estimate.[2] If, in an age that was coming to take doctrines and teachers more seriously, the uncritical might be prone to overvalue the philosopher behind the throne, there was a contrary danger, and greater: malice or ignorance would darken the truth with posterity. Without the testimony of Tacitus, Seneca the statesman could hardly exist.[3] Seneca's own writings furnish no adequate clue. But Seneca mattered. Along with personal prestige among the educated he had allies of some use[4]—and even a policy.

Seneca's policy was the best available. It derived from recognition of a fact, the monarchy. With that admitted (and no awkward questions asked), the government proceeded to operate through diplomacy, persuasion, and pretence. Not much was achieved—or attempted. The minister held no authority in his own right, only by grace and favour of Caesar. He could never oppose to the end, but must give way and be thankful; and he learned, as others before him, how impermanent is the friendship of princes.

Compromise is inherent in the nature of civil government. A contradiction between sermons and statecraft would not distress a Roman consular unduly. Whatever value be set upon the moral essays of Annaeus Seneca (and they were far from dogmatic),[5] in Thrasea Paetus, it should seem, was a man who ordered his life by the tenets of an established creed and school.

Philosophy encountered a deep distrust among the Romans—it dealt in words and ratiocination, it might lead to subversive opinions or mystical aspirations. The name embraced the high and the low, taking in all manner of sects and pursuits. It covered magic or theosophy. Street preachers were also noxious, for they exploited social discontent and troubled the peace of the cities. But skill or sanctity could rise high, and philosophers, like other experts or charlatans from the gifted peoples of the Greek East, win admittance to the mansions of the aristocracy as spiritual directors, and are suitably

---

[1] It has been argued that Tacitus could not make up his mind about Seneca, or deal successfully with him, because he did not fit into the 'Tacitean biographic scheme' (W. H. Alexander, *Univ. of Cal. Pub. in Class. Phil.* xiv, 8 (1952), 269 ff., esp. 377). But what if Tacitus' portrayal be pronounced a masterpiece, indicating an advance in technique and in historical imagination?

[2] cf., deprecating exaggerations, J. Crook, *Consilium Principis* (1955), 119 ff.

[3] Suetonius, for example, is miserable (*Nero* 7. 1; 35. 5; 52).

[4] below, p. 591 (the army commanders).

[5] Quintilian x. 1. 129: 'in philosophia parum diligens, egregius tamen vitiorum insectator.'

installed, along with doctors and astrologers, in the palace of the Caesars.[1]

Some kept a reputation for honesty and sagacity, friends of the dynasty and useful agents of the government. Others were found out. The allegations range from repulsive habits to crime, vice, and conspiracy. The general charge was hypocrisy. When claims to ethical superiority collapse, the vulgar exult. Satire and declamation scored easy triumphs from the shaggy beards and the intimidating eyebrows.[2] At the same time, sober and respectable critics were not loath to speak out. Quintilian bears witness. The profession easily became a disguise for idleness, a refuge for the ignorant and pretentious. Quintilian utters a just pronouncement—'philosophia enim simulari potest, eloquentia non potest'.[3]

Quintilian was defending the educational primacy of style and rhetoric: the enemies were petty lawyers or arrogant and superficial moralists. He wrote at a season when philosophy incurred something more than suspicion and dislike. The government proscribed it, and many of the professors went into exile.

Tacitus (it appears) strains almost to parody various traditional attitudes of the Roman. His hostility to doctrines and their addicts recalls Cato the Censor or that newer type of the old Roman, the parent of Seneca, rigorously guarding wife or son from temptation.[4] In Tacitus care for choice language works to the same end as prejudice, and he is revealed in both. The standard and inoffensive term 'professor' is used once in the *Agricola* and then discarded;[5] he exploits 'professorius' for derision;[6] 'philosophia' is not found in the *Annales*, and 'philosophus' is there admitted only once, when Suillius Rufus launches a diatribe against Seneca.[7]

Tacitus has a keen flair for the spurious and the pretentious. Nero, so he records, admitted philosophers to his company. Not from curiosity or benevolence, but to enjoy their wrangles. They were brought in after dinner, and men of grim demeanour did not disdain to purvey palace entertainment.[8]

---

[1] p. 507 f. [2] Juvenal II. 1 ff.

[3] Quintilian XII. 3. 12. He had been describing persons 'pigritiae arrogantioris . . . subito fronte conficta immissaque barba . . . in publico tristes domi dissoluti.' Also *praef.* 15: 'vultum et tristitiam et dissentientem a ceteris animum pessimis moribus praetendebant.' Further, Pliny (*Epp.* I. 22. 6; III. 11. 6)—the venerable Euphrates, of course, was very different (I. 10. 6 f.).

[4] *Ad Helviam matrem* 17. 3; *Epp.* 108. 22. For Cato, doctrines were no better than dirges, 'mera mortualia' (cited by Gellius XVIII. 7. 3).

[5] *Agr.* 2. 2.

[6] XIII. 14. 3 (Agrippina on Seneca). [7] XIII. 42. 4.

[8] XIV. 16. 2: 'nec deerant qui ore vultuque tristi inter oblectamenta regia spectari cuperent.'

Many were ridiculous, but some were sinister. When Barea Soranus, consul and proconsul of Asia, stood on trial, the chief witness was an adherent of the Stoic sect, Egnatius Celer, suborned to destroy his patron and friend. Egnatius was a crafty fellow—grave and convincing in word and garb, but venal, corrupt, and licentious. An example and a lesson, so Tacitus solemnly proclaims, that men may detect hypocrisy and crime—and especially the false friend that can lurk under the disguise of religion and morality.[1]

If morality and public order were not impaired, it was in general a matter of indifference to the Roman historian, as to the Roman government, what beliefs were held by foreigners or by persons of low degree. Like alien religions, philosophical doctrines may take on a different meaning when they attract members of the governing class. On a rigorous or traditional estimate, any exclusive devotion to a sect or creed might seem not quite proper for a Roman knight. The senator laid himself open to a double reproach: either quietism, with neglect of the duties of rank and station, or the spirit of contumacious opposition, scorning the sad but necessary compromise between monarch and Senate.

Tacitus made his protestation in the *Agricola*. When he came to write history, anger abated (or rather was diverted into other channels), equity asserted a more than intermittent right, and admiration could not be withheld.

Tacitus cannot resist a fling at Musonius Rufus, a knight who forced himself on an embassy of senators, an exponent of the Stoic doctrines who read a lecture to armed men.[2] Other members of a motley tribe, such as Demetrius the Cynic, no doubt incurred derision in later books of his *Historiae*.[3] The central theme of the clash between opinion and authority, quickly and firmly brought in at the beginning of Book IV, is illustrated at once by a character sketch of Helvidius Priscus, strongly sympathetic in colouring.[4] A note of criticism is admitted. It is very faint—some thought that Helvidius was more than a little eager for fame.[5]

In the *Annales* the conflict did not break out openly and fiercely until the twelfth year from Nero's accession. The causes and nature are liable to be misconstrued. Any alleged influence of either philoso-

---

[1] XVI. 32. 3. The word 'Stoicus' appears in the *Annales* only here—and on the lips of Tigellinus (XIV. 57. 3).

[2] *Hist.* III. 81. 1 (p. 206).

[3] Demetrius (*PIR²*, D 39) seems to have exceeded limits in attacking Vespasian.

[4] *Hist.* IV. 5. 2: 'civis senator maritus gener amicus, cunctis vitae officiis aequabilis, opum contemptor, recti pervicax, constans adversus metus.'

[5] 6. 1: 'erant quibus adpetentior famae videretur, quando etiam sapientibus cupido gloriae novissima exuitur.' Cf. p. 99.

phical doctrine or Republican sentiments needs to be carefully scrutinized; and due attention will be given all through to the language and to the literary technique of Cornelius Tacitus.

The first hint that the Stoic sect might be a danger to Nero emerges unobtrusively, with Rubellius Plautus. When a comet appeared, portending (the vulgar belief) a change of ruler, everything seemed to point to Rubellius. Nero was apprehensive, and a portent confirmed the comet.[1] Rubellius, in the degree of his descent on the maternal side from Caesar Augustus, was the peer and equal of Nero, so it could be asserted.[2]

Tiberius Caesar in the year 33 decided that he must find husbands for three princesses. Agrippina, the daughter of Germanicus, was already married to Domitius Ahenobarbus. Her two sisters had to be provided for, also Julia, the daughter of his own son Drusus (who had been betrothed to Aelius Seianus). As bridegroom for Julia this paradoxical emperor elected no scion of the old families but Rubellius Blandus, the grandson of a Roman knight.[3]

From that marriage sprang Rubellius Plautus. Modest and discreet in his way of living, the young man honoured the standards of ancient days.[4] He dissembled his fears, but he could not escape the consequences of good fame and dynastic blood. Nero urged him to go abroad to avoid calumny and peril to the public peace. Rubellius therefore went to live in Asia, where he owned ancestral property.[5]

Scarcely two years passed, and a centurion arrived bearing the order that Rubellius must die. Ofonius Tigellinus had ousted Seneca from the counsels of the prince. Nero, he insisted, could never be secure as long as certain eminent exiles remained alive: Cornelius Sulla at Massilia, Rubellius in the province of Asia. Sulla might seem a torpid creature—but his name was historical and ominous, and he was dissembling genuine energy and talents.[6] There was no pretence about Rubellius Plautus. He took the old Romans for model, and he had adopted the arrogant, ambitious, and dangerous tenets of the Stoics.[7]

Such is the earliest notification of that creed in the *Annales*. It is declared by the infamous Tigellinus, to ruin his master's dynastic rival. Nor are philosophical tenets the primary offence of Thrasea

---

[1] XIV. 22. 1.

[2] XIII. 19. 3 (the allegation that Agrippina designed to marry him and seize the power).

[3] VI. 27. 1.

[4] XIV. 22. 1: 'ipse placita maiorum colebat, habitu severo, casta et secreta domo.'

[5] ib. 3.

[6] XIV. 57. 3, cf. XIII. 57. 1. This is Faustus Sulla Felix (*PIR²*, C 1464), *cos.* 52, son of the consul of 31.

[7] ib.: 'adsumpta etiam Stoicorum adrogantia sectaque quae turbidos et negotiorum adpetentes faciat.'

Paetus. Though Paetus was a person of some consequence when Nero's reign began, the historian keeps him off the stage until the year 58. The occasion of his entrance was trivial—gladiators at Syracuse. Thrasea spoke against a proposal for exceeding the statutory limit. Thrasea's action may (or may not) have excited adverse comment. Tacitus can produce critics of Thrasea. He also refutes them in the reasoned defence which Thrasea offered to his friends. Thrasea argued for the dignity of the Senate: attention even to small matters would demonstrate its sense of responsibility.[1]

When the memory of Agrippina was being condemned in due form, Thrasea rose and walked out. Which, as Tacitus observes, was dangerous to himself, and could not lead to independent behaviour on the part of others.[2] His next action, however, provided both an example and a tonic to the high assembly. In the year 62 a senator stood on trial for having written and recited a libellous poem about the Emperor. Some were for a sentence of death. Thrasea intervened—the legal penalty, and nothing more. Thrasea's speech was complimentary to Nero, who was forced to accede, though annoyed.[3]

The same year registered another success. At the prosecution of a Cretan magnate called Claudius Timarchus, a deplorable fact came out—the fellow had boasted that he could make or mar the province's official vote of thanks to the proconsul. Thrasea saw an opportunity: the practice ought to be totally abolished. The historian allows him a firm and dignified speech, with appeal to the ancient relations between mandatories of the imperial people and their subjects.[4] Thrasea was heard with approbation; and, although the consuls at first hesitated to accept his proposal, it was given force of law by Nero.

However, the next year shows Thrasea in deep disgrace. No new motive is adduced: Nero forbids him to attend the obsequies of Poppaea's infant. Undismayed, Thrasea took the affront as a sign that he would not have long to live. Yet Nero soon afterwards told Seneca that he had made his peace with Thrasea. Seneca thereupon congratulated the prince, which (according to Tacitus) enhanced the renown of Thrasea and Seneca, and also their peril.[5]

The reconciliation did not last. Thrasea for his part was not appeased. With no fresh cause of irritation diagnosed by the historian, Thrasea now adopted a deliberate policy of abstention from all public business. He lapses from the narrative, his name is not so

---

[1] XIII. 49. 4—perhaps deriving from the biography by Junius Rusticus.
[2] XIV. 12. 1: 'sibi causam periculi fecit, ceteris libertatis initium non praebuit.'
[3] 48 f.   [4] XV. 20 f.
[5] 23. 4: 'unde gloria egregiis viris et pericula gliscebant.'

much as mentioned in the whole story of the Pisonian conspiracy, and he only comes back a year after that affair, to be indicted about the same time as Barea Soranus. Tacitus links the two cases.[1]

Nero was resentful. Thrasea had a personal enemy, Cossutianus Capito, with a known grudge.[2] This was the man who went to Nero and inflamed him against Thrasea. Cossutianus went through the catalogue of Thrasea's acts of protest or contumacy, as demonstrating hostility to ruler and government. He reviled Thrasea and his school for their censorious and aggressive demeanour, he declaimed about Cato and Cassius and Brutus.

The language is conventional, and so are the themes.[3] What measure and weight of relevance ought they to be accorded? Thrasea had in fact written a life of Cato.[4] At this late date reverence for Cato need not in itself connote a Republican allegiance and policy. The great names passed from politics into literature, being annexed in support of social pretensions or moral edification. Hence a perversion of past history.[5] Cato avowed himself an adherent of the Stoic doctrine, to the admiration or mockery of contemporaries. But Cato was a political leader; he controlled a great nexus of alliances in the *nobilitas*; he possessed clear discernment and a policy—namely, the fight against those 'extraordinariae potestates' which, he so firmly proclaimed, would mean the end of the Republic; and, when he departed from that policy, compelling Pompeius Magnus to make his choice between the Catonian party and Caesar, he hastened, if he did not provoke, the armed conflict between the dynasts.[6]

Cato's nephew inherited his mantle. Marcus Brutus had a philosophical allegiance—not the Stoa but the Academy. Brutus engrosses the glory of the conspiracy against Caesar the Dictator. The originator was Cassius, by conviction an Epicurean.[7] Cassius and Brutus might have lacked full confidence had they not been able to win over the

[1] XVI. 21 ff. According to R. S. Rogers he does much more, suppressing the real charges against each (*TAPA* LXXXIII (1952), 290; 296).

[2] 21. 3, cf. XIII. 33. 2 (in 57, when it did not suit Tacitus to introduce Thrasea).

[3] 22 (p. 332 f.). Included is the stock charge 'rigidi et tristes'.

[4] Plutarch, *Cato* 25; 37. For 'Virtus ipsa', applied by Tacitus to Thrasea, cf. Velleius (on Cato) II. 35. 2: 'homo Virtuti simillimus.' The name of Cato, used for praise or blame, is admitted by the historian only in speeches (*Hist.* IV. 8. 3; *Ann.* IV. 34. 4; XVI. 22. 2).

[5] Seneca did his best to convert Cato from a politician into a sage. He rebukes Cato for taking part in the Civil War (*Epp.* 14. 13).

[6] R. Syme, o.c. 26; 46.

[7] ib. 57. Observe that Tacitus, almost alone of the Latins, insists on the order 'Cassius et Brutus'. Not only three times in the oration of Cremutius Cordus (IV. 34 f.), but, speaking in his own person, 'Cassius atque Brutus' (III. 76. 2). Cf. also 'Cassii et Brutorum exitus' (I. 10. 3). The author's hostility to convention and to 'ideologies' could not be more emphatically paraded. The form 'Remus Romulusque' (XIII. 58), however, is not due to anti-suggestibility: it is good archaic usage, cf. Cassius Hemina, fr. 11; Cicero, *De legibus* I. 8, &c.

Caesarian marshals—in the forefront D. Brutus, than whom none more remote from books and theory.[1]

Cato and the Liberators stood for the honour and predominance of their own order. They invoked 'Libertas'. Always flexible, the term changed with the times.[2] Thrasea Paetus may be described as the heir of those noble Romans, with a difference. The monarchy had the power, yet the Senate was not devoid of use in the new system which army, empire, and provinces imposed. The reign of Nero announced a fair profession: the Senate might gain if it took the government at its word.

Thrasea's interventions in public business showed sagacity and restraint—he avoided the portion of Caesar, namely foreign policy, the armies, and finance. His proposal to forbid provincial votes of thanks was no doubt flattering to the pride of senators, but did not lack justification. As Thrasea pointed out, it is not a good thing that a governor should have to curry favour with foreigners.[3] The earliest of his actions as chronicled by Tacitus belongs to the year 58. It was still perhaps not too late for Seneca's policy. Dynastic murders, it is true, had ushered in the new reign: M. Silanus in the province of Asia, Claudius' son Britannicus in the imperial palace. That was all. There had been no sequels of bloodshed—and some men might condone, mindful of past history and the lessons of pitiless expedience.[4]

It was not so easy to accept and explain away the superfluous crime of Agrippina's removal in 59. The events of 62—Seneca discarded and more murders—abolished all pretence. Thrasea soon made up his mind.[5] His conduct both before and after that date becomes intelligible. Not creed or dogma, but the dignity of the governing class, personal honour, and the paramountcy of free speech.[6]

Something more can be said about Thrasea Paetus. Origin and family stand in strict relevance to his principles and to his fate. The zone of Italy beyond the Po kept and guarded the ancient standards: Patavium enjoyed high credit for material prosperity, for moral worth—and for an attachment to Republican allegiances.[7] Thrasea, who belonged to an old Patavine family, did not disdain to dress up and perform at local pageants.[8] Also from the North were a number of

---

[1] With the armies abroad, hardly a break since 56 B.C. (or perhaps 58).

[2] Ch. Wirszubski, *Libertas as a Political Idea at Rome during the Late Republic and Early Principate* (1950), 125 ff.

[3] XV. 21. 1: 'at nunc colimus externos et adulamur.' Not quite, however, a 'narrow Italian nationalism' (as Ch. Wirszubski, o.c. 140). Observe that Thrasea is made to refute an enthusiastic asseveration of Pliny about the value of provincial testimonials (*Pan.* 70. 9).

[4] XIII. 17. 1: 'facinus cui plerique etiam hominum ignoscebant, antiquas fratrum discordias et insociabile regnum aestimantes.'

[5] He had not entered the Curia for three years (XVI. 22. 1).

[6] Ch. Wirszubski, o.c. 138 ff.   [7] p. 137.   [8] XVI. 21. 1.

his relatives and associates.[1] Helvidius Priscus, however, to whom he gave his daughter in marriage, came from an older Italy, out of the recesses of the Samnite country.[2]

The party of Thrasea Paetus was proudly and notoriously a family group. After his death Helvidius led it. No less significant the antecedents. Thrasea married the daughter of the consular Caecina Paetus.[3] Now Caecina was an adherent of Arruntius Camillus, the aristocrat who made an armed proclamation against Claudius Caesar. Arrested and taken to Rome, Caecina committed suicide in prison, by injunction and example of his heroic wife.[4]

The pretender Arruntius raised the standard of Senate and People.[5] Which may have pleased some of his associates. It meant little. There is no sign that this descendant of Pompeius Magnus was ever taken for a Republican. The men who prosecuted Thrasea Paetus could perhaps have alleged a stronger charge than dissent or contumacity: an hereditary feud with the dynasty.[6]

Thrasea held the consulate early in Nero's reign,[7] and many years elapsed before his conduct brought him to grief. Similarly, it will be noted, the final catastrophe of the group under Domitian did not come until the year 93.[8] The time and season of such transactions will repay scrutiny. Chance or feud intervenes; and men who adopt moral attitudes may get carried further than they ever intended.

Nero attacked 'Virtus' itself in the persons of Thrasea Paetus and Barea Soranus. From Piso's conspiracy to that act led a sequence of deaths or prosecutions on various charges of treason, astrology, or magic. Six men of consular rank were involved. Three are important and may yield a hint or clue.[9] Cassius Longinus, the great jurist, was sent into exile (along with him went his wife's nephew, L. Junius Silanus);[10] Antistius Vetus, anticipating condemnation, took his own

---

[1] Perhaps Junius Rusticus and his brother Mauricus, cf. G. E. F. Chilver (*Cisalpine Gaul* (1941), 104, arguing from 'illa nostra Italia' in Pliny, *Epp.* I. 14. 4 (addressed to Mauricus). Further, Fannia, the daughter of Thrasea, was related to a Vestal called Junia (*Epp.* VII. 19. 1); and C. Fannius (*Epp.* v. 5) will not be forgotten.

[2] *Hist.* IV. 5. 1.

[3] Arria, daughter of A. Caecina Paetus, *suff.* 37 (*PIR*², C 103). Thrasea's full name is P. Clodius Thrasea Paetus (*PIR*², C 1187). That Caecina family might also be Patavine.

[4] Pliny, *Epp.* III. 16. 13: 'Paete, non dolet.'   [5] Dio LX. 15. 3.

[6] cf. XVI. 28. 1: 'Paconium Agrippinum, paterni in principes odii heredem.' There is no warrant, however, for the view that Thrasea had been 'advocating the overthrow of the government by force,' as argued by R. S. Rogers, *TAPA* LXXXIII (1952), 290.

[7] In 56, perhaps through Seneca's patronage (and design of conciliating favour for the dynasty). Thrasea was also a *quindecimvir* (XVI. 22. 1).

[8] Junius Rusticus was consul in September, 92; and T. Avidius Quietus, a friend of the group, belongs to the first pair of *suffecti* in 93.

[9] The other three are Petronius, Junius Gallio (Seneca's brother), and P. Anteius Rufus: Anteius, however, may have links with Thrasea's group (cf. p. 561).

[10] XVI. 7 ff.

life;[1] and a centurion brought the fatal mandate to Ostorius Scapula, then residing on his distant estates in Liguria.[2]

A great conspiracy had recently failed. Nero had been lucky, on various counts. Piso was a *nobilis*, but frivolous and incompetent. Nero's enemies might build up against him a coalition of triple strength —the leading men of principle and authority in the Senate, a candidate endowed with birth and energy, and a group of the army commanders.

Four years earlier, Rubellius Plautus, learning of his danger, solicited the great general Domitius Corbulo to make a proclamation, so some averred. Tacitus will have none of this story. He reports, however, that Antistius Vetus, the father-in-law of Rubellius, sent a message, urging him not to submit tamely to his doom.[3] Barea Soranus (it can be added) was also a friend of Rubellius.[4] Further, both Antistius and Barea when proconsuls of Asia had the opportunity to get into touch with Corbulo;[5] and, although no known facts of the years 65 and 66 directly incriminate Corbulo, he had connexions of one kind or another with several of Nero's victims. His daughter was married to Annius Vinicianus (the son of an eminent partisan of Arruntius Camillus);[6] and the brother of Annius Vinicianus was the son-in-law of Barea Soranus.[7] Before the year was out Annius perished on a charge of conspiracy at Beneventum.[8]

Corbulo's own fate followed quickly. Nero on the Hellenic tour summoned to his presence the general who for a dozen years had maintained the prestige of Empire and dynasty in the eastern lands. Corbulo received the command to die, and he obeyed.[9]

Corbulo was highly connected through his mother's numerous marriages.[10] The identity of his wife has not been preserved: she might be a daughter of the jurist Cassius Longinus.[11] Cassius, himself a

---

[1] xvi. 10 f.   [2] 14 f.   [3] xiv. 58. 3 f.   [4] xvi. 23. 1.

[5] Corbulo's name is kept out of the narrative by Tacitus after 63: there would soon be ample compensation, and perhaps certain revelations (believed or not) about Antistius, Barea, and others.

[6] This young man was with Corbulo in 63 (xv. 28. 3). For his father, L. Annius Vinicianus, presumably of consular rank, one of the conspirators in 41 and prominent after the assassination of Caligula, see *PIR*,[2] A 701. The degree of his relationship to M. Vinicius (*cos.* 30, *II ord.* 45) cannot be ascertained.

[7] xvi. 30. 3. This man (Annius Pollio, *PIR*[2], A 678) had been exiled for complicity (unproven) in the Pisonian conspiracy (xv. 71. 3).

[8] The 'coniuratio Viniciana' of Suetonius (*Nero* 36. 1), not otherwise recorded: clearly in the course of Nero's journey to Greece.

[9] Dio LXIII. 17. 2; 5 f. In the winter of 66/7, perhaps even before the end of 66.

[10] For the six husbands of Vistilia (Pliny, *NH* VII. 39) see C. Cichorius, *Römische Studien* (1922), 429 ff. Above, pp. 373, 386.

[11] App. 83. Corbulo's daughter, later consort of an emperor, is Domitia Longina (*PIR*[2], D 181). The *cognomen* might, however, derive not from the Cassii but from the family of C. Pompeius Longinus Gallus (*cos.* with Q. Veranius in 49), about whom nothing is known.

descendant of the tyrannicide, had married Junia Lepida, of the blood of Augustus.[1] Finally, Ostorius Scapula. The links fail that might attach him to this company. But Ostorius ought not to be neglected. Of the new imperial nobility, he possessed the repute of valour and arms, won under his father in Britain. Nero feared his courage and bodily strength—and he had a horoscope.[2]

If the conjectures are waived and the bare facts of origin, blood, and propinquity are admitted, an even stronger reason emerges for discounting the influence of philosophical teachings. On a plain statement, Thrasea Paetus, the Roman senator, stood for 'dignitas' and 'libertas'. Those were traditional virtues of the governing class. Their force and content had changed. If the times forbade such power and glory as aristocrats strove for under the Free State, dignity, honesty, and the freedom of speech might still be asserted. Thrasea was an impressive champion. With a proper care for his own renown, he was anything but a fanatic, or ostentatious.[3] When zealous friends wished him to go to the Senate and confront his accusers (no doubt about Thrasea's 'constantia', and he could not fail to enhance his 'gloria'), Thrasea refused;[4] and he prevented an enthusiastic young adherent from incurring danger uselessly.[5]

Thrasea proclaimed an allegiance to 'fides' and 'constantia'.[6] But he was not rigorous or obstinate. If he spoke for reform, and thus became vulnerable, he was no grim censor but an advocate of modest amelioration.[7] He was both sensible and humane.[8]

---

[1] XVI. 8. 2—daughter of M. Silanus (*cos.* 19), and sister of M. Silanus (*cos.* 46). According to Tacitus, C. Piso the conspirator was apprehensive of the rival claims of her nephew, L. Junius Silanus (XV. 52. 2). Tacitus may have seen or known Cassius Longinus, who was back from exile under Vespasian (p. 300).

[2] XVI. 14 f. The consular Anteius Rufus (*PIR*[2], A 731) is linked with Ostorius in allegations about astrology and horoscopes (14. 2 f.). Note that the younger Helvidius Priscus married a woman called Anteia (Pliny, *Epp.* IX. 13. 4).

[3] If Tacitus says 'Thrasea sueta firmitudine animi et ne gloria intercideret' (XIV. 49. 3), the censure is so faint as not to matter. U. Knoche was able to write about the Roman concept of glory without mentioning Thrasea or citing the *Annales* (*Philologus* LXXXIX (1934), 102 ff.).

[4] XVI. 25 f. Some of the notions of Thrasea's friends (as cruelly reported by Tacitus) are damaging and fanciful, e.g., 'posse ipso miraculo etiam Neronem permoveri' (25. 2).

[5] 26. 4 f.

[6] XV. 20. 4: 'dignum fide constantiaque Romana capiamus consilium.'

[7] Observe the echo from 'emendatio' (XIII. 49. 3) to 'emendari', used by Cossutianus Capito (XV. 20. 3). See further App. 52.

[8] Pliny describes him as 'vir mitissimus' and cites his maxim 'qui vitia odit, homines odit' (*Epp.* VIII. 22. 3). To be set against all that Suetonius can report, 'tristior et paedagogi vultus' (*Nero* 37. 1). The sympathies of Tacitus are patent. It is therefore an aberration to state that Thrasea is 'the subject of some of Tacitus' most taunting criticisms' (B. Walker, *The* Annals *of Tacitus* (1952), 229).Tacitus even has 'ipsius Thraseae venerabilis species' (XVI. 29. 2). Elsewhere in the *Annales* the adjective is confined to Germanicus—'visuque et auditu iuxta venerabilis' (II. 72. 2).

The times were evil, and inimical to those qualities also. Nor did all members of the aristocracy possess the character and equipment. When life could no longer be maintained with honour and for use, suicide offered a way out. Some converted their exit into a dramatic protest, or boldly anticipated the command to die. Others went down without a word or act of defiance. Something more heroic might have been predicted of a man like Ostorius Scapula. The shameful wastage moves Tacitus to express his fatigue and sorrow. Not that he wishes the reader to believe him hostile to those who died without spirit.[1] Illustrious men are singled out from the vulgar by the manner and parade of their obsequies, and they deserve an abiding commemoration.[2]

Preoccupation with the fate of noble Roman families does not have to be excused in an historian.[3] If the old names appealed to sentiment and memory, they were also the substance of Roman annals, continuous from the Republic to the monarchy of the Caesars. The *nobiles* survived the ordeal of the civil wars but were involved with the dynasty (itself an aristocratic faction) and brought down by it in parallel degeneration to a common and final catastrophe.

The *Historiae* betray no excessive tenderness for birth and pedigree.[4] If the *Annales* seem different, there is a reason. Tiberius and the matter of the Tiberian books drew the historian to the names of ancient power. He saw the grandeur of the old *nobilitas* (and a few men not unworthy of the tradition, though in a changed season), and he felt the tragedy of its decline and fall.

Something else, however, has been discovered in Tacitus, and sharply censured—the tone and sentiments of a man enslaved to the standards of class and rank.[5] Several instances are adduced. Tacitus adopts the language of violent prejudice when he refers to the humble and sordid origin of Vibius Crispus and Eprius Marcellus, who surpassed in public notoriety all other orators and politicians in the time of Vespasian: they were born, or said to be born, the one at Vercellae, the other at Capua.[6] Most striking is his denunciation

---

[1] XVI. 16. 2: 'neque aliam defensionem ab iis quibus ista noscentur exegerim quam ne oderim tam segniter pereuntes.'

[2] ib.: 'detur hoc inlustrium virorum posteritati ut, quo modo exsequiis a promiscua sepultura separantur, ita in traditione supremorum accipiant habeantque propriam memoriam.'

[3] cf. Ammianus XXVIII. 1. 14: 'non omnia narratu sunt digna quae per squalidas transiere personas.'

[4] On the contrary, cf. I. 88. 2: 'segnis et oblita bellorum nobilitas.'

[5] R. Reitzenstein, *Neue Wege zur Antike* IV (1926), 6: 'der adelsstolzeste Römer den wir kennen'; M. L. W. Laistner, *The Greater Roman Historians* (1947), 131: 'the snobbery of the historian.' Hence incautious assumptions about the birth and origin of Tacitus: see Ch. XLV and App. 89.

[6] *Dial.* 8. 1.

of the princess who was seduced by Aelius Seianus—she disgraced her ancestry and all posterity by an intrigue with a 'municipalis adulter'.[1]

More might be added on this count. For example, when another princess lost caste by marrying Rubellius Blandus (whose grandfather men remembered as a Roman knight from the town of Tibur), it was reckoned among the calamities of a year that had witnessed the deaths, if not the murders, of Agrippina and Asinius Gallus, state criminals held in official custody.[2] After these exhibitions of an historian's horror and indignation, it is hardly necessary to bother about the scandalous folly of Musonius Rufus, who, by rank only a knight, thrust himself upon an embassy of senators,[3] or the ridiculous intervention of Togonius Gallus, after the 'magna nomina' of nobles and consulars had been heard in debate.[4]

Togonius was a low-born intruder. His nomenclature cried aloud an alien extraction.[5] Some alleged that the consular *novus homo* Curtius Rufus was the son of a gladiator. The shameful truth was far worse. Tacitus refuses to disclose it.[6] Tiberius Caesar saw merit in this man, supporting his candidature to the praetorship. Curtius subsequently became consul and proconsul of Africa—in fulfilment of a vision vouchsafed during his impecunious youth when a hanger-on of the provincial quaestor.[7] In the high season of his worldly success the upstart comported himself intolerably: when he was not insolent, he was servile.[8]

Tone and language may be deceptive. The writer has wrapped himself in his subject. None of the Roman historians can refuse an allegiance to tradition. Conformity does not prove them narrow and conservative. Tacitus allows the eminent lawyer Cassius Longinus to expound an impressive defence of old Roman practices—Cassius is

---

[1] IV. 3. 4: 'seque ac maiores et posteros municipali adultero foedabat.'

[2] VI. 27. 1: 'tot luctibus funesta civitate pars maeroris fuit.' Tacitus is doing his best to reproduce contemporary atmosphere, cf. II. 43. 6: 'contra Druso proavus eques Romanus Pomponius Atticus dedecere Claudiorum imagines videbatur'; III. 29. 4: 'adversis animis acceptum quod filio Claudii soper Seianus destinaretur. polluisse nobilitatem familiae videbatur.'

[3] *Hist.* III. 81. 1.   [4] VI. 2. 2 (p. 284).

[5] Celtic, cf. Togodumnus, the brother of Caratacus (Dio LX. 20. 1); 'Togius' (*CIL* XII, 1257), and 'Togiacius' (3217 = *ILS* 6978; 3960).

[6] XI. 21. 1: 'neque falsa prompserim et vera exsequi pudet.' This consular (*suff.* c. 43) may well be identical with the Q. Curtius Rufus noted by Suetonius, *De rhet.* 9. The latter, despite much controversy, is presumably the historian who wrote about Alexander, cf. A. Stein, *PIR*², C 1619.

[7] Tacitus here corrects Pliny, who stated 'tenuis adhuc et obscurus obtinenti Africam comes haeserat' (*Epp.* VII. 27. 2).

[8] XI. 21. 3: 'adversus superiores tristi adulatione, adrogans minoribus, inter pares difficilis.'

convinced that all change is for the worse.[1] The personality of Cassius (but not perhaps his argument in this instance) commanded the esteem of the historian. Jurists under the Principate were often the servants of expedience or power. Cassius, like the famous Antistius Labeo, was Republican by family and sentiment.

Averse from the new order of Caesar Augustus, Labeo in his teaching stood by the witness of the old books.[2] Cassius, when demanding that the slaves in the household of Pedanius Secundus, the Prefect of the City, should all be put to death, appealed to the rigour of a 'vetus mos'. It is not clear that he was correct.[3] Moreover, recent legislation had taken the contrary course.[4] Cassius, as the historian is careful to indicate, was feared for his 'severitas'[5]—and his example might be pernicious. When the slaves had been executed, another senator went so far as to propose that the freedmen should also be punished, by deportation. The government had to intervene.[6]

The Romans were inordinately addicted to embellishing the national past. Augustus, by system and programme, superadded a fresh layer of deceit. He was able to enlist the complicity of senators, especially such as had recently come to station and riches. Senators under the Empire were hostile to change, and they would have liked to be obstructive. Claudius Caesar knew that they would shudder at the idea of any innovation.[7]

It was not easy for a *novus homo* to be liberal in outlook. Tacitus saw through social pretence and conventional attitudes. Aware of long perspectives in history, and fortified by the study of style in its varieties and development, he was redeemed from a blind devotion to antiquity —and from idle fancies about the steady decline of Roman morality from century to century.[8]

An oration from the son of Messalla Corvinus conveys a graceful plea that the times change, and not always for the worse.[9] And

---

[1] XIV. 43. 1: 'melius atque rectius olim provisum et quae converterentur ⟨in⟩ deterius mutari.'

[2] Gellius XIII. 12. 2 (citing remarks by his adversary, Ateius Capito).

[3] The practice is deduced from Cicero, *Ad fam.* IV. 12. 3, which is hardly valid. When the unspeakable Hostius Quadra was murdered, Augustus refused to take any action whatsoever (Seneca, *NQ* I. 16. 1).

[4] XIII. 32. 1 (of 57), cf. *Dig.* XXIX. 5. 3. 17. For difficulties in Tacitus' account, R. H. Barrow, *Slavery in the Roman Empire* (1928), 56 ff. The hypothesis that the third hexad was not completed may help (cf. App. 60).

[5] XIII. 48: 'quia severitatem eius non tolerabant' (the townsfolk of Puteoli).

[6] XIV. 45. 2: 'id a principe prohibitum est ne mos antiquus quem misericordia non minuerat per saevitiam intenderetur.'

[7] *ILS* 212, col. i, l. 3 f.: 'ne quasi novam istam rem introduci exhorrescatis.'

[8] Such fancies still obtain: for example, to vindicate the veracity of a satirist, 'the long degeneration of Roman morals' (G. Highet, *Juvenal the Satirist* (1954), 102). The testimony of Tacitus and of Pliny tends to be ignored.   [9] III. 34.

Tacitus speaks in his own person for his own epoch of imperial Rome 'nec omnia apud priores meliora'.[1] He there affirms not only a sounder morality than hitherto, but a proud achievement in arts and letters. Nor will it be safe to assume him an unqualified admirer of the noble houses. When Roman historians appeal to the ancient glories of the *nobiles*, it is commonly to review and arraign the pretensions of their descendants. They attack the aristocracy with its own weapons.

---

[1] III. 55. 5 (after a digression on the rise and fall of luxury). Seneca was hostile to conventional notions about decadence, cf. *De ben.* I. 10. 1: 'hoc maiores nostri questi sunt, hoc nos querimur, hoc posteri nostri querentur' &c.

XLII. *NOVUS HOMO*

M. PORCIUS CATO, an energetic upstart from Tusculum, waged
steady warfare against birth and class. When he turned author in his
old age, he perpetuated the conflicts of his career in Forum and
Senate. The seven books entitled *Origines* are the first historical work
in the Latin language. A peculiar conglomerate—local antiquities
and Hellenic erudition, the annals of the Roman wars, and not a
little autobiography.

Cato attacked and rebutted the claims of the aristocracy by various
devices. He wrote about Italy as well as about Rome; he left out the
names of the generals in order to enhance the 'gesta populi Romani';
and he put in some of his own speeches, impugning the *nobiles* for
cupidity and oppression.

Yet Cato was not a declared enemy of the traditional order. Though
inspired by rancour as well as conscious virtue, he might plausibly
claim that he wished to purge and strengthen the governing class.[1]
The challenge that shook the *nobilitas* had a very different origin. The
first impulsion came from their own ranks. The irritation of the
Spanish campaigns, a fiercer rivalry among the parties (with a split in
the Scipionic group), a young nobleman's angry resentment, and an
ambitious plan of military and social reform—all combined to
produce the Gracchan sedition, ushering in a century of tribulation.
Before long another foreign war, in Numidia, gave rise to internal
conflicts, issuing in the secession of the Italian allies and a complicated
civil war. The *nobilitas* fought its way back to power under the
leadership of Sulla. The struggle had been savage. Marius and his
party, so it could be represented, had made a revolutionary onslaught
on birth and privilege, a deliberate defiance of 'dignitas';[2] and that
party was large and formidable, drawing its strength from the
financial interests, from the municipal aristocracy, and from the
newly enfranchised Italians.[3]

Though defeated, that cause was not silenced. Cicero by class and
origin had links with it, and his earlier career is not lacking in words
or actions to the detriment of the restored oligarchy. Nor was the new
man from Arpinum loath to claim Cato or Marius for model and
predecessor. Another role might alternate or prevail in his fancy.
Cicero saw himself not any longer as a critic of the *nobiles*, an enemy of

---

[1] For an acute and balanced estimate, D. Kienast, *Cato der Zensor* (1954).
[2] Cicero, *Pro Sex. Roscio Amerino*, 16; 136.   [3] R. Syme, *Rom. Rev.* (1939), 86 ff.

Scipiones or Metelli, but now a senior statesman, suitably enrolled beside the princes of the aristocracy. The epoch and entourage of Scipio Aemilianus had a strong appeal. Though Cicero might hesitate, for all his vanity, to impersonate in rank and renown the leader of the group, the mantle of a Laelius could fit, honoured as a friend and a counsellor.[1] Or again, a generation later, in the great age of the Metelli, an exemplar offered in some ways more impressive: Aemilius Scaurus, the *Princeps Senatus*, for long years the acknowledged master and manager of conservative statesmanship.[2]

Such were the consolations open to one who lacked the power and resources of the noble families—and also their 'virtus' and their 'magnitudo animi'. Cicero was made to suffer acutely by the arrogance of a Claudius, a Metellus, or a Lentulus; and the constancy of the younger Cato in asserting principle and honour was a perpetual reproach. These were Cicero's wounds and grievances. Not all of them were allowed to come out in his public speeches or theoretical treatises; and, had he written history, as his brother and his friend advised, exalting Pompeius Magnus and defending his own career,[3] there is no certitude that he would have been frank, courageous, and ruthless. It fell to Sallust to arraign that oligarchy which, menaced by Marius and the 'municipales', was restored by Sulla, but was crumbling already because of its inner vices before it was overthrown by Caesar.

In the first monograph Sallust portrays Sulla as the author of all evil in the Roman Commonwealth. Catilina is introduced as a natural product of Sulla's system; and, after a digression on the corruption, rapacity, and vice which that system engendered, the author goes on to expound the subversive attempt of the patrician demagogue. It was too simple that it should arise merely from an electoral defeat in the year 63. Sallust antedates the conspiracy by a year (and more), to enhance its significance.[4]

Three men receive full-length portraits—Catilina, Cato, and Caesar. Also one woman—the gay, elegant, and criminal Sempronia.[5] Yet this lady intervenes nowhere in the action, no facts bear out her title to fame, and her precise identification remains a question.[6] Sallust has boldly produced a counterpart to Catilina, a female type and pattern of corruption in the aristocracy.

With Cato he adopts a more insidious and deadly technique. Cato

---

[1] *Ad fam.* v. 7. 3 (to Pompeius).
[2] Not, indeed, that Cicero cares to exploit Scaurus very much.
[3] *De legibus* I. 8 (p. 133).
[4] *Cat.* 17. 1 (before the elections of 64).
[5] 25.
[6] The reader would know that she was the mother of D. Brutus, a favourite of Caesar—and one of the assassins.

was a leader of the *Optimates*, and Cato by his death became a hero, a legend, and a symbol. Into Cato's mouth therefore Sallust places a noble appeal to the virtues that made Rome great in ancient days— and a stern denunciation of the oligarchy for its greed, luxury, and sloth.[1] And finally, Cato, matched with Caesar for 'virtus', shows up the mediocrity of their coevals and of their seniors in the governing order.[2]

Sallust's next work, the *Bellum Jugurthinum*, announces its subject —not only a great war, but the first effective challenge to the arrogant regiment of the *nobilitas*.[3] The leader of the ruling faction, Aemilius Scaurus, is quickly brought on the scene and mercilessly delineated— avid, ambitious, and crafty.[4] One aristocratic general follows another, corrupt and incompetent in the field; while the good qualities of Metellus are impaired by his class feeling and refusal to acknowledge the claims of a *novus homo*.[5] In culmination, the electoral harangue of Marius attacks the pretensions of birth and station in all particulars.[6]

At the same time the historian allows the defects of Marius to be discerned—he was rancorous and ruthless, a boastful demagogue, and an unscrupulous intriguer. Nor are other enemies of the dominant party given credit for disinterested patriotism.[7] Sallust is already pervaded by that general pessimism, that sombre or malignant impartiality which he advertises in the preface to his *Historiae*. There was little to choose between the Senate's champions and the Senate's enemies. Both were equally infected with the lust for domination: only the 'pauci potentes' mattered—and the defenders of the existing order had the advantage of nomenclature.[8] If in this respect the political partisan seems to surrender to the acrid moralist, the municipal man has not perhaps forgotten his social resentments or relaxed his hostility towards the aristocracy of the capital.

The subject of the *Historiae* was the decline and fall of the Sullan oligarchy, with Pompeius Magnus as the chief agent, now its enemy, now its false friend.[9] Aemilius Lepidus launches the action with a call to freedom, denouncing tyranny, murder, and the profits of murder.[10] A splendid exordium—but all was hollow and corrupt.

[1] 52.

[2] 53. 6: 'sed memoria mea ingenti virtute diversis moribus fuere viri duo, M. Cato et C. Caesar.'

[3] *Jug.* 5. 1: 'quia tunc primum superbiae nobilitatis obviam itum est.'

[4] 15. 4: 'homo nobilis inpiger factiosus, avidus potentiae honoris divitiarum, ceterum vitia sua callide occultans.'

[5] 64. 1: 'tamen inerat contemptor animus et superbia, commune nobilitatis malum.'

[6] 40. 3.

[7] 85.

[8] *Hist.* I. 12: 'uti quisque locupletissimus et iniuria validior, quia praesentia defendebat, pro bono habebatur.'

[9] Ch. XII.

[10] I. 55.

The patrician Lepidus owed enrichment and the consulate to Sulla's predilection for a pedigree.[1] No sign of energy, sagacity, or patriotism —and the revolution failed, ignominiously.

Sallust's Lepidus is double-edged, condemning Sulla and himself. Further, Sallust uses the oration of Marcius Philippus as a device to arraign the government for inertia and incapacity.[2] Not that Philippus, the most versatile of politicians, need elsewhere have been commended or spared by Sallust; and other nobles, so the fragments reveal, are labelled with derogatory epithets.[3] To Metellus Pius, as to his father Numidicus, honesty and ability could not be denied. Sallust imputes pomp and vanity, describing with relish how at a pageant in Spain a mechanical contrivance deposited a laurelled crown upon the head of the *imperator*, and incense was burned before him, to the disgust of 'veteres et sancti viri'.[4]

Lucullus, again, might be a great general, and not indifferent to the dignity of the Empire or the well-being of its subjects. But Lucullus was greedy of fame and profit, a harsh taskmaster to the soldiers.[5] Against this dark or ambiguous background stood forth the shining virtue and patriotism of a municipal Roman from the Sabine country, Q. Sertorius.[6]

Asinius Pollio took up the tale.[7] The Italian *novus homo* had no cause for indulgence towards the Roman aristocracy. He knew it too well. The leaders of the *Optimates* who threw in their lot with Magnus in a desperate gamble to save their predominance were a highly vulnerable group. And he could also find material on the Caesarian side, notably the flimsy and pretentious Aemilius Lepidus, who was to end as the failed Triumvir.

Though he had followed Caesar, and for a few years M. Antonius, the consular historian was nobody's partisan. He asserted a ferocious independence. Sallust had succumbed to the spell of Cato; and Pollio spoke well of Cassius and Brutus. Livy in his earlier books might take over from his annalistic predecessors the figure of some arrogant or tyrannical patrician without intending to vilify a contemporary Claudius, and without incurring blame or danger. When, in the prosecution of his long labours, he came to deal with the civil wars, their memory had receded, and the tone of Augustan society became

---

[1] So, at least, it could be conjectured, on the hypothesis that the sources antedate Lepidus' hostility to Sulla: cf. p. 144 (Sallust's placing of the invective).
[2] I. 77.
[3] III. 3 (M. Antonius, *pr.* 74); IV. I (Cn. Lentulus Clodianus, *cos.* 72).
[4] II. 70.
[5] IV. 70.
[6] From Nursia (Plutarch, *Sertorius* 2)—a fact not always sufficiently estimated when the bias of Sallust is discussed (from Amiternum himself).
[7] Ch. XII.

ever more Republican—and also more aristocratic. Caesarians, if not Caesar Augustus himself, could hardly refuse to honour the defeated cause as the symbol, not only of 'libertas' but of 'dignitas'. The last books of Livy, it may be conjectured, acknowledged an enthusiasm for birth and rank as did the last instalment of the *Odes* of Horace.[1]

Caesar Augustus repaired the fabric of the Republic. At Rome men and families had always mattered more than rules and institutions. The old families were back. Hence an effulgence of historic names on the consular *Fasti*. Many houses had languished in obscurity for generations, for centuries even. Most striking, yet not paradoxical, is the oldest aristocracy of all, the patricians, now renascent under the monarchy. Though worsted in the race for power by the dynastic houses of the plebeian nobility, such as the Caecilii Metelli, and depressed for long periods, the patricians remembered their claim to primacy at Rome. After one civil war the victorious leader was Cornelius Sulla. After another, Julius Caesar. Each was eager to rehabilitate the patrician order. When the monarchy came, it was established as the principate of one man, Caesar's heir, but embraced a group of noble families and was perpetuated as the dynasty of the Julii and Claudii. Among the chief allies of that dynasty were Aemilii, Fabii, and Valerii.[2]

Under the aristocratic monarchy pedigree came to count for more than during the last generation of the Republic; and the new families who entered the circle of privilege were not disposed to challenge the pretensions of the *nobilitas*, the canons of polite society—and the sacred legend of the Roman tradition. The age was prosperous. Few critics annoyed its complacency. Yet books had to be burned by order of the Senate. Among them was the history written by Labienus, whose name and family denoted enmity to the Caesarian cause.[3] Perhaps because of something very noxious. Mere Pompeian loyalties need not now prove dangerous. Labienus may have attacked the aristocracy as well as the monarchy. The great orator Cassius Severus got into trouble for publishing libels about persons of rank, such as Paullus Fabius Maximus, a noble in high favour with Caesar Augustus.[4]

A more typical child of the age is Velleius Paterculus. Obsequious towards names and titles, he gathers a choice anthology of ready-made phrases, some so vague as to be almost devoid of meaning, others

---

[1] Book IV opens with a poem dedicated to Paullus Fabius Maximus (*cos.* 11 B.C.). Next comes Iullus Antonius (10 B.C.), while the fourth and fourteenth are devoted to the Claudii.

[2] R. Syme, o.c. 376 ff.; 419 ff.; 493 ff.   [3] Seneca, *Controv.* x, *praef.* 8.

[4] ib. II. 4. 11 (citing Cassius' remarks which show up the 'centum puer artium' of Horace, *Odes* IV. 1. 15).

false and refuted by the facts. When Velleius has to concoct an en-comium for a *novus homo* (for he is lauding Aelius Seianus), the thing can be done without discomfort—no disparagement anywhere of blood and lineage.[1]

A time-server like Velleius deceived nobody. The regular idealiza-tion of the Republic was another matter. It was congenial to a society which acknowledged its own changed condition not least by the fervour of its allegiance to past grandeurs. Seneca yields to the consensus of educated opinion. But not for all the time. Doctrine or a truism might preserve the philosopher—only the mind, he affirms, can make a man noble, not pedigree or collections of family portraits.[2] A sharper reminder was the personal experience of the eminent parvenu whose talent and success excited envy and hatred. Seneca could strike back at aristocratic detractors. Birth, he concedes, is a valid claim in this, that Rome owes a debt to great men, and repays it to their descendants.[3] Birth is a shield to cover their debilities, a light to irradiate their obscurity.[4] Thus honour and preferment go to the vilest persons, to degenerate noblemen of patrician stock like Fabius Persicus and Aemilius Scaurus. The credit of Fabius had been earned by a fighting clan long ago, and the consulate of Scaurus denoted a commemoration of his great-grandfather, the *Princeps Senatus*.

The vices of Persicus and Scaurus were avowed and cynical, a theme for scandal and anecdote.[5] Seneca mentions other *nobiles* with malice or distaste.[6] A robust moralist would not worry about such failings as a notorious over-indulgence in wine—it might go with integrity and capacity.[7] But he can be merciless towards the stupid or the preten-tious. One of the Cornelii Lentuli was heavily subsidized by Augustus. Yet he never stopped complaining: the service of the State left him no time for perfecting his oratorical gifts. This Lentulus was a mean avaricious fellow, with no talent whatsoever.[8]

Seneca's criticism is searching but sporadic. Cornelius Tacitus presents the full indictment, reverting to the spirit of Sallust, and to

---

[1] Velleius II. 127 f.

[2] Seneca, *De ben.* III. 28. 2; *Epp.* 44. 5: 'non facit nobilem atrium plenum fumosis imaginibus.'

[3] *De ben.* IV. 30. 1.

[4] ib. 4: 'sub umbra suorum lateat. ut loca sordida repercussu solis inlustrantur, ita inertes maiorum suorum luce resplendeant.'

[5] ib. 2: 'Fabium Persicum cuius osculum etiam impudici devitabant.' Cf. 31. 3 (Scaurus). Also II. 21. 5 f., where help from Persicus and from Caninius Rebilus is spurned by Julius Graecinus. Tacitus cannot fail to have mentioned Persicus (*cos.* 34) in the lost books. Rebilus (*suff.* 37), who was a jurist (App. 68), earns a brief and damaging obituary, con-trasted with L. Volusius (XIV. 30. 2).

[6] *Epp.* 70. 10 (M. Libo, *pr.* 16); *Apocol.* 11. 2 (M. Crassus Frugi, *cos.* 27).

[7] *Epp.* 83. 14, on the habits (and value to Tiberius) of L. Piso and Cossus Lentulus.

[8] *De ben.* II. 27. 1 f. (Lentulus the Augur, *PIR*², C 1379).

his technique. An emperor can be enlisted in his design. With Tiberius Caesar for his Cato, the historian scourges the aristocracy for sloth, incapacity, and servility. A phrase or a random incident will suffice—but there is also a whole speech in denunciation of Hortensius, the grandson of the orator.[1]

When competition was fierce and free, the *nobilis* had need of all his energy to maintain the 'dignitas' of his family in the oligarchy of the 'principes'. For the consulate, birth was requisite (with rare exceptions). But birth alone could not prevail. An aristocrat might have to struggle, tenacious and resourceful, like any *novus homo*. Otherwise rank and station lapsed. Many families dropped out—a single political error condemned them to obscurity, a disaster in the field, loss of honour or property, lack of vigorous heirs, or an accidental death. But failure did not always mean extinction. The political dynasts in the closing epoch of the Free State found eager and rapacious partisans among the submerged aristocracy.

When the last of the dynasts seized possession of the 'res publica', with central control and the abatement of competition, the *nobilitas* now renascent and subsidized was able to assert and advertise the prerogatives of birth, irrespective of merit. Its weaker members were now protected. The *nobiles* had always been arrogant, and some with reason. But many were a byword for stupidity, or for emptiness. Both types are now conspicuous, the 'stolidi' no less than the 'vani'.[2]

The Roman nobility had once been a fighting aristocracy: 'ex virtute nobilitas coepit.'[3] In the early Principate the men of blood and pedigree still held great commands, and aristocrats could earn military distinction in the wars of Caesar Augustus.[4] But wars became fewer, and it was by a rare chance that a Furius Camillus, when proconsul of Africa, revived the laurels of his family.[5] More and more the *nobiles* are crowded out by the *novi homines* whom the Caesars promote. Nor could they prevail in the arts of peace. The best speakers and the best lawyers came from the new stocks, rising by energy and ambition. From resentment and in protest the *nobilis* might disdain to compete in a field where he could so easily be defeated. Hence the pose and cult of leisure, inducing torpor—and torpor seemed often safety in Rome of the Caesars. An able man might adopt this disguise. Some-

---

[1] II. 38 (p. 325). Not that Tiberius' attitude is here commended. For that emperor's promotion of *novi homines* see pp. 428, 563, 589.
[2] Sallust scored a double hit against a patrician with 'perincertum stolidior an vanior' (*Hist.* IV. 1). Cinna Magnus and M. Libo were both 'stolidi' (Seneca, *De Clem.* I. 9. 2; *Epp.* 70. 10). For the reverse side of the *nobilitas* under Augustus see R. Syme, o.c. 510 f.
[3] Sallust, *Jug.* 85. 17.
[4] e.g. L. Piso in Thrace, M. Lepidus in Illyricum.   [5] II. 52. 5.

times, however, it was not a disguise—a certain Cornelius Sulla was found out to be a genuine nonentity.[1]

The *nobiles* might no longer spend for power. They fell back upon display. The exorbitant luxury prevailing in the epoch of the Julii and Claudii both corrupted the aristocracy and drained its wealth.[2] Caesar would not always grant subsidies, and poverty was the extremest of evils. Hence venality and all manner of shameful expedients. The descendants of consuls could be hired to adorn the pageants of Nero.[3]

They had lost their honour long before the money went. The subservience of senators nauseated Tiberius Caesar—he never left the Curia (it is alleged) without a word of contempt.[4] New men could not always be outspoken, for they had their way to make. But obsequiousness was unpardonable in an aristocrat. Tacitus, when registering certain adulatory decrees along with their sponsors, is explicit—he means to demonstrate that the infection developed early.[5] The incident belongs to the third year of Tiberius. The historian was not intending to exculpate the previous reign.[6]

As a form of government the Principate was essentially equivocal, and the *nobilitas* was called to play a false role therein, forfeiting power but ostensibly retaining honour and prestige. Messalla Corvinus, in his own person a link with 'Libertas', might gracefully advertise the gestures of independence; and the superior parvenu Asinius Pollio could indulge his congenial truculence. The attitudes were impressive, but not wholly convincing—unfriendly criticism could argue that both Messalla and Asinius were profiteers of the Revolution.[7] The next generation imitated the parental demeanour. While Asinius Gallus asserted the rights of free criticism but was tactless and ineffective, the sons of Messalla got a bad name for subservience. The elder, Messallinus, is introduced early in the *Annales*, urging that the

[1] His was a 'socors ingenium', and a 'nullius ausi capax natura' (XIII. 47. 1; 3), despite Nero's fears and the allegations of Tigellinus (XIV. 57).

[2] III. 55. 2: 'dites olim familiae nobilium aut claritudine insignes studio magnificentiae prolabebantur.' They had to compete with the huge fortunes of certain *novi homines* among the partisans of Augustus.

[3] XIV. 14. 3: 'nobilium familiarum posteros egestate venales in scaenam deduxit: quos fato perfunctos ne nominatim tradam maioribus eorum tribuendum puto.'

[4] III. 65. 3: 'Graecis verbis in hunc modum eloqui solitum "o homines ad servitutem paratos".'

[5] II. 32. 2 (p. 279).

[6] Tacitus on 'adulatio' is valid only for the Flavian Senate, it has been alleged, because 'to attribute a similar servility to men who had grown up during the Augustan age is simply to imagine the unbelievable' (M. L. W. Laistner, *The Greater Roman Historians* (1947), 135). By contrast, Wilamowitz—'κόλακες μεγαλοφυεῖς zu heißen verdienten die Senatoren der ersten Dynastie' (*Der Glaube der Hellenen* II (1932), 547).

[7] XI. 7. 2 (in the guise of reported speech).

oath of allegiance to Tiberius Caesar be annually renewed;[1] and, after the prosecution of Cn. Piso, he proposed the consecration of a golden statue in the temple of Mars Ultor.[2] The younger brother, Cotta Messallinus, earned the greater notoriety—crafty, cruel, and unscrupulous. The poet Ovid praised the nobility of his character, not omitting his deep devotion to the imperial household.[3] Tacitus allows nothing for commendation.[4]

Another *nobilis* of this type, alert and ingenious to devise new honours for Caesar, and merciless against enemies of the government, was P. Cornelius Dolabella, whom able conduct as a governor of provinces did not guard from dishonour at Rome.[5] It was Dolabella who proposed that Tiberius should enter Rome in martial pageantry after a tour in Campania. That stung Tiberius to scornful anger.[6]

To stigmatize the conduct of subservient nobles the historian evokes the honourable figure of M. Lepidus.[7] Few, it appears, had sought to emulate him in sagacity and dignity—and for some of the *nobiles* the best performance might be the manner of their death. Thus the infamous Scaurus ended, 'dignum veteribus Aemiliis'.[8]

As the *Annales* unfold, step by step the doom of the ancient houses is consummated. Various reasons contributed. Most effective and murderous was their entanglement in the family politics of the dynasty. After Nero, hardly any survived. Nero, himself a Domitius Ahenobarbus by birth, had in his veins the blood of Julii, Claudii, and Antonii: the Julio–Claudian house presents the central episode in the decline and fall of a whole aristocracy. Their rivals and peers perish also, the descendants of the dynasts Cinna, Sulla, Crassus, and Pompeius. Despite intrigue or conspiracy they had not been able to bring forth a substitute for the Caesars.

When a plot formed against Nero, with C. Piso as candidate for the purple, the chance of the aristocracy seemed to have arrived after all. Tacitus regards many of the participants with favour. Not, however, the ostensible protagonist. Piso had all the easy and amiable accomplishments, but no strength of character, no capacity for affairs. In

---

[1] I. 9. 5.   [2] III. 18. 2.

[3] See the *testimonia* in *PIR²*, A 1488. He sent Ovid imperial busts or statuettes of silver for his domestic shrine (*Ex Ponto* II. 8. 1 ff.).

[4] V. 3. 3: 'promptissimo Cotta Messallino cum atroci sententia'; VI. 5. 1: 'saevissimae cuiusque sententiae auctor'; 7. 1: 'egens ob luxum, per flagitia infamis.'

[5] Dolabella (*cos.* 10) was legate of Dalmatia in 14 (Velleius II. 125. 5; *ILS* 938).

[6] III. 47. 4. As a prosecutor in the company of Domitius Afer, 'suam ipse nobilitatem suum sanguinem perditum ibat' (IV. 66. 2).

[7] IV. 20 (where Cotta Messallinus is contrasted).

[8] VI. 29. 4. He is described as 'insignis nobilitate et orandis causis, vita probrosus' (ib. 1). Cf. also III. 66. 2; 'ille Scaurus quem proavum suum obprobrium maiorum Mamercus infami opera dehonestabat.'

short, an inoffensive Nero. A resplendent lineage and influential connexions were supported by the credit, or at least the semblance, of many virtues. Piso was eloquent, generous, and gracious; and he was commended by a handsome physique. Yet for all his magnificence he was only a lover of pleasure, a frivolous fellow.[1]

The narrative, as designed by Tacitus, bears out the character sketch: by almost suppressing any mention of Piso himself, it confirms his nullity. Other persons capture the interest, with lavish detail about their movements and the manner of their deaths. Piso in fact did nothing. How and when he met his end is barely noticed.[2] Conspicuous by contrast is the fate of the consul Julius Vestinus, a bold and witty man who had often made fun of Nero.[3] Vestinus had not even been admitted to the plot—they feared his independent temper. Seneca was not in it either, and Seneca dominates the scene, firm and courageous to the last.[4]

Seneca had no craving for the power. Seneca and others would ask whether the change from Nero to Piso was worth the disruption of a long dynastic stability, the risk of trouble from the generals and the armies. There were prudent and vigilant men among the counsellors of Nero.[5]

The second and ultimate chance of the old aristocracy came with the patrician Sulpicius Galba. His line was notorious for rigour and cruelty. Caesar Augustus retrieved the Sulpicii, hence a consul with no support of merit.[6] The son of that consul paraded pedigree and exploited the favour of the dynasty. The historian, hostile to conventional notions of antique virtue, shows him up as a calamitous failure.

Galba, who had no son, adopted a Piso and sought to transfer the Principate to the line of Crassus and Pompeius.[7] The next three rulers in their rapid sequence show the power passing to much newer stocks. The parents of Otho and Vitellius owed ennoblement to Tiberius Caesar for loyal service, and continued to enjoy high honour from the dynasty. Vespasian's father was not even a senator.

The brief experiment of Galba abolished once and for all the claims of Republican ancestry. Thirty years later it became evident with Cocceius Nerva that the equestrian and municipal families which broke into the governing class in the years of the Revolution or arrived by the patronage of Caesar Augustus were also a spent force.

---

[1] xv. 48. 2 f. His motives are impugned in 52. 4 f.

[2] 61. 4 f., with the note 'testamentum foedis adversus Neronem adulationibus amori uxoris dedit, quam degenerem et sola corporis forma commendatam amici matrimonio abstulerat.'

[3] 68 f.　　　　　　　　　　　　　[4] 60–64. No fear (61. 2); no subservience (62. 1).

[5] If Cocceius Nerva was active in detecting the plot against Nero (cf. xv. 72. 1), that need not be wholly to his discredit.

[6] R. Syme, o.c. 511.　　　　　　　　　[7] For the pedigree, p. 385.

The Cocceii came from Narnia, an ancient Latin colony in the border zone between Sabines and Umbrians.[1] Nerva's father married a daughter of Octavius Laenas, a *novus homo* from the Marsi in the heart of the Appennines, while a son of this Octavius formed a connexion with the dynasty—his wife was Rubellia Bassa, the great-granddaughter of Tiberius Caesar.[2] The Octavii Laenates lapsed into an almost total obscurity, missing the consulate for two generations, while the Rubellii also declined, and were perhaps extinct. But the pedigree and the kinsfolk of Nerva, as of other aristocrats, leapt into sudden and ephemeral notoriety in 96 and 97.[3]

What Tacitus thought of Cocceius Nerva may perhaps be divined from the way he deals with Galba's rule—and with Galba's choice of a successor. There is something else. In the *Annales* he recounts the death of Nerva's grandfather, the eminent jurist.[4] A few lines lower down comes the marriage of Rubellius Blandus to Julia, the granddaughter of Tiberius Caesar. The match aroused public grief and indignation, so the historian alleges.[5] Further, two other princesses (daughters of Germanicus) were betrothed in this same year, but the notice is inserted in another place, disjoined from Julia and Rubellius. One princess (Drusilla) was to marry L. Cassius Longinus, the other (Julia Livilla), M. Vinicius. Now the father and grandfather of Vinicius had been consuls, but his extraction was municipal. Tacitus supplies the facts and extenuates them. Anger is absent.[6]

The son born to Rubellius and Julia should have silenced criticism. Tacitus conjures up all his resources to embellish, and to magnify, Rubellius Plautus, admirable in the conduct of his life, courageous and constant at the end.[7] Other descendants of this match may not have been exemplary for virtue and achievement.

In his satire on pedigree Juvenal produces as the prime exhibit a Rubellius Blandus, son of Julia.[8] No merit or quality, no sign of life or spirit—this Rubellius is a lump of living statuary.[9] To succour him in the courts of law he will need a low-born advocate and eloquence coming up out of the people.[10] The satirist might have added that

[1] Victor, *De Caes.* 12. 1, cf. *Epit.* 12. 1.

[2] *ILS* 281 (Nerva's mother); 952 (Rubellia Bassa). See further App. 1.

[3] App. 1. Thus Calpurnius Crassus. Also certain Asinii (p. 302), descended from Gallus and Vipsania. For their stemma, J. H. Oliver, *AJP* LXVIII (1947), 157. Ser. Cornelius Dolabella Petronianus, the consul of 86, may still have been alive, cf. *PIR*[2], C 1351: the son of Galba's kinsman (p. 151).

[4] VI. 26. 1 f.   [5] 27. 1.

[6] 15. 1: 'Vinicio oppidanum genus: Calibus ortus, patre atque avo consularibus cetera equestri familia erat, mitis ingenio et comptae facundiae.' The consul of 30, and of 45.

[7] p. 555.   [8] VIII. 39 ff.

[9] 53 ff.: 'nil nisi Cecropides truncoque simillimus Hermae. | nullo quippe alio vincis discrimine quam quod | illi marmoreum caput est, tua vivit imago.'

[10] 47 ff.

Rubellius was doubly degenerate. He was not merely a scion of the nobility. His stupidity and torpor dishonoured the 'bonae artes' of an energetic ancestor, precisely the municipal knight from Tibur who had taught the art of speech at Rome.[1]

Juvenal's Rubellius is not otherwise certified. He may be genuine, he may be only a malignant invention.[2] Contemporaries could discern in Cocceius Nerva many of the authentic features of an effete stock. With Nerva Caesar ended a family that established its *nobilitas* in war and enhanced its repute by juristic excellence.[3] Nerva was not a jurist, not even a public speaker.[4]

Birth, the subtle arts, and court influence since the Neronian days, that was not enough. Nor could Nerva find and use *nobiles* for his allies in government. Five names are attested.[5] Nobody in that group had a consular parent, and each (so far as known) was the first senator in his family. The list of second consulates under Trajan tells the same story.[6]

If the descendants of Triumviral and Augustan consuls seem an anomaly when Trajan ruled and Tacitus wrote, Republican *nobiles* are portentous in their rarity. They benefited from Trajan's indulgence, so it is asserted. He gave back their mansions and built up their fortunes;[7] and he was eager to rescue from oblivion the ancient names, bringing them rapidly to honour in the Commonwealth.[8]

The facts stand in contrast. Measured by consulates Trajan appears less a friend than Domitian. That emperor permitted a number of aristocrats to inaugurate a year with their names.[9] Birth, however, is debarred from the earliest honours that Trajan awards (publishing the new ruler's allies and true policy), still less could there be prospect of an iterated tenure of the *fasces*.[10] The first *ordinarius* of rank and family comes in 104.[11] Then a gap till 111, which produces one of the *nobiles* that recall the Republic.[12]

To be preserved and exhibited as historical relics was their sole utility. In dread of the Caesars, the feeble heirs to a name of power

---

[1] *PIR²*, R 80. He is frequently cited by the elder Seneca.

[2] App. 1.

[3] M. Cocceius Nerva (*PIR²*, C 1224) is the ancestor, consul in 36 B.C. Tiberius' friend, the illustrious jurist (*suff.* 21 or 22), is perhaps his grandson.

[4] Fronto, p. 123 N = Haines II, p. 136: 'et Nerva facta sua in senatu rogaticiis verbis commendavit.' Martial's praise of his 'facundia' (VIII. 70. 2) is cautious and revealing.

[5] p. 3. Three Transpadani, two Narbonensians.　　　　　　[6] p. 599.

[7] Pliny, *Pan.* 50. 3: 'ergo in vestigia sedesque nobilium inmigrant pares domini.'

[8] 69. 6: 'sunt in honore hominum et in ore famae magna nomina ⟨revocata⟩ ex tenebris oblivionis indulgentia Caesaris, cuius haec intentio est ut nobiles et conservet et efficiat.'

[9] e.g. 91, 92, 94, 96 (the last three Triumviral or Augustan nobility). For aristocrats coeval with Tacitus, App. 24.

[10] For the iterations, p. 599.　　　　　　[11] M. Asinius Marcellus.

[12] C. Calpurnius Piso.

shunned the Senate and the Forum, crept into the shelter of their palaces and lurked in the seclusion of their country houses.[1] It was not easy to reassure their fears, and it was not always safe. A great name echoed back to the great age of Rome.[2] Calpurnius Crassus carried the lineage of the Licinii Crassi as well as that of the Calpurnii Pisones, with descent also from Pompeius Magnus on the female side. Innocuous, so far as is known, and mindful of what the times permitted, this aristocrat could not evade the repeated suspicion of conspiracy: he was sent into exile, and in the end he was executed.[3]

No less melancholy was the destiny of another Piso. He devoted himself to the writing of elegiac verse on mythological subjects; and he recited his compositions with touching grace and modesty.[4] Pliny was unable to restrain an ingenuous enthusiasm. He embraced the author, exhorting him to go on as he had begun and transmit to posterity the torch he had received from his ancestors.

Pliny extols erudite and frivolous versification as an accomplishment worthy of the historic Pisones; he prays to heaven that similar documents of excellence may be vouchsafed among young men of birth and breeding; and he dwells upon the conduct proper to 'nobiles nostri' in a tone of smug and possessive condescension. So low have the scions of the nobility fallen. They can now be patronized by a self-satisfied upstart. Pliny in his exuberance discloses the standards of praise and blame conventionally honoured in the society of his time.

When Trajan supplanted Nerva, and 'virtus' conquered pedigree, there was no denying the fact—and every reason to cover it up. The official panegyrist behaves with proper discretion—no depreciation of the *nobilitas* or praise of the new stocks. In Trajan he acclaims a worthy peer of the military heroes in the ancient days, a Fabricius, a Camillus, a Scipio.[5] One of them, it is true, was a *novus homo*, Fabricius. But Fabricius now belonged to legend and rhetoric, innocuous were he not laudable. The orator does not name the authentic predecessors, C. Marius or M. Vipsanius Agrippa.

The author of the *Annales* knew no such impediments; and he discerned, in the vicissitudes of the governing oligarchy under the Julii and Claudii, the foreshadowing of what was to stand out and predominate in his own time and generation. The claims and qualities of *novi homines* would be accurately and conspicuously registered.

---

[1] Pliny, *Pan.* 44. 5.

[2] 69. 5: 'illos ingentium virorum nepotes, illos posteros libertatis.'

[3] pp. 9, 241, 477, 485. Not perhaps identical with the man mentioned by Fronto, p. 151 N = Haines II, p. 76: 'ut nostra hic memoria Crassus lucem fugitabat.'

[4] Pliny, *Epp.* v. 17. Possibly C. Piso (*cos.* 111), who might be a grandson of the Neronian conspirator.

[5] *Pan.* 13. 4.

At the lowest, plain merit, steady service, and the patronage of Caesar. Thus Poppaeus Sabinus, who held a great command for long years: he is coolly designated as 'par negotiis neque supra'.[1] Memmius Regulus (who had Moesia after Poppaeus) rose higher in worldly success—three priesthoods and the hand of Lollia Paullina.[2] Sagacity and balance put him almost on a level with certain noblemen who in the days of Tiberius Caesar had found and followed the middle path in politics. When Nero fell ill, and courtiers freely spoke their grim forebodings, the Emperor reassured them: the 'res publica' would be safe with Memmius Regulus.[3]

Despite the testimonial to his eminence, Memmius died in his bed. He was preserved by 'quies'. No affectation of 'quies' would have availed to save Valerius Asiaticus. If nothing else, his bold demeanour after Caligula's assassination marked him out as a dangerous man. His was a courage and dignity that most of the aristocracy had forfeited— and a splendour of living that surpassed them.[4]

The reign of Nero, opening with the murder of M. Silanus, a nobleman of dynastic blood, caused a great carnage of the aristocracy. Many noble houses were extinguished utterly. In the conception of the historian Tacitus, however, the principal victims of Nero are three *novi homines*, precisely Seneca, Thrasea, and Corbulo.[5] Their virtues were varied—supreme literary and oratorical talent in the one, in the other dignity and independence. The third, with military renown excessive in a senator, was plainly 'capax imperii'.[6]

Perhaps the historian has made too much of these three characters. Seneca was not the sole counsellor and minister in the early years of the reign; the campaigns of Corbulo, in purpose or achievement, hardly deserve the space they occupy; and it is not clear that the party of Thrasea Paetus was a direct menace to the government. Tacitus had his reasons. The most obvious is the need for dramatic contrast. More important, his insistence that the history shall not be just a history of Nero. Yet it might (and should) be claimed that Seneca, Corbulo, and Thrasea possess a wider significance in the design and thoughts of the author, a validity not exhausted by their time and place and actions.

However it be, Tacitus is careful not to dwell exclusively upon their

---

[1] VI. 39. 3.   [2] *ILS* 8815 (Delphi); *I. l. de Gaule* 683 (Ruscino), &c.

[3] XIV. 47. I. The historian shows an especial interest in, and favour towards, Memmius Regulus (App. 60; 82). Some episodes in his career could have earned a different interpretation (cf. App. 82).

[4] XI. I ff.

[5] The *suffectus* of 39 might be the general (not his father, *PIR²*, D 141). In any case, a new family, cf. App. 83.

[6] For his links with the aristocracy and with enemies of Nero, above, p. 560; for his *legati*, App. 84.

good qualities. A few hints put the reader on his guard about Corbulo; criticism of Thrasea is admitted from time to time; and he supplies all the arguments for detractors of Seneca.

A facile antithesis contrasted *nobiles* and *novi homines*. On the one side, luxury and inertia; on the other, energy and integrity. The formulas were devised by *novi homines* of the Republic in the struggle for office and advancement. The Empire took them over, careerists or their patrons exploited them—and the uncritical concur.

Tacitus brings the corrective. A series of summary portraits reveals the qualities that political success under the Caesars demanded or produced. Military merit, oratory, and proficiency in legal studies, such were the channels of advancement for *novi homines* according to the traditional prescription at Rome, which the monarchy inherited.[1] A trio of detestable old men surviving into the reign of Tiberius exemplify the system—and demolish any comforting generalizations about the solid worth of Augustan consulars.

From humble origins in a small town of Latium, Sulpicius Quirinius rose by military talent to the consulate, with high commands thereafter and signal services to Augustus. Unlike some hasty careerists, he was careful to pay court to Tiberius at Rhodes, and he benefited all through—wealth, honours and influence, resplendent marriages, and a state funeral. A footnote to the obituary notice adds that Quirinius was bitterly hated for his greed and rancour.[2]

Q. Haterius, that fluent orator, was bold and free in the schools of rhetoric, where he would declaim against despotism and deplore the extinction of liberty.[3] But nowhere else. To make up for a lack of tact in debate, Haterius grovelled before Tiberius Caesar.[4] And he once proposed that certain decrees should be inscribed in letters of gold, for permanent exhibition in the Curia. Such was Haterius, 'senex foedissimae adulationis'.[5] His descendants conform—the son cruel and vicious, the grandson a wastrel.[6]

---

[1] IV. 6. 2 (Tiberius' practice): 'mandabatque honores nobilitatem maiorum, claritudinem militiae, inlustres domi artes spectando.' Cf. Livy on Cato, 'ad summos honores alios scientia iuris, alios eloquentia, alios gloria militaris provexit' (XXXIX. 40. 5).

[2] III. 48. Before Aemilia Lepida (once betrothed to L. Caesar, cf. III. 22 f.), Quirinius had been married to a Claudia, 'Ap. f.' (*CIL* VI, 15626, cf. 37865). For his career, R. Syme, o.c. 399. The home town of Quirinius (Lanuvium) was presumably stated by Tiberius himself in his oration to the Senate.

[3] Seneca, *Suas.* 6. 1: 'Cicero, quid in alieno saeculo tibi? iam nostra peracta sunt'; 7. 1: 'quod ad me quidem pertinet, multum a Cicerone absum: tamen non taedet tantum me vitae meae sed pudet.' For the damning obituary (*Ann.* IV. 61) see p. 324.

[4] I. 13. 6: 'constat Haterium, cum deprecandi causa Palatium introisset ambulantisque Tiberii genua advolveretur, prope a militibus interfectum, quia Tiberius, casu an manibus eius impeditus, prociderat.'　　　　　　　　　　　　　　　　　　　[5] III. 57. 2.

[6] p. 324; for the description of the son, Haterius Agrippa (VI. 4. 4), p. 345.

No less notorious for subservience to the government was the learned lawyer Ateius Capito, whose grandfather had been a centurion in Sulla's army. Augustus gave him the consulate, passing over his rival, whose scholarship was equal if not superior—and whose sentiments were independent and Republican.[1] The historian exhibits Ateius in action. When Tiberius Caesar quashed an indictment for treason, Ateius put up a show of virtuous indignation, deceiving nobody. Wickedness, he protested, ought not to go unpunished. Caesar might be magnanimous, but was it right to condone an offence against the 'res publica'? Tiberius saw what he was about; and the expert (human law and divine ritual) incurred reprobation and dishonour.[2]

New men thrusting forward to wealth and honours were avid, unscrupulous, obsequious, if nothing worse: Quirinius, Haterius, and Ateius Capito might seek cover under that plea. But there was something much worse. The orator of talent, turning prosecutor to make a career or win the favour of court and ministers, dealt in confiscation and exile, in judicial murder or constrained suicides. The greatest of all the orators, Domitius Afer, earned an evil repute. Suillius Rufus fell short of Afer in success as in eloquence; and L. Vitellius was not so much a speaker as a diplomat and a manager of patronage. Matched with these men, his coevals, Seneca comes out very creditably—his earlier career did not march through prosecutions to fame and opulence; and when he held power as chief minister for Nero, he was temperate in its exercise—and, enormous though his profits might be, profit was not his incentive.[3]

The great *novus homo* of the age was also its great literary figure, 'princeps eruditorum'.[4] Seneca's writings, as well as his public role and performance, came in for damaging criticism.[5] Depreciation was easy, and there were few or none to defend. A family, a faction, and a cause might cherish the memory of Thrasea Paetus. Seneca, also a victim of Nero, was yet not a martyr to liberty. Comparable in this to Cicero (whom true and strict Republicans refused to reckon among

---

[1] III. 75. It was Ateius Capito who interpreted the Sibylline Oracles as requisite for Augustus' celebration of 17 B.C., producing (so it appears) justification for a (new) cycle of one hundred and ten years (Zosimus II. 4, cf. M. P. Nilsson, P–W I A 1710). The historian's allegation ('consulatum ei adceleraverat Augustus') can hardly stand, cf. App. 68.

[2] III. 70. 2: 'Capito insignitior infamia fuit quod humani divinique iuris sciens egregium publicum et bonas domi artes dehonestavisset.' Like 'dehonestamentum', 'dehonesto' is a rare and powerful word, used by Tacitus for effect.

[3] *De vita beata* 23. 1: 'habebit philosophus amplas opes, sed nulli detractas nec alieno sanguine cruentas.'

[4] Pliny, *NH* XIV. 51.

[5] For Quintilian's verdict, p. 336. In style Seneca was against Cicero (*Epp.* 114. 16); also against the archaists (17 f.), and therefore not liked by the contemporaries of Cornelius Fronto.

their own), he lacked Cicero's claims upon posterity.[1] The historian Tacitus redressed the balance. His sympathetic understanding reveals something of his own personality and ideals—in short, the man of letters who serves the 'res publica' to the best of his ability, without illusions and with little hope.[2]

The name of Seneca evoked fame, fashion, the hazards of survival— and the long warfare unabating that talent is forced to wage against birth and privilege, envy and detraction. Tacitus went on with that warfare. His first steps in the career of honours brought the young orator against the entrenched positions, and rivals from families either old or recent (the latter not always much superior in rank to his own). If he met disappointment in his path then and later, and took offence, he may not have discarded all the set beliefs that served to protect and embellish the fame of the Roman aristocracy in times before his own. When, however, he came to the *Annales* and studied the conduct of *nobiles* in the reign of Tiberius, what he discovered was enough to dispel any residual prepossessions about the 'magna nomina'. Taking courage from things said or done by Tiberius Caesar, the historian indicted the *nobilitas* for its failings, but was able at the same time, like Sallust, to assess his own class without indulgence, not sparing the whole senatorial order.

It was a good thing for an historian to be a *novus homo*. His origin would not in itself tempt him to write local or regional history—that was antiquarian or trivial. In the larger and central theme he could understand Italy as well as Rome, the provinces no less than Italy.[3] Many of the newer Romans, it is true, honouring the past, and suscep- tible to the creeds and observances of high society, might be unduly deferential to tradition in the persons of the surviving relics of aristo- cracy. Yet genius or confidence could break free. The judgements of the *novus homo*, like his status, derived from his own efforts. In pride of achievement, putting himself on a level with the older stocks when they first won rank by merit, he might look their descendants in the face—or pass them by. The contemporary Asinii were negligible. It was their ancestor that Tacitus honoured—and outdistanced in the writing of Roman history.[4]

---

[1] The heroes of Marcus Aurelius are Cato, Brutus, Helvidius, and Thrasea (*Ad se ipsum* I. 14).

[2] For the equity of Tacitus towards Seneca, R. Waltz, *Vie de Sénèque* (1909), 15. But perhaps it is a little more than equity. On the other side, hostility is assumed by B. Walker, *The* Annals *of Tacitus* (1952), 222 ff.; E. Paratore, *Tacito* (1951), 669; 689.

[3] Like Cato the Censor—or, better, the poet who wrote *Annales*, Ennius with his 'tria corda' (Messapian, Greek, and Roman), cf. Gellius XVII. 17. 1.

[4] Pollio, p. 136.

First and last, the theme of Cornelius Tacitus in *Historiae* and *Annales* is not merely the story of ten emperors from the death of Caesar Augustus to the assassination of Domitian. It is the struggle between the imperial power and the Roman Senate. Oligarchy is the enduring fact of all Roman history, whether Republican or imperial, and constant in most things, save in its composition. The recruitment of that oligarchy, its titles to rank, its behaviour and its vicissitudes, such is the constant preoccupation of the historian Tacitus.

In political contests the protagonists are not always the real adversaries, still less the eventual victors. When the strife of aristocratic factions at Rome developed and changed, involving Italy and the whole world, forces were unloosed that made an end of the Republican system of government and brought forth the monarchy. And the monarchy, while it imposed concord and preserved the *nobilitas* for a season, none the less wrought its ruin steadily in the years of peace. Caesar needed agents and ministers; and *novi homines* saw every avenue open at last for talent and ambition, and all barriers down.

The clients of the Caesars took over the inheritance of the *nobilitas*. They seized control of patronage, and the ruler of the world was caught up in their meshes; they managed the imperial dominions of Rome, they excelled in all arts, they even set the tone of society. On the face of things merit prevailed. Reflection might engender misgivings. Would the new classes prove equal to their task?

Aristocratic tradition was not enough to guard the old families from the perils or the temptations of life under the Caesars. The new men had not known liberty; they advanced through conformity with the imperial system; native energy might not hold out against the blandishments of success or the routine habits of a bureaucratic system. Under the Republic open competition had been valuable and invigorating. The memory of that spirit persisted into the Empire. But competition was curbed through the 'disciplina Caesaris', and the career of a senator became in the end a safe occupation. 'Securitas' took the place of 'libertas'. Something had been lost in the process. The Empire and its servants might soon be needing all their strength, whether to resist the northern barbarians, if they came again in force and fury, or to maintain the Roman spirit intact against the steady invasion of the resurgent East.

The typical *novus homo* was now a provincial. After Italy the western lands came to power at Rome, and men from Spain wore the purple of the Caesars. Thus terminated the latest chapter of the central theme in the history of the Roman People. Tacitus, it might seem, has missed an opportunity. He ought to have written that chapter. Perhaps he did, in his own fashion. The theme is not explicit —but it emerges through a quiet hint, an evocative name, or the choice and emphasis of single but related incidents. The triumph of the provincial Romans was the consummation of a long development, and it calls for an inquiry far back into the past. What explains Trajan and Hadrian may also explain Cornelius Tacitus.

PART IX

THE NEW ROMANS

XLIII. THE RISE OF THE PROVINCIALS

THE Caesars preserved and exploited the Free State. The fabric was there, and the formulas. The true continuity, however, is not discovered in the Roman constitution. It resides in the governing class. A Roman emperor explained the matter in an allocution to the Praetorian Guard: the Senate, ordained by Romulus in the beginning, was perpetual from the kings to the emperors, and immortal.[1]

The primeval Senate was mixed in origin: Latin, Sabine, and Etruscan. As the Roman State extended its dominion in Italy, it brought the other peoples into subjection or alliance, and frequently drew their leading families to Rome. Under the Caesars the first men from among the nations by birth and wealth and excellence enter the imperial Senate. The movement began before Italy itself became Roman, and it develops in natural sequence from the advance of Italian *novi homines*. To explain which, three reasons concur—the geography of Italy, the dispersal to the provinces, and the character of the Roman citizenship.

That Italy would come late to unity was determined by the structure of the land, the diversity of its peoples, and the cautious policy of the Roman government. The process is accelerated by accident and by violence. When the allies revolted in 91 B.C., wide regions still lay outside the Roman State: most of Etruria, Umbria, the central highlands, Samnium, and Lucania were autonomous. And, though the grant of the franchise after the *Bellum Italicum* brought the citizen territory northwards, not only to the Appennines but to the river Po, the whole tract between the Appennines and the Alps kept the humiliating status of a province until 42 B.C.[2] That was not the main obstacle to the consummation of 'tota Italia'. Local loyalties persisted, alien tongues, and the memory of old feuds. It took another great

---

[1] *Hist.* I. 84. 4 (p. 155).　　　　[2] App. 93.

upheaval. Italy emerged from the Revolution resembling a nation in order and concord, keeping local liberties but obeying a central authority, under the rule of Caesar Augustus.

In the meantime the Populus Romanus had spread far and wide beyond the boundaries of Italy. While much of Italy was still foreign, while the Transpadani were a mere collection of native tribes, nuclei of Roman life had been forming in the provinces. The roots lay deep embedded in the past. Since the second war against the Carthaginians Roman legions stood on garrison duty in the two Spains. Roman veterans and Italian allies were persuaded to forget the hardships of poverty at home. They stayed behind in the rich territories of easy life, along the coast of Hispania Citerior from Tarraco down to Carthago Nova, and in the valley of the river Baetis. Trade and the mines lured adventurers. When the Italian War broke out, with civil strife in its train and sequel, various political refugees escaped to the far West—Samnite insurgents whom Sulla persecuted, the Etruscans, the municipal partisans of Marius.[1]

Sicily had long been exploited by tax collectors and business men, trading communities sprang up across the Adriatic on the coast of Dalmatia, lands in Africa were thrown open to settlement, and in southern Gaul a Roman colony had been founded at Narbo in 118 B.C. when the 'provincia' was constituted. Finally, to crown the process, Caesar, the Triumvirs, and Augustus planted many colonies of veterans in the western lands.[2]

In most of those foundations natives of the better sort were associated with the soldiers.[3] At the same time, and apart from colonies, the Roman citizenship made rapid strides in the more civilized regions. The capitals of native tribes became towns of the Latin right. The *ius Latii*, with citizenship for the magistrates, meant a regular and automatic promotion of loyal and wealthy families. Before long most of Narbonensis and various parts of Spain succeeded to the place of Transpadane Italy—and to like prospects.

The proconsuls who led the armies of the Roman People and fought the wars of the imperial Republic, arbitrary and despotic in their exercise of the *imperium*, augmented their own power and influence by taking towns and princes, tribes and whole provinces, under their protection and into their *clientela*. The notables of the provinces became the clients of the proconsuls, acquiring the Roman franchise, and often the family names of their patrons. The forerunners of the

---

[1] For the Romans in Spain ('Hispanienses') and the partisans of Sertorius see E. Gabba, *Athenaeum* XXXII (1954), 297 ff.

[2] F. Vittinghoff, 'Römische Kolonisation und Bürgerrechtspolitik unter Caesar und Augustus', *Akademie der Wissenschaften u. der Literatur*, Abh. 14 (Mainz, 1951).

[3] *Ann.* XI. 24. 3, cf. *Hist.* IV. 65. 2 (Colonia Claudia, a later foundation).

provincial invasion are a pair of Cornelii. The one is Balbus, an opulent magnate from Punic Gades on the far edge of the western world. A partisan of Pompeius and then of Caesar, Balbus became the agent of Caesar's heir and was made consul in 40 B.C. The other is Gallus, the poet and adventurer, a general in the revolutionary wars and first viceroy of Egypt after the conquest. Gallus came from Forum Julii in Gallia Narbonensis, of native dynastic stock, it will be presumed. Nor is it vain to speculate how Balbus and how the parent of Gallus acquired citizenship and *gentilicium*. The same answer avails: Cornelii Lentuli in official posts under Pompeius Magnus in the provinces of the West.[1]

Defending Balbus in a court of law, Cicero proclaims that the Romans do not mind, they never minded, where a man comes from. Therefore they brought into the ambit of their citizenship men of valour from all quarters, and not seldom preferred energy without birth to birth without energy.[2] The consular advocate, vindicating the alien born, adds a hint about the *novus homo* he had been himself, with a strong appeal to 'virtus' against 'nobilitas'.

The bare possession of the franchise would not take a man very far in the aristocratic Republic; and the franchise itself was now cheapened when all free men had it in Italy south of the Po. The poor citizen was nothing. Distinctions of class and wealth prevailed—and continued to prevail when the political structure changed, the monarchy superseding the Republic. To make his mark at Rome the new arrival, be he Italian or extraneous, needs talent and industry, money and education—and a patron.

Prosperity and vitality were conspicuous in Italia Transpadana when most of its towns had only the imperfect privilege of Latin rights. The names of Catullus, Virgil, and Livy stand as testimony. As for the Spains, there were already poets at Corduba—perhaps elsewhere in the land of Baetica or in Hispania Citerior.[3] The Narbonensian province, permeated for centuries by influences from Massilia, was now passing from Greek and native to Roman civilization; and the families of the chieftains were mostly in possession of the citizenship when Julius Caesar became proconsul.[4]

The excellent culture of men and towns in the western lands was not created by the Roman government; and the grant of a higher legal status is only the recognition of facts. If history in its assessments puts the emphasis on the policy and acts of Caesar and of Caesar Augustus,

[1] R. Syme, *CQ* xxxii (1938), 39 ff. For Cornelii see further App. 79; 94.
[2] *Pro Balbo* 51.
[3] For Corduba, *Pro Archia* 26. Egnatius the 'Celtiberian' (Catullus 39. 17) may be the Egnatius who wrote 'de rerum natura' (cited in Macrobius VI. 5. 2 and 12).
[4] cf. the frequency of the *nomina* 'Valerius', 'Cornelius', 'Pompeius' (App. 79).

it obscures, through biographical fancies or legalistic prepossessions, the slow work of ages and the operation of innumerable factors.

Citizenship for citizenship, the law of Rome knew no disparity between the rights enjoyed by the alien of yesterday and the scion of the patriciate, by the Roman from Italy and the Roman from a province. Race and geography are alike irrelevant. Rank in society is another matter, and so is prejudice. Those disabilities were overcome by the new men through talent and energy. The force of events carried them forward, and the power of their patrons.

Victorious over Pompeius Magnus and the chief men of the *nobilitas*, Caesar drew to himself the *clientelae* of the defeated leaders. When he augmented the Roman Senate, he brought in his partisans—men of substance and repute from the *municipia*, bankers and officers, merchants and adventurers. Among them were grandsons of the insurgents who led the confederate armies of Italia in the great rebellion. Also new Romans from the provinces.[1]

The proconsul had conquered the tribes of Gaul. Lampoons asserted that the Dictator imported natives wearing trousers into the Curia.[2] The truth is not so exhilarating—these Gallic senators came (it will be presumed) not from Tres Galliae, but from Gallia Cisalpina (especially the Transpadane zone) and from the old 'provincia' of Narbonensis.[3] And there were now Spanish senators, of colonial or refugee stock.[4] With the élite of the western provinces many of the rough sons of Appennine Italy could never hope to compete in education and the social graces.

Caesar overthrew the Republic, but the autocrat himself perished before he could show the quality of a conservative statesman. The wars began again. The abrogation of the Free State was confirmed by the military despotism of the Triumvirs. Confiscation, proscription, and the contests of the dynasts, involving the whole world in Roman quarrels, gave a violent impetus to change. Foreigners or freed slaves might command fleets and armies; and all manner of men thrust forward and forced an entry into the Roman Senate.

Terminating the wars, the heir of Caesar went on to consolidate the revolutionary process. Unchallenged in power, he was able to affect the show of moderation and reconcile policies that appeared contradictory. Duplicity marked his career as a revolutionary leader, and duplicity seals his success as a statesman. Caesar Augustus restored the Republic without impairing his own primacy; he honoured birth

---

[1] R. Syme, *BSR* xiv (1938), 12 ff.; *Rom. Rev.* (1939), 79 f.

[2] Suetonius, *Divus Iulius* 80. 2, cf. 76. 3.

[3] R. Syme, *JRS* xxv (1935), 130 f.

[4] ib. 132 f., discussing L. Decidius Saxa (*tr. pl.* 44). Julius Caesar had once composed a speech 'pro Deci⟨di⟩o Samnite' (*Dial.* 21. 6). Cf. *Pro Cluentio* 161.

and rank, but served plutocracy; he fought for Italy and the West against the princes of the East, but employed them like satraps after the victory to rule in the kingdoms. If Augustus exalted Italy, it did not mean that he depressed the loyal provinces of the Roman West.

The Revolution had lasted for twenty years. Stability and dignity now became the watchwords. Since the classes and individuals who had gained wealth and status in the wars were victorious at the end, the new order which their leader established can hardly be called reactionary. A partisan here and there had to be thrown over—thus for one reason or another Cornelius Gallus incurred disgrace.[1]

The Senate, now to be reduced in size, is suitably purged by the expulsion of unworthy, disloyal, or impoverished members; the consulate puts on the semblance of its traditional honour; and, when trusty partisans and agile renegades have been provided for, the sons of the *nobiles* come back. If no provincial consul disturbs the decorous *Fasti* of the renovated Republic, neither does any *novus homo* from Transpadane Italy.[2]

That adherents of Caesar and the Triumvirs were removed from the Senate merely because they were provincial there is no evidence. The nephew of Cornelius Balbus governs the province of Africa and celebrates a spectacular triumph.[3] Provincial senators of lower rank can be discovered under Augustus and in the first years of Tiberius Caesar.[4]

It might have been Tiberius who in the exordium of a proud discourse to an illiberal Senate made pointed reference to the alien antecedents of his own house, the Claudii from the Sabine land—and it was in fact Tiberius who in a joke passed off the humble origin of Curtius Rufus.[5] Provincials were not set back if they had qualities to commend them. Domitius Afer, the illustrious orator from Nemausus, avid for advancement at any cost, and sacrificing good repute in his haste, became praetor in the year 25.[6] Earlier perhaps in fame, but not equal in success, was the Spanish declaimer Junius Gallio.[7] Spain is conspicuous in the record of the Augustan schools of

---

[1] *Rom. Rev.* (1939), 309 f.

[2] P. Alfenus Varus (*cos.* A.D. 2) is the son or grandson of a consul, the *suffectus* of 39 B.C., who is said to come from Cremona (Porphyrio on Horace, *Sat.* I. 3. 130), an ancient colony of the Latin right.

[3] *PIR*², C 1331. Possibly *suffectus* in 31 B.C.—but never consul if Velleius is right, who styles him 'ex privato consularis' (II. 51. 3).

[4] *Rom. Rev.* (1939), 367; S. J. de Laet, *De Samenstelling van den Romeinschen Senaat* (1941), 279 f. Of the eight instances claimed by the latter scholar for the reign of Augustus, four are dubious.

[5] *Ann.* XI. 21. 2: 'videtur mihi ex se natus.' Cf. *Pro Plancio* 67: 'a me ortus'.

[6] *Ann.* IV. 52. 1. From Nemausus (Jerome, *Chron.* 179 H).

[7] *PIR*¹, J 493. Spanish origin is not directly attested but can be surmised, cf. P–W x, 1035 f.

rhetoric as compiled by the Roman knight Annaeus Seneca, a tireless and fanatical adept. He was born at Corduba. One of his three sons became quaestor towards the end of the reign of Tiberius. Splendid promise was seconded by discreet influence—his aunt had married a prefect of Egypt.[1]

Other provincials might be detected or surmised. The startling fact is Valerius Asiaticus, suffect consul in the year 35.[2] From Narbonensis, but not a colonial—he came from Vienna, the town of the Allobroges, of native dynastic stock. Valerius Asiaticus could show all the proud spirit of a Republican noble, and the fine manners of a great gentleman: a second consulate (46) was to put him in the forefront of public fame.[3]

The brief and fantastic interlude of Caligula's reign is not without significance. Caligula visited Gaul.[4] It also happens to be recorded that he granted the *latus clavus* to a number of provincials;[5] and the second Narbonensian consul is registered, Domitius Afer (in 39). The Emperor, something of a wit himself, was ready to honour style and eloquence in others—even though it be alleged that both Afer and Seneca went in fear for their lives.[6] Under Caligula and in the first years of Claudius there ensued an unobtrusive advance of provincial senators—and even several consuls emerging, if inferences from nomenclature are permitted. Among the Narbonensian notables the names 'Domitius', 'Valerius', and 'Pompeius' stand out, recalling early grants of the franchise.[7] Spain, and especially Baetica, exhibits a contrast. Many of the senators have rare and peculiar names, not Latin but Etruscan, Oscan, or Illyrian, labelling unequivocally the immigrants—the Italian allies of the Roman Republic or the old colonial families.[8]

Claudius in the year 48, holding the censorship, replenished the Roman Senate by adlection. If that act was decisive for the fortunes of Narbonensians and Spaniards, the evidence does not reveal it. Not one of them can be proved to have been adlected. They had been advancing by the normal channel.[9]

The next year was perhaps more momentous. Agrippina, to instruct the young Nero, brought Seneca back from exile; and in 51 she secured the command of the Guard for Afranius Burrus, a Narbonen-

---

[1] C. Galerius (p. 536). [2] p. 455 f.

[3] In the run of second consulates from 43 to 46, after L. Vitellius, Passienus Crispus, and M. Vinicius (the last two, husbands of princesses).

[4] p. 459. Vienna's elevation to the rank of a Roman colony (*ILS* 212, col. ii, ll. 15 ff.) is presumably his doing.

[5] Dio LIX. 9. 5. [6] ib. 19. [7] App. 78 f.

[8] e.g. 'Annaeus', 'Dasumius', 'Ulpius' (App. 80).

[9] For the adlection of notables from Tres Galliae, above, p. 459 f.

sian from the town of Vasio.[1] The control of dominant positions safe-guarded the transmission of the power when Claudius died.

Rome under Claudius had endured the rule of courtiers, freedmen, and females. The new régime announced a reform—the household and the government were to be kept strictly apart.[2] What happened fell short of the proclamation. The freedmen and the Emperor's mother gave place to the Emperor's tutor and the commander of the Praetorians. The latter post was military in rank, but political in significance. Tacitus amicably commends the military repute and experience of Afranius Burrus.[3] In fact he had only been a tribune. His service to the dynasty was personal and financial—a procurator of Livia, of Tiberius, of Claudius.[4]

Seneca and Burrus, firmly pushing Agrippina aside and diverting Nero into harmless recreations, proceeded, under show of deference to the Senate, to manage the Empire in their own way and build up through patronage a body of allies. The results are seen in consulates and army commands.

Domitius Corbulo they dispatched to the East, on pretext of an emergency.[5] To the Lower Rhine went Duvius Avitus, a citizen of Burrus' own town, soon after his consulate, there to command four legions;[6] his predecessor had been Pompeius Paullinus from the colony of Arelate, whose sister Seneca married.[7] Seneca himself took a consulate and gave one to his brother, previously proconsul of Achaia, whom the eloquent Junius Gallio, a friend of the family, had adopted as his son.[8] When the post of *praefectus urbi* fell vacant, it was given to a Roman from Spain, Pedanius Secundus.[9]

The death of Burrus in 62 broke the backbone of Seneca's influence.[10] Seneca saw that he would have to retire, and Nero accepted his offer. Various changes ensued. Though the advance of provincial senators received a strong impulsion from the confederated efforts of Seneca and Burrus, they were not the sole counsellors of the Princeps, and their removal, though leaving Nero open to various and mostly evil

---

[1] *ILS* 1321. [2] xiii. 4.

[3] xii. 42. 1: 'egregiae militaris famae.' [4] *ILS* 1321.

[5] His origin is nowhere stated. Conceivably Narbonensian, cf. App. 83.

[6] *ILS* 979, cf. *I. l. de Gaule* 206: *suffectus* at the end of 56.

[7] Pliny, who served under him, attests the origin (*NH* xxxiii. 143). Consulate (? c. 53) not attested. The parent is the Paullinus, *praefectus annonae*, to whom Seneca dedicated *De brevitate vitae*.

[8] Seneca's consulate falls in 56, that of L. Junius Annaeus Gallio (known from Pliny, *NH* xxxi. 62) is not attested. Gallio was proconsul of Achaia in 52 (*SIG*³ 801: Delphi).

[9] Presumably in 56, on the death of L. Volusius Saturninus (*Ann.* xiii. 30. 2). Pedanius (*suff.* 43) is the earliest verifiable Spanish consul since Cornelius Balbus. The Pedanii came from Barcino (App. 80).

[10] So at least Tacitus alleges (xiii. 52. 1). For a new group emerging, with consulates in 61 or 62, see the five names, all Italian, in App. 60.

influences, did not sensibly retard the process, or impair the prospects of Spaniards and Narbonensians. They appear, along with Italian *novi homines* and a sprinkling of *nobiles*, on the consular *Fasti* from 62 to 68. Altogether, in the brief span of thirty-one years from the accession of Caligula to the fall of Nero, there are more than a dozen consuls from Spain and Narbonensis.[1]

The insurrection of Julius Vindex started a sequence of wars and proclamations, and fresh waves of senators advance. The city of Vienna, it is reported, helped Vindex—not only from neighbourly enmity to imperial and Neronian Lugdunum or the memory of ancient tribal links.[2] Other cities may have come out on the side of Galba and the Senate in the war against the tyrant. Forum Julii, for example, once a naval station, was a point of strategic importance, lying where the road from Italy leaves the coast and plunges into the interior of Narbonensis.[3] The 'provincia' was noted for reverence towards the Roman Senate. The paradoxical victory of Galba saved it from penalization, and ensured conspicuous signs of honour, with several consulates for citizens of Vienna and Nemausus.[4] Partisans prospered, and the scandalous Antonius Primus of Tolosa regained his rank as a senator, with command of a legion.[5]

As for Spain, Galba in his eight years' tenure of Tarraconensis had acquired friends among the educated classes. For the conduct of the war against Nero, he organized a kind of senate of the notables.[6] Some of his provincial adherents he brought in his train to Rome. Such was Fabius Quintilianus, who was to become a famous teacher of rhetoric.[7] To some he gave commissions in the Praetorian Guard.[8] Others were introduced into the Roman Senate.[9]

---

[1] App. 82.   [2] p. 463.

[3] App. 30. Also App. 33: on Cornelius Fuscus, 'pro Galba dux coloniae suae' (*Hist.* II. 86. 3).

[4] C. Bellicius Natalis of Vienna (*PIR*[2], B 101) was *suffectus* in the last three months of 68. Some of the consuls of 69 were Galba's nominees (cf. *Hist.* I. 77. 2), among them presumably Arrius Antoninus and Marius Celsus (App. 32).

[5] *Hist.* I. 86. 1 f. For his 'patria', Suetonius, *Vitellius* 18; Martial IX. 99. 3.

[6] Suetonius, *Galba* 10. 2: 'e primoribus prudentia atque aetate praestantibus velut instar senatus.' The class and type is patent—high priests of the provincial cult at Tarraco, e.g. Q. Licinius Silvanus Granianus (*ILS* 2714), whose son is consul in 106, or Pliny's friend (C. Licinius Marinus) Voconius Romanus (*PIR*[1], L 144), cf. *Epp.* I. 13. 4. Contemporary with Galba's action is 'Sex. Pomponius praetorii viri pater, Hispaniae citerioris princeps' (Pliny, *NH* XXII. 120).

[7] Jerome, *Chron.* p. 186 H.

[8] Thus Pompeius Longinus, 'non ordine militiae sed e Galbae amicis' (*Hist.* I. 31. 3).

[9] Thus (P.) Licinius Caecina, 'novus adhuc et in senatum nuper adscitus' (*Hist.* I. 53. 1): his father in Spain poisoned himself with opium (Pliny, *NH* XX. 199). Also Q. Pomponius Rufus (*suff.* 95), who had held a command for Galba on the coasts of Tarraconensis and Narbonensis (*IRT* 537). Also perhaps the Narbonensian Sex. Julius Frontinus (cf. App. 84).

Not that Galba's acts matter much, nor do those of the next two pretenders. Sudden and brief in their occupancy of the imperial power, Otho and Vitellius perished before they could do much to modify, even by battle and murder, the composition of the governing class. The victor Vespasian was able to establish a dynasty, and plan a whole system of government.

The year 69 witnessed four emperors and fifteen consuls, among them several Narbonensians. And now Vespasian had his own partisans to promote. Not, however, Antonius Primus, who won the war for the Flavian cause by the daring invasion of northern Italy and the signal victory at Cremona. Primus was pretentious, and perhaps dangerous. Vespasian's chief ally, Licinius Mucianus, soon arrived at Rome, a master without equal in all the arts of diplomatic guile. By deceitful promises he subdued Antonius and quietly edged him aside. There was also Cornelius Fuscus, the procurator of Pannonia and Dalmatia, who, son of a senator, had declined a senatorial career in his youth. If Fuscus now seems to fade out, he was destined to hold the stage again as Prefect of the Guard under Domitian and perish in Dacia at the head of a Roman army.[1]

Speedy consulates now came to the sound men among the legionary legates of the Danubian and eastern armies.[2] Some were provincials, and some had been legates under Corbulo, who in a dozen years of the high command won numerous adherents. From their company Vespasian drew many governors of the military provinces.[3]

The proclamation of Vespasian was the work of Corbulo's men, and their revenge. In the forefront, Licinius Mucianus and Ti. Julius Alexander. Other agents will be suspected among the legionary commanders in the different armies: Aurelius Fulvus, who had come to Moesia from Syria, and perhaps Ulpius Traianus in Judaea.[4]

The consular legates of Dalmatia, Pannonia, and Moesia contributed very little to Vespasian's victory. They were not debarred from honours or further employment. Pompeius Silvanus and Tampius Flavianus, that pair of 'divites senes', torpid and timorous, are found a few years later in the conjoint distinction of a second consulate.[5]

[1] On Fuscus see further App. 33.

[2] Thus M. Ulpius Traianus (*suff.*? 70, cf. p. 30); T. Aurelius Fulvus (? 70); L. Annius Bassus (71); Sex. Vettulenus Cerialis (c. 73); Cn. Pompeius Collega (c. 72); C. Dillius Aponianus (c. 73).

[3] For the role of Corbulo's men, App. 84.   [4] p. 166.

[5] Probably in 75 (App. 12). Pompeius (*suff.* 45) and Tampius (*anno incerto*) held the *cura aquarum* in succession, 71–73 and 73–74 (Frontinus, *De aquis* 102). Tampius' proconsulate of Africa (Pliny, *NH* IX. 26) could be put, not under Claudius or Nero as commonly, but in 70/71 or 72/73, cf. R. Syme, *Rev. ét. anc.* LVIII (1956), 236 ff. For these persons, *PIR*[1], P 495; T 5. Omitted from P–W.

K

Nor was Aponius Saturninus denied a chance to refurbish his reputation.[1] Easy credit accrued to a government when it brought back some worthy consular who had been shabbily treated by an earlier ruler.[2] But Caesennius Paetus, who is discovered as Vespasian's first governor of Syria, was the author of that shameful capitulation in Armenia.[3]

Rulers change, not the system. New ministers perhaps, but behaving like their predecessors—'magis alii homines quam alii mores'.[4] And often the ministers are the same. Vespasian's government avowed its needs by the choice of its allies. Eprius Marcellus and Vibius Crispus passed serenely through all hazards. Not only skilful orators, mediating between the Emperor and the Senate—they had capacity for affairs, and could be employed in the governorship of provinces. Eprius after a change of air (the proconsulate of Asia, prolonged for three years), returns to hold a second consulate and a place next to Mucianus in the esteem and counsels of Vespasian.[5] Vibius, who managed to keep the coveted post of *curator aquarum* through the vicissitudes of changing emperors, becomes proconsul of Africa and governs the province of Tarraconensis.[6] Vespasian's reign saw at least eight men benefit from iterated consulates.[7]

Other Neronian consulars were on call, eager to repair their credit: Silius Italicus and Paccius Africanus (compromised through prosecutions), and Galerius Trachalus, who composed the orations of Otho. All three go on to proconsulates.[8] Behind them follow smooth and acceptable persons (birth, eloquence, or court favour) such as Cocceius Nerva, Fabricius Veiento, and Catullus Messallinus: useful in Senate or cabinet but not (so far as known) governors of any consular province.[9]

Vespasian created a stable order, resting on the support and consent

[1] Proconsul of Asia (*ILS* 8817), perhaps in 73/74. Aponius (*PIR*², A 938) is probably related to Dillius Aponianus (D 89), and from Baetica (App. 80).

[2] Thus Ti. Plautius Silvanus Aelianus (*cos.* 45), governing Tarraconensis (70–73), *praefectus urbi* and *cos. II* 74 (*ILS* 986: nr. Tibur).

[3] Legate of Syria in 70–72 (Josephus, *BJ* VII. 59; 219 ff.).

[4] *Hist.* II. 95. 3 (Mucianus and Eprius).

[5] *ILS* 992 (Capua) reveals his proconsulate (70–73), *AE* 1956, 86 (Paphos), his early career.

[6] The *cura aquarum* from 68 to 71 (Frontinus, *De aquis* 102); Africa (Pliny, *NH* XIX. 4); Tarraconensis, during the census, as is revealed by the inscription of his *adiutor*, Sex. Attius Suburanus (*AE* 1939, 60: Heliopolis). The reader of the *Dialogus* gains no hint of the provincial employment of Eprius and Vibius.

[7] App. 12.

[8] viz. Silius Italicus in Asia (Pliny, *Epp.* III. 7. 3, cf. the inscr. from Aphrodisias, *CR* XLIX (1935), 217); P. Galerius Trachalus (Africa, *CIL* v, 5812); C. Paccius Africanus (Africa, *IRT* 342).

[9] Veiento (*suff.* c. 73) is presumably the adopted son of A. Didius Gallus (*suff.* 36), cf. App. 5, whereas the main portion of the nomenclature of L. Valerius Catullus Messallinus (*cos.* 73) suggests the Veronese family (not perhaps a blood descendant).

of municipal Italians and provincial aristocrats. After the proclamation by the legions of Egypt, Judaea, and Syria, Vespasian at once gave senatorial rank to a number of officers in the eastern armies: excellent men who subsequently rose high, and some whose only merit was luck.[1] Next, his censorship in 73, crowning the Flavian Peace, was suitably marked by the adlection of men from the towns of Italy and the Roman West.[2] Vespasian also augmented the patriciate, and provincial luminaries like Ulpius Traianus and Julius Agricola add their splendour to the highest rank in Roman society.[3] Certain other Spaniards and Narbonensians who rose to great eminence under the Flavian emperors had already entered the Senate under Claudius or Nero.[4]

Neronian in its origins, the administrative oligarchy supporting the Flavian dynasty is a heterogeneous amalgam. Local friends of Vespasian are notable, the kinsmen by blood and the connexions by marriage, several of whom gain second consulates.[5] Alliances extended the family group from the Sabine land westwards into Etruria and northwards through Umbria into the old Ager Gallicus about Pisaurum and Ariminum.[6]

The influence of other families from central Italy may be surmised, promoting adherents in their turn. And so, for a season at least, the period might even seem to exhibit a certain reaction against the provincial and foreign tendency that had been so marked under Nero.

The internal history of the reign of Domitian, beginning with a tranquil and dynastic succession, with a circle of friends and kinsfolk, and even with some prospect that an amicable compromise between the ruler and the Senate would be firmly perpetuated, degenerates after a time into suspicion and hostility. What has been preserved amounts to little more than the habits of the tyrant, the list of his

---

[1] *Hist.* II. 82. 2: 'egregios viros et mox summa adeptos: quibusdam fortuna pro virtutibus fuit.'

[2] For the adlections (69 and 73) see p. 69.

[3] Also Annius Verus (*HA, Marcus* I. 2); Lucanus and Tullus, the two brothers (themselves Narbonensian) whom the orator Cn. Domitius Afer adopted (*ILS* 990 f.); P. Calvisius Ruso Julius Frontinus (*AE* 1914, 267); the parent of Pedanius Fuscus (cf. Pliny, *Epp.* VI. 26. 1); the parent of P. Manilius Vopiscus (*cos.* 114, deduced from *ILS* 1044); and perhaps Aurelius Fulvus (*suff.* ? 70), or his son.

[4] Ch. XLIV.

[5] Thus the Petillii (*Hist.* III. 59. 2), and M. Arrecinus Clemens (IV. 68. 2). L. Caesennius Paetus (*cos.* 61) was married to a Flavia Sabina (*ILS* 995). He did not earn (or survive to) a second consulate.

[6] The Petillii may well be Sabine or Picene (though E. Swoboda (P–W XIX, 1149) argues for Aquileia); Sex. Vettulenus Cerialis (*suff.* c. 73) and his brother Civica Cerialis (c. 76) are probably Sabine, cf. the rare *nomen* and another senatorial Vettulenus who has the tribe 'Quirina' (*CIL* VI, 31773); M. Arrecinus Clemens comes from Pisaurum (*AE* 1947, 40); while the Caesennii, who have the tribe 'Stellatina', are an old family of Tarquinii (*C. I. Etr.* 5526, cf. Cicero, *Pro Caecina* 12; 27).

enormities, and the roll of his victims, with casual or frivolous charges to explain their fate. The true and political history of the reign, namely the vicissitudes of different factions in the competition for honours and influence, must ever baffle inquiry.

Consuls from Transpadane Italy had emerged to govern the armed provinces, such as Rutilius Gallicus, Vestricius Spurinna, and Corellius Rufus. The Transpadani seem to fall back a little under Domitian. Evidence or appearances may be deceptive. Rutilius Gallicus obtained a second consulate and the Prefecture of the City.[1] If Spurinna and Corellius hoped to be consuls again, there is no sign that their merits warranted that honour; and Verginius Rufus could not expect to rise higher save through special arts or special favour. The momentous events attending the fall of Nero designated him either to extinction or discreet retirement.[2]

Spain and Narbonensis, with legionary legates on the right side in 69, duly furnish a number of army commanders. One of them received a second consulate, Aurelius Fulvus.[3] Others not, for all their worth— Ulpius Traianus in Syria, Frontinus and Agricola in Britain. And none of them comes into notoriety for victory or defeat in Domitian's Dacian Wars. An Italian group can be discerned at that time.[4] It was not strong enough to exercise a monopoly everywhere—and many names and facts are missing.[5]

In 89 came the proclamation of Antonius Saturninus, no noble and not from any of the solidly established provincial groups, but the newest of the new, owing senatorial rank to Vespasian.[6] The loyal adherents of the dynasty are revealed by the lengthy consular list of the next year. The Emperor Domitian leads, with M. Cocceius Nerva for colleague. Eleven names follow. Provincials are conspicuous, but not of any one type or region.[7]

Another crisis, in 93, brought the government into conflict with the party which drew its tradition and continuity from Thrasea

---

[1] Statius, *Silvae* I. 4. 90 ff.; *ILS* 1007.

[2] For northern consuls in the period see G. E. F. Chilver, *Cisalpine Gaul* (1941), 95 ff. T. Atilius Rufus (*suff.* c. 75) might be one (p. 75), also L. Mestrius Florus (c. 73), Plutarch's friend and patron.

[3] *Cos. II ord.* in 85 (cf. App. 8): now known to have been governor of Hispania Citerior (*AE* 1952, 121).

[4] cf. p. 24 (L. Funisulanus Vettonianus and L. Tettius Julianus).

[5] A strong provincial influence early in Domitian's reign is suggested by the name of Julius Ursus, Prefect of Egypt and of the Guard (App. 7). Also perhaps the *praefectus urbi*, Pegasus (App. 94).

[6] Aelian, fr. 112 H. Perhaps from Hispania Citerior, cf. *CIL* ii, 4194; *Eph. Ep.* ix, p. 450, no. 200 (Tarraco).

[7] Of the *suffecti* the first three are L. Cornelius Pusio (from Gades, cf. his father, *PIR²*, C 1425); L. Antistius Rusticus (Spanish, cf. *PIR²*, A 765); Ser. Julius Servianus (cf. App. 7).

Paetus and Helvidius Priscus. It was a mixed aggregation (doctrine as well as family ties), the components being, however, mainly Italian.[1] All in all, 'maiestas' or factional rivalries brought death to no fewer than twelve men of consular rank during the reign of Domitian.[2] No Spaniard or Narbonensian appears on that register.

Nor was the year 93 a fatal blow to Transpadane Italy. Though Patavium incurs reproach in the eyes of autocracy, the Transpadani are variegated—alert careerists along with antique morality and admiration for the Republic. Patavines can still win advancement, and other sons of the northern zone are in no way retarded.[3] Vibius Crispus will have kept influence till his death, but other consulars lapsed into retirement, contented or sullen—Silius Italicus, Vestricius Spurinna, and Corellius Rufus.

Political catastrophes disencumbered the path to honours, and new regions began to show their consuls. It was no scandal if old families from the Roman colonies in Africa or in the eastern lands furnished officers, procurators, and senators in due sequence.[4] But Asia itself and the foreign aristocracies now enter the lists (with consuls in 92 and 94).[5] Not at all a symptom of security in the ruler.[6]

Accident or an assassin might subvert the dynasty, putting the purple into competition again. After the Flavii anybody was eligible. The sudden fortune exalting a new family from the Sabine country could not depress or disparage the men of quality from Corduba, Nemausus, or Vasio.[7] Romans from the western lands, active or discreet, were well forward on the road to power before the Julii and Claudii went down in ruin. The ministers of state Annaeus Seneca and Afranius Burrus had managed the empire of the world. They came too early to take over the inheritance of the Caesars.

---

[1] p. 558 f. [2] Suetonius, *Dom.* 10 f.; 15.

[3] L. Silius Decianus (*suff.* 94) is presumably a son of Silius Italicus, while P. Ducenius Verus (*suff.* 95) and Ti. Catius Caesius Fronto (*suff.* 96) should also be Transpadane.

[4] A Pactumeius was the first consul from Africa (*ILS* 1001 : Cirta), probably Q. Aurelius Pactumeius Fronto (*suff.* 80). The eastern parallel is C. Caristanius Fronto (*suff.* 90), from the colony of Pisidian Antioch (*ILS* 9485). Further, L. Stertinius Avitus (*suff.* 92) might be from Africa (Groag, P–W III A, 2452 f.).

[5] Ch. xxxviii (Ti. Julius Celsus and A. Julius Quadratus).

[6] And relevant to the recent emergence of a false Nero.

[7] Luck or fate in the elevation of Vespasian is strongly (and properly) emphasized by Tacitus (*Agr.* 13. 5; *Hist.* iv. 81. 3; *Ann.* xvi. 5. 3).

XLIV. THE ANTECEDENTS OF EMPERORS

WHEN Domitian had been reigning for fifteen years, the principal figures among the Narbonensian notables were old men now, inactive by disposition or mainly decorative in function. Yet they had some influence and patronage. The Narbonensians and the Spaniards kept clear of entanglement with outspoken critics of autocracy; admiration for the old Republic did not blind their vision to the imperial needs of centralized authority; and their intellectual interests found an outlet in oratory or verse rather than in doctrine.

Younger members were now pressing forward, with high promise and high hopes. The outcome surpassed all calculation. The removal of the Flavian dynasty cleared the way for its clients; the weakness of the new and makeshift ruler encouraged, and the threat of anarchy enforced, a disguised proclamation. When fate beckoned, a powerful group in the governmental hierarchy was ready with a 'vir militaris', one of the ten consular legates.

Some but not all of the scenes and events of 68 and 69 were now enacted anew. In the civil wars after the fall of Nero, Licinius Mucianus could have put up his candidature. The family and origin of Mucianus lacks attestation, but there is a chance that he came from Spain.[1] To Mucianus there stands a parallel in Licinius Sura—and perhaps something more than a parallel. Sura in Domitianic Rome enjoyed a social distinction hardly to be predicted of the first generation in a family from the provinces: he is named as a patron of literature in the company of two famous consulars, and of the Emperor himself.[2] Mucianus, a diplomat rather than a soldier, was the maker of an emperor, and Sura had a share in the proclamation of Trajan. The honours to which Sura subsequently acceded stamp him as 'capax imperii', with a premium above Julius Servianus.

How and why the power went to Trajan and not to Servianus or to Sura may in part be divined. Trajan outshone Servianus in birth and distinction, with a consular and patrician parent; and there is no evidence that Sura stood at the head of an army in October, 97. Sura died prematurely, but Servianus survived to the age of ninety.

It is not merely a few individuals or families that now rise and prosper, but a mass of men. The bulk and the names are revealed by

[1] App. 85.
[2] Martial VI. 64. 10 ff. (Silius Italicus and Aquillius Regulus).

the consular *Fasti* of the first decade. First the praetorian governors in office in 96 and 97; then the legionary legates of those years, certain of whom are destined to hold consular commands not many years later; and, in due course, the legionary legates distinguished in the Dacian Wars.[1]

From 98 to 113 fourteen men enjoyed an iterated tenure of the *fasces*.[2] New men and provincials predominate heavily. One only of these consuls had a consular father.[3] Origins are instructive. The four persons singled out for honours in 98 and 100 appear to be decorative survivors, but may be something more.[4] Only one of them is Italian, Vestricius Spurinna from the Transpadane zone. As for the other ten (between 102 and 113), Glitius Agricola is also a northerner;[5] Cornelius Palma's home is Volsinii in Etruria,[6] while Laberius Maximus comes from the *municipium* of Lanuvium.[7] Publilius Celsus, with whom the series closes in 113, cannot be linked to any town or region, but might well be Italian. The rest derive from the provinces.[8] Conversely certain Italian senators of outstanding achievement fail to reach a second consulate, such as the brothers Neratius Marcellus and Neratius Priscus.[9]

What the Italians thought about this seizure of power and honour has to be divined. No sign anywhere betrays a protest, by word or act, against the invasion from Spain and Narbonensis. It may be pure accident that the only marshal who came into conflict with Trajan (or with some of Trajan's friends) is Laberius Maximus, a son of old Latium.[10]

Trajan was secure, but a chance might offer to dislodge his successor in the first precarious months. If it could with safety be believed that four of the consulars made a conspiracy (it is easier to suppress a plot than prove its existence), their identity and origins might prompt a speculation. Three (it seems) were Italian, namely Avidius Nigrinus, Cornelius Palma, and Publilius Celsus.[11] Were they perhaps driven

---

[1] Ch. V. Among the most notable early Trajanic consuls are Sosius Senecio and Cornelius Palma (99), Fabius Justus and Publilius Celsus (*suff.* 102). Cf. p. 53.

[2] App. 12.

[3] viz. Ti. Julius Candidus Marius Celsus (*suff.* 86, *II ord.* 105)—if the son of a consular Marius Celsus (cf. App. 32).

[4] Julius Frontinus, Vestricius Spurinna, Domitius Tullus, and Julius Ursus.

[5] *ILS* 1021 (Augusta Taurinorum).

[6] *PIR*², C 1412, adducing *CIL* XI, 2697 (an earlier member of the family).

[7] *ILS* 6194 (Lanuvium) reveals the local magistrate L. Laberius Maximus, presumably his grandfather.

[8] The origin of Sosius Senecio will be presumed provincial; and Sex. Attius Suburanus is Narbonensian, to judge by name and tribe (*AE* 1939, 60).

[9] p. 230. Also Cilnius Proculus of Arretium (*PIR*², C 732), who had earned consular military decorations, and who survived into Hadrian's reign.   [10] p. 231.

[11] Nigrinus came from Faventia on the Aemilia (*HA, Verus* 1. 9, cf. *Hadr.* 7. 2).

to use Lusius the Moor against the new ruler and against the group that produced and supported him?[1]

The names of the first *consules ordinarii* under Hadrian register the most important of his allies and relatives. The Emperor leads off in 118 with Pedanius Fuscus, the husband of his niece Julia. His colleague in the next year is Dasumius Rusticus, son of L. Dasumius.[2] In 120 Catilius Severus, consul for the second time, shares the *fasces* with Aurelius Fulvus (the third of that name). In 121 the aged Annius Verus emerges from his virtuous obscurity to hold a second consulate. From the list of honours one name is conspicuously absent, that of Julius Servianus; and Annius Verus anticipates Servianus with a third consulate in 126.

Nothing is heard of Pedanius Fuscus after his consulate, and nothing of his wife.[3] Further, Hadrian's sister, Domitia Paullina, was not allowed to bear the title of 'Augusta'; and even when she died (about the year 132), she had no especial commemoration[4]—that would have exalted unduly her husband, Julius Servianus. An ancient grudge, or new annoyances, poisoned the relations between Hadrian and Servianus. When the old man at last became consul for the third time (in 134) the honour was delusive. No doubt he hoped that his grandson would have the power, the young son of Pedanius Fuscus.[5]

Hadrian, having returned this year after a lengthy absence, began to think about the transmission of the power. Various senators are named (on imperfect report) as potential successors, all of whom he came quickly to dislike.[6] Two years later a serious illness made the problem urgent—and he was now sixty. Hadrian made a decision—which sealed the fate of Servianus and his grandson.[7] Both were executed. Servianus in his last hour cursed his kinsman and enemy, who would linger in anguish and long for deliverance.[8]

About this time Hadrian composed (or revised) his autobiography. The document conveyed an elaborate apologia, with curious excuses and allegations. Hadrian sought to dispel the notion that Licinius Sura might have been a preferred rival, or less than a friend: Sura before he died made the revelation that Trajan would adopt his young kinsman.[9] As for Avidius Nigrinus the conspirator, he must have been culpable, precipitate, and thankless, for it was Hadrian's design to nominate him as heir to the throne.[10] Against Julius Servianus the

---

[1] A plot, however, is hardly to be credited (pp. 244, 485).
[2] cf. *PIR*², D 13 and 15. For L. Dasumius (? Hadrianus) see further App. 80.
[3] p. 488.
[4] Dio LXIX. 11. 4.
[5] Born in 118 (Dio LXIX. 17. 1).
[6] *HA, Hadr.* 23. 6.
[7] He adopted Ceionius Commodus shortly before the end of 136, cf. *PIR*², C 605.
[8] Dio LXIX. 17. 2.
[9] *HA, Hadr.* 3. 10.
[10] 7. 1.

author brought up an act of spite and envy long ago;[1] and Servianus' hasty presumption was cited to justify his removal.[2]

Hadrian's choice had fallen upon a person of no outstanding capacity, a certain Ceionius Commodus.[3] The reasons are obscure. Perhaps a tardy reparation for a crime and an error: Ceionius' wife was the daughter of Avidius Nigrinus.[4]

The act was useless, for Ceionius died not long after becoming Aelius Caesar. Hadrian now elected for the succession a much older man, the amiable and sedentary Aurelius Fulvus, who was instructed to adopt in his turn both the son of Ceionius and the grandson of Annius Verus.[5] Hadrian died bitterly hated, and barely escaping a posthumous indignity unparalleled for any Caesar who had died a natural death—excepting only Tiberius. The Senate would have denied consecration but for the urgent request of the new ruler, Aurelius Fulvus, whom posterity knows as Antoninus Pius.[6]

The new dynasty, which is Spanish with Trajan and Hadrian, emerges as Narbonensian with Antoninus Pius, and the strains are blended in the grandson of Annius Verus (otherwise Marcus Aurelius). Those rulers are the successive products of a group of families allied and interlocked long since, first in their countries of origin and then at Rome. To recover its shape and texture, odd facts about names and kinship combine with conjecture; and conjecture is not vain when it operates with the solid substance of family politics.

The first object of matrimony among the gentry, whether Italian or provincial, was to link families of wealth and standing, to concentrate their resources, spread influence, and acquire predominance in a town or a region. The same principles tended to operate when a stock had to be perpetuated by the device of adoption. Even when a family had risen from equestrian rank to senatorial, from local repute to metropolitan fame, its sons might still look for their brides in their own country, so strong was the tie of home, the habit of alliance in a congenial circle, and the attraction of joining estate to estate. An opulent local heiress might well outweigh the birth and distinction of an extraneous connexion.[7]

---

[1] 2. 6.   [2] 23. 8.

[3] *Cos.* 136, son of the consul of 106. Perhaps from Bononia (cf. App. 87).

[4] *HA, Hadr.* 23. 10. For the stemma see under *PIR²*, A 1408. Further, P. Charneux, *Bull. corr. hell.* lxxxi (1957), 130. An adventurous conjecture opines that Ceionius was really a son of Hadrian, through adultery (J. Carcopino, *Rev. ét. anc.* li (1949), 290 ff.).

[5] The latter had already been betrothed to a daughter of Ceionius (*HA, Marcus* 4. 5) —whom he was soon to exchange for Faustina, the daughter of Aurelius Fulvus, and his own cousin.

[6] Dio LXIX. 2. 5; *HA, Pius* 5. 1.

[7] Pliny's third wife, Calpurnia, was the granddaughter of a knight, L. Calpurnius

Migrating to the capital, the *élite* of the western lands took station beside their predecessors from the Italian towns, whom they emulated in ousting the *nobiles*, and then went on to supplant. Wealth came with them, often ancestral, whereas many Italian fortunes were very recent, deriving from civil war and the proscriptions. Some of the invaders were harsh and frugal, answering to a conventional label, but others magnificent. Valerius Asiaticus acquired the gardens of Lucullus;[1] the palace of Julius Vestinus dominated the Forum;[2] Pedanius Secundus had an enormous establishment;[3] and Licinius Sura was already installed in a mansion beside Diana's temple on the Aventine, long before his fame and power.[4]

A fashionable resort near Rome such as Tibur with its villas might congregate a whole cluster of magnates from one and the same region.[5] If the new-comers were ready to pay for comfort and display, they did not all abate the appetite for gain. Eminent speculators bought country estates which they improved by superior skill (none could rival the viticultors of Narbonensis or the oil men from Spain).[6] Matrimony and inheritance caused fortunes to pile up, and, few males surviving in certain groups, vast possessions reverted to women or lucky heirs like the descendants of Aurelius Fulvus and Annius Verus.

New ties of friendship formed at Rome in the schools and salons or in the service of the Caesars, with advantageous marriages, and support thence accruing for lofty ambitions. Court favour brought a man close to the dynasty in more ways than one. Thus Valerius Asiaticus and Julius Vestinus. Each found a wife among the powerful houses established and endowed by the marshals of Augustus. Asiaticus married a sister of the beautiful Lollia Paullina,[7] while Vestinus acquired that stylish lady Statilia Messallina, whom Nero

---

Fabatus, of Comum (*ILS* 2721). For a presumable link with Hispulla, the wife of Corellius Rufus, see p. 86.

[1] *Ann.* XI. I. I.

[2] xv. 69. I. M. (Julius) Vestinus Atticus (*cos.* 65) was the son of Claudius' friend from Vienna (*ILS* 212, col. ii, l. 11).

[3] XIV. 43. 3.   [4] Martial VI. 64. 13. The Aventine was now becoming very stylish.

[5] The Spaniards are notable there—thus L. Cornelius Pusio, consul under Vespasian (*PIR²*, C 1425), cf. *AE* 1915, 60; Manilius Vopiscus (Statius, *Silvae* I. 3), and his son (or grandson), the consul of 112 (*ILS* 1044); L. Minicius Natalis (*suff.* 139), cf. *ILS* 1061; M. Accenna Saturninus (*CIL* XIV, 3585); and others, whose Spanish origin is attested or surmised.

[6] A man from Gades, L. Junius Moderatus Columella, had estates at Ardea, Carseoli, Alba, and Caere (*De re rustica* III. 3. 3; 9. 2); his uncle was 'diligentissimus agricola Baeticae provinciae' (v. 5. 15). As viticultors note Agricola's father (above, p. 20), and Julius Atticus (Columella I. 1. 14). Seneca paid a huge price at Nomentum, but it is not implied that he made a bad bargain (Pliny, *NH* XIV. 51, cf. Columella III. 3. 3). Note also the estates of Septimius Severus, a knight from Lepcis (Statius, *Silvae* IV. 5. 54 ff.).

[7] Lollia Saturnina (*CIL* VI, 21473a): the marriage was deduced by Groag from the nomenclature of the Valerius Asiaticus *suffectus* in 94 (P–W XIII, 1395).

coveted and took, whom Otho (so the rumour ran) destined for his Empress.[1]

Seneca could have aspired as high, if he looked for splendour and hazard. The identity of his first wife has not been preserved. His second was Pompeia Paullina, from the colony of Arelate in Narbonensis. Her father was a knight, from the most illustrious kind, at the top of the administration; her brother became consul and governed a military province.[2]

No theory can legislate in these matters. Not every provincial family would reach out to exotic alliances until its own rank in the senatorial order was triumphantly established—that is to say, by the consulate. Fidelity to local attachments held back the Transpadane Italians on the road to power. Some of the colonial Romans from Spain were bolder, and they carried with them the Narbonensian notables. The Flavian period witnesses the creation of a formidable nexus, uniting new Romans and the descendants of old colonial families.[3]

There is much that remains obscure about the Ulpii from Italica. Their first known senator is M. Ulpius Traianus, consul and legate of Syria. He married a woman called Marcia, whose origin and family is not verifiable. There were two children: the daughter, Ulpia Marciana, went to a senator from Vicetia in northern Italy, a certain Matidius.[4] This man, however, died before achieving any notable distinction: his daughter, Matidia, married L. Vibius Sabinus, whence Vibia Sabina, the wife of Hadrian.

The Aelii, also from Italica, had made an early start, if an item in Hadrian's autobiography is correct and correctly transmitted: the senator Aelius Marullinus would take them back to Caesar or the Triumvirs.[5] A gap may have intervened. Then an Aelius takes to wife (so it is inferred), a sister of M. Ulpius Traianus. The son, P. Aelius Hadrianus Afer, reached the praetorship but died in his fortieth year, leaving two children (a son and a daughter) by his wife, a lady called Domitia, from the ancient city of Gades.[6]

In Hadrian's own circle of friends and allies, connexions might be surmised with opulent families of other towns in Baetica, such as the Annii of Uccubi.[7] The Dasumii of Corduba are also promising. In the year 108 the consular L. Dasumius drew up an elaborate testament, with a long string of legatees. Next after the son (whom by this act he took in adoption) and the daughter, stands the name of Julia, daughter

---

[1] *PIR*[1], S 625.   [2] p. 591.
[3] Brief data about most of these people will be found under the twenty names in App. 87.
[4] viz. C. Salonius Matidius Patruinus (*PIR*[1], S 81).
[5] *HA*, Hadr. 1. 2.   [6] *PIR*[1], A 185.   [7] App. 86.

of Servianus; and to Julius Servianus himself is entrusted the super-
vision of the obsequies.[1]

Servianus had married Hadrian's sister (perhaps not his first wife).[2]
Servianus, it appears, was related to Dasumius the testator, whose
stock supplied another link elsewhere in the group.[3] Further, Servianus
had recently betrothed his daughter, the child of Hadrian's sister,
to a young man of distinction and promise, Pedanius Fuscus, whose
family derived from another part of the peninsula, from the colony of
Barcino in Tarraconensis.[4]

Early immigration is revealed by nomenclature—and sometimes by
the claims of families (not all perhaps authentic) to derive from a
specific people or town of ancient Italy. With the Aelii it is the Latin
colony of Hadria in Picenum;[5] the Dasumii discovered an ancestor
among the princes of the Messapians;[6] and the ultimate origin of the
Ulpii (a solitary writer attests it) was the city of Tuder, renowned for
martial valour, on the Etruscan border of the Umbrian territories.[7]

The kin of the Ulpii have been indicated. They disclose no tie with
Narbonensis. There remains the wife of Trajan. She was called
Pompeia Plotina—and, it would seem, already related to the Ulpii,
though it cannot be said whether she was close in propinquity.[8]

Pompeia Plotina, the consort of Trajan, probably came, like many
other Pompeii in the new aristocracy, from the province of Narbonensis. The city of Nemausus might be the home of her family.[9] The
praenomen of her father can be established—he was L. Pompeius—
but that is all.[10] The presumption remains of connexions, significant
no doubt but far beyond the reach of conjecture, with other families
in Nemausus and throughout the 'provincia'.[11]

Narbonensis comes out earlier than Spain on the imperial roll of
consuls, and the native dynasts precede the colonials of Latin or
Italian stock: Vienna and Nemausus had once been tribal capitals.
Of the first two consuls Valerius Asiaticus was cut short in his glory,

---

[1] *CIL* VI, 10229, l. 6; 110.

[2] Servianus (*suff.* 90), born c. 47 (Dio LXIX. 17. 1), is a whole generation younger.

[3] App. 86.   [4] App. 80.   [5] *HA, Hadr.* 1. 1.

[6] *Marcus* 1. 6, cf. App. 86.   [7] Victor, *Epit.* 13. 1 (cf. App. 81).

[8] A lady called 'Ulpia M. f. Plotina' is revealed on the wax tablets of Herculaneum
belonging to the period 60–79 (published in *La Parola del Passato* I (1946), 383 f.); further,
one dated to 70 (*AE* 1955, 198). Conceivably a sister of Trajan's father, or daughter by an
earlier wife.

[9] Because of the basilica built there in her honour (*HA, Hadr.* 12. 2).

[10] App. 87.

[11] Perhaps with Arrius Antoninus, with his wife Boionia Procilla, or with the successful
D. Terentius Scaurianus (*suff.* ? 102 or 104), whom Groag plausibly claims as Narbonensian
(P–W v A, 669). Note also Pompeia Marullina, sister, wife, or mother of the unidentified
consularis with military decorations (*CIL* XII, 3169: Nemausus): registered in App. 14 as
Ignotus C.

but Domitius Afer went gaily on, adding commercial gains to his profits from the bar: he developed extensive brickworks in the neighbourhood of the capital.[1] His enormous fortune passed to a pair of Narbonensian brothers whom he adopted. The two Domitii, Tullus and Lucanus, lived in concord, administered the property in common, enjoyed honours and public distinction—and were much disliked.[2] The daughter of Lucanus inherited it all, Domitia Lucilla, whom Tullus adopted. She married Calvisius Tullus.[3] That match produced a second Domitia Lucilla.[4]

The city of Nemausus continues to be prodigious as the home of senators. Aurelius Fulvus, a legionary legate in the East under Domitius Corbulo, and later on the Danube (in 69), got a consulate from Vespasian, a second from Domitian, and also the post of Prefect of the City.[5] His son achieved honour as consul ordinarius in 89.[6] He married the daughter of that elegant and distinguished person Arrius Antoninus (also twice consul).[7] Born in the year 86, and consul in 120, the son of this match was destined to become an emperor, the successor of Hadrian.[8]

Baetica and Narbonensis enter into successive alliances. Two significant stages can be verified. The first is the marriage of Trajan and Pompeia Plotina. In the second a single Spanish family, the Annii, acquires a double reinforcement from Narbonensis. M. Annius Verus, about whom the records of Trajan's reign are all but silent, owes more to matrimonial politics and to his descendants than to personality or any achievements. As bride for his son Annius Verus secured the second Domitia Lucilla;[9] and he gave his daughter, Annia Faustina, in wedlock to Aurelius Fulvus, the grandson of the two eminent Narbonensian consulars Aurelius Fulvus and Arrius Antoninus.[10]

The matches were devised by Annius Verus at the end of Trajan's reign or early under his successor, and the texture of a whole dynasty is revealed. Certain links are missing in this Hispano–Narbonensian group. The local origins of Julius Servianus and of the Calvisii remain unattested, no man can say precisely where Catilius Severus

---

[1] CIL xv, 979–83, &c.   [2] Pliny, Epp. 8. 18.

[3] PIR², C 357. For him, and his father, Calvisius Ruso, see App. 87. Lucilla had had an earlier husband and children (cf. Pliny, Epp. viii. 18. 2 f.).

[4] D 183 (the mother of M. Aurelius).

[5] A 1510 (which needs correction and supplement, cf. App. 87).   [6] A 1509.

[7] A 1086. To be presumed Narbonensian, and perhaps from Nemausus (cf. App. 32, on Marius Celsus).

[8] A 1513. By his full style 'T. Aurelius Fulvus Boionius Arrius Antoninus'.

[9] A 696, marrying D 183.

[10] The next generation tightened the link when two cousins married, young Annius Verus (i.e. the future emperor) and Faustina, the daughter of Aurelius Fulvus (otherwise Antoninus Pius).

comes in, and there are other figures on the fringe of the complex. The consular magnates promoted friends and adherents from their own towns or regions. One man who clearly had a following of his own among the consuls early in Trajan's reign was Licinius Sura.[1] Yet for Sura, by paradox, no link of blood or propinquity is known with anybody.

Such is the group that comes to power with Trajan and furnishes the dynasty of the Antonines. The personalities and the inner rivalries remain for the most part obscure. The true story could not be related by any historian in that season.

The long ascension of the provincial notables began in the last age of the imperial Republic. That epoch in Rome's history was turbulent, and it is sometimes arraigned as corrupt and decadent. The charge is superficial. On the contrary, energy and vitality. The age that produced the oratory of Cicero, the poems of Lucretius and Catullus, needs no defence; and it created, or rather allowed to grow, the whole civilization of the new Romans in Transpadana, Narbonensis, and the two Spains.

If the provinces seem neglected by the Roman government under the Republic, it meant that they could develop in their own way, without impediment. Hierarchic grades in Roman society were an incentive to action, and prejudice acted as a stimulus to the virtue and energy of the new stocks. Finally, the strife of factions and leaders at Rome, while deplorable (and fatal to many of the participants), broke down barriers and swept the provincials forward. Their advance is a natural sequel to the admission of alien stocks of Italy into the Roman governing class during the Revolution. The provincials tread close on their heels and begin to draw level before the Julio–Claudian dynasty ends.

The role and agency of the different Caesars has been variously assessed, and commonly misconceived. Preoccupation with the biography of emperors, fancied oppositions of personality, and artificial contrasts in policy are largely to blame. When combined with ignorance about dynastic politics at Rome and neglect of patronage in its manifold operations, whether Republican or imperial, the results can be disastrous. Thus a schematic contrast, both in character and in policy, between Caesar the Dictator and Caesar Augustus, cleaves a chasm between the Republic and the Principate and obscures the whole rhythm of the Revolution.

Far too much attention goes to the emperors as individuals. They may accelerate or retard the social movement. They seldom do much

[1] e.g. L. Minicius Natalis (*suff.* 106): from Barcino (*ILS* 1029).

to modify it. The exception is Claudius. The steady line is the promotion of municipal aristocrats, but Claudius deviates by admitting tribal chieftains to the Roman Senate. Claudius' act was impermanent. Accident redressed the balance, and history resumed a more normal course, an almost predictable development.[1]

It is a question not always asked, how powerful is an autocrat. He may often be merely the name for a government, or the creature of a syndicate, with a restriction of his licence to do good or evil. The State needs Caesar for its head, and Caesar needs friends and ministers —but the servants are not sorry to manage without their master, to exploit his youth or his absence, his kindness or stupidity.

From the beginning the *clientela* of the Caesars overrode the distinctions of birth, rank, and nationality; and the favour of the ruler opened an avenue for provincials and foreigners to posts in the household or places in the cabinet. One branch of the dynasty itself is strongly cosmopolitan. While Tiberius Caesar spent the last ten years of his reign at Capreae, his brother's widow, Antonia the daughter of M. Antonius the Triumvir, maintained a court at Rome, supervising her grandson Caligula along with a collection of foreign princes, and commanding no small political influence.[2]

Through all grades and ramifications of the governmental service the ministers of the Caesars dispense patronage and promote their adherents—centurionates, officer posts and procuratorships, the *latus clavus*; and for the senator, magistracies, provinces, and priesthoods. Two paths lie open to the highest honours. The one is law and oratory, with diplomatic arts that manage the Senate for the Princeps, with loyal talent to defend Caesar's friends and destroy his enemies in the high court of justice. The other is the administrative or military career. The sons or grandsons of the procurators tend to monopolize the consular commands. They are the principal supports of the dynasty—and they hold the arbitrament, should it come to civil war.

Military and civilian, the contrast is facile and imperfect. In the higher strata of society, Rome knew no distinct military caste. The senator governing a province unites in his one person the functions of judge and general; and equestrian officers wear no insignia unless with the troops. The Caesars of the Julian and Claudian line affected a standard of polite accomplishments that was to excite the wonder of later ages.[3] And they made exacting demands upon their ministers and favourites: court officials shine as men of letters, the secretariat

---

[1] p. 462.

[2] Both L. Vitellius and Valerius Asiaticus had cultivated Antonia (*Ann.* XI. 3. 1).

[3] Victor, *De Caes.* 8. 7: 'adeo litteris culti atque eloquentia fuere ut, ni cunctis vitiis absque Augusto nimii forent, tantae artes profecto texissent modica flagitia.'

bristles with erudition, and the procurator abroad will alternate fiscal duties with scientific research.[1]

The consular legates who supervise the imperial armies are none the less orators or writers—Pomponius Secundus the tragedian, the elegant Cluvius Rufus on his way towards historical compositions, or Licinius Mucianus eagerly registering the curiosities of nature. A generation later intellectual interests become more pervasive with men like Fabius Justus whom the friendship of Cornelius Tacitus illuminates, and Sosius Senecio, the patron of Plutarch; and no estimation of the governing oligarchy in its tastes and quality will neglect the enigmatic figure of Licinius Sura.

The provincial schools and instructors in the last age of the Republic were far from contemptible. Already formed and inspired, the young men who take the road to the capital rise by talent and alacrity, prominent in the new literary movements of each age, whether it be poetry, with Catullus and his friends, or rhetoric at the Augustan prime of the great artists in declamation, whose memorials the elder Seneca compiled. The provincials go on as vigorous innovators, in the person of Seneca's son, who marked and symbolized a whole period; and provincials are still in the lead when innovation descends to preciosity and reverts to archaism. Spain and Gaul end by seizing the political power. When Corduba or Italica, Nemausus or Vasio prevail, it is the triumph of wealth, energy, and opportunism: it is also the triumph of the educated classes.

There were good provincials, and bad. Competition made them ruthless, they were subservient to the Caesars, and success bred ostentation and insolence. Received opinions monotonously commemorate the antique honesty or provincial parsimony of the new governing class. Casual and disquieting facts emerge. Domitius Afer, for all his wit and oratorical renown, can earn no commendation at the ultimate verdict, even though the historian suppresses the gross authentication of his greed.[2] When Afer's son died, a social commentator well trained in tact and delicacy is not afraid to reveal more than would be expected about the squalid accompaniments of a resplendent fortune. A man's last will and testament, so Pliny avers, is sometimes, but not always, the mirror of his character.[3] Domitius Tullus was a repellent old man in every way (the details of his physical decrepitude are registered) but he redeemed himself at the end: the

---

[1] Apart from notorious instances like Pliny and Suetonius, observe Pompeius Planta, Titinius Capito, and Vibius Maximus. Also Seneca's friend Lucilius Junior (*PIR¹*, L 286), himself a writer (*Epp.* 19. 3), and expected to make profitable investigations when procurator of Sicily (79. 1 ff.).

[2] He perished 'ex cibi redundantia in cena' (Jerome, *Chron.* 179 H.).

[3] *Epp.* VIII. 18. 1.

adopted daughter got the inheritance (Domitia Lucilla), disappointing a numerous pack to whom Tullus had artfully held out brilliant inducements.

Sex. Marius, who owned mines in Baetica, the wealthiest man in all Spain, was a depraved person;[1] Marius Priscus when proconsul behaved criminally;[2] and provincial names stand out in the group that joined with Antonius Primus in forging the will of an opulent and childless old senator.[3]

Nothing is known to impugn the cultivated leisure of Arrius Antoninus or the quiet years of Annius Verus; Aurelius Fulvus holds the prefecture of the City without mistake or misdemeanour recorded; the testamentary dispositions of Dasumius bear witness to the comprehensive generosity of a man of property from Corduba; the Pedanii have lived down the scandal of a Pedanius murdered not perhaps without provocation; and only a stray hint in a Greek writer incriminates the morals of Licinius Sura.[4]

Men of the time might have had another story to tell, if comment had been free and safe, registering intrigue, torpor, and complacency. In what survives of literary record the provincial magnates from Spain and Gaul benefit from a highly favourable presentation. It is not surprising. Most of the writers had no other origin.

Quintilian furnishes a list of the six orators predominant in his own time and knowledge.[5] With Seneca and Domitius Afer go two Gauls, Julius Africanus and Julius Secundus. There are two Italians, Vibius Crispus from Vercellae in the North and Galerius Trachalus (whose town was Ariminum).[6] Central Italy and Campania are lacking.

Other branches of literature confirm. In the age between Nero and Hadrian what writer is there of any consequence save Statius (and his claims will be variously estimated) who is not provincial? The provincial zone of Italy has the elder Pliny and the younger, also Silius Italicus. The others, so far as ascertained, belong to the western lands.[7] Seneca and Lucan, Quintilian and Martial, derive from Spain. Also the historian Fabius Rusticus.[8]

Juvenal could have turned the edge of his satire against the successful upstarts from the western provinces. Seneca was a gift, and the enormously wealthy men like Domitius Tullus or L. Dasumius. Juvenal

---

[1] *Ann.* VI. 19. 1.   [2] *Epp.* II. 11 (p. 70).   [3] *Ann.* XIV. 40 f. (p. 479).
[4] Arrian, *Diss. Epicteti* III. 17. 4 (p. 41).
[5] Quintilian X. 1. 118 f.; XII. 10. 11.   [6] *PIR²*, G 30.
[7] The author of the *Argonautica*, C. Valerius Flaccus Setinus Balbus (if not identical with Flaccus the Patavine poet, Martial I. 61. 4, cf. 76. 2), may be provincial. Observe L. Julius Ursus Valerius Flaccus (*PIR¹*, J 418, cf. Groag in P-W x, 881): perhaps identical with L. Valerius Flaccus (*suff.* 128).
[8] p. 179.

refrains, seeking easier topics, and more congenial—decayed noble-men or indigent Greek adventurers. Junius Juvenalis, though his family lives at Aquinum, may be provincial himself.[1]

Cornelius Tacitus, with an historian's equity or malice, discloses the dark side as well as the light when he writes about men from Spain and Narbonensis. By paradox, the friendlier view is most in evidence. It illuminates the larger figures in his narrative such as Annaeus Seneca and Afranius Burrus. The minister of state, vulnerable to malice on manifold counts, is shielded from detraction; and the Prefect of the Guard is magnified to be a worthy partner, embellished in performance and repute.[2] Elsewhere odd details are significant. Not in a single place is an origin from Spain or Narbonensis brought up against a man for contumely or dispraisal. On the contrary. Valerius Asiaticus is glorified—bold and generous, surpassing the *nobiles* of Rome. He openly avowed his share in the conspiracy that removed Caligula; and the dignity of his life was matched by the elegant composure of his end when he fell a victim to the intrigues of Messal-lina, the perfidy of L. Vitellius, and the dull apathy of Claudius Caesar. The consul Julius Vestinus, who despised Nero, loved free-dom, and was not wanted by the adherents of the aristocratic Piso, made a quick decision for a quick death; and Dillius Vocula plays a heroic part as a Roman general on the Rhine, not perhaps answering wholly to his military success, but immortalized by an oration of antique and Roman grandeur.[3]

[1] App. 74. And Suetonius might come from Hippo Regius in Africa (*AE* 1953, 73, cf. App. 76).

[2] For doubts about the virtuous Burrus, H. de la Ville de Mirmont, *Rev. phil.* xxxiv (1910), 73 ff.; in defence, R. Waltz, ib. 244 ff. It will not be forgotten that an historian could have his reasons for a favourable presentation of Seneca or of Burrus, whatever their origin.

[3] Hist. iv. 58 (highly Livian, cf. App. 34). Like C. Dillius Aponianus (*PIR*[2], D 89), he comes from Corduba (App. 80).

XLV. THE ORIGIN OF CORNELIUS TACITUS

IF an historian claims to be better than an antiquarian or a purveyor of received truths, it is expedient to know something about the country of his origin and his rank in society—all the more when he happens to be bound up with the process he describes, not merely narrating the record of events but in his own person an historical document. Cornelius Tacitus was a senator and a consul. The *Historiae* recount what happened in his own time and experience. And, although in the *Annales* he went back and began with the accession of Tiberius Caesar, his narrative was designed to link the two compositions. The man, the methods, and the preoccupations are the same. Taken together, the *Annales* and the *Historiae* were suitably regarded as a single work in thirty books.[1]

Tacitus writes according to the spirit and the categories of the past. What is his relation to the present? Does he come from the old aristocracy or the new? And if the new, will his 'patria' be sought in Italy or in the provinces?

Some argue that the ancestry of Tacitus is illustrious, deriving not merely from the *nobilitas* of the Republic, but from the patriciate itself, the ultimate aristocracy of the city of Rome; and they suppose him to belong to a branch of the Cornelii that had languished in obscurity for long generations.[2]

The miracle of supreme literary genius emerging among the patricians at that late season, or at any season, would stagger the best disciplined of credulities. War and politics, honour and privilege, such were the preoccupations of the patricians in their great age; and in their decline they kept up the fight for wealth and dignity. Literature was never their business, not even a refuge and consolation. Poetry and history are supplied by imported talent: Italian under the Republic, provincial under the Empire.

That is not the major embarrassment. It takes search and effort to identify a patrician among the contemporaries of Cornelius Tacitus. The class is all but obsolete. Cornelii, Fabii, Valerii, and patrician *gentes* of lesser fame, coming back to honour in the alliance of the

---

[1] Jerome, *Comm. in Zach.* III. 14, cf. App. 35.

[2] R. Reitzenstein, *Neue Wege zur Antike* IV (1926), 7; E. Ciaceri, *Tacito* (1941), 47. And others. For an anthology of opinions claiming Tacitus as a 'Stadtrömer', a 'Stockrömer', or an 'Italico', see App. 89.

Caesarian dynasty, enjoyed a brief renascence, but hazardous and calamitous, verging to total extinction when the line of Caesar Augustus terminated with Nero.

Only one of the patrician houses is registered on the consular *Fasti* under the Flavian emperors. It happens to be the Cornelii, the family that once produced the glory of the Scipiones, the ambition of Cinna and of Sulla, the long line of the dull Lentuli. Several branches survive, but inferior, of no consequence save to the student of genealogy. As would be expected and postulated, they have inherited and distinctive *cognomina*.[1] No family of the patrician Cornelii ever owned to the *cognomen* 'Tacitus'.

Though more numerous, the plebeian *nobilitas* of the Republic succumbs to a comparable destiny, and even the descendants of Triumviral and Augustan consuls are sadly reduced. Tacitus belongs, not to the decayed and impotent *nobilitas*, but to the class now dominant at Rome and managing the Empire.

On what grounds has it been denied? The argument depends upon sundry remarks of the historian. He speaks with scorn and distaste of upstarts; and his animadversions on men of equestrian rank and municipal origin are taken as a strong presumption that he cannot be the son of a mere knight.

Hence the easy persuasion that Cornelius Tacitus must be an aristocrat of the bluest blood and purest prejudice. Undue credence has been given to the language of social disparagement at Rome, traditional in its ferocity. A *novus homo*, though he might count as noble in his own town, was obscurely born, and a nonentity, 'ignobilis', at Rome—and they told him so. The tone and colouring of Tacitus comes from the traditions of Roman history—and the dramatic genius of an historian who composed the annals of the Empire in the spirit of the Republic.

One extreme opinion about the antecedents of Cornelius Tacitus has now been challenged. The other conjectures a servile extraction, with a strong hint at the ten thousand Cornelii liberated from bondage and enfranchised by Sulla the Dictator.[2] The appeal to the monstrous company of Sulla's freedmen is familiar and misleading. Tacitus himself must take his part of the blame: a discussion in the *Annales* brings up the assertion that most of the equestrian order and many of the senators are of libertine stock.[3] The citation has become canonical. To believe it does less than justice to the art of the historian, who,

---

[1] App. 94.   [2] A. Stein, *Neue Jahrbücher* xxxv (1915), 361 ff.

[3] XIII. 27. 1: 'et plurimis equitum, plerisque senatoribus non aliunde originem trahi.' A notorious contemporary instance was Larcius Macedo, murdered by his slaves. According to Pliny, this senator's father had been a slave (*Epp.* III. 14. 1).

employing speeches to dramatize a person or expound a theme, claims his full liberty and achieves plausibility by adding what speeches normally contain: that is to say, distortion and deceit.

An inspection of the Roman Senate under the rule of the Julii and Claudii fails to support the contention that any great number of the 'patres' had come up from slavery. The Revolution accelerated the process of social change, rapid and menacing. Yet, while civil war and the proscriptions benefited the libertine class, spoil and profit were not disdained by careerists of free birth and good condition; and noble partisans of the great dynasts shared with municipal worthies in the distribution of private land and public funds. If some *novi homines* rose by their own efforts, through financial skill and the trade of warfare, not all were sordid and despicable in their origin. They might derive from reputable local families—some, indeed, the pride and flower of the Italian gentry, of ancient lineage and inherited primacy in the towns. The reign of Caesar Augustus, consolidating the revolutionary process, installs the municipal magnates in the circle of the Roman governing aristocracy.

If the descendants of freed slaves were numerous among the new senators, their domiciles and their nomenclature might confirm the fact. They might be expected to come from commercial cities in some preponderance (Rome among them), and to bear the *gentilicia* of aristocratic houses that possessed great riches and a host of slaves. The contrary emerges. Small and remote *municipia* are strongly in evidence; while rare and peculiar names, Etruscan, Umbrian, Oscan, Illyrian, exemplify the linguistic and tribal mosaic that is called Italy, and reveal the indigenous aristocracy of the land.[1]

Under the Empire the families of the Republican *nobilitas* fade and perish. By paradox their names, both the patrician and the plebeian, become more frequent on the consular *Fasti*—new Cornelii, Valerii, and Fabii, new Licinii and Domitii. The new arrivals that carry this type of nomenclature are not freedmen, not even Italians, but provincials for the most part. The noble *gentilicia* go back to the proconsuls who granted the citizenship to their forefathers.

Extreme views being discarded, the argument can converge on the class and country of Cornelius Tacitus. It is clear that the Roman knight of that name, financial agent of the government in Gallia Belgica and the two Germanies, is the parent of the senator. In the preface to the *Historiae* Tacitus plainly states that he owes his rank to the Emperor Vespasian.[2] These Cornelii are a new family, rising through the service of the Caesars and discovered at the moment of transition.

[1] R. Syme, *Rom. Rev.* (1939), 82 ff.; 362 ff.   [2] *Hist.* I. I. 3 (quoted, p. 63).

Tacitus exhibits a keen interest in the Rhineland; he has accurate knowledge or odd details about Colonia Claudia; and he carefully registers certain transactions round about the years 55–58.[1] The elder Pliny was then passing his third and last period of equestrian service with the armies on the Rhine. Pliny records that he had seen a son of the procurator who died in infancy.[2] Another son may have seen the light of day somewhere in Belgica or in the Rhineland, perhaps at Augusta Trevirorum or Colonia Claudia. It does not matter much. The place where a man happens to be born is a mere accident, telling nothing about rank or origin. It is not his 'patria'.[3]

'Tota Italia' triumphed with Caesar Augustus. Before long, first with officers and procurators and then with senators and consuls, an impressive contingent comes from three territories—from the Transpadane tract of northern Italy, from Gallia Narbonensis, and from Spain. These regions, showing wealth and vitality in the last age of the Republic, furnished decisive resources of power in the struggle for mastery at Rome. Dragged into faction and civil war in the train of the monarchic party-leaders, the new Romans (colonial, native, and mixed in origin) find scope for talent and ambition. They surge irresistibly forward under the patronage of the Caesarian dynasty.

Transpadane Italy, Narbonensis, or Spain—somewhere in that provincial and dynamic zone is the home of Cornelius Tacitus. To narrow the quest, various arguments can be invoked. First, his marriage. The procurator's son, making his start in the career of honours, may have required, when he took a wife, the backing of influential senators from his own country; and Julius Agricola, looking for character, education, and promise in a son-in-law, may have preferred not to look beyond the borders of Narbonensis.[4]

Next, the friends of Cornelius Tacitus. The *Dialogus* might furnish some guidance. Four persons appear in that treatise. One of them is Curiatius Maternus, senator and dramatic poet. His origin lacks attestation, nothing connects his name or family with any of the of the Gallic provinces.[5] The second is Julius Secundus, an orator of repute. A Gaul, it is true, but not from Narbonensis. He comes from somewhere in Tres Galliae:[6] the distinction between Gallia Comata and Narbonensis was primordial in the conception of the Romans.[7] Similarly the third character in question, M. Aper—probably a Gaul rather than a Narbonensian, and perhaps a Julius.[8]

---

[1] p. 452.   [2] *NH* VII. 76 (quoted, p. 60).

[3] Hadrian was born at Rome (*HA, Hadr.* 1. 3), but Italica is described as his 'patria' (2. 1).

[4] Agricola's own occupations between 70 and 77 would not favour his coming to know the young Tacitus. His own wife was Narbonensian (p. 21).

[5] Probably Spanish, see App. 90.   [6] App. 91.   [7] Ch. xxxiv.   [8] App. 91.

The fact that Julius Secundus and M. Aper are prominent in the *Dialogus* has no relevance to the origin of Cornelius Tacitus. It attests the singular fame and proficiency attained in the field of oratory by provincials—and by Gauls especially. The young Tacitus attached himself to the leading forensic speakers, precisely Secundus and Aper. Like the official career, the pursuit of education took a man far outside his regional friendships, into the company of teachers and students from every land. The fourth character in the *Dialogus* is Vipstanus Messalla, immeasurably superior to the others by distinction of birth. Though his stock was ultimately municipal, it had risen to the consulate two generations before, and had been found worthy of a matrimonial alliance with a house of the old patriciate.[1] To round off the argument about the *Dialogus*, and indeed to dispose of it, will be added the dedicant, Fabius Justus (who forswore oratory and elected the career of provinces and armies). Like most other Fabii of note under the Empire after the extinction of the patrician Fabii, he might be Spanish.[2]

Fabius Justus and the four interlocutors in the *Dialogus* permit no decision between Narbonensis and Transpadane Italy. Apart from the *Dialogus*, the sole source of knowledge about friends of Tacitus is the correspondence of Pliny. That Tacitus, like Pliny, was a son of Italia Transpadana is an attractive and reasonable notion.[3] There is no proof. The letters fail to yield any single item that can convince. Pliny publishes no fewer than eleven missives to the address of Cornelius Tacitus: nothing about 'Italia nostra' as a common loyalty, no mention of any mutual friends as linked by a common origin in the North.[4] Though Pliny asks Tacitus for advice when seeking a schoolmaster for the town of Comum, no regional claims reinforce the appeal to the mature judgement of the educational expert.[5] Again, Pliny describes to a friend the obsequies of the great Verginius Rufus, with emphasis on the fact that Verginius was his own guardian, that the territories of their towns marched, and so did their estates. An eloquent speaker delivered the funeral eulogy, none other than the consul Cornelius Tacitus.[6] Pliny does not say that the choice of the

---

[1] Their first attested member (*suff.* 18), is only a name; but the nomenclature of the second, L. Vipstanus Messalla Poplicola (*cos.* 48), implies descent from the Valerii Messallae on the maternal side (p. 101). Hence a singular appropriateness in the role of Vipstanus Messalla in the *Dialogus*.

[2] But Narbonensis is not at all excluded. Narbo shows a cluster of L. Fabii, mostly libertine (*CIL* XII, 4791, 4794–6, 4798, 5218), and there are six other instances in the *provincia* (e.g. 694: Arelate).

[3] J. Asbach, *Römisches Kaisertum und Verfassung bis auf Traian* (1896), 128; G. E. F. Chilver, *Cisalpine Gaul* (1941), 104 f. Not, however, that 'his style and thought can be shown to contain Gallicisms' (ib. 105).

[4] Italy is not among the 'tot vincula' that bound the two friends (*Epp.* VII. 20. 7).

[5] *Epp.* IV. 13. [6] II. 1. 6.

orator had any geographical point or propriety. Nor need it have: a state funeral explains the consul.

The argument from silence cannot go very far. An author does not have to mention facts with which his readers may be presumed familiar. Pliny nowhere documents the northern origin of his consular friends Corellius Rufus and Vestricius Spurinna; and his language towards Cornelius Tacitus, who was senior in years and renown, is suitably marked by distance and deference.

Not but what the lack of personal links between Tacitus and Pliny's circle of northern friends calls for remark. Patriotism and vanity ought to have testified somewhere. In all the correspondence there are only two passages that bring Tacitus into relation with any known and named third person. Though not conclusive, they tell against Transpadana.[1]

Inferences of this kind cannot but be faint and flimsy. The historian's own writings might disclose some arguments in support. When Nero in the progress of his enormities exhibited his histrionic and vocal talent before the public, Tacitus records how indignant were visitors from the remote towns and from that Italy which still kept the rigorous habit of the old morality.[2] The words recall Pliny's tribute to the virtue of 'illa nostra Italia', but offer no guidance.[3] The thing had become a commonplace, the Transpadana superseding the Sabine land as domicile and paragon of the ancient ways.[4] Nor would it perhaps be fair to invoke Tacitus' account of the campaigns of the year 69, and especially the difficulty about the battle near Bedriacum, as contributing to disprove a northern origin.[5]

So far the discussion has been confined in the main to miscellaneous and fragmentary items. A more adventurous interpretation may delve into the style and thought of Tacitus, there to discover the qualities and essence of the Celt. Of old the natives of Gaul, fervently addicted to oratory, affected a manner of discourse both majestic and epigrammatical;[6] and their eager talent soon put them among the masters of

[1] viz. Asinius Rufus (IV. 15) and Julius Naso (VI. 6; 9). See App. 92.

[2] *Ann.* XVI. 5. 1: 'sed qui remotis e municipiis severaque adhuc et antiqui moris retinente Italia', &c.

[3] *Epp.* I. 14. 4: 'patria est ei Brixia ex illa nostra Italia quae multum adhuc verecundiae frugalitatis atque etiam rusticitatis antiquae retinet ac servat.'

[4] And elsewhere the historian does not seem to infuse 'Italia' with a heavy message of emotion. It is not very significant that he should denounce an admiral at Ravenna 'quod . . . velut infimam nationum Italiam luxuria saevitiaque adflictavisset' (*Ann.* XIII. 30. 1). 'Italia' is used sentimentally in the speech of Tiberius (III. 54. 4), and in two passages that may derive from Claudian orations (XI. 15. 1; XII. 43. 2). Cf. the opening words of the *senatus consultum ILS* 6043, which may embody Claudian language (App. 40).

[5] p. 163 f., with App. 30. For an enigmatic statement about the incorporation of northern Italy (XI. 24. 2 f.) see App. 93.

[6] Diodorus V. 31. 1: κατὰ δὲ τὰς ὁμιλίας βραχυλόγοι καὶ αἰνιγματίαι, πολλὰ δὲ λέγοντες ἐν

rhetoric at Rome. The pride, the passion, and the invective of the Celt, blending with the temper and the traditions of the Roman governing order, might go a long way towards explaining the genius of Cornelius Tacitus.[1]

The invocation of the Celtic spirit is a familiar device in criticism and in biography. The poet Valerius Catullus is taken as a prime example, for his fire and passion, his tenderness and pathos, the spontaneity of his loves and hates. Nor is Mantua's poet omitted.[2] Catullus came from Verona, and the *cognomen* may be Celtic.[3] Mantua, however, is an ancient foundation of the Etruscans. Not that it matters much. Even if it be proved that the name 'Vergilius' is Etruscan, the nomenclature of the North is so tricky, its ethnic amalgam so complex, that no valid conclusions about the stock of the poet in relation to his writings (or anything else) are likely to emerge.[4]

Arguments have sometimes been based upon the race of the historian Livy—Patavium was the capital of the Veneti, a nation whose language was certainly not Celtic.[5] It would be more pertinent to draw attention to the things that Livy and Virgil have in common, despite all that separated their cities in origin and history, in speech and in customs.[6]

That is not to deny the survival of local divergences north of the Po, or elsewhere in Italy, still less to depreciate the force of local patriotisms. There was something in Livy that could be opprobriously designated as 'Patavinitas'.[7] How much the inner 'Patavinitas' of the historian had to do with race or region is another matter. Nor will a prudent man try to assess what is Umbrian in Propertius, what is Paelignian in Ovid.[8]

The facile and delusive play with racial origins in Latin literature has been almost entirely concentrated upon the Celtic strain in poets

ὑπερβολαῖς ἐπ᾽ αὐξήσει μὲν ἑαυτῶν, μειώσει δὲ τῶν ἄλλων, ἀπειληταί τε καὶ ἀνατατικοὶ καὶ τετραγῳδημένοι ὑπάρχουσιν.

[1] cf. M. L. Gordon, *JRS* xxvi (1936), 150 f.

[2] Thus, on both Catullus and Virgil, H. W. Garrod in *The Oxford Book of Latin Verse* (1912), xix ff.

[3] Celtic, cf. 'Caturix', 'Catuvolcus', &c.; but perhaps Celto-Illyrian, for 'Cato' is Illyrian, cf. H. Krahe, *Lexikon altillyrischer Personennamen* (1929), 29. M. Schuster, asserting that the Celtic origin of the poet should be relegated 'in den Fabelbereich', prefers to believe that he belongs to an old Roman colonial family (P–W vii A, 2354 f.). Verona was not a Roman colonial foundation.

[4] The poet's mother was Magia, a name *prima facie* Oscan. Observe N. Magius of Cremona (Caesar, *BC* i. 24. 4)—an old Latin colony.

[5] R. S. Conway, *New Studies of a Great Inheritance* (1921), 190 ff. (on the 'Venetian point of view in Roman history').

[6] R. Syme, o.c. 465.   [7] p. 202.

[8] E. Norden discovered in Propertius an affinity with Virgil, 'mit dem er das umbrische Geblüt teilt' (*R. Literatur*[5] (1954), 72).

from the North, as though it were certain what 'Celtic' meant. Spain might engender doubts about operations of this kind. If Spanish characteristics were sought in members of the Seneca family, it would be well to recall that the Annaei are of Italian colonist stock.[1] Their town is Corduba, in the south-west, in Baetica. Celtiberia is a very different part of Spain. Both Quintilian and Martial were born in that country—of native ancestry, it may be presumed.[2] Nobody has been able to isolate a Celtiberian element in the language, style, and thought of Quintilian or Martial. Martial gives full and loving detail about the mountains and rivers in his own region.[3] But who could have surmised the origin of Quintilian if it were not attested? That author mentions Spain only once—and then it is with the curious affectation of not knowing much about a certain local word.[4]

The supreme examples of the new Roman from the western provinces are the Emperor Trajan and the rulers of the Antonine dynasty. In the estimate of their personality as men and emperors, zealous speculation has run riot with the supposed influences of race and blood, of soil and landscape—Umbro-Illyrian in the Italian ascendance of Trajan, the Gaditane mother of Hadrian, the Narbonensian climate for Antoninus Pius, the fable of a Sabine descent from Numa Pompilius in the genealogy of Marcus Aurelius.[5] It is all vanity. The things that matter are education and national spirit, wealth and energy and rank.

To return to Cornelius Tacitus. No erudition or fancy has yet devised a criterion for deciding between Narbonensis and Italia Transpadana. The assumption that Tacitus came from the Celtic zone does not depend upon inferences from style or personality. It derives from external evidence, from his relationship with Julius Agricola and his friendship with Pliny. Not from those facts alone. Otherwise, Spain would be a fair guess. Martial addresses a poem to Pliny:[6] he does not anywhere name the orator and consul Cornelius Tacitus, senior in rank and reputation to Pliny. The verses of Martial would not endear him to a man of grave habit, preoccupied with the problems of education and morality. Had Tacitus been a

---

[1] App. 80.

[2] The *gentilicia* 'Fabius' and 'Valerius' are indicative. Their towns, Calagurris and Bilbilis, were not *coloniae*.

[3] Martial I. 49; IV. 55, &c. Cf. A. Schulten, *Neue Jahrbücher* XXXI (1913), 462 ff. That scholar, however, outran the evidence (and confused the question) by scouting Iberian blood on the grounds that Martial's parents were both 'Römer' (ib. 463).

[4] Quintilian I. 5. 57: 'et *gurdos*, quos pro stolidis accipit vulgus, ex Hispania duxisse originem audivi.'

[5] W. Weber, *CAH* XI (1936), 325; *Rom: Herrschertum und Reich im zweiten Jahrhundert* (1937), 228; 284.

[6] Martial X. 20, cited in *Epp.* III. 21. 5.

Roman from Spain, there is no guarantee that Martial must have mentioned him.[1]

The truth is almost revealed in an incident which Tacitus himself reported to his friend. At the games he found himself seated next to a Roman knight. Their converse was varied and literary. After a time the knight was emboldened to ask his companion whether he was Italian or provincial. Tacitus gave a veiled answer—'your acquaintance with Roman oratory should tell you who I am'. At once the man rejoined 'are you Tacitus or Pliny?'[2]

If the mention of oratory enables the Roman knight to defeat the evasiveness of Cornelius Tacitus and identify his interlocutor as one of two persons, that may not have been the only thing he went by. Manner and accent might give a clue—something that Tacitus shared with Pliny. That something need not have been confined to Transpadana, but may be common to Transpadana and Narbonensis.

'Italicus es an provincialis?' The terms are mutually exclusive, but the alternatives need not imply any great difference. If they did, the Roman knight would not have had to put his question. The resemblances between Transpadana and Narbonensis are patent. Of the 'provincia' it was with truth proclaimed 'Italia verius quam provincia'.[3] By the same token, the Transpadane tract of the Cisalpina is provincial rather than Italian. Almost every one of its towns had been in origin the capital of some native people—Celtic, Raetian, Venetic, or Illyrian.[4] Nomenclature suggests that the indigenous elements survived in preponderance.

In so far as concerns Cornelius Tacitus, external reasons weaken the case for a north Italian origin; and some might be disposed to believe that his diffidence when questioned at the games indicates the provincial rather than the Italian.[5]

Transpadane or Narbonensian, the distinction does not count for much. Immigrants from central Italy may be detected among the local aristocracies of the northern towns.[6] Yet the criteria are often

---

[1] Martial I. 35. 1 ff.: 'versus scribere me parum severos | nec quos praelegat in schola magister, | Corneli, quereris.' Perhaps a real person, possibly Tacitus.

[2] *Epp.* IX. 23. 2 f.: 'hunc post varios eruditosque sermones requisisse: "Italicus es an provincialis?" se respondisse: "nosti me et quidem ex studiis." ad hoc illum: "Tacitus es an Plinius?"'

[3] Pliny, *NH* III. 31 (quoted, p. 455).

[4] The most notable exceptions are the old Latin colonies of Cremona and Aquileia and the Augustan veteran colony of Augusta Praetoria.

[5] A man of consequence would not care to make the avowal 'provincialis sum'. It may (or may not) be held significant that the historian did not reproduce or adapt from Claudius' oration the passage beginning 'quid ergo? non Italicus senator provinciali potior est?' (*ILS* 212, col. ii, ll. 5–8).

[6] Thus C. Pontius Paelignus (*ILS* 942: Brixia). And M. Arruntius Aquila (*suff.* ? 77)

deceptive, especially where names of an Etruscan type are concerned; and most of the Transpadane senators seem to come from the various and mixed indigenous stocks. As for the 'provincia', Roman settlement, though intense in some places, modified but did not overpower the native substratum. Narbonensis exhibits a signal paradox. It might have been expected that the Roman colonies would account for the great majority of senators in the first century of the Empire. It turns out not to be so. The ancient colony of Narbo cannot show a senator until the time of Hadrian—and he is a person of no consequence.[1] By contrast the tribal capitals Nemausus, Vienna, and Vasio are triumphant and overwhelming. Furthermore, some of the colonial notables such as Julius Agricola from Forum Julii and Pompeius Paullinus from Arelate had native ancestors, enfranchised before ever the colonies existed, and incorporated when they were founded.[2]

Consuls and emperors, poets and orators, it is the same story. To explain their character and talent, there is no call to speculate about the questionable influences of race and blood and climate. Not that the town or region is indifferent. On the contrary. The new Romans of the North and the West derive from zones of prosperity and energy. Cornelius Tacitus is a part of the process that carries them forward to the conquest of the Empire, superseding both the Roman aristocracy and the aristocratic Caesars.

Spain and Narbonensis also out-distanced the native sons of Italy, whom they excelled in various ways. A number of the Italian *novi homines* could not face the test of birth and education (being flagrantly of low extraction, sordid gains, or recent enrichment) when set against the class of property holders in the western lands, resident in Spain long since or descended from chieftains in Narbonensis. The historian, recording the deaths of Augustan consulars, is alert for facts of discredit—Ateius Capito grandson of a mere centurion, Sulpicius

has the 'Teretina' (*ILS* 980: Patavium), which is the tribe of Atina, the home of L. Arruntius (*cos.* 22 B.C.), cf. *PIR*[1], A 1129. For L. Arruntius Stella of Patavium (*suff.* ? 101), see App. 25.

[1] *ILS* 1064 (L. Aemilius Arcanus, an equestrian officer and local magistrate, adlected by Hadrian). Lugdunum (only geographically in Tres Galliae) offers a supporting parallel: nobody before the senator with the mutilated name 'Fidus A[. . . . .] Gallus [P]acc[' (*CIL* XIII, 1803, cf. *PIR*[2], F 153), and even he may not be from Lugdunum. The reason is clear—Lugdunum with its small *territorium* had few magnates. Relevant to Claudius' assertion 'ex Luguduno habere nos nostri ordinis viros non paenitet' (*ILS* 212, col. ii, l. 29), cf. p. 460.

[2] There is no reason to suppose Agricola's ancestor a mere veteran soldier. The *colonia* was founded probably c. 36 B.C., but Forum Julii existed before that—and had produced C. Cornelius Cn. f. Gallus (*ILS* 8995), presumably of reputable local stock, cf. R. Syme, *CQ* XXXII (1938), 39 ff. According to Pliny, who could know, Pompeius Paullinus of Arelate was 'paterna gente pellitus' (*NH* XXXIII. 143). For admixture in *coloniae*, p. 453.

Quirinius a small-town upstart.[1] In his own time or memory, those parvenu orators and political managers, Eprius Marcellus and Vibius Crispus, came from no known families in their places of origin.[2] Seneca the Corduban had been their superior in social rank. Similarly, Agricola and Trajan were much more presentable than Vespasian.

In earlier days Italy had its own dignity for protection against the arrogance of Rome. The better sort despised the Roman plebs or soldiery, and might disdain to seek office and honours at the metropolis. But Italy sagged in strength and wealth and honour as other regions rose; and Italy was reduced under the monarchy very close to the condition of a province. The old towns faded before the splendid and prosperous cities of the western world, and suffered affront. The persons whom Tacitus rebukes for their lowly or municipal origin are Italian, with hardly an exception.[3] The historian's pose is dramatic and mimetic, reproducing Roman tradition and annexing the manner of the *nobilitas*. It is not only that. The pride of the provincial aristocracy finds expression, and a compensatory revenge.

Origins were known or patent by various signs. Though reticent or even evasive, Cornelius Tacitus could not wholly baffle an interlocutor. Posterity can turn its scrutiny upon the shape and colour of a Roman name, often with sudden and startling recognition.

First, a man's *gentilicium*, which may be rare and regional. 'Cornelius' is too common to be of any value, being transmitted and spread, not merely by the enfranchisement of slaves and aliens, but through fashion and imitation. Nothing can be got from the search for early municipal Cornelii, in Italy or abroad. Nor will it help to compile the record of equestrian and senatorial Cornelii in this age. Some might be kinsmen of the historian, but there is no proof to be had anywhere.[4]

The *cognomen* is another matter. Although 'Tacitus' has a meaning in Latin, there is no reason to suppose it a Latin word by origin any more than 'Vindex', the *cognomen* of the Aquitanian noble Julius Vindex.[5] Nor is Etruscan plausible for guess or argument, however wide and various that term may be. Region and social status plainly indicate that the name is native, indigenous to northern Italy and to the barbarian fringe. The easy assumption is that 'Tacitus' is

---

[1] *Ann.* III. 75; 48 (pp. 580 f.).   [2] *Dial.* 8. 1 (p. 101).
[3] p. 562 f. The historian refuses to disclose the antecedents of the unspeakable Curtius Rufus (XI. 21. 1). A Q. Curtius Rufus can be adduced, *duumvir* at Arausio (*CRAI* 1951, 238), but the nomenclature is not distinctive.
[4] See, however, App. 94 (on 'some Cornelii', among them Cornelius Fuscus and (? T. Cornelius) Pegasus).
[5] Names of persons and places with the root 'vind-' (meaning 'white') need no exemplification. On the same principle *cognomina* such as 'Tutor' or 'Verax' are not to be explained from Latin if borne by natives.

Celtic; and a Celtic derivation can be duly furnished.[1] If doubt be conceived (as well it may be) about etymologies, the regional indication may suffice, and the limits of science can be respected by a modest hint at the terms 'Celto-Ligurian' or 'Celto-Illyrian'. A negative clue may be added. There is a strong Celtic element in the nomenclature of northern and western Spain. Yet Spain furnishes not a single example of the name 'Tacitus'.

It has been supposed from time to time and for various reasons, not all of them adequate, that Cornelius Tacitus was native by ultimate extraction. Precise inquiry strengthens the case, and practically confirms it, putting his origin somewhere in Cisalpine Gaul or Gallia Narbonensis. It would be tempting to go further, to balance Narbonensis against the Transpadane zone of Cisalpina. Two of the three instances of the *cognomen* in Transpadane cities are instructive— they are borne by members of families notable among the local aristocracies in the last age of the Republic.[2] Narbonensis has four Taciti, all from towns or regions that are not colonial but native.[3] One of them deserves to be singled out. At the capital of the Vocontii a man called Tacitus set up a dedication, to the god of war and to the town itself, Vasio.[4]

The high civilization of Vasio in the early imperial epoch is attested by the splendour of its monuments. More impressive is the record of the Vocontii in the arts of peace and war, in letters, in politics, and in government. Chieftains of the Vocontii led the cavalry of their tribe in the campaigns of Pompeius Magnus, and gained the Roman citizenship as the reward of their loyalty. The son of a chieftain became the confidential secretary of Caesar; and his son was the historian Pompeius Trogus.[5] The next notice about the men of Vasio shows them high in office and influence at the capital. After long service as a procurator to members of the dynasty, Afranius Burrus

[1] M. L. Gordon, *JRS* xxvi (1936), 147 f. For the register of instances of 'Tacitus', 146 f.

[2] viz. P. Sepullius P. f. Fab. Tacitus (*CIL* v, 3037: Patavium); Aufillena Tacita (3507: Verona). In northern Italy Sepullii are found only at Patavium (three other instances): P. Sepullius Macer was *monetalis* at Rome in 44 B.C. An Aufillena of Verona occurs in Catullus 100; 110 f. The third instance is the *sevir* P. Valerius P. l. Tacitus (5895 = *ILS* 6734: Mediolanium).

[3] *CIL* xii, 3515 (Nemausus); 5691[8] (an oculist's stamp at Nemausus); 1301 (Vasio); 1517 (the eastern Vocontian territory). For confirmation observe the derived *gentilicium* 'Tacitius'—*I. l. de Gaule* 496 (Nemausus); *CIL* xii, 2803 (territory of Nemausus).

[4] *CIL* xii, 1301 = *ILS* 4841: 'Marti / et Vasioni / Tacitus.' Several Cornelii make dedications to Mars at Vasio, among them Sex. Cornelius Sacratus (1300 = *ILS* 4542) and T. Cornelius Pegasus (1297). For the use of the bare *cognomen* by a man of station, cf. *CIL* iii, 1081 = *ILS* 3594 (Sarmizegethusa): 'I. o. m. / et dis Pe/natibus/Scauria/nus.' D. Terentius Scaurianus was the first governor of Dacia—and probably a Narbonensian (App. 14).

[5] Justin XLIII. 5. 11 f. Further, Burrus' ancestor presumably got his *nomen* from Pompeius' partisan L. Afranius (*cos.* 61 B.C.).

emerges as Prefect of the Guard; and, not unrelated as a fact, the senator Duvius Avitus becomes consul and passes at once to command the army of Lower Germany.[1] Decisive promotion in the career of the knight Cornelius Tacitus, the procurator of Gallia Belgica, probably falls in this period when patronage was so generously and so patently managed by two provincial ministers of state, Afranius Burrus and Annaeus Seneca.[2]

The historian is amicably disposed towards Burrus, whose role in counsel and government he enhances, with nowhere so much as a hint that honest Burrus was flagrantly lacking in 'fides' and 'pietas' towards Agrippina, the author of his elevation. When introducing Burrus and when taking leave of him, Tacitus neglects to register the town and origin. A writer will often by inadvertence omit precisely those items that are most familiar to him personally.[3] Not all readers are so well placed. Writing in the *Annales* about Seneca, Tacitus could dispense with annotation about Corduba—the world knew it, and all posterity, as long as Latin letters would endure. Afranius Burrus was an ephemeral phenomenon.[4]

Tacitus writes of the Gallic lands with knowledge, discernment, and sympathy.[5] Were his origin thence derived, nobody would expect to see it announced by a writer who discards personal concerns, insisting upon the majesty of history and the validity of his own exposition. Any allusion will be discreet, or even ironical.

When the counsellors of Claudius Caesar attempt to dissuade their imperial master from admitting the Gallic 'principes', they take refuge in a farrago of protestations. Italy, they plead, is not decadent. That is a calumny—Italy furnished Rome with senators in old days, and the Republic is good enough for anybody.[6] It was shameful enough

---

[1] p. 591.

[2] Tacitus was born in 56 or 57 (p. 63)—possibly in Belgica (p. 614).

[3] Thus, perhaps, the *colonia* of Cornelius Fuscus (*Hist.* II. 86. 3), or the origin of the consular pair Arrius Antoninus and Marius Celsus (I. 77. 2, cf. App. 32).

[4] The preceding remarks (along with the evocation of a Tacitus at Vasio) are not quite strong enough to prove the historian's 'patria'. It might have been some other city of Narbonensis, possibly the 'vetus et inlustris Foroiuliensium colonia' (*Agr.* 4. 1)—which, indeed, could be the *colonia* of Cornelius Fuscus, whom Tacitus treats favourably, when he could easily have represented him otherwise (App. 33).

[5] Ch. xxxiv. For his familiarity with Narbonensis, App. 95. Not at all out of keeping with this origin would be a remark here and there in dispraisal of the Gallic addiction to oratory. Thus Petillius Cerialis begins—'neque ego umquam facundiam exercui et populi Romani virtutem armis adfirmavi: sed quoniam apud vos verba plurimum valent', &c. (*Hist.* IV. 73. 1). That, of course, is conventional. Another matter when Agricola is made to prefer the untutored talents of the insular Celts—'ingenia Britannorum studiis Gallorum anteferre' (*Agr.* 21. 2).

[6] *Ann.* XI. 23. 2: 'non adeo aegram Italiam ut senatum suppeditare urbi suae nequiret. suffecisse olim indigenas consanguineis populis nec paenitere veteris rei publicae.'

that Insubres and Veneti from the Transpadana broke into the Curia. What dignity will be kept intact for the surviving Roman *nobiles*, and Latium's impoverished senators? The new invaders bring with them a deluge of wealth. They are the vanquished of old—and a pack of foreigners. Their ancestors besieged Divus Julius at Alesia—and think of the consecrated memory of Romans who fell in battle to defend the Capitol against the Gallic hordes!

Anger and pathos are helped out (it happens often) by the appeal to race or history, with arguments crude, feeble, or spurious. So Tacitus intended.[1] He made them up, to refute them majestically. The historian also invented a sentence to strengthen and ennoble the spineless oration of Claudius Caesar, echoing and refuting the invocation of Italy and the Republic. 'The Balbi are good enough, who came from Spain, and men no less illustrious from Gallia Narbonensis; their descendants are among us, they do not yield to us in devotion to Rome.'[2]

The irony is restrained and impressive. When Tacitus wrote, colonials and provincials from the Latin West occupied the place of the Caesars. There was only one higher pinnacle: literary renown. To that also the epoch of Trajan and Hadrian might confidently aspire. Men and dynasties pass, but style abides.[3]

---

[1] Compare the technique employed in the invectives of Suillius Rufus (XIII. 42) and Cossutianus Capito (XVI. 22).

[2] XI. 24. 3: 'num paenitet Balbos ex Hispania nec minus insignis viros e Gallia Narbonensi transivisse? manent posteri eorum nec amore in hanc patriam nobis concedunt.'

[3] IV. 61: 'meditatio et labor in posterum valescit.' Clearly Tacitus' testimony to his own quality—he condemns the ephemeral notoriety of the fluent Haterius. For another veiled and personal claim, III. 55. 5: 'nec omnia apud priores meliora; sed nostra quoque aetas multa laudis et artium imitanda posteris tulit' (p. 339).

APPENDIXES

A. THE YEAR 97

1. THE KINSMEN OF NERVA

THE ancestor is M. Cocceius Nerva, consul in 36 B.C. (*PIR*², C 1224).[1] Then, one generation probably missing, comes the great jurist, consul suffect in 21 or 22. As for his son (the parent of the Emperor), also a jurist but in no way comparable, there remains a doubt whether he reached the consulate.[2] He married a lady called 'Sergia Laenatis f. Plautilla' (*ILS* 281), who may be identified as a daughter of C. Octavius Laenas (*suff.* 33): that man was a *novus homo*, and he succeeded the parent of his son-in-law as *curator aquarum* in 34 (Frontinus, *De aq.* 102). The Octavii Laenates are clearly Marsian by origin (cf. *ILS* 5364, a magistrate of Marruvium). Indeed, the family may earlier have produced that Antonian partisan, Octavius the Marsian, 'sceleratus latro atque egens' (Cicero, *Phil.* XI. 4).

Through the Octavii Laenates, Nerva acquired a link with the dynasty. It is deduced from indirect evidence.[3] A consul under Hadrian, Sergius Octavius Laenas Pontianus (*cos.* 131) set up a dedication to his grandmother, 'Rubellia Blandi f. Bassa Octavi Laenatis' (*ILS* 952). This Rubellia Bassa must be a daughter of the match contracted in 33 between C. Rubellius Blandus (*suff.* 18) and Julia, daughter of Drusus Caesar, grand-daughter of the Emperor Tiberius (*Ann.* VI. 27. 1). Her husband, Octavius Laenas, will presumably be a son of the *suffectus* of 33, hence brother of Sergia Plautilla and maternal uncle of Nerva.

This Octavius Laenas is not otherwise attested, and after him there is a gap of a generation before the *ordinarius* of 131—whose *cognomen* 'Pontianus' arouses curiosity but cannot satisfy it.[4] As for the missing generation, it happens to be recorded that Nerva in 97 had kinsfolk alive (Dio LXVIII. 4. 1). Who could they be? A fragment of the *Fasti Ostienses* reveals the fact that one of the *suffecti* of 97 had a colleague with the *praenomen* 'Se['.[5] That is to say, a Sextus, or a Servius, or a Sergius (that name being employed as *praenomen*, as by the consul of 131). Conceivably a Sergius Octavius Laenas—but there is a better candidate, Sex.

---

[1] For the three Cocceii of that time see R. Syme, *Rom. Rev.* (1939), 200; 267, &c.

[2] The consular pair M. Cocceius Nerva with C. Vibius Rufinus (*ILS* 1795) is put c. 40 by Degrassi (*I Fasti Consolari* (1952), 11). Cf. also W. Kunkel, *Herkunft u. soziale Stellung der r. Juristen* (1952), 120; 130; 378 ff. (appendix by C. Meier).

[3] cf. the reconstruction of E. Groag, *Jahreshefte* XXI / XXII (1924), Beiblatt 425 ff., with a stemma in some items conjectural (ib. 435).

[4] The only consular Pontius in the first century was P. Petronius Pontius Nigrinus (*cos.* 37), perhaps parent of T. Petronius Niger (*suff.* c. 62). Note the Roman matron Pontia Postumina, murdered in 58 by her lover Octavius Sagitta (*Ann.* XIII. 44, cf. *Hist.* IV. 44. 2). The *nomen* is common and indistinctive.

[5] Published by G. Barbieri, *Studi Romani* I (1953), 367, with photograph on Pl. I, facing p. 370.

Hermetidius Campanus, who had been governor of Judaea in 93 (*CIL* XVI, App. no. 12).[1]

Descendants may also have survived of Rubellius Blandus and the princess. Juvenal stigmatizes a degenerate *nobilis* called Rubellius Blandus (VIII. 39 ff., cf. p. 576). He is described as a son of Julia. Perhaps an invention—but perhaps an unattested brother of the irreproachable Rubellius Plautus (*Ann.* XIV. 22, &c.), therefore a known figure in Roman society and named somewhere in the *Historiae* of Cornelius Tacitus.[2]

Rubellius Plautus had children (*Ann.* XIV. 59. 1). A lead pipe recently discovered at Rome reveals the name of a Sergius Rubellius Plautus (*AE* 1954, 70). Perhaps a son (hence adult under the Flavians), perhaps the man himself, for his *praenomen* has not been recorded. A son of Rubellius Plautus would be a cousin of Nerva's presumed cousin Octavius Laenas (the parent of the consul of 131).

To conclude, a small fact that has not been exploited. Otho's brother (or half-brother) Titianus (*cos.* 52) had a son called L. Salvius Otho Cocceianus (*PIR*[1], S 110). The son's *cognomen* suggests that the father had married a Cocceia: a sister, presumably, of Nerva (what other Cocceii were there?). Otho, born in 32, was a close coeval with Nerva: his brother must have been a good fifteen years older.

Salvius Cocceianus perished, a victim of the tyrant (Suetonius, *Dom.* 10. 3, cf. Tacitus, *Hist.* II. 48. 2; Plutarch, *Otho* 16). The smooth man, who may be his uncle, survived.

2. THE REIGN OF NERVA

THE reign of Nerva, auspiciously leading on the happy epoch of the Antonines, could not fail to benefit from an optimistic presentation. One of the epitomators in late antiquity accords Nerva more space than Trajan (Victor, *Epit.* 12); Julian the Apostate commends his personal appearance;[3] and the modern age numbers a plethora of well-wishers, with few to gainsay.

Nerva and Otho belong to the same milieu. They were close coevals (born in 35 and 32 respectively). Otho found his way to Nero's friendship through a 'congruentia morum' (Suetonius, *Otho* 2. 2). The same could be said of Nerva. The imperial poet respected his fine judgement of verse—'lascivum iuvenis cum tibi lusit opus' (Martial IX. 26. 10). Which genre of erotic poetry knew Nerva as an expert is not a theme to linger on.[4]

---

[1] App. 10.

[2] Some have fancied that Juvenal was referring to Plautus under the name 'Blandus'. Cf. opinions cited by G. Highet (*Juvenal the Satirist* (1954), 273), who is inconclusive. It is not likely. Note further that, while some identify the consul Lateranus of the poet (VIII. 146 ff.) with the Plautius Lateranus of Tacitus (*PIR*[1], P 354), *cos. des.* in 65 (and executed), that does not have to be so. Plautius Lateranus had children (*Ann.* XV. 60. 1).

[3] *Caesares* 311b.

[4] At least if Nero, hailing Nerva as Tibullus (Martial VIII. 70. 7 f.), meant the poems about Marathus (Tibullus I. 4; 8 f.).

The historian Tacitus by quiet juxtaposition of documentary items intends the reader to assume that Nerva had a hand in the unmasking of Piso's conspiracy (*Ann.* xv. 72. 1, cf. p. 2). Most regrettable. Scholars incline to dissemble or extenuate.[1] One suggests that Nerva rendered services of a legal nature.[2] But Nerva for all his ancestry was not a jurist,[3] and other techniques were now in play to make or quell a plot. Another waxes sentimental over Nerva's friendship with his august patron—and invokes his deficiency in will-power.[4] The effort is out of place. There is a defence, if a sagacious man saw no advantage but only peril in removing Nero to have Piso (p. 575). On a surface appraisement, Nerva was mild and benevolent.[5] Other qualities were requisite for survival and long influence with the Caesars.

What matters is the character of his government. A brief reign, and badly documented. The inquiry must range backwards and forwards, and there is room for divergence of opinion.

Domitian (it can be argued) was a careful administrator.[6] He was faced with heavy expenses—some his own, some inherited. Perhaps he did not do enough to repair the governmental finances, compromised as they had been by Titus.[7] What of Trajan? It has been contended that he was desperately short of funds in the first years: the gold of Dacia brought affluence and the means for a vast building programme.[8] Yet it cannot be proved that Trajan was in difficulties in his first years.[9] Perhaps Nerva was a financier of genius.[10]

Nerva needed cash—*congiarium* and *donativum* to pay at once. And he went on to a programme that involved expenditure (policy, not mere kindliness). If there was a financial stringency, ought not its source and cause to lie precisely in Nerva's reign?[11] An Economy Commission was set up by the Senate (Pliny, *Pan.* 62. 2, cf. Dio LXVIII. 2. 2). At what stage, it might be worth divining. Not at the outset. Verginius Rufus slipped and broke his thigh 'cum vocem praepararet acturus in consulatu principi gratias', hence a lengthy illness, 'aditus tantum mortis durior longiorque', and he died when Cornelius Tacitus was suffect consul (Pliny, *Epp.* II. 1. 4 ff.).[12] In the course of that illness he refused nomination to the Economy Commission then being constituted (ib. 9). The Commission can therefore be disjoined from an empty or depleted Treasury of September 96.

What, in the end, did it achieve? The economies were trivial, so far as reported

---

[1] B. W. Henderson, *Five Roman Emperors* (1927), 169; R. P. Longden, *CAH* XI (1936), 188; A. Garzetti, *Nerva* (1950), 23.

[2] H. Schiller, *Gesch. der r. Kaiserzeit* (1883), 539.

[3] Though some unconsciously assume it, e.g. M. P. Charlesworth, *CAH* XI (1936), 32.

[4] R. Paribeni, *Optimus Princeps* I (1926), 124.

[5] B. W. Henderson, o.c. 169 ff.; H. Götze, *Mitt. des d. arch. Inst.* I (1948), 139 ff.

[6] Th. Mommsen, *Provinces of the Roman Empire* I (1886), 108.

[7] S. Gsell, *Essai sur le règne de l'empereur Domitien* (1894), 334.

[8] J. Carcopino, *Dacia* I (1924), 28 ff. = *Points de vue sur l'impérialisme romain* (1934), 73 ff.

[9] R. Syme, *JRS* XX (1930), 55 ff.   [10] A. Stein, P-W IV, 143.

[11] R. Syme, o.c. 59 ff. Against, C. H. V. Sutherland, *JRS* XXV (1935), 150 ff.; R. P. Longden, *CAH* XI (1936), 194 f.; G. Biraghi, *La Parola del Passato* VI (1951), 257 ff.

[12] That is, late in the year (App. 10). Despite Sutherland (o.c. 151), the survival of an octogenarian senator with a broken thigh presents no strain on belief. The speech may have been intended for the first day of 97—perhaps for later (cf. Fronto, p. 25 N = Haines I, p. 110). It does not matter.

—some sacrifices and horse races abolished (Dio LXVIII. 2. 3). Too much has been made of the thing, whether to argue financial skill or, against that, a deficit. It might have been well to bear in mind Tacitus' cool comment on one of the measures of the year 70—'verane pauperie an uti videretur' (*Hist.* IV. 47). Moreover, the *aerarium* is in question, not the *fiscus*. The 'res publica' could be poor, and Caesar rich.

Domitian increased the pay of the soldiers. He fought three wars, the last of them in 92. He constructed many edifices—some of necessity after the great conflagration under Titus—and most of the more important had been terminated by 93.[1] The buildings are invoked to explain a shortage.[2] Other items have been roped in.[3] Facts and figures for estimate or comparison are missing. It is therefore impossible to refute the opinion that the *fiscus* was at a low ebb when Domitian was assassinated—but strong doubt is legitimate.[4]

Nerva on his accession found the money there for large and necessary disbursements. How long was the position cheerful, or tolerable? The Economy Commission, even if not to be taken too seriously, is a symptom. Difficulties may be surmised as the year wore on, with rumours about the army commanders, with the chance for peculation or distrainment of state funds at Rome and abroad. It was not a strong and prosperous government that Casperius and the Praetorians assaulted. It will not do to discount the danger of civil war; and it cannot with safety be believed that Nerva was a free agent when he adopted the legate of Upper Germany.[5]

Sharp and menacing, the crisis recalled the events of 68 and 69. There were inescapable parallels, the past influencing a man's judgement on the present. Galba as emperor instead of Nero, that might have seemed all that was desired. But Tacitus shows no liking, or even indulgence. He had seen through Galba. A question should be put even if it cannot be answered: what opinion did he have of Nerva?

There might have been a calamity. It was averted—and Nerva redeemed himself by escaping Galba's error in the choice of a successor.[6] There is no sign that Tacitus set a high value on the capacities of Nerva. He was familiar with his character, his past record—and his pedigree, to which he alludes in the *Annales* in a manner not exempt from malice.[7] At the same time he was in a position to make allowances for the ruler in his unhappy plight, knowing what cannot now be known: whose interest Casperius served (or thought he served) when he stirred the Guard to mutiny, and how near Trajan came to making an armed proclamation against Nerva before he was named a son and a colleague.

---

[1] R. Syme, o.c. 69. Some items against this are adduced by D. M. Robathan, *TAPA* LXXIII (1942), 130 ff. Not conclusively.

[2] Suetonius, *Dom.* 12. 1: 'exhaustus operum ac munerum impensis stipendioque quod adiecerat.'

[3] Thus the subsidy to Decebalus, C. H. V. Sutherland, o.c. 156; R. P. Longden, o.c. 195. Rome was now subsidizing Dacians—but instead of the Germans of Bohemia (cf. *Germ.* 42. 2), and presumably the Sarmatae Jazyges.

[4] cf. A. Garzetti, o.c. 61; 65.

[5] As, for example, by C. H. V. Sutherland (o.c. 154) and by A. Garzetti (o.c. 89). Henderson can even say 'after enjoying a placid rule of sixteen months, he died quietly' (o.c. 170).

[6] cf. Pliny, *Pan.* 8. 5.   [7] VI. 27. 1, cf. above, p. 576.

Nerva was something of an anachronism, his reign episodic. On the larger perspective it can be seen as an interruption in the development of the Roman government in the Flavio-Antonine period.

3. SYRIA IN 97

PLINY's attack on Publicius Certus made prudent men give heed to the attitude of the governor of Syria, who was a friend of Certus (*Epp.* IX. 13. 10 f.). The incident probably falls fairly early in 97. Domitius Apollinaris is described as 'consul designatus' (ib. 13). His tenure can hardly be earlier than May or later than August (App. 10).

That was not the end of suspicion, or much worse, about Syria. A certain A. Larcius Priscus, legate of IV Scythica, acted as 'pro legato consulare provinc. Syriae' (*AE* 1908, 237, cf. *ILS* 1055: Thamugadi). Clearly the *suffectus* of 110—and a fact to be exploited.[1] The commander of IV Scythica, the legion closest to Antioch, is the normal deputy for the governor. Thus Cn. Pompeius Collega in 69/70 (Josephus, *BJ* VII. 58 ff., cf. E. Ritterling, P–W XII, 1562). Also C. Julius Severus in 132 (*ILS* 8826). Larcius Priscus, however, was quaestorian in rank and a new arrival, coming from the quaestorship of Asia.[2]

Another item can fit in. If the order of his posts is correct, C. Julius Proculus (*suff.* 109) was 'tr. leg. IIII Scythic.' after having been 'q. Augustorum' (*ILS* 1040: Antium), that is, quaestor of Domitian and of Nerva (in succession in 96), or of Nerva and Trajan. That is so anomalous as to appear improbable. Yet Julius Proculus could have acted as deputy-commander of the legion when its legate was governor of Syria; compare a tribune in 69/70, attested by *ILS* 1000 (Arretium), where one could read 'tr. mil. leg. IIII / [Scyth. v]ic. leg. Aug. Vesp.' The two young men, Larcius Priscus and Julius Proculus, might have been dispatched to Syria at the same time.

Furthermore, a transference from Cappadocia. An unknown senator commanded XVI Flavia under Nerva, VI Ferrata (in Syria) under Trajan (*ILS* 1020: Aventicum).[3] He is quaestorian in rank, which is abnormal after 70, nor is iteration in the command of legions at all common.[4] This man—or his predecessor—may have taken the place of an unsatisfactory legionary commander in Syria.

Who was the mysterious consular? Possibly L. Javolenus Priscus the jurist (*suff.* 86), legate of Syria at some time between 90 and 101 (*ILS* 1015: Nedinum).[5]

---

[1] E. Groag, *Jahreshefte* XXIX (1935), Beiblatt 190 ff.; R. Syme, *Philologus* XCI (1936), 238 ff.

[2] Compare in 69 the parent of Priscus, A. Larcius Lepidus, summoned by Vespasian from the quaestorship of Crete and Cyrene to Judaea, to command X Fretensis (*ILS* 987: Antium) in place of M. Ulpius Traianus, needed elsewhere (cf. p. 30).

[3] A different person from the *Ignotus* of *IGR* III, 558 (Tlos), who also held those legions in that order, and who might be Mettius Modestus (*suff.* 103).

[4] cf. R. Syme, *Laureae Aquincenses* I (1938), 282 f.

[5] S. Gsell, *Essai sur le règne de l'empereur Domitien* (1894), 332; and (with reserves) R. Syme, *Philologus* XCI (1936), 243 f.

But, for sundry reasons, not very likely. His tenure could go in 92–95, or in 98–100 (preceding his proconsulate of Africa, which can be in 101–2). The latter date is not implausible. Pliny commends Voconius Romanus to an army commander called Priscus (II. 13), who has been holding his office for some time—'longum praeterea tempus quo amicos tuos exornare potuisti'. The letter should belong to 100 or 101. That rules out L. Neratius Priscus (suggested in *PIR¹*, N 46), whose governorship of Pannonia cannot have begun before the end of 102 (because of Glitius Agricola's tenure, cf. App. 14). Moreover, Syria would be more suitable than one of the northern armies (compare Pliny's occupations there, VII. 31. 2) for Voconius Romanus, a quiet man and probably an Epicurean (cf. IX. 28. 1), resident for most of the time at Saguntum by the sea, his home town (p. 83). There is no sign that Pliny's request was granted. It is precisely to Voconius that he reports gleefully an alleged gaffe of Javolenus Priscus some years later (VI. 15).[1]

The consular of 97 is perhaps to be sought among the army commanders of the previous six years. Syria was not normally a man's first post after his consulship, though the thing could happen, as witness L. Ceionius Commodus, the *ordinarius* of 78 (cf. *PIR²*, C 603). Domitian was insecure—and Trajan's first directly attested choice is A. Julius Quadratus (*suff.* 94), from 101 to 104, a man who had never seen an army hitherto (*ILS* 8819: Pergamum).

4. UPPER GERMANY IN 97

A RECENT theory produces a rebellion in Upper Germany, crushed by Trajan, who was thus in a strong position to enforce his claims. It depends on the burnt stratum in the legionary camp at Argentorate, in which a gold coin of Nerva was found.

A detailed reconstruction is offered, with definite roles for certain legions.[2] There were five at this time in Germania Superior (the author assumes), two of them, XIV Gemina and XXI Rapax being 'sur le *limes*'. XXI Rapax broke loose, and, accompanied by a horde of Suebi (i.e. the Suebi Nicretes), marched on Argentorate and burned it. Trajan promptly came down from Moguntiacum with I Adiutrix and defeated the rebels.

The theory has earned acclamation.[3] It also provokes disquiet. It is clear that the *Bellum Suebicum* under Nerva (*ILS* 2720), whence the appellation 'Germanicus' for the Princeps and for his adopted son (*Pan.* 8. 2, cf. 9. 2), has nothing to do with the Rhine: it was an expedition against the Germans of Bohemia (who had been at war with Domitian in 89).[4]

As for the legions Upper Germany (like Lower Germany) had (and needed) only three at this time. I Adiutrix had probably departed for the Danube a dozen years before; then XXI Rapax, to be destroyed by the Sarmatae Jazyges in 92;

---

[1] For Javolenus and Neratius see further App. 68.
[2] J. J. Hatt, *CRAI* 1949, 132 ff.; *Gallia* VII (1949), 161 ff.; *Historia* II (1953), 234 ff.
[3] J. Carcopino, cited in *CRAI* 1949, 134; cf. *Rev. ét. anc.* LI (1949), 271 f.
[4] cf. M. Durry, *Mémorial d'un voyage d'études en Rhénanie* (1953), 197.

then XIV Gemina, to take its place.[1] It is not to be fancied that Pannonia and the two provinces of Moesia had only seven legions between them in 97.

Local mutiny or turbulence in 97 is a possibility not to be lost from view. It needs to be proved. To support the notion that Trajan went very close to a *coup d'état*, a garbled statement in a late epitomator could be adduced (not with any confidence)—'cum extrema aetate apud Sequanos, quo tyranni defecit metu, imperium arbitrio legionum cepisset' (Victor, *De Caes.* 12. 2). The author, writing about Nerva, may be conflating Nerva and Nerva Traianus. In the fourth century Sequania or Maxima Sequanorum embraced the greater part of the old Germania Superior, taking in the territories of the Rauraci and the Helvetii.[2]

A minor puzzle is the 'pia fidelis' of I Adiutrix, not on *ILS* 2720 (of 97 or soon after) or on 1379 (before 103), but attested on *CIL* III, 1004 (Sarmizegethusa) before the year 114.[3] The appellation is generally granted for loyalty in civil war or against a rebel.[4]

5. FABRICIUS VEIENTO

VEIENTO (*PIR²*, F 91) was praetor at some time early in the reign of Nero (Dio LXI. 6. 2). There is no record of his first consulate, but his second has now been revealed by a diploma (*AE* 1948, 56 = *CIL* XVI, 158). He took the place of the Emperor Titus on the Ides of January 80. The fragment of Statius, *De bello Germanico* names Veiento together with Vibius Crispus as a consul for the third time (quoted above, p. 5). The dedication at Moguntiacum (*ILS* 1010) confirms Veiento's third consulate. The dramatic date of the poem (and of Juvenal's parody) being 83, the only years possible are 82, when Domitian's colleague was his cousin T. Flavius Sabinus, and 83, when it was Q. Petillius Rufus II Perhaps 83. Veiento's second consulate followed upon a crisis in the government, namely, the catastrophe of Eprius Marcellus. In 82 Domitian had trouble with his consort (see App. 7).

Vibius Crispus (*suff.* c. 62) was senior in rank to Fabricius Veiento, and older—if Juvenal (IV. 92 f.) be taken literally, he reached eighty. His second tenure of the *fasces* might well have come before the death of Vespasian. It cannot be taken as certain that he shared them with Veiento the third time, but it might be so.

Only the dedication and the diploma (*ILS* 1010; *CIL* XVI, 158) disclose the full nomenclature of Veiento, which is A. Didius Gallus Fabricius Veiento. It may be inferred that he was adopted by A. Didius Gallus (*PIR²*, D 70), suffect consul in 36 and a personage of note under Caligula and Claudius, ending as governor of Britain. Attica, the wife of Veiento (*ILS* 1010), cannot be linked to any group or family.

---

[1] E. Ritterling, P-W XII, 1277 ff.; 1387 ff.; 1736; 1789 f.; R. Syme, *JRS* XVIII (1928), 44 f.

[2] Relevant, for example, to *HA, Marcus* 22. 10: 'res etiam in Sequanis turbatas.'

[3] A gap precludes certainty about the full title of the legion on *ILS* 1016 (Nemausus) set up c. 107.   [4] E. Ritterling, o.c. 1389 f.

6. VESTRICIUS SPURINNA

BORN about 25 (Pliny, *Epp.* III. I. 10), Vestricius Spurinna is first discovered in 69, holding a command subordinate to the consular Annius Gallus (Tacitus, *Hist.* II. 11. 2, cf. p. 159). His consulate presumably falls in the reign of Vespasian, and his active career ends before the last years of Domitian—'quoad honestum fuit, obiit officia, gessit magistratus, provincias rexit' (*Epp.* III. I. 11). Spurinna was at Rome in December of 96 (*Epp.* I. 5. 8), and was appointed a member of the Economy Commission in the course of 97 (*Pan.* 62. 2). Two unnamed senators received each a second consulate from Nerva, a third from Trajan (*Pan.* 60. 5; 61. 7). One is patently Julius Frontinus. Mommsen divined the other—Spurinna.[1] Not everybody agreed. However, the *Fasti Ostienses* have revealed him as 'cos. II' on April 1, 98, and established his *praenomen* as 'T.'.[2] The third consulate is therefore reasonably certain, succeeding that of Frontinus in 100.

A vexatious problem subsists. The Senate, 'auctore principe' (probably Nerva), voted him a 'triumphalis statua'. The grounds are specified—'nam Spurinna Bructerum regem vi et armis induxit in regnum ostentatoque bello ferocissimam gentem, quod est pulcherrimum victoriae genus, terrore perdomuit' (*Epp.* II. 7. 2). Furthermore, another aspect (or rather phase) of the same operation might be referred to by Tacitus when he describes how the Bructeri were massacred by their neighbours, in the sight and presence of a Roman army (*Germ.* 33, cf. p. 46). Hence the theory that Vestricius Spurinna was legate of Lower Germany in 97.[3] He was now about seventy-three years old. Exceptionally vigorous in body, however. It could be argued that he was sent in urgency from the capital to appease the troops or forestall treason: on past performance (*Hist.* II. 18 f.) Spurinna was the man to curb, or at least cajole, an unruly army. If he chose to conduct the troops into hostile territory, a modest exploit was more than welcome to Nerva's government.

None the less, the man's age, and other things, inspires a strong doubt. Dessau (in *PIR*[1], V 308) suggested that Spurinna's exploit belongs to the reign of Domitian, and many concur.[4] Indeed, a suitable date and occasion could be found: it need not be supposed that Domitian's pacification of Germany in 83 (and the years following) was confined to the conquest of the Chatti.[5] Finally, against a military command in 97 (or 98) may be adduced what Pliny says about third consulates conferred on Spurinna and Frontinus: they were 'in toga meriti', not 'bellorum socii' or 'proeliorum consortes' (*Pan.* 60. 5).

For the tardy triumphal honour will be compared Vespasian's action, compensating a former legate of Moesia for Nero's neglect (*ILS* 986). The Senate also voted a statue to Spurinna's son Cottius, 'quem amisit absens' (*Epp.* II. 7. 3).

---

[1] *Hermes* III (1869), 39 f. = *Ges. Schr.* IV (1906), 374 f.

[2] *FO* XIV, first published in 1939.

[3] Mommsen, l.c.; thus J. Asbach, *R. Kaisertum u. Verfassung* (1896), 140. Others opted for 98, F. Münzer, *Klio* I (1901), 314.

[4] E. Ritterling, *Fasti des r. Deutschland unter dem Prinzipat* (1934), 61 ff., with Groag's opinion there cited; A. Garzetti, *Nerva* (1950), 57 f.

[5] cf. R. Syme, *JRS* XVIII (1928), 43; *CAH* XI, 158 f.

When was that absence? At first sight, when Spurinna was at the head of an army. Dessau proposed a different interpretation: perhaps Spurinna was a member of the senatorial embassy that went (it will be assumed) to congratulate Trajan in the late autumn of 97. Cf. p. 16.

The origin of Vestricius Spurinna is nowhere documented. The name of his wife Cottia (*Epp.* III. 10) is Celtic, and he is related to a northern bard, Sentius Augurinus of Verona (*Epp.* IV. 27. 5). Presumably a Transpadane, like Verginius and Corellius.[1] The *nomen* 'Vestricius', Etruscan like the *cognomen*, is exceedingly rare. All Italy furnishes a single instance on its inscriptions, a woman at Florentia.[2]

7. URSUS AND SERVIANUS

DOMITIAN, angered with his consort because of her affair with the dancer Paris, wanted to kill her, but a certain Ursus intervened (Dio LXVII. 3. 1). The incident belongs early in the reign (82 or 83). Then, after Domitian's return from the war against the Chatti, Ursus was himself in peril. Julia, the daughter of Titus, rescued him, and he was given the consulship (ib. 4. 2). In fact the *Fasti Ostienses* exhibit an '[U]rsus' as consul suffect in 84, perhaps from May 1 (*FO* XIII*s*). The emphasis on the consulship is peculiar, if Ursus was a senator. The two anecdotes show him in high favour with court and dynasty. Surely a prefect of the Praetorian Guard.[3]

Promotion from Egypt to the Guard becomes normal in this period (it went the other way previously), and can be attested for four prefects between 70 and 96. An Ursus was Prefect of Egypt,[4] certified as Julius Ursus by the dedication in honour of Sex. Attius Suburanus—'adiut. Iuli Ursi / praef. annonae, eiusdem in praefect. / Aegypti' (*AE* 1939, 60: Heliopolis). Let it be added that his *praenomen* is 'Lucius'.[5]

A Latin papyrus (*P. Berl.* 8334) casts a flood of light. An emperor, addressing 'mi Maxime', alludes to the virtues of that person and to their previous recompense, and announces further promotion. That promotion arises from something that has been done for a man called Julius—'se[d cum et] Iuliu[m Ursum suis / precibus u]sum in amplissimum ordinem transtu[lissem iam diu / id des]iderantem' (11. 3 ff.). Maximus is to be appointed colleague to a '[F]uscus' (11. 8 f.).

Now L. Laberius Maximus was prefect of Egypt (attested on June 9, 83: C. Septimius Vegetus being there on February 8, 85). Maximus, it is clear, is

---

[1] G. E. F. Chilver, *Cisalpine Gaul* (1941), 103. Q. Corellius Rufus (*suff.* ? 78) is attested as legate of Germania Superior on September 20, 82 (*CIL* XVI, 28).

[2] *CIL* XI, 7056.

[3] E. Groag divined it (cited by A. Stein in P–W, Supp. VII, 1624, who disagreed).

[4] A. Stein, *Die Präfekten von Ägypten* (1950), 42 f., who put him in 84, after L. Laberius Maximus. He could belong to an earlier date, as predecessor of C. Tettius Africanus (attested on February 12, 82), cf. R. Syme, *JRS* XLIV (1954), 117.

[5] As revealed by the much worn Latin inscription on the road to Berenice, published in *Chronique d'Égypte* XXIX (1954), 284, whence *AE* 1956, 57. The date 'anno IIII' is not secure. It depends on Wilkinson's MSS. copy of 1826 (photograph on p. 285).

being summoned to take the place of Julius Ursus, whose demotion is suitably veiled in bland and diplomatic phraseology. Maximus will share the command of the Guard with Cornelius Fuscus.[1] The date is presumably late in 83 (conceivably at the beginning of 84).

Fuscus occurs among the Emperor's counsellors in Juvenal's famous satire (IV. III f.). The dramatic date is 83, in the earlier part of the year. No colleague of Fuscus is there named. Some, it is true, suppose that the Egyptian Crispinus twice mentioned in the poem (1 ff.; 108 f.) was prefect of the Praetorians.[2] That is not very likely—and Crispinus could have been *praefectus annonae*. Julius Ursus, if Guard Prefect, ought to have been present at the imperial conclave. He is not there. The satirist might have discreetly omitted a man whose name and family stood high in later reigns.

A L. Julius Ursus was suffect consul early in 98, after Frontinus and before Spurinna (*FO* XIV). Surely an iterated consulate (see App. 11).[3] There is even a chance that he held the *fasces* for a third time in 100.[4]

The *Fasti Potentini* have disclosed Ser. Julius Servianus, *suffectus* in 90. He can be identified without discomfort as the Servianus who was legate of Germania Inferior early in 98 (*HA, Hadr.* 2. 5 f.): the husband of Hadrian's sister was born c. 47 (ib. 23. 8, cf. Dio LIX. 17. 1), which would give him the standard consular age.[5] By his second consulate of 101 he has become 'Ursus Servianus' (e.g. *ILS* 4965: Rome), the full style being 'L. Iulius Ursus Servianus'. To explain which, testamentary adoption could be invoked.

Servianus and Ursus may already have been related. Servianus was perhaps connected with the opulent Dasumii of Corduba (p. 604), and he gave his daughter in marriage to a Pedanius from Barcino (p. 480). If the above reconstruction is accepted, an earlier stage can be detected in the fortunes of a powerful group supporting Trajan and Hadrian.

To judge by the *gentilicium*, Julius Ursus is provincial. One might wonder whether there is any link with enigmatic persons like Ti. Julius Lupus, Prefect of Egypt in 71/72,[6] or the consular P. Julius Lupus, who married Arria Fadilla, the widow of T. Aurelius Fulvus (*cos.* 89).[7] Ursus and Lupus are not inappropriate in the same family.[8]

---

[1] The papyrus was first published in 1940. For this reconstruction, A. Piganiol. *CRAI* 1947, 376 ff. Against, H. G. Pflaum, *Latomus* x (1951), 474 f.; in favour, R. Syme, *JRS* XLIV (1954), 117. Uncertainties cannot fail to subsist. The improvement '[suis / precibus u]sum' for '[pre / cibus tuis u]sum' is due to E. Birley.

[2] A. Passerini, *Le coorti pretorie* (1939), 290; G. Highet, *Juvenal the Satirist* (1954), 78; 260; J. Crook, *Consilium Principis* (1955), 50.

[3] A. Stein, however, disagreed, preferring to distinguish three persons, viz. the Prefect of Egypt, the *suffectus* of 84, and the *suffectus* of 98 (P–W VII, 1623 ff.; *Aegyptus* XX (1940), 51 ff.).

[4] That is, if Vestricius is not the only *cos. ter* among the *suffecti* of 100. See App. 11.

[5] cf. R. Syme, *JRS* XLIV (1954), 156. A. Degrassi registers L. Julius Ursus Servianus as consul for the first time in an unknown year (*FC* (1952), 27).

[6] A. Stein, o.c. 40.   [7] App. 87.

[8] *CIL* XI, 1777 (Volaterrae) exhibits three brothers, Ursus, Lupus, and Aper.

B. CONSULS AND GOVERNORS

8. THE CONSULAR *FASTI*

TRAJAN and Tacitus were coeval within about three years, and it is desirable to place them firmly in the social and political context of the time. The consular roll of 85–96 now stands almost entire; and, by various devices, thirty-seven imperial legates of consular rank can be established in the period 92–106. That list will disclose some of the army commanders in the critical season after the fall of the Flavian dynasty (though many facts are missing), and Trajan's principal adherents during the first half of his reign will emerge. Further, the consuls of Tacitus' own year 97 excite a proper curiosity; the next year is politically revealing; and it will be convenient to register the iterated consulates and prefectures of the City right through from Vespasian to Hadrian inclusive.

A brief note on documentation is required. The evidence is highly heterogeneous—epigraphic calendars, military *diplomata*, other documents on stone, bronze, wood, or papyrus, and dates preserved in literary sources or thence divined.[1] Thanks to two recent discoveries, the list of consuls for 85–96 is all but complete. (1) New fragments of the *Fasti Ostienses* came to light in 1939.[2] One

---

[1] The epigraphic calendars have been edited by A. Degrassi, *Inscriptiones Italiae* XIII, 1 (1947). In *I Fasti Consolari dell' Impero Romano* (1952), the same scholar reconstructs the list of consuls for each year from 30 B.C. (whatever be the source); and he registers all other known consulates that cannot be tied to any year. The military *diplomata* were collected by H. Nesselhauf in *CIL* XVI (1936, Supplement 1955). The latter documents carry consular datings, by month and by day of the month, which, however, do not always tally with the year indicated by the imperial titulature (cf. notably *CIL* XVI, 38 f.); and it cannot always be taken as certain that the provincial governor named on a *diploma* was still in office when it was issued at Rome (i.e. on the consular date).

As for senators a register was drawn up by B. Stech, 'Senatores Romani qui fuerint inde a Vespasiano usque ad Traianum', (*Klio*, Beiheft X, 1912). Stech also investigated origins, not always with sufficient alertness and precision. A more recent list, but rather limited in time, is provided by A. Garzetti, *Nerva* (1950), 103 ff.

For consular governors of the imperial provinces see especially E. Ritterling, *Fasti des r. Deutschland unter dem Prinzipat* (edited by E. Stein, 1932); A. Stein, *Die Legaten von Moesien* (1940) and *Die Reichsbeamten von Dazien* (1944).

This series of appendixes (8–16) has been carefully designed for ready reference. To make the primary and decisive items of evidence stand out clearly, citation has been cut to a minimum; and some polyonymous senators have been abbreviated. The entries by letter and number in the *Prosopographia Imperii Romani* make for brevity. Perhaps the best label is a man's consular date (whether precise or approximate), for it conveys an historical fact: a mark of interrogation added denotes that the year, even when reasonably certain, lacks precise documentation.

[2] G. Calza, *Epigraphica* I (1939), 151 ff., whence *AE* 1940, 92 f. Now in *Inscr. It.* XIII, 1 (1947), p. 192 (*FO* XIIIs); 194 (*FO* XIIId and XIV).

tablet (found in three pieces) carries in parallel columns the *Fasti* of two series of years, namely, 84–86 (beginning about half-way through 84) and 94–96: of the former, on the left side of the block, only the last letter or letters in each line is preserved, but the latter, though broken on the right edge, is complete enough for certitude (*FO* XIIIs and XIIId). (2) Observed for the first time in 1946, rather than discovered, a large slab from Potentia in Picenum has on its left side the list of consuls from mid 86 down to a point in 93: the bottom right side of this series is truncated at 92 and 93, but other evidence (*FO* XIId) supplements the year 92.[1]

Defective for 85, 86, and 93, the record can be improved by certain conjectures. Degrassi (the editor of *Inscr. It.* XIII, 1) interprets *FO* XIIIs as introducing the year 85 with Domitian consul for the eleventh time with the colleague ']r. Mess. II'— that is L. Valerius Catullus Messallinus (*cos.* 73). So far so good. But there is a difficulty. Some written calendars (Mommsen, *Chron. Min.* I, 57, 222, 284, 416; II, 139) produce as Domitian's colleague in 84 a 'Fulvus' or 'Rufus'.[2] Now in *FO* XIIIs the preceding line terminates with ']vos II'. Degrassi takes this to be the name of a municipal magistrate at Ostia.[3] Surely, however, the desiderated second consulate of T. Aurelius Fulvus (*suff.* ? 70), the Prefect of the City (*HA, Pius* 1. 2).[4] Furthermore, another *cos. II* can be recovered, holding office with ']atus' (*FO* XIIIs). It is known that M. Arrecinus Clemens held a second consulate (*AE* 1947, 40)—and precisely with L. Baebius Honoratus (*CIL* XII, 3637). The remaining point of uncertainty is the colleague of Valerius Messallinus. Possibly C. Rutilius Gallicus (*suff.* 70 or 71), consul again and Prefect of the City (attested in 89). Otherwise Arrecinus Clemens might have shared the *fasces* for a time with Messallinus after the Emperor resigned, then yielding place to another *suffectus*.

If these conjectures are accepted, the gaps in the register of 85–96 are as follows. (1) in 85: two *suffecti*, viz. the one discussed above (whether a *cos. II* or not), and, after the pair M. Arrecinus Clemens and L. Baebius Honoratus, the missing colleague of '[Po]llio f.' (*FO* XIIIs). (2) in 86: a colleague for Q. Vibius Secundus (*Fasti Potentini*). (3) in 93: the hiatus between the *Potentini* and *FO* XIIId. After the *ordinarii* stands one suffectus, '[T.] Avidius Q[uietus]', colleague missing, and four letters 'Corị[' from the beginning of the next pair. The latter can be identified as C. Cornelius Rarus Sextius Na[?so], proconsul of Africa c. 107 (*IRT* 523).[5]

One could add (? L.) Julius Marinus, legate of Moesia Inferior in 97 (App. 14). Perhaps also L. Dasumius (? Hadrianus), whose proconsulate of Asia may fall in 106/7 (App. 23, cf. 87). Note further that a small Ostian fragment (*FO* XXXI) contains the name 'Vibius', and seems to indicate that an 'Um[midius]' died in office in the second half of December. Perhaps 93—an unhealthy year (cf. Tacitus, *Agr.* 44. 1).[6]

---

[1] N. Alfieri, *Athenaeum* XXVI (1948), 110 ff., whence *AE* 1949, 23.

[2] For the problem of the Fulvi *ordinarii* in 85 and 89 see Groag, *PIR²*, A 1509 f.; Degrassi, *Inscr. It.* XIII, 1, p. 221.   [3] cf. *Inscr. It.* XIII, 1, p. 193; *FC* 25.

[4] As argued by R. Syme, *JRS* XLIII (1953), 155; H. Nesselhauf, *Gnomon* XXVI (1954), 270. In criticism of this view see now Degrassi, *Athenaeum* XXXIII (1955), 112 ff.

[5] R. Syme, o.c. 153.

[6] ib. 160. Degrassi suggested that the 'Vibius' was a local magistrate, that 'Um[midius]'

The year after the last of Domitian's wars may have had a long string of *consules suffecti*. Compare 90, with eleven—or 100, with eight at least. It would be impracticable in this place to seek to apportion a large number of consulates, known or inferential, between 93, 97, and the early years of Trajan.

What is here presented (App. 9) is not a reconstruction of epigraphic documents, but only a list of the consuls of the twelve years 85 to 96. A blank in the second line of certain years denotes the Emperor's resignation, one of the *consules suffecti* moving up to take his place; and several polyonymous senators have been entered under their shortest or most familiar nomenclatures. Further, there is an uncertainty about the structure of 85 (cf. above); the 'M. Tullius Cerialis' in 90 could be 'Tuccius Cerialis' attested as consular at the end of 99 (Pliny, *Epp.* II. 11. 9); the *praenomen* of D. Plotius Grypus (*suff.* 88) might be 'L.' (cf. *ILS* 5161*k*); and that of Metilius Nepos (*suff.* 91) is reproduced by the *Fasti Potentini* as 'L'.

9. THE CONSULS, 85–96

85 Imp. Domitianus XI
    Ignotus ? II
    M. Arrecinus Clemens II
    Ignotus
    D. Aburius Bassus

    T. Aurelius Fulvus II
    L. Valerius Catullus Messallinus II
    L. Baebius Honoratus
    [. . . . . . . Po]llio f.
    Q. Julius Balbus

86 Imp. Domitianus XII
    C. Secius Campanus
    Ignotus
    Sex. Octavius Fronto
    A. Lappius Maximus

    Ser. Cornelius Dolabella Petronianus

    Q. Vibius Secundus
    Ti. Julius Candidus
    L. Javolenus Priscus

87 Imp. Domitianus XIII
    C. Calpurnius Piso Licinianus
    C. Bellicus Natalis Tebanianus
    C. Cilnius Proculus

    L. Volusius Saturninus

    C. Ducenius Proculus
    L. Neratius Priscus

88 Imp. Domitianus XIV
    D. Plotius Grypus
    M. Otacilius Catulus

    L. Minicius Rufus
    Q. Ninnius Hasta
    Sex. Julius Sparsus

89 T. Aurelius Fulvus
    P. Sallustius Blaesus
    A. Vicirius Proculus

    M. Asinius Atratinus
    M. Peducaeus Saenianus
    M'. Laberius Maximus

resigned office (*Inscr. It.* XIII, 1, p. 239). Vibius might be a Vibius Varus; and it would be desirable to have the parent of C. Ummidius Quadratus (*suff.* 118). For a 'Vibius Va[rus]', consul suffect in November of an unknown year, *CIL* XVI, 172.

90 Imp. Domitianus XV   M. Cocceius Nerva II
    L. Cornelius Pusio
    L. Antistius Rusticus   Ser. Julius Servianus
    Q. Accaeus Rufus   C. Caristanius Fronto
    P. Baebius Italicus   C. Aquillius Proculus
    L. Albius Pullaienus Pollio   Cn. Pompeius Longinus
    M. Tullius Cerialis   Cn. Pompeius Catullinus

91 M'. Acilius Glabrio   M. Ulpius Traianus
    D. Minicius Faustinus   P. Valerius Marinus
    Q. Valerius Vegetus   P. Metilius Nepos

92 Imp. Domitianus XVI   Q. Volusius Saturninus
    L. Venuleius Montanus Apronianus
    L. Stertinius Avitus   Ti. Julius Celsus Polemaeanus
    C. Julius Silanus   Q. Junius Arulenus Rusticus

93 Sex. Pompeius Collega   Q. Peducaeus Priscinus
    T. Avidius Quietus   *Ignotus*
    C. Cornelius Rarus Sextius Na[? so]   *Ignotus*

                 . . .

94 L. Nonius Asprenas   T. Sextius Magius Lateranus
    M. Lollius Paullinus   A. Julius Quadratus
    L. Silius Decianus   T. Pomponius Bassus

95 Imp. Domitianus XVII   T. Flavius Clemens
    L. Neratius Marcellus
    A. Lappius Maximus II   P. Ducenius Verus
    Q. Pomponius Rufus   L. Baebius Tullus

96 C. Manlius Valens   C. Antistius Vetus
    Q. Fabius Postuminus   T. Prifernius [Paetus]
    Ti. Catius Fronto   M. Calpurnius [. . . . .]icus

10. SOME CONSULS OF 97

THE year opened with the Emperor Nerva and L. Verginius Rufus, consuls for the third time. A lengthy list would be expected. One or more of the *suffecti* might be iterations, compare 98. Arrius Antoninus is almost certain. Observe the consular pair 'Sabinus et Antoninus' which Mommsen rejected (*Chron. Min.* I, 255; *Ges. Schr.* IV, 381), but which Groag regards with more favour (*PIR²*, A 1086). Arrius was a friend of Nerva (Victor, *Epit.* 12. 3), and certainly twice consul (Pliny, *Epp.* IV. 3. 1). The colleague could be L. Vibius Sabinus, husband of Trajan's niece Matidia (App. 87).

A welcome fragment from Ostia reveals the first consuls of three successive pairs and enables a fourth name to be supplied.[1] As follows:—

[M.] ANNIVS VERVS	[L. NERATIVS PRISCVS]
[L. DO]MITIVS APOLLINAR.	SE[ ]
Q. ATILIV[S AGRICOLA	]

As for Annius Verus, see App. 86 f. His colleague is beyond doubt (*Dig.* XLVIII. 8. 6). To be identified as L. Neratius Priscus the jurist (cf. App. 68). Domitius Apollinaris (*PIR*², D 133) is named as 'consul designatus' in the earlier part of 97 (*Epp.* IX. 13. 13, cf. App. 3). He had been legate of Lycia-Pamphylia (*IGR* III, 559), and seems to have reached Rome by December 96 (cf. Martial XI. 15). His colleague might be a Sergius Octavius Laenas: better, Sex. Hermetidius Campanus, attested as legate of Judaea in 93 (*CIL* XVI, App. no. 12).[2] As for Q. (Glitius) Atilius Agricola, he was still in Gallia Belgica after the accession of Nerva (*ILS* 1021), departing (one might assume) in the spring of 97 (it would be worth knowing who took his place). Who shared the *fasces* with Glitius Agricola? Perhaps Cornelius Tacitus.[3] But it is not at all certain that the three pairs indicated by the new fragment exhaust the *Fasti* of this notable year. Like 98 it probably had two pairs of *suffecti* in the last four months. Not to mention various possibilities earlier, after the *ordinarii*.

Two names can be adduced. First, M. (Ostorius) Scapula, proconsul of Asia (App. 23), presumably in 114/15: on the coin attesting the proconsulate Trajan is Ἄριστος but not yet Παρθικός. Not a Julius, as some suppose (cf. P-W II A, 354), but an Ostorius, son of M. Ostorius Scapula (*suff.* 59): not noticed in P-W XVIII, 1670.

Next, L. Licinius Sura (*II ord.* 102, *III ord.* 107). The difficult problem of his first consulate[4] has been simplified but not solved by recent discoveries. The evidence of Martial tells against 93. A poem in a book that was published in December 92 welcomes Sura's recovery from a dangerous illness (VII. 47), but Martial gives no sign that Sura will soon be consul. In the present state of knowledge 97 seems the best guess. It might be well to leave out of account the acephalous *elogium* of a 'vir militaris' who had been legate of Belgica before his consulship (*ILS* 1022). Universally attributed to Sura, it could belong to somebody else (cf. App. 14). Yet, if the *Ignotus* is Sura, a rapid tenure of Belgica (after Glitius Agricola) and a consulate at the end of the year (perhaps in *absentia*) are not impossible. But again, 93 is not excluded for Sura.

For 97, as for 93, further speculation will be unprofitable, even though it could

---

[1] The fragment was first published by Degrassi, *FC* (1952), in his 'Aggiunte', p. 288, whence *JRS* XLIII (1953), 150. It was then assumed to be the right-hand side of a block, but the publication by the discoverer, G. Barbieri, showed that it was the left (*Studi Romani* I (1953), 367, with pl. 1). See now *AE* 1954, 220.

[2] R. Syme, *JRS* XLIV (1954), 81 f.

[3] So G. Barbieri, o.c. 367 f. That scholar, however, assumed that there were only three pairs of *suffecti* in 97, following directly on Nerva and Verginius Rufus. Also A. Garzetti, *Aevum* XXVII (1953), 549 ff.

[4] cf. E. Groag, P-W XIII, 475 f.

bring in such characters as Aufidius Umber, the legate of Cappadocia (App. 14),[1] the orator Lucceius Albinus (*Epp.* III. 9. 7), or Libo Frugi (ib. 33). And sundry other persons.[2]

11. THE CONSULS OF 98

ANOTHER fragment from Ostia (*FO* XIV) reveals 98 almost entire. A most anomalous year.[3] After the *ordinarii*, Nerva and Trajan, there follow down to May 1 five men with whom Trajan shared the *fasces* in turn (cf. *AE* 1936, 66), then two pairs of *suffecti* (incomplete but recoverable from other sources).

Certain comments may be added. Of the five successive colleagues of Trajan, the second and the fourth, namely, Sex. Julius Frontinus and T. Vestricius Spurinna, were certainly *consules iterum*; but not the fifth, C. Pomponius [Pius] (cf. *AE* 1936, 66). The second, taking office on January 13, is a 'Cn. Domiti[us]'. Who precisely? Groag suggested Domitius Apollinaris (*PIR*[2], D 133, Addenda, p. xi), whose *praenomen*, however, should rather be 'L.'. This man is now certified in 97. An emendation of *HA, Marcus* 1. 3 (cf. App. 87) can recover a second consulate for the eminent Cn. Domitius Tullus (*suff.* c. 79).

The third name is that of the enigmatic L. Julius Ursus (App. 7). It is preserved entire and followed by a space before the break in the stone. Yet the sign of iteration may have been there.[4]

Hence four iterated consulates for *suffecti* in January–April 98. After the end of June the *Fasti* become normal again, with a regular pair on July 1, and a second presumably on September 1. That is not the end. A pair for November–December could be surmised in 98 as in 97 (and as certified in 100, cf. *ILS* 3619). In fact a tiny fragment with 'K. No[v.]' joins to *FO* XIV.[5] Conjecture can supply two names. A condemned inscription, one of the *Ligorianae*, ends with a consular date 'III non. Decembr. / Vettio Proclo / Iullo Lupo cos.' (*CIL* VI, 616*). It might embody material ultimately genuine. Q. Fulvius Gillo Bittius Proculus (*PIR*[2], F 544), *praefectus aerarii Saturni* in 97, secured designation for a consulate when his colleague Publicus Certus did not (Pliny, *Epp.* IX. 13. 23). His proconsulship of Asia should fall in 115/16 (*IGR* IV, 172, with the eleventh acclamation of Trajan). That accords with a consulate in 98: if 97, the interval would be eighteen years, one year longer than any so far on record for Trajan's reign. The colleague of Bittius Proculus could be the mysterious P. Julius Lupus, second husband of the daughter of Arrius Antoninus (App. 87).[6]

---

[1] Omitted by Degrassi from his *Fasti Consolari* (1952).

[2] It would not be safe to insert A. Caepio Crispinus and Q. Asinius Marcellus. A fragmentary inscription copied by Helbig (*Röm. Mitt.* I (1886), 128) exhibits this pair with the *ordinarii* of 96 preceding: *PIR*[2], A 1235; C 150.

[3] *Epigraphica* I (1939), 157 = *AE* 1940, 93.

[4] As Groag assumed, in a letter to Stein cited in P-W, Supp. VII, 1624. The possibility is not discussed by Degrassi in *Inscr. It.* XIII, 1, p. 224—or admitted in *FC*.

[5] *FO* XXXII, cf. G. Barbieri, *Studi Romani* I (1953), 370, with Pl. I, 2 facing.

[6] This conjecture was advanced, with diffidence, in *JRS* XLIII (1953), 154. Mommsen rejected *CIL* VI, 616* (*Ges. Schr.* IV (1906), 373; cf. *PIR*[1], J 262), and the inscription was not noted in P- W[x], 664 or in *PIR*[2], A 1119.

So far the consuls of 85–96, of 97, of 98. Different sections of Trajan's reign exhibit wide divergences of documentation. Five *suffecti* of 99 are known, whereas 100 certainly had at least eight, among them one *cos. ter*, T. Vestricius Spurinna.[1] There is space for conjectural attributions in 101, 102, 104, and 106. A recent discovery gives the structure of 103—seven *suffecti*, two of them already known and three others that can be both supplemented and identified (viz. Q. Baebius Macer, C. Mettius Modestus, and P. Calpurnius Macer).[2] The years 105 and 107 are complete (*FO* XIX and XX), 108 almost so (XXI). There follows a clean run, 109–13 inclusive (XXII), a gap, and another full year, 116 (XXIII). Further, Potentia now comes to the help of Ostia. The *Potentini*, though here very fragmentary, overlap at 113, and give names (entire or truncated) for the first item in each consular pair of 114 and 115. If no consuls have been omitted, only two vacancies now remain in those years.[3] Finally, 117 is mainly a blank.[4]

12. ITERATED CONSULATES

70	C. Licinius Mucianus (*suff.* c. 64)
72	C. Licinius Mucianus III : with T. Flavius Sabinus (69)
74	*Ti. Plautius Silvanus Aelianus (45)
	Q. Petillius Cerialis (70) : with T. Clodius Eprius Marcellus (62)
? 75	M. Pompeius Silvanus (45) : with L. Tampius Flavianus (*anno incerto*)
? c. 77	Q. Vibius Crispus (c. 62)
80	A. Didius Gallus Fabricius Veiento
83	*Q. Petillius Rufus (? c. 73)
? 83	Q. Vibius Crispus III
? 83	A. Didius Gallus Fabricius Veiento III
85	T. Aurelius Fulvus (? 70)
	L. Valerius Catullus Messallinus (*cos.* 73)
	M. Arrecinus Clemens (73)
? 85	C. Rutilius Gallicus (70 or 71)
90	*M. Cocceius Nerva (*cos.* 71)
95	A. Lappius Maximus (86)
97	*L. Verginius Rufus III (*cos.* 63, *II suff.* 69)
? 97	Arrius Antoninus (69)
98	Sex. Julius Frontinus (? 73)
	T. Vestricius Spurinna (c. 73)
?	Cn. Domitius Tullus (c. 79)
?	L. Julius Ursus (84)

[1] Perhaps even two more, if Barbieri is right in assigning an enigmatic new fragment to 100 (o.c. 371, with Pl. I, 1 facing, whence *AE* 1954, 222). Possibly L. Julius Ursus and A. Lappius Maximus. An anonymous *cos. ter*, deduced for 99 by Degrassi (*FC* 30) from Pliny, *Pan.* 58. 1, is only Fabricius Veiento.

[2] G. Barbieri, o.c. 373 (with Pl. II), whence *AE* 1954, 223.

[3] One might suspect that the structure of the *Potentini* for 115 (two pairs of *suffecti*) is not correct. P. Valerius Priscus, proconsul of Africa in 127/8 (*IRT* 361), could not be later than 115.

[4] But taking in Trajan's generals Sex. Erucius Clarus and Julius Alexander—and Lusius the Moor (p. 242).

100 *Sex. Julius Frontinus III
 T. Vestricius Spurinna III
102 *L. Julius Ursus Servianus (90): with L. Licinius Sura (? 97)
103 *M'. Laberius Maximus (89)
 Q. Glitius Atilius Agricola (97)
104 *Sex. Attius Suburanus Aemilianus (101)
105 *Ti. Julius Candidus Marius Celsus (86): with C. Antius A. Julius Quadratus (94)
107 *L. Licinius Sura III with Q. Sosius Senecio (*cos*. 99)
109 *A. Cornelius Palma Frontonianus (*cos*. 99)
113 *L. Publilius Celsus (102)
120 *L. Catilius Severus Julianus Claudius Reginus (110)
121 *M. Annius Verus (97)
125 *M. Lollius Paullinus D. Valerius Asiaticus Saturninus (94)
126 *M. Annius Verus III
128 *L. Nonius Calpurnius Torquatus Asprenas (*cos*. 94)
129 *P. Juventius Celsus (c. 117): with L. Neratius Marcellus (95)
134 *L. Julius Ursus Servianus III

The foregoing list omits members of the imperial dynasties. Iterated *ordinarii* are marked by asterisks. Several uncertainties subsist.

The pair Pompeius Silvanus and Tampius Flavianus (*CIL* IV, 2560): Flavianus is here entered ?75, and might well belong to that year. For Fabricius Veiento and Vibius Crispus see App. 5. As for Rutilius Gallicus (*ILS* 1007), 85 is only a possibility: he cannot be later, and he might be earlier. For the consuls of 85, with a proposal about *FO* XIII*s*, see App. 8; for Arrius Antoninus, App. 10; for two conjectures about 98, App. 11. In 100 the third consulate of T. Vestricius Spurinna is deduced from Pliny, *Pan*. 61. 6 f.; 62. 1 f. For the chance of two other *consules tertio* in that year see App. 11. As for L. Julius Ursus Servianus, it will be recalled that he presumably began as Ser. Julius Servianus (*suff*. 90), cf. App. 7.

13. PREFECTS OF THE CITY

70– 73 *Ignotus*
73– Ti. Plautius Silvanus Aelianus (*suff*. 45, II ord. 74). *ILS* 986
 83 Pegasus (? c. 73). Juvenal IV. 76 f.
– 89 C. Rutilius Gallicus (70 or 71, II ?85). Statius, *Silvae* I. 4. 90 f. He died in 91 or 92 (*CIL* VI, 1984)
 T. Aurelius Fulvus (? 70, II ord. 85). *HA*, *Pius* 1. 2. Either before or later than Gallicus. He was certainly alive after 89
 Q. Glitius Atilius Agricola (97, II 103). *CIL* V, 6980
–117 Q. Baebius Macer (103). *HA*, *Hadr*. 5. 5
 M. Annius Verus (97, II ord. 121, III ord. 126). *HA*, *Marcus* 1. 2; *ILS* 2117.
 M. Lollius Paullinus D. Valerius Asiaticus Saturninus (94, II ord. 125). *ILS* 2117
–138 L. Catilius Severus (110, II ord. 120). *HA*, *Hadr*. 24. 6; *Marcus* 1. 4
 138 Ser. Cornelius Scipio Salvidienus Orfitus (*cos*. 110). *HA*, *Pius* 8. 6

No Prefect of the City is attested at the time of Domitian's death, or under Nerva, and there are gaps in Trajan's reign. Groag suggested Ti. Julius Candidus Marius Celsus (*suff.* 86, *II ord.* 105) because of the second consulate (P-W x, 541); also Q. Fabius Postuminus (96), adducing the fragmentary inscription *CIL* xiv, 2933a (*PIR²*, F 54). Add perhaps Sex. Attius Suburanus (101, *II ord.* 104), the former Guard Prefect, who re-heard a case which had been before Julius Servianus as *iudex* (Pliny, *Epp.* vii. 6. 10): Groag (P-W x, 884 f.) and Stein (*PIR²*, A 1366) assign the incident to Suburanus' consulate in 104.

14. CONSULAR LEGATES, 92-106

1. Q. Acutius Nerva (*suff.* 100). *PIR²*, A 101. Germania Inferior from 101, cf. *CIL* iii, 7697; 7715 f. (Brohltal quarries)

2. L. Antistius Rusticus (90). *PIR²*, A 765. Cappadocia (*AE* 1925, 126: Pisidian Antioch), succeeding Ti. Julius Candidus Marius Celsus (*suff.* 86), who is attested by *CIL* iii, 250. He died there in 93 or 94 (Martial ix. 30). From Spain, to judge by the tribe 'Galeria'

3. Aufidius Umber (*anno incerto*). *PIR²*, A 1395. Cappadocia, 100/1 (coins). Probably Umbrian, from Pisaurum (cf. A 1393)

4. T. Avidius Quietus (93). *PIR²*, A 1410. Britannia in 98, replacing (P. Metilius) Nepos (*CIL* xvi, 43), cf. p. 51. From Faventia

5. A. Caecilius Faustinus (99). *PIR²*, C 43. Moesia Inferior on May 13, 105. (*CIL* xvi, 50)

6. P. Calvisius Ruso Julius Frontinus (?79). *PIR²*, C 350. Cappadocia in 105 (*MAMA* vii, 193: Philomelium), and 106/7 (coins), cf. *AE* 1914, 267 (Pisidian Antioch). For origin and family, App. 87

7. C. Cilnius Proculus (87). *PIR²*, C 732. Moesia Superior on May 8, 100 (*CIL* xvi, 46). Previously legate of Dalmatia; consular decorations for the Dacian War (*Not. Scav.* 1925, 224). From Arretium

8. A. Cornelius Palma Frontonianus (*cos.* 99, *II ord.* 109). *PIR²*, C 1412. Hispania Citerior in 100 or 101 (Martial xii. 9. 1); Syria from 104 to 108. From Volsinii (cf. *CIL* xi, 2697)

9. L. Fabius Justus (102). *PIR²*, F 41. Syria in 109 (*AE* 1940, 210). But add a previous military command (?106) on the basis of Pliny, *Epp.* vii. 2, addressed to a man called 'Iustus'. From Narbonensis or Spain (cf. p. 615)

10. Q. Fabius Postuminus (96). *PIR²*, F 54. Moesia Inferior in 103 (*CIL* iii, 14451: Tomi)

11. Q. Glitius Atilius Agricola (97, *II* 103). *PIR²*, G 181. Pannonia, attested on November 19, 102 (*CIL* xvi, 47), cf. *ILS* 1021a: consular decorations for the Dacian War. From Augusta Taurinorum

12. L. Herennius Saturninus (100). Not in *PIR¹*. Moesia Superior at some time between 104 and 106 (*CIL* xvi, 54)

13. *Ignotus A.* Governor of Syria in 97. (Pliny, *Epp.* ix. 13. 11). See App. 3

14. *Ignotus B.* A general when Trajan 'gentem Dacor. et regem Decebalum / bello superavit', and honoured with a double set of consular military decorations (*ILS* 1022: Rome). Usually and plausibly identified with L. Licinius Sura. Conceivably Sosius Senecio

15. *Ignotus C.* A senator with consular military decorations, previously legate of a legion under Nerva and Trajan and governor of a (praetorian) province under Trajan (*CIL* XII, 3169: Nemausus). Related to a woman called Pompeia Marullina. Perhaps D. Terentius Scaurianus (as suggested in *JRS* XXXVI (1946), 160); perhaps L. Fabius Justus

16. L. Javolenus Priscus (86). *PIR*[1], O 40. Germania Superior on October 27, 90 (*CIL* XVI, 36): Syria at some time between 91 and 100 (App. 3). Cf. his *cursus* (*ILS* 1015: Nedinum). From Iguvium in Umbria (cf. App. 68)

17. (? L.) Julius Marinus (? 93). *PIR*[1], J 273. Moesia Inferior in January 97 (*CIL* XVI, 41). The diploma has 'sub Iulio Mar['. The name is deduced from that of L. Julius L. f. Fab. Marinus Caecilius Simplex (*ILS* 1026), *suffectus* probably in 101 (*ILS* 6106), who had been legate of Bithynia-Pontus 'proconsulatu patris sui' (i.e. c. 89)

18. A. Julius Quadratus (94, *II ord.* 105). *PIR*[1], J 338. Syria from 101 to 104, cf. *ILS* 8819, &c. (see P–W x, 425). By his full name C. Antius A. Julius A. f. Volt. Quadratus. From Pergamum

19. C. Julius Quadratus Bassus (105). General in the Second Dacian War, later governor of Cappadocia, of Syria, of Dacia (in 117/18) where he died: revealed by the inscription from Pergamum first published by W. Weber, whence *AE* 1933, 268, but better interpreted by A. v. Premerstein (*Bayerische S–B*, 1934, Heft 3). Weber conflated this man with A. Julius Quadratus (94, *II ord.* 105). Premerstein showed that he is the *suffectus* of 105, but also (o.c. 13) assumed identity with C. Julius Bassus, the delinquent proconsul of Bithynia (Pliny, *Epp.* IV. 9; *AE* 1939, 294: Nicaea). Various scholars have concurred; against: E. Groag, P–W, Supp. VII, 311 f. (briefly): R. Syme, *JRS* XXXVI (1946), 162 f. Bassus has for tribe the 'Fabia'. Of royal stock, cf. his kinsfolk (*OGIS* 544 (Ancyra))

20. Ser. Julius Servianus (90) = L. Julius Ursus Servianus (*II ord.* 102, *III ord.* 134). See App. 7. Germania Superior in February 98 (*HA, Hadr.* 2. 6), passing thence to Pannonia (Pliny, *Epp.* VIII. 23. 5), and with Trajan for a time during the First Dacian War (cf. III. 17). Presumably provincial, cf. App. 7

21. M'. Laberius Maximus (89, *II ord.* 103). *PIR*[1], L 4. Moesia Inferior, attested in October 25, 100 (*SEG* I, 329, ll. 62 ff.: Istros); commanding an army in the campaign of 102 (Dio LXVIII. 9. 4). From Lanuvium (cf. *ILS* 6194)

22. A. Lappius Maximus (86, *II* 95). *PIR*[2], A 949 (now obsolete). Germania Inferior in 88/89 (Victor, *Epit.* 11. 10; Dio LXVII. 11. 1). The new evidence for his consulates confirms Pichlmayr's emendation in Victor ('per Norbanum ⟨L⟩appium'), corrects Dio, and improves *ILS* 1006. Lappius also held the other Germany for a time after his victory over L. Antonius Saturninus (cf. *CIL* XIII, 12168[7–9] &c.: tiles of VIII

Augusta). A later consular command (? Pannonia) might be deduced from Martial IX. 84 (of 94 or 95) which extols the 'sancta fides' of a certain Norbanus at a time of civil war, and welcomes his return to Rome after an absence of six years—unless this be Norbanus the Prefect of the Guard in 96 (*PIR*[1], N 132). Probably Italian: the *nomen* 'Lappius' is very rare (W. Schulze, *LE* 358)

23. L. Licinius Sura (?97, *II ord.* 102, *III ord.* 107. *PIR*[1], L 174. Germania Inferior, presumably from 98 to 100/1 (*AE* 1923, 33: Brohltal quarries); with Trajan in the First Dacian War (Dio LXVIII. 9. 2), and presumably in the Second. For the dating of his first consulate, App. 10; for the attribution of *ILS* 1022 see under *Ignotus B*. From a town of Tarraconensis (App. 85)

24. Macer (*anno incerto*). *PIR*[1], M 6. Dalmatia, going there precisely in 98 (Martial x. 78); perhaps the Macer already named among some fairly senior persons (v. 28. 5). Not to be identified with Q. Baebius Macer (*suff.* 103). Perhaps polyonymous

25. P. Metilius Nepos (91). *PIR*[1], M 381. Britannia in 97, superseded by T. Avidius Quietus (cf. *CIL* xvi, 43). From Novaria, cf. *CIL* v, 6503; a later member of the family has the 'Claudia', the tribe of Novaria (*ILS* 1053)

26. P. Metilius Sabinus Nepos (103). *PIR*[1], M 389. A military province in 105, Pliny, *Epp.* IV. 26. 2, cf. *CIL* VI, 2075. Groag suggests Pannonia (P–W xv, 1401), because of a kinsman's military tribunate in a legion there (*ILS* 1053). Add perhaps Pliny *Epp.* IX. 2, to a Sabinus, mentioning 'tuae occupationes' and 'arma vestra'

27. L. Neratius Marcellus (95). *PIR*[1], N 43. Britannia on January 19, 103 (*CIL* xvi, 48), cf. Pliny, *Epp.* III. 8. 1 (probably in 101, at the beginning of his tenure). Brother of the jurist. From Saepinum in Samnium (*ILS* 1032)

28. L. Neratius Priscus (97). *PIR*[1], N 46. Pannonia (*ILS* 1033 f.: Saepinum). For his identity with the jurist, and for two homonyms, the *suffectus* of 87 and the son of the jurist, see App. 68

29. Sex. Octavius Fronto (86). *PIR*[1], O 25. Moesia Inferior on June 14, 92 (*CIL* xvi, 37). Acclaimed by Martial c. 85 as 'clarum militiae, Fronto, togaeque decus' (I. 55. 2)

30. Cn. Pompeius Longinus (90). *PIR*[1], P 469. Moesia Superior on September 16, 94 (*CIL* xvi, 39), Pannonia on February 20, 98 (42). Perhaps the Longinus commanding troops in occupied Dacia in 105 (Dio LXVIII. 12. 1), cf. Fronto, p. 217 N = Haines II, p. 214: 'in Dacia captus vir consularis'. By his full style Cn. Pinarius Aemilius Cicatricula Pompeius Longinus —i.e. Cn. Pompeius Longinus, legate of Judaea in 86 (*CIL* xvi, 33), adopted by the *suffectus* of 79

31. T. Pomponius Bassus (94). *PIR*[1], P 530. Cappadocia from 95 to 100 (coins and milestones, and cf. especially E. A. Sydenham, *The Coinage of Caesarea in Cappadocia* (1933), 53 f.; 72)

32. Q. Pomponius Rufus (95). *PIR*[1], P 561. Moesia Inferior on August 14, 99 (*CIL* xvi, 44 f.). The inscription from Lepcis shows him 'leg. Aug. pro

pr. provinc. [M]oesiae Dalmat. Hisp.' (*ILS* 1014+*IRT* 537). The order is anomalous, and in fact Pomponius held Dalmatia as a praetorian, cf. *CIL* XVI, 38, with the date July 13, 94. His governorship of Tarraconensis could fall before 99—or, possibly, after 101. Probably from Spain, cf. p. 592

33. L. Publilius Celsus (102, *II ord.* 113). *PIR*[1], P 782. Consular military commands are implied by the public statue (he is named along with Cornelius Palmo and Sosius Senecio in Dio LXVIII. 16. 2), the second consulate—and his subsequent fate

34. Sallustius Lucullus (*anno incerto*). *PIR*[1], S 63. Britannia (Suetonius, *Dom.* 10. 3). Possibly in 88/89 (*CAH* XI (1936), 174), perhaps rather c. 94, for he may be identical with P. Sallustius Blaesus (*suff.* 89). The latter person might be a *polyonymus*, with (e.g.) 'Velleius' for his second *gentilicium*, cf. 'Velleius Blaesus ille locuples consularis' (Pliny, *Epp.* II. 20. 7). Italian, observe Cicero's faithful friend Cn. Sallustius, who had a relative P. Sallustius (*Ad Att.* XI. 11. 2)

35. Q. Sosius Senecio (*cos.* 99, *II ord.* 107). *PIR*[1], S 560. Governor of a military province (and not at the beginning of his tenure) c. 103 (Pliny, *Epp.* IV. 4). Perhaps Moesia Superior or Inferior. Stein, who neglects this passage, puts him in Moesia Inferior, later, succeeding A. Caecilius Faustinus, who is attested in 105 (*Die Legaten von Moesien* (1940), 62 f.). The second consulate and public statue (Dio LXVIII. 16. 2) suggest a high command in the Second Dacian War

36. D. Terentius Scaurianus (?102 or 104). *PIR*[1], T 68. Trajan's first governor of Dacia (*CIL* XVI, 57; 160; 163), perhaps after a consular command. Probably from Narbonensis, cf. E. Groag, P-W V, 669 (adducing *CIL* XII, 5211: Narbo; *I. l. de Gaule* 497: Nemausus). Perhaps *Ignotus C* (XII, 3169: Nemausus), cf. R. Syme, *JRS* XXXVI (1946), 160

37. M. Ulpius Traianus (*cos.* 91). Germania Superior (deduced from *HA, Hadr.* 2. 5 f.). Sent there by Nerva (Pliny, *Pan.* 9. 5; 94. 4)

15. CONSULAR AND PRAETORIAN PROVINCES

OF the consular legates catalogued in the preceding appendix, one, C. Julius Quadratus Bassus, is described on his inscription as a general in the war that conquered Decebalus; and, it can be surmised, as many as half a dozen others were leaders of armies in the four campaigns against the Dacians (101 and 102, 105 and 106), not governors of provinces. Most of them are eminent personages who had already held one consular command, or two.

The following arrangement of the items by provinces will illustrate the sequence of governors—and certain gaps in knowledge:

Britannia, 34, 25, 4, 27
Cappadocia, 2, 31, 3, 6, 79
Dalmatia, 32, 7, 24
Germania Inferior, 22, 23, 1

Germania Superior, 22, 16, 37, 20
Hispania Citerior, 32, 8
Moesia Superior, 30, 7, 12
Moesia Inferior, 29, 17, 32, 21, 10, 5
Pannonia, ? 22, 30, 20, 11, 28, ? 26
Syria, 13, 16, 18, 8, 9, 19

Eight in number at the death of Nero, the consular commands rise to ten by Vespasian's creation of Cappadocia–Galatia in permanence, and by Domitian's division of Moesia (in 86). Dalmatia lost its legion, IV Flavia, called to the Danube in 85/86, but did not, so far as known, forfeit its rank. One praetorian legate is in fact revealed by a diploma with the imperial titulature of 93 and the consular dating to July 13, 94 (*CIL* xvi, 38). Probably an emergency measure, caused by a death or deaths somewhere else, or by a shortage of suitable candidates. Q. Pomponius Rufus, the man in question, was a senior praetorian with military experience (*IRT* 537). No other instance has to be assumed.

Consular legates are drawn in the main from the governors of the imperial praetorian provinces. Under the Flavian emperors there were eight of those posts, viz. Lusitania, Belgica, Lugdunensis, Aquitania, Lycia–Pamphylia, Cilicia, Judaea, Numidia (the last two combined with the command of a legion). Trajan adds four—Arabia, Pannonia Inferior (each with a legion), Thrace (previously procuratorial), and Galatia (severed from Cappadocia after the conquest of Armenia). And, with two changes (Dacia degraded, but Judaea made consular), the total subsists under Hadrian and Pius.

The post is vital, carrying a clear promise of the consulate: observe the language used about Aquitania (*Agr.* 9. 1). A governor can receive the title 'cos. des.', e.g. Larcius Priscus (*suff.* 110) in Numidia (*ILS* 1055): the earliest example is a legate of Cilicia in 77 or 78 (*IGR* III, 840). In the Antonine system a governor may continue in office, holding the *fasces* abroad. Precedents offer in the late years of Trajan — L. Acilius Strabo Clodius Nummus (*suff.* 114) in Numidia (*PIR²*, A 83), Lusius Quietus (*suff.* 117) in Judaea (Ch. XX).

There is no record of the praetorian posts held by most of the men on the list. Eight can be proved to have passed through this form of promotion (11, 14, 15, 16, 18, 19, 30, 32), three not (2, 6, 28). However, some of the younger Trajanic marshals provide good evidence (App. 16).

16. THE YOUNGER TRAJANIC MARSHALS

THERE are oldish and even elderly men among the governors of the consular provinces in the early years of Trajan's reign (Ch. V). A new generation can be quickly discerned, namely, persons attested or surmised as legionary legates or as praetorian governors during the critical years of transition, 96–98. The details happen to be scanty. Nothing is known about the previous careers of the remarkable *ordinarii* of 99, Sosius Senecio and Cornelius Palma; and other 'viri militares' excite curiosity only to baffle it—Fabius Justus (*suff.* 102), Publilius Celsus (102), Terentius Scaurianus (?102 or 104).

By a singular chance, documentation offers for the next group, men about six to eight years junior to Pliny, holding the quaestorship in the period 94–97. Seven epigraphic careers supply full details, and four of them show consular provinces:

> C. Julius Quadratus Bassus (*suff.* 105). See App. 14
> L. Minicius Natalis (106). *ILS* 1029
> Q. Pompeius Falco (108). *ILS* 1035 f.
> C. Julius Proculus (109). *ILS* 1040
> A. Larcius Priscus (110). *ILS* 1055; *AE* 1908, 237
> L. Catilius Severus (110). *ILS* 1041; *AE* 1913, 229
> T. Julius Maximus (112). *ILS* 1016[1]

The first five belong to the favoured class of 'viri militares' with rapid promotion, reaching the consulate at thirty-seven or thirty-eight (App. 18): Catilius Severus and Julius Maximus are slower in their advance (the former holds no fewer than five praetorian posts). On their earlier showing consular commands might have been expected for Julius Proculus and Larcius Priscus, but are nowhere attested. It can, however, be conjectured that Julius Maximus is Maximus the consular legate who was defeated and killed in Mesopotamia.[2] Minicius Natalis and Pompeius Falco were not given commands in the East (for their employments, p. 243).

Of the seven, only one seems Italian by origin, namely, A. Larcius Priscus, son of A. Larcius Lepidus (*ILS* 987): for Priscus, see further App. 3. Julius Quadratus Bassus comes from Pergamum, of regal ancestry. The colony of Barcino in Tarraconensis is the home of Minicius Natalis, while Julius Maximus comes from Nemausus, and the tribe 'Voltinia' indicates a Narbonensian origin for Julius Proculus. For the enigmatic Catilius Severus see App. 87; and Pompeius Falco, who married the daughter of Sosius Senecio, is most mysterious —at some time subsequent to 116 the item 'Julius Eurycles Herclanus' emerges in his nomenclature (*ILS* 1035: not in 1036).

This younger group contains names of no little import for military (and political) history in the last years of Trajan. Notably certain friends of Hadrian are now discovered in the high commands (Ch. XX). Two, but only two, are among the correspondents of Pliny, viz. Pompeius Falco and Catilius Severus.

For relevance both to Pliny and to Roman history may be added two members of the same age-group: C. Minicius Fundanus (107), that highly cultivated person (pp. 114, 468), survived to become proconsul of Asia (? 122/3): an inscription discloses, along with several items of his earlier career, the fact that he was imperial legate governing Dalmatia.[3] Then C. Bruttius Praesens, who had been military

---

[1] A praetorian post after his command of two legions in succession has recently emerged, namely Pannonia Inferior in 110 (*CIL* xvi, 164).

[2] p. 239. The reading of E. Hauler in Fronto (p. 209 N = Haines II, p. 214) produced 'Appius Santra', whence *PIR*[2], A 950 and Degrassi, *FC* 112 ('Appius Maximus Santra'). One might conceive doubts about 'Santra'; and, even admitting an Appius there, the 'vir consularis' (p. 217 N = Haines II, p. 21), equated with the Maximus of Dio LXVIII. 30. 1, can be T. Julius Maximus, cf. R. Syme, *Laureae Aquincenses* I (1938), 218; *JRS* XLIII (1953), 158.   [3] See the inscription from Šipovo in Bosnia quoted in App. 92.

tribune in 89, emerges tardily and paradoxically as a legionary legate in Armenia in 114, proceeds to the consulate (118, or very soon after), governs military provinces, and ends, after the death of Hadrian, as *cos. II*, 139.[1] Minicius Fundanus could have been conjectured a Transpadane: his tribe, the 'Papiria', indicates Ticinum.[2] Bruttius Praesens is described by Pliny as 'Lucanus' (VII. 3. 1), and his tribe is the 'Pomptina'. But his full name is 'C. Bruttius L. f. Praesens L. Fulvius Rusticus', the second member of which suggests Comum or Mediolanium (cf. *PIR*², F 557 f.): perhaps a Fulvius adopted by a Bruttius.

Sex. Erucius Clarus (117), parallel in certain respects to Bruttius Praesens, is a little younger (quaestor about 100).[3] Nephew of the successful knight, C. Septicius Clarus: local origin not verifiable.

---

[1] *IRT* 545 (Lepcis), cf. *AE* 1950, 66 (Mactar). See p. 242. *PIR*², B 161 and 164 must be amalgamated.

[2] App. 92. [3] *PIR*², E 96. See pp. 242, 477.

C. SENATORS AND ORATORS

17. THE SENATORIAL CURSUS

A MAN might become quaestor when twenty-five, praetor when thirty (Dio LII. 20. 1 f.). That is not the end of the matter. Much remains obscure about the precise working of the system, along with the various complications—allowance for the possession of children (*Dig.* IV. 4. 2); the reckoning of a year begun in a man's life as a year completed (inferred from *Dig.* L. 4. 8); the intervals between office and office; and the confusion between cardinal and ordinal in the ancient evidence or in modern estimates.[1] The data about Julius Agricola are generally invoked as a standard. He was born in 40 (there are textual problems).[2] Now Agricola was quaestor in 64, tribune of the plebs in 66, praetor in 68: one child appears to gain him a year before the quaestorship, a second takes off a year before the tribunate.[3] For the consequent short interval (three entire years) between quaestorship and praetorship compare Ummidius Quadratus, quaestor in 14 (*ILS* 972), aedile, and then praetor in 18 (*CIL* VI, 1496 = *Inscr. It.* XIII, 1, p. 306). Further, intervals may be not only abbreviated but abolished, as when Vespasian, aedile in 39, becomes praetor in 40 (Suetonius, *Divus Vesp.* 2. 3, cf. *PIR²*, F 398).

However, concentration upon minimum ages and intervals may be misleading. Q. Veranius, quaestor in 37, is not tribune till 41 (*IGR* III, 703; Josephus, *AJ* XIX. 234): Veranius, the son of Germanicus' legate, and *quaestor Augusti* when Tiberius died, should not have incurred retardation under Caligula. Again, P. Aelius Hadrianus, born in 76, duly enters upon the quaestorship in 101, but if the *HA* date is correct (and it is supported by *ILS* 308, cf. *PIR²*, A 184), his tribunate of the plebs falls in 105.[4]

Such, at its briefest, is the information requisite for establishing the early stages in the official careers of Tacitus and Pliny. Some latitude will have to be allowed. Tacitus states that his 'dignitas' was 'a Tito aucta' (*Hist.* I. 1. 3). Clearly the quaestorship.[5] Therefore, at the latest in 81—but perhaps 82, under Domitian, supposing him designated before Titus died. If Tacitus' birth be put in 56,

---

[1] Mommsen, *R. Staatsrecht* I³ (1887), 534 ff.; 572 ff. See also his classic study of Plinian chronology, *Hermes* III (1869), 31 ff. = *Ges. Schr.* IV (1906), 366 ff.

[2] cf. Anderson's note on *Agr.* 44. 1. Some have argued firmly for 39, reading in *Agr.* 45. 1, 'Gaio Caesare ⟨i⟩ter⟨um⟩ consule', cf. K. Nipperdey, *Opuscula* (1877), 511.

[3] cf. Mommsen, *Ges. Schr.* IV, 414 f.

[4] *HA, Hadr.* 3. 4. He proceeds to the praetorship in 107 (ib. 8, where the nomenclature of the consuls is erroneous), or rather in 106, cf. P. W. v. Rohden, P-W I, 498. The anomaly in Hadrian's career, apart from the command of a legion in 105-6 (cumulated with tribunate and then praetorship), is the rapid advance (after brief tenure of the new province of Pannonia Inferior) to a suffect consulate in the summer of 108. That has a political significance (cf. p. 232 f.).

[5] Groag in *PIR²*, C 1467 is unduly agnostic about the meaning of 'dignitas nostra.'

he became quaestor at twenty-four or twenty-five, praetor (in 88, cf. *Ann.* XI. 11. 1) at thirty-one. There is no reason to fancy him a later beginner, or unduly retarded.[1]

Similarly Pliny, who, moreover, was *quaestor Augusti*. The year of birth is either 61 or 62, for Pliny was in his eighteenth year (*Epp.* VI. 20. 5) at the time of the eruption of Vesuvius (August 24, 79). The quaestorship presumably falls between 86 and 89. Pliny might have been held back by sickness (note a later malady in 97, *Epp.* x. 8. 3). Again, it might be worth waiting a year to be *quaestor Aug.*: there was competition about this time, observe Pliny's coeval L. Roscius Aelianus, with military decorations for his military tribunate in 83 (*ILS* 1025). If Pliny was born in 62, then 88 or even 89 for the quaestorship is just possible, though 89 (Mommsen's date) seems too late.[2]

Pliny's own statement is useful but not conclusive. Writing about his friend Calestrius Tiro he says 'simul militavimus, simul quaestores Caesaris fuimus. ille me in tribunatu liberorum iure praecessit, ego illum in praetura sum consecutus, cum mihi Caesar annum remisisset' (VII. 16. 2). Mommsen argued that Pliny was quaestor in 89, tribune in 92, praetor in 93.[3] This produces a very rapid passage from quaestorship to praetorship, like that of Ummidius (14–18) and Agricola (64–68). Observe, however, Tacitus (81 or 82–88), and Aelius Hadrianus (101–6). Mommsen may not be correct in all particulars. The quaestorship could go in 87 or 88; and, even with a year remitted, a year could perhaps still have intervened between tribunate and praetorship. The latter office cannot be prior to 93.[4] Indeed, 94 is not absolutely excluded. But Pliny ought not to accede rather late to the praetorship. The like argument holds for the aristocrat Cocceius Nerva, praetor in 66 (*Ann.* xv. 72. 1), whose birth should fall in 35.[5] Another factor now intervenes (though commonly ignored)—how quickly can a *novus homo*, however successful, reach the consulate?

18. THE AGE FOR THE CONSULATE

MOMMSEN briefly stated that thirty-two was the minimum consular age in the time of Augustus.[6] Indiscriminate application of that norm can be harmful and

---

[1] Fabia's discussion of Tacitus' career (*Journ. des Savants* 1926, 193 ff.) was eloquent but established nothing. It was easy to invoke 'l'inconnu total où nul indice ne provoque la curiosité, nul espoir ne sollicite la sagacité' (ib. 195). Retardation and a late consulate was assumed by Mommsen, *Ges. Schr.* IV, 422; Dessau, *Gesch. der r. Kaiserzeit* II, 1 (1926), 96; Reitzenstein, *Neue Wege zur Antike* IV (1926), 7. Hence the notion that Tacitus had no prospect of the consulate from Domitian (E. Paratore, *Tacito* (1951), 73).

[2] The narrative (Ch. VII) admits this possibility.   [3] o.c. IV, 414 ff.

[4] The attempt of R. H. Harte (*JRS* xxv (1935), 51 ff.) to put the praetorship in 90 or 91 has found no favour.

[5] The ancient evidence about the date of his birth is markedly discrepant. Boissevain (on Dio LXVIII. 4. 2) arranged and interpreted it to produce the year 30, which has been widely approved, cf. R. P. Longden, *CAH* XI (1936), 188; A. Stein, *PIR²*, C 1227; A. Garzetti, *Nerva* (1950), 17. Yet Nerva was a favoured person, and a patrician (*ILS* 273): it is difficult to believe that he was not praetor until he had passed his thirty-fifth birthday. One should therefore revert to 35 as the year of birth, as indicated by Victor (*Epit.* 12. 11), and as previously argued by Stein (P–W IV, 148).

[6] R. *Staatsrecht* I³ (1887), 574: 'das laufende 33. Lebensjahr.' The vital question of the

misleading. Birth and rank have to be allowed for. Though members of consular families can hold the *fasces* at this early age (and a number do), the *novus homo* generally has to wait after his praetorship for a decade at least.[1] It would be preferable to posit the standard age of forty-two, taken over from the Republic, noting the kind of remissions conceded to various favoured classes of senators.

The term 'nobilis' was never defined by any legal enactment. None the less, its connotation is clear. In the late Republic the *nobilitas* is a restricted order, the descendants of consular houses.[2] The Empire sets a problem: who are the people called 'nobiles' now that the Republic is no more? The usage of Tacitus is instructive and conclusive. For example, *Ann.* XIII. 18. 2: 'nomina et virtutes nobilium qui etiam tum supererant.' Further, this rank can now be inherited through the female line, as by Piso Licinianus, *Hist.* I. 14. 2: 'nobilis utrimque'. Similarly, Pliny on a Piso talks of 'nobiles nostri' (*Epp.* v. 17. 6); and he designates the whole class as 'illos ingentium virorum nepotes, illos posteros libertatis' (*Pan.* 69. 5). Obviously, therefore, the Republican *nobilitas*.[3] But when is the Republic deemed to have terminated? Technically speaking, Caesar the Dictator and the Triumvirs curbed or suspended rather than abolished the Republic, and Caesar Augustus kept the traditional fabric. The year 14, however, proclaims the demise of the Republic: not so much by the transmission of the power to an heir as by the removal of the consular elections from the People (cf. p. 369). Triumviral and Augustan consuls may therefore be held to qualify as ancestors for the *nobiles* of the Empire.[4]

This class enjoys high preference in the career of honours. Similarly the social *élite* of the imperial aristocracy, the new patricians created by the Caesars.[5] Next, the new nobility itself, i.e. the descendants of the imperial consuls. They will normally become consuls well before their forty-third year;[6] and, along with *nobiles* and patricians, they tend to monopolize the eponymous consulate.[7]

For other senators, a standard consular age of forty-two may be postulated. It is useful for sorting out, comparing, and evaluating the careers of senators in the first two centuries of the Empire; it emerges from facts, and is confirmed by them; and the failure to notice it invalidates most assumptions about the public

consular age in the early Empire is sometimes totally neglected, e.g. in *CAH* x, and by M. Hammond, *The Augustan Principate* (1933).

[1] cf. R. Syme, *Rom. Rev.* (1939), 369.

[2] As was established by M. Gelzer, *Die Nobilität der r. Republik* (1912). Not all have accepted it, e.g. H. Dessau, *Gesch. der r. Kaiserzeit* I (1924), 103.

[3] M. Gelzer, *Hermes* L (1915), 395 ff. Gelzer, however, neglected to define his date for the end of the 'Republic'. The sole indication is that a consul of 42 B.C. is assumed to qualify as parent of a *nobilis* (ib. 405).

[4] E. Stein, *Hermes* LII (1917), 264 ff. Others have been more generous. W. Otto argued that *nobiles* are descendants of any curule magistrates of the Republic (*Hermes* LI (1916), 73 ff.), and E. Groag suggested that the term came to cover any families senatorial before the Dictatorship of Caesar (*Strena Buliciana* (1924), 253 ff.). One cannot believe that the descendants of Republican consuls would have conceded such a claim under the early Principate—and, a little later, the evidence from Tacitus and Pliny tells against it.

[5] e.g. Nerva consul at thirty-five (assuming him born in 35), Trajan at thirty-seven. Early consulates may also be assumed for P. Calvisius Ruso (? 79) and L. Neratius Marcellus (95).

[6] Thus A. Vitellius, born in 15 (Suetonius, *Vitellius* 3. 2), *cos. ord.* in 48.

[7] E. Groag, *Wiener Studien* XLVII (1929), 143 ff.

life of Tacitus and of Pliny.[1] This standard age comes out in various but converging data: for example, about twenty-two years from the military tribunate, seventeen from the quaestorship, a dozen from the praetorship. An epoch of remarkable stability and regularity, that of Antoninus Pius, provides the most convincing results. For the Flavio-Trajanic period a few instances will suffice to exemplify:

L. Tettius Julianus (*suff.* 83): *pr.* 70 (*Hist.* IV. 40. 2)
Q. Baebius Macer (103): *pr.* c. 92, cf. App. 25
M. Vitorius Marcellus (105): *pr.* c. 92, cf. App. 25
T. Julius Maximus (112): *tr. mil.* 89 (*ILS* 1012)[2]

Also, a little retarded:

Q. Glitius Atilius Agricola (97): *q.* 78 or earlier (*ILS* 1021)
L. Maecius Postumus (98): *q.* 79 (*AE* 1934, 248)
L. Julius Marinus (? 101): *pr.* c. 87 (*ILS* 1026)[3]

Though close datings can seldom be had, further parallels may be discovered among the consular coevals of Pliny and Tacitus (for a selection of whom see App. 24 f.). And it will be recalled that there were plenty of people who took much longer to reach the consulate, as is evident from dated posts or from their presumed ages.[4]

And now, a contrast. In the imperial system the tenure of a praetorian province develops as sign and promise of the consulate for *novi homines* (App. 15). An exceptional and favoured category can be established, the 'viri militares' who, with only the command of a legion and a praetorian province intervening, proceed in a straight run to the consulate, which they seem to reach at thirty-seven or thirty-eight. An interval of some seventeen years from the military tribunate and twelve or thirteen from the quaestorship marks and confirms this class. An early instance might be Q. Veranius (*cos.* 49), quaestor in 37 (if his legionary command were attested): not an old man, therefore, when governor of Britain in 57 or 58 (*Ann.* XIV. 29. 1).[5]

[1] cf. App. 17. The differential in consular ages is not discussed in certain works devoted to the imperial Senate, e.g. for 28 B.C.–A.D. 68, S. J. de Laet, *De Samenstelling van den Romeinschen Senaat*, &c. (1941); for the Flavio-Trajanic period, B. Stech, *Klio*, Beiheft X (1912); for 117–92, P. Lambrechts, *La Composition du Sénat romain*, &c. (1936). The 'calcolo dei normali intervalli' of A. Garzetti, *Nerva* (1950), 103, is much too short: he assumes that a consul of 105 would normally have been quaestor c. 95–97 (i.e. a consular age of thirty-three to thirty-five).

[2] The very rapid career assumed by R. Syme, *Laureae Aquincenses* I (1938), 281 ff., was a mistake, deriving from comparison with the highly anomalous case of D. Terentius Gentianus (*ILS* 1046), suffect consul in 116. It now emerges that Julius Maximus held a praetorian province, viz. Pannonia Inferior in 110 (*CIL* XVI, 164).

[3] He was consul with L. Arruntius Stella in October (*ILS* 6106), either 101 or 102. Groag prefers the latter year, *PIR*[2], A 1151. Martial's allusion (XII. 2. 10) to Stella's consulate accords better with the former: the dedicatory epistle refers to a 'trienni desidia'— that is, since Martial's departure from Rome in 98.

[4] Compare Pliny's elderly friends Verginius Rufus (*cos.* 63), Vestricius Spurinna (*suff.* ? c. 72), Corellius Rufus (*suff.* ? 78, cf. *PIR*[2], C 1294), born respectively c. 14 (*Epp.* II. 1. 4), c. 24 (III. 1. 10), c. 31 (I. 12. 11).

[5] See now the long inscription published by A. E. Gordon, *Univ. of California Pub. in Class. Arch.* II (1952), 321 ff., whence *AE* 1953, 251. His praetorship will fall in 42 or 43, probably the former. Cf. also E. Birley, *Proc. Brit. Ac.* XXXIX (1953), 203.

The following examples are more or less clear:

    Cn. Julius Agricola (*suff.* 77): *tr. mil.* 60 (*Agr.* 5. 1. cf. p. 20)
    C. Julius Proculus (109): *q.* 96 or 97 (*ILS* 1040)[1]
    Q. Pompeius Falco (108): *tr. pl.* 97 (Pliny, *Epp.* 1. 23. 1, cf. IX. 13. 19). His
        cursus, ILS 1035

Note also the two *Ignoti, ILS* 1022 and *CIL* XII, 3169 (App. 14, nos. 14 f.); C. Julius Quadratus Bassus (ib., no. 19); and, presumably, L. Roscius Aelianus (100), *tr. mil.* in 83, whose selective inscription lists no praetorian posts (*ILS* 1025); and A. Larcius Priscus (110), *q.* ?97 (cf. App. 3) is comparable for the interval, though he has more praetorian employments. It may be assumed that the remarkable *ordinarii* of 99, Q. Sosius Senecio and A. Cornelius Palma, conform to this superior class of *novi homines*. Perhaps also Tacitus' friend L. Fabius Justus (*suff.* 102).[2] Promotions were no doubt rapid at this time: see also App. 16 on the younger Trajanic marshals.

On comparison Tacitus and Pliny make a good showing. Expecially Pliny. With the two civilian posts and the short interval (93–100) between praetorship and consulate he equals a 'vir militaris'; and oratory and politics bring him in ahead of his coeval L. Arruntius Stella (*suff.* ?101),[3] who was a patrician (see p. 666). A decade later another *novus homo*, L. Catilius Severus, accedes to the consulate by way of the same two posts as Pliny (namely the *aerarium militare* and the *aerarium Saturni*); but Catilius moves much more slowly— he holds three other posts after the praetorship (*ILS* 1041, cf. *I. l. d'Afrique* 43).[4]

19. PROBLEMS IN PLINY'S CAREER

THE earlier posts have been discussed (App. 17). For the praetorship Mommsen established 93, to the general contentment (cf. *PIR*[1], P 370). The date has since been pertinaciously contested by Otto, arguing for 95, and many have concurred.[5] The main points at issue concern the prosecution of Baebius Massa in 93, and its sequel: the trial led to an indictment for treason against one of the prosecutors,

---

    [1] Proculus was 'q. Augustorum'—perhaps Domitian and Nerva rather than Nerva and Trajan. His post of 'leg. Aug. p.p. region. Transpadanae' can count as a praetorian province.   [2] p. 53.
    [3] For the date of his consulship see above under L. Julius Marinus (his colleague).
    [4] Note also M. Acilius Priscus A. Egrilius Plarianus (*PIR*[2], E 48), now known to have held not only the first prefecture (*CIL* VI, 31678; XIV, 4444), but the second (in 105, *Not. Scav.* 1953, 259, whence *AE* 1955, 171, cf. 173): after four other praetorian posts.
    [5] W. Otto, *Bayerische S–B, phil.-hist. Kl.* 1919, Abh. 10; also ib. 1923, Abh. 4; *Phil. Woch.* XLVI (1926), 732 ff. and XLVII (1927), 511 f. The disputant was W. A. Baehrens, *Hermes* LVIII (1923), 109 ff.; *Phil. Woch.* XLVII (1927), 171 ff. Otto's dating was accepted by M. P. Charlesworth, *CAH* XI (1936), 31, by C. Hosius in Schanz–Hosius, *Gesch. der r. Literatur* II[4] (1935), 657, by R. Hanslik in Bursian's *Jahresberichte* CCLXXXII (1943), 41, and by others. F. Oertel tried to reinforce it, *Rh. Mus.* LXXXVIII (1939), 179 ff. M. Schuster, however, after a full exposition of Otto's views (P–W XXI, 442 ff.), briefly agrees with Baehrens against the year 95 (ib. 445).

Herennius Senecio (Pliny, *Epp.* VII. 33. 7), then against his friends and allies, notably Junius Rusticus, upon which followed the expulsion of the philosophers.[1]

Otto's attack was threefold. (1) Pliny, after becoming *praefectus aerarii Saturni*, affirms that he has given up practising as an advocate—'omnibus advocationibus, quibus alioqui nunquam eram promiscue functus, renuntiavi' (x. 3a. 1). Compare also his attitude when tribune (I. 23. 2). Therefore he cannot have been praetor when he appeared against Baebius Massa (VII. 33. 4). (2) The *Chronicle* of Jerome in the Latin version (p. 192 H) puts the expulsion of the philosophers in 94/95. (3) It was all over, prosecutions, deaths, and banishments, when Pliny visited the philosopher Artemidorus in the suburbs—'septem amicis meis aut occisis aut relegatis' (III. 11. 3). The visit took place when Pliny was praetor (ib. 1). Surely there is not room for all of these transactions in 93, for when Agricola died on August 23 the Baebius Massa case was still proceeding—'et Massa Baebius etiam tum reus erat' (*Agr.* 45. 1).

None of these arguments is conclusive. Nothing that Pliny said precludes his having undertaken a prosecution at the bidding of the Senate when praetor—and in fact he does accept two cases when holding the treasury post (see below). The datings in Jerome are notoriously hazardous. Finally, though proceedings against proconsuls might drag on for years, the ruin of Senecio, Rusticus, and the whole group could easily have come as swift as it was savage, 'velut uno ictu'.

The controversy is barren. Otto's whole reconstruction of Pliny's career defies probability: for example, he puts the quaestorship intolerably late, in 92, and he ignores the external and parallel data about contemporary senators.[2] Indeed, since Otto, his principal adversary, and some of his convinced disciples all assumed without doubt or compunction that a civilian *novus homo* at this time would pass from a praetorship as late as 95 to the consulate in 100 (or even 97), the matter can be dropped.[3] Pliny might, it is true, have been praetor in 94 (cf. App. 17). That hypothesis could not quite be disproved. Yet it will be best to keep him in 93.

With a short interval (or none at all) Pliny became *praefectus aerarii militaris*, as the epigraphic records of his career reveal (*ILS* 2927, &c.): the correspondence is mute, the author of the *Panegyricus* (cf. 95. 3 f.) far from honest. This post was triennial and shared with two colleagues (Dio LV. 25. 2). Pliny therefore was prefect either in 94–96 or 95–97 (assuming a full triennium).[4] The former alternative

---

[1] The causal nexus between the prosecution of Rusticus and the expulsion of the philosophers is clearly stated by Suetonius, *Dom.* 10. 3, and Dio LXVII. 13. 3.

[2] cf. Pliny's career as tabulated by Otto, o.c. 98.

[3] Otto argued from *Pan.* 90. 6 that Nerva was actually proposing to give Pliny the consulate (o.c. 56 ff.); and Oertel assumed that Pliny, praetor in 95, could have been consul in 97 (*Rh. Mus.* LXXXVIII (1939), 184). Similarly Baehrens (arguing for the praetorship in 93), 'auf Grund des damaligen *ordo magistratuum* hätte Plinius schon 95 Consul werden können' (*Hermes* LVIII (1923), 111). Thus both sides can (and do) defend Pliny's credit when he said 'longius iter malui' (*Pan.* 95. 3).

One could concede abnormal promotions in a season of change and crisis. Sex. Julius Frontinus, praetor in 70 (*Hist.* IV. 39. 1) becomes consul presumably in 73—perhaps more elderly than his praetorship would indicate, see App. 84. Note also the elevation of Sex. Attius Suburanus, Trajan's first Prefect of the Guard, suffect consul in 101.

[4] A further possibility may be touched on in passing—a biennial tenure covering 95 and 96. Pliny might have been persuaded to resign the prefecture, to make way for somebody else—and not without the hope or prospect of compensation.

is surely preferable. In 97 Pliny is ostensibly without employment, compare the reference to 'otium' in *Epp.* II. 2. 2 : also perhaps I. 13. 6 and x. 8. 3. The 'occupationes' referred to in I. 10. 9—'subnoto libellos, conficio tabulas'—could belong to the second treasury post, which began in 98, for these letters are by no means in strict sequence. Which brings up the next problem, the length of tenure of *praefecti aerarii Saturni*. It is reasonable to conjecture a triennium (for an isolated case of four years cf. *CIL* VI, 1495). Claudius replaced the praetors of the treasury with quaestors, who, however, held office for three years (Dio LX. 24. 2, cf. *ILS* 966). The same term could therefore be assumed for the prefects whom Nero appointed in 56 (*Ann.* XIII. 28. 3). Since the post is magisterial in origin (and note a temporary reversion to praetors, *Hist.* IV. 9. 1), let it be supposed that the prefects normally entered upon their charge on January 1, and much trouble will be saved. Pliny and Cornutus followed Publicius Certus and (Q. Fulvius Gillo) Bittius Proculus. Pliny describes the result of his attack upon Publicius Certus in a compressed phrase—'obtinui tamen, quod intenderam: nam collega Certi consulatum, successorem Certus accepit' (IX. 13. 23). This does not have to mean that the pair were compelled to resign at once or before their time——only that one of the two failed to gain designation to the consulate.[1]

Pliny was appointed by Nerva and Trajan—'indulgentia vestra' (x. 3a. 1 cf. 8. 3)—and, along with his colleague, received designation for the consulate before two years had elapsed: 'nondum biennium compleveramus in officio laboriosissimo et maximo' (*Pan.* 91. 1). That is to say, at some time in the second half of 99. (Complications have been imported, and persist, because of Mommsen's statement that the *suffecti* of any year were designated on January 9 of that year.[2])

While holding this post, Pliny agreed to undertake two senatorial prosecutions. The dates have been not a little in dispute.[3] The following summary reconstruction may be offered. First, against Marius Priscus the proconsul of Africa: if (as is probable) his tenure was 97/98, Pliny could have been solicited in the late summer of 98, and Pliny's letter to Trajan on the matter (x. 3a) can stand at this date. Secondly, against Caecilius Classicus, proconsul of Baetica contemporaneous with Priscus in Africa (III. 9. 2). It was Pliny's third official case, 'munere hoc iam tertio' (III. 4. 8)—that is to say, counting in Baebius Massa. The appeal came when he had set out on leave to visit his estate at Tifernum Tiberinum (III. 4. 2), therefore in a September, either 98 or 99 (cf. his petition to Trajan for leave, x. 8). It is best to opt for the former year: one notes (I. 4) a journey to a place beyond Perusia, and (perhaps connected) I. 7. 4: 'me circa Idus Octobres spero Romae futurum'.[4] The case of Priscus terminated in January, 100 (II. 11. 10), but the other dragged on, 'fuit enim multiplex actaque est saepius cum magna varietate'

---

[1] cf. Otto, o.c. 64. Merrill attempted to keep them in office for a great part of 98 as well (*AJP* XXIII (1902), 405).

[2] Mommsen, *Ges. Schr.* IV, 423, followed by Otto (o.c. 55), and by most scholars. The date comes from the Calendar of Polemius Silvius, of A.D. 448, *CILT*², p. 257.

[3] cf. especially Mommsen, o.c. 376, &c.; Otto, o.c. 70 ff.

[4] In this letter Pliny assures a friend that he will take no part in a prosecution that the 'Baetici' are trying to promote against a certain Gallus. Not noticed in *PIR*¹ or in P–W, this Gallus might be a proconsul of Baetica whose tenure was 96/97 (i.e. the predecessor of Caecilius Classicus).

(III. 9. 1), and, as the placing of the letter suggests, may well have lasted into 101.[1]

The consulate itself (September–October 100) presents no difficulties. Pliny in an involved sentence seems to be saying that the two prefects of the treasury continued in office both during and after the consulate (*Pan.* 92. 1).[2] Which could be believed. If so, to the end of the calendar year; but not (as some have held) later.

Pliny's augurship (IV. 8) should belong about 103. Then comes his *cura alvei Tiberis et riparum et cloacarum urbis*. The date is inferred from III. 6. 6 f., which shows him holding an 'officium' at a time when he meditates a journey to Comum. This is the enterprise announced in IV. 1, referred to as 'proxime cum in patria mea fui' (IV. 13. 3, cf. 30. 1), and described in V. 14. For various reasons it should belong to 104.[3] Now Pliny when at Comum learns with satisfaction that his friend Cornutus Tertullus has likewise been given an 'officium', namely, the charge of the Via Aemilia (V. 14. 1 f.). Pliny in his own post is surely the direct successor of Ti. Julius Ferox (*suff.* 99), who is attested both in 101 and 103 (*CIL* VI, 31549 f.). Hence a hint that the employment was at this time triennial. Pliny was still holding it in 106, possibly 107 (VII. 15. 1). The next known *curator* is L. Minicius Natalis (*suff.* 106). It was his first (and only) consular position before he became legate of the great military province of Pannonia c. 116 (*ILS* 1029).

Last of all, the mission to Bithynia–Pontus, where Pliny died (App. 20).

20. PLINY IN BITHYNIA

WHEN was Pliny sent to Bithynia–Pontus? The canonical date is 111—but Mommsen only said 'etwa 111'.[4] Now 109 or 110 is not excluded.[5] Pliny in one of the latest of his epistles seems to be expecting something, and so does his friend Voconius Romanus—'cum certius de vitae nostrae ordinatione audieris, futurum te fugitivum rei familiaris statimque ad nos evolaturum, qui iam tibi compedes nectimus quas perfringere nullo modo possis' (IX. 28. 4).

Whichever the year, Pliny entered his province on September 17 (X. 17a. 2). The dispatches to Trajan register 'vota' for anniversaries in a January (X. 35; 52), a September (88), another January (100 ff.), but do not go as far as the second September date (Trajan's birthday, on the eighteenth of the month). No sign indicates the termination of the mandate. The governor will have died in spring or summer, before two years of his mission were completed.

The only piece of external evidence is provided by P. Calpurnius Macer

---

[1] Otto (o.c. 81) suggests early in 100. It does not matter much. The vital point in which Otto controverted Mommsen was the dating of the letter X. 8—and consequently the date at which Pliny agreed to undertake the prosecution.

[2] Mommsen, o.c. 424: contested by Merrill, o.c. 410, and by Otto, o.c. 85 ff.

[3] He appears to have gone to Tifernum Tiberinum in the next year (V. 6. 1, cf. 18. 2).

[4] Mommsen, o.c. 393. The detailed chronology has also been discussed by U. Wilcken, *Hermes* XLIX (1914), 120 ff.; O. Cuntz, ib. LXI (1926), 192 ff.

[5] Cuntz asserted (o.c. 192) that 110 is impossible. The proof is not adequate.

(*PIR*², C 273), legate of Moesia Inferior (x. 42, &c.). He is attested as governor in 112.[1] His tenure could have begun several years earlier.[2]

The volume of official correspondence with Trajan cannot have been published by Pliny or in the lifetime of the Emperor. The devoted interest of scholarly friends surviving may be suspected. Voconius Romanus was a friend of Plotina (ix. 28. 1), but there is no sign that he in fact went to Bithynia. More important the dedicant of the *Epistulae*, C. Septicius Clarus, who became Prefect of the Guard under Hadrian (119–22). Better, perhaps, the imperial secretary C. Suetonius Tranquillus, who (it could be argued) had been with Pliny on his staff (x. 94. 1, cf. App. 76). Suetonius may have inherited (or sequestrated) the papers of his friend and patron, to issue later on this novel and peculiar supplement.

21. THE CHRONOLOGY OF PLINY'S LETTERS

THE dedicatory epistle to Septicius Clarus proclaims an elegant disdain for strict sequence—'collegi non servato temporis ordine (neque enim historiam componebam), sed ut quaeque in manus venerat' (1. 1. 1). The principle may be applicable, as the dedication itself surely belongs, not to the whole series of nine books, but rather to the first published section: Pliny gives a strong hint of more to come—'ita enim fiet ut eas quae adhuc neglectae iacent requiram et, si quas addidero, non supprimam' (ib. 2). The author would be primarily intent upon variety. Yet related events had to be told in their proper order, and, as his purpose developed (namely, to provide a running commentary on current affairs, combined with autobiography), care would be needed to place public transactions fairly accurately—and Pliny was a person of methodical habits. External evidence offers confirmation (some of it only recently accruing, from the *Fasti Ostienses*); and, although a margin of doubt must be conceded, although a number of letters can be shown out of sequence, the framework stands the test and permits a tolerable dating of the most important affairs. The whole subject is intricate, and could easily lure one into a lengthy discussion. What follows is a brief summary, indicating for guidance a few salient dates.

None of the letters can be proved earlier than Nerva's accession or later than the end of 108. Most of the items in Book I appear to belong to 97, but a certain number (e.g. 4, 7, 10, 12) can or should be assigned to the next year. The first letter of Book II (the funeral of Verginius Rufus) is still in 97, also perhaps the second, and the emperor referred to in the letter about Vestricius Spurinna (7) is probably Nerva,[3] but the trial of Marius Priscus (January 100) is soon reached (11), and what is said about the slow progress of Sex. Erucius (Clarus) in his

---

[1] *CIL* III, 777. Macer is now revealed as 'P. Calpurn[ius . . . .]' *suffectus* in 103 (*AE* 1954, 223).

[2] The name of the legate in 109 ended, in the ablative, with -'e' (*CIL* III, 12467). Possibly Ti. Julius Ferox (*suff.* 99), cf. *Epp.* x. 87. 3.

[3] App. 6, supposing Vestricius absent on the embassy to Trajan (late autumn 97).

career (9) should be as late as 101.[1] As for Book III the end of the Classicus trial (9) can be put in 101, and the concluding item, the death of the poet Martial, can belong to 102.[2]

Book IV contains letters embracing the years 103–5. For the trial of Julius Bassus winter 102/3 is suitable, cf. IV. 9. 14: 'dixit in noctem atque etiam inlatis lucernis'—and 'Baebius Macer, consul designatus' (ib. 16) is now attested as suffect consul early in 103.[3] Then one proceeds quickly to a later date, 'C. Caecilium, consulem designatum' (IV. 17. 1): this is C. Caecilius Strabo, entering office on September 1, 105 (FO XIX). Further, Licinius Nepos the praetor (IV. 29) must belong to that year.[4]

In Book V the reader finds himself still in 105, with Licinius Nepos (4), and a later stage of the same affair exhibits Afranius Dexter as 'cos. des.' (13. 4): Cn. Afranius Dexter, consul on May 1, 105, was assassinated on June 24 (FO XIX). Finally, one is carried into 106 with the first stage of the proceedings against the proconsul Varenus Rufus, for 'Acilius Rufus, consul designatus' (V. 20. 6) is surely the '[L. Acilius] Rufus' who assumed the fasces on March 1, 107 (FO XX).

Book VI continues with Varenus (5 and 13), the tenth year from the decease of Verginius Rufus is registered (10. 3), and a Severus is addressed as 'designatus consul' (27. 1), presumably C. Vettenius Severus, consul on May 1, 107 (FO XX, cf. CIL XVI, 55). Pliny attends the Emperor's 'consilium' at Centumcellae (31)—not before autumn 106. In VI. 13. 2 Trajan was still absent (in Dacia).

As for Book VII, the case of Varenus terminates (6 and 10), presumably early in 107. A letter addressed to a Minicius adverts upon 'istas occupationes' (12. 5). Now C. Minicius Fundanus is the consular colleague of C. Vettenius Severus on May 1 (above): the subject-matter (style and criticism) suits this man admirably.

Data are not abundant in VIII and IX. Observe, however, the death of Junius Avitus (VIII. 23). His name occurs on the testament of Dasumius (CIL VI, 10229, l. 20), which was drawn up in the summer of 108. The autumn of that year is indicated by IX. 15. 3, where Pliny incites Falco to send him the 'urbana acta': Q. Pompeius Falco, still abroad (in Judaea, cf. ILS 1035) when he received the missive VII. 22, became consul on September 1, 108 (FO XXI).

Finally, to illustrate the period of time covered, or ostensibly covered, by Books VI–IX, the facts supplied about Calestrius Tiro, proconsul of Baetica (107/8, so it appears) are instructive—the allocation of the province (VI. 22. 1), his journey, touching Ticinum on the way (VII. 16; 23; 32), and his comportment when proconsul (IX. 5).

So far the chronology in outline. There are advantages in exploiting it. Thus the army commander Priscus (II. 13) could be kept in 100—otherwise he would have

---

[1] A lapse of time (98–101) is demanded by the stages reported by Pliny—'ego Sexto latum clavum a Caesare nostro, ego quaesturam impetravi, meo suffragio pervenit ad ius tribunatum petendi' (II. 9. 2).

[2] Martial's last book was probably published late in 101, cf. XII. 2. 10, referring to the consulate of Arruntius Stella (ILS 6106, cf. App. 18; 25), but 102 is not excluded.

[3] Probably from March 1, cf. a new fragment from Ostia (AE 1954, 223).

[4] cf. VI. 5. 1 (of 106, describing the Varenus case) where he is no longer labelled as praetor—but (P.) Juventius Celsus is (ib. 4).

to go in or after 103 (cf. App. 14, under Javolenus Priscus and Neratius Priscus). It is appropriate that the governorship of Neratius Marcellus (Britain, cf. App. 14) should begin in 101 (III. 8. 4). A consular province for Sosius Senecio in 102 or 103 is plausible (IV. 4). Again, the letter commending a man for a job to Vibius Maximus (III. 2). Vibius became Prefect of Egypt in the summer of 103. Yet Vibius could have been holding a different office earlier, in 101—i.e., be it conjectured, that of *praefectus annonae*, succeeding C. Minicius Italus (*ILS* 1374) whom he succeeded in Egypt.[1]

Not but what there are clear cases of inadvertence. For example, Licinius Nepos is already praetor (v. 4) before his first day of office is described (v. 9); among letters of 105 occurs a premature reference to the expected consulate of Minicius Fundanus (IV. 15. 5) which will not be till 107;[2] and a 'delayed letter' (IX. 37. 1) alludes to the imminent taking office of (C. Valerius) Paullinus—which had happened on September 1, 107 (*FO* xx, cf. *CIL* xvi, 56). Pliny is also careless about the journey to Comum (in 104, cf. App. 19). It is firmly announced in IV. 1, to the grandfather of Pliny's wife, but there was already a hint of it in III. 6, which has got inserted among the letters of 101.

In essentials the above scheme corresponds with that established by Mommsen.[3] He operated, however, with excessive rigour, and critics were able to indicate a number of letters that refused to conform. H. Peter offered useful contributions.[4] The most thorough onslaught came from Otto.[5] With this encouragement, Premerstein went a long way further in denying chronological sequence. He put the prosecution of Julius Bassus in 100, that of Varenus Rufus in 102.[6] Various scholars have given assent.[7]

The new dates imported intolerable complications.[8] The death-blow was given by the discovery of *FO* xx which, revealing the consulate of [L. Acilius] Rufus, dated the inception of the Varenus case (*Epp.* v. 20) to 106.[9] The laborious argumentations proved largely illusory.

One question remains, the date of publication. Mommsen made an assumption, but did not see that he had to prove it, namely, that the nine books were issued

---

[1] Pliny wanted for his friend something 'quod sit splendidum nec molestum' (III. 2. 5). Perhaps a post like that of Sex. Attius Suburanus, 'adiut. Iuli Ursi / praef. annonae, eiusdem in praefect. / Aegypti' (*AE* 1939, 60).

[2] It could happen that a consulate was postponed, as in 69 (*Hist.* II. 71. 2): Trajan may have desired to promote rapidly some 'vir militaris' during the Second Dacian War, in place of Fundanus.   [3] *Ges. Schr.* IV, 366 ff.

[4] H. Peter, *Sächsische S-B, phil.-hist. Kl.* 1901, Abh. 3, using and developing the results of earlier scholars such as C. Peter, Asbach, and Stobbe.

[5] W. Otto, *Bayerische S-B, phil.-hist. Kl.* 1919, Abh. 10, 17 ff.

[6] A. v. Premerstein, *Bayerische S-B, phil.-hist. Kl.* 1934, Heft 3, 72 ff. As the author wished to prove that the general C. Julius Quadratus Bassus (*suff.* 105, see App. 14) was none other than Julius Bassus, the proconsul of Bithynia, it was desirable to throw back the prosecution as far as possible before 105.

[7] Thus R. Hanslik in Bursian's *Jahresberichte* CCLXXXII (1943), 62: previously, objecting to Mommsen's date, he had argued that the trial of Varenus began in 105 at the latest, *Wiener Studien* L (1932), 194 ff. Groag also favoured Premerstein's dating for the Varenus affair—'a. fere 102 ut videtur' (*PIR²*, C 1420).

[8] cf. R. Syme, *JRS* xxxvi (1946), 163.

[9] And now *AE* 1954, 223, dates the trial of Julius Bassus to 102/3.

separately and in quick succession, beginning with Book I in 97.[1] This cannot be correct. There is no sign that Pliny had published any letters prior to 104. Various scholars raised objection, and H. Peter argued for publication in groups of three books—I–III in 104, IV–VI towards the end of 108, and VII–IX (which is mainly a selection of earlier epistles) soon after, in 109.[2]

Nobody would be so incautious as to believe that every item represents a genuine letter, written as and when it purports to have been written.[3] The author, when editing (and supplementing) his previous output, was able to arrange the material in the light of subsequent events. In III. 14 (ostensibly in or about 101) he describes how Larcius Macedo was attacked by his slaves. A warning is appended—'vides quot periculis, quot contumeliis, quot ludibriis simus obnoxii, nec est quod quisquam possit esse securus, quia sit remissus et mitis' (ib. 5). This letter might have been composed after the murder of the consul Afranius Dexter (summer 105, cf. above).

Evidence might also be sought in the letters about Regulus. Derided in Books I and II but absent from III, he is ostensibly still alive in IV. 2 and 7 (i.e. presumably 104). His death is referred to for the first time in VI. 2. It may have occurred in 104 or even 105. The odious and spiteful tone might raise a doubt whether Regulus was still alive when these compositions were given to the world.[4]

Let it be conjectured that no letters were published before 105 (and perhaps late in that year), and a satisfactory theory can be worked out. Books I and II might have appeared together (a neglect of chronological order within and between those books has been pointed out above), quickly followed by Book III or supplemented by it to form a triad. The last item in Book III, on Martial, quotes the poet's eulogy of the orator and conveys an author's modest claim to immortality (cf. p. 97), and Book IV at once introduces the theme of Pliny's visit to Comum.

The rest of the collection may have appeared in the form of two triads, as H. Peter suggested. Yet pairs of books are not wholly out of the question. Books IV–V and VIII–IX might seem in some ways to go together. Then the following scheme might be suggested: I–III, 105–6; IV–V, 107; VI–VII, 108; VIII–IX, 109. These details are not important: indeed, the publication in triads is more attractive. What matters is the probability that the issue of the nine books falls in a short compass of time, 105 or even 105/6 to 109. Approximately the period of the *Historiae* of Cornelius Tacitus, of which there is a premonitory hint in 105 (v. 8, cf. Ch. X). Did the work of his friend furnish Pliny with an added spur to

[1] o.c. 371 ff. Similarly Schanz–Hosius, *Gesch. der r. Literatur* II[4] (1935), 664—separate books or groups published in succession between 97 and 110.

[2] o.c. 107 ff.

[3] There has been room for differences of opinion. Thus Peter (o.c. 101 ff.) argues for a large proportion of 'genuine' letters: against, W. Kroll, *Studien zum Verständnis der r. Literatur* (1924), 238 f. Compare also, for the extreme artifice of Pliny's procedure, A.-M. Guillemin, *Pline et la vie littéraire de son temps* (1929), 128 ff.; M. Schuster, P-W XXI, 448.

[4] A further possibility may be relevant to the date of publication: did Pliny include in a group of books any missives to persons who had died? Observe that there is no letter at all to Julius Frontinus, deceased in 102 or 103; and the last addressed to Arrius Antoninus and to Vestricius Spurinna are v. 15 and 17 respectively.

acquire literary fame in an original fashion—not history but autobiography, subtly blended with the depicture of contemporary social life?

22. THE SACERDOTAL COLLEAGUES OF TACITUS

M. Ulpius Traianus (*suff.* ?70). *ILS* 8970
A. Fabricius Veiento (c. 72). *ILS* 1010
A. Caesennius Gallus (c. 76). *CIL* III, 12218
M. Arruntius Aquila (?77). *ILS* 980
P. Calvisius Ruso Julius Frontinus (?79). *AE* 1914, 267
C. Bellicus Natalis Tebanianus (87). *ILS* 1009
C. Valerius Flaccus Setinus Balbus. *Argonautica* I. 5 f.
L. Arruntius Stella (?101). Statius, *Silvae* I. 2. 176 f. (c. 89)
Ti. Julius Celsus Polemaeanus (92). *ILS* 8971
C. Cornelius Rarus Sextius Na[?so] (?93). *IRT* 523
M. Pompeius Macrinus Neos Theophanes (100 or 101). *IG* v, 1, 151
Q. Pompeius Falco (108). *ILS* 1035 f.
C. Julius Proculus (109). *ILS* 1040
Ignotus (?). *ILS* 1039
C. Bruttius Praesens (c. 118). *AE* 1950, 66
Sex. Julius Severus (127). *ILS* 1056

The above list of *quindecimviri sacris faciundis*, with consular dates in brackets, is drawn up roughly in order of seniority. Trajan's father may have died before Tacitus joined the college. Observe the early entry of Arruntius Stella, a cultivated person of patrician family; while the *ignotus* of *ILS* 1039 was also only quaestorian, and Julius Severus not yet quaestor (if the posts on his inscription are in correct order: almost certainly not, cf. *AE* 1950, 45).

All on this list were consuls or became consuls except for Valerius Flaccus, who died prematurely (Quintilian x. 1. 90). A consulate should be assumed for the *Ignotus* of *ILS* 1039, given the type of his career, viz. praetorship, legionary command, and imperial praetorian province (App. 18).

23. TACITUS' PROCONSULATE OF ASIA

THE proconsulate is attested by an inscription of Mylasa, [ἀνθυπά]τω Κορνηλίω Τακίτω (*OGIS* 487, improved by R. Meister, *Jahreshefte* XXVII (1932), Beiblatt 233). The year should be either 112/13 or 113/14, cf. *PIR²*, C 1467. The register between the dated proconsulates of 103/4 and 120/1 is now almost complete. See the latest list, D. Magie, *Roman Rule in Asia Minor* II (1950), 1583. That list, however, is not provided with the consular datings (exact or surmised) which are a valuable guide, and it needs to be modified in more ways than one.

The proconsul Hadrianus (*BMC, Lydia* cxxii) is probably the same person as the Corduban magnate L. Dasumius (*CIG* 2876), cf. E. Groag, *PIR²*, D 14 + Addenda, p. xi: below, App. 87. Dasumius is put by Magie towards the end of Trajan's reign. There is a place in 106/7, assuming him *suffectus* in 93.

Furthermore, an Ephesian inscription reveals Αὖλος Οὐικίρι[ος] (communicated by H. Lieb, who is editing Groag's text, *Die Fasti von Asien*). Groag (under *PIR²*, F 544) identifies him as A. Vicirius Martialis (*suff.* 98), hence proconsul presumably in 113/14. That would confine Cornelius Tacitus almost for a certitude to 112/13. However, there is a faint chance that the person might be A. Vicirius Proculus (*suff.* 90).

The following list carries in each case the single (and the best) item of evidence requisite for confirming a proconsulate. In addition to 103/4 and 120/1 the years 114/15, 115/16, and 119/20 can be taken as certain; but none of the eight names in 104–12 can be independently dated to a year. A vacancy has been left (112–14) for Cornelius Tacitus and for A. Vicirius Martialis.

103/4   C. Aquillius Proculus (*suff.* 90). *Forsch. in Ephesos* II, 131, n. 27, ll. 134 f., cf. *PIR²*, A 999

104/5   L. Albius Pullaienus Pollio (90). *ILS* 4046

105/6   Ti. Julius Celsus Polemaeanus (92). *ILS* 8971

106/7   L. Dasumius (? Hadrianus) (?93). *CIG* 2876, cf. *BMC, Lydia* cxxii

107/8   L. Nonius Calpurnius Asprenas Torquatus (*cos.* 94). *Forsch. in Ephesos* II, 150, n. 29, l. 24

108/9   M. Lollius Paullinus D. Valerius Asiaticus Saturninus (94). *OGIS* 481

109/10   C. Antius A. Julius Quadratus (94). *ILS* 8819

110/11   L. Baebius Tullus (95). *OGIS* 478, cf. *PIR²*, B 29

111/12   Q. Fabius Postuminus (96). *IGR* IV, 572, cf. *PIR²*, F 54

112/13

113/14

114/15   M. (Ostorius) Scapula (?97). *BMC Phrygia*, 166, n. 40 (unique)

115/16   Q. Fulvius Gillo Bittius Proculus (?98). *IGR* IV, 172, cf. *PIR²*, F 544

116/17   Ti. Julius Ferox (?99). Coins, cited in P–W x, 587

117/18   ?C. Julius Cornutus Tertullus (100). *ILS* 1024 (Asia *or* Africa)

118/19   Ti. Caepio Hispo (?101). *SEG* IV, 532; 117/18 or 118/19, cf. *PIR²*, E 83

119/20   C. Trebonius Proculus Mettius Modestus (103). *SIG³*, 833

120/21   (? L.) Cornelius Priscus (? 104). *SIG³*, 833, cf. *PIR²*, C 1420

The widening interval between consulate and proconsulate will be noted. Also the fact that only three of these proconsuls had held a consular military command, viz. Julius Quadratus and Fabius Postuminus (App. 14), and Julius Ferox (Pliny, *Epp.* x. 87. 3: province not discoverable).

24. CONSULAR COEVALS OF TACITUS

Persons of varying notoriety are registered among the consuls of 97 (App. 10), the *quindecimviri* (22), and the proconsuls of Asia in the period 103–21 (23); also below, the contemporary orators (27). For estimating the speed of Tacitus' career, the data about Q. Glitius Agricola (*suff.* 97), L. Maecius Postumus (98), and L. Julius Marinus (?101) may be adduced (App. 18). Further, a selection from the *Fasti* of 92–97 can put on record predecessors and rivals of Tacitus. They do not quite constitute an age-group. Some of them were much older than

Tacitus. On the other hand, certain aristocrats out-distanced the *novus homo*, and, though prior in the consulate, would be close to his age. The following notes reveal the disparities of age, ancestry, and accomplishment. Also the hazards of survival—though the freak consulate of C. Manlius Valens in 96 (a nonagenarian, cf. Dio LXVII. 14. 5) proves nothing.

The oriental senators Ti. Julius Celsus Polemaeanus (92) and A. Julius Quadratus (94), adlected by Vespasian, were already praetorian in 74 (*ILS* 8791; 8819). T. Avidius Quietus (93) was also elderly—he knew Thrasea Paetus (Pliny, *Epp.* VI. 29. 1), and had commanded a legion as long ago as 82 (*ILS* 6105). Q. Pomponius Rufus (95) had held a military commission under Galba (*IRT* 537). Q. Glitius Agricola (97) was three or four years older than Tacitus; the same will hold for T. Pomponius Bassus (94)—he was legate to M. Ulpius Traianus, proconsul of Asia in 79 (*ILS* 8797)—possibly for Q. Fabius Postuminus (96). L. Licinius Sura (?97) is enigmatic in most things. The brothers L. Neratius Marcellus (95) and L. Neratius Priscus (97), adlected into the patriciate by Vespasian, will be fairly youthful consuls.

With the exception of Julius Celsus these men all governed military provinces early in Trajan's reign. Motley in origin (see under App. 14), they have, except the Neratii, one thing in common, the lack of attested or surmised consular parents.

At the other extreme, five high aristocrats. T. Sextius Lateranus (*cos.* 94) is ostensibly descended from an ancient house of the plebeian *nobilitas* (cf. Groag in P–W II A, 2039). The others all derive from Triumviral or Augustan consuls, L. Nonius Calpurnius Torquatus Asprenas (*cos.* 94), whose Pisonian lineage comes through the female line, L. Volusius Saturninus (*cos.* 92), C. Antistius Vetus (*cos.* 96), and the polyonymous suffect of 94 who unites the nomenclature of M. Lollius (*cos.* 21 B.C.) and of D. Valerius Asiaticus (*suff.* A.D. 35), the first consul from Gallia Narbonensis. This man and Nonius Asprenas survive to hold second consulates under Hadrian. Otherwise bare names and dates—but known as persons to Cornelius Tacitus, and, like certain Asinii Marcelli, not absent from his thoughts when he wrote about their ancestors in the *Annales* (p. 302). At that season it would not have been wholly fanciful to divine a splendid destiny for the family of one of the historian's own coevals among the *novi homines*, the unobtrusive but highly favoured Annius Verus (*suff.* 97: on whom, App. 86).

25. CONSULAR COEVALS OF PLINY

FOR Pliny closer parallels offer. The two friends, C. Julius Cornutus Tertullus and Calestrius Tiro, deserve separate notice (Ch. VII). Calestrius was Pliny's exact coeval (*Epp.* VII. 16. 1 f.), but fell behind. The following persons (two of whom, Baebius Macer and Fabius Justus, receive epistles from Pliny) were among the praetors of the years 90–94, it can be argued or proved:

L. Arruntius Stella (*suff.* ?101). Praetor in 93, cf. Martial VIII. 78. A patron of Martial and Statius; neo-patrician, from Patavium, cf. *PIR*², A 1151.

Q. Baebius Macer (103). To be identified (despite the hesitations of *PIR*², B 20) with Macer, *curator viae Appiae* c. 95 (Martial x. 18. 6) and with Macer, proconsul of Baetica in 100/1 (ib. XII. 98. 7). Prefect of the City in 117 (*HA, Hadr.* 5. 5). Perhaps from Comum, cf. *Epp.* VI. 24—unless this is P. Calpurnius Macer (*suff.* 103, legate of Moesia Inferior in 112). Note that P. Baebius Italicus (*suff.* 90) has the 'Oufentina' (*ILS* 8818), which is the tribe of Comum (and of Mediolanium)

Ti. Caepio Hispo (?101). His *cursus* (abbreviated), *ILS* 1027 (Ravenna), cf. *CIL* v, 5813 (Mediolanium, set up by the Patavini). Prefect of the *aerarium militare*, and proconsul of Baetica (?98/99 or 99/100). To be identified with Galeo Tettienus Severus Ti. Caepio Hispo, attested as proconsul of Asia in 118 (*SEG* IV, 532), cf. Groag in *PIR*², E 83, revoking his doubts in P–W V A, 1103 ff. Local origin unverifiable: note that 'M. Eppuleius Proculus' and the tribe 'Claudia' belong to his nomenclature (*ILS* 1027). The Tettieni come from Asisium in Umbria

L. Fabius Justus (102). The friend of Cornelius Tacitus: for career and origin (? Spain or Narbonensis), App. 14, and pp. 53, 74, 615.

M. Junius Homullus (102). Something of an orator (App. 27); legate of Cappadocia in 114 (Dio LXVIII. 19. 1)

M. Maecius Celer (101). Proceeding to the command of a Syrian legion c. 93 (Statius, *Silvae* III. 2. 121 ff., cf. *praef.*)

M. Pompeius Macrinus Neos Theophanes (100 or 101). His *cursus*, *IG* v, 1, 151. *Curator viae Latinae* c. 93, then legate of VI Victrix (in Germania Inferior), legate of Cilicia, proconsul of Sicily and consul; proconsul of Africa (?116/17). Descendant of Cn. Pompeius Theophanes of Mytilene (App. 62)

L. Roscius Aelianus Maecius Celer (100). His *cursus* (without praetorian posts), *ILS* 1015. Tribune of IX Hispana in 83, decorated in Domitian's war against the Chatti, also *q. Aug.* (c. 87). Origin and relationships uncertain. The other Maecius Celer (above) is designated as Italian by Statius, *Silvae* III. 2. 20

M. Vitorius Marcellus (105). *Curator viae Latinae* c. 95 (Statius, *Silvae* IV. 4. 60). The poet predicts that he will go on to command a legion somewhere (ib. 61 ff.). Quintilian dedicated his great work to Vitorius (*Inst. Or., praef.* 6, &c.). He came from Teate Marrucinorum (Statius, l.c. 85), and was connected with the Hosidii Getae (a consular house from Histonium), cf. Statius (l.c. 73) and the nomenclature of his son (*PIR*¹, V 518)

26. FLAVIAN ORATORY

ORATORY under the Julian and Claudian Caesars may be studied through the works of the elder Seneca and of Quintilian—and perhaps best through the *Annales* of Tacitus (Ch. XXV). Seneca, for one reason or another, fails to mention certain notable speakers such as L. Fulcinius Trio (*suff.* 31). Moreover, between the reigns of Nero and Trajan a grievous hiatus intervenes. Quintilian, who was born about 33, registers the greatest orators he had heard, six in number, with a careful estimate of their quality and powers (X. 1. 118 ff.), and he recapitulates his verdict—'copiam Senecae, vires Africani, maturitatem Afri, iucunditatem Crispi, sonum Trachali, elegantiam Secundi' (XII. 10. 11). When Quintilian wrote, the first three names belonged to an already distant past. As for the others, Galerius Trachalus (*cos.* 68) is last heard of as proconsul of Africa c. 78 (*CIL* v, 5812), while Julius Secundus died comparatively young. Vibius Crispus, however, consul suffect c. 62, prolonged his life well into Domitian's reign.

The *Dialogus* reckons Julius Secundus and M. Aper (who is otherwise unattested) as the leading barristers early in Vespasian's reign; and the prime political speakers are Vibius Crispus and Eprius Marcellus. Eprius, who had incurred disaster, was discreetly omitted by Quintilian from his catalogue, and convention forbade him to mention the living. Their performance will have been adequately reported in the *Historiae* of Tacitus—and some no doubt also earned a place in the record of prosecutions towards the end of Nero's reign.

To bridge the gap, seven consular orators, advocates, or politicians, may be invoked:

(1) Ti. Catius Asconius Silius Italicus (*cos.* 68). See also p. 88 f. His Neronian activities were redeemed by 'laudabile otium' under Vespasian and an exemplary proconsulate of Asia (*Epp.* III. 7. 3). This need not imply a total cessation of Silius' senatorial or forensic eloquence

(2) C. Paccius Africanus (*suff.* c. 67). Believed responsible for denouncing to Nero the brothers Scribonii, hence vulnerable in 70 (*Hist.* IV. 41. 3). Proconsul of Africa, 77/78 (*IRT* 342)

(3) A. Didius Gallus Fabricius Veiento. See App. 5

(4) L. Valerius Catullus Messallinus (*cos.* 73, *II. suff.* 85). A person of no little social distinction (for a conjecture about family and kin see *PIR*¹, S 626); notorious for his services to Domitian (*Epp.* IV. 22. 5; Juvenal IV. 113 f.), and still alive in 93 (*Agr.* 45. 1)

(5) C. Salvius Liberalis Nonius Bassus (*suff.* c. 84). A municipal worthy from Picenum, adlected by Vespasian (*ILS* 1011); an advocate (Suetonius, *Divus Vesp.* 13); provincial posts, including that of *iuridicus* in Britain; prosecution and exile, after 87 (cf. *PIR*¹, S 105); attested as a powerful speaker in 100 (*Epp.* II. 11. 17, cf. App. 27)

(6) M. Aquillius Regulus (*anno incerto*). The great barrister, surviving till 104 or 105. Presumably consular, cf. *Hist.* IV. 42. 5

(7) Pompeius, a 'delator' (Juvenal IV. 110). Presumably to be identified with Cn. Pompeius Catullus, suffect consul in 90

The names do not take one very far. Nor is much to be got from Valerius Licinianus, 'inter eloquentissimos causarum actores' (*Epp.* IV. 11. 1), who was exiled for adultery with a Vestal Virgin (justly, it appears): from Spain, to judge by nomenclature, but not to be confused with Licinianus of Bilbilis, 'vir Celtiberis non tacende gentibus | nostraeque laus Hispaniae' (Martial I. 49. 1 f.). Nothing can be said about Mettius Carus and Publicius Certus, the notorious prosecutors. But there might be curiosity about the talents of Satrius Rufus, 'cui non est cum Cicerone aemulatio, et qui contentus est eloquentia saeculi nostri', as Regulus remarked (*Epp.* I. 5. 11). He intervenes on behalf of Publicius Certus in 97 (IX. 13. 17).

27. PLINY AND THE ORATORS

QUINTILIAN extols the oratorical achievement of the late Domitianic period (X. 1. 122). Yet Tacitus' predecessors among the great 'patroni' baffle inquiry; and Pliny names only Tacitus as his own guide and model (*Epp.* VII. 20. 4). If the oratorical annals of the eighties and nineties are almost a blank, the series of prosecutions under Trajan compensates a little. Pliny reports four trials—Marius Priscus (100), Caecilius Classicus (terminating in 100 or 101), Julius Bassus (102/3), and Varenus Rufus (106 and 107). Various consulars participated in one way or another. Six of them (apart from Tacitus) are labelled and characterized. The comment may be instructive:

Ti. Catius Caesius Fronto (*suff.* 96): 'insigniter' (*Epp.* II. 11. 18); 'mirifice' (IV. 9. 15); 'graviter et firme' (VI. 13. 3); his command of pathos (II. 11. 3)[1]

(? M.) Herennius Pollio (*anno incerto*): 'instanter et graviter' (IV. 9. 14)

M. Junius Homullus (102): 'mirifice' (IV. 9. 15); 'callide, acriter, culte' (V. 20. 6)

(? Cn.) Lucceius Albinus (*anno incerto*): 'vir in dicendo copiosus, ornatus' (III. 9. 7); cf. also IV. 9. 13

C. Pomponius Rufus (98): 'vir paratus et vehemens' (IV. 9. 3); cf. also III. 9. 33.[2]

C. Salvius Liberalis Nonius Bassus (c. 84): 'vir subtilis, dispositus, acer, vehemens' (II. 11. 17); 'ut est vehemens et disertus' (III. 9. 36). Cf. App. 26

It is worth nothing that only one of these six consular 'patroni' figures among the recipients of Plinian epistles, namely Lucceius Albinus (VI. 10), his partner in the Classicus case, 'quem ego cum olim mutuo diligerem, ex hac officii societate amare ardentius coepi' (III. 9. 7). As for Pliny's close coevals (see App. 25), Junius Homullus belongs to that company; there is no means of telling whether Vitorius Marcellus (like Pliny, a disciple of Quintilian) came up to expectation; but Baebius Macer and Caepio Hispo might have had some talent.

There was rivalry among the orators, and doctrinal antagonism. Not everybody liked Pliny's brand of Ciceronianism. Sending a composition for the criticism of C. Minicius Fundanus (*suff.* 107), Pliny knows that it might be judged 'tumidius'. To spare his friend trouble and distaste, Pliny deliberately inserts 'pressius quiddam et exilius' (VII. 12. 4). Fundanus stands for an 'Attic' tendency in style—compare the hit at 'tenuitas vestra' (ib. 5). Various details about Fundanus (among other things a friend of Plutarch) combine to make a living and attractive character.[3]

One senatorial orator of lower rank is accorded by Pliny a treatment otherwise reserved for consulars. A certain Nigrinus displayed energy when tribune of the plebs in 105 (*Epp.* V. 13. 6 f.); and, next found among the prosecutors of Varenus Rufus, he spoke 'presse, graviter, ornate' (V. 20. 6). The terms might fit some disciple of Cornelius Tacitus. Who can this Nigrinus be? Perhaps C. Avidius Nigrinus (*PIR*² A1408, *suff.* 110), the friend of Hadrian (and his victim), despite the interval between tribunate and consulate, which seems anomalously brief.

Pliny was not quite happy about the younger generation—'statim sapiunt, statim sciunt omnia, neminem verentur, imitantur neminem atque ipsi sibi exempla sunt' (VIII. 23. 3). That did not prevent him from becoming ecstatic about a pair of youths not yet of quaestorian standing, who showed brilliant

---

[1] Presumably a relative of Silius Italicus (p. 668). He voiced criticism of Nerva's government (Dio LXVIII. 1. 3).

[2] To be distinguished from Q. Pomponius Rufus (*suff.* 95).

[3] cf. E. Groag, P–W xv, 1820 f.

promise and imitated the best models—'me aemulari, meis instare vestigiis videbantur' (VI. 11. 2). Unfortunately, nobody can tell their true quality or how they developed: another historical gap intervenes. These 'clarissimi iuvenes' had claims above mere eloquence. The one was Pedanius Fuscus, soon to be chosen by Julius Servianus as husband for his daughter (VI. 26), Hadrian's niece—and *ordinarius* in 118. The other, Ummidius Quadratus (*suff.* 118), was perhaps already connected in some way with this dynastic group: his son, *suff.* c. 139, married Annia Cornificia Faustina (*PIR*², A 708), a sister of Marcus.[1]

28. THE DATING OF THE *DIALOGUS*

THE treatise has called forth an enormous volume of discussion. Transmitted by the lost *Codex Hersfeldensis* along with the *Agricola* and the *Germania* (and the fragments of Suetonius, *De gram.* and *De rhet.*), it is not, however, authenticated by the name of Cornelius Tacitus. Beatus Rhenanus doubted, and so did Justus Lipsius. The latter scholar toyed with the name of Quintilian, but dropped it.[2] In more recent days some have consigned their fancies to the younger Pliny;[3] and Pliny's author-friend of equestrian rank, Titinius Capito, has even been invoked.[4] It is all vanity. There is no solid reason against Tacitean authorship. To call it in question strains (and perhaps discredits) the fair name of scholarly caution.[5]

Two problems subsist. First, of minor moment, the dramatic date. The author registers the sixth year of Vespasian's reign—'sextam iam felicis huius principatus stationem qua Vespasianus rem publicam fovet' (17. 3). A question arises, from what initial point would the author compute that 'felix principatus'? Vespasian reckoned as his 'dies imperii' the first day of July 69, when he was proclaimed in the East, in the first instance by the army of Egypt (*Hist.* II. 79. 1); and his *tribunicia potestas* was back-dated to begin on that day. In fact, Vespasian was not recognized at Rome until late in December, after the defeat and death of Vitellius (*Hist.* IV. 3. 3). It would therefore be intelligible if a writer took Vespasian's reign to begin with the years of peace, that is, by calendar years from 70 (which the language of the passage supports). Moreover, Vespasian (so it happened) was consul for the sixth time in 75, a useful coincidence. Hence it might be permissible to put the dramatic date of the *Dialogus* in 75, not in 74/75 (on the reckoning from July 1, 69).

Some have disputed this meaning of 'statio', it is true.[6] Moreover, the computation adduced in the same context, 120 years from the death of Cicero, is at variance (ib., cf. 24. 3). It would indicate the year 77/78. The reckoning may

---

[1] For Pedanii and Ummidii, p. 479 f.
[2] The notion has been revived by L. Herrmann, *Latomus* XIV (1955), 349 ff.
[3] C. Landi, *Athenaeum* XVII (1929), 489 ff.; C. Gallavotti, ib. XIX (1931), 35 ff.
[4] E. Paratore, *Tacito* (1951), 233 ff. Against, H. Bardon, *Latomus* XII (1953), 166 ff.; 485 ff.; R. T. Bruère, *Class. Phil.* XLIX (1954), 166 ff.
[5] Thus E. E. Sikes, *CAH* XI (1936), 738: 'the author whom we must call Anonymous.'
[6] E. Norden, *Die antike Kunstprosa* I (1898), 325 f.; E. Koestermann, *Philologus* LXXXVII (1932), 363.

have gone wrong somehow.¹ Several reasons tell in favour of 74 or 75. First, the author describes himself as 'iuvenis admodum' (1. 2) when the discussion took place. That phrase carries more precise connotation than might seem likely. It can be argued that it belongs to the early pre-quaestorian years of a young man's life. Thus, in general, referring to Helvidius Priscus and to Aquillius Regulus (*Hist.* IV. 5. 1 and 42. 2); and, precisely datable, a man aged eighteen—'iuvene admodum Domitiano' (*Agr.* 7. 4). The same term when elsewhere used can be instructive: Quintilian was 'iuvenis admodum' in relation to the dramatist Pomponius Secundus (VIII. 3. 31), the one born c. 33, the other probably not surviving long after 50. Secondly, the *Dialogus* conceives Licinius Mucianus as still alive (37. 2): he was dead by 77 (*NH* XXXII. 62). Thirdly, but not conclusive: the alarm caused by the *Cato* of Curiatius Maternus (2. 1) fits 74 most pertinently, for that was probably the year in which the modern Cato, Helvidius Priscus, was prosecuted and banished (Dio LXV. 12. 2, cf. p. 212).

The second problem is the date of composition. Tacitus in the *Agricòla* (3. 2 f.) does much more than merely imply that the biography is his first publication. The *Dialogus* should be later. Yet it has been argued that it is an early work of Tacitus, belonging to the reign of Titus, or perhaps of Domitian.² That thesis could only be supported by perverse argumentation; and it is kept alive by tired or uncritical acquiescence in a fancied 'communis opinio'.³

The whole setting of the *Dialogus* conveys a past long distant (1. 2 f.). The interlocutors, all four, were surely no longer among the living. Nor would an author writing under Titus, or Domitian, have been able to describe so freely Vibius Crispus and Eprius Marcellus (8. 2 ff.). Quintilian, indeed, had to omit Eprius altogether.

There is something else, and decisive against a date under Titus. Would Tacitus, then aged about twenty-four, refer to himself when half a dozen years younger as 'iuvenis admodum'? A prosopographical point can here be inserted. Tacitus alludes to frequent discussions with his friend about the high and important topic of the cessation of great oratory—'saepe ex me requiris, Iuste Fabi' (1. 1). Fabius Justus was consul suffect in the year 102. In the reign of Titus he was perhaps barely adolescent: there is a good chance that he belongs to the favoured class of 'viri militares' who reach the consulate young, at thirty-seven or eight (cf. App. 18). Fabius may have been born as late as 64 or 65: that is to say, 'iuvenis admodum' himself under Titus.

The *Dialogus*, as is generally recognized, shows knowledge of the *Institutio Oratoria*.⁴ That work belongs to the end of Domitian's reign. Moreover, the *Dialogus* has a mature and authoritative tone. It is not the product of a youth; and it exhibits a writer who can think and argue like an historian. It should therefore be put in the years when Tacitus was preparing or writing his *Historiae*.

¹ For suggestions and remedies see A. Gudeman in his (second) edition (Berlin, 1914), 55 ff.; Schanz–Hosius, *Gesch. der r. Literatur* II⁴ (1935), 608.

² Thus, respectively, the editors A. Gudeman (Berlin, 1914), 29 ff.; W. Peterson (Oxford, 1893), XVI ff.

³ An early date is argued or assumed, for example, by J. Wight Duff, *A Literary History of Rome in the Silver Age* (1927), 565 f.; C. Marchesi, *Tacito*⁴ (1944), 45; M. L. W. Laistner, *The Greater Roman Historians* (1947), 103, cf. 177; M. P. Charlesworth, *OCD* (1949), 876.

⁴ cf. especially R. Güngerich, *Class. Phil.* XLVI (1951), 159 ff.

What plea could be raised against? Only that of style—and of style imperfectly understood. The Ciceronian manner of the *Dialogus* has incautiously been assumed to be an early stage in the development of Cornelius Tacitus. Yet the style is determined by the genre.[1] It affords no evidence of date.[2] As far as style goes, the *Dialogus* could quite well belong in or close to 98, about the time of the *Agricola* and the *Germania*.[3]

That is not the end of the matter. The treatise could (and perhaps should) be dated a few years later.[4] A poem or a book might appropriately be dedicated to a senatorial patron about the time of his consulate—thus Virgil with the *Fourth Eclogue* to Pollio, Velleius Paterculus to M. Vinicius (*cos.* 30), or Martial with Book XII, cf. the second poem there, to L. Arruntius Stella (*suff.* ?101). Ought not the *Dialogus* to be dated by the consulate of Fabius Justus—that is, to 101, for Fabius assumed the fasces early in 102?[5] It is a temptation to exploit this date, cf. p. 112.

One might perhaps go further down. Indications in Pliny suggest a later date. There are two references to a book that Tacitus has sent to his friend (*Epp.* VII. 20. 1; VIII. 7). Tacitus, it appears, had used the phrases 'ut magistro magister' and 'ut discipulo discipulus'. Hence clearly a speech or a work on oratory, not an historical book (cf. p. 113). It might be the *Dialogus*, about the year 107.[6]

That conjecture could be supported. There is no hint or trace of the *Dialogus* in the earlier letters of Pliny. But a hint comes after all, quite late—'itaque poemata quiescunt, quae tu inter nemora et lucos commodissime perfici putas' (IX. 10. 2). Few have been able to deny the allusion to *Dial.* 9. 6. (cf. 12. 1): 'in nemora et lucos.'[7] Note perhaps also the story (in a letter that mentions Tacitus) of the man who pointed out Pliny at a dinner party to a newly arrived fellow-townsman (IX. 23. 4). It illustrates *Dial.* 7. 4: 'advenae quoque et peregrini iam in municipiis et coloniis suis auditos, cum primum urbem attigerunt, requirunt ac velut adgnoscere concupiscunt.'

To sum up. It looks as though the *Dialogus* was composed either about the time of Fabius' consulate or some four or five years later. Either way the treatise stands in close relation to the historical studies of Tacitus and to his renunciation of oratory. When he came to narrate the reign of Vespasian (*Hist.* IV–VI) he was

---

[1] As demonstrated by F. Leo, *Gött. gel. Anz.* 1898, 169 ff. (reviewing Gudeman's first edition); E. Norden, *Die antike Kunstprosa* I (1898), 322 ff.

[2] But, properly investigated, speaks for Tacitus, cf. A. Gudeman, o.c. 20 ff.; H. Bardon, *Latomus* XII (1953), 485 ff.

[3] R. Reitzenstein, *Gött. gel. Nachr.* 1914, 173 ff. Also a number of more recent writers, e.g. M. Schuster, *Wiener Studien* XLVI (1928), 234 ff.

[4] A Trajanic date is assumed (but not specified) by E. Koestermann, *Hermes* LXV (1930), 421 and by F. Klingner, *Die Antike* VIII (1932), 151 ff. = *R. Geisteswelt* (1943), 310 ff. A certain time subsequent to the *Agricola* and *Germania*, according to K. Barwick, *Sächsische S-B, phil.-hist. Kl.* 1954, Heft 4, 31—even after 105.

[5] A. Kappelmacher, *Wiener Studien* L (1932), 121 ff. Also R. Güngerich, *Festschrift Bruno Snell* (1956), 145 ff. That scholar argues that Pliny, revising the *Panegyricus* in 101, imitated passages in the *Dialogus*.

[6] H. Wagenvoort, *Mnemosyne* XLVII (1919), 359 ff.; ib. LIV (1926), 416 ff.

[7] See the acute discussion of these passages by R. T. Bruère, *Class. Phil.* XLIX (1954), 166 ff. He also suggests that *Epp.* I. 6. 2 is an echo of *Dial.* 36. 1.

back among the scenes and friends of his youth—and he had already used Vipstanus' memoirs for the campaign of 69 (III. 28. 1). There was Regulus as an
exciting figure (IV. 42). Above all, the great orators and ministers of state,
Eprius Marcellus and Vibius Crispus, sharpened the contrast with the speakers
in the early years of Trajan and with the present condition of public eloquence.
The *Dialogus* can perhaps be regarded as a by-product of the *Historiae*.[1]

[1] For a useful classification of opinions about date and authenticity see now J. Frot,
Rev. ét. lat. XXXIII (1955), 120 ff.

D. THE *HISTORIAE*

29. TACITUS AND PLUTARCH

THE concordances between Plutarch in his *Galba* and *Otho* and certain portions of *Historiae* I–II are numerous and notable.[1] Two explanations offer. Either Plutarch followed Tacitus, or there was a common source.

The first alternative cannot stand without qualification. Plutarch provides a full account of Nymphidius Sabinus, and elsewhere has details and names not in Tacitus. Therefore, in any case, another source. Did Plutarch also use Tacitus? That has been contended, e.g. by Borenius and by Momigliano, on various criteria.[2] To prove the case items are needed that could not come from a source earlier than the first two books of the *Historiae* (c. 105). One such has been claimed. Otho in his last words exhorted his nephew Salvius Cocceianus to remember him, not too little—but not too much (II. 48. 2; *Otho* 16). This, it might seem, is a *vaticinium ex eventu*, for Cocceianus was put to death by Domitian because he celebrated Otho's birthday (Suetonius, *Dom.* 10. 3). Therefore, it is suggested, the remarks cannot have been published previous to the death of Domitian. The conclusion is tempting, but not peremptory.[3] Otho's words might be authentically reported and widely known. Various persons were present, such as Julius Secundus, his secretary, who is named by Plutarch's source (*Otho* 9).

Moreover, there is a further problem. The *Galba* and the *Otho* are an adaptation of an historical narrative. They do not belong to the series of *Parallel Lives*. They are what survives from the biographies of eight Caesars, from Augustus to Vitellius (attested by the *Catalogue* of Lamprias). The work might have been composed before the publication of *Historiae* I–II—perhaps very soon after 96, when the end of the Flavian dynasty made the history of the earlier rulers an attractive theme. It is best to assume that Tacitus and Plutarch are independent.

There remains the common source, and that is the theory which has generally been adopted.[4] Next, identity. An author is required who wrote about Nero (cf. *Galba* 2: ὥσπερ εἴρηται) and also about Vitellius, because of the concordances between Book III of the *Historiae* and Suetonius' life of that emperor: Suetonius used this *Ignotus*, Tacitus, and yet a third source.[5]

---

[1] They are conveniently listed by E. G. Hardy in his edition of the two *Lives* (1890), XXXVII ff.; also the discrepancies, XXIX ff. For the lengthy bibliography of the controversy, Schanz–Hosius, *Gesch. der r. Literatur* II⁴ (1935), 629 ff.

[2] C. E. Borenius, *De Plutarcho et Tacito inter se congruentibus* (Diss. Helsingfors, 1902); A. Momigliano, *Stud. it. fil. cl.* IX (1931), 117 ff., appendix on sources, 171 ff.

[3] cf. Ph. Fabia, *Les Sources de Tacite dans les* Histoires *et les* Annales (1893), 207; E. Groag, *Jahrbücher für cl. Phil.*, Supp.-Band XXIII (1897), 761.

[4] Indeed, it is unavoidable, cf. E. Hohl, *Klio* XXXII (1939), 312.

[5] E. Groag, o.c. 766 ff.

Mommsen opted for the consular historian Cluvius Rufus, but not many have concurred.[1] It is not at all certain that Cluvius covered the events of 69.[2] Plutarch, it is true, cites Cluvius as authority for official documents being sent to Spain with the title 'Nero Otho' (*Otho* 3, cf. Suetonius, *Otho* 7, while Tacitus omits the story). This notice could have occurred in Cluvius' narrative of 68 (to illustrate the posthumous popularity of Nero), or might have come verbally to Plutarch's source. Another particular, however, seems decisive—the colloquy between Vitellius and Flavius Sabinus. Cluvius was there. Tacitus reports the matter, citing no authority, but only 'ut fama fuit' (III. 65. 2). It was not the habit of Tacitus to miss an authentic record (when it could be had) of secret negotiations.

The general favourite has been Pliny—so Nissen, Gercke, Fabia, and others.[3] The mere fact that Pliny should be cited for an episode at Cremona (III. 28) is not enough. On the other side, it can be claimed that the quality of Pliny as an historian (and his utility to Tacitus) has been overestimated. Certain remarks of Groag and Peter will provide a corrective.[4] Further, Groag produced an item to demonstrate that Pliny cannot be the *Ignotus*. It is the portrayal of Caecina Alienus as he advanced through cities of Italy, to their great distaste, 'quod versicolori sagulo, bracas, barbarum tegumen, indutus togatos adloqueretur' (II. 20. 1; *Otho* 6).[5] That cannot have been published before the year 79— and that was the year of Pliny's death. Pliny could make free with Antonius Primus (in disgrace) but not with Caecina. (It could, of course, be objected that Pliny might have given vent to his opinions about that person in a work which he intended anyhow to be posthumous, *NH, praef.* 20.)

The *Ignotus* remains elusive. Groag in his careful investigation suggested Fabius Rusticus, who would fill the bill on many counts.[6] Proper attention has not been given by scholars to Groag's study (which concerns Tacitus' methods as well as his sources).[7]

It is safer to confess ignorance. Those transactions were dealt with by many historians, so Flavius Josephus affirms (*BJ* IV. 496), and there would be no harm (but not much gain) in supposing that Marius Celsus wrote a narrative (cf. App.

[1] *Hermes* IV (1870), 295 ff. = *Ges. Schr.* VII, 224 ff. He had been anticipated by H. Peter, who later retracted, cf. *HRR* II (1906), CLII. However, arguments for Cluvius have been advanced by F. R. B. Godolphin, *AJP* LVI (1935), 324 ff.

[2] Fabia, o.c. 171 ff.; Groag, o.c. 776. H. Peter is inconclusive (o.c. CLXVIII).

[3] H. Nissen, *Rh. Mus.* XXVI (1871), 497 ff.; A. Gercke, *Jahrbücher für cl. Phil.*, Supp.-Band XXII (1896), 159 ff.; Ph. Fabia, o.c. 199 ff.; A. Momigliano, *Stud. it. fil. cl.* IX (1931), 187. The last writer, having disposed of Cluvius Rufus, finds himself left with the choice between Vipstanus Messalla and Pliny, whom he therefore chooses: observe, however, a brief statement more recently, 'the usual identification with the elder Pliny is very doubt-ful', *OCD* (1949), 377.

[4] E. Groag, o.c. 777 ff.; H. Peter, *HRR* II (1906), CLV. On the defects of Pliny's annalistic history see further Ch. XXIII (on the sources for Nero's reign).

[5] Groag, o.c. 772, accepted by H. Peter, o.c. CLIII. The story about the Gallic insurgent Julius Sabinus, whose hiding-place was not discovered until 79 (*Hist.* IV. 67. 2), is best omitted from discussions about sources. Tacitus did not have to learn about it from a written source, any more than did Plutarch (*Amat.* 25). That it is also in Dio (LXVI. 16. 1 f.) is irrelevant to the study of Tacitus' sources, despite the elaborate arguments of J. Martin, *Würzburger Studien* IX (1936), 53 ff.

[6] Groag, o.c. 787 ff.

[7] His views were not cited or discussed by Momigliano, *Stud. it. fil. cl.* IX (1931), 171 ff.

32). The known historians of the period are barely attested as such—Pliny only by himself, by his son, and by Tacitus; Fabius Rusticus only by Tacitus (for Quintilian's reference is anonymous); and, but for two notices in the *Annales* and an anecdote in the younger Pliny, nobody would be aware that Cluvius Rufus wrote history.

Erudite preoccupation with *Quellenkritik* has tended to obscure what matters most—the quality of Tacitus, his technique, and his choice of material. Also the quality of the *Ignotus* (as revealed especially in Plutarch), for he is a valuable link in the line of the lost annalists between Livy and Tacitus.

For the study of Roman historiography a principle or dogma was decreed by Nissen—each writer generally selected one source and followed it slavishly. Nissen showed in his pioneer work on Livy how that author transcribed Polybius for eastern affairs.[1] Nissen appealed to those results when estimating Tacitus;[2] and Mommsen went so far as to assert that Tacitus and the *Ignotus* correspond to Livy and Polybius.[3] Fashion hardened into tradition. Fabia in his lengthy volume applied 'Nissen's Law' to the *Annales* as well as to the *Historiae*—with much learning and pertinacity, and most harmfully. Protests were made, but not always heeded.[4]

30. THE STRATEGY OF OTHO

TACITUS' account of the civil war waged between the generals of Otho and Vitellius betrays various inadequacies. An elaborate assault upon his credit and judgement was launched by B. W. Henderson, who, with copious appeal to modern manuals, sought to establish the design behind the action, and, believing his method valid, claimed that Otho himself possessed remarkable strategic gifts.[5] Henderson's notions about the sources employed by Tacitus were most peculiar,[6] and he denounced the senatorial historian for addiction to rhetoric and for total ignorance of warfare. Henderson's methods quickly incurred severe censure, from E. G. Hardy.[7] The subject continues to engage attention.[8]

One of the minor operations is instructive. Otho sent an expedition against the coast of Gallia Narbonensis (*Hist.* 1. 87; 11. 12 ff.). There might have been a model and precedent the year before. Nero was confronted with a similar

[1] H. Nissen, *Kritische Untersuchungen über die Quellen der 4. und 5. Dekade des Livius* (1863).
[2] *Rh. Mus.* XXVI (1871), 500.
[3] *Ges. Schr.* VII, 244. As Groag points out (o.c. 762 f.), neither Nissen nor Mommsen had made a sufficiently thorough comparison of Tacitus and Plutarch.
[4] cf. the sagacious paper of G. H. Stevenson, *Journ. Phil.* XXXV (1920), 204 ff.
[5] *Civil War and Rebellion in the Roman Empire* (1908).
[6] o.c. VIII: 'his information represents little but the common gossip of the camp, the talk of the private soldier or subordinate officer.'
[7] *Journ. Phil.* XXXI (1910), 123 ff.
[8] See especially A. Momigliano, *Stud. it. fil. cl.* IX (1931/2), 117 ff.; A. Passerini, *Studi di antichità classica offerti ... a Emanuele Ciaceri* (1940), 178 ff. The former scholar taxes the historian with an 'inesperienza talvolta perfino ingenua di operazioni militari' (o.c. 131).

problem—the Gallic rebellion and Galba proclaimed in Spain. Scattered evidence reveals the large concentrations of troops ordered by Nero in northern Italy.[1] No trace, however, survives of any plan or action by the fleet. Galba for his part had not been wholly inactive. A recently discovered inscription shows that Q. Pomponius Rufus was appointed 'praef. orae marit. Hispan. citer. Gallia[e] N[a]rbon. bello qu[od] imp. G[a]lba pro [re p.] gessit' (*AE* 1948, 3 = *IRT* 537). The dominant strategic place on the Narbonensian coast was Forum Julii, where the main artery of Narbonensis (the road from Spain by Narbo and Arelate) reached the coast. Forum Julii had played a part in an earlier civil war, being occupied by M. Antonius after his retreat from Mutina (Cicero, *Ad fam.* x. 17. 1). It was a naval base for a time under the early Principate; and Tacitus, noting an incident later in 69, can call the place 'claustra maris' (III. 43. 1). To secure Forum Julii could have been vital for Galba, or for Nero; was this perhaps the colony that Cornelius Fuscus won for Galba (II. 86. 3: see App. 33)?

The Othonian force, however, got nowhere near Forum Julii. It never entered Narbonensis. Operations began in the small frontier zone of the Alpes Maritimae (II. 12). The expedition attacked the town of Albintimilium (II. 12 f.). Yet the town of Albintimilium which the fleet took and sacked (II. 13) belonged in fact to Italy, to the Ninth Region (Liguria). Nor did this foray detach any considerable body of troops from the column which Fabius Valens was leading to the crossing of the Alps.[2] Though the Othonians were victorious in two skirmishes, they achieved nothing more, but retreated a long way back, to Albingaunum in Liguria, 'velut pactis indutiis' (II. 15. 2).

Otho has been praised for designing the first operation as part of a magnificent strategic plan, which only the incapacity of his commanders ruined.[3] After their victory they might have 'dared to push up country in the direction of Briançon'.[4] It is not explained by what route an army could march from the vicinity of Albintimilium to Brigantio (Briançon). The sober narrative of Tacitus and the hard facts of geography are an adequate deterrent. On the other hand, sound strategy (if Otho had it) would have enjoined an attack on Forum Julii in the first instance—and Fabius Valens was aware of that danger (II. 14. 1).[5]

The principal matter, however, is the Battle of Bedriacum. It is advisable to start with the narrative of Plutarch, who had a good source, and no occasion to alter or supplement it. His account is clear and straightforward (*Otho* 11). Otho wanted a battle, and the soldiers were keen. The army marched out from Bedriacum and encamped fifty stades on. The intention was to advance upon the enemy, a march of not less than a hundred stades more, but on the next day Suetonius Paullinus raised objections: they ought to stay where they were, and not expose themselves to attack while proceeding on that long march. Dispute

---

[1] cf. R. Syme, *AJP* LVIII (1937), 10 f.

[2] II. 14. 1: 'duas Tungrorum cohortis, quattuor equitum turmas, universam Trevirorum alam cum Iulio Classico misit, e quibus pars in colonia Foroiuliensi retenta.'

[3] B. W. Henderson, o.c. 77 ff.   [4] ib. 78.

[5] The judgement of Momigliano, 'azione abile e fortunata' (o.c. 128) appears too indulgent. Nor is Passerini justified in concluding 'l'operazione era ben concepita' (o.c. 190).

arose among the generals, but a Numidian courier arrived with a message from Otho: they must not stop or delay, but proceed immediately against the enemy. The army therefore struck camp and moved forward, and a battle ensued.

Plutarch's figures are round numbers. Added together, they put the intended goal of the second day's march about fifteen miles from Bedriacum (if ten stades are reckoned to a mile), or (better) eighteen (eight stades to the mile). Cremona is about twenty miles from Bedriacum, and the clash in fact came, so it appears, a few miles (perhaps four) short of Cremona.

So far so good. The difficulty emerges in the Tacitean account. The Othonian army marched out—'ad quartum a Bedriaco' (II. 39. 2). There was discussion and doubt about the plan—'ibi de proelio dubitatum'. A dispatch from Otho discountenanced any delay; the soldiers, however, wanted him to be there for the battle; and many argued that the troops on the other side of the Po should be summoned.

However, the march proceeded on the next day, and its goal is indicated, sixteen miles further on—'non ad pugnam sed ad bellandum profecti confluentis Padi et Aduae fluminum, sedecim inde milium spatio distantis, petebant' (II. 40. 1). Now comes more discussion. Paullinus and Celsus were critical—the army would incur danger of attack, while marching or forming their camp, and the enemy would have barely four miles to advance. Titianus and Proculus, however, insisted—and there was Otho's order, the Numidian courier 'cum atrocibus mandatis'.

In what is narrated between the Othonian army's departure from Bedriacum and the final rout, it is clear that Tacitus (II. 39–44) is using the source which Plutarch reproduces (*Otho* 11 f.). The discrepancies become important. It is necessary to see how and why they arise. The main discrepancy is Tacitus' definition of the goal for the second day's march, 'confluentis Padi et Aduae fluminum'. But for that detail, there would hardly be a problem—and attention concentrates upon it.

There is something else. Plutarch has one debate among the generals. It occurs before the second day's march begins—and it is terminated by the arrival of the Numidian courier. In Tacitus, however, there are two. The first is reported before the setting out on that day. No generals are named, but a dispatch from Otho is referred to. The second, however, is placed after the army has started for its named destination. Paullinus and Celsus are overruled, with appeal to Otho's missive brought by the Numidian courier.

There is nothing in itself to disprove two discussions and two messages from Otho (Plutarch omits and abbreviates). None the less, the suspicion of a doublet arises, introduced by Tacitus when he had recourse to another source to provide an additional detail of presumed value, namely, the goal of the march—and perhaps introduced in the wrong place, hence the overlap. Tacitus says 'non ad pugnam sed ad bellandum profecti'. That indication of strategic plan is not false where it stands—but ought it not to have been placed where it properly belongs, namely, as the reason for the march out from Bedriacum the day before?

If Tacitus has conflated two sources unskilfully, a further consequence might be drawn. Perhaps the item of sixteen miles (in Tacitus' second source) indicated the distance from Bedriacum to the ultimate goal, and not, as it stands in Tacitus, the distance from the encampment after the march of four miles on the first day. That would take one to a point about four miles short of Cremona. Paullinus and Celsus (in Tacitus' account) urge that the enemy would have barely four miles to advance to the attack; and Cremona was twenty miles from Bedriacum, at least on the reckoning adopted by Pompeius Planta, who wrote the story of this battle (*Schol.* on Juvenal II. 99). This would fit the figure in Plutarch—150 stades from Bedriacum (i.e. a total distance of fifteen or eighteen miles). Pompeius Planta might well be the writer whom Tacitus at this point used to supplement the source which he and Plutarch both follow.

On this interpretation the distances in Plutarch and in Tacitus bring the Othonian army more or less to the point on the Via Postumia at which the clash occurred. Tacitus, however, equates his sixteen miles with the point at which the Adua ran into the Po. That item could only be explained on an extreme and violent hypothesis, for the Adua now enters the Po about seven miles upstream from Cremona (see below).

Enough has been said to suggest that the problem concerns 'Quellenkritik' no less (and perhaps more) than topography: compare Hannibal's march from the crossing of the Rhone to the Alps in Livy (XXI. 31 f.), where two (or perhaps rather three) versions are blended. The one source (reproduced in Plutarch) is clear. How and why Tacitus brought in the 'confluentis Padi et Aduae fluminum' cannot be discovered from anything in his own narrative. When composing Book II of the *Historiae* Tacitus may have had no helpful critics to hand: perhaps he was never familiar with the topography of Transpadane Italy.

A note may be added on modern reconstructions of the campaign. Mommsen argued that Tacitus confused the ultimate goal of the Othonian army with the goal of the second day's march.[1] The figure of sixteen miles is correct: the Othonians were to leave the Postumia, marching north-westwards, and put themselves astride the road from Brixia to Cremona, cutting the Vitellian communications with Brixia.

Henderson developed and elaborated this theory.[2] The Othonians were to make a detour round Cremona and establish themselves on the west, precisely at the confluence of Adua and Po, hemming in the enemy around Cremona; meanwhile Danubian troops coming up from the rear would face Cremona from the east. To support his case, however, Henderson was reduced to violent expedients. He proposed to alter the text of Tacitus to produce fourteen miles instead of four for the march of the first day.[3] That is an illicit device— it neglects Plutarch, *Otho* 11 (fifty stades). Moreover, were the Danubian troops near and numerous enough? Henderson cites (but does not quote)[4] Suetonius, *Divus Vesp.* 6. 2. That passage proves that the Moesian *vexillationes* were still the other side of Aquileia. The theory collapses.

A modified form of Henderson's reconstructions has recently emerged. Passerini in his careful and thorough study assumes that the figure of sixteen miles in Tacitus is incorrect, but retains the goal indicated, 'confluentis Padi et Aduae

[1] Mommsen, *Ges. Schr.* IV (1906), 361.
[2] o.c. 100 ff.; 340 ff.
[3] o.c. 345.
[4] o.c. 96, cf. 101.

fluminum'.[1] It was intended, he argues, that the army should leave the Postumia, and, by cutting or threatening the Vitellian communications with Ticinum and Mediolanium (Brixia is unimportant) force a battle speedily—but not on the day on which the battle actually occurred. One night's camp at least would intervene, it being necessary to have the troops fresh for the attack.

It is a signal merit of Passerini's study that he goes into the question of numbers thoroughly, building up the Othonian forces so as to offer some prospect of success in a pitched battle (cf. App. 31). A difficulty remains—the flank movement of an army with baggage across country intersected by rivulets, ditches, clumps of trees, and vineyards. Compare what is said about the terrain on the northern fringe of the Postumia—'per locos arboribus ac vineis impeditos' (II. 42. 2). On the other side, towards the Po, there was open country—'patenti campo' (II. 43. 1), where some stiff fighting ensued.

Other scholars, perplexed by the mention of the Adua, deduce the strategic plan (so far as there was one) from the actual site of the battle—astride the Via Postumia, perhaps three or four miles short of Cremona, and between the Postumia and the Po. It is an advantage of this view that it brings in the Othonian troops south of the Po. In fact the gladiators crossed in boats, but were defeated, and the victors thereupon attacked and enveloped the left flank of the Othonian line of battle (II. 43. 2).

Hardy discovered a small river, the modern Adra, which runs into the Po a few miles below Cremona, from the southern (i.e. right) bank;[2] and under the form 'Ardae' this stream has crept into the Oxford text of the *Historiae* (C. D. Fisher, 1911). The device will not serve. The Adra is inadmissible as the goal of an army marching on the opposite (i.e. left) bank of the Po. (Similarly, the battle named after the Allia: it must have been fought on that side of the Tiber where the Allia joined the Tiber, i.e. the left bank.)

An extreme remedy is to change, not the text of Tacitus, but the hydrography of the region: the Adua in antiquity might have joined the Po a few miles below Cremona, not seven miles above that city. This explanation has not lacked supporters.[3] No proof is available. The puzzle remains.

31. THE OTHONIAN STRENGTH AT BEDRIACUM

BOTH Annius Gallus and the Emperor took troops from Rome to the North (*Hist.* II. 11).[4] Annius had the legion I Adiutrix, five cohorts of the Guard, and two thousand gladiators; with the Emperor went 'speculatorum lecta corpora cum ceteris praetoriis cohortibus, veterani e praetorio, classicorum ingens

---

[1] A. Passerini, o.c. 228 ff. [2] E. G. Hardy, o.c. 139.

[3] G. Niccolini, *Rend. Acc. Lincei* xv (1906), 278 ff.; A. Momigliano, o.c. 139 f. Against, A. Passerini, o.c. 220.

[4] Neglected by many scholars, the problem of the Othonian forces has been discussed at some length by A. Passerini, o.c. 200 ff., and by Ph. Fabia, *Rev. ét. anc.* XLIII (1941), 192 ff.

numerus'. The Guard at this time numbered twelve cohorts, each possibly with a nominal strength of a thousand; and there were four urban cohorts, also another at Ostia (I. 80. I). The unknown factor is the size of the fleet expedition—'addidit classi urbanas cohortis et plerosque e praetorianis, viris et robur exercitus atque ipsis ducibus consilium et custodes' (I. 87. I). If it were legitimate to argue from the actual operations and from the size of the column sent against this force by Fabius Valens (II. 14. I), the Praetorian contribution need not have been very large.

Next, the marines. The 'ingens numerus' is explained away by Passerini,[1] who assumes that they are mainly accounted for by the thousand who were taken prisoner between Ticinum and Placentia (II. 17. 2). That episode, however, occurred early in the campaign, before Otho went north. It could be assumed that the 'classici' amounted at the very least to the total of a legion. Such a legion, indeed, was in process of formation, cf. I. 87. I: 'reliquos caesorum ad pontem Mulvium et saevitia Galbae in custodia habitos in numeros legionis composuerat, facta et ceteris spe honoratae in posterum militiae'. This rudimentary Othonian legion (neglected in modern calculations) is clearly different from I Adiutrix (I. 6. 2; 31. 3; 36. 3; II. 11. 2, &c.).

The two Italian fleets were lavishly manned (cf. for Ravenna, III. 50), and Otho could have drawn upon Ravenna as well as Misenum. Finally, one notes the detachments from the Danubian armies present at Rome in January, originally summoned by Nero (I. 6. 2; 26. 1; 31). All in all, Praetorians (perhaps ten cohorts), I Adiutrix, marines, and oddments, the total perhaps approached twenty thousand.

Otho had summoned forces from the armies of Moesia, Dalmatia, and Pannonia. The *auxilia* marched ahead of the legions, and a number of regiments should be allowed for at Bedriacum.[2] An otherwise unattested incident is noted later in a speech by Antonius Primus—'duae tunc Pannonicae ac Moesicae alae perrupere hostem' (III. 2. 4). As for legions, there were three in Moesia: III Gallica, VII Claudia, VIII Augusta. Two of them would have had a long distance to come, being stationed in what was later Lower Moesia.[3] As it happened, the Moesian *vexillationes* were still far away, on the other side of Aquileia (II. 85. 1, cf. Suetonius, *Divus Vesp.* 6. 2).[4]

There were four legions in Pannonia and Dalmatia, on the march, and each preceded by a *vexillatio* of two thousand men. A detachment of XIII Gemina, which came from the nearest garrison (Poetovio in Pannonia), fought in the engagement at Ad Castores, while the whole legion under its legate (Vedius Aquila) was present at the Battle of Bedriacum (II. 24. 3; 43 f.). Also at Bedriacum was a part of XIV Gemina (II. 43. 2, cf. 66. 1)—the main bulk of it was alleged to be not far behind (II. 32. 2, cf. 54. 1). Its provenance is not attested—probably Pannonia.[5] It had been withdrawn from Britain by Nero for his eastern expedition,

---

[1] o.c. 192.
[2] As properly emphasized by Passerini, o.c. 201 ff.
[3] E. Ritterling, P–W XII, 1521; 1649 (III Gallica and VIII Augusta).
[4] Hence the report of their arrival at Aquileia, brought to Otho at Brixellum the day after the battle (II. 46. 3), was false.
[5] R. Syme, *AJP* LVIII (1937), 11 (discussing Nero's muster). Most scholars prefer Dalmatia, cf. E. Ritterling, P–W XII, 1732.

and was in northern Italy along with other troops at the time of Nero's fall (II. 27. 2).

As for the Seventh Legion (recently enrolled by Galba in Spain) it later emerges that the legate at least, the redoubtable Antonius Primus, was of no service to Otho in the war (II. 86. 2). This legion was at Carnuntum, in Pannonia. Finally, XI Claudia, stationed at Burnum in Dalmatia.

All four are reported in northern Italy after the battle (II. 66 f.). Perhaps portions of legions VII and XI should be added to the Othonian total at Bedriacum. Some, indeed, argue for their presence in full strength, giving Otho three whole legions (VII, XI, XIII), and a detachment of the other (XIV).[1]

About the three legions of Moesia Tacitus confines himself to reporting argument or rumour (II. 32. 2; 44. 3; 46. 3). They were too far away to matter. Very different the four legions of Pannonia and Dalmatia. To understand both the strategy and the action one would need to know if they were present at the battle, or could have been counted on in a few days.

32. MARIUS CELSUS

MARIUS CELSUS, consul designate in 69, comes early into the narrative. He is present at Galba's council (I. 14. 1), goes to reason with a detachment of Danubian troops at the Porticus Vipsania, but in vain (31; 39. 1), incurs danger from the soldiery after the killing of Galba but is protected by being taken into custody (45. 2), and is later liberated by Otho, welcomed and enrolled among his closest friends—'clementiae titulus e viro claro et partibus inviso petebatur' (71. 1).

Celsus is appointed as one of the generals (87. 2; 90. 2; II. 23. 4); he earns credit at the engagement at Ad Castores (II. 24 f.), is present at the council of war, supporting the opinion of Suetonius Paullinus (33), with whom he is named as being no longer valued, in contrast to Licinius Proculus and Salvius Titianus (39. 1: 'inani nomine ducum alienae culpae praetendebantur'); and, like Paullinus, he protests, before the second day's march, against those generals for insisting on an advance (40). Celsus makes his way to Bedriacum after the defeat (44. 2), but is not named at all in the discussions there, or at the capitulation. Subsequently Celsus is allowed to hold his consulship, despite the machinations of a certain Caecilius Simplex, which in fact were exposed in the Senate—'sed creditum fama obiectumque mox in senatu Caecilio Simplici, quod eum honorem pecunia mercari, nec sine exitio Celsi, voluisset' (60. 2: not perhaps a detail likely to come from the *acta senatus*).

Celsus is treated throughout in a favourable and friendly way. The character and role of the honest man (if he could be found) in a civil war, was attractive to Tacitus—'mansitque Celso velut fataliter etiam pro Othone fides integra et infelix' (I. 71. 2).

Celsus is likewise prominent in the narrative of Plutarch and notably in the

---

[1] A. Passerini, o.c. 205 ff.; Ph. Fabia, *Rev. ét. anc.* XLIII (1941), 203, cf. 214.

full and clear story of what happened at Bedriacum after the defeat. The summary account of Tacitus (II. 45) reports the gist of what Annius Gallus then said to pacify the troops. No word or action, however, of Marius Celsus. Plutarch has a speech addressed to the commanders, recalling earlier civil wars and urging a cessation of hostilities. Whereupon the sentiments of the troops are sounded; Celsus and Gallus (it is decided) shall go as envoys to the Vitellian generals, and, after some vicissitudes (Celsus' life being endangered, and Salvius Titianus momentarily changing his mind), the capitulation ensues.

Tacitus preferred to concentrate the interest upon Otho, his oration and his suicide (II. 46–9). In Plutarch Celsus argued for surrender, ὡς ἐπὶ συμφορᾷ τηλικαύτῃ καὶ φόνῳ τοσούτῳ πολιτῶν μήδ᾽ Ὄθωνος, εἴπερ ἀνὴρ ἀγαθός ἐστιν, ἐθελήσοντος ἔτι πειρᾶσθαι τῆς τύχης (*Otho* 13). Tacitus puts that argument in Otho's own mouth (II. 47).

It is reasonable to claim Marius Celsus as one of the sources of information drawn upon by the common source of Tacitus and Plutarch. Similarly, Vestricius Spurinna, given the full account both writers preserve of his actions at Placentia. There could also have been a written narration by Marius Celsus: he had been close to the action, both political and military.

What else can be known about this person (*PIR*[1], M 223)? He brought the legion XV Apollinaris from Pannonia to join Corbulo in 63 (*Ann.* xv. 25. 3). He should therefore be identified with that Κέλσος ὁ Ῥωμαῖος τακτικός who stated the best way of dealing with the Parthians, and alluded to Corbulo (Lydus, *De mag.* III. 33). After 63 there is no trace of this man till 69—and nothing after 69. Yet he may well be the Marius Celsus attested as legate of Syria in 72/3 (*ILS* 8903: south of Samosata), despite Dessau, who decides for P. Marius Celsus (*PIR*[1], M 224), *cos.* 62, *curator aquarum* 64–66 (the articles in P–W xiv, 1823 f. may be neglected).

These people might be provincial, from Narbonensis. Observe a C. Marius Celsus, municipal magistrate at Nemausus in the early Principate (*ILS* 6977). Celsus' colleague in the consulship in 69 was Arrius Antoninus (*Hist.* I. 77. 2). Tacitus, who has just commented on the consulship of L. Pompeius Vopiscus ('plerique Viennensium honori datum interpretabantur'), does not annotate the pair. No fact attests what most scholars assume, a Narbonensian origin for Arrius Antoninus, *cos. II* and familiar to Tacitus and his readers. Perhaps from Nemausus (p. 605). As for Celsus, relationship with a family of new Romans is attested by the nomenclature of a senator prominent in the early years of Trajan, Ti. Julius Candidus Marius Celsus (*PIR*[1], J 164), *suff.* 86, *II ord.* 105: possibly, as Groag suggests (P–W x, 541), *praefectus urbi*.

33. CORNELIUS FUSCUS

INTRODUCING Antonius Primus with a vigorous and lurid character-sketch and summarily noting the consular legates of Pannonia and Dalmatia, 'divites senes', Tacitus brings on Cornelius Fuscus (II. 86. 3)—'sed procurator aderat Cornelius

Fuscus vigens aetate, claris natalibus. prima iuventa quietis cupidine senatorium ordinem exuerat; idem pro Galba dux coloniae suae, eaque opera procurationem adeptus, susceptis Vespasiani partibus acerrimam bello facem praetulit: non tam praemiis periculorum quam ipsis periculis laetus pro certis et olim partis nova ambigua ancipitia malebat.'[1]

The presentation seems amicable, and no act or motive is subsequently alleged to the discredit of Cornelius Fuscus. For a partisan in a civil war where only Vipstanus Messalla (the friend of Tacitus) contributed 'bonae artes' (III. 9. 3), the phrase 'nova ambigua ancipitia malebat' is the mildest of censures. Tacitus (it may be assumed) knew this man, and did not dislike him.

Fuscus was to have a place later in the *Historiae* as commander of the Guard (as early as 83, cf. Juvenal IV. 111 f.) and leader of a Roman army with which he perished in Dacia in 86 or 87 (cf. especially Orosius VII. 10. 4, citing Tacitus). His rashness proved his ruin, cf. *Agr.* 41. 2; 'temeritate aut per ignaviam ducum.'

Tacitus knew, but does not name, the 'colonia' of Cornelius Fuscus. Perhaps he was reserving it for the obituary notice—yet enough is said here to render such a notice superfluous (compare the case of L. Vitellius, who is accorded no necrology since he had been characterized in *Ann.* VI. 32. 4). A vexatious problem remains. A Roman colony is required, the allegiance of which was important for Galba at the time of his proclamation, or later, during the interval of uncertainty before he was recognized by the Rhine armies. Cichorius, identifying as Fuscus the unnamed *praefectus* of the Altar at Adamclisi in the Dobrudja (*ILS* 9107), proposed Pompeii; Domaszewski, however, Vienna.[2] Now Pompeii is ruled out, a mere 'Ulubrae', whereas Vienna, being already strong for Vindex, so at least it is alleged (I. 65. 2), did not have to be won over to the cause of his ally Galba. Both Spain and northern Italy could be admitted as well as Narbonensis—and especially northern Italy because of the troops mustered there by Nero for the war against Galba. Hence a suggestion that one of the colonies on the great roads was the colony of Fuscus—perhaps Aquileia.[3]

Somebody ought to have thought of a place on the high road to Spain, or on the coast of Gallia Narbonensis: Baeterrae, Narbo, or Arelate,[4] or better, Forum Julii. The place must have been important in the war (however abortive that war) between Nero and Galba, as in Otho's war the year after (see App. 30). Fuscus as a Cornelius of senatorial family from Forum Julii might open various entertaining perspectives (see Ch. XLV).

---

[1] Some scholars have been unnecessarily puzzled by 'quietis cupidine'. Hence 'quaestus' (Grotius, favoured by A. Stein in *PIR²*, C 1365) or 'inquies cupidine' (Meiser). It is enough to mention Pliny, *Epp.* I. 14. 5 ('honesta quies').

[2] C. Cichorius, *Die r. Denkmäler in der Dobrudscha* (1904), 21; A. v. Domaszewski, *Rh. Mus.* LX (1905), 158 f. Also, for Pompeii, J. Colin, *Latomus* XV (1956), 57 ff.

[3] R. Syme, *AJP* LVIII (1937), 13 f. The case for Aquileia itself was not there strongly pressed, the argument being designed to disprove the thesis of Cichorius, cf. ib. 18: 'Vienna, Corduba or Aquileia; anywhere but Pompeii.'

[4] Baeterrae, a *colonia*, happens to show a 'C. Cor. Fu[scus]' (*CIL* XII, 4267, described as 'optimis litteris saeculi primi'). Not, however, a person of any consequence.

34. LIVIAN STYLE IN THE *HISTORIAE*

THE influence of Livy upon the language of Tacitus was the subject of a detailed study, the results of which do not seem to have become common knowledge.[1] However, a whole episode or an oration will reveal more than any collection of words and phrases. One of the most splendid of Livy's products is the speech of Scipio to the mutinous troops (XXVIII. 27–29)—and indeed the theme of the young military leader quelling the soldiery possessed a certain contemporary relevance.[2]

Tacitus knows the speech, and puts it to use more than once.[3] Above all in the appeal of Dillius Vocula when deserted by his army (*Hist.* IV. 58). Dillius is eloquent and impassioned, he uses rhetorical questions and ample phraseology, with frequent resort to pairs of nouns and verbs. The peroration deserves to be quoted—'te, Iuppiter optime maxime, quem per octingentos viginti annos tot triumphis coluimus, te, Quirine, Romanae parens urbis, precor venerorque ut, si vobis non fuit cordi me duce haec castra incorrupta et intemerata servari, at certe pollui foedarique a Tutore et Classico ne sinatis, militibus Romanis aut innocentiam detis aut maturam et sine noxa paenitentiam'.

The invocation of the gods of Rome lacks parallel in Tacitean orations. A solemn archaic phrase would not be out of place, cf. Scipio in Livy, 'ne istuc Iuppiter optimus maximus sirit' (XXVIII. 28. 11). Tacitus has 'si vobis non fuit cordi', a phrase from the speech in Livy just after the capitulation of the Caudine Forks (IX. 8. 8). The word 'cordi' had passed out of normal prose usage. The only other occurrences in Tacitus are therefore notable, suggesting pomp with an ironical hint, namely, when Mucianus makes a statement, 'sibi salutem securitatemque Italiae cordi fuisse' (III. 53. 3), and when the doctors at Alexandria give an opinion, 'id fortasse cordi deis' (IV. 81. 2).

Again, when Vocula asks 'etiam vetera exempla deficiunt, quotiens Romanae legiones perire praeoptaverint ne loco pellerentur?' (IV. 58. 2). The verb 'praeopto', not elsewhere admitted by Tacitus, occurs a number of times in Livy (it is not Ciceronian).

A dramatic or rhetorical turn may decline into a conventional formula. Thus 'horret animus' which Dillius is allowed to use, just before the peroration—and which is found in Scipio's speech (XXVIII. 29. 4).[4] Otherwise Tacitus bans the formula. Note also that the histrionic (and hypocritical) Otho exclaims 'horror animum subit' (I. 37. 3): the word 'horror' occurs nowhere else in Tacitus.

Tacitus' evocation of Livy is very skilful, and, were not the theme most

---

[1] G. Andresen, *Wochenschr. für cl. Phil.* 1916, 210 ff.; 401 ff.; 688 ff.; 758 ff. The second of these articles is devoted to the *Historiae*. See also G. B. A. Fletcher, *CR* LIX (1945), 45 ff. (for the *Historiae*, 47 ff.).

[2] *Ann.* I. 42. 3: 'divus Augustus vultu et aspectu Actiacas legiones exterruit.'

[3] The exordium of Scipio's speech, namely a military man's disclaimer of eloquence, is employed for Petillius Cerialis (IV. 73. 1); and Scipio's opening objurgation of the soldiers will be reproduced in Germanicus' address to the mutineers on the Rhine (*Ann.* I. 42). See App. 54.

[4] For the formula cf. *TLL*, 'horreo', II B, 1 b. Observe Livy II. 37. 6; Seneca, *Ag.* 5; Quintus Curtius IX. 6. 12; Lactantius, *Div. Inst.* VII. 15. 11.

solemn, might appear to verge upon parody. After the doom of Dillius Vocula follows the capitulation of the Roman garrison at Vetera (IV. 62), suggesting to any Roman an inevitable precedent (Livy IX. 5 ff.). There are many resemblances in word and phrase and tone. Two may suffice as examples. After grim thought, the soldiers receive the enemy's order to leave their camp, IV. 62. 2: 'haec meditantibus advenit proficiscendi hora exspectatione tristior'; Livy IX. 5. 11: 'haec frementibus hora fatalis ignominiae advenit, omnia tristiora experiundo factura quam quae praeceperant animis.' They go out in silence: 'silens agmen et velut longae exsequiae'; Livy IX. 6. 11: 'silens ac prope mutum agmen.' Finally, for the deep shame of the legionaries later at the town of the Treveri (IV. 72), compare Livy IX. 7. 2 ff.

35. THE TOTAL OF BOOKS

THE total being recorded as thirty books,[1] how do they divide? Wölfflin insisted that there ought to have been twelve in the one work, eighteen in the other.[2] A structure in hexads can be supported by the analogy of Roman epic and historical poetry. Thus the *Annales* of Ennius, or, no less relevant to Tacitus, the *Aeneid*.[3]

If that is so, how were the twelve books of the *Historiae* apportioned? Wölfflin was not certain whether the first hexad should end with Vespasian, or embrace Vespasian and Titus. Hence Domitian would have either six books or five. Some scholars have opted for the first alternative.[4] For vague reasons, or inadequate. The surviving evidence (it is asserted) shows that very little happened between 71 and 81, therefore that decade could have been polished off in a single book.[5] Such a notion does little justice to the design, and to the resources, of Cornelius Tacitus. The second alternative is preferable, Book VII for Titus, Books VIII–XII for Domitian (Ch. XVIII).

Not all scholars have been prepared to concede the hexadic structure and the twelve books; and standard works of reference are found to affirm that fourteen is the probable or generally accepted total for the *Historiae*.[6] For the most part, assertion has sufficed. There have been few attempts to apply the theory. One of them stands condemned by its anomalous distribution, three books (VII–IX) for the years 71–79, one for the reign of Titus—and only four (XI–XIV) for the fifteen years of Domitian.[7] On the other hand, assuming the total of twelve, the five books for Domitian fit the proportions of the whole work—and the different phases and crises of that reign (Ch. XVIII).

[1] Jerome, *Comm. ad Zach.* III. 14, cited above, p. 211.
[2] H. Ritter in his edition of the *Annales* (Cambridge, 1848) I, xxii ff.; E. Wölfflin, *Hermes* XXI (1886), 157 f.
[3] cf. H. Oppermann, who argues for twelve books down to 197 B.C. as the original design of Ennius (*Gymnasium* LXI (1954), 531 ff).
[4] S. Hammer, *Eos* XXXII (1927), 545 ff.; W. Weber, *Princeps* I (1936), 20*.
[5] W. Weber, o.c. 20*: 'die erhaltene Überlieferung zeigt', &c.
[6] Schwabe, P–W IV, 1576; Schanz–Hosius, *Gesch. der r. Lit.* II⁴ (1935), 625. Cf. also R. Reitzenstein, *Gött. gel. Nachr.* 1914, 250; O. Seel, *R. Denker u. r. Staat* (1937), 48 ff.; C. Marchesi, *Tacito*³ (1944), 297; E. Paratore, *Tacito* (1951), 439 f.
[7] F. G. Moore, *TAPA* LIV (1923), 5 ff.

Further, there is a corollary, and very painful: sixteen books for the *Annales*. The events from the suicide of Thrasea Paetus in 66 (*Ann.* XVI. 35) to the end of Nero's reign would have to be confined and terminated in Book XVI. Those events were considerable—in themselves, for Tacitus, and for the structure. To say nothing of what happened at Rome, there is the Jewish revolt, the tour in Hellas, and the risings in the West: pageantry, tumult, and doom.[1] There is no way out, unless one ignores the history of 66-68.[2] The mere total of years in a reign is no clue to proportions;[3] and it does not help to suppose that Tacitus, being an old man, was in a hurry, and so compressed his finale.[4] There are no signs of compression in what survives of Book XVI.

Tacitus cannot have intended to finish off Nero in Book XVI. It would be better to suppose that death or collapse prevented him from carrying the third hexad to its foreseen conclusion (hence fourteen books for the *Historiae*, not twelve). Various and converging indications could be invoked. There is his change in style—which, however, admits other explanations (Ch. XXVII). But there are signs of weakness in the style towards the end (App. 59). Also odd phenomena that could be brought into relation: an incoherence, a promise unfulfilled, a weak suture, a provisional nexus, a speech in full perfection but the context not properly worked up. These clues might lead a long way (App. 60)— but not perhaps enough to prove that the author himself was arrested at XVI. 35.

So far the arguments from structure, proportion, and material. There is another approach. The scribe who wrote *Codex Mediceus* (*Ann.* I-VI) took the words 'ab excessu divi Augusti' to be a part of the text, not the title. Why was this? It has been suggested that the phrase represents a sub-title in the 'hyparchetype'.[5] That is to say, what posterity calls the *Annales* was only a part of one work, i.e. the thirty books attested by Jerome, *Comm. ad Zach.* III. 14. Further, there is evidence for such a 'consolidated edition'. The *Codex Mediceus II* (*Ann.* XI-XII and *Hist.* I-V) numbers the books continuously: thus *Hist.* II is labelled 'liber octavus decim.' This arrangement (it is argued) presumably goes back to an ancient edition, which contained no book of the *Annales* beyond XVI. On that showing, Tacitus did not complete his last work.[6]

How old was that edition, and (supposing 'ab excessu divi Augusti' to be the sub-title of the one part), what was it called? The author of the theory here summarized suggests that it may derive from the third century.[7] The next step is slippery. He invokes the *Historia Augusta* and the beneficent activities of the Emperor Claudius Tacitus. That is fable.[8]

---

[1] p. 264. Cf. Ph. Fabia, *Rev. ét. anc.* XXXIV (1932), 139. Whether Tacitus be supposed to terminate with Nero's death, with the proclamation of Nymphidius, or with the end of 68, is here irrelevant.　　　　　　　　　　　　[2] As O. Seel, o.c. 49.

[3] Thus four books for Nero because four for Claudius, the two reigns being of equal length (E. Paratore, o.c. 440).

[4] Schwabe describes this as 'psychologisch wahrscheinlicher' (P-W IV, 1577).

[5] R. P. Oliver, *TAPA* LXXXII (1951), 232 ff., at 258.

[6] o.c. 259.　　　　　　　　　　　　　　　　　[7] o.c. 260 f.

[8] *HA, Tacitus* 10. 3 (paraphrased above, p. 59). Oliver objects to Hohl's judgement on this passage (*Hermes* LV (1920), 300 f.) as 'quite gratuitous scepticism.' On the value of *HA* see App. 88.

E. THE SOURCES OF THE *ANNALES*

36. TACITUS AND DIO

THE death of Augustus and the accession of Tiberius are related by Tacitus (*Ann.* I. 4–15) and by Cassius Dio (LVI. 30. I–LVII. 3. 4, here the entire Dio except for one short passage). With the two historians goes Suetonius (*Tib.* 21–25). The evidence is precious. It has been frequently and fully discussed.[1]

What stands out at first sight is the divergence of the three writers. Each follows his own path in choice or in omission of facts, in arrangement, and in emphasis. Hence valid conclusions about their methods, their aims, and their quality. Tacitus comes off best. There is far too much innuendo, it is true; and two of his digressions, namely, Augustus' alleged visit to Agrippa Postumus on the island (I. 5. I f.) and the anecdote about the 'capaces imperii' (I. 13. 2 f.) deserve stern censure (cf. App. 37). None the less, Tacitus sets out events in their true order. He distinguishes sharply between the two sessions of the Senate, that which decided about the ceremony of the funeral (I. 8), and that which voted the consecration and discussed the position of the new ruler (I. 10. 8–15. 3). Furthermore, there is welcome authentication by names, three eminent senators coming forward in the discussion about the funeral honours, four intervening at the second session. Finally, Tacitus' account permits it to be affirmed that the position of the new ruler was regulated (or recognized) in some way or other at the second session, although he is imprecise (perhaps wilfully so).

Suetonius in this part of the biography keeps surprisingly clear of scandal and rumour. Not a word about the journey to Planasia; and it is a fact for him that Augustus was still alive when Tiberius, summoned in haste, came to Nola (21. 1). Suetonius can adduce valuable details like the opening phrase of Augustus' testament (23); he states that Tiberius after hesitations and debate finally 'recepit imperium'—not that he tells in what that consisted; and he then cites the words of Tiberius—'dum veniam ad id tempus quo vobis possit aequum videri dare vos aliquam senectuti meae requiem' (24. 2). Suetonius, however, lapses badly at the end. He assigns reasons for the hesitations of Tiberius, namely various dangers: the false Agrippa (the slave called Clemens), the secret plotting of Libo Drusus, the mutinies on the Rhine and in Pannonia (25. 1).[2]

Dio is careless in small matters as in great. He retails the journey to Planasia as a fact (LVI. 30. 1). More serious, he believes that Augustus left four state papers, all of which were duly read out by Drusus the son of Tiberius at the first meeting

---

[1] e.g. by Ph. Fabia, *Rev. phil.* XXXIII (1909), 28 ff.; F. B. Marsh, *The Reign of Tiberius* (1931), 272 ff.; W. Weber, *Princeps* I (1936), *passim*.

[2] Note also that in Tacitus (I. 35. 3) the soldiers' offer of the power to Germanicus arises only late and accidentally: by contrast, Suetonius, *Tib.* 25. 1; *Cal.* I. 1; Dio LVII. 5. 1.

of the Senate, before the funeral (LVI. 32. I ff.). There were only three, viz. the 'mandata de funere suo', the 'index rerum a se gestarum', and the 'breviarium totius imperii' (Suetonius, *Divus Aug.* 101. 4). The third paper was produced by Tiberius during the debate at the second meeting (*Ann.* I. 11. 3 f.). Subjoined to it were certain 'consilia' of Augustus: that is, what Dio takes to be a separate, and fourth, document.[1]

Again, Dio invokes the mutinies as an explanation of Tiberius' behaviour. He serves up a trivial motive—Tiberius hoped that, being a private citizen and not emperor, he might still survive if the insurrection succeeded (LVII. 3. 2). Further, Tiberius did not frankly and explicitly accept the power until the disturbances had abated (7. 1).

Dio, like Suetonius, may have been misled by the (necessary) interval elapsing between the death of Augustus (August 19) and the consecration (September 17), as certified by the *Fasti Amiternini, CIL* I², p. 244), and induced to overestimate and prolong the hesitations of Tiberius. His version has led a number of modern inquirers along strange paths, assuming that Tiberius delayed his acceptance of the power until late September or early October.[2] Yet it should be clear that the 'constitutional' question was settled at the debate which ensued immediately on the consecration—and at which *imperium proconsulare* was conferred on Germanicus. Drusus was present at that debate (*Ann.* I. 14. 3). The mutiny was still raging at the summer camp of the Pannonian legions when he arrived, the day before the eclipse (which fell on September 27).

Some of the clear or important variants have now been registered. Next, the resemblances, which have been variously appraised. What is the relationship between the three writers?

Suetonius would not fail to read the work of the consular historian—if it was available (see App. 77).[3] How far he put it to use is another matter. Not much, it seems, if at all. His purpose was different—rather to supplement Tacitus. And emulation might even be surmised (cf. p. 502). In support will be adduced his treatment of the year 69: the search for traces of the *Historiae* in the biographies of Galba, Otho, and Vitellius yields nothing, or next to nothing. As for the chapters of his *Tiberius* here relevant (21–25), one might be tempted to discover, in one particular, covert criticism of the great man. Tacitus allows the 'prudentes' at the funeral to assign a sinister motive for Augustus' adoption of Tiberius—'comparatione deterrima sibi gloriam quaesivisse' (I. 10. 7). Suetonius notes this—'ne illud quidem ignoro, aliquos tradidisse', &c. (21. 2). He enters firm protest—'adduci tamen nequeo quin existimem circumspectissimum et prudentissimum principem, in tanto praesertim negotio, nihil temere fecisse'— and he goes on to quote at some length from Augustus' letters to Tiberius.

---

[1] W. Weber argued that it is in fact a separate document (o.c. 67 ff.). Against, E. Hohl, *Klio* xxx (1937), 323 ff.

[2] e.g. A. Lang, *Beiträge zur Geschichte des Kaisers Tiberius* (Diss. Jena, 1911), 11 ff.; M. Gelzer, P-W x, 496; A. v. Premerstein, *Bayerische Abh., phil.-hist. Kl.* 1937, Heft 15, 58; J. Béranger, *Recherches sur l'aspect idéologique du Principat* (1953), 24; F. Klingner, *Bayerische S-B, phil.-hist. Kl.* 1953, Heft 7, 33.

[3] It was probably not.

A sustained critical excursus in Suetonius is most unusual. It will be recalled, however, that Tacitus did not invent the 'comparatio deterrima'. It also occurs in Dio (LVI. 45. 3), presumably independent of Tacitus.

Dio professes great industry (LXXII. 23. 5). It was normal good sense to go first to the writers nearest the events. Not that he would omit to look at Tacitus, sooner or later—perhaps when he had finished Book LVI and was engaged upon the next book, with which the reign of Tiberius begins, opening with the elaborate character-sketch. Dio would have found the early chapters of the *Annales* compressed and enigmatic—and he was interested in the funeral ceremonial and the like (not in Tacitus). To prove (and not merely surmise or assume) that Dio has used Tacitus demands a rigorous method. All resemblances must be ruled out that might derive from common sources. What is needed is the reflection in Dio of some specifically Tacitean digression or comment.

Tacitus interpolates comment between Tiberius' edict (I. 7. 3) and the consequent summoning of the Senate (I. 8. 1). The passage deals with Tiberius' prompt exercise of the military functions of the Principate—it was only when speaking in the Senate that he betrayed hesitation—and notes his fear of Germanicus. It ends with the following two sentences: 'dabat et famae ut vocatus electusque potius a re publica videretur quam per uxorium ambitum et senili adoptione inrepsisse. postea cognitum est ad introspiciendas etiam procerum voluntates inductam dubitationem: nam verba vultus in crimen detorquens recondebat' (I. 7. 7). Whatever be thought of the whole passage, the last two sentences look like the historian's own invention—possibly even an addition to his first draft.[1] Now they turn up in Dio (LVII. 3. 3 f.), blunted and opaque. The entry is prefixed with the words ἤδη μὲν γὰρ ἤκουσα ὅτι. That indicates a subsidiary source—compare a note on Livia, the widow of Drusus, ἤδη δ' ἤκουσα (LVIII. 11. 7).

At the best, Tacitus was only a subsidiary source for Dio. In fact, barely noticed, let alone exploited. A negative test may be applied. Dio recounts Tiberius' suggestion that the supreme power might perhaps be divided, and with it Asinius Gallus' intervention, in a fashion notably divergent from Tacitus.[2] Tacitus subjoined a digression about Augustus' last conversations, concerning the 'capaces imperii' (I. 13. 2 f., cf. p. 380 and App. 37). A theme that might have appealed to Dio, who chronicles Trajan's verdict on the quality of Julius Servianus (LXIX, 17. 3, cf. p. 486). Dio has neglected it.

There is no sign of Dio's having used Suetonius. It follows that the three writers can be treated as virtually independent witnesses. Comparison can therefore be employed to disentangle some strands in the tradition. A passage in Dio's necrological comment on Augustus is instructive (LVI. 44. 2 ff.). Tacitus used the same source, but dispersed the material, in three places, viz. I. 9. 5: 'pauca admodum vi tractata quo ceteris quies esset'; 2. 1: 'cum ferocissimi per

---

[1] See further App. 37.

[2] According to Dio, τρία μέρη were named by Tiberius, viz. ἐν μὲν ᾗ τε Ῥώμη καὶ ἡ ἄλλη Ἰταλία, ἕτερον δὲ τὰ στρατόπεδα, καὶ ἕτερον οἱ λοιποὶ ὑπήκοοι (LVII. 2. 5 f.). This is different from Tacitus (who implies partnership rather than division) and looks anachronistic. Cf. E. Hohl, *Hermes* LXVIII (1933), 113. But Dio (with ἐς μηδένα ἕνα ἀναρτᾶν αὐτά) reflects the original of 'non ad unum omnia deferrent' (I. 11. 1), cf. F. Klingner, o.c. 28 f.

acies aut proscriptione cecidissent, ceteri nobilium', &c.; 3. 7: 'quotus quisque reliquus qui rem publicam vidisset'.

Arguing from Dio's 'necrology' and from his character-sketch of Tiberius (LVII. 1), Eduard Schwartz produced his famous theory—the single unknown annalist who formed and dominated the historical tradition about Tiberius.[1] Some scholars have given enthusiastic support, or even provided a name.[2] There are strong reasons against so simple a view (p. 273).

Not all have been willing to concede that Dio is reproducing writers earlier than Tacitus. It has been pertinaciously contended that Tacitus created the conception of Tiberius that is to be found in Dio.[3] That theory in its turn is vulnerable. It must force the resemblances between Tacitus and Dio;[4] it neglects the plain evidence about common sources;[5] and it fails to allow for the testimony of Suetonius (who is not dependent on Tacitus).[6]

In other portions the divergences between the two writers can be remarkable. Tacitus sets down in order the urban events of the year 15 (*Ann.* I. 72–81). The last three items (79–81) are the discussion about the flooding of the Tiber, the provinces assigned to Poppaeus Sabinus (with comments), the consular elections (likewise with comments). Dio devotes one section only to the whole year (LVII. 14). At first sight one would hardly suspect that the same year is being chronicled. For example, not a word in Dio about certain (abortive) prosecutions for *maiestas*, which Tacitus singles out. Along with other material, mainly about Drusus, Dio has two items about provinces (not in Tacitus anywhere). Further, a patent discrepancy that may prove profitable. According to Tacitus, the motion of Piso being adopted, nothing was done about the Tiber. Dio, however, reports the institution of a board of five senators. What is the solution? Tacitus here follows the *acta*. The *curatores* of the Tiber were not established in 15, but soon after. Dio follows an historian who wound up the matter of the Tiber by recording what was done subsequently.[7]

Comparison is also available for the last years of the reign.[8] Early in the year 32 Tacitus notes and describes fully the proposals made in the Senate by Togonius Gallus and by Junius Gallio (VI. 2 f.). Dio has these items (omitting the former name). His account (LVIII. 17. 3–18. 4) looks like a blurred summary of Tacitus. A little later Tacitus has the oration of the Roman knight M. Terentius (VI. 8). He seems to be presenting it as a product of his own researches ('nobis

---

[1] P–W III, 1716 f.

[2] Thus, acclaiming Aufidius Bassus, F. A. Marx, *Klio* XXIX (1936), 99. Fabia had asserted that Aufidius was the main (and almost the sole) source of Tacitus down to XII. 24.

[3] D. M. Pippidi, *Ephemeris Dacoromana* VIII (1938), 280 ff. = *Autour de Tibère* (1944), 77 ff.

[4] As does J. Bergmans, *Die Quellen der Vita Tiberii (Buch 57 der Historia Romana) des Cassius Dio* (Diss. Heidelberg, Amsterdam 1903), to whom Pippidi appeals.

[5] Pippidi omits to take into account the fact that comments occurring together in Dio LVI. 44. 2 ff. are dispersed in Tacitus.

[6] cf. J. P. V. D. Balsdon, *JRS* XXXVI (1946), 168 ff.

[7] Similarly Tacitus omits the transference of Seius Strabo from the Guard to Egypt, in 15 (not of course to be found in the *acta*), whereas Dio knows about it (LVII. 19. 6.).

[8] For concordances, H. Jaeger, *De Cassii Dionis librorum 57. et 58. fontibus* (Diss. Berlin, 1910), 58 ff.

pleraque digna cognitu obvenere', VI. 7. 5), and he proceeds to introduce the episode with the words 'nam ea tempestate'. Dio has a brief version of this speech (LVIII. 19. 3 f.). It is difficult to resist the conclusion that Dio had Book VI before him. Observe further that Tacitus (VI. 20. 2) attaches to Galba's consulate the story of Tiberius' prediction that Galba would one day have the power. Dio also has it, in similar language, but in another part of the reign (LVII. 19. 4). That cannot have come from an historian writing before the fall of Nero, but it does not quite prove that Dio used Tacitus.[1] Finally, Dio has a lot of trivial or anecdotal matter, presumably coming from his principal source (above, p. 318); also dates divergent from Tacitus, e.g. the false Drusus put in 34 (LVIII. 25. 1), the phoenix in 36 (27. 1).

Dio's book on Caligula (LIX) is preserved entire down to the beginning of 40. For Claudius, from 41 to 46, there is Book LX, mutilated at beginning and end; but when the *Annales* resume in 47, Dio is in so fragmentary a condition that inquiry about sources becomes extremely hazardous.[2] Among other things the terminal date of Aufidius Bassus is involved (App. 38). In this situation little of value can be expected to emerge; while for Nero's reign Tacitus and Suetonius, taken with what there is of Dio, show a general concordance, which is clearly due to the use of common sources, but a multitude of variant details.[3] For the Flavian period, however, Tacitus was a primary authority, and must have been used by Dio (p. 215), however faint be the traces.

37. SIGNS OF REVISION IN I–VI

SENTENCE or whole episode, Tacitus has the gift of managing his transitions. A lack of sequence, an imperfect joint, or a disproportionate parenthesis, should therefore excite curiosity. Phenomena of this kind may enable one to divine the intrusion of material from a subsidiary source, or the author's second thoughts, provoked by facts emerging in the course of his operations or even influenced by extraneous events in his own time. The inquiry demands extreme caution and restraint.

First, the inartistic parenthesis. Augustus' health began to fail—'gravescere valetudo Augusti' (*Ann.* I. 5. 1). In a factual narrative the next sentence would be 'vixdum ingressus Illyricum Tiberius properis matris litteris accitur' (3). The author, however, with the words 'et quidam scelus uxoris suspectabant' introduces a digression: Livia found out about the journey Augustus made to Planasia to visit Agrippa Postumus; Fabius Maximus went with him; Fabius told his wife Marcia, she revealed it to Livia, and Marcia, when her husband died,

---

[1] As Fabia suggested, *Les Sources de Tacite dans les* Histoires *et les* Annales (1893), 388.

[2] See the detailed studies of A. Momigliano, *Rendiconti dell' Accademia dei Lincei*[6] VIII (1932), 293 ff.; J. Martin, *Würzburger Studien zur Altertumswissenschaft* IX (1936), 21 ff., with a list of parallels and resemblances right through from A.D. 14 (34 ff.).

[3] They are to be regarded as independent of one another, cf. A. Gercke, *Jahrbücher für cl. Phil.*, Supp.-Band XXII (1896), 159 ff.; K. Heinz, *Das Bild Kaiser Neros bei Seneca, Tacitus, Sueton und Cassius Dio* (Diss. Bern, 1948).

blamed herself as the cause of his decease. This episode, which Tacitus could not resist, does him no credit as an historian. He knows that it is a 'rumor'. Not only does it interrupt the narrative—it disperses the interest by naming two characters, Fabius and his wife, not mentioned hitherto, and not to recur anywhere in the *Annales*.

A subsidiary (and scandalous) source has been woven into the story. It was also used by Dio (or by one of the writers he followed), but in a different fashion, specifying the 'scelus uxoris', that is, poison.[1] Again, the next chapter, concerning the execution of Agrippa Postumus. Tiberius, according to Tacitus, tried to make out that the responsibility went back to Augustus. The next and natural stage in the exposition would be Tiberius' answer to the centurion that he, Tiberius, had not issued the order. The author, however, in between adds his own comment, exculpating Augustus, and blaming, as 'propius vero', Tiberius and Livia (I. 6. 2, from 'multa sine dubio saevaque Augustus' to 'caedem festinavisse').

These two instances show the author's way of working on his source. They could be (but need not be) examples of later revision, later even than the obituary notice of Livia in v. 1; but it is not legitimate to invoke them to support elaborate theories about the influence of contemporary events on the writer (Livia being here incriminated because of another woman, Plotina, cf. p. 482).

A third instance is also instructive. In the record of the year 15 Tacitus has the prosecution of a proconsul—'Granium Marcellum praetorem Bithyniae quaestor ipsius Caepio Crispinus maiestatis postulavit, subscribente Roman⟨i⟩o Hispone, qui formam vitae iniit', &c. (I. 74. 1).[2] There follows the highly stylized portrait of a 'delator'. To whom does the relative clause (introducing a long parenthesis) refer? At first sight, to Romanius Hispo, one might think.[3] Caepio Crispinus happens not to be otherwise attested, whereas Romanius is named frequently by the elder Seneca, as notable and notorious.[4] He was a savage speaker—'erat natura qui asperiorem dicendi viam sequeretur' (*Controv.* IX. 3. 11). Moreover, Caepio Crispinus was a quaestor, whereas the 'delator' here characterized is called 'egens ignotus', and the 'subscriptor' in a prosecution might well be a person of lower status —'venalis adscriptor et subscriptor tuus' (Cicero, *De domo* 48). Finally, why should the 'subscriptor' be named here at all, if not for the character-sketch? However that may be, as one reads on one discovers that the subject of the sketch must be Caepio Crispinus, not Romanius Hispo, for the narration resumes with the words 'sed Marcellum insimulabat' (74. 3), the next sentence thereafter beginning with 'addidit Hispo'. What has happened is clear. Tacitus wished to introduce a 'delator' as soon as possible in the *Annales* (not waiting for Fulcinius Trio),[5] and the name of Caepio Crispinus

---

[1] LVI. 30. 2 f.—the story of the poisoned figs, following the brief statement that Augustus had been to Planasia.

[2] The 'Romanus' of the *Codex Mediceus*, reproduced by all modern editors, should be changed to 'Roman⟨i⟩us'. For that *nomen* cf. *JRS* xxxix (1949), 14 f.

[3] So Furneaux; Ph. Fabia, *Onomasticon Taciteum* (1900); H. Gerth, P-W I A, 1063: on the other side, Nipperdey.

[4] cf. *PIR¹*, R 57.

[5] Brought on the next year as already notorious—'celebre inter accusatores Trionis ingenium erat avidumque famae malae' (II. 28. 3). An important character (later consul), cf. Ch. XXV.

drew him.[1] But, operating on his source (presumably the *acta* as all through from I. 72 to 81), he was not quite skilful enough with the suture.[2]

Another and longer parenthesis has an especial claim for its manifold implications. At the second session of the Senate Asinius Gallus intervened in the debate, angering Tiberius who already had cause to hate him (I. 12. 4, cf. Dio LVII. 2. 5 ff.). He was followed by another consular—'post quae L. Arruntius haud multum discrepans a Galli oratione perinde offendit, quamquam Tiberio nulla vetus in Arruntium ira' (13. 1). The next stage in the discussion brings on two more senators—'etiam Q. Haterius et Mamercus Scaurus suspicacem animum perstrinxere' (13. 4). Observe the connexion of thought, the motive being resentment in Tiberius, with 'ira' leading on to 'suspicacem animum'. In between, however, the historian has interpolated a digression. Attached to the name of Arruntius are the words 'sed divitem promptum artibus egregiis et pari fama publice suspectabat. quippe Augustus supremis sermonibus', &c. (13. 1 f.). There follows the anecdote about Augustus, discussing the quality of certain aristocrats and their claims to the power—M. Lepidus, Asinius Gallus, and L. Arruntius; and a variant is mentioned, not Arruntius but Cn. Piso. All of these men, except Lepidus, adds Tacitus, were in due course to succumb to the machinations of Tiberius.

One thing is clear, the anecdote is not good history, and it does not agree with what subsequently emerges about all of these characters in the *Annales* (p. 381 f.). What is the explanation? It has been suggested that when Tacitus penned these words he had not yet studied the later history of Tiberius' reign;[3] or else the historian simply forgot what he had written, and so was not aware of any inconsistencies.[4]

There may be another reason—a hasty insertion inspired by the accession of Hadrian. A dead emperor's speculations about 'capaces imperii'—and the fate of men thus singled out—had suddenly become an exciting and damaging subject (cf. p. 486). This item is not only bad history: it is clumsy, because it brings in two new and additional names, M. Lepidus and Cn. Piso. Neither took any part in the debate, and there is no annotation to explain their rank and importance. The reader might know about Piso, hardly about Lepidus. That is to say, bad artistry, not to be expected of Cornelius Tacitus —but finding an explanation if the historian had already written the books in which he makes so much of Marcus Lepidus. Where he got the story is irrelevant. Suetonius and Dio ignored it—or rather, missed it.[5]

A Tacitean digression that comes in its proper place, with no disturbance to the narrative, may be found in Book IV. After the death and funeral of Drusus the historian examines and refutes, with careful method, a scandalous legend

---

[1] No doubt because of two consulars in the time of Tacitus (cf. p. 326).

[2] Hence the remedies of some modern scholars—'insimulabant' (Nipperdey); 'insimulabat ⟨Caepio⟩' (F. Ritter, *Rh. Mus.* XVII (1862), 103).

[3] Ph. Fabia, *Les Sources de Tacite dans les Histoires et les Annales* (1893), 428; R. Reitzenstein, *Neue Wege zur Antike* IV (1926), 30.

[4] E. Löfstedt, *JRS* XXXVIII (1948), 6.

[5] For a full discussion of the item see now *JRS* XLV (1955), 22 ff.

still current in his own time (IV. 10 f.). This item encourages one to examine a later passage, where he has not been so skilful. Tiberius leaves Rome—'inter quae diu meditato prolatoque saepius consilio tandem Caesar in Campaniam, specie dedicandi templa apud Capuam Iovi, apud Nolam Augusto, sed certus procul urbe degere' (IV. 57. 1). The next stage in the story of his departure is 'profectio arto comitatu fuit: unus senator consulatu functus Cocceius Nerva, cui legum peritia', &c. (58. 1). The author, however, has chosen to interrupt this sequence. He had assigned Tiberius' departure to the influence of Seianus. That was the opinion of most of the writers: he now wonders whether other reasons were not more potent, notably such as resided in the character of Tiberius himself. Hence a digression, in the middle (IV. 57. 2 f.). Perhaps it would have been better after IV. 58. 1.

The digression throws some light on the author's methods of composition: it does not have to be assumed that it belongs to a second draft, or to a revision (though it might). There is something else, however, in the body of this passage. Tacitus alludes to Tiberius' cruelty and vices—'saevitiam ac libidinem cum factis promeret locis occultantem'. He then goes on to discuss the Emperor's physical decline or repulsiveness—'quippe illi praegracilis et incurva proceritas, nudus capillo vertex, ulcerosa facies ac plerumque medicaminibus interstincta'. Then follows the sentence 'et Rhodi secreto vitare coetus, recondere voluptates insuerat'. The next item refers to the domineering nature of Livia. Something has gone wrong. The allusion to Rhodes and secret pleasures is not in the right place. It ought to come after the first of the sentences quoted above, after 'locis occultantem'.[1] What has happened? Perhaps (it is suggested) the author's order has been disturbed in the transmission of the text.[2] More likely, the author's own marginal addition, inserted not carefully enough.

And why should this be so, why the addition? The reason can be divined. Tacitus began to write the *Annales* without having given deep enough study to the reign of Augustus. Above all, he failed to make proper allowance for the earlier life and vicissitudes of Tiberius. As he went forward, he came to see the significance of that subject—and notably the years of self-willed exile in Rhodes as the origin of enmity or rancour. Thus the ungrateful conduct of Archelaus, the king of Cappadocia (II. 42), or the villainy of M. Lollius, brought up when Tiberius asked the Senate to vote a public funeral for Sulpicius Quirinius (III. 48). Or again, a neutral item—the funeral of Lucilius Longus, the only friend of senatorial station who was with him on the island (IV. 15. 1).

Vice, and secret vice, is a late motive in Tacitus' case against Tiberius (cf. VI. 1, recording abominations on Capreae). Perhaps it was taken from a subsidiary source which he did not light upon until he had written a large part of the first hexad. The retreat to Capreae made the historian look back to the retreat on Rhodes. The past ought to be used to explain the present. Hence the sentence about Rhodes inserted in IV. 57.

Furthermore, discovering this motive, he would wish, for coherence, to establish it somewhere at an early stage in the *Annales*. When Augustus grows old and

---

[1] cf. J. P. V. D. Balsdon, *CR* LXI (1947), 44 f.—who notes that the same idea had also occurred, independently, to H. Cron in 1874 and to K. Zacher in 1883.

[2] ib. 45: 'a sentence which has slipped out of the place where Tacitus wrote it.'

weak, and the end is near, speculation makes play with the next ruler. The pride and cruelty of Tiberius are noted. Then comes 'hunc et prima ab infantia eductum in domo regnatrice: congestos iuveni consulatus triumphos. ne iis quidem annis quibus Rhodi specie secessus exulem egerit aliud quam iram et simulationem et secretas libidines meditatum. accedere matrem muliebri impotentia', &c. (I. 4. 4). Here too can be discerned an interruption in the natural order. Rhodes, the resentment, and the 'secretae libidines' ought to follow the 'superbia' and 'sae-vitia', not the consulates and triumphs. Presumably, therefore, a later addition to fit and corroborate the sentence in IV. 57.

Another, and similar, motive can be detected in the gradual formation of the historian's view about the character of Tiberius, namely, disagreements with his mother. According to Tacitus there were none as late as the year 22, or they were concealed—'sincera adhuc inter matrem filiumque concordia sive occultis odiis' (III. 64. 1). Yet one finds under 15, subjoined to a brief history of 'maiestas', the remark 'hunc quoque asperavere carmina incertis auctoribus vulgata in saevitiam superbiamque eius et discordem cum matre animum' (I. 72. 4). It might be doubted whether these libellous poems are quite so early in date—compare the specimens in Suetonius, *Tib*. 59.

At the least it can be maintained with some confidence that the two sentences about Rhodes and secret vice were inserted by the historian subsequently in their context. They are second thoughts, an effort to make his Tiberius more coherent. The other passage deserving careful scrutiny is the digression about the 'capaces imperii'. Perhaps, but not certainly, motivated by what happened at the time when Tacitus was writing the *Annales*.

Without the art or artifice of an historian, the parallels between Tiberius and Hadrian when they came to the power were close enough, and deadly enough. Were they sharpened by Tacitus, either composing Book I in 117/18, or adding suitable comments to what he had already written? The question is relevant to the date of the *Annales*, but admits no firm and single answer (Ch. xxxvi). It is easy (but it proves nothing) to single out items that appear significant when set against events at the outset of Hadrian's reign. Thus a murder (that of Agrippa Postumus) and the allocation of responsibility (cf. p. 485). None the less, one cannot help wondering about the two consecutive sentences which Cassius Dio did not find in his principal source but took over from Tacitus—the 'senilis adoptio' furthered by a woman's intrigue, and the dissimulation adopted by the new ruler in order to discover what was in the minds of the leading senators, as 'postea cognitum est' (I. 7. 7, whence presumably Dio LVII. 3. 3 f., cf. App. 36).[1] They look like an added comment. Perhaps also, in the same context, 'nusquam cunctabundus nisi cum in senatu loqueretur'. One thinks of Hadrian's plight (p. 484).

The traces of revision touch the date and manner of composition, also (but without deciding it) the question of publication. The first half of the hexad is marked off by the emphatic termination of Book III (Cassius' widow and the

---

[1] Missed by most, if not all, scholars, the sinister relevance of the phrase about 'senilis adoptio' was observed by P. L. Strack, *Untersuchungen zur r. Reichsprägung des zweiten Jahrhunderts* II (1933), 52.

memory of the Republic), by the fresh beginning of Book IV (the ninth year, the turn to despotism, and Seianus). Cross-references sometimes furnish a clue, indicating sections of a work conceived by the author as separate units. Observe, for example, that IV. 21. 1 carries a full, express, and resumptive reference back to the character and actions of L. Piso (the brother of Cn. Piso) related in II. 34. If Books I–III were in fact published separately, later insertions might have been made when Tacitus was writing IV–VI, or after he had completed that instalment. Some of the remarks about Tiberius and about Livia may therefore be posterior to the obituaries on those persons (VI. 51; V. 1)—with which, in fact, they are not in complete harmony.

38. THE HISTORIAN AUFIDIUS BASSUS

IT is reasonable to assume that the monograph, the 'libri belli Germanici' (Quintilian X. 1. 103), came first.[1] It was therefore written during the reign of Tiberius. What was its compass? At the widest, the campaigns that started with Drusus' invasion of Germany in 12 B.C., were prosecuted by Tiberius (8 and 7), and terminated in the victory won by Germanicus in A.D. 16. At the narrowest, the operations of Germanicus only.[2] What arguments avail? In the Augustan books of Livy's history the campaigns of Drusus marked the peak, and the end. No need and no excuse to rewrite that episode so soon after Livy. Nor was the next portion of much profit—after two campaigns Tiberius was not seen again on the Rhine until a decade had elapsed.

If he wished to rival Livy, Aufidius could find a comparable subject, but new, in the exploits of Germanicus. To celebrate Germanicus without Tiberius, however, might not be tactful. The Emperor would have to take the general credit. Better, by starting at A.D. 4 so as to include the campaigns of Tiberius, the writer could exalt his performance in the field and justify one panegyric with another.

The beginning, then, is clear. Also the end. It would be ridiculous to terminate with the last operations of Tiberius in 11 or 12, with Varus and the legions still unavenged.[3] The conclusion of the *Bellum Germanicum* was officially celebrated at the end of 16 when the Senate voted a triumphal arch at Rome 'ob recepta signa cum Varo amissa' (*Ann.* II. 41. 1).

Tone, colour, and tendency are not beyond surmise. The technique employed by Velleius Paterculus to praise the generalship of Tiberius can furnish some hints (p. 274). Also Tacitus on the exploits of Germanicus. Tacitus may well have drawn upon Aufidius. Traces of that writer have also been sought elsewhere, both in Velleius and in Dio—and some claim to have found them.[4] Caution is requisite.

The full-length history is beset with problems. The elder Seneca cites the various 'historici' on the death of Cicero—Livy, Pollio, Aufidius Bassus, Cremutius Cordus, and Bruttedius Niger (*Suas.* VI. 18 ff.). Hence the general

---

[1] cf. Ph. Fabia, *Les Sources de Tacite dans les* Histoires *et les* Annales (1893), 358.
[2] For an anthology of opinions see Schanz–Hosius, *Gesch. der r. Lit.* II⁴ (1935), 645.
[3] As suggested by B. R. Motzo, *Studi Cagliaritani* I (1927), 58 ff.
[4] F. A. Marx, *Klio* XXIX (1936), 202 ff. He affirmed that his result is 'sicher' (ib. 208).

assumption that Aufidius' work began with 44 or 43 B.C. A faint doubt could be expressed. The fate of Cicero was a favoured theme for declaimers, as the copious extracts in Seneca attest. Aufidius might have acquired in the schools of rhetoric the notion of treating the theme in a similar fashion, but historically. Cicero had invited Lucceius to write about his consulship and subsequent vicissitudes down to his return from exile, pointing to the various advantages of the monograph (*Ad fam.* v. 12. 4). The last and heroic year of Cicero's life was even better.

There is therefore a chance that Aufidius put his exordium at a later point, perhaps, like Claudius Caesar, 'a pace civili' (Suetonius, *Divus Claudius* 41. 2), perhaps even at 8 B.C., continuing Livy. However that may be, Aufidius must come into discussion about the sources for the reign of Augustus. Livy (it can be conjectured) made one section of his work terminate with Book CXXXIII, which recounted the triple triumph of 29 (p. 366). Now Dio's use of Livy cannot be traced after 30.[1] Soon after that a fresh source can be allowed for.[2] Perhaps Aufidius Bassus. Perhaps not—there is Cremutius Cordus to be kept in mind.

Some will have it that Aufidius was the principal authority followed by Dio for the whole of Augustus' reign.[3] A full and proper investigation would be needed; and it would have to be recalled that Dio is much more personal and independent on Augustus than on the late Republic or on the successors of Augustus. It is only in the later years that a clue offers—Dio's scrappy treatment of the German wars in A.D. 4–6 (p. 275), best explained on the assumption that Aufidius had been brief, not wishing to rewrite his own monograph. Similarly, though Dio is entire down to a point in the year 17 (LVII. 17. 8), he does not allude to the campaigns of Germanicus. They were presumably to be registered and summarized on the occasion of Germanicus' triumph in that year.

Next, the terminal date, from which Pliny's uncle took up the story, 'a fine Aufidi Bassi triginta unus' (*Epp.* III. 5. 6). That formulation, most scholars argue, shows that Aufidius cannot have ended with the end of a reign. At what point, therefore? Perhaps the catastrophe of Seianus. Cassiodorus in his *Chronicle*, after taking his consular dates from Livy, went on to use Aufidius for the same purpose from 8 B.C. to A.D. 31 (*HRR* II (1906), 96). Hence, according to Mommsen, the terminal date.[4] A number of scholars concurred.[5]

Others, however, prefer a point in the reign of Claudius, between 47 and 52. The inquiry needs sharp eyes—and much faith as well. The seekers look for a sign that Tacitus or Dio (who is here fragmentary) has changed his main source, that a new source is there, identifiable on various criteria as Pliny. The year 47 seems not unpromising. Tacitus and Dio diverge widely in their accounts of Valerius Asiaticus (*Ann.* XI. 1–3; Dio LX. 29. 4–6). Shortly afterwards, however, there is a point of contact about Corbulo. Tacitus cites his utterance 'beatos

---

[1] cf. E. Schwartz, P–W III, 1698 ff.

[2] M. A. Levi puts the suture in 27 B.C., before LIII. 17, where Dio embarks on considerations about the general nature of imperial history (*Athenaeum* XXV (1937), 22 = *Il Tempo di Augusto* (1952), 433.

[3] F. A. Marx, *Klio* XXIX (1936), 217.

[4] *Abh. der sächsischen Ges. der Wiss.* VIII (1861), 558 f. = *Ges. Schr.* VII (1909), 677 ff.

[5] H. Peter, *HRR* II (1906), cxxvi; W. Pelka, *Rh. Mus.* LXI (1906), 620 ff.; C. Cichorius, *Römische Studien* (1922), 414.

quondam duces Romanos' (XI. 20. 1). This is also in Dio.[1] Hence Momigliano's theory. Both writers (he argues) turn to Pliny in 47; and there are concordances between the two from now on. The former had previously stood by Aufidius, the latter by Cluvius Rufus.[2]

Others have preferred a slightly later date. For Grigull it is in the year 48, after the death of Messallina.[3] Fabia carries Aufidius down to the end of 49 (i.e. as far as *Ann.* XII. 24: Tacitus now opted for Cluvius).[4] Münzer discovered the earliest certain trace of Pliny in the year 52.[5] Nipperdey, noting that Tacitus begins to report *prodigia* from 51 onwards, surmised that this was due to Tacitus' use of Pliny, but was ready to admit 54 (the death of Claudius).[6] The latest inquirer, F. A. Marx, suggests 50 or 54.[7]

It is time to ask whether other criteria would be of any value. Supposing Aufidius to have dealt with any part of Claudius' reign (and to have been free to choose where he would stop), two matters are relevant (cf. p. 288). First, an effective and historical conclusion to an historical work. The conquest of Britain would do, with Claudius' triumph thereafter early in 44. Otherwise, the *Ludi Saeculares* of 47, marking the eight-hundredth anniversary of Rome. Secondly, the point of discretion and safety for a contemporary author: how could he recount the destruction of Messallina a dozen years at most from that event?

Yet it is not at all certain that Aufidius narrated any part of Claudius' reign. That he did is an assumption, based probably upon the title of Pliny's work: he would not have chosen it, if Aufidius had ended with the reign of an emperor. Let it be observed that Pliny's choice has something to do with the prestige of Aufidius and his own literary ambitions. Furthermore, Pliny's own work went on to cover the year 69 and to end (so it appears likely) with the Jewish triumph of Vespasian and Titus in 71. Whether or no his history began with the accession of a ruler, it would scarcely have been possible to devise a title that should indicate its compass better than 'a fine Aufidi Bassi' (whatever the date).

And now, to bring this question itself to an end. Tacitus in his first surviving reference to Pliny's histories calls him 'Plinius', not 'C. Plinius' (XIII. 20. 2). That may mean that this authority had been cited before, i.e. earlier than the episode of Valerius Asiaticus in 47 with which Book XI (as extant) begins.

The name of Aufidius Bassus has engrossed much attention. Aufidius appeals to those who assume that Tacitus was normally content to follow a single source only. That fact in itself should excite suspicion. For Fabia it is Aufidius all the way, from the accession of Tiberius down to the end of 49;[8] and for Momigliano

---

[1] LX. 30. 5: ὦ μακάριοι οἱ πάλαι ποτὲ στρατηγήσαντες.

[2] *Rendiconti della R. Accademia dei Lincei* [6] VIII (1932), 310.

[3] *De auctoribus a Tacito in enarranda Divi Claudii vita adhibitis* (Diss. Münster, 1907), 8, cf. 30.

[4] o.c. 392 ff. [5] *Rh. Mus.* LXII (1907), 161 ff.

[6] In his edition (ed. 11, revised by G. Andresen, 1915), 33.

[7] *Klio* XXIX (1936), 94, cf. 100.

[8] o.c. 397: 'les onze premiers livres *des Annales* tout entiers étaient donc une dérivation d'une seule source principale.' After that, Cluvius Rufus. Similarly O. Clason, *Tacitus und Sueton* (Breslau, 1870), 75 f.—down to the end of XII.

the one source is also Aufidius (at least for Claudius' reign down to a point in 47).[1]
One must ask, and ask again, how and why must Aufidius on Claudius be deemed
to carry greater weight with Tacitus than, for example, the consular historian
Servilius Nonianus? That eminent personage died in 59 (*Ann.* XIV. 19). The death
of Aufidius (his senior by a few years) falls about 60, or not much later (Seneca,
Epp. 30). Man for man, each is as likely as the other to have narrated some part
of the reign of Claudius Caesar. And finally, if Servilius for the sake of argument
be let fall, the other consular remains, Cluvius Rufus.

The scholars most pertinaciously addicted to the theory of the 'single source'
are at the same time (and naturally enough) the advocates of another dogma:
Tacitus seldom consulted the *acta senatus*, perhaps never. Against them stands
the powerful evidence from the first hexad (Ch. XXII); and it can further be
demonstrated that Tacitus went to the *acta* for the pronouncements of Claudius
Caesar, exploiting them in manifold ways (App. 40 f.).

39. THE SPEECHES OF TIBERIUS

TIBERIUS took Messalla Corvinus for model, without, however, reproducing
his grace and clarity—'sed adfectatione et morositate nimia stilum obscurabat'
(Suetonius, *Tib.* 70. 1). Several specimens are cited (28 f.; 67). The longest comes
from the speech in refusal of the appellation *pater patriae*. It has a balanced
construction, though broken by a parenthesis; alliteration is frequent; the tone is
dignified, deferential—and ironical.[2]

Messalla's manner could not be described as archaic—'Cicerone mitior
Corvinus et dulcior et in verbis magis elaboratus' (*Dial.* 18. 2). But Tiberius went
in for old-fashioned and unusual expressions. Augustus blamed him for it
(Suetonius, *Divus Aug.* 86. 2). When the historian produces a version of the
speech on divine honours (*Ann.* IV. 37 f.), he duly equips Tiberius with a pair of
archaisms, viz. 'duint', and 'fungi' with the accusative.[3]

When Tacitus makes up a speech, he naturally employs a number of the normal
rhetorical turns to produce an illusion of spoken discourse. Structure and style is
not at all like that of his narrations. The difference can be seen most clearly in the
vocabulary. Words occur that he elsewhere avoids, of various types, namely, the
Ciceronian or the standard and contemporary; and especially compound verbs
and abstract nouns (cf. App. 50). Hence a clue to his devices for verisimilitude,
notably in the rendering of different kinds of eloquence. The orations of L.
Vitellius (XII. 5 f.) and of Seneca (XIV. 53 f.) will be found highly instructive in
choice of words (Ch. XXV). Moreover, as in the narrative, the recurrence of certain
expressions is worth watching (p. 345 f.).

If it was for facts that Tacitus first went to the *acta senatus* (a few items after
the decease of Augustus, but a pretty full record for the year 15, viz. I. 72–81), he

---

[1] o.c. 310. After that, the elder Pliny.

[2] cf. H. Bardon, *Les Empereurs et les lettres latines d'Auguste à Hadrien* (1940), 113.

[3] Note 'fungi' once elsewhere, in a Tiberian context (III. 2. 1). Similarly, 'quis' for
'quibus' (III. 53. 4) is anomalous in speeches.

quickly saw the startling value of Tiberius' speeches. The first to be reproduced in direct discourse is the Emperor's answer to the petition of M. Hortensius Hortalus, the grandson of the great orator (II. 38). It looks highly authentic.[1] The exordium is harsh and brutal—'si quantum pauperum est venire huc et liberis suis petere pecunias coeperint, singuli nunquam exsatiabuntur, res publica deficiet'. Strong language follows. Tiberius denounces the request of Hortensius —'non enim sunt preces istud, sed efflagitatio'. It is an attempt to break into the Treasury—'velut perfringere aerarium'.

Now the word 'exsatio' is not in itself a rarity; but Tacitus has it only once again, in a rhetorical passage (III. 17. 2—reported criticism of Tiberius). 'Efflagitatio' is strong, but colloquial. Three instances in the Ciceronian correspondence —Cicero himself, Munatius Plancus, and M. Brutus.[2] Otherwise nothing till very late writers.[3] As for 'perfringo' in the metaphorical sense, it does not occur anywhere else in Tacitus.

Tiberius Caesar, for all his control and circumspection, was prone to outbursts of anger, with unbridled language (cf. IV. 71. 3). The historian even uses the word 'inclementia' (IV. 42. 3). The written messages of the Emperor could be terrifying. Thus a consular, forbidden to enter the competition for a province 'tristibus Caesaris litteris' (VI. 40. 2), took his own life. They so much impressed Tacitus that he introduced a reference to 'cruentae epistulae' out of place and season (III. 44. 3). Elsewhere he is careful to emphasize the strain of violence in Tiberius. Thus 'perrumpo' (metaphorically) is employed twice, in the letter to Seianus (IV. 40. 5) and in a context concerning the Emperor (III. 15. 2). Compare further the reference to an edict 'ne quis quietem eius inrumperet' (IV. 67. 1): the usage ('inrumpo' as a transitive verb) is striking and poetical (cf. Lucan I. 470).

Other orations show a different Tiberius—solemnity (IV. 8), balance (III. 12), good sense (III. 53 f.), dignity (IV. 37 f.); and, after dignity, consummate craft in the response to Seianus (IV. 40).

The historian by his various devices is not merely rendering speech in contrast to narrative. He is reproducing a personality, with its characteristic manner. Observe the alliteration (III. 53. 4; IV. 38. 2), or the strong asyndeton, 'foveret attolleret' and 'suscipite regite' (IV. 8. 4 f.). Most significant is an accumulation of compound verbs, vigorous and explicit, e.g. III. 12. 5: 'sed neque reum prohibeo quo minus cuncta proferat quibus innocentia eius sublevari aut, si qua fuit iniquitas Germanici, coargui possit, vosque oro ne, quia dolori meo causa conexa est, obiecta crimina pro adprobatis accipiatis.'

Several compound verbs in the *Annales* occur only in speeches of Tiberius (direct or reported), e.g. 'conformo' (IV. 8. 4), 'denoto' (III. 53. 1), 'desidero' (IV. 37. 2), 'detego' (III. 12. 2), 'exonero' (III. 54. 5), 'suscenseo' (III. 12. 4).

---

[1] Otherwise H. Bardon, o.c. 113: 'un discours dont le style est, de toute évidence, dû à l'historien.'

[2] *Ad fam.* v. 19. 2; x. 24. 6; *Ad M. Brutum* I. 16. 11.

[3] It might have occurred in the remarkable and enigmatic inscription referring to Seianus' canvass: 'Seiani sce[lerata / . . . . .]itatio et inprobae comitiae' (*ILS* 6044: Rome). Compare what Munatius Plancus said about Octavian's ambition for the consulate 'insulsa cum efflagitatione' (*Ad fam.* x. 24. 6). But 'flagitatio' (which Tacitus has once, XIII. 50. 1) suits the space better, cf. R. Syme, *Hermes* LXXXIV (1956), 259.

It is not fanciful to suppose that the historian took over authentic expressions from the imperial orator. Thus the archaisms (above), and the word 'peregrinatio' (III. 24. 4; 47. 4), which he subsequently employs himself, once only, but very suitably (VI. 14. 2).[1] Similarly, a Tiberian alliteration—'nam quae saxo struuntur, si iudicium posterorum in odium vertit, pro sepulcris spernuntur' (IV. 38. 2). It is carried on in the comment 'perstititque posthac secretis etiam sermonibus aspernari talem sui cultum' (ib. 3).

Perhaps the historian could be detected in his operations. Tiberius hesitated much before making a pronouncement on sumptuary legislation—'saepe apud se pensitato an coerceri tam profusae libidines possent' (III. 52. 3). The reasons are given, and the Emperor's dispatch follows (in the form of a speech). The verb 'pensito' might come from the original exordium.[2] Again, after a summary of Tiberius' remarks about the *flamen Dialis*, the next sentence exhibits the word 'demuto', archaic and very rare.[3]

Tacitus' vocabulary was liable to be influenced. Certain 'Tiberian' words occur in speeches, recur once in the hexad, and never again. Thus 'compello' (II. 38. 3; IV. 70. 4), 'diiudico' (III. 12. 1: 69. 1), 'exsatio' (II. 38. 1; III. 17. 2).

To render Tiberius, Tacitus made a careful choice of words—not only the rare and arresting, but also less obtrusive words, alien from his own manner (and sometimes repeated with telling effect, cf. p. 345). The *Annales* have the following verbs uniquely in reference to actions of Tiberius: 'cohonesto' (III. 76. 2), 'commonefacio' (VI. 12. 2), 'eloquor' (III. 65. 3; IV. 31. 2), 'eluctor' (IV. 31. 2).

The letter to Seianus (IV. 40) was invented by the historian. It would not be the masterpiece it is if he had not studied authentic documents with loving care. The originals of the speeches and summaries were in the *acta*.

In support of the general fidelity of Tacitus a remarkable fact can be adduced: his versions sometimes conflict with his own interpretations of Tiberius' intentions, policy, and character.

Claudius was a different matter. The oration about the Gallic notables (*ILS* 212, cf. *Ann.* XI. 24) had to be treated very drastically (p. 318). None the less, Tacitean summaries of other speeches show traces (it can be argued) of Claudian language (cf. App. 40). Tacitus seems to have acquired familiarity with those documents long before he completed the first hexad (p. 286). What the archives told him about Tiberius may have whetted his curiosity about the psychology of other emperors.

The present inquiry has been restricted to a few points, mostly suggested by a single speech. The others will each have something to disclose about Tiberius, from the brief summaries to the long dispatch on sumptuary legislation (III. 53 f.). A revaluation of that ruler could do worse than start from the speeches and utterances as reported by Tacitus. The process might indicate another problem: the influence of the Emperor on the historian.

---

[1] p. 284.

[2] Likewise presumably 'diiudico' in the summary which precedes the oration in III. 12. The verb 'adtrecto' in III. 52. 3 could be Tiberian: elsewhere in Tacitus only in Tiberius' rebuke to Germanicus (I. 62. 2).

[3] In Plautus and Cato—but not again until late writers (cf. *TLL*).

Not all historians tried to bring out the individuality of the speaker by style and vocabulary. Livy produces an oration on the *Lex Oppia* that is not noticeably archaic or Catonian (XXXIV. 2 ff.). Nor is Sallust Caesarian in the speech of Caesar (*Cat.* 51). On the contrary, as a careful study has demonstrated.[1] Characteristic traces might be discoverable in the context. Caesar may have invoked 'mansuetudo et misericordia' (rather than 'clementia', for good reasons). Now Cato in his oration takes up that phrase (52. 11; 27), and it occurs in Sallust's comparison of the two statesmen (54. 2).[2]

Tacitus (as has been argued above) goes far beyond any normal practices of Roman historians in his renderings of Tiberius. Further, in confirmation, 'Tiberian' words can be detected in the vicinity of Tiberian orations.

40. SOME CLAUDIAN ORATIONS

THE speech about the *principes* of Tres Galliae, preserved almost entire on the Lugdunum tablet (*ILS* 212, cf. *Ann.* XI. 24), is well known and seldom fails to be fully discussed in its various aspects.[3] There are other documents, revealing this unorthodox emperor in his policy and acts, his manner and his language.[4] Edicts show him interjecting personal comment about previous rulers (*ILS* 206) or rebuking the 'nequitia hominum' (*ILS* 214).

Claudius Caesar can also be discovered in decrees of the Senate. When a measure was promoted by the Princeps, there might be discussion and further proposals, as in the honouring of Pallas, the imperial freedman (*Ann.* XII. 53, cf. Pliny, *Epp.* VIII. 6). Or there might not, as in the Gallic business— 'orationem principis secuto patrum consulto' (*Ann.* XI. 25. 1). Either way something of an emperor's own utterances would tend to be incorporated in the *senatus consultum*. A clear example is the decree (c. A.D. 45) designed to prevent the demolition of buildings by speculative purchasers (*ILS* 6043). The preamble opens with due laudation—'cum providentia optumi principis tectis quoque urbis nostrae et totius Italiae aeternitati prospexerit', &c. Before long, however, terms of unusual violence emerge—'deberentque apstinere se omnes cruentissimo genere negotiationis'. Surely the manner and words of Claudius Caesar.[5]

---

[1] H. Schnorr von Carolsfeld, *Über die Reden und Briefe bei Sallust* (1888), 34 ff.; 79 f.

[2] cf. remarks by E. Wölfflin incorporated in Carolsfeld (o.c. 42 f.).

[3] cf. especially Ph. Fabia, *La Table claudienne de Lyon* (1929); *Rev. ét. anc.* XXXIII (1931), 117 ff. and 225 ff.; J. Carcopino, *Journal des Savants* 1930, 69 ff. and 116 ff., modified and enlarged in *Points de vue sur l'impérialisme romain* (1934), 159 ff.; A. Momigliano, *Claudius: the Emperor and his Achievement* (1934), 10 ff.; F. Vittinghoff, *Hermes* LXXXII (1954), 348 ff. For the constitutional point at issue (not always grasped), H. F. Pelham, *Essays on Roman History* (1911), 152 ff.

[4] Notably *ILS* 206 and 214; the three edicts in Josephus, *AJ* XIX. 280 ff., 286 ff. and XX. 11 ff.; *BGU* 611; *P. Lond.* 1912. See the convenient collection of M. P. Charlesworth, *Documents illustrating the Reigns of Claudius and Nero* (1939).

[5] The phrase in question is taken over and toned down in the later *s.c.* of 56—'ut apstinerent se a tam foedo genere negotiation(is).' (*ILS* 6043, l. 41). For the style of Claudius, J. Stroux, *Bayerische S-B, phil.-hist. Kl.* 1929, Heft 8, 82 ff.; H. Bardon, *Les Empereurs et les lettres latines d'Auguste à Hadrien* (1940), 138 ff.

Scholars are drawn strongly to the documentary evidence (some of it new and recent). As a result, Tacitus suffers. A number of valuable passages have been unduly neglected—or simply ignored. Apart from the one speech rendered by the historian in *oratio recta* (XI. 24), there are three explicit addresses in the Senate, much condensed (one assumes), and mercifully so.

Claudius voiced his concern that the art of divination had fallen into decay (XI. 15). The *haruspices* were an ancient and necessary institution, as both Etruria and Rome testified. Although, providentially, all was going well, alien religions were a menace, and something would have to be done to strengthen the 'collegium haruspicum'. The next summary concerns policy in the East (XII. 11). Claudius was in the happy position of providing a ruler over the Parthians. He exalts his own action (rated by him level with Augustus); he duly admonishes the prince Meherdates, retailing for his benefit the standard principles of civil government, and urging him to practise 'clementia ac iustitia'; and he adds advice for the Parthian envoys—they must put up with their monarch, whatever his character, and frequent changes are a bad thing. Thirdly, a petition from a Greek island, supported by the Princeps—'rettulit deinde de immunitate Cois tribuenda multaque super antiquitate eorum disseruit' (XII. 61. 1). Mythology is followed by a history of medicine, with a catalogue of its exponents in the descent from Aesculapius (Tacitus omits the names), down to Xenophon, the court doctor, whose value Claudius asseverates. The Emperor did not bother (so Tacitus points out) to adduce the other (and valid) merits of Cos.

In addition, as deriving from speeches, will be registered the imperial dispatch about Mithridates, the ruler of Bosporus (XII. 20. 2), and the remarks concerning Lollia Paullina—Claudius spoke of her family and personal history, mentioned the fact that she had been the wife of Memmius Regulus, but (so Tacitus is careful to note) no word of her marriage to Caligula (XII. 22. 2).

And further, brief statements by the Emperor cropping up in the course of senatorial business. Thus, for example, the clemency advertised towards the son of Arruntius Camillus—'idque ad clementiam trahebat Caesar, quod stirpem hostilem iterum conservaret' (XII. 52. 2). Or, better, the grotesque testimonial on behalf of an imperial freedman to whom the Senate has voted a large sum of money—'adseveravit Claudius contentum honore Pallantem intra priorem paupertatem subsistere' (XII. 53. 3).[1]

So far speeches in Tacitus, or their clear traces. Next, three learned digressions. The first recapitulates the whole history of the alphabet: it is appended to the notice about the three new letters introduced by Claudius during his censorship (XI. 14). In fact, Claudius in his earlier existence had composed a treatise on the subject (Suetonius, *Divus Claudius* 41).

The second carries the history of the quaestorship (XI. 22). The erudition is peculiar. Thus the origin of the office—'sed quaestores regibus etiam tum imperantibus instituti sunt, quod lex curiata ostendit ab L. Bruto repetita'. The author (let him frankly be called Claudius Caesar) is arguing that the *lex curiata* installing the first consuls of the Republic is the same as that used for the Kings,

---

[1] Compare the funeral monument of Pallas, which moved Pliny to inspect and dilate upon the *s.c.*, *Epp.* VII. 29; VIII. 6.

hence the Kings too must have had the privilege of nominating quaestors. Next, he can furnish a date (447 B.C.) for the first election of quaestors by the People— it is the date of no other authority. And further, he expresses a view discrepant from the other traditions surviving—military quaestors were prior to civilian quaestors. The classic history of Livy gave no help or guidance. Quaestors turn up in his narrative, unheralded and unexplained, in 485 B.C. (II. 41. II).[1]

The third excursus is provoked and justified by the enlargement of the *pomerium* of Rome (XII. 23–24). It follows on items patently deriving from the *acta*, viz. the prosecution of Lollia Paullina (with remarks by Claudius), the condemnation of a proconsul, a privilege for Gallia Narbonensis, an addition to the province of Syria, and the *Augurium Salutis*. Nobody hitherto, it is stated, had extended the sacred precinct, save Sulla and Augustus. Such presumably was the considered opinion of Claudius. There could be dispute, on more points than one, as a contemporary writer attests.[2] Claudius omits Caesar the Dictator, though there was reputable testimony in support.[3] Caesar's extension may have been quickly disallowed or suppressed by Caesar Augustus—who, however, makes no claim for himself in the *Res Gestae*.[4] Caesar would not have been regarded by Claudius as a good precedent. Caesar's doubling of the total of quaestors is left out (XI. 22)—and, more important because durable in its effects, his role in bringing Italians into the Roman Senate.[5]

It is a fair assumption that these three digressions come from imperial orations by way of the *acta senatus*.[6] A fourth may be added, the excursus (a part if not the whole of it) on the *equester ordo*. In the year 53 the Emperor was frequently heard to say that his procurators must have judicial authority—'eodem anno saepius audita vox principis', &c. (XII. 60. I). And, to make sure that he meant what he said, 'ne forte prolapsus videretur', a decree of the Senate was passed. The phrases quoted make one suspect that the historian is here using the exordium of the speech: 'saepe numero, patres conscripti'. Compare his technique when introducing Tiberius' speech on moral and sumptuary legislation. He furnishes the Emperor's motives—'Tiberius saepe apud se pensitato', &c. (III. 52. 3). Surely taken from Tiberius' opening phrases (cf. App. 39).

Certain brief antiquarian notices should also be scrutinized. Claudius augmented the patriciate (XI. 25. 2). The 'gentes minores' are here defined in a

---

[1] For the early history of the quaestorship (obscure and controversial to the Romans) see Mommsen, *R. Staatsrecht* II³ (1887), 523 ff., or Furneaux's notes on this passage.

[2] Seneca, *De brevitate vitae* 13. 8: 'Sullam ultimum Romanorum protulisse pomerium, quod nunquam provinciali, sed Italico agro adquisito, proferre moris apud antiquos fuit.'

[3] Dio XLIII. 50. I, cf. XLIV. 49. 2—not to say Messalla the augur, cited by Gellius (XIII. 14. 4).

[4] The *Lex de imperio Vespasiani* (*ILS* 244) is silent (it only cites Claudius). Also Suetonius. Yet the fact of Augustus' extension is stated by Dio (LV. 6. 6). J. H. Oliver opts for Augustus, *Mem. Am. Ac. Rome* x (1932), 178; but J. Guey for Caesar, *Mélanges* LIV (1937), 165 ff.

[5] Omitted by Claudius (*ILS* 212, col. ii, ll. 1 ff.), cf. R. Syme, *BSR Papers* XIV (1938), 8.

[6] Leo argued that Tacitus took the matter for all his digressions on Roman antiquities from a single handbook, in the school and tradition of Ateius Capito (*Gött. gel. Nachr.* 1896, 191 ff.). Against, Th. Grigull, *De auctoribus a Tacito in enarranda Divi Claudii vita adhibitis* (Diss. Münster, 1907), 31 ff.; E. Hahn, *Die Exkurse in den Annalen des Tacitus* (Diss. Munich, 1933), 90 ff. Grigull, however, prefers to derive the excursus on the alphabet from Claudius' separate treatise (ib. 27 f.).

fashion without parallel, as the families added in the first year of the Republic. This may represent a peculiar view of the Emperor. The head of the *gens Claudia* was never reluctant to obtrude his scholarship. The notice also refers to a *lex Cassia* and a *lex Saenia*, not elsewhere attested (but easily to be identified).[1] The concluding words convey Claudius' extreme gratification at what he was doing— 'laetaque haec in rem publicam munia multo gaudio censoris inibantur'. The next measure follows, introduced by the Emperor's perplexity—'famosos probris quonam modo senatu depelleret anxius', &c. Not wishing to behave with 'severitas prisca', he suggests a merciful remedy and promises to publish on a single list the names of those expelled and of those who asked leave to retire. Also an oration, presumably. Claudius on a later occasion varied with severity of action and language his benevolence towards unsatisfactory senators.[2] He always took pride in his conscientious search for 'remedia', as one of the edicts openly proclaims.[3]

Claudius' doubts and Claudius' motives find expression in another passage (XII. 20. 1). Although 'nobilitatibus externis mitis', he was not sure whether to accept the surrender of Mithridates of Bosporus or insist upon his being captured. Resentment and vengeance pointed one way. But there were contrary arguments. 'Disserebatur contra.' By whom, we are not told, or where: the Senate did not discuss foreign policy. However that be, the arguments are given, rendered in Sallustian language—'suscipi bellum avio itinere, importuoso mari', &c.[4] They influenced Claudius. He therefore wrote a dispatch to Eunones (the ruler of the Aorsi). It begins with firm, not to say violent, words—'meritum quidem novissima exempla Mithridaten, nec sibi vim ad exsequendum deesse'. The first phrase is tantamount to calling the ruler of Bosporus a common criminal: thus does the Roman plebs think of the Christians, 'sontis et novissima exempla meritos' (xv. 44. 5). But there is mercy at the end—'beneficentia adversus supplices'.

Claudius in a threatening attitude is familiar from a document that carries his authentic words, the *Letter to the Alexandrians*. He warns the Greeks and the Jews. Unless they mend their ways, he will be forced to show them the other side of a benevolent ruler—righteous anger.[5] It can be argued that the whole of this Tacitean passage concerning Mithridates (and not merely the dispatch in conclusion) is based on an imperial oration: that is, the Emperor scrupulously expounds his reasons and also tells the Senate what answer he proposes to send. The historian, abbreviating, suitably contributes Sallustian colouring, as in parts of the narrative of eastern affairs.[6]

---

[1] Under Caesar, and in 30 B.C. (L. Saenius being *cos. suff.*).

[2] XII. 52. 3: 'laudati dehinc oratione principis qui ob angustias familiaris ordine senatorio sponte cederent, motique qui remanendo impudentiam paupertati adicerent.'

[3] *ILS* 214: 'c[um sati]s multa remedia invenisse m[ihi viderer, p]otu[it ta]men nequitiae hominum [non satis per ea occurri].'

[4] cf. App. 53.

[5] *P.Lond.* 1912, col. 4, ll. 79 ff.: ἁπλῶς δὲ προσαγορεύω ὅτι, ἂν μὴ καταπαύσητε τὴν ὀλέθριον ὀργὴν ταύτην κατ' ἀλλήλων αὐθάδιον, ἐκβιασθήσομαι δεῖξαι οἷόν ἐστιν ἡγεμὼν φιλάνθρωπος εἰς ὀργὴν δικαίαν μεταβεβλημένος. The Emperor in an edict once drew the distinction between 'ira' and 'iracundia' (Suetonius, *Divus Claudius* 38. 1).

[6] e.g. XII. 12. 1 (Cassius Longinus, the legate of Syria); 14. 3 (the mutilation of Meherdates).

Tacitus operates with a bold hand, as his version of the speech about the Gallic notables demonstrates (cf. p. 318). He throws out the Etruscan erudition (Caeles Vibenna, and Mastarna, identified as Servius Tullius), and he furnishes a new peroration. In Tacitus the speech leads off with 'maiores mei, quorum antiquissimus Clausus, origine Sabina'. Highly plausible, but not perhaps used by Claudius on this occasion. Tacitus may have taken the reference to Attus Clausus from the speech about the adoption of Nero (XII. 25. 2, cf. below). Again, the statement about sons of *libertini* in the Roman Senate, 'non, ut plerique falluntur, repens, sed priori populo factitatum est' (XI. 24. 4). That may have had no parallel in the lost portion of Claudius' address: it could come from a different oration, delivered when Claudius himself adlected such persons (cf. Suetonius, *Divus Claudius* 24. 1).

It can be suspected that the historian quietly transferred material from the orations, several times. The freedman Pallas urges Claudius to adopt Nero, for the sake of the 'res publica', and for the protection of the young Britannicus; and he cites precedents from the history of the dynasty (XII. 25. 1). Claudius complies, and reproduces the arguments of his mentor—'habita apud senatum oratione eundem in quem a liberto acceperat modum'. Tacitus could easily have invented the arguments and precedents he attributes to Pallas, had it been necessary. But they were presumably ready to hand, in the oration of Claudius. This episode reveals another type of transference. According to Suetonius it was Claudius himself who affirmed (repeatedly) that nobody had hitherto entered the Claudian House by adoption. In Tacitus, however, that is the comment of the audience—'adnotabant periti nullam antehac adoptionem inter patricios Claudios reperiri, eosque ab Atto Clauso continuos duravisse' (XII. 25. 2).

Similarly when Caratacus is brought to Rome. Claudius can hardly have failed to orate upon that historic theme. In Tacitus it is the senators who relate 'multa et magnifica', evoking captive princes like Syphax and Perses (XII. 38. 1).

One should therefore be on the watch for other specimens of this device. After Claudius had bestowed privileges on Cos, the next petitioners were the people of Byzantium, who recapitulated their past services to Rome (XII. 62). This piece of history furnishes an excuse for a geographical excursus (63). The historical section might be a lecture of Claudius. It was his habit to answer embassies with a regular speech (in Greek) in the Senate (Suetonius, *Divus Claudius* 42. 1). And why not the geography, in part at least? Tacitus has turned it into a Sallustian digression, quoting for guidance from the famous excursus *De situ Ponti*.[1]

Somewhere in Books IX–XII the Emperor should have spoken (and perhaps more than once) about a subject close to his heart, the food supply of Rome (cf. a whole chapter in Suetonius, *Divus Claudius* 18). There was famine in 51, and a riot. Tacitus reports that there were supplies for fifteen days only, but Rome was providentially saved 'magnaque deum benignitate et modestia hiemis' (XII. 43. 2). The phrase 'deum benignitas' deserves comment. It is conventional (and sometimes hypocritical). It is used by Tacitus in three other places,[2] but never when speaking in his own person. One of the instances occurs in the summary of Claudius' oration on the *haruspices*—'et laeta quidem in praesens

---

[1] Sallust, *Hist.* III. 66, cf. App. 53.　　[2] *Hist.* IV. 85. 2; *Ann.* XI. 15. 2; XIV. 6. 2.

omnia, sed benignitati deum gratiam referendam' (XI. 15. 2). That is not all. The historian goes on and concludes thus: 'at hercule olim Italia legionibus longinquas in provincias commeatus portabat, nec nunc infecunditate laboratur, sed Africam potius et Aegyptum exercemus, navibusque et casibus vita populi Romani per-missa est.' Now the expletive 'at hercule' is direct, personal, and rhetorical. It is alien to normal historical narrative. It occurs in four other places in the *Annales*, once in a strongly worded objection (I. 3. 5: 'at hercule Germanicum', &c.), twice in reported or imagined discourses (I. 17. 4; 26. 2), once in an imperial oration. Not of Claudius, however, but of Tiberius. That Emperor exclaims 'at hercule nemo refert quod Italia externae opis indiget, quod vita populi Romani per incerta maris et tempestatum cotidie volvitur' (III. 54. 4). The verbal resemblance is remarkable—so much so that one might doubt after all whether Tacitus is here drawing upon Claudius.

41. FURTHER TRACES OF CLAUDIUS

VARIOUS clues can be followed: the placing and the structure of episodes in Tacitus, digressions with peculiar erudition, manifestations of the Claudian idiosyncrasy (viz. paternal benevolence, anger, impatience, and ineptitude), and even vocabulary. When Tacitus composes speeches, the style is notably divergent from that of his narration. Furthermore, he often delicately suggests the speaker, either by a word taken from an actual discourse, or by a word foreign to his own manner, though not in itself a rarity: there are a number of common and Cice-ronian words that he normally avoids.[1]

Claudius in the speech on the Gallic *principes* uses the verb 'paenitet' (*ILS* 212, col. ii, l. 23). Tacitus employs it in his own version (XI. 24. 3)—and also in the invented objections of the Emperor's counsellors (23. 2). Observe also that 'inveterasco' (24. 7) comes nowhere else in Tacitus. Similarly, 'beneficentia' is found in the summary of Claudius' dispatch (XII. 20. 2), and nowhere else in all the writings of Tacitus. Again, the verb 'propago', in the remarks on the *haru-spices* (XI. 15. 1) and in the excursus on the *pomerium* (XII. 23. 2), but never before, and only once again (XV. 59. 5).[2] In confirmation one notes the way Tacitus operates when producing a parody of Claudius, put into the mouth of L. Vitellius (XII. 5 f., cf. p. 331).

If the above arguments are admitted, Tacitus must have exploited the archives of the Senate much more thoroughly than many scholars believe.[3] The *acta* are thus the principal, if not exclusive, source for certain continuous portions of the narrative. Thus XI. 22–25 (from the digression on the quaestorship down to the

---

[1] App. 42; 50.

[2] Note further, in Claudian contexts, 'conservo' (XII. 52. 2), the sole instance in all Tacitus, and 'impudentia' (ib. 3) the sole in the *Annales*.

[3] Momigliano, for example, will not allow Tacitus to draw any of the Claudian anti-quarian material direct from the *acta* (*Rendiconti della R. Accademia dei Lincei*[6] VIII (1932), 319). Furthermore, he insists that XV. 74. 3 ('reperio in commentariis senatus') is inad-missible, being an isolated reference—and Tacitus might have taken it over from his source (ib. 320).

end of Claudius' measures as censor); XI. 22–24; XI. 52 f.; or indeed, XII. 58–63, where the year 53 is filled out by the digression on the *ordo equester*, by Cos, and by Byzantium. Speculation about the lost books can hardly be resisted—orations on all manner of subjects, from the ancient ritual of the *fetiales* to the taverns and cookshops of Rome as they were in Claudius' earlier days.[1]

And something further. The historian (so it appears) already knew one at least of the Claudian orations when he was writing about Tiberius. He used it for the digression on the Mons Caelius (IV. 65), as the material certifies (the Etruscan adventurer Caeles Vibenna), also the word 'appellitatus'.[2] One is therefore entitled to wonder about the digression on the *praefectura urbis* appended to the funeral of L. Piso (VI. 11). It contains two statements unique of their kind. First, three *praefecti* appointed by the Kings, viz. Denter Romulius, Numa Marcius, and Sp. Lucretius: Livy and the standard tradition know only Lucretius (I. 59. 12, cf. Dion. Hal. IV. 82). Secondly, 'Cilnius' as a part of the regular nomenclature of C. Maecenas.[3] Here speaks a scholar with views of his own about things Etruscan as well as Roman, the scholar who asserted that Servius Tullius was really Mastarna, a companion of Caeles Vibenna (*ILS* 212).[4] If Claudius appointed a *praefectus urbi*, he would not spare the Senate a lecture.[5]

That is not all. The digression on legislation (III. 26 ff.) has a strong Sallustian colouring, naturally enough (cf. App. 53). It could be argued that it contains three clues leading to Claudius, viz. peculiar erudition about the Kings of Rome, an echo of Claudius on the Gauls, and an echo of the Tacitean version. First, an especial prominence is given to Servius Tullius as a legislator, at the expense of Romulus, and deviating from standard Roman tradition—'sed praecipuus Servius Tullius sanctor legum fuit quis etiam reges obtemperarent' (III. 26. 4).[6] Next, 'quidam statim aut postquam regum pertaesum leges maluerunt' (ib. 3): compare

[1] Suetonius, *Divus Claudius* 25. 5 (the fetial formula); 40. 1: 'cum de laniis ac vinariis ageretur, exclamavit in curia: *rogo vos, quis potest sine offula vivere?* descripitque abundantiam veterum tabernarum, unde solitus esset vinum olim et ipse petere.' It is not certain that Tacitus was the only author to use Claudius as excuse and material for an excursus. Observe his edict explaining eclipses in the year 45, with Dio's long commentary (LX. 26. 1 ff.).

[2] *ILS* 212, col. i, l. 22, cf. Furneaux in his note on IV. 65. 1; J. Carcopino, *Journal des Savants* 1930, 118 f.; *Points de vue sur l'impérialisme romain* (1934), 183 f.; L. Pareti, *Studi etruschi* V (1931), 156.

[3] His official style is 'C. Maecenas L. f. Pom.' (*ILS* 7848). Tacitus has 'Cilnium Maecenatem' (i.e. inverted nomenclature), which implies that Maecenas has a *cognomen*, 'Cilnius'. That was the *nomen* of a family of old renown at Arretium (Livy X. 3. 2), his ancestry (it is assumed) on the maternal side: Augustus addressed his friend as 'Cilniorum smaragdus' (Macrobius II. 4. 12). Now Claudius is the likely source for this notion about Maecenas' true and complete nomenclature. Nor should it be forgotten that there was an Arretine Cilnius in Tacitus' own day, C. Cilnius Proculus (*suff.* 87), who lasted into Hadrian's reign (cf. *PIR*², C 732).

[4] For his Etruscological studies cf. now J. Heurgon, *Latomus* XII (1953), 402 ff.; *CRAI* 1953, 92 ff.

[5] L. Volusius Saturninus (*suff.* A.D. 3) was *praefectus urbi* when he died (Pliny, *NH* VII. 62). He could have been appointed by Claudius (and not by Caligula). Tacitus was interested in the Volusii (p. 302).

[6] cf. F. Leo, *Gött. gel. Nachr.* 1896, 198 f. Not, indeed, that the tradition about Romulus is as uniform as Leo assumed, cf. E. Hahn, *Die Exkurse in den Annalen des Tacitus* (Diss. Munich, 1933), 17 ff.

ILS 212, col. i, l. 26: 'nempe pertaesum est mentes regni.' Thirdly, 'accitis quae usquam egregia' (27. 1): compare XI. 24. 1: 'transferendo huc quod usquam egregium fuerit.'[1]

Claudius when a young man took up history-writing at the encouragement of Livy (Suetonius, *Divus Claudius* 41. 1); his style owes something to that model;[2] and scholars have marked and emphasized the notion of historical development expounded both in the oration about the Gallic notables and in the Livian speech of the tribune Canuleius (Livy IV. 3 ff.).[3] If Tacitus was not familiar with the latter document, he could find the appropriate language without effort. Referring to the immigrant kings, he makes Claudius say 'advenae in nos regnaverunt' (XI. 24. 4): compare Livy IV. 3. 13: 'cum maiores nostri advenas reges non fastidierint.' The word 'advena' occurs in only one other place in the *Annales*: precisely the digression on the Mons Caelius (IV. 65), which the historian took from Claudius Caesar.

The Emperor (it is abundantly clear) was eager to parade recondite facts beyond the reach of his old tutor, or discrepant with the vulgate tradition.[4] Fresh evidence from Tacitus now accrues (if the above argument be accepted) to complete and round off the picture of Claudius Caesar the scholar and emperor.[5] At the same time, the sources of Tacitus are revealed, his methods of work, and his stylistic devices (down to the choice of a single word).[6] To pile summary on summary of Claudian orations would be clumsy—and it would accord that ruler a prominence in history which Tacitus of set purpose denies him. Instead, the author distributes, transfers, or disguises the material. The style he could not reproduce, but he sometimes leaves a sign or hint of his operations. And there was a faint and posthumous compliment—'nec in Claudio, quotiens meditata dissereret, elegantiam requireres' (XII. 3. 2). Tacitus put Claudius to good employ.

---

[1] These parallels have been neglected by most, if not all, of the scholars who discuss *Ann.* XI. 24 and the Lugdunum tablet.

[2] E. Norden, *Die antike Kunstprosa* I (1898), 236.

[3] e.g. F. Leo, o.c. 193; A. Momigliano, o.c. 16 f.

[4] Hence Camerium as the 'origo' of the Coruncanii (*Ann.* XI. 24. 1) will derive from Claudius' erudition, not that of Tacitus. The standard version in the late Republic had Tusculum, not Camerium (Cicero, *Pro Plancio* 20).

[5] For the Emperor's erudition (Suetonius, *Divus Claudius* 41 f.) see H. Bardon, o.c. 125 ff.; A. Momigliano, o.c. 6 ff. The latter scholar's picture is incomplete, for his assumptions about Tacitus' sources precluded him from seeing how much in the historian comes straight from Claudius. Of this material he discusses the digression on the alphabet (not, in his opinion, from the *acta senatus*) and notes (but only in passing) the speech about Cos (o.c. 10, cf. 84).

[6] Not but what some scholars are reluctant to admit that Tacitus used the original version of the speech about Gallic senators. Thus F. Vittinghoff suggests that he might have found a satisfactory version in an earlier historian (*Hermes* LXXXII (1954), 363).

F. STYLE AND WORDS

42. WORDS TACITUS AVOIDS

THE historian's developed manner is so startling that it attracts attention to what is choice and rare. There is another approach, by way of the unobtrusive words which the lexica define as 'frequent and classical'. It is remunerative all through. It illustrates the progress from the two monographs to the *Historiae*, from the *Historiae* to the *Annales*: in the *Annales* it exemplifies the divergence in vocabulary between orations and narrative—and it brings out the great change in style towards the end.

The *Dialogus* is not the starting-point of Tacitus' development, or of this inquiry. It belongs to a literary genre different from the other works, and there is no point in a detailed examination. Two phenomena can be briefly noted. First, it contains seventy words appropriate to literary criticism, only five of which occur elsewhere in Tacitus.[1] Secondly, a number of ordinary words, not found in the other works, for example:

abundo	excogito	perturbo
adcumulo	importo	sordeo
admirabilis	improbus	studeo (3)
comprehendo	insanus	studiosus (3)
concludo	insulsus	subministro
delecto (4)	introduco	suspicor
dimico	iucunditas (5)	temerarius
elaboro (3)	perturbatio	vitupero

At the same time there is another feature that can be noted in passing. Although the style of the treatise is Ciceronian, one looks in vain for certain common and Ciceronian words that might have been expected to occur there—'declaro', 'exhibeo', 'intellegentia', and others (cf. App. 43).

None the less, the *Dialogus*, which is contemporaneous with historical writings of Tacitus (perhaps roughly with the *Historiae* as extant), admits of exploitation—for types of words, irrespective of the precise date. It has a number of words in common with the other works, and it is instructive to see what happens to them.

The *Germania* has its own marked peculiarities of vocabulary. It will be convenient to leave out of account a number of the poetical and precious words in the

[1] See A. Gudeman (ed. 2, 1914), 21.

Germania which the historian (wisely, be it said), preferred not to employ subsequently. For example:

eduro	hortamen	obliquo
eiectamentum	ingemo	praetracto
excresco	inlaboro	raresco
hebeo	lentesco	velamen
hebeto	monstrator	

Two lists, viz. words absent from Tacitus and words dropped after the *Agricola* and *Germania* (App. 43 f.), suggest the following classification:

(1) Shape and structure. For example, compound verbs, especially those formed with 'cum'. Also adjectives in '-osus'. Their employment calls for delicate discrimination.[1]

(2) Oratorical and ethical words. 'Humanitas' and 'integritas' are thrown out.

(3) The typically Ciceronian, e.g. 'singularis'. And, naturally, many of the compound verbs and ethical terms.

(4) Normal, unemphatic, and prosaic words. Thus 'exhibeo' and 'opinor'. It will be observed that 'arbitror' drops out before the *Annales*, while 'aestimo', 'existimo', and 'iudico' are not there in high favour.[2]

(5) Feeble, crude, or vulgar words. Thus 'calvus', 'ebrius', 'piger'.[3]

(6) Words spoiled by politics, e.g. 'pius'.[4] 'Fidelis', once in the *Dialogus*, occurs only once again (*Ann.* xv. 67. 2—in the mouth of a tribune of the Guard).

The process goes on. More are discarded before the *Annales* (App. 45), also some that had cropped up for the first time in the *Historiae* (App. 46).

Now avoidance of 'Ciceronian' words is a congenital habit in the historical prose of the Romans, and a traditional necessity. Tacitus not only conforms, but is ready from the outset to go further. He soon rejects a number of those words which had been admitted by Livy, or even by Sallust, that declared and flagrant anti-Ciceronian.[5]

Tacitus is a decisive and wilful writer. How far are his verbal dislikes (shape, strength, atmosphere, or connotation) to be regarded as deliberate, how far unconscious? It is a large question. His animosities make the idiosyncrasy of the writer stand out in sharp relief. They may also furnish clues to his psychology. Tacitus exhibits a marked distaste for words of a kindly, optimistic, or improving nature: 'iucundus' and 'urbanitas' are discarded before the *Annales*, while 'benignus' and 'blandus' each appear in the *Historiae* once, and never again; and there is one example all though of 'tranquillus' (*Ann.* i. 3. 7).

---

[1] A. Ernout, *Les Adjectivs latins en -osus et en -ulentus* (1949). That scholar gives no separate treatment to Tacitus (it would have been highly instructive).

[2] B. Axelson points out that poets avoid 'arbitror', 'existimo', 'iudico' (*Unpoetische Wörter* (Lund, 1945), 64). Naturally enough, given also the metrical value of most of them. Note also that 'puto' is an unattractive word—only seven occurrences in the *Annales*.

[3] p. 342 f.   [4] p. 415.

[5] Thus the following, in Sallust, but not in Tacitus after the minor works:—concito, iniustus, integritas, vehemens. Cf. further App. 53.

Various hazards and uncertainties must be allowed for.[1] Is the bulk of material adequate for comparisons and conclusions? More than the half of the *Historiae* is missing, there are the gaps in the *Annales*. In pages the extant works add up as follows:[2]

Dial. (43)	*Ann.*: I–VI (199)
Agr. (31)	XI–XII (56)
Germ. (26)	XIII–XVI (127)
Hist. (219)	

The books in the *Historiae* are longer than those in the *Annales*, and the proportion between the two works as extant comes to about 11:19.

43. SOME WORDS NOT IN TACITUS

abalieno	derelinquo	lasso
abstinentia √	devinco	lassus
calamitosus	disiungo	loquax
calvus	disturbo	machinor
capto	ebrius	mendax
celo	elevo	mirabilis
celsus	exaequo	obsecro
coacervo	excludo	odiosus
commisceo	exhibeo	perspicuus
commoneo	exopto	pristinus
communitas	facetus	religiosus
condono	factiosus	repraesento
consolatio	fastidiosus	reprehendo
consolor	furiosus	sagacitas
conspicor	incommodus	sano
consuesco	indignitas	singularis
contemplor	indoctus	sollicito
contribuo	ineptus	spondeo
convoco	ingeniosus	suffragor
declaro	inlucesco	supervacaneus
decresco	insania	suscito
demens	insidiosus	suspiciosus
deperdo	intellegentia	timiditas
deploro	investigo	turpitudo
depravo	iracundus	verax
depugno √	lassitudo	verecundus

[1] The lists here presented are selective and exemplificatory, not exhaustive. Let it, however, be added that the avoidances and rejects are instructive for Latin semantics in general as well as for Tacitus: sometimes obviously, but some surprises (cf. App. 52).

[2] In old-Teubner pagination.

44. WORDS DROPPED AFTER THE MINOR WORKS

	Agr.	Germ.	Dial.		Agr.	Germ.	Dial.
accuratus	..	..	2	inlacessitus	1	1	..
antecedo	..	1	3	inritatio	..	1	..
astutus	..	1	..	integritas	1	..	..
augustus	..	..	2	laudator	..	1	..
bellicosus	..	1	..	lenocinor	..	1	1
cohaereo	..	1	..	lucrosus	1	..	1
commigro	..	2	..	numerosus	1	1	1
communico	1	..	..	operosus	..	1	..
comploro	1	..	..	opinor	..	1	5
concito	1	..	2	percipio	..	..	2
definio	..	1	..	piger	1	2	..
diligens	2	1	2	pius	2	..	..
disputo	..	..	3	prosperitas	1	..	..
efficax	..	1	1	recedo	1	2	4
gratiosus	..	1	..	robustus	..	2	1
humanitas	1	1	..	sanus	..	..	1
iactatio	2	1	..	temerarius	..	..	1
iniucundus	1	..	..	vario	..	2	1
iniustus	1	..	1	vehemens	1	..	1

45. WORDS DROPPED AFTER THE *HISTORIAE*

	Agr.	Germ.	Dial.	Hist.		Agr.	Germ.	Dial.	Hist.
adfectatio	..	1	..	1	inquietus	..	..	2	1
adsuesco	2	..	2	2	insequor	2	..	3	1
amplitudo	..	1	1	1	instigo	..	..	1	4
arbitror	4	5	6	5	iucundus	..	1	2	1
blandior	1	..	..	3	marceo	..	1	..	1
cautus	2	..	..	5	mitesco	1	..	..	2
committo	..	1	1	1	necesse	..	1	2	3
consequor	1	..	6	2	nobilito	..	1	1	1
cresco	..	..	1	3	obligo (*met.*)	..	2	1	1
cupiditas	1	2	1	6	obtrectatio	1	..	1	2
depono	1	1	..	5	offensa	..	..	3	10
excusatio	2	..	1	1	opportunitas	2	..	..	1
exiguus	1	..	..	1	oppugno	1	..	..	6
extendo	..	2	..	1	pasco	1	..	..	1
faveo	..	..	1	2	paucitas	1	1	..	2
feritas	..	2	..	1	permuto	..	1	..	1
gloriosus	..	..	1	2	perpetuitas	..	..	1	1
horreo	..	2	..	4	persevero	..	1	..	1
incompositus	..	..	1	3	persuadeo	..	1	3	1
indignor	..	..	1	1	petulantia	1	..	..	3
infirmus	3	1	1	2	praecurro	..	..	2	2
inlustro	1	..	2	1	quiesco	1	2	..	7
innotesco	..	..	1	1	redundo	..	..	1	2

	Agr.	Germ.	Dial.	Hist.		Agr.	Germ.	Dial.	Hist.
reformido	..	..	1	1	torpor	1	1	..	2
sono	..	1	..	1	tumeo	..	..	1	4
splendeo	..	1	1	1	urbanitas	..	..	1	2
splendor	..	..	2	1	vitabundus	1	..	..	1
sublimis	2	..	1	1	vocito	..	..	1	2

46. WORDS ONLY IN THE *HISTORIAE*

abunde
adoro
adsertor
aemulator
antecapio
aufugio
blandus
confodio (6)
confusio (3)
conicio (2)
conlaudo
considero (2)
consummo
contemptim (3)
contumeliosus (4)
convalesco
convecto
conveho
credulus (5)
crudesco
culpo (4)
debilitas (2)
deflagro
delitesco
deprecator (2)
deses (4)
desiderabilis
despectus
destituo (2)
detrectatio
deverto (3)
diffidentia
diffugium
dirumpo
domitor (3)
ducto
eblandior

elanguesco (2)
enotesco
evanesco
evilesco
exarmo (2)
existimatio
exoro
expavesco
exspiro (2)
firmamentum
fraudator
frustratio
grandaevus
gratulatio
haesito
horror
hortamentum
increbresco
indignatio (2)
indigus (4)
indiligentia
induresco
induro
inexplebilis (3)
infesto
ingravesco
inhumanus (2)
inquieto
inscius
instigator
instinctor (2)
integro
interimo
inutilis
invalesco
langueo
languor

lenimentum
lenocinium
levamen
lucrum
luxuriosus (2)
maculo (2)
mulceo (4)
nequitia
noscito
obscuritas (2)
obsecratio
observantia
obstinatio (3)
obtrunco (6)
oppugnator (4)
ordino
pando (4)
pauperies
perrogo
pertinax (4)
petulans (2)
praefinio
praeopto
praetextum (4)
principalis (6)
prodigiosus
rapax
rapina
reclamo
recurso
redempto
relucesco
renascor
reprehensio
reputatio
resipisco (2)
retento (4)

sagax
sagina (4)
scriptito (2)
sedo (3)
separatio
serenus (2)
sollicitus (3)
sopio
sopor
spectator (3)
stimulatio

suasor
substituo (2)
superiacio (2)
supersto (3)
supervenio
superventus
supervolito
supprimo (4)
taeter
temno
temptamentum

tero (4)
timidus
torpedo
torpesco
torvitas
transitio (3)
turbamentum
turbulentus
turpo
venditator

47. FROM *HISTORIAE* TO *ANNALES*

	Agr.	Germ.	Dial.	Hist.	Ann.
ardesco	..	..	..	1	8
cerno	..	..	..	2	10
claritas	1	1	..	3	2
claritudo	..	..	..	3	31
cognomentum	..	..	..	1	17
cresco	..	..	1	3	..
glisco	..	..	..	4	19
cupiditas	1	2	1	6	..
cupido	1	..	..	30	47
dictito	..	..	..	3	21
fatisco	..	..	..	1	4
firmitudo	..	..	..	..	6
grator	..	..	..	1	6
imperito	..	1	..	6	20
incuria	1	..	..	1	7
invenio	8	2	7	9	10
reperio	1	1	..	7	80
memoro	4	4	..	20	74
mirus	1	2	4	8	36
modicus	3	1	..	20	40
patro	..	..	..	5	19
perimo	..	..	..	1	5
polliceor	..	..	..	2	10
praevaleo	..	..	1	2	12
priscus	..	1	1	1	18
properus	..	..	..	3	14
reor	1	..	..	21	50
sector	..	1	2	1	7
senecta	..	..	..	4	20
senectus	3	3	..	4	10
subdolus	..	..	..	1	7
suboles	..	..	1	1	7
suspecto	..	..	..	2	8
sustento	..	..	..	1	12

	Agr.	Germ.	Dial.	Hist.	Ann.
tracto	..	..	4	5	20
tutor	..	..	..	1	8
vanesco	..	..	1	1	4
vetustus	..	1	..	6	29
vigeo	..	..	..	4	13

48. WORDS DROPPED AFTER HEXAD I

	Agr.	Germ.	Dial.	Hist.	Ann. I–VI
adlicio	..	..	..	6	2
adpropinquo	1	..	..	1	1
aequalitas	1	..	..	1	4
ambitiosus	3	1	..	8	4
augesco	1	..	..	4	1
aviditas	1	..	..	5	1
calamitas	..	..	..	2	1
careo	..	..	3	2	2
castigo	1	..	..	2	2
circumspecto	1	..	..	5	1
comparo	3	..	6	2	2
congrego	..	..	..	8	4
contemptor	..	1	..	2	1
crebresco	..	..	..	4	2
custodio	1	1	..	1	1
decipio	..	..	..	4	2
dego	..	1	..	..	2
demo	..	1	..	5	3
deposco	1	..	..	3	1
desidero	1	..	3	4	1
diuturnus	..	..	..	1	4
excito	..	..	3	6	2
flagitiosus	..	..	..	5	5
fluito	..	1	..	4	1
honorificus	..	..	1	2	1
ignominiosus	..	2	..	1	1
ignorantia	2	1	..	1	1
incito	..	..	..	2	1
inclutus	..	1	..	6	2
incolo	1	1	..	1	1
inertia	4	3	..	3	1
insimulo	..	..	..	1	2
insolesco	..	..	..	1	2
instinguo	2	..	1	1	1
intermitto	..	..	1	2	3
intumesco	..	1	..	2	1
irascor	..	1	1	5	2
itero	1	..	..	2	2
levo	..	..	..	2	8

	Agr.	Germ.	Dial.	Hist.	Ann. I–VI
linquo	..	..	..	1	3
locuples	1	1	3	2	3
mediocris	..	..	1	..	2
meo	..	..	..	1	2
miseriae	1	..	..	4	4
nolo	..	..	4	5	4
notabilis	1	1	3	6	1
obsto	..	1	..	8	3
obturbo	..	..	..	2	3
occurso	..	..	..	3	5
operor	..	..	..	1	3
opto	..	..	2	2	1
palor	1	..	..	6	4
patesco	..	1	..	3	1
penso	1	..	1	3	1
perdomo	1	..	..	3	2
periclitor	..	1	4	1	6
periculosus	2	1	1	2	4
perimo	..	..	..	1	5
persuasio	1	1	1	2	1
pertempto	..	..	..	3	1
pone	..	..	..	4	2
praesto	1	3	3	2	3
precarius	1	1	..	1	1
prudentia	3	..	1	2	2
pulso	1	..	..	2	1
restituo	1	1	..	7	1
reveho	1	..	..	4	1
salvus	1	1	..	3	2
senesco	..	..	..	1	3
senium	..	..	..	3	3
sincerus	..	1	1	1	3
sollers	..	..	..	1	3
splendidus	2	1	2	6	2
stolidus	..	..	..	3	2
stultus	..	1	2	4	1
surgo	..	..	2	3	1
taceo	2	..	1	1	1
temero	..	..	..	3	2
transfugium	..	..	..	3	1
trudo	..	..	..	1	3
vanesco	..	..	1	1	4
vastus	2	..	..	5	5
velox	2	..	..	2	1
vereor	2	..	4	3	2
veritas	..	..	2	2	6
vexo	..	..	5	1	1
vigilantia	..	..	..	1	3
vigor	2	1	..	4	1
vindico	1	1	..	1	3

49. WORDS ONLY IN HEXAD I

adcumulator, III. 30. 1

adrepo, I. 74. 2; III. 50. 3

advecto, VI. 13. 2

antehabeo, I. 58. 3; IV. 11. 3

antevenio, I. 63. 4; IV. 18. 3

auctito, VI. 16. 1

belligero, II. 5. 2; III. 73. 3; IV. 46. 1

comperior, IV. 20. 2

condemnator, IV. 66. 1

consultor, IV. 24. 3; VI. 10. 2

contionabundus, I. 17. 1

dedeceo, II. 43. 6

dehortor, III. 16. 3

demuto, IV. 16. 3

denseo, II. 14. 3

deruptus, II. 80. 3; IV. 45. 1; VI. 21. 1

exsors, VI. 10. 1

exspes, VI. 24. 2

fastus, II. 2. 3; IV. 74. 4

firmator, II. 46. 5

genticus, III. 43. 2; VI. 33. 2

honorus, I. 10. 7; III. 5. 1; IV. 68. 3

incelebratus, VI. 7. 5

inclementia, IV. 42. 3

incultus, IV. 46. 1

indolesco, II. 72. 2; III. 73. 2; IV. 17. 2

innutrio, VI. 48. 2

insenesco, IV. 6. 3

instar, I. 20. 1; II. 61. 1; III. 36. 2

libidinosus, VI. 4. 4

lucar, I. 77. 4

ludificor, I. 46. 1; III. 21. 4

marcidus, VI. 4. 4

nanciscor, III. 32. 2

oppeto, II. 24. 2; IV. 50. 3

percutio, IV. 24. 2

perdisco, IV. 33. 2; VI. 45. 3

perstimulo, IV. 12. 4

pervigeo, IV. 34. 4

pessum, I. 9. 4; 79. 2; III. 66. 4

plecto, IV. 20. 4

positus, IV. 5. 3; VI. 21. 2

postscribo, III. 64. 2

praedatorius, IV. 24. 3

praefestino, V. 10. 3

praegracilis, IV. 57. 2

praelego, II. 79. 1; VI. 1. 1

praeverto, II. 55. 6; IV. 19. 4; 32. 1

provivo, VI. 25. 1

recepto, III. 60. 1; IV. 41. 1

receptor, IV. 23. 2

saltuosus, IV. 45. 1; VI. 34. 2

sanctor, III. 26. 4

secundo, II. 24. 3

subversor, III. 28. 1

superbio, I. 19. 5; II. 36. 3

suspicax, I. 13. 4; III. 11. 2

truculentia, II. 24. 1

turbator, I. 30. 1; 55. 2; III. 27. 2

vaniloquentia, III. 49. 1; VI. 31. 1

50. WORDS ONLY IN SPEECHES[1]

adminiculum, XII. 5. 3; XIV. 54. 2

adnumero, XIV. 53. 5

adsuefacio, XII. 5. 3; 10. 2

aestimatio, XV. 21. 1

aeternitas, XI. 7. 1

compesco, I. 42. 3

*conformo, IV. 8. 4

*conservo, XII. 52. 2

contemplatio, XV. 63. 1

*continentia, XIV. 56. 2

*contradictio, XIV. 43. 2

*contrecto, III. 12. 4; XIV. 35. 1

*dehortor, III. 16. 3

*demereor, XV. 21. 3

[1] The category takes in reported discourse, even of persons not named. Words occurring nowhere else in the writings of Tacitus are marked by an asterisk.

denoto, III. 53. 1
*derogo, XIII. 27. 3; XV. 20. 4
desidero, IV. 37. 2
detego (*met.*), III. 12. 2
detrudo (*met.*), XIII. 43. 2; XIV. 54. 3.
dilacero (*met.*), II. 71. 1
*efflagitatio, II. 38. 2
emendo, XV. 20. 3
eniteo, XIV. 53. 5
excelsus, III. 53. 3; IV. 40. 7
exonero (*met.*), III. 54. 5
exsatio, II. 38. 1
exubero, XIV. 53. 5
felicitas, XIII. 42. 4; XIV. 53. 2
fulgor (*met.*), IV. 39. 2; XIV. 54. 3
hebesco (*met.*), III. 69. 2
*inausus, I. 42. 2
ignorantia, I. 59. 5
inclaresco, XII. 37. 3
*insatiabiliter, IV. 38. 5
*inveterasco, XI. 24. 7
*labefacto, XIII. 21. 4
liveo, XIII. 42. 3
marito, XII. 6. 1

*nefandus, III. 13. 2
*nefarius, III. 50. 1
nescio, III. 53. 2; XVI. 31. 2.
oppleo (*met.*), XI. 23. 4
*perfringo (*met.*), II. 38. 2
*pervigeo, IV. 34. 4
pio, I. 42. 1
praeparo, XI. 7. 1; XIII. 21. 3
praestringo (*met.*), XIV. 54. 3
*recido, III. 53. 4
*residuus, XI. 23. 3
restinguo (*met.*), III. 54. 1
rudimentum, XIV. 53. 4
*saepe numero, XIV. 43. 1
scelestus, II. 71. 4; III. 50. 2
*secessio, XVI. 22. 2
splendidus (*met.*), III. 54. 1
sublevo (*met.*), III. 12. 5
submoveo, I. 42. 1
*suppeto, XIV. 55. 4
*suscenseo, III. 12. 4
tranquillitas, IV. 40. 6
*transfundo, IV. 52. 2

51. THE VOCABULARY OF THE *ANNALES*

THE development between *Historiae* and *Annales* is patent, and so are the historian's various devices (Ch. XXVI). The difference in vocabulary is very striking (especially for the first hexad), and comparison by statistics is there legitimate, for the bulk is almost the same as that of the *Historiae* (proportion 10:11).

Lists of words can exemplify:

(1) Words dropped after the *Historiae* (App. 45). Tendencies already observed (App. 42) become stronger. Thus 'arbitror' and 'cupiditas' go. Similarly, a sharp decline in some instances: 'remaneo' (*Hist.* 12) and 'trepidatio' (13) are absent from *Ann.* I–VI, 'resumo' (9) appears twice there.

(2) Words first appearing in the *Historiae* but not used again (App. 46). Some dull and indistinctive, like 'confusio', 'considero', 'existimatio', 'substituo'. Others by contrast poetical—'deses', 'indigus', 'temno', 'pauperies'. Sallustian items like 'ducto', 'torpedo', and 'turbamentum' were presumably rejected because too startling and ornamental (App. 53). Similarly, a falling off in the frequency of typically Livian words could be surmised (cf. App. 54). Finally, the shape and form of certain words. At least ten in '-atio' are found only in the *Historiae*; some frequentative verbs ('haesito',

'infesto', 'noscito', 'retento', 'scriptito'); also a number of verbal substantives and inchoative verbs (see below).

(3) Emphatic or archaic words in growing favour (App. 47). Thus the predilection for 'claritudo', 'cupido', 'glisco', 'reperio', and 'senecta', with a sharp decline in their synonyms.[1]

(4) Words emerging first in the *Annales*. For twenty-four examples, thirteen of which are Sallustian (of various types), see App. 53 (on Sallust).[2]

(5) Some words that Tacitus employs only in the first hexad (App. 49). A number of rarities are among them.

(6) Rare words that have been claimed to be unique (below, p. 722).

Not that the development from *Historiae* to *Annales* is uniform, or simply to be defined by categories of words. The author's discrimination leads him to forswear some Sallustian words (for nine examples see App. 53). Tacitus likes the verbal substantives in '-tor' (p. 342). Yet some of them, found in the *Historiae*, are discarded later: adsertor, aemulator, deprecator (2), domitor (3), instigator, oppugnator (5), spectator (3), suasor. Perhaps of the more commonplace. But 'instinctor' (2) is rare and precious, and even more so 'venditator'.[3]

Again, inchoative verbs. Some, such as 'ardesco', 'fatisco', 'vanesco', are on the increase (App. 47). But there is a contrary tendency: no fewer than eighteen occur only in the *Historiae*, most of them once only (App. 46). The author came to have doubts. Many inchoatives are unduly poetical or conspicuous. Tacitus had shunned altogether 'defloresco', 'desuesco', and 'marcesco' (all of which are found in Livy).

Lastly, normal prose words, that is, 'classical' and 'Ciceronian'. Two phenomena. The one is in accordance with Tacitus' selectiveness—a number of them employed exclusively in speeches in the *Annales*, twenty of them occurring nowhere else in all his works (App. 50). The other is contrary—their first emergence in the *Annales*. The list is instructive (or rather, not a little enigmatic). As follows:

*adseveratio (7)	devincio (10)	lamentor (6)
*aegritudo (3)	*diligentia (2)	*maleficium (3)
cesso (3)	discidium (7)	*maleficus (4)
*clandestinus (2)	*dubitatio (4)	*obitus
*commonefacio	*exagito	oboedio (5)
*conor (2)	exanimo (7)	offensio (29)
*consenesco (2)	*excrucio (2)	*peregrinatio (3)
damnatio (11)	firmitudo (6)	*persolvo (3)
defleo (7)	fluvius (4)	*pertimesco (2)
*dementia	*gratificor	*reicio (4)
deporto (7)	inrogo (5)	*sempiternus (2)
detrimentum (3)	*insolentia (3)	vividus (4)

Some of these, marked by an asterisk, occur only in the first hexad.

[1] The comparative table in App. 47 is based on Löfstedt, *Syntactica* II (1933), 276 ff., but largely supplemented.

[2] Some of the others might be Sallustian: 'apiscor' (twelve times) is Livian but strangely not in Sallust.

[3] The former word is found six times in late writers, 'venditator' (*Hist.* I. 49. 3) only in Gellius V. 14. 3; XVIII. 4. 1 (information from the Direction of *TLL*).

As for vocabulary, two comments are called for—the one a doubt, the other a warning. First, the verifiable change in style and in choice of words. So large a portion of the *Historiae* having perished, might it not be hasty and illegitimate to put the change at the inception of the next work? An answer can be given. If the lost books exhibited (as will readily be conceded) a number of words that happen not to be on record before the *Annales*, for example either ordinary and unobtrusive words such as the first hexad of the *Annales* tends to shun, or some Sallustian expressions (there was presumably an excursus on the Dacians), nothing encourages the notion of a wide divergence between the beginning and the end. The history of the Flavian dynasty was one theme, and contemporary, proceeding from civil war to tyranny, a conception present to the mind of the writer, and (it may be conjectured) brought out in the structure, the first triad balancing the last (p. 214). On the other hand, Tiberius and the 'res publica', that was ancient history.

Secondly, the rarity of words. The following short selection of the ostensibly unique (or solely Tacitean) specimens will exemplify some of the verbal types that Tacitus favours:

adcumulator	perstimulo	professorius
aemulatus	pervigeo	provisus (6)
antehabeo (2)	postscribo	provivo
infenso (3)	praegracilis	regnatrix
peramoenus	praeumbro	
persimplex	prodigentia (3)	

Now some of these, let it be said in passing, might be Sallustian; and others are easy or obvious formations. Commentators have often taken over obsolete pieces of information, making the style of Tacitus thereby much more peculiar than it is, or could be. Careful inquiry shows that sundry words and expressions find parallel or precedent.[1] At the same time, however, a contrary danger emerges— the assumption, without need, of 'echoes' and 'borrowings' from earlier writers. Many of the instances cited can be dismissed, being natural resemblances (and some perhaps inevitable).

To catalogue Tacitean rarities is legitimate, useful, and necessary. What is needed is a sense of proportion—and a thought for all that is lost of Sallust and Livy, for all the lost historians between Livy and Tacitus. One of the lists most easy of access registers no fewer than sixty-five words in the *Annales* which 'appear to have been invented' by Tacitus.[2]

Some of the claims are manifestly false. Thus 'incelebratus' (VI. 7. 5) is taken from Sallust (*Hist.* I. 88), avowedly one might say; and 'appellito' (IV. 65) was used by Livy and by Claudius Caesar (cf. App. 41). And it would be most surprising if a century of imperial Rome left to Cornelius Tacitus the dubious honour of coining 'gladiatura' (III. 43. 2), or 'histrionalis' (*Dial.* 26. 2; 29. 3; *Ann.* I. 16. 3), or 'professorius' (XIII. 14. 3).[3]

---

[1] For a wealth of pertinent examples, G. B. A. Fletcher, *AJP* LXVI (1945), 13 ff.

[2] H. Furneaux (ed. 2, 1896) I, 63 f.

[3] Similarly, Fletcher (o.c. 14) was able to adduce three later instances of the allegedly unique 'adulatorius' (VI. 32. 4).

On the other side, it is evident that the compounds with 'per-' and 'prae-' could be created with the utmost facility. Especially the former. Sporadic evidence from a variety of Latin writers shows that Tacitus is only exploiting a normal licence of the language.[1] Similarly, the verbal substantive in '-tor'. It appealed, to be sure, to Sallust, the great 'novator verborum'. It appealed to other creative writers. Cicero has 'adiunctor', which is unique; also 'delenitor' (elsewhere only in Apuleius) and 'deliberator' (only in Martianus Capella).[2] The singularity of Tacitus therefore abates. Given 'regnator', 'domus regnatrix' (1. 4. 4) does not deserve to cause much excitement. Further, 'repertor' (*Ann.* four times) was already in Sallust (*Hist.* IV. 69. 7); 'turbator' (three times) may have been there, and happens to occur in Livy. Nor did 'defector' (*Hist.* four times) and 'exstimulator' (once) have to wait for the intensified stylistic effort of the *Annales*. Eight others, first attested in that work, recur in writers of late antiquity:[3]

concertator	detractor	sanctor
condemnator	patrator	subversor
cupitor	profligator	

But there is one specimen unique in all Latinity—'adcumulator' (III. 30. 1).

Four other rarities of diverse types can be noted. Tacitus has 'prodigentia' three times;[4] and 'provisus' (but only in the form 'provisu') no fewer than six times (two of them in the *Historiae*).[5] And it is strange but true that the normal-looking 'antehabeo' (twice) and 'postscribo' cannot be matched anywhere else.[6]

To conclude. The selective vocabulary of the *Annales* stands out on a negative test—a mass of words the work eschews (App. 42–46). And the peculiar quality of the first hexad is revealed if two further lists be added (App. 55 and 57).

With the first hexad the Tacitean manner reaches its highest level. It cannot quite be said to fall off, but it is no longer the same afterwards. Discarding has gone on, but not only of the normal and unemphatic (App. 48). There is a continuous experimentation—and a number of the new words first appearing in Hexad I also fade out (App. 48). They belong to different types (among them some Sallustian words). The discards could be classified under the following heads:

(1) The indistinctive (as before). Thus 'diligentia', 'inertia', 'persuasio'.[7]

(2) The poetical and over-ornamental: 'exsors', 'exspes', 'honorus', 'marcidus'.

---

[1] Thus 'perdives' (Cicero, *In Verrem* II. iv. 59; *Ad Att.* VI. 1. 3); 'perincertus' (Sallust, *Hist.* IV. 1); 'peringratus' (Seneca, *Epp.* 98. 11); 'percopiosus' (Pliny, *Epp.* IX. 31. 1; Sidonius, *Epp.* I. 1. 4).

[2] Cf. *TLL.*

[3] As for 'profligator' (XVI. 18. 1), it is saved from being unique by Ennodius, *Dictiones* 18. 5; likewise 'sanctor' (III. 26. 4) by the scholiastic *Synonyma Ciceronis* 413. 13b. (information supplied by the Direction of *TLL*).

[4] VI. 14. 1; XIII. 1. 3; XV. 37. 1. Confined to Tacitus (information from *TLL*).

[5] See App. 53—it might be Sallustian. Cf. 'incultu' (IV. 46. 1).

[6] He has 'posthabeo' (*Hist.* IV. 7. 1; *Ann.* II. 86. 2)—which occurs in Caesar as well as in Virgil.

[7] Much better than 'inertia' were the Sallustian 'ignavia' and 'socordia'—or 'incuria' (not attested in Sallust). Sallust has 'inertia' only in *Cat.* and *Jug.*

(3) The conventionally ornate, like 'inclutus'.[1]
(4) The over-archaic: 'belligero', 'demuto', 'pessum', 'truculentia'.

These heads, however, do not exhaust the count, and there are many puzzles in Tacitus' changing predilections (see App. 52). In general what has been going on is a mixed process, both towards majesty and away from too much of the poetical and archaic. The marked and dominant development in the third hexad is, however, of a different nature (App. 58).

52. TACITUS' SELECTION OF WORDS

THE *Dialogue* seeks to convince through logic, sobriety, and elegance. If the style is quiet, it is far from timid; and in style, as in other respects, Curiatius Maternus discloses something about Cornelius Tacitus. The poet condemns in bold and ornate language the murderous oratory of the prosecutors and all that was repulsive in the habits of the Roman Forum.[2]

Maternus can risk unusual words. For example, 'clientulus' (*Dial.* 37. 1). It is rare—once in the *Annales* (XII. 36. 3), and three instances in writers of late antiquity.[3] Proclaiming his divorce from public speaking, Maternus uses 'deiungo' (11. 3). At first glance the verb looks normal and unobtrusive: before Tacitus it can be attested only in Varro (three times), and in Statius (once).[4] That being so, there is no reason to question or reject the unique 'depaco' of Maternus, describing how the firm peace of Caesar Augustus conquered and tamed Roman eloquence—'et maxime principis disciplina ipsam quoque eloquentiam sicut omnia depacaverat' (38. 2).[5]

In the *Annales* Tacitus exploits uncommon locutions for startling effects. He can also operate with words which, not rare in themselves, are rarely admitted by him save in speeches (App. 50). Similarly, the repetitions. L. Vitellius in his oration echoes both Valerius Messallinus and Claudius Caesar; and Vitellius in his turn is echoed by Eprius Marcellus (Ch. XXV).

There are other instances, felicitous if not deliberate. Germanicus in his dying words makes appeal to the ties of blood and kinship—'si quos propinquus sanguis' (II. 71. 2). The identical words recur at no long interval, on the lips of Tiberius Caesar (III. 12. 6), when he delivers an injunction to those who will defend the enemy of Germanicus (he alludes to the brother of Cn. Piso, namely L. Piso the *augur*, cf. III. 11. 2).

The wild rocks near Tiberius' villa at Rhodes, 'per avia ac derupta' (VI. 21. 1) were well suited for a murder: the phrase (identical but for the order of the words)

---

[1] For 'inclutus' in Tacitus, with some observations on Livy, see App. 54. For the history of the word, O. Prinz, *Glotta* XXIX (1942), 138 ff.
[2] *Dial.* 12. 2; 'lucrosae huius et sanguinantis eloquentiae usus'; 13. 5: 'nec insanum ultra et lubricum forum famamque pallentem trepidus experiar.'
[3] cf. *TLL*.   [4] cf. *TLL*.
[5] The word is admitted by Peterson and Gudeman (ad loc., the latter with a slight reserve); reproduced by Koestermann (Teubner, 1949); but rejected by Furneaux (Oxford, 1899) in favour of 'pacaverat' (inferior Mss.), and not in *TLL*, or the *Lexicon Taciteum* of Gerber and Greef.

had been used for a scene of violence in the remote parts of Spain (IV. 45. 1). Valerius Asiaticus in the last hours did not neglect his customary routine— 'usurpatis quibus insueverat exercitationibus, lauto corpore, hilare epulatus' (XI. 3. 2): the pastimes of Claudius Caesar are indicated by the phrase 'duas paelices quarum is corpori maxime insueverat' (XI. 29. 3). Both Mithridates of Bosporus and the Christians are held to deserve exemplary treatment—'novissima exempla' (XII. 20. 2, cf. XV. 44. 5). The prince Tiridates asks for time before his journey from Armenia to Italy, 'tantum itineris aditurus' (XV. 30. 2): Nero, meditating a peregrination in the eastern lands, must delay, his loyal citizens being grieved 'quod tantum ⟨itineris⟩ aditurus esset' (XV. 36. 3). The prosecutor Suillius Rufus refers to those 'qui . . . eloquentiam tuendis civibus exercerent' (XIII. 42. 3). He meant himself, the plea was dishonest as well as conventional. Of C. Piso (a conventional and empty character) it is stated 'facundiam tuendis civibus exercebat' (XV. 48. 3).

Reported criticism of Thrasea Paetus for a proposal of reform makes play with the word 'emendatio' (XIII. 49. 3). Nowhere else in Tacitus—and nowhere else in the *Annales*—is 'emendo', which is used by Thrasea himself in his oration (XV. 20. 3). The theme is taken up by Cossutianus Capito, denouncing Thrasea to Nero—'censeret quid corrigi aut mutari vellet' (XVI. 28. 2). Thrasea was in danger of being held a moralistic 'improver', cf. Suetonius, *Nero* 37. 1: 'tristior et paedagogi vultus'. It was not good to be an 'emendator senatus' (Pliny, *Epp.* VI. 5. 4).

A single word will be repeated with deadly effect. The speeches show notable examples. The device can be seen elsewhere. Suillius Rufus was 'terribilis ac venalis' (XIII. 42. 1): the imperial freedman Polyclitus, making his pompous appearance in Britain, is described as 'militibus quoque nostris terribilis' (XIV. 39. 2). The *Annales* show no other instance of the word. Nero feared the torpid nobleman Cornelius Sulla, believing him a 'simulator' (XIII. 47. 1). Tigellinus duly takes it up, denouncing Sulla as 'simulatorem segnitiae' (XIV. 57. 2).

Tacitus' unerring sense for words comes out most clearly in his portrayal of Tiberius. In two ways—the speeches, with their Tiberian phraseology (App. 39), and the narration, describing the manner or actions of the enigmatic ruler (Ch. XXVI).

Tacitus shows marvellous discrimination all through. Thus the archaic phrase 'Remus et Romulus' (XIII. 58).[1] He has 'percutio' only once, 'principes Musulamiorum . . . securi percutit' (IV. 24. 2)—it is a Republican and consecrated term.[2] 'Deleo' is admitted in the *Annales* only for the destruction of a city, Artaxata (XIII. 41. 2; XIV. 23. 1), 'proles' only for Parthian princes (II. 1. 2; XI. 10. 4; XII. 18. 2), 'aequor' only in the Virgilian description of the Ocean (II. 23. 2), the poetical 'fastus' only for a Parthian (II. 2. 3), and for the haughty demeanour of janitors (IV. 74. 4); while 'vates' (meaning 'poet') occurs only in reported discourse, and 'pango' is restricted to Nero's productions (XIII. 3. 4; XIV. 16. 2). The panegyrists of Germanicus at Antioch laud the dead hero as a 'proeliator' (II. 73. 2): the poet Maternus (and nobody else) is allowed to employ 'proeliator', and

---

[1] Observe Naevius (cited by Donatus on Terence, *Ad.* 537); Cassius Hemina, fr. 11; Cicero, *De legibus* I. 8; Servius on *Aen.* VI. 777; Varro in Festus 332 L.

[2] cf. Cicero, *In Pisonem* 84 (Balkan chieftains).

very suitably—'pluris tamen bonos proeliatores bella quam pax ferunt' (*Dial.* 37. 7).[1]

Poetical language was permitted in historical writing, but an author had to be on his guard. Tacitus did not care to repeat a number of words he had ventured in the *Germania* (App. 42), or several in the *Historiae*. Long lists of poetical words can be drawn up, or short and selective; and other writers can be brought in for illustration, such as Ammianus Marcellinus. A brief catalogue registers the following in Tacitus:[2]

> convecto, crudesco, denseo, grandaevus,
> inaccessus, innumerus, inopinus, intemeratus,
> lapso, oppeto, praescius.

What Tacitus has the good sense to avoid is worth noting:

> letalis, longaevus, praecelsus, molimen.

The reasons for many of Tacitus' likes and dislikes can easily be divined. Some are less obvious (but instructive for the study of Latin semantics), others enigmatic. 'Fluvius' (4) and 'oboedio' (5) first crop up in the *Annales*, which alone have 'offensio' ('offensa' being exclusive to the *Historiae*); 'culpo' is admitted only in the *Historiae* (four times), 'celo' nowhere. The simple verb might be expected to appeal for vigour and brevity (thus 'rapio', 'traho'). There are surprises—'carpo' once in all Tacitus (*Ann.* XII. 32. 1), 'vado' twice (*Hist.* III. 41. 2; *Ann.* XIV. 8. 1), 'tango' only in the form 'tactus', of objects struck by lightning (XIII. 24. 2; XIV. 12. 2); 'surgo' (*Hist.* 12) appears only four times in the *Annales*; others are infrequent or fade out after the first hexad—'levo', 'surgo', 'vexo'; also 'careo', 'doleo', 'taceo' (App. 48).

And other odd phenomena—the rarity of 'debeo' (*Dial.* 4; *Hist.* 4; *Ann.* 8) and of 'nolo' (*Dial.* 4; *Hist.* 5; *Ann.* 4—all in hexad I); 'conor' (2), 'clandestinus' (2), and 'sempiternus' (2) occur in I–VI for the first time and the last. 'Cogito' (mainly in speeches) is not found after XII. 11. 2, 'temere' after XII. 39. 2, 'obviam' after XIII. 2. 1. 'Dives' is frequent, 'divitiae' eschewed (only in *Dial.* 8. 4 and *Ann.* XVI. 3. 1), while 'locuples' drops out after VI. 16. 2, 'opulentus' after XII. 63. 3.[3] 'Crudelis' occurs once (VI. 4. 4), 'tranquillus' once (I. 3. 7), 'fidelis' twice (*Dial.* 34. 5; *Ann.* XV. 67. 2). It is not until very late that 'lascivus' (XIV. 2. 1), 'scurrilis' (XV. 34. 2), 'obscenus' (XV. 37. 3), and 'aegrotus' (XV. 60. 3) slip in; while 'fugo' (XV. 5. 3) and 'fraudo' (XIV. 37. 3) likewise make their sole appearance in the third hexad.

Compositions like the Emperor's letter to Aelius Seianus or the speeches of L. Vitellius and of Seneca reveal a parodist as well as an artist. Exploiting Sallust, Tacitus annexes and develops the Sallustian manner. He can echo other writers. Alluding with distaste to Haterius' flow of ephemeral eloquence, he employs a

---

[1] A rare word, cf. Justin XV. 4. 19: 'proeliator insignis.'

[2] H. Hagendahl, *Studia Ammianea* (Diss. Uppsala, 1921), 21.

[3] 'Opes' is more ample and suggestive: nearly five columns in Gerber–Greef. The ugly 'pecuniosus' emerges for the first time in the *Annales* (III. 55. 3; XIII. 6. 4; 52. 2): all instances worth attention.

Ciceronian phrase, 'canorum illud et profluens' (IV. 61, cf. p. 324). Haterius was very Ciceronian. It is therefore singularly appropriate that on his first presentation he should objurgate Tiberius with the Ciceronian exordium 'quo usque patieris, Caesar, non adesse caput rei publicae?' (I. 13. 4)—especially if the text (here corrupt) in fact carried the word 'tandem' after 'caput'.[1]

The Tacitean adaptations of Livy, among them 'stolide ferox' (I. 3. 4) are instructive on various counts (App. 54). Tacitus comes very close to Ovid's description of the oratory of Valerius Messallinus (III. 34. 1, cf. *Tristia* IV. 4. 3 ff.). But nothing can surpass the Virgilian phrase adapted to the unhappy Julia (I. 53. 2, from *Aen.* VI. 442, cf. p. 358). It is therefore hardly necessary to document the affinity of their common predilection for certain words. The standard example is 'infensus' in proportion to 'infestus'—different from all other Latin writers.[2]

The arguments about fame put into the mouths of those who criticized Tiberius (IV. 38. 5) suitably serve up the stock examples of the Augustan poets—which discloses Tacitus' own attitude in the matter (cf. p. 315). Then comes the phrase 'unum insatiabiliter parandum, prosperam sui memoriam'. The word 'insatiabiliter' is rare, and wholly alien to the kind of rare words that Tacitus normally favours. It is charged with emotion, exaggerated if not insincere. Compare the eloquent protestations of the mourners in Lucretius, 'at nos horrifico cinefactum te prope busto | insatiabiliter deflevimus', &c. (III. 906 f.).[3] Note therefore phrases like the Ciceronian 'immortaliter gaudeo' (*Ad Q. fr.* III. 1. 9).

Prose or poetry, Tacitus had a subtle ear and a memory for words that never failed. He can blend echoes of different writers without danger of incongruity. Thus Livy and Virgil in Germanicus' address to the mutinous troops (I. 42); and summaries of Claudian orations or other material from the *acta senatus*, like the reports of Roman generals, take on a convincing Sallustian hue (cf. App. 41 and 53).

The range of his reading must have been vast. The *Dialogus* reveals a close and verbal familiarity with many of the writings of Cicero (p. 116). The *Annales*, by casual but relevant items about obscure or forgotten practitioners, show how well he knew the register of the Roman orators from Cicero down to his own time or memory (Ch. XXV). Moreover, when the topic of sumptuary legislation arose in the reign of Tiberius, the historian recalled, or looked up, a famous debate of 55 B.C. (II. 32. 2, cf. Dio XXXIX. 37. 2).

Attention to words need not mean neglect of facts. Precision becomes a habit. Tacitus was diligent in consultation of the senatorial archives, and the manner of his writing is a result of industry as well as of exigent taste. Such is the man who, when he composed history, was content to reproduce for the most part a single source—so some believe.

---

[1] The *Codex Mediceus* has 'aput tē'. Modern texts take no account of the 'tē'. Lenchantin de Gubernatis in the *apparatus* of his edition (Rome, 1940) suggested 'tandem', which is attractive for the reason given above, cf. R. Syme, *JRS* XXXVIII (1948), 128. Against, C. O. Brink, *JRS* XLI (1951), 40.

[2] *TLL*, s.v. 'infestus' (with a table).

[3] It was difficult to use the word seriously. Pliny has it once, deliberately, and indeed epigrammatically, but in a trivial context (*Epp.* IX. 6. 3).

53. SALLUSTIAN LANGUAGE

THE style of Sallust has been much studied, though not always properly assessed.[1] The influence on Tacitus can readily be recognized—syntax, vocabulary, and diction. It stands out clearest in the two monographs with their restricted compass, and especially in the military and geographical portions of the *Agricola*. As for the *Historiae*, imitation is direct and open (Ch. XVII). Hence a tendency to underestimate what that work owes to Livy—or to take the thing for granted and not go further, to the *Annales*. Yet the *Annales*, it can be contended, yield evidence of a deeper familiarity, a much more subtle technique. So sure is the taste of Tacitus that, echoing a passage of Sallust, he amends it to reproduce the later manner of his model, substituting 'socordia' for 'inertia'.[2] Tacitus shows himself veritably 'unicum lectorem esse enarratoremque Sallustii'; he has been able 'neque primam tantum cutem ac speciem sententiarum, sed sanguinem quoque ipsum ac medullam verborum eius eruere atque introspicere penitus'.[3]

Single words or typical devices point the way.[4] But it is not a matter of mere borrowing—the manner has been adapted and extended, in manifold ways. It can be detected in the appropriate (and often predictable) contexts, namely, foreign wars and exotic geography, digressions, character-sketches, and orations— notably the orations of admired or old-fashioned senators. Indeed, whole episodes appear to be selected and exploited by Tacitus largely because they would immediately recall Sallust (Ch. XXVII). A number of 'Sallustian' passages have in fact escaped the notice of collectors and commentators, though obvious: for example, a Roman governor called Piso, assassinated by a native in Spain (IV. 45, cf. *Cat.* 19).[5]

Sallust's early writings on Catilina and Jugurtha furnish numerous clues. The results are striking—much more so when it is recalled how little survives of Sallust's *Historiae*. The subject-matter of that work encourages one to search more widely in the *Annales*. So much emerges that it is desirable to eschew in this place a number of obvious borrowings and proceed 'per difficilius'. The inquiry might even permit surmise about a few words not directly attested as Sallustian. Various criteria can be invoked. For example, the type of episode or comment; indubitable Sallustian phraseology in the vicinity; the shape of the phrase (disharmonious or deliberately plain); turns of accidence or syntax; words of a shape and colour that Sallust fancies; and an archaic atmosphere. With this guidance

---

[1] As W. Kroll points out, *Glotta* xv (1927), 280. For a list of typical words, ib. 301 ff.

[2] I. 9. 4 (on Lepidus and Antonius), cf. *Jug.* I. 4. Sallust's *Historiae* show no specimen of 'inertia': the stronger word 'socordia' is employed sixteen times in his works.

[3] Gellius XVIII. 4. 2—where, however, the person who made those claims, a 'iactator et venditator Sallustianae lectionis' was cruelly exposed. The word 'venditator' is choice, cf. App. 51.

[4] For details cf. E. Wölfflin, *Philologus* XXVI (1867), 122 ff.; G. Schönfeld, *De Taciti Studiis Sallustianis* (Diss. Leipzig, 1884). The parallels cited by A. Draeger, *Über Syntax und Stil des Tacitus*[3] (1882), 125 ff., come from Wölfflin; and H. Furneaux in his edition of the *Annales* (ed. 2, 1896) I, 72 f. is also derivative.

[5] Furneaux's notes on this chapter mention Sallust only once, and the moral is not drawn.

half a dozen passages of narrative or digression (from among those noted or cited at the beginning of Ch. XXVII) may be put to the test.[1]

(1) The judgement on Pompeius Magnus (III. 28. 1). This comes towards the end of the digression on legislation (III. 26 f.), where the mention of L. Sulla and the 'turbidae Lepidi rogationes' inevitably calls up their chronicler. Nor has anybody failed to recognize that this is a 'Sallustian' digression, whatever be its ultimate source or sources (see App. 41). Not merely a phrase, like 'suopte ingenio' (26. 1); or 'largitor' and 'turbator' (27. 2), the former of which is attested in Sallust.[2] Observe the atmosphere suggested by 'provenere dominationes multosque apud populos aeternum mansere'.[3] Now Magnus is styled 'suarumque legum auctor idem ac subversor'—deliberate and derisive echo of Servius Tullius, 'sanctor legum' (26. 4). The word 'sanctor' is all but unique, and 'subversor' is elsewhere found only in ecclesiastical Latin (p. 723). Either or both might have been coined by Sallust.

(2) L. Piso, governor of Hispania Citerior (IV. 45), cf. Cn. Piso (*Cat.* 19). The assassin duly exhibits Spanish defiance when put to torture.[4] He had tried to escape from the scene of his crime—'pernicitate equi profugus, postquam saltuosos locos attigerat, dimisso equo per derupta et avia', &c. Tacitus has 'pernicitas' elsewhere (*Germ.* 46. 2; *Hist.* I. 79. 2; *Ann.* II. 68. 1; III. 20. 1; XII. 51. 1); 'saltuosi loci' again in VI. 34. 2 (cf. 'saltuosa loca', *Jug.* 38. 1; 54. 3); 'per avia ac derupta' in VI. 21. 1, and 'colle arduo et derupto' in II. 80. 3. There is a chance that Sallust used both 'pernicitas' and 'deruptus'. Further, both episodes are wound up in a very similar fashion.[5]

(3) The campaign of Poppaeus Sabinus in Thrace (IV. 46–51). The whole episode is instructive, showing use of Sallust on the operations of P. Servilius against the Isaurians.[6] For present purposes the first chapter can suffice. It exhibits a rare and Sallustian expression, 'montium editis incultu atque eo ferocius agitabant'. Some editors have wished to emend 'incultu', but cf. *Cat.* 55. 4; *Jug.* 2. 4. Note the phrase 'adversum accolas belligerare' (46. 1). The verb may be Sallustian; the noun certainly is.[7] Tacitus has two other instances of 'belligero', both in the first hexad (II. 5. 2; III. 73. 3).

---

[1] None of these six passages occurs among those specially singled out by G. Schönfeld, o.c. 51 ff.

[2] For 'largitor', *Jug.* 95. 3. Elsewhere in Tacitus only *Hist.* II. 86. 2 (the character of Antonius Primus). Livy has 'turbator' several times.

[3] cf. XII. 28. 2: 'Cherusci, cum quis aeternum discordant.' The only other instance in Tacitus of 'aeternum' thus used.

[4] For the τόπος compare the assassin of Hasdrubal (Livy XXI. 2. 6).

[5] Sallust, *Cat.* 19. 3: 'sed is Piso', &c.; 4: 'sunt qui ita dicant imperia eius iniusta superba crudelia barbaros nequivisse pati', &c. Cf. *Ann.* IV. 45. 3: 'sed Piso Termestinorum dolo caesus habetur; quippe pecunias e publico interceptas acrius quam ut tolerarent barbari cogebat.'

[6] Sallust, *Hist.* II. 87, cf. W. Heraeus, *Archiv für lat. Lex.* XIV (1906), 273 ff.

[7] IV. 27: also in I. 107, if the supplement of Kritsch be accepted. Tacitus likes the word (four times in the *Historiae*, nine in *Annales*).

(4) C. Cassius, the governor of Syria (XII. 12. 1). The notice contains a verb first attested in Sallust ('praemineo') and an aphorism in the manner of the master—'industriosque aut ignavos pax in aequo tenet'. Cassius is meant to suggest Metellus in the *Bellum Jugurthinum* (45). He pays strict attention to discipline—'cura provisu perinde agere ac si hostis ingrueret'. The word 'provisu', in that form only, is not found elsewhere than in Tacitus (twice in the *Historiae*, three other instances in the *Annales*).[1] Sallust may be the precedent as well as the model.

(5) Mithridates of Bosporus (XII. 20. 1). The hazards of warfare are set forth— 'sed disserebatur contra suscipi bellum avio itinere importuoso mari; ad hoc reges ferocis, vagos populos, solum frugum egenum; taedium ex mora, pericula ex properantia', &c. The description is taken from Africa, cf. Sallust, *Jug.* 54. 9: 'aviis itineribus'; 17. 5: 'mare saevom importuosum.' Further, 'properantia' occurs in all Latin only in *Jug.* 36. 3—apart from two instances in late authors.[2] As for 'importuosus', Tacitus has one other example of it, in the brief and highly stylized digression on Capreae (IV. 67. 2); but he has a strong predilection for 'avius'.[3] What then should be said about 'solum frugum egenum'? The word 'egenus' is archaic and poetical. Once in Livy (IX. 6. 4), it is not attested in Tacitus before the *Annales*. The instances are all worth noting (I. 53. 2; IV. 30. 1; XII. 46. 1; XIII. 56. 3; XV. 3. 2; 12. 1). Strange that it should be absent from Sallust.

(6) The excursus on Byzantium (XII. 63). The author gives a lead by referring to the fish, 'vis piscium immensa Pontum erumpens' (63. 2), cf. Sallust, *Hist.* III. 66: 'qua tempestate vis piscium Ponto erupit.' Indeed, he improves on his model. Further speculation is therefore justifiable. Byzantium is designated as 'fertili solo fecundo mari'. The word 'fecundus', favoured in geographical contexts (*Agr.* 12. 5; *Germ.* 5. 1; *Hist.* I. 11. 1; IV. 50. 4; *Ann.* IV. 65; XIII. 57. 1), ought to be Sallustian.[4] Furthermore, the Byzantines gained profit from the fisheries—'quaestuosi et opulenti'. The adjective 'quaestuosus' occurs only once again in Tacitus, where the prosperous appearance of the soldiers in Syria is described—'nitidi et quaestuosi, militia per oppida expleta' (XIII. 35. 1). That is not all. The survey of Byzantine history put into the mouths of the envoys leads up to the geographical excursus with a phrase about the site—'quando ea loca insiderent quae transmeantibus terra marique ducibus exercitibusque, simul vehendo commeatu, opportuna forent' (XII. 62). There is no other case of 'transmeo' in Tacitus. Then the digression begins 'namque artissimo inter Europam Asiamque divortio', &c. The word 'divortium' might come from Sallust on the Pontus—or on the Pillars of Hercules.[5]

---

[1] One of the instances, characterizing Mucianus, is suggestive (*Hist.* II. 5. 1).

[2] viz. Julius Valerius I. 43; Martianus Capella VI. 607 (information supplied by the Direction of *TLL*).　　　　　[3] *Agr.* twice, *Hist.* twice, *Ann.* eight times.

[4] He has both 'infecundus' and 'infecunditas', which are rarer than one might expect (cf. *TLL*): 'infecundus' occurs in the account of Africa (*Jug.* 17. 5). Observe how Tacitus describes the Garamantes, *Hist.* IV. 50. 4: 'gentem indomitam et inter accolas latrociniis fecundam.'

[5] cf. the *schol.* on Juvenal x. 1: 'angustissimo divortio inter columnas Herculis.'

There is another way of approach. One of the changes in Tacitus' style from the *Historiae* to the *Annales* is the increasing frequency of certain 'Sallustian' words. For example, 'memoro', 'patro', 'polliceor', 'sustento' (cf. App. 47). More remarkable perhaps is the emergence of words he had not used before. Some of them, rare and startling in any case, are employed only once (like 'sanctor' and 'subversor' noted above). Others are more instructive:

antehabeo (2)	*gravesco (3)	*praeverto (3)
*antevenio (2)	imitamentum (3)	prodigentia (3)
apiscor (12)	infenso (3)	*prolato (*met.* 4)
belligero (3)	*inquies (6)	*repertor (4)
*consultor (2)	*insuesco (7)	*saltuosus (2)
dehonesto (5)	notesco (6)	*satias (4)
deruptus (3)	*pessum (3)	turbator (3)
egenus (7)	*praemineo (4)	*vecordia (6)

Several in this list (marked by an asterisk) are Sallustian. Others might also be, e.g. 'egenus'[1] and 'dehonesto'.[2] The context is often worth inspecting.

Negative indications will not be neglected. Some 'normal and classical' words occur not infrequently in Sallust. For example:

exaequo (3)	machinor (4)	saucio (6)
exopto (4)	pristinus (4)	vehementer (10)
factiosus (9)	remoror (4)	

They were not 'Sallustian' enough for Tacitus—and they are found nowhere in all his works. Similarly 'rapina' (9)—once only (in the *Historiae*); and 'existimo' (37)—very rare in Tacitus (*Dial.* once, *Hist.* once, *Ann.* three times).

Imitators of Sallust easily incurred criticism through their too obvious predilections. Seneca takes to task the historian Arruntius, with pertinent examples (*Epp.* 114. 17 ff.). A number of Sallustianisms were archaic or poetic to excess. Tacitus balked at the following:

dedecor	discordiosus	missito
defenso	festinus	musso
desenesco	gnaritas	negito

And his taste grew more exacting. Some that occur in the *Historiae* are not repeated in *Annales*. Sallust was never so much himself as in 'vitabundus per saltuosa loca exercitum ductare' (*Jug.* 38. 1). Of the three typical and striking words in that passage, Tacitus will now admit only one, 'saltuosus'.[3] A short list

---

[1] Here as elsewhere, however, the debt to Livy and to Virgil should not be left out of account. Note 'egenus' in Virgil (*Aen.* I. 599; VI. 91; VIII. 365). For the common elements in Sallust and Livy, see E. Skard, 'Sallust und seine Vorgänger' *Symbolae Osloenses*, Supp. xv (1956), 8 ff.

[2] Tacitus avoids 'dedecoro' (which is classical), but has the rare 'dedecorus' (III. 32. 2; XII. 47. 3), which occurs only twice elsewhere in Latin (Plautus, *Bacch.* 1191, where Ritschl emended; Orosius III. 23. 28).

[3] Quintilian observes that some found 'ducto' obscene (VIII. 3. 44). Livy has 'vitabundus', Tacitus not after *Agr.* 37. 5; *Hist.* III. 37. 2.

of discards gives:

abunde	hortamentum	torpesco
antecapio	indigus (4)	turbamentum
ducto	torpedo	vitabundus[1]

The Sallustian influence and colouring is most pervasive in the first hexad. Thus, words not occurring in Tacitus before or afterwards:

antevenio (2)	denseo	praedatorius
comperior	incelebratus	praeverto (3)
consultor (2)	pessum (3)	

One will also note 'cassus' (*Hist.* III. 55. 2), not repeated after the emphatic and solitary 'in cassum' of I. 4. 2.

Elsewhere the subject-matter often decides. Book XII, as has been shown, was propitious (e.g. XII. 12; 60; 63). Further instances can be discovered in the oriental narrations: thus the atrocities committed by Gotarzes, 'dum socors domi bellis infaustus ignominiam saevitia tegat' (10. 1), and his mutilation of Meherdates, 'auribus decisis vivere iubet, ostentui clementiae suae et in nos dehonestamento' (14. 3).[2] Nor would one search in vain the warfare in Britain. One example can suffice—'atque illi . . . multa et clara facinora fecere' (31. 4).[3]

Comparison with the third hexad might prove instructive in various ways. There seems to be less of the Sallustian manner in the story of Corbulo's campaigns than one would have expected. Given the verifiable change in Tacitus' style and vocabulary (cf. especially App. 58) the later books ought to be scrutinized. Unmistakable specimens can easily be found, it is true. Thus 'adversa in inscitiam Paeti declinans' (XV. 26. 3, cf. Sallust, *Hist.* II. 15), or 'plebi volentia fuere' (36. 4, cf. *Hist.* IV. 42), followed soon after by 'senatus et primores in incerto erant procul an coram atrocior haberetur', with which compare *Jug.* 46. 8: 'ut, absens an praesens . . . perniciosior esset, in incerto haberetur.' Again, XIV. 51. 3 (Faenius and Tigellinus): 'atque illi pro cognitis moribus fuere.' None the less, a change can be detected.

The last four character-sketches are relevant—Vatinius (XV. 34. 2), C. Piso (48. 3), Petronius (XVI. 18. 1 f.), Egnatius Celer (32. 3). They exhibit a deviation: balance, and a more flowing style, fewer disharmonies or omitted verbs. This in spite of the presence of rare or significant words (which the genre demands), e.g. 'praemineo' in the description of Vatinius, 'perseverus' in that of Piso. Again, Petronius is suitably introduced—'pauca supra repetenda sunt' (cf. *Jug.* 5. 3)—and described as 'non ganeo et profligator' (the second noun is all but unique, cf. App. 51); while 'adfluentia' (cf. III. 30. 2), though classical, is not common. As for Egnatius, he is described as 'perfidiosus' (nobody else in Tacitus earns that ugly label); but 'commaculatus', though found in Sallust (*Hist.* I. 55. 21), is also rhetorical and Ciceronian, alien to Tacitus' favourite manner.

---

[1] It is worth noting that Sallust risks 'torpedo' only in speeches—*Hist.* I. 77. 19; III. 48. 20; 26. Similarly 'musso' (I. 77. 3; III. 48. 8).

[2] For 'dehonestamentum' cf. p. 341.

[3] Sallust has the turn 'facinus facere' seven times.

54. LIVIAN STYLE

LIVIAN words and expressions are frequent in the writings of Tacitus.[1] The contrary would surprise. They had become the common stock of the Latin historical style. It is not helpful to talk of 'borrowings' from Livy.

But there are clear echoes and adaptations. It was a habit in ancient ethnographical writing to transfer descriptive terminology from one barbarian people to another. Likewise in history the neat and epigrammatical label. Thus 'liberator haud dubie Germaniae' (*Ann.* II. 88. 2, cf. Livy III. 53. 2) and 'plura consilio quam vi' (II. 26. 3, cf. Livy XXI. 2. 5).[2]

Whole scenes and episodes from an earlier author would be present to the mind of an historian. Thus, to illustrate Germanicus' peregrination of the East, it is legitimate to adduce Livy's account of the tour of Aemilius Paullus among the renowned sites of the Greek lands (XLV. 27. 5 ff.), even though the resemblances of motive or phrase may not be very close.[3] Livy can also help the interpretation of vital passages in Tacitus.[4]

Germanicus on and beyond the Rhine should show a Livian colouring, and something more.[5] Scipio's oration to the mutinous soldiers in Spain (XXVIII. 27–29) had already been exploited for Dillius Vocula in the *Historiae* (App. 34). Germanicus in a like emergency indignantly asks the troops how shall he address them: are they 'cives', 'milites', or 'hostes' (I. 42. 2, cf. Livy XXVIII. 27. 4)? The vocabulary of the speech is noteworthy—the verbs 'compesco' and 'pio' not elsewhere in the *Annales*. Further, Virgilian shades in 'inausum intemeratumve' (ib. 2): both adjectives occur in that poet for the first time, and the first of them is unique in Tacitus. Also 'egregiam duci vestro gratiam refertis' (ib. 3), which might be illustrated by *Aen.* IV. 93: 'egregiam vero laudem et spolia ampla refertis.' Conversely, the marvellously Virgilian picture of the storm in the Ocean (p. 357) contains a Livian motive—soldiers impeding the operations of the sailors (II. 23. 2, cf. Livy XXII. 19. 10), but in very different language.

Tacitus' echoes of other writers (as of himself) tend to be precise as well as subtle. He describes the relegated Agrippa Postumus as 'robore corporis stolide ferocem' (I. 3. 4). Commentators duly register and repeat the borrowing from Livy VII. 5. 6—'stolide ferocem viribus suis'.[6] The startling value of it should be added. Livy was referring to a brutish son of the patriciate, a Manlius cast off by his family and sent away.

---

[1] See the valuable (but not complete) studies of G. Andresen, *Wochenschr. für cl. Phil.* 1916, 210 ff.; 401 ff.; 688 ff.; 758 ff. The second of those papers compares items in the first decade and in *Ann.* I–VI. See also G. B. A. Fletcher, *CR* LIX (1945), 45 ff.

[2] The second instance is not in Furneaux's note ad loc., and seems to have escaped Andresen and Fletcher.

[3] Andresen, o.c. 691. Observe that one of the two cases of 'inclutus' in the *Annales* occurs in Germanicus' travels (II. 53. 2), whereas Livy's account has three instances, rather too close together (XLV. 27. 6; 9; 28. 3). The word had been admitted six times in the *Historiae*.

[4] Thus 'rubrum ad mare patescit' (II. 61. 2, cf. App. 71).

[5] Andresen, o.c. 211; 759.

[6] Strangely absent from Andresen, o.c. 210 ff.

Another and comparable felicity seems to have escaped notice altogether. Recounting the sacred legend, how Romulus when he disappeared from mortal view was taken up into the heavens, Livy observes that there was a different and less edifying version—'fuisse credo tum quoque aliquos qui discerptum regem patrum manibus taciti arguerent' (I. 16. 4). When Tiberius Caesar asked the Senate to grant a dispensation to the eldest son of Germanicus and cited Augustan precedents, the historian duly puts in his comment—'sed neque tum fuisse dubitaverim qui eius modi preces occulti inluderent' (III. 29. 2).

In the *Historiae* there was no lack of the Livian fluency, and even redundancy. The *Annales* exhibit a strong movement away from rhetoric.[1] It might well prove possible to document the change by the progressive abandonment of a number of the words favoured by Livy. Some are of the 'normal and classical' type which Livy shares with Cicero, e.g. compound verbs (App. 45 f.). The following, of a more ornamental kind, and rare, Tacitus allows only in the *Historiae* (App. 46):

> contemptim (3), deses (4), horror, hortamentum,
> levamen, noscito, sopio, sopor.[2]

For comparison, a few that Tacitus has shunned altogether:

> confestim, defloresco, hisco, letum, marcesco, missito,
> molimen, mussito, musso, peregrinabundus, territo, vesanus.

55. NEW WORDS IN HEXAD III

abiudico	constitutio	emptito
abutor	continentia	eneco
adpropero	contradictio	exprobratio (2)
adsimulatio	deerro	expurgo
adtraho	demereor	fraudo
asporto	depopulor	gratulor
celeritas (3)	derogo (2)	imaginatio
commaculo	dissimilitudo (2)	imaginor
commuto (2)	dissipo	immortalitas
condemno (3)	dissociatio	impertio (2)
confio	dissolutio (2)	infirmo (2)
confuto	dissuadeo (4)	infitiae
coniveo	dito	infrequentia (3)
conscelero	doctrina (2)	intercīdo
consono (2)	effemino	intercurso
conspiro	emendatio	interiaceo

[1] As can be documented by the progressive abandonment of synonyms and hendiadys, from the minor works to *Hist.*, from *Hist.* to *Ann.*, cf. the table drawn up by K. Jax, *Studi in Onore di U. E. Paoli* (1956), 431.

[2] For the peculiar 'contemptim', suddenly used and dropped (*Hist.* III. 9. 5; 47. 3; 58. 4), cf. *TLL*. For 'horror' (and also for the highly Livian 'praeopto') see App. 34.

intromitto
inverto
malitia (2)
mansito (2)
merso
nuncupatio
obscuro (2)
perorno
praecaveo (2)
praemeditor
praeumbro

praevaricor
queritor
rebellatio
remuneror
restringo (4)
retego
reviso
secessio
subripio
subvectio
subvecto

subvectus
succurro
superpono
supersedeo
suppeto
supplico
traditio
traiectus
transmoveo

56. INCREASING FREQUENCY IN HEXAD III

| | Agr. | Germ. | Dial. | Hist. | Ann. | | |
					I–VI	XI–XII	XIII–XVI
accommodo	..	..	2	..	1	1	3
adduco	2	..	..	2	1	..	3
adfirmo	3	2	1	13	..	1	1
adnoto	1	..	..	1	..	1	5
adquiro	..	1	1	2	..	2	2
adsentior	..	..	..	1	1	..	2
amoenitas	..	..	..	2	1	..	5
celebritas	1	..	..	2	1	..	1
circumspicio	..	..	..	1	..	1	3
concupisco	2	2	3	7	..	1	2
conglobo	1	..	..	1	1	2	4
conitor	1	..	..	1	..	1	4
conqueror	..	..	..	3	2	..	4
consocio	..	..	..	..	1	..	4
criminatio	..	..	..	3	1	..	5
deceo	1	..	2	1	1	..	4
deprendo	4	..	6	4	1	..	3
destinatio	..	..	..	3	..	1	1
detego	..	1	2	3	1	..	2
deterreo	..	..	1	4	1	1	3
dissolvo	1	..	..	..	1	..	4
dulcedo	1	1	..	..	1	..	3
existimo	..	..	1	1	..	..	2
expendo	..	..	..	1	..	1	4
expono	..	1	1	8	2	..	6
expromo	..	..	1	1	..	2	2
exuro	1	..	..	..	1	..	4
facetiae	..	..	..	..	2	..	4
factito	..	..	..	1	3	..	5
familiaritas	..	..	..	1	1	..	4
grassor	..	..	..	4	2	..	4
impunitas	..	..	..	7	1	..	5
inrisus	..	..	..	2	2	..	3

	Agr.	Germ.	Dial.	Hist.	Ann.		
					I–VI	XI–XII	XIII–XVI
inscitia	2	1	1	5	..	1	4
intellectus	..	1	2	..	1	..	2
interpretatio	1	1	1	3	1	..	3
nequeo	1	..	..	11	3	3	5
novitas	..	..	..	1	1	..	3
obnitor	..	..	..	1	1	..	4
obsidio	1	..	..	2	1	3	5
obsigno	..	..	..	..	1	1	5
obversor	..	..	..	2	..	2	4
occasio	2	3	..	7	2	4	7
occurro	2	1	..	18	3	..	8
oportet	..	1	..	5	..	1	2
perfungor	..	..	..	..	1	1	3
perpetro	..	..	..	2	1	3	6
proclamo	..	..	..	2	1	..	2
promitto	..	..	1	10	4	2	10
resumo	..	..	..	9	2	1	3
revoco	3	..	1	6	2	1	6
separo	2	6	1	3	2	1	4
suppedito	1	..	..	3	1	1	3
tarditas	..	..	..	1	1	..	2
testificor	..	..	..	..	..	2	5
timor	3	..	..	3	1	1	7
tractus	..	..	..	..	1	..	3
transeo	5	1	7	16	2	3	8
transmitto	..	..	..	10	2	..	11
vanitas	1	..	..	4	1	..	4
ventito	1	..	..	1	1	2	5

57. RECURRENCE OF WORDS

	Agr.	Germ.	Dial.	Hist.	Ann. XIII–XVI
abscondo	..	1	..	1	1
adfingo	..	..	..	1	1
adgrego	..	1	1	9	2
adnumero	..	..	..	2	1
adquiesco	..	..	..	1	1
adsigno	..	2	3	4	1
advoco	..	..	1	4	1
aequitas	..	..	1	..	2
aestimatio	..	..	1	..	1
antecello	..	..	..	1	1
audentia	..	2	..	..	1
blanditiae	..	..	..	3	2
brevitas	..	..	1	2	1
commemoratio	..	..	1	..	1
commodo	2	..	1	..	1

	Agr.	Germ.	Dial.	Hist.	Ann. XIII–XVI
comprobo	..	..	..	I	I
confirmo	..	I	2	..	I
confugio	..	..	I	2	I
coniectura	..	..	..	2	I
consuetudo	I	I	4	..	2
contemplatio	I	..	..	..	I
cruento	..	..	..	I	I
decerto	..	..	..	I	I
delego	I	2	2	2	I
denego	..	..	2	..	3
descendo	..	..	..	4	3
desperatio	..	..	..	8	I
distinctio	..	I	..	..	I
diversitas	..	2	I	6	I
divitiae	..	..	I	..	I
domo	4	..	..	I	I
emendo	..	..	I	I	I
eniteo	..	..	I	..	I
enumero	..	I	..	I	2
erudio	2	..	2	..	I
escendo	I	..	..	..	2
evalesco	..	2	..	I	I
everto (met.)	..	..	..	2	4
evulgo	..	..	..	I	3
exhortatio	..	..	..	5	I
expello	3	3	I	I	2
expio	..	..	..	2	I
exspectatio	..	..	..	2	I
exubero	..	..	..	I	I
felicitas	3	..	..	5	2
fortitudo	I	I	..	2	2
frequentia	I	..	I	I	I
gesto	I	4	..	3	4
glorior	..	..	..	I	I
gratulor	..	..	..	I	I
imitatio	..	I	..	I	I
immanitas	..	..	..	I	3
imprudentia	..	..	..	2	2
indulgentia	I	..	I	2	I
infamo	..	..	..	2	I
inhibeo	..	..	..	I	I
iniungo	I	I	..	..	I
inscribo	..	I	3	..	2
inservio	..	..	I	I	I
inspicio	I	..	..	2	2
invito	..	I	I	I	2
iracundia	I	..	..	8	2
lenitas	..	..	..	I	4
lentitudo	..	..	I	..	3

	Agr.	Germ.	Dial.	Hist.	Ann. XIII–XVI
luxuria	2	1	..	8	2
meditamentum	..	..	..	1	1
misereor	1	..	..	1	1
neglegentia	..	..	1	..	1
notitia	2	..	6	1	2
oblectamentum	..	..	1	..	4
observatio	..	1	..	1	1
obsido	..	..	..	1	2
parco	1	..	1	1	3
percontatio	..	..	1	..	1
pervulgo	..	..	1	..	2
placamentum	..	..	..	1	1
praeripio	..	..	..	1	4
probitas	..	1	2	2	1
proconsulatus	1	..	..	2	2
procuratio	..	..	..	3	1
pronuntio	..	..	..	1	3
propugno	1	..	1	..	1
providentia	..	..	..	2	1
querela	1	..	..	1	1
reconcilio	..	1	..	1	1
recordor	1	..	..	1	3
reservo	2	1	..	7	1
revalesco	..	..	..	1	1
rudimentum	1	..	..	..	1
satisfactio	..	1	..	..	1
scando	..	..	..	5	2
sciscitor	..	..	..	4	3
spolio	1	..	1	8	2
superfundo	1	..	..	4	1
supergredior	1	..	..	1	3
torqueo	..	..	..	2	2
tremo	..	..	..	1	2
vado	..	..	..	1	1
vastatio	..	..	..	1	1
vendito	..	..	..	1	1
verecundia	1	..	1	..	1
vociferor	..	..	..	2	1

58. THE STYLE OF HEXAD III

THE stylistic enhancement from the minor works to the *Historiae*, from *Historiae* to *Annales*, was quickly and firmly put on record.[1] There could be no dispute. Many years passed, however, before attention was paid to change and difference within the *Annales*. It was the peculiar behaviour of 'forem' that first

[1] E. Wölfflin, *Philologus* xxv (1867), 92 ff., &c.

attracted notice, with 'ni' showing a similar development.[1] The almost complete occlusion of 'quis' (for 'quibus') was a welcome confirmation.[2] The statistics are vocal:

	Agr.	Germ.	Dial.	Hist.	Ann. I–XII	Ann. XIII–XVI
essem	8	2	10	17	31	29
forem	4	..	..	51	62	1
quibus		passim		71	45	50
quis	1	..	..	23	54	7
ni	4	..	..	30	36	1

Other phenomena fitted in. 'Apud' (meaning 'in') shows a sharp decline in the third hexad (33:14), and there is a change in the relative frequency of 'quamquam' (34:6) and 'quamvis' (6:11). Moreover, the adjective 'grandis', banished from the *Annales* hitherto, comes back with five instances.[3]

The contrast lies between the first hexad and the third. What survives of the second (XI–XII) is not enough to permit firm deductions, yet it can be said that it occupies an intermediary stage in the development.[4] Here as elsewhere the relative bulk of the different portions will not be neglected.[5]

A careful inquiry into Tacitus' use of synonyms has produced striking results.[6] The historian, it is clear, turned from the choice and decorative to the quieter and the normal: fewer 'Tacitean' words, more 'Ciceronian'. For example:[7]

	I–VI	XI–XII	XIII–XVI
consulo	16	8	19
consulto	15	5	5
contemptio	..	1	1
contemptus	3	1	..
formido	14	2	2
pavor	8	2	11
timor	1	1	7
necessitas	17	5	13
necessitudo	5	1	..
transmitto	2	..	5
tramitto	11	1	6

It is much to be regretted that no systematic and exhaustive analysis of the vocabulary of the third hexad has ever been attempted. In the meantime it may be of some use to present three illustrative lists of nouns and verbs, viz:

(1) Increasing frequency in Hexad III (App. 56).

---

[1] H. C. Nutting, *Univ. of Cal. Pub. in Class. Phil.* VII (1923), 209 ff.
[2] E. Löfstedt, *Syntactica* II (1933), 285 f.   [3] ib. 286; 292 f.
[4] N. Eriksson, *Studien zu den Annalen des Tacitus* (Lund, 1934), 107.
[5] viz. in old-Teubner pages, 199:56:127.   [6] N. Eriksson, o.c.
[7] The instances are taken from Eriksson. Others could be added, e.g. 'polliceor' and 'promitto'.

(2) Words recurring that were absent from Hexad I (App. 57).

(3) New words (App. 55).

The lists are selective, not exhaustive; and especial attention has been given to 'normal' or unobtrusive words (for they often provide useful clues, cf. App. 42). One cannot fail to be struck by the abundance of abstract nouns and compound verbs, such as the historian previously eschewed (or admitted only in speeches, cf. App. 50).

The cumulative evidence is very powerful. Not, it is true, that the style changes in all particulars. The author is still keen on the practice of 'variatio'.[1] He can come out with an unusual word like 'mercimonium' (xv. 38. 2), which is Plautine, 'deprecabundus' (xv. 53. 2), 'indutus' (xvi. 4. 3), 'concertator' (xiv. 29. 2), or 'profligator' (xvi. 18. 1).[2] And he appears to have created a novelty in syntax, the genitive of the gerund used instead of the infinitive.[3]

There are other phenomena. One of the arrangements of words typical in polished prose is the extended *dicola* and *tricola*, e.g. 'per Africam etiam ac Siciliam et Italicas colonias' (vi. 12. 3). The device is frequent in the first hexad, but falls off later on.[4]

Tacitus comes more and more to fancy 'dehinc' (12 : 4 : 19), a word not used by him before the *Annales*; and 'abusque (2) and 'adusque' (1) appear for the first time. And a strange predilection emerges for 'ergo' at the beginning of a sentence in narrative passages. Two instances in the *Annales* before xiii. 51. 1, then five in xiv, ten in xv, and two in xvi. The perfect form '-ere' for '-erunt' lends dignity. Hence, it would appear, a valuable clue.[5] Yet it does not lead where one might expect. The relative frequency is strongest in III, VI, XI, and XIV : and, taken together, XV and XVI come next.[6] Observe, however, that there are only three instances in the last twenty-two chapters of XVI.

The new (but unemphatic) words seem to pile up towards the end of the *Annales* as extant. No single item can prove anything. But a doubt creeps in : did the author revise these books, or live to complete the hexad?

59. STYLISTIC WEAKNESSES

To suggest resemblances of scene or person Tacitus will repeat a word or an expression, most insidiously. Thus the Caesars and their ministers echo one

[1] cf. R. H. Martin, *Eranos* li (1953), 89 ff.

[2] 'Deprecabundus' is not attested elsewhere in all Latin, 'indutus' previously only in Varro, cf. *TLL*; and 'profligator' once in a late writer (Ennodius).

[3] xiii. 26. 3: 'nec grave . . . retinendi libertatem'; xv. 5. 3: 'Vologaesi vetus et penitus infixum erat arma Romana vitandi'; xv. 21. 2: 'decernaturque et maneat provincialibus potentiam suam tali modo ostentandi.' Cf. E. Löfstedt, *Syntactica* I² (1942), 106; ΔΡΑΓΜΑ . . . *M. P. Nilsson dedicatum* (1939), 297 ff. Some scholars doubted the construction, and the text. It is strange that two of the three instances occur in speeches (where Tacitus shuns the abnormal).

[4] E. Lindholm, *Stilistische Studien. Zur Erweiterung der Satzglieder im Lateinischen* (Lund, 1931), 196 ff.

[5] E. Löfstedt, *Philologischer Kommentar zur Peregrinatio Aetheriae* (1911), 36 ff.

[6] cf. in criticism of Löfstedt's statistics and opinions, R. H. Martin, *CR* lx (1946), 17 ff.

another—not so much the choice and startling phrase as the unobtrusive and conventional word, elsewhere in scant favour with the historian (p. 345: also, on the selection of words, App. 52).

Repetition may be a sign not of art but of ineptitude. Quintilian had to point out that Livy is prone to redundancy; and an emperor damned him as 'verbosus in historia neglegensque'.[1] The charge of carelessness can be extended from history to style. The author tends to iterate unemphatic words. Thus 'satis', five times in XXII. 4. 4–5. 1, four times in XXIII. 17. There is something else—forms or expressions that he takes up for the first time, repeats in close proximity, but then drops.[2]

Tacitus, it should seem, is the last author liable to be censured for redundance or for inadvertence. His more fluent style towards the end is a challenge. One discovers a number of verbal repetitions. The word 'coniuratio' shows fourteen instances in XV and XVI; and 'coniuratus' (a solitary case in the *Historiae*) is present five times in XV. The expression 'carmina factitare', once in the first hexad (VI. 39. 1), recurs four times in the third (XIV. 48. 1; 52. 3; XVI. 14. 1; 28. 1); and the verb 'conitor', once previously in the *Annales* (XI. 31. 3) comes back four times at short intervals in Book XV (42. 2; 51. 1; 57. 2; 66. 2). Similarly, certain words not previously attested in the *Annales*—e.g. 'denego' (XV. 42. 1; 57. 1; 62. 1), 'recordor' (XV. 57. 1; 70. 1; XVI. 7. 1).

How grave a view is to be taken of those repetitions? It is hard to say. But who can commend or approve the feeble 'se ostendere', twice in the *Historiae* (IV. 49. 2; V. 1. 1), banished from the *Annales* until Book XVI (10. 4; 18. 2; 22. 1)?

A number of flat and indistinctive words seem to be gaining in ascendancy (App. 56). And, whereas the author had anxiously avoided or paraphrased the technical and administrative terms, there now crop up for the first time in the *Annales* 'procuratio' (XVI. 17. 3) and 'proconsulatus' (XVI. 23. 1; 30. 1). Observe also 'institutio' for a philosophical sect (XVI. 34. 1). That is not in the Tacitean manner. By contrast, the few novel and decorative words like 'deprecabundus' and 'profligator' seem to stand out too sharply from this context.

It is negligent to have an ablative absolute, the subject of which is the subject or object of the main sentence. No fewer than five instances occur in Hexad III (XIV. 10. 1; XV. 30. 1; 51. 1; XVI. 14. 3; XVI. 17. 4). The last of those may be quoted —'quo interfecto dum rem familiarem eius acriter requiret'. The same chapter has the unemphatic pronoun 'is' a little too often (cf. 'eius' five times in c. 14).

The penultimate chapter (XVI. 34) exhibits three items worth a comment— 'queritor' for the first time in Tacitus;[3] 'facesso' likewise, in the sense of 'depart';[4] and a Graecism hard to parallel anywhere in prose— 'ut coniectare erat'.[5]

With every allowance made for a style changing as the history changed, it

---

[1] Quintilian VIII. 3. 53; Suetonius, *Cal.* 34. 2.

[2] K. Gries, *Class. Phil.* XLVI (1951), 36 ff.

[3] Some editors (not the most recent) wished to emend to 'quiritantes'.

[4] Elsewhere in Tacitus only with 'periculum' as the object (*Hist.* IV. 43. 1; *Ann.* I. 74. 2; VI. 30. 2).

[5] Given these items, it is hardly necessary to add 'dissociatio'—only here and in the elder Pliny (cf. *TLL*).

becomes hard to believe that all parts of the third hexad had been properly worked up.[1] And there are sundry defects in matter and structure (App. 60).

60. SIGNS OF INCOMPLETENESS

A NUMBER of phenomena raise a doubt whether Tacitus put the finishing touches to the third hexad. Citing the variant versions of his principal authorities early in Book XIII, he makes a promise to follow that practice in the future (20. 2). He fails to redeem it. Where is the explanation—did he forget, or find the thing not worth while? Or again, it may be, the references to Cluvius Rufus, Fabius Rusticus, and Pliny represent a stage short of the final elaboration, destined ultimately to be expunged for artistic reasons. Somewhere in the course of the second hexad Tacitus had probably mentioned the eminent Cluvius Rufus, it is true. Specification of sources is foreign to his normal and predictable manner. In the first hexad the principal historians of the period, Servilius and Aufidius, are nowhere even named.[2] Tacitus there operates with anonymities, deliberately.

Next, documentary information. Much of the material in I–VI comes from the archives of the Senate—not that the author anywhere says so. The third hexad, which owes much less to the *acta*, carries a casual and isolated citation (xv. 74. 3). Would Tacitus have let it stand in the finished version?

The chronological framework of the British insurrection presents a serious difficulty—too many events have been inserted under the year 61. It will have to be assumed that Tacitus was careless: the thing began in 60 (App. 69).

At the end of 62 three annalistic items are reported: Nero's gymnasium struck by lightning, an earthquake in Campania, and the decease of a Vestal Virgin (xv. 22. 2). The first item probably caused the author to go back and put in a sentence about the gymnasium at the end of 61 (xiv. 47. 2), where otherwise the death of the eminent consular Memmius Regulus would have made a more effective termination. As for the earthquake, on the testimony of Seneca (*NQ* vi. 1. 2), it ought to belong to 63. Seneca has day and date—'nonis Februariis hic fuit motus, Regulo et Verginio consulibus'. Which is correct—the historian or the contemporary witness who goes on to describe (and to assess) the damage?[3]

The year 63 also ends with three items: Latin rights for the communities of the Alpes Maritimae, a decision about the seating of Roman knights at the Circus, and a report about gladiatorial contests (xv. 32). What was done for the Alpes Maritimae cannot be regarded as very important. That small province subsisted. On the other hand, the author has missed two annexations that occurred in or about 64—the Alpes Cottiae and Pontus Polemoniacus. The fact comes from

[1] And it will not be easy to follow F. Klingner, who registers emphatically his impression that Tacitus is not less 'Tacitean' in the last books (*Hermes* LXXXIII (1955), 188).

[2] They might have been cited in Book V in a clash of testimony about the conspiracy of Seianus.

[3] The discrepancy causes much debate. See R. Lecocq, *L'Antiquité classique* XVIII (1949), 85 ff. That scholar argues that the consular date in Seneca is an interpolation ('Regulo et Verginio consulibus').

Suetonius (*Nero* 18), taken over by sundry later authors.[1] Tacitean omissions are often deliberate. A fact will be reserved for later treatment in a suitable context. It need occasion no disquiet that transactions on and beyond the Danube in Nero's reign are not noticed in the *Annales* as extant.[2] Similarly the decease of Polemo and the fate of his principality could have found an entry among eastern affairs in 67 or 68. Hardly, however, the incorporation of the Alpes Cottiae.

The year 64 ends with a report of 'prodigia' (xv. 47). Two notices deriving from the *acta* are employed to terminate the year 65 (XVI. 13. 3). The first is of a type unique in Tacitus—it specifies certain senatorial provinces in which levies are ordered for the legions of Illyricum. The second is a reference to a catastrophe at Lugdunum, 'clades Lugdunensis', which some critics find unduly curt and cryptic. It was in fact a fire, which must have occurred recently, not long after the conflagration at Rome (July 64), since Seneca mentions it (*Epp.* 91. 1 ff.), and Seneca perished in April 65.

Certain persons are introduced for the first time without proper elucidation. The great Vibius Crispus has an entry at the end of 60, but only in annotation on somebody else, his brother, who escaped the worst consequences of a prosecution, 'Vibii Crispi fratris opibus enisus' (XIV. 28. 2). More remarkable the note two years later on Cossutianus Capito—'qui nuper senatorium ordinem precibus Tigellini soceri sui receperat' (XIV. 48. 1). To the historian, Tigellinus was a familiar character. But, at the first mention (it is hardly a presentation), he ought to have labelled the man properly and given his *gentilicium*, 'Ofonius'.[3] Compare the trouble he takes with names and characters when beginning a new section of the work in the first two chapters of Book XIII (e.g. 'Afranius Burrus et Annaeus Seneca', though each had occurred in Book XII).

If Tacitus had cast an eye on the consular *Fasti* of these years, he could have observed the emergence of a cluster of names, permitting a guess (and something more) about the identity of the persons who were supplanting Seneca and Burrus in the counsels of Nero. He would discover, along with Vibius Crispus (*suff.* c. 62) his future peer, partner, and ally in oratory and in the favour of Vespasian, namely, Eprius Marcellus (*suff.* 62). Also T. Petronius Niger (*suff.* 62)—who may be the 'elegantiae arbiter' (XVI. 18. 2). The process can already by detected in the persons of the *ordinarii* of 61, Caesennius Paetus and Petronius Turpilianus, rapidly appointed to the commands in Cappadocia and in Britain. Turpilianus (*PIR*[1], P 233), who superseded Suetonius Paullinus, was one of Nero's friends and agents to the end.

The penultimate item of the year 61 is the decease of Memmius Regulus (*suff.* 31), containing the anecdote with Nero's tribute to Regulus on the occasion of Nero's illness (XIV. 47. 1). The historian states 'vixit tamen post haec Regulus quiete defensus'. If the illness of Nero was the 'anceps valetudo' of XIV. 22. 4, it occurred the year before, and the anecdote loses much of its force. To judge

---

[1] For Polemo's Pontus, *PIR*[1], P 406; D. Magie, *Roman Rule in Asia Minor* (1950), 561; 1417.

[2] Ph. Fabia, *Rev. ét. anc.* XXXIV (1932), 139 ff.

[3] When he recurs soon after (51. 2), Tacitus omits the fact that he had been *praefectus vigilum* (*Hist.* I. 72. 1), though he registers the previous employment of his colleague Faenius Rufus, the charge of the *annona*.

by the year of his consulate, this *novus homo* was a very old man anyhow. What is noteworthy is not his survival after Nero's compliment, but his survival into Nero's reign. Regulus had not been named in the Neronian books—or in the Claudian, save in an annotation on Lollia Paullina (XII. 22. 2) which carries no sign that he was still alive. The anecdote has been dragged in, thoughtlessly. The historian's friendly interest in Memmius Regulus deserves attention.[1]

That item is also the last of the obituary notices with which Tacitus honours illustrious survivors. At the end of 56 he had registered Caninius Rebilus and L. Volusius (XIII. 30. 2), at the end of 59 Domitius Afer and Servilius Nonianus (XIV. 19). The notices are all unusually brief, although none of these four consulars had been named hitherto in the third hexad, and one would have expected to be told that Volusius was holding the office of *praefectus urbi* when he died (Pliny, *NH* VII. 62). Rapid jottings, perhaps, to be rounded off later. These were all persons that interested Tacitus for various reasons. The question arises, were there no other suitable deceases in the following years (after Regulus in 61) —or were the peaceful deaths swallowed up and submerged by Nero's murders?

Two public transactions are not properly explained. The status of freedmen and slaves was a matter of some concern to Tacitus and his contemporaries. Under the year 56 he reports (or rather invents) a discussion about freedmen in the imperial privy council, with eloquent arguments for and against (XIII. 26 f.).

The question at issue—and the original proposal in the Senate—is nowhere clearly stated.[2] In the next year the historian goes to the trouble of registering a decree of the Senate which, so the reader is led to believe, ought to become relevant when a senator is murdered by his slaves—'ultioni iuxta et securitati, ut ii quoque qui testamento manu missi sub eodem tecto mansissent, inter servos supplicia penderent' (XIII. 32. 1). In 61 Pedanius Secundus, the *praefectus urbi,* is duly assassinated. Recounting the debate in the Senate, Tacitus supplies the oration of the jurist Cassius Longinus (XIV. 43 f.)—who based his appeal, not upon the legislation of the Principate but upon an alleged Republican precedent, the 'vetus mos'. The legal situation is not elucidated by Tacitus; and the presuppositions of the *senatus consultum* of the year 57 (extending punishment to 'testamento manu missi') do not come into the debate at all, though in the aftermath there is a proposal for deporting 'liberti . . . qui sub eodem tecto fuissent' (45. 2).

Again, makeshift motivation. The most glaring instance concerns the removal of Agrippina in 59—Poppaea's insistence on lawful wedlock with Nero, and Agrippina's incestuous overtures to her son, brought in anachronistically with a role for the freedwoman Acte (XIV. 1 f., cf. p. 377). The story was vouched for by the sources, Cluvius Rufus in the first instance. A proper revision might have modified it.

Also from one of the sources ('ferebatur') is the report (under 64, after the great fire) that Seneca wanted to retire from Rome so as not to be held responsible for the stripping of shrines in Asia and Achaia carried out by two agents of Nero— 'quo invidiam sacrilegii a semet averteret' (XV. 45. 3). There follows an attempt of

---

[1] App. 82.

[2] For the inadequacies of the Tacitean account, A. M. Duff, *Freedmen in the Early Roman Empire* (1928), 41 f. He incautiously assumes that there was a 'debate' with 'motions'.

Nero to have Seneca poisoned, which Seneca evaded: this is introduced by 'tradidere quidam'. Later, after the detection of Piso's conspiracy, the story becomes a fact, Nero being eager to have Seneca killed 'quando venenum non processerat' (60. 2).[1]

In two instances the links from book to book are unsatisfactory. Concluding Book XIII with a series of events on the Rhine frontier, Tacitus realized that the last item (a mysterious fire in the territory of Colonia Claudia, which he wanted to have for some reason or other) was not a suitable termination. He added the report of a portent at Rome, brief, isolated, and meaningless, and left it there (XIII. 58).

The final notice of Book XIV exhibits the other extreme. It foreshadows future developments most ominously—and erroneously. One of Nero's freedmen denounced Seneca to his master for being an associate of C. Piso, whereupon Seneca turned the charge more powerfully against that freedman, hence the apprehensions of Piso and the origin of the conspiracy—'unde Pisoni timor et orta insidiarum in Neronem magna moles et improspera' (XIV. 65. 2).

Yet the plot takes nearly three years to come to a head. It does not originate with Piso (the prime movers are specified), and, so little suspicion had Nero, that he would regularly resort to Piso's palace at Baiae without ceremony or guards, there to bathe and dine (XV. 52. 1).

On the lowest count, a number of inconsequences have been laid bare. Some portions of these books are presented in a finished form, e.g. the Corbulonian narrative, Boudicca's rebellion, the orations of Thrasea and of Cassius Longinus, the interview between Seneca and his ex-pupil. Other portions were not revised by the author.

Novelties in expression or inadvertences of style seem to pile up towards the end (App. 59). The final episode might supply a clue. It was the 'quaestor consulis' who brought the fateful command to Thrasea Paetus (XVI. 34. 1). Other names are registered in the context (Demetrius, Domitius Caecilianus, Arria), but not that of the quaestor. His identity might have been worth knowing, for he is the recipient of Thrasea's last message to the world. It was also a personal message—'libemus (inquit) Iovi liberatori. specta, iuvenis; et omen quidem di prohibeant. ceterum in ea tempora natus es quibus firmare animum expediat constantibus exemplis' (35. 1). Thrasea's injunction may be not irrevelant to the subsequent vicissitudes of the young man. Compare his words of warning to Junius Rusticus—'illi initium magistratuum et integra quae supersint. multum ante secum expenderet quod tali in tempore capessendae rei publicae iter ingrederetur' (26. 5). The memory and example of Thrasea Paetus was to prove fatal to Rusticus many years later.

Ought not the historian to have furnished the name of the quaestor? It is his way to let a name speak for itself, to make his point by significant allusion, eschewing the detail of annotation.

---

[1] Is this all taken, too rapidly, from Fabius Rusticus, the friend and apologist of Seneca?

G. THE MATTER OF THE *ANNALES*

61. MISTAKES IN THE *ANNALES*

MANY of the errors are trivial. An historian could easily make a slip on chronology. Thus 'priore aestate' (III. 20. 1), under 20, for the operations of Furius Camillus—who, however, was proconsul of Africa in 17/18 (II. 52) The author is wrong about the age of Octavia (XIV. 64. 1, cf. *PIR*², C 1110), inconsistent about that of Nero (XII. 25. 2; 58. 1; XIII. 6. 2). And it is strange that Tacitus should term M. Hortensius Hortalus, the grandson of the orator, a 'nobilis iuvenis' (II. 37. 1), for he cannot have been less than fifty-six years old.[1]

Some scholars resort to emendation, generously transferring to the historian their own inerrancy. Tacitus, beginning the narration of 21, refers to the consuls of 18 as 'biennio ante' (III. 31. 1). Nipperdey helpfully corrected to 'triennio ante'. Most editors concur.[2] They failed to observe the same type of reckoning in the 'triennio ante' of VI. 38. 1. Tacitus registers the burning of the Capitolium 'sociali bello' (VI. 12. 3). It occurred, however, in a civil war, in the year 83. Again, some have emended.[3] Better suppose a mistake of the historian. The date at which L. Piso was appointed *praefectus urbi* is a notorious crux, involving various problems.[4] Tacitus has 'xx per annos' for his tenure of the office when he died in 32 (VI. 11. 3). Some have the confidence to alter the figure.[5] Which presupposes knowledge that nobody can claim.

The opening chapters present various unsatisfactory features, some due to abbreviation or recourse to allusion. In I. 3. 3 the *tribunicia potestas* of Tiberius is put after the deaths of the princes Gaius and Lucius. In fact a renewal, the original grant having been made in 6 B.C. Again, in I. 10. 7 we have 'Augustus paucis ante annis, cum Tiberio tribuniciam potestatem a patribus rursum postularet'. Is this in A.D. 4? Or, as can be argued from Suetonius (*Tib.* 16. 1), in A.D. 9? Note also the vagueness caused by abbreviation in III. 56. 2: 'Marcum deinde Agrippam socium eius potestatis, quo defuncto Tiberium Neronem delegit ne successor in incerto foret.'

To proceed to patent errors. The historian is incorrect with 'adiectaque ex Germania legio' (XIII. 35. 2): it was not IV Macedonica (on the Rhine) but IV

---

[1] His father fell at Philippi (Livy, *Per.* CXXIV).

[2] e.g. C. D. Fisher (Oxford, 1906), G. Andresen (Teubner, 1913), E. Koestermann (Teubner, 1952), H. Fuchs (*Ed. Helv.* 1946). Not, however, Lenchantin de Gubernatis (Rome, 1940).

[3] Thus 'civili bello' (Lipsius) or 'Sullano bello' (C. Heraeus), while Nipperday excised. Similarly, Tacitus may have made a mistake about the period during which the office of *flamen Dialis* was vacant after the death of Cornelius Merula (III. 58. 2): of the recent editors, Fuchs and Koestermann print emendations in their texts.

[4] cf. E. Groag, *PIR*², C 289, who argues that the historian is correct.

[5] Fuchs and Koestermann print Nipperdey's 'xv per annos'.

Scythica (in Moesia). A minor inadvertence assigns the *consularia insignia* to Rufrius Crispinus, commander of the Guard under Claudius (XVI. 17. 2), instead of the *praetoria* (XI. 4. 3).

Two items concerning the history of Judaea are puzzling. Under 49 stands the brief notice 'Ituraeique et Judaei defunctis regibus Sohaemo atque Agrippa provinciae Syriae additi' (XII. 23. 1). Now Herod Agrippa had acquired some notoriety for his services to Claudius in the two critical days following the assassination of Caligula. He died in 44, Judaea being then annexed and put under the procurator Cuspius Fadus (*PIR²*, C 1636). That fact ought surely to have been registered in the lost books. One wonders therefore whether the historian may not have confused him with his brother, Herod of Chalcis, who died in the eighth year of Claudius (Josephus, *AJ* XX. 104): Chalcis was in fact given to the son of Herod Agrippa a year or two later (the date inferred from *BJ* II. 284). Then there is Tacitus' account of the division of Judaea between Ventidius Cumanus and Antonius Felix (XII. 54). Incompatible with Josephus. Yet Tacitus is explicit—note especially the intervention of the legate of Syria and the indictment of Cumanus. His account can probably stand (cf. *PIR²*, A 828).

More serious, Claudius' transference of the *aerarium* to quaestors—'sed deerat robur eum primum magistratum capessentibus' (XIII. 29. 2). It appears that the pair of quaestors was chosen to hold office for three years (Dio LX. 24. 1 f.). One of them was none other than Domitius Decidius, the parent of Agricola's wife (*ILS* 966).

A senator would be careful about names and identities.[1] Some of the errors in the *Annales* are scribal; others have been assumed prematurely by critics who gave insufficient study to the rarities of Roman nomenclature.[2] It is another matter when the same person is called 'Latinius Latiaris' (IV. 68. 2), and 'Latinius' (71. 1), but 'Lucanius Latiaris' (VI. 4. 1). What is the remedy? 'Lucanius' is probably correct:[3] but the inconsistency should not be corrected out of existence.[4] The historian (not a scribe) may be responsible; and the *nomina* might derive from different sources ultimately.[5]

An historian's errors may prove variously instructive. In the passage 'ad amnem Visurgim' (I. 70. 5) there is clearly a gloss, as was seen by a scholar long ago, anonymous and approved by Justus Lipsius.[6] The item about Tigranocerta —stated to be thirty-seven miles from Nisibis (XV. 5. 2)—baffles elucidation (p. 396).[7] But 'Epidaphnae quo in loco vitam finierat' (II. 83. 2) furnishes a clue. The

[1] He can be condoned an easy confusion between Furii Camilli of the fourth century B.C. (IV. 52. 5).

[2] cf. R. Syme, *JRS* XXXIX (1949), 6 ff.

[3] One L. Lucanius Latiaris is attested by *CIL* XV, 1245.

[4] Andresen, Fuchs, and Koestermann correct to 'Lucanius' but Fisher prefers 'Latinius'. Lenchantin rightly leaves the discrepancy standing.

[5] R. Syme, o.c. 13, cf. above, p. 277. 'Lucanius' (VI. 4. 1) may come from the *acta*.

[6] It is bracketed by Fisher, Fuchs, and Koestermann. For the justification see F. Ritter, *Rh. Mus.* XVII (1862), 100; C. O. Brink, *JRS* XLII (1952), 39 ff. Perhaps the only certain gloss in the *Mediceus I* (*Ann.* I–VI); but should not one follow Nipperdey and excise 'Amisiae' (II. 8. 2)?

[7] Dessau suggests that the mistake goes back to the 'Urbericht' (*Gesch. der r. Kaiserzeit* II (1926), 195). However it be, the item ought not to be used to support a localization of Tigranocerta south of Mons Masius, on the Mesopotamian plain.

suburb of Antioch is called Daphne. It follows that Tacitus was never in Syria, not even on a senatorial embassy to Trajan.[1]

Not all of the oversights in the *Annales* have been detected or properly assessed. Tacitus' version of the *Oratio Claudi Caesaris* appears to carry a peculiar statement about the incorporation of the Transpadana (XI. 24. 3, cf. App. 93). Moreover, his dating to 61 of Boudicca's revolt (XIV. 29. 1), though generally accepted, can hardly stand (see App. 69). In fact sundry discrepancies in the later books ought to be carefully scrutinized (App. 60). The author failed to revise that portion of his work. Perhaps he did not live to complete it.

62. POSSIBLE ERRORS ABOUT PEDIGREE

TACITUS may have made mistakes about persons and pedigrees. Lollia Paullina is styled daughter 'M. Lollii consularis' (XII. 1. 2). This lady could hardly be the daughter of M. Lollius (*cos.* 21 B.C.), who died in A.D. 1 or 2 (Velleius II. 102. 1); and Pliny, who had seen her, speaks of 'avitae opes' (*NH* IX. 117), plainly indicating the rapacities of her grandfather. Hence a homonymous consular son of M. Lollius is assumed (*PIR*,[1] L 227). When, however, is a son of Tiberius' enemy likely to have been honoured with a consulship? It is a problem.[2] There is no other trace of this Lollius.[3] Tacitus had already mentioned his parent (III. 48. 2). To an historian of the early Empire (be he ancient or modern) 'M. Lollius consularis' clearly means the notorious Marcus Lollius (in distinction, if need be, from one who was not consul). Perhaps the text is wrong.[4] Or has Tacitus made a careless assumption about the parentage of Lollia Paullina? That is a way out. Yet it will be noted that precise details about her family are furnished a little further on—Cotta Messallinus was her 'patruus magnus', a sister of L. Volusius her mother (XII. 22. 2, from a speech of Claudius Caesar).[5] Tacitus was interested in the Volusii (p. 302). Moreover, in his own day the name of the Lollii was perpetuated by a suffect consul of 94, M. Lollius Paullinus D. Valerius Asiaticus Saturninus (*PIR*[1], L 233).

There is also a difficulty about a famous Greek family. In 33 the descendants of Theophanes the Mytilenaean, the client and historian of Pompeius Magnus, incurred calamity. Pompeia Macrina was exiled, while her brother, a senator of praetorian rank, and her father, an 'inlustris eques Romanus', both committed suicide. Theophanes is here designated 'proavus' of the brother and sister (VI. 18. 2). The question is, how many generations intervene between Theophanes and the Q. Pompeius Macer (*PIR*[1], P 471), who was praetor in A.D. 15 (*ILS* 9349).

---

[1] There is a faint possibility he may have been on embassy to congratulate Trajan's successor. Observe the digression on Byzantium (XII. 62 f., cf. p. 449).

[2] Degrassi suggests A.D. 13, *Epigraphica* VIII (1946), 36; *Fasti Consolari* (1952), 7. But Tiberius did not lack influence in that year, and Augustus had no reason to cherish the memory of Lollius.

[3] Unless it be in Horace, *Epp.* I. 2. 1; 18. 1 (on whom, *PIR*[1], L 231).

[4] Hence Ritter's solution—'⟨neptem⟩ M. Lollii consularis'.

[5] For the mysterious connexion with the house of the Valerii Messallae see E. Groag, P-W XIII, 1378.

Strabo states that Theophanes left a son, whom Augustus made procurator of Asia—and who now (καὶ νῦν, clearly an addition by the author on his last revision) ranks among the principal friends of Tiberius Caesar (XIII. 618). If the procurator of Asia (*PIR¹*, P 472) were identical with the 'inlustris eques' of Tacitus, Tacitus would be in error. Most scholars, however, assume him correct —two generations between historian and praetor.[1] Some contend that the historian made a late marriage, his son being approximately coeval with the Emperor Tiberius (who was born in 42 B.C.).[2] If this were accepted, one might still have cause to wonder: for the great-grandson of Theophanes (praetor in A.D. 15) cannot have been born earlier than 15 B.C.[3]

It is worth adding that there was a descendant in the time of Tacitus: M. Pompeius Macrinus Neos Theophanes (*PIR¹*, P 475), consul suffect in 100 or 101, proconsul of Africa c. 117 (*AE* 1913, 168 = *IG* v, 1, 151): a member of Tacitus' sacerdotal college (App. 22, cf. 25). The *suffectus* of 115 revealed by the *Fasti Potentini* might be his son: Degrassi (*FC* (1952), 34) has 'M. Pom[', but the inscription justifies 'M. Pomp['.

63. TIBERIAN PROSOPOGRAPHY

THE deaths of illustrious survivors from the reign of Augustus suggested the valuable device of obituary notices. Not all of the consuls could so be treated. Tacitus did not wish to encumber his narrative. At the same time, his knowledge about the aristocratic families under Tiberius was incomplete. He was not likely to confuse Marcus Lepidus and Manius, the consuls of 6 and of 11 (App. 64), but elsewhere he sometimes appears (and is) guilty of inadvertence. Identity as well as nomenclature can be in question.

Valerius Messalla is one of the three consulars who come out with proposals about the funeral ceremonial (1. 8. 4). This is the elder son of Messalla Corvinus, consul in 3 B.C. and legate of Illyricum in A.D. 6 (*PIR¹*, V 93). He is later styled Valerius Messallinus (III. 18. 2; 34. 1). In fact, he bore both *cognomina*. No obituary, despite his distinction.

M. Aurelius Cotta was consul in 20 (III. 17. 4, cf. 2. 3), the younger son of Corvinus (*PIR²*, A 1488). He also turns up under the name of Cotta Messallinus, the author of 'sententiae' in the Senate (II. 32. 1; IV. 20. 4; V. 3. 2), and unsuccessfully prosecuted (VI. 5).[4] He took the *cognomen* 'Messallinus' after the death of his brother (Velleius II. 112. 2): it is attested when he was proconsul of Asia, year uncertain (*IGR* iv, 1508; *Forsch. in Ephesos* iii, p. 112, n. 22). He may have outlived Tiberius—and so have qualified for an entry somewhere in Books VII–X.

---

[1] e.g. R. Hanslik, P–W XXI, 2276 ff.

[2] R. Laqueur, P–W v A, 2099; accepted by R. Hanslik, o.c. 2276.

[3] Another solution has been propounded—to make the 'vir praetorius' of Tacitus different from, and a generation later than, the praetor of A.D. 15: see J. Schwartz, *Rev. phil.* LXXVII (1951), 185.

[4] Borghesi argued for the identification, and it is accepted by Degrassi, *Epigraphica* VIII (1946), 38. Groag expressed strong (but superfluous) doubts (*PIR²*, A 1488). He is named before ex-consuls in 16 (II. 32. 1): presumably *praetor designatus*, cf. R. Syme, *JRS* XLVI (1956), 18.

Cn. Lentulus is mentioned several times (I. 27. 1; II. 32. 1; III. 68. 2; IV. 29. 1) down to his death in 25, with obituary (IV. 44. 1). That obituary may have been found useful by the author to elucidate what he had said about Lentulus on his first introduction—'ante alios aetate et gloria belli' (I. 27. 1). Lentulus, who held a Danubian command under Augustus and fought a war, can be identified as the consul of 14 B.C. (*PIR*², C 1379): distinguished from his homonym of 18 B.C. by being styled 'augur' (*Res Gestae* 8; *SIG*³ 781). Therefore the same as 'augur Lentulus' (III. 59. 1). Various perplexities that have vexed modern scholars[1] are here irrelevant, however. Only one of the two Lentuli is named by Tacitus: the other was probably dead.

The Calpurnii Pisones are much more troublesome. The reader is presented with 'in sententiam Pisonis' in I. 79. 4. Perhaps the *praenomen* has fallen out. Hence some editors, following Nipperdey, read 'Cn.', for that person (the consul of 7 B.C.) had been mentioned a little earlier (I. 74. 5). This is better than conjecturing that the *praenomen* might have been 'L.' There were two consulars of that name. The one is a very famous man indeed, L. Piso the *pontifex*, consul in 15 B.C. (*PIR*², C 289), son of the consul of 58 B.C.: *praefectus urbi* under Tiberius, he receives a resplendent necrological commemoration (VI. 10. 3), from which it emerges that something had been said about him in Book V. He can hardly be the 'L. P⟨iso⟩' who is named among the *consulares* who decreed thanksgivings after the death of Scribonius Libo (II. 32. 2);[2] but he is clearly the author of the merciful 'sententia' in III. 68. 2. In contrast for character stands L. Piso the *augur*, consul in 1 B.C. (*PIR*², C 290). He was the brother of Cn. Piso (*cos.* 7 B.C.), the truculent governor of Syria (III. 11. 2); and, as he is described as 'nobilis ac ferox vir' (IV. 21. 1), the incidents in II. 34 could leave no doubt about who was meant. A third L. Piso is registered as *PIR*², C 292, where he is assumed to be a consul of unknown date. This is the governor of Hispania Citerior in 25, whom Tacitus, using an archaism, styles 'praetorem provinciae' (IV. 45. 1). It is not easy to find a place for him on the *Fasti*.[3] Indeed, it would be justifiable to conjecture that he was only praetorian, the consular legate (L. Arruntius) being kept at Rome by Tiberius (p. 442). This Piso baffles identification: perhaps a son of the *pontifex*.

Marcellus Aeserninus was one of the 'patroni' who refused to defend Cn. Piso in 20 (III. 11. 2). He is referred to (in reported discourse) among those 'ad summa provectos incorrupta vita et facundia' (XI. 6. 2). Hence Borghesi's assumption (accepted by Groag in *PIR*², C 928) that he reached the consulate. That is most dubious.[4] More should have been heard of him in the *Annales*. Since M. Clau-

---

[1] See Groag's full discussion under *PIR*², C 1379, preferring the consul of 14 B.C.: accepted in *Rom. Rev.* (1939), 381; 400 f.

[2] The supplement is standard, adopted in all modern texts of Tacitus. In view of what Tacitus says of L. Piso the *pontifex*, 'nullius servilis sententiae sponte auctor' (VI. 10. 3), one might be tempted to ask whether 'L. P⟨lancus⟩' be not preferable, i.e. L. Munatius Plancus, the consul of A.D. 13: independence did not run in that family. For this emendation, *JRS* XLVI (1956), 19.

[3] Degrassi briefly doubts whether he was consul (*Epigraphica* VIII (1946), 37), but admits him below the line in his *Fasti Consolari* (1952), 8, with the remark 'se fu governatore della Spagna citeriore nel 25.' See *JRS* XLVI (1956), 20 f.

[4] Degrassi refuses to admit him, even with a query, anywhere in his *Fasti Consolari*.

dius Marcellus Aeserninus was a grandson of Pollio on the maternal side, and an orator of great promise, it is strange that Tacitus should have said so little. Aeserninus was praetor in 19 (*CIL* I², p. 70). He should have come quickly to the consulate. Decease may be presumed. Tacitus may have missed the fact, if and because it was not in the *acta senatus*: no public funeral.

64. MARCUS LEPIDUS

WHICH was the 'capax imperii' (I. 13. 2)? Marcus the consul of 6, or Manius, the consul of 11? Where, and how often, does the text of Tacitus have to be altered?[1]

Both men come into the narrative of the year 21, where the consular provinces are concerned; and in one of two places the *praenomen* must be emended. Tiberius in a dispatch to the Senate suggested that the recrudescence of trouble in Africa called for a proconsul with military experience and in sound bodily health. That was seized as a chance for a personal attack by one of the consulars—'quod initium Sex. Pompeius agitandi adversus Marcum Lepidum odii nanctus' (III. 32. 2). He described Lepidus as slothful and impoverished, a disgrace to his ancestors, not good enough for Asia, let alone Africa. The Senate, however, took Lepidus under its protection—a quiet decent man, who had done no harm, 'mitem magis quam ignavum'.

The attack and the defence are equally ludicrous, if Marcus Lepidus is in question. Corrupt, oppressive, or vicious—anything, but not 'ignamis' or 'mitis'. The consul of 6 had fought in the war in Illyricum and had received the *ornamenta triumphalia* (Velleius II. 114. 5; 115. 2 f.; 125. 5; Dio LXVI. 12. 2).

The remedy is patent. Read 'Manium'. In the only other passage in the *Annales* which indubitably and incontestably mentions the consul of 11, that *praenomen* is also written out in full—'defendente ream Manio Lepido fratre' (III. 22. 1).[2]

Despite the unpleasantness, the man went to Asia (32. 2). A M'. Lepidus happens to be certified as proconsul of Asia (*CIL* III, 398 = 7089: Ephesus)— and ten years from the consulate seems to be the normal interval about this time.[3]

Africa and the war still had to be provided for, and the Emperor put forward two names—'M. Lepidum et Junium Blaesum nominavit' (III. 35. 1). M. Lepidus naturally, for he had served under Tiberius in Illyricum. The historian nowhere mentions the Scipionic ancestry of Lepidus: it may have occurred, appropriately, in Book V, when the betrothal (or the marriage) was registered between Lepidus' daughter and Drusus, the son of Germanicus (cf. VI. 40. 3).

If the above account is accepted, it follows that only one emendation is needed in the *Codex Mediceus*. On the other hand, 'M. Lepidus' must be restored in I. 13. 2—and in no fewer than seven other passages where the current doctrine (all modern editions), which began with Lipsius and was elaborated by Borghesi and by Nipperdey, substitutes 'M'. Lepidus' for 'M. Lepidus'.[4] The consequences

---

[1] For a full statement of the problem, R. Syme, *JRS* XLV (1955), 22 ff.
[2] o.c. 26.   [3] o.c. 27.
[4] viz. III. 11. 2; 35. 1; 50. 1; IV. 20. 2; 56. 3; VI. 5. 1; 27. 4.

are serious. Manius, the consul of 11, an inconspicuous character, is left with two entries only in the *Annales* (III. 22. 1; 33. 2). Everything else goes to Marcus Lepidus, the 'vir triumphalis'.

There happens to be external and independent proof. Both Manius and Marcus held the proconsulate of Asia. But Marcus cannot be the man who went there in 21. An inscription shows that Marcus' tenure was biennial (*AE* 1934, 87: Cos).[1] Now 21–23 is ruled out: Marcus was certainly in Rome in 22, for he then asked the permission of the Senate to repair a family monument, the Basilica Aemilia (III. 72. 1). His appointment to Asia is registered by Tacitus, in 26 (IV. 56. 3).[2] That was late—but is not inexplicable. He had been elsewhere employed in the period when his name would normally have come into the balloting for Asia or Africa.[3]

65. THE CONSPIRACY OF SEIANUS

TACITUS knew that the craft and the influence of Seianus were liable to be magnified (IV. 11. 2; 57.1). As for the death of Drusus Caesar, he dismissed one atrocious legend (IV. 10 f.). He did not try to subvert the whole tradition. The revelations about adultery and poison were not disclosed until eight years had elapsed. They may be authentic, or may not.[4] As for the events of 31, it is not easy to discover how far the historian may have gone in scepticism. He could recall from his youth the alleged plot of Caecina Alienus and Eprius Marcellus; and the destruction of four men of consular rank (in 118) may precede the composition of Book V or the publication of the first hexad.

The letter from Capreae, as reported by Cassius Dio (LVIII. 10. 1 ff.), does not, it is true, carry any definite accusation that Seianus plotted to murder Tiberius and seize power. Too much should not be made of that ostensible omission.[5] It cannot prove that such charges had not been conveyed to Capreae—or were not produced in the immediate sequel, with suitable names and details, once Seianus had been executed as a 'perniciosissimus hostis p. R.' (so he is styled on a loyal dedication at Interamna, *ILS* 157). Josephus states that there was a great conspiracy, Tiberius being warned in time by a message from Antonia, his

[1] Registered by Groag in the *addendum* to *PIR*[2], A 369 (III, p. xi)—but incautiously adduced for the (impossible) tenure of Asia in 21–23.

[2] It is unfortunate that this passage was mistranslated as well as misunderstood by D. Magie, *Roman Rule in Asia Minor* (1950), 1362. The whole problem has become unnecessarily confused (cf. ib. 1363; 1581).

[3] The only alternative would be to invent a M. Aemilius Lepidus, *cos. suff.* 13, proconsul in 26.

[4] Most scholars accept the story, e.g. M. P. Charlesworth, *CAH* x (1934), 638. For strong doubts, H. Dessau, *Gesch. der r. Kaiserzeit* II (1926), 32; E. Paratore, *Maia* II (1949), 113 f.

[5] F. B. Marsh exaggerates its value, *The Reign of Tiberius* (1931), 304. Note that, according to Dio, Seianus repented of not having carried out a coup when still consul (LVIII. 8. 2).

brother's widow (*AJ* XVIII. 181 f.).[1] Suetonius describes Seianus as 'res novas molientem', and uses the phrase 'oppressa coniuratione' (*Tib.* 65. 2).

Cassius Dio would be cautious. Not only does he issue a general warning about 'conspiracies' (LIV. 15. 1 ff.). He knew about the destruction of Severus' Prefect of the Guard, the great Fulvius Plautianus, in 205, and he mentions him in this context (LVIII. 14. 1), though he is usually sparing of references to contemporary persons. The parallel was inescapable. It may have determined and distorted Dio's portrayal of Seianus. There was no conspiracy of Plautianus—it was all a σκευώρημα (LXXVI. 3. 3). Hence Dio may have suppressed evidence that pointed to there having been, at some stage, a conspiracy of Seianus.[2]

Tacitus would also be cautious. There is no means of knowing what distinctions he drew or what doubts he expressed when narrating the fall of Seianus. He has several subsequent references, which deserve close scrutiny. He reports an allegation that P. Vitellius, in charge of the *aerarium militare*, was ready to help Seianus with funds for 'res novae' (V. 8. 1). The consul Memmius Regulus, on provocation, attacked his colleague Fulcinius Trio for being 'noxium coniurationis' (V. 11. 1)—but with no danger to the latter. Three Roman knights succumbed 'coniurationis crimine' (VI. 14. 1). The knight M. Terentius in his oration refers to himself and others as 'cunctos qui novissimi consilii expertes fuimus' (VI. 8. 3) and refers to 'insidiae in rem publicam, consilia caedis adversum imperatorem' (ib. 6). Finally, Tacitus is careful to adduce a name. In 36 a certain woman was charged with treason—'multorum amoribus famosa Albucilla, cui matrimonium cum Satrio Secundo coniurationis indice fuerat' (VI. 47. 2).[3] Her husband, Satrius Secundus, was also mentioned in the speech of Terentius (VI. 8. 5): 'etiam Satrium atque Pomponium venerabamur'. Was the information he gave authentic? And did he survive his patron by many days? Satrius Secundus was a client of Seianus, he had indicted the historian Cremutius Cordus six years earlier (IV. 34. 1).

Was there a conspiracy of Seianus? Many scholars believe in it.[4] A few are sceptical.[5] The proper questions have not always been asked: when precisely did it take shape, with what purpose, and with what allies (cf. p. 405)?

Governmental acts and professions tended to create unwarranted scepticism at Rome. The historian Tacitus may have found it necessary to refute opinions that there had not at any time been any kind of plot (compare the observations about the Pisonian conspiracy, XV. 73. 2). The imperial minister, towards the end, may have started to plan some counterstroke, whatever be the 'novissimum consilium' to which M. Terentius is made to allude.[6]

The doom of Aelius Seianus fell on October 18 of the year 31 (*ILS* 157). The Emperor's suspicions had begun to form many months earlier, as is clear from the

---

[1] It would help to know what it conveyed—and when it came. M. P. Charlesworth dates it quite early in the year (o.c. 636).

[2] See now E. Koestermann, *Hermes* LXXXIII (1955), 350 ff.

[3] Badly misinterpreted by Marsh (o.c. 307 f.).

[4] Especially the apologists of Tiberius. Thus R. S. Rogers, *Criminal Trials and Criminal Legislation under Tiberius* (1935), 114 ff.; E. Ciaceri, *Tiberio*[2] (1944), 314 f.

[5] e.g. H. Furneaux in his edition of the *Annales*, (Oxford, 1896) I, 150 f.; H. Dessau, o.c. 74 f.; F. B. Marsh, o.c. 304 ff.

[6] Thus, explicitly, M. P. Charlesworth, o.c. 637.

account of Cassius Dio (LVIII. 7. 3 ff.). For Suetonius, Seianus is a conspirator. But he is also the dupe whom Tiberius destroyed—'spe adfinitatis ac tribuniciae potestatis deceptum inopinantem criminatus est pudenda miserandaque oratione' (*Tib.* 65. 1). According to Tacitus the minister succumbed to the superior craft of the Emperor (IV. 1. 2).

66. IMPERIAL VIRTUES

THIS engaging topic has not gone short of exponents. The legends on coins furnish visible guidance to the policy of the Roman government, or at least to its professions; and a number of valuable studies are available, discussing the various ethical qualities that were advertised on the coinage as attributes of the Caesars.[1] Some of the edifying assertions tend to be taken at face value, but others ought to excite immediate suspicion. Indeed, CONCORDIA EXERCITVVM must have disturbed contemporaries, as suggesting the contrary;[2] CLEMENTIA is not devoid of sinister connotations;[3] and PROVIDENTIA might attest the suppression of a conspiracy.[4] Others again have to be carefully assessed in relation to the facts of history. Not all stand the test, but some come off without reproach, such as the MODERATIO of Tiberius Caesar.[5]

Little, it might seem, now remains to be said. Yet there are two aspects that can repay attention. First, the derivation of sundry governmental virtues in a straight line from the political language of the late Republic (which coloured or even tainted them for ever).[6] Secondly, imperial literature. The *Panegyricus* of Pliny yields a spontaneous and bountiful harvest: many chapters of that speech could bear coin legends for their title.[7] More instructive, however, is the negative evidence of an anti-governmental writer.

Tacitus furnishes startling exemplifications. Some 'virtues' he will hardly ever admit in relation to emperors. Thus 'pietas' only for Nero, ironically (XIII. 5. 2; XIV. 3. 3), 'providentia' for Claudius, in derision (XII. 3. 1).[8] 'Providentia' occurs

---

[1] Especially the pioneer work of H. Mattingly in the introduction to *BMC, R. Emp.*; also C. H. V. Sutherland, *Coinage in Roman Imperial Policy 31 B.C.–A.D. 68* (1951), *passim.* For a lucid general survey, M. P. Charlesworth, *Proc. Brit. Ac.* XXIII (1937), 105 ff.; for a list of sixteen personifications explicitly defined as properties of the ruler (the word 'Augusti' following), M. Grant, *Roman Imperial Money* (1954), 167. In general see now L. Wickert, P–W XXII, 2222 ff.; J. Beaujeu, *La Religion romaine à l'apogée de l'empire* I (1955).

[2] p. 7 (Nerva).

[3] M. P. Charlesworth, *Proc. Brit. Ac.* XXIII (1937), 112 f.

[4] Id. *Harv. Th. Rev.* XXIX (1936), 111 f.; M. Grant, *Roman Anniversary Issues* (1950), 62 f. (on the PROVIDENTIA series of Tiberius). Observe *ILS* 157 f. (commemorating the destruction of Seianus).

[5] C. H. V. Sutherland, *JRS* XXVIII (1938), 129 ff.; *Coinage in Roman Imperial Policy 31 B.C.–A.D. 68* (1951), 97 ff. That author argues that the parallel *dupondii* with CLEMENTIAE and MODERATIONI were issued in 22 or 23—and under the inspiration of Seianus (which is hard to credit). For a later dating, M. Grant, *Roman Anniversary Issues* (1950), 47. For the quality of 'moderatio' see also R. S. Rogers, *Studies in the Reign of Tiberius* (1943), 60 ff.

[6] *Rom. Rev.* (1939), 154 ff.; 169 f.; 516 f.

[7] See the catalogue of 'lieux communs' in the edition of M. Durry (Paris, 1938), 35 ff.

[8] p. 416.

nowhere else in the *Annales*. Indeed, the historian seems to regard a number of the words with extreme distaste. They are seldom allowed, save in speeches, and these serve to illustrate his deliberate choice, his delicate feeling for language.[1]

From an early date 'aeternitas' had come to be predicated of Rome's dominion—and associated with the ruler.[2] Ovid even calls Caesar Augustus 'aeternus' (*Fasti* III. 421 f.; *Ex Ponto* II. 2. 48). Tacitus allowed 'aeternitas' once in the *Historiae* (I. 84. 4: Otho on the Empire, cited on p. 155). The word occurs once in the *Annales* (XI. 7. 1: 'aeternitatem famae', in a reported speech). A kindred notion is 'perpetuitas'—nowhere in the *Annales*, and he does not like 'perpetuus' either.[3] More remarkable perhaps is the evidence about 'felicitas', inherited by the Caesars from the generals of the Republic.[4] It was promptly applied to the blessings of their rule: Ovid has 'felicia saecula' (*Tristia* I. 2. 103).[5] Tacitus did not avoid the word 'felicitas' in his earlier writings (three times in the *Agricola*, sixteen in the *Historiae*), and he duly paid his tribute to the 'felicitas temporum' that dawned after the tyranny of Domitian (*Agr.* 3. 1; *Hist.* I. 1. 4). Yet 'felicitas' is employed only twice in the *Annales*, in speeches—Suillius Rufus about Seneca (XIII. 42. 4), Seneca in deprecation about himself (XIV. 53. 2). The adjective 'felix' shows only two instances there, 'faustus' only four—because each was associated with official prayers or professions. Hence 'feliciter' only once, and most ironically.[6]

'Iustitia' was one of the virtues on the golden shield of Augustus (*Res Gestae* 34, cf. p. 414), and it appeared on the Roman coinage under Tiberius.[7] Tacitus exhibits no liking for the word. It is attested three times in the *Annales*, twice in reported speech (XII. 11. 2; XIV. 20. 5), and once applied to an individual—not an emperor, but a victim of the Neronian tyranny, the virtuous Barea Soranus (XVI. 23. 1). Again, 'aequitas' emerged as an official legend under Vespasian;[8] it was dropped by Domitian, but at once installed again by Nerva.[9] The word is found only twice in the *Annales* (XV. 2. 3; XVI. 33. 1). Hadrian was the first ruler to proclaim 'indulgentia Augusti'[10]—benevolent, but conveying the benevolence of a master (cf. 'clementia'). The word occurs once in the *Annales* (XIII. 57. 1, of the gods, in a foreign context).

---

[1] For the types of words he avoids see App. 42; for the vocabulary of the speeches, App. 50.

[2] M. P. Charlesworth, *Harv. Th. Rev.* XXIX (1936), 107 ff.; H. U. Instinsky, *Hermes* LXXVII (1942), 313 ff. Cf. p. 208.

[3] He has 'perpetuus' only in *Dial.* 5. 4 and *Ann.* XIV. 21. 2. For the numismatic history of these words see M. Grant, *Aspects of the Principate of Tiberius* (1950), 83 ff.

[4] J. Gagé, *Rev. arch.* XXXII (1930), 1 ff.; M. Grant, o.c. 76 f.

[5] cf. *ILS* 112 (Narbo): 'saeculi felicitas.'

[6] III. 17. 2—a reference to an alleged poisoning.

[7] *BMC, R. Emp.* I (1923), 131. It is a surprisingly rare legend. As Mattingly points out (ib. III (1936), xxxviii), discussing the IVSTITIA AVGVST. of Nerva, Trajan did not use IVSTITIA, but it returns with Hadrian.

[8] ib. II (1930), 112; 150 ff., &c.

[9] ib. III (1936), 1, &c. Like IVSTITIA, AEQVITAS lapsed with Trajan but was restored by Hadrian.

[10] ib. III, 305; 310 f., &c.

Not all of the imperial 'virtues' fell under the interdict of the senatorial historian. 'Moderatio' was not spoiled by Tiberius, or 'constantia' by Claudius.[1] And it would be excessive to claim that the words here singled out were eschewed or discarded by Tacitus solely and precisely because they had been annexed as attributes of the Caesars. A deeper cause was working to the same end. The Roman historians were repelled by the noble and improving phraseology that lent itself so readily to political oratory and political deceit. Thus Sallust (cf. p. 135), thus Tacitus (p. 344). The phenomenon is in accord with other anti-Ciceronian features of their style and thought. Tacitus went to extreme lengths in his distrust; measured by vocabulary, his pessimism grows more intense. After the minor works he does not again employ 'integritas' and 'humanitas'; while 'prudentia' and 'veritas' are dropped after the first hexad of the *Annales*. Tacitus elected a bleak world for his habitation (cf. p. 545).

The process of attaching various personifications to the Emperor went on steadily. The coinage of Hadrian exhibits no fewer than six new specimens: 'disciplina', 'hilaritas', 'indulgentia', 'liberalitas', 'patientia', 'tranquillitas'.[2] Some of them are highly instructive. 'Disciplina' has its origin in the military sphere, but the legend had no long survival on the coins.[3] As for 'hilaritas', Velleius Paterculus (II. 127. 4) had evoked in laudation the 'prisca hilaritas' of Aelius Seianus. Tacitus eschews that word, and 'tranquillitas' is admitted only once in the *Annales*, in Tiberius' letter to his minister (IV. 40. 6).

67. THE *TABULA HEBANA*

WHEN Augustus died, the consuls for 15 had already been elected, but not the praetors. The list had been drawn up (twelve names this time for twelve places) and it was ready to go before the electoral body. Tiberius read out that list to the Senate—'candidatos praeturae duodecim nominavit' (I. 14. 4).

To explain what the new ruler's action signified, the historian interpolates a note: 'tum primum e campo comitia ad patres translata sunt', &c. (15. 1). Similarly, the year after, he reports the first consular elections to be held under the new system, and goes on to confess his uncertainty about the exact procedure followed by Tiberius in the presentation of candidates—'de comitiis consularibus, quae tum primum illo principe ac deinceps fuere, vix quicquam firmare ausim', &c. (81. 1).

Thus was abolished the last pretence of free election by the Populus Romanus; and the change was made (it can be assumed) under injunction from the dead Princeps, whose *Res Gestae* proclaimed that he gave sovereign power back to Senate and People. Not indeed that the assembly of the Comitia Centuriata was abolished in 14. Various traditional ceremonies had to be gone through before a consul was well and truly elected. Pliny praised Trajan for the exemplary

---

[1] For the latter quality cf. M. Grant, *Num. Chron.*[6] x (1950), 23 ff. It had valuable and Stoic connotations.

[2] J. Beaujeu, o.c. 424.   [3] ib. 164.

patience with which he endured 'longum illud carmen comitiorum' (*Pan.* 63. 2); and Cassius Dio (under the year 32) refers to the symbolical survival in his own day, ὥστε ἐν εἰκόνι δοκεῖν γίγνεσθαι (LVIII. 20. 4).

So far the change. The process of limiting the powers of the Comitia Centuriata had been carried some distance before the death of Augustus, in fact if not in law, as the historian discreetly indicates, 'nam ad eam diem, etsi potissima arbitrio principis, quaedam tamen studiis tribuum fiebant' (15. 1). And indeed, the bronze tablet found at the colony of Heba in Etruria discloses a law, the *Lex Valeria Cornelia* of A.D. 5, concerning the 'destinatio' of candidates for consulate and praetorship. It is embedded in the *rogatio* about the funeral honours in memory of Germanicus Caesar in 19, one of the items of which is five new *centuriae* added to the existing ten named after the Caesars Gaius and Lucius: '[utiq. ad X] / centur. Caesarum quae de cos. pr. destinandis suffragium ferre solent adiciantur V centur[iae].'[1]

The *Lex Valeria Cornelia* enjoined that the senators along with the knights on the jury panels should constitute ten *centuriae*, to select candidates, before the final vote and ratification by the Comitia Centuriata. The immediate purpose of the law seems clear enough—the new body was to function very much as a *centuria praerogativa*, to influence (if it had not already decided) the elections.

The new document raises many problems, with abundant discussion, though not so much about the historical bearing of the law for the Principate of Augustus and for the year 5 in particular.[2] That is not so easy to divine.

There is room for differences of opinion about the procedure of election previously employed, and about the measure of freedom permitted by Caesar Augustus.[3] On the face of things the *Lex Valeria Cornelia* appears to mark a decisive stage in the degradation of the Comitia Centuriata. It might not be so. The previous decade had been a critical period for the Roman government, with need for tight control. Competition for the consulate will not have been free and easy, for example, in the year following the exile of Julia and the destruction of Iullus Antonius. One might wonder whether more candidates than two were normally permitted to get as far as having their names accepted by the magistrate presiding at the elections.

The law was passed in the year after Ti. Claudius Nero came back to power and influence, now Ti. Caesar, the son of Caesar Augustus. The reform was perhaps much less objectionable than what had gone before. Not 'auctoritas' (that is, 'potentia'), but a constitutional provision, with the added advantage that, combining senators and knights in the predominant electoral body, it could be advertised as 'concordia ordinum'. Nor was it inappropriate to employ the names of Gaius and Lucius. Being 'principes iuventutis', they had been the leaders of the 'ordo equester'. And Augustus insisted on commemorating them.

---

[1] The document was first published in *Not. Scavi* LXXII (1947), 49 ff. A revised text and apparatus is furnished by J. H. Oliver and R. E. A. Palmer, *AJP* LXXV (1954), 225 ff., whence V. Ehrenberg and A. H. M. Jones, *Documents Illustrating the Reigns of Augustus and Tiberius*² (1955), no. 94 a.

[2] See the lengthy bibliographies in G. Tibiletti, *Principe e magistrati repubblicani* (1953), 283 ff.; Oliver and Palmer, o.c. 225 ff.

[3] A large measure of liberty is postulated by A. H. M. Jones, *JRS* XLV (1955), 9 ff.

There is a further, and a different problem: Tacitus and the change he reports in A.D. 14. How does he stand when confronted with the new evidence emerging from the *Tabula Hebana*?

It is hasty to assume that he is totally in error. Can the historian and the *Tabula* be combined, or correlated? One careful investigation tries to rescue something of his credit. In A.D. 14 (it is suggested) the ten *centuriae* of the *Lex Valeria Cornelia* (senators and knights) now become the main electing body, superseding the Comitia Centuriata. Tacitus says 'e campo comitia ad patres translata'. Speaking of 'patres' he is not quite adequate—for the body comprised knights as well as senators.[1]

There is a difficulty. The ten *centuriae* (even if convoked somewhere else) belong to the mechanism of Comitia Centuriata, to the Campus, whereas 'patres' in a senatorial writer should mean (must mean) the Senate, in the Curia, not just a collection of senators somewhere else—still less a mixed body in which senators are only a minority. Other evidence indicates that the main and decisive part of the elections was now and henceforth conducted in and by the Senate (see below). Moreover, if the arrangement devised in A.D. 5 for 'destinatio' subsisted after 14, a precise date will have to be found for its supersession. Mere 'desuetudine' will not do, if the thing mattered.[2] The record of Tacitus is extant down to the beginning of 29.

Perhaps it would be better for the present to keep the *Tabula Hebana* out of the question and refrain from combining heterogeneous pieces of evidence. One piece is baffling, and may be unimportant. Not so the other. Profit can accrue from a closer scrutiny of the historian.

Born not long after the beginning of Nero's reign, Tacitus in his youth had known men who could tell him about the events of 19 and 20 at least (cf. III. 16. 1). The precise date at which direct election by the People was abrogated could be ascertained, and it ought to have attracted a senator's attention when he came to write about the successors of Augustus.

Tacitus (it can be argued) went to the *acta senatus*. The structure of his writing is revealing. After the note explaining the transfer of the elections (15. 1), he reverts to senatorial business with the words 'inter quae tribuni plebei petivere' (15. 2). It is an annalistic item—ceremonial games in honour of the deceased ruler, and where the money is to come from. Deliberate, and it is almost bathos. It is not certain that the predecessors of Tacitus would have bothered to record that detail. Further, under 15, he refers to the imperial orations for guidance about the consular elections (1. 81. 1). That is the last item in a sequence (from 1. 72 onwards). Comparison with Cassius Dio (LVII. 14) shows that Dio for the year 15 followed an annalist who had made a remarkably different selection of senatorial business (cf. App. 36).

That is not all. Tacitus under the year 19 puts on record a selection of the

---

[1] G. Tibiletti, o.c. 169, cf. 176. Apparently approved, or at least not criticized, by H. M. Last in his discussion of Tibiletti's book (*JRS* XLIV (1954), 121). Against, A. H. M. Jones, *JRS* XLV (1955), 18. The express testimony of Tacitus (1. 15. 1) ought never to have been doubted or infringed.

[2] Tibiletti (o.c. 186) suggests that possibility for the exclusion of knights from the 'assemblea destinatrice.'

'honores' voted for Germanicus (II. 83). The account is interrupted by a sarcastic observation from the Emperor, modifying and abating one proposal (p. 279). Tacitus knows what he is talking about. No mention of the five *centuriae* (as revealed by the *Tabula Hebana*), but he can sum up: 'pleraque manent, quaedam statim omissa sunt aut vetustas oblitteravit' (83. 4).

The change carried out in 14 was unobtrusive (and made little difference). An inattentive writer could miss it. Nothing in Suetonius—and nothing in Dio, though Dio's subsequent remarks about the elections under Tiberius imply it (LVIII. 20). If necessary, an inscription proves that under Tiberius the Senate selected the consuls—'per *commendation.* | Ti. Caesaris *Augusti* | ab senatu *cos. dest.* | patrono'.[1]

Even a contemporary says less than might have been expected. Velleius Paterculus and his brother were on the list drawn up by Caesar Augustus and bequeathed to Tiberius. What interests Velleius is that unique felicity, and the social prestige of the other candidates. Velleius mentions the 'ordinatio comitiorum', but his words, examined without prepossessions, give no sign that he was putting on record a novel method of election.[2]

New documents such as the *Tabula Hebana* run the risk of being estimated above and beyond their due. What was in fact the fate of the *Lex Valeria Cornelia*?

The device promulgated in A.D. 5 may not have lasted very long. According to Dio there was rioting in 7, and Augustus appointed (ἀπέδειξε) all the candidates (LV. 34. 2). This is the first record of any electoral disturbances since 19 B.C. Was the *Lex Valeria Cornelia* still in operation?[3]

The evidence of a careful and reputable historian indicates that the decisive stage in the election of consuls and praetors was transferred to the Senate in 14. If the ten *centuriae* subsisted thereafter, they can only have been a part of the ceremonial, of the 'longum illud carmen comitiorum', on which they had been superimposed by the law of A.D. 5. That is, of no importance whatsoever.

All in all, it might be safest to suppose that the operation of the ten *centuriae* for elections was suspended by a *senatus consultum* in A.D. 14. Those *centuriae* bore the names of the Caesars Gaius and Lucius. Identical honours (or at least no less) had to be voted when Germanicus died. Again, in 23, after the death of Drusus, the son of Tiberius. They are in fact attested.[4] The next occasion would have come in 37, on the decease of the young Ti. Caesar, the son of Drusus Caesar, equal heir with Caligula, and in fact adopted by him as his son.

---

[1] *ILS* 944 (Allifae). The words in italics depend on the copy of Antonius Augustinus. The person honoured (his name is missing) had either not yet entered on office, or died before his consulate.

[2] Velleius II. 124. 3 f.: 'primum principalium eius operum fuit ordinatio comitiorum, quam manu sua scriptam divus Augustus reliquerat. quo tempore mihi fratrique meo, candidatis Caesaris, proxime a nobilissimis ac sacerdotalibus viris destinari praetoribus contigit', &c. For 'ordinatio comitiorum', cf. Pliny, *Pan.* 72. 1. Velleius a little later, in a general panegyric of the new reign, has 'summota e foro seditio, ambitio campo, discordia curia' (II. 126. 2).

[3] It is denied by M. Gelzer, *Festschrift für Rudolf Egger* I (Klagenfurt, 1952), 84 ff.

[4] *AE* 1952, 80 (Ilici in Tarraconensis).

Suspended by *senatus consultum* in 14 (so it could be argued), the mixed *centuriae* ordained by the *Lex Valeria Cornelia* could easily have been revived for the elections at any time. So could the integral Comitia Centuriata. No man can tell what forms and pageantry were adopted in 30 when Aelius Seianus was proclaimed on the Aventine (of all places), if credit be given (and there is nothing against it) to an inscription most peculiar that alludes to the 'inprobae comitiae / [q]uae fuerunt in Aventino ubi / [Sei]anus cos. factus est'.[1] Caligula brought back free elections in 38, it is recorded, but dropped them in 39, reverting to the practices of Tiberius (Dio LIX. 9. 6; 20. 4 f., cf. Suetonius, *Cal.* 16. 2).

Caligula wished to publish a reaction and advertise τὸ σχῆμα τῆς δημοκρατίας. There was nothing in it. It would be fanciful to suppose that Caligula went back to the Comitia Centuriata because he did not wish to create five more *centuriae* in honour of the young Ti. Caesar, thus perpetuating the name and memory of the boy he had murdered. It is also fanciful to discard a consular historian in favour of ephemeral arrangements, dutifully commemorated on tablets of bronze by the loyal zeal of small towns.

68. TACITUS AND THE JURISTS

RECORDING at the end of the year 22 the decease of Ateius Capito, Tacitus evokes for damaging comparison the other luminary of Augustan days, Antistius Labeo (III. 75). Posterity claimed them as founders of rival schools of jurisprudence (*Dig.* I. 2. 2. 47 ff.). Without due warrant: and nobody has been able to justify the dichotomy.[2]

Rivalry there certainly was, and a succession of jurists. It is expedient to note the names furnished by the *Digest*.[3] The Proculian school derived from Antistius Labeo through M. Cocceius Nerva (*suff.* 21 or 22). Next came Proculus, whose nomenclature, status, and personality baffle inquiry. His successor was Pegasus, consul under Vespasian and *praefectus urbi* early in the reign of Domitian. There followed Juventius Celsus, and after him the younger Juventius (*pr.* 106, *suff.* c. 117) along with Neratius Priscus (*suff.* 97).

The other school, ostensibly descending from Ateius Capito, takes shape with Masurius Sabinus, or rather with C. Cassius Longinus (*suff.* 30). The next representative is Cn. Arulenus Caelius Sabinus (*suff.* 69), then Javolenus Priscus (*suff.* 86), who lived long enough to be the teacher of P. Salvius Julianus (*cos.* 148).[4]

The historian Tacitus nowhere discloses any abnormal preoccupation with the science of jurisprudence. The men, however, were variously noteworthy. He exploits and denounces Ateius Capito as the type of jurist subservient to power

---

[1] *ILS* 6044, cf. R. Syme, *Hermes* LXXXIV (1956), 257 ff.

[2] F. Schulz, *Roman Legal Science* (1946), 119 ff.

[3] For details of rank and origin see W. Kunkel, *Herkunft u. soziale Stellung der r. Juristen* (1952).

[4] *Dig.* XL. 2. 5. Along with Julianus in the succession to Javolenus are named Aburnius Valens and Tuscianus (I. 2. 2. 53), probably of no great consequence.

(*Ann.* III. 70. 3), parallel in abasement to Q. Haterius among the orators (p. 581). A further fact drew him: Capito was a famous sacerdotal lawyer and member of the *XV viri s.f.* Indeed, in the obituary (III. 75) the historian goes too far—'consulatum ei adceleraverat Augustus ut Labeonem Antistium isdem artibus praecellentem dignatione eius magistratus antiret'. Now it happens to be recorded that Augustus offered the consulate to Labeo, who refused it (*Dig.* I. 2. 2. 47). There can have been no marked acceleration for Capito, already a notable expert at the time of the *Ludi Saeculares* in 17 B.C. (cf. Zosimus II. 4. 2). He only became *suffectus* in A.D. 5. Was not that through the favour of Tiberius (who came back to power and influence the year before)?

Cocceius Nerva, an intimate friend of Tiberius Caesar, was the only senator who accompanied him to Capreae, and he died there (IV. 58. 1; VI. 26. 1 f.). The low social status of Masurius Sabinus made it unlikely that he could appear in the pages of the *Annales*, and the same reason may have debarred Proculus.[1] Cassius Longinus was a *nobilis*, of an historic family; he governed Syria, and earns praise for insisting on the military discipline of ancient days (XII. 12. 1). The note of severity recurs (XIII. 48); his good sense deprecates lavish victory honours for Nero (XIII. 41. 4); and he is accorded a powerful oration in the Senate (XIV. 43 f.). Nero suspects him, and he is sent into exile (XVI. 7 ff.).

Cassius Longinus enjoyed the author's interest for various reasons. He can further produce an aristocratic jurisprudent unknown to the *Digest*—'Caninius Rebilus, ex primoribus peritia legum et pecuniae magnitudine' (XIII. 30. 2), stigmatized 'ob libidines muliebriter infamis', and contrasted with the excellent L. Volusius. This was the man (*suff.* 37) who offered to assist with money Julius Graecinus, the parent of Agricola, and was repulsed (Seneca, *De ben.* II. 21. 6). No other author names him.

Closer to his own time, Tacitus had personal acquaintance with several great lawyers. He could have seen the venerable Cassius Longinus, back in Rome: he died in Vespasian's reign (*Dig.* I. 2. 2. 52). Of the more recent masters of jurisprudence, there was Cn. Arulenus Caelius Sabinus, whose rare *gentilicium* recurs in the official nomenclature of Junius Rusticus.[2] Pegasus was a portent, not only for his erudition (they called him 'liber, non homo'), but for his lowly extraction: the son, it is said, of a ship's captain in the imperial navy (*Schol.* on Juvenal IV. 76). He became Prefect of the City, perhaps nominated by Domitian at the very outset of the reign, compare Juvenal IV. 77: 'attonitae positus modo vilicus urbi'. His *gentilicium* is nowhere attested, and the *cognomen* is exceptionally rare.[3]

The *Historiae* would have a place for Pegasus, also for Javolenus Priscus (*suff.* 86), who was still alive when the work was published (cf. p. 91). This man, by his full style 'C. Octavius Tidius Tossianus L. Iavolenus Priscus', held important provincial posts (*ILS* 1015, cf. App. 14): presumably of non-senatorial stock and 'adlectus inter praetorios' by Vespasian. Iguvium in Umbria was his home: 'Iavolenus' (very rare) and 'Tidius' (not common) occur there.[4] His friend the poet, Passennus Paullus, belongs to the neighbour city of Asisium (p. 91).

---

[1] For speculation about the identity of Proculus, W. Kunkel, o.c. 123 ff.

[2] The latter, suffect consul in 92, is styled 'Q. Ar[' (*FO* XIId); 'Q. Arulenus Rust[' (*Fasti Potentini*).   [3] W. Kunkel, o.c. 133 f. Perhaps a 'Cornelius', see App. 94.

[4] W. Kunkel, o.c. 138 ff. That scholar's statement of the case could be made more

The Neratii come from Saepinum in Samnium, an old local family (*AE* 1927, 118): adlected into the patriciate by Vespasian, cf. *ILS* 1032, which, though acephalous, is convincingly attributed to L. Neratius Marcellus (*suffectus* in 95, taking the place of the Emperor). Now the jurist L. Neratius Priscus was the brother of Marcellus (*Dig.* xxxiii. 7. 12. 43). He should therefore be identified with the man of that name *suffectus* as colleague of M. Annius Verus in 97. He was legate of Pannonia (*ILS* 1033 f.).[1] Legend accrued to the memory of Neratius Priscus—it is alleged that Trajan thought of him for the succession (*HA, Hadr.* 4. 8)[2].

As for the two Juventii Celsi, the elder is little more than a name in the *Digest*. The younger, by full nomenclature 'P. Iuventius Celsus T. Aufidius Hoenius Severianus', was to have a long career. Consul suffect presumably about 117, he was consul again as *ordinarius* in 129, sharing the *fasces* with L. Neratius Marcellus (now aged about seventy). His region and town are not attested.[3] There may have been something in his earlier years to bring him into the *Historiae*: a certain Juventius Celsus, accused of conspiracy towards the end of Domitian's reign, gained immunity by promising to act as an informer, and so outlived the tyrant (Dio LXVII. 13. 3 f.). Malice would combine with morality or paradox to ensure that the incident was not forgotten.

69. BOUDICCA'S REBELLION

TACITUS' narration (XIV. 29–39) has been impugned, from various points of supposed vantage. First of all, the cause of the rising in Britain. Cassius Dio supplies something different (LXII. 2. 1): the procurator Decianus Catus laid claim to sums of money that the Emperor Claudius had bestowed upon the leading men among the natives, and Seneca, who had forced them to contract loans (to a total of ten million denarii), extracted repayment all at once, oppressively. It was Boudicca (continues Dio), a woman of royal stock, who stirred up discontent and led the revolt.

Dio assigns no other cause. Seneca's usury has proved too tasty a morsel for scholars to pass over. Few omit it. Some even affirm that Dio's statement is sober,

positive. Some have argued, from *ILS* 1015, for Nedinum, in Dalmatia: against, R. Syme, *Serta Hoffilleriana* (1940), 227.

[1] The consular year of the jurist was long in doubt, and the problem was not always adequately treated (e.g. by A. Berger, P–W xvi, 2549; A. Garzetti, *Nerva* (1952), 146). The *Fasti Potentini*, first published in 1948, showed a L. Neratius Priscus suffect in 87, whom some identify with the jurist (W. Kunkel, o.c. 144; G. Barbieri, *Studi Romani* I (1953), 368). But the new Ostian fragment (*AE* 1954, 220, cf. App. 10) necessitates another, who is preferable, cf. A. Garzetti, *Aevum* xxvii (1953), 551; R. Syme, *JRS* xliii (1953), 159. There is a third homonym (omitted by Degrassi from his *Fasti Consolari*), namely the man who governed Pannonia Inferior and Pannonia Superior (with his parent on *ILS* 1034), *suffectus* probably under Hadrian.

[2] Not very plausible, cf. p. 233 f.

[3] See W. Kunkel (o.c. 147), who lays emphasis on the rare *nomen* 'Hoenius' which has two examples at Fanum Fortunae (*CIL* xi, 6263 f.). Note also that Juventii are numerous and important at Brixia (*PIR*[1], J 587; 595–8).

accurate, and valuable.[1] It can serve to supplement Tacitus, or correct him.[2] That historian did not register the item about Seneca. Why? Because (it is contended) he is here transcribing Fabius Rusticus, notoriously the friend and client of Seneca.[3] Dio, however, reproduces the elder Pliny.[4]

To waive for the moment the question of sources. Tacitus (it is fair conjecture) was familiar with the story about Seneca —and dismissed it. He had let fall a hint previously—'Italiam et provincias immenso faenore hauriri' (XIII. 42. 4). It occurs, as is appropriate, in the diatribe which Tacitus composes for Suillius Rufus, Seneca's bitter enemy. Before Dio is played against Tacitus, it would be well to note and assess the allegations against Seneca which that writer elsewhere serves up with such relish (LXI. 10. 1 f.; 12. 1), many of them monstrous. Dio found abundant scandal in his sources, and he was animated by a double prejudice against Seneca (p. 551).

When Tacitus composed the life of Agricola, he was content to describe the insurrection in the most general terms (*Agr.* 5. 3 f.; 15–16. 2): no tribe or town is there named. Further, he allows the Caledonian chieftain Calgacus to make a startling reference to it in his oration: a Brigantian rising led by a woman, and the capture of a legionary camp.[5] In the *Annales* he is full and precise (XIV. 31). After the death of King Prasutagus (he states) the vassal principality of the Iceni was incorporated in the province. Centurions and fiscal agents proceeded to work their will, rapacious and violent, not sparing from outrage Boudicca the widow and her daughters. The Iceni took up arms, and the Trinovantes quickly joined, having grievances of their own (Camulodunum and its veteran colonists).

Dio has none of these things, and no name of any tribe or town.[6] His account is verbose, and miserable. Much of it is taken up by an oration of Boudicca inciting the Britons to revolt. From first to last there is perhaps only one item that could be safely used, the statement that Suetonius Paullinus was compelled to fight a pitched battle (LXII. 8. 1). Tacitus (XIV. 34. 1) attributes the general's decision to his own choice of time and place. Not perhaps a serious discrepancy.

Tacitus, it should seem, furnishes the necessary facts. It has been asserted, however, that his account is dominated by conventional themes (native liberty against Roman oppression), coloured and overlaid with literary elaborations; the actions of robbery and violence he reports come from rhetorical stock-in-trade; there is no reason to believe that the incorporation of Prasutagus' kingdom led to a deterioration in imperial administrative methods or that the Roman colonists of Camulodunum (founded a decade earlier) suddenly took to evil ways.[7]

---

[1] G. Walser, *Rom, das Reich und die fremden Völker in der Geschichtsschreibung der frühen Kaiserzeit* (1951), 92; 130; 133.

[2] Thus C. E. Stevens, who links it to Nero's intention of evacuating Britain (Suetonius, *Nero* 18)—which he dates to 58 (*CR* LXV (1951), 4 ff. This is a double paradox: for the value of Suetonius' story see p. 490.   [3] G. Walser, o.c. 131.

[4] ib. 130. Among the reasons advanced is the invective against Nero in Boudicca's speech.

[5] *Agr.* 31. 5: 'Brigantes femina duce exurere coloniam expugnare castra, ac nisi felicitas in socordiam vertisset, exuere iugum potuere.' The author knew that no camp was captured (cf. 16. 1), and 'Brigantes' may be deliberate—a boastful Caledonian's error.

[6] It should of course be borne in mind that 'Dio' here is Xiphilinus' version. But Xiphilinus cannot be blamed for monstrosities like Boudicca's oration.

[7] G. Walser, o.c. 135.

These objections miss the mark. Critics of Tacitus are themselves influenced by conventional themes, but of another sort, viz. the excellence of Roman rule or the ravages of rhetoric among Roman historians. Certain facts should be recalled. Annexation tended to provoke immediate rebellion in vassal kingdoms. Thus Judaea in A.D. 6, Mauretania under Caligula, Thrace under Claudius. Even a hint of Roman methods was enough to alarm the natives. When it was reported that their ruler was about to introduce a census on the Roman model, the tribesmen of Cietis in Cilicia Aspera took to the mountains (VI. 41. 1).

Next, the operations of warfare. This episode drew from Mommsen his celebrated verdict, damning Tacitus as a military historian.[1] Many have concurred. Thus it can be alleged that Tacitus 'cared nothing for and knew nothing of geography or strategy'.[2] Not all of the critics are judicious—or even accurate. Mommsen in his own reconstruction of what happened innocently took over from the Caledonian chieftain (*Agr.* 31. 5) the storming of a legionary camp (i.e. that of IX Hispana) by the Brigantes; and he cast doubt on Tacitus' statement that Suetonius Paullinus marched to London. Again, a recent critic inadvertently assumes that Paullinus went to Camulodunum.[3] Since, however, that same writer, complaining about the *Agricola*, asserted that the 'military and topographical details compare unfavourably with the information supplied by Pliny',[4] his strictures do not deserve to be taken seriously. It is enough to look at Pliny's description of Britain (IV. 102 f.). That strange medley contains no military detail, no town, river, or estuary.

On the contrary, it can be maintained that Tacitus' narrative of the great rebellion is admirable. It should be accepted with confidence.[5] The historian has left out a number of things, it is true. He has not furnished the precise localization of the battle (how could he, and for what purpose?). He names the four legions in Britain at that time, but not the camps they occupied: presumably Glevum (II Augusta), Viroconium (XIV Gemina and XX Valeria Victrix—if the latter legion was not somewhere else), Lindum (IX Hispana). Tacitus did not wish to pester and confuse the reader with irrevelant data; and in his own day the camps were different (Isca, Deva, and Eboracum). On the other hand, he mentions three cities, being careful to specify their status—the *colonia* Camulodunum (XIV. 31. 3), the *municipium* Verulamium (33. 2), a precious fact, and Londinium, 'cognomento quidem coloniae non insigne sed copia negotiatorum et commeatuum maxime celebre' (33. 1).

Only two officers are named, because only two (he decided) mattered for history, Petillius Cerialis, the legate of IX Hispana (32. 3), and Poenius Postumus, the disobedient *praefectus castrorum* in charge of II Augusta (37. 3). The legate of that legion (it follows) was not there, but perhaps with Paullinus on Mona when the revolt broke out. Likewise the *tribunus laticlavius*, who is the senior officer in the absence of the legate: perhaps Cn. Julius Agricola, who had been

---

[1] *The Provinces of the Roman Empire* I (1886), 181. See further p. 157.

[2] B. W. Henderson, *The Life and Principate of the Emperor Nero* (1903), 478.

[3] M. L. W. Laistner, *The Greater Roman Historians* (1947), 130.   [4] ib. 112.

[5] As it seems to be by R. G. Collingwood in *Roman Britain and the English Settlements* (1936), 98 ff. That scholar, however, was subsequently able to proclaim Tacitus' 'remarkable ignorance of the actualities of warfare' (*The Idea of History* (1946), 39).

chosen earlier by Paullinus as his 'contubernalis'.[1] The historian's attention to names and persons can be illustrated from other parts of his British narrations. He refuses to name a mere *praefectus castrorum* who, along with eight centurions, was killed in the land of the Silures (XII. 38. 3). But he duly notes M. Ostorius, the son of the governor P. Ostorius Scapula (31. 4), and the legionary legate Manlius Valens (40. 1): both characters known to history. The former (*suff.* 59) was to recur in the *Annales* (XIV. 48. 14 f.; XVI. 14 f.);[2] while the latter had been mentioned in the *Historiae* (I. 64. 4), and was to be consul in extreme old age, in 96.[3]

The notion that Cornelius Tacitus went to Fabius Rusticus for his account of the British insurrection may be dismissed: there is no sign that the man was a senator or had seen an army. Pliny would perhaps have been more useful.[4] Suetonius Paullinus may have written memoirs.[5] In that case, less need to consult the *acta senatus*. Or again, Tacitus may have known somebody's funeral oration in praise of the general under whom his father-in-law had served.

However that may be, it appears that he operated with insufficient care when fitting this episode (perhaps previously composed) to the annalistic structure of his work. He dates the outbreak explicitly to 61, to the consulate of Caesennius Paetus and Petronius Turpilianus (XIV. 29. 1). Yet the successor of Paullinus, precisely Turpilianus, turns up in the same year, fresh from his consulate (39. 3).

One must observe the total of events that ostensibly belong to the one year. Paullinus, after defeating Boudicca, proceeds to stamp out the insurrection, keeping the army in the field; reinforcements come from the Rhine; and the auxiliary troops are disposed in new camps for the winter. Further, the procurator Julius Classicianus (successor to Decianus Catus) quarrelled with the legate and sent an unfavourable report to Rome. Thereupon the government dispatched a person of confidence, the freedman Polyclitus. His report was temperate, and Paullinus was kept in charge of operations. He was later superseded because of a mishap to the fleet.

It is clear that Tacitus has been guilty of an inadvertence in dating. The revolt must have begun in 60. Hence a paradox. Scholars have been at pains to interrogate and challenge the narrative of Tacitus. Hardly anybody observed the error of chronology.[6]

How much does it matter? Q. Veranius, the predecessor of Suetonius Paullinus,

---

[1] *Agr.* 5. 1.

[2] Tacitus must have known his son, *suffectus* in 97 (App. 10).

[3] One might therefore feel curious about the legionary legate Caesius Nasica (XII. 40. 4), elsewhere unrecorded.

[4] It is apparent that the *prodigia* (XIV. 32. 1, cf. Dio LXII. 1. 2) derive from the same source ultimately. Speculation is unprofitable.

[5] As about his campaign in Mauretania (Pliny, *NH* v. 14). Pliny, discussing the length of the summer nights in Britain and in Thule, concludes with the item 'quidam vero et in Mona, quae distat a Camaloduno Britanniae oppido circiter ducentis milibus, adfirmant' (II. 187). Possibly, but not necessarily, from Paullinus. The distance between the two points is, in a straight line, about two hundred and fifty miles: some are inhuman enough to blame Pliny for his estimate.

[6] It was pointed out by J. Asbach, *Analecta historica et epigraphica Latina* II (Bonn, 1878), 8 ff. Cf. B. W. Henderson, o.c. 206; 477 f. It is not easy to find another adherent.

looked forward to a triennial tenure (xiv. 29. 1), but died before a year had
passed (*Agr.* 14. 3). His governorship will have begun in 57, not 58.[1] As for
Paullinus, 'biennio prosperas res habuit' (*Agr.* 14. 4) before his attack on Mona:
presumably 58 and 59.

The new date, 60, has no direct bearing on imperial policy in other regions, so
far as can be ascertained. But the disaster in Britain may have impaired the credit
and influence of Seneca, and of Burrus. Various persons were no doubt already
alert for a chance to displace Seneca in the counsels of the prince (cf. p. 387). One
result of the events in Britain in 60 might have been the choice of Petronius
Turpilianus and Caesennius Paetus as consuls for the next year. It happened
that both men were sent out to enact new policies in their respective commands.

70. TACITUS AND THE EMPIRE

MANY students of history and literature discover a narrow range of subjects in
the *Annales* and voice their disappointment. 'It may be said with virtual truth
that the book ignores the Empire.'[2] The thing has become a commonplace. Hence
an easy censure on the historian: he was obsessed with Rome, the Caesars, the
Senate.[3]

His vision was also narrow, and his sympathies. Tacitus is indifferent (it is
claimed) towards all that the provinces contributed to Rome in men and in
letters.[4] He was not moved towards the provincials.[5] He felt no interest in the
Gallic notables who sought from Claudius Caesar admission to the Roman
Senate.[6]

Even the acute and sagacious Boissier allowed himself to chide the historian.
Tacitus (he suggests) ought to have travelled more widely. A change from the
tainted air of the metropolis would have done him good. Moral health abode in
municipia and in the provinces.[7]

Narrow also was his personal experience. Outside Italy perhaps only Asia, so

[1] As generally assumed, e.g. A. E. Gordon, *Univ. of Cal. Pub. in Class. Arch.* 11,
5 (1952), 241 f. Observing the notably divergent estimates of Q. Veranius offered by
R. G. Collingwood (o.c. 98) and C. E. Stevens (o.c. 4 ff.), that writer is moved to 'wonder
again how reliable Tacitus| himself was in his own interpretations' (o.c. 242). See
further E. Birley, *Roman Britain and the Roman Army* (1953), 1 ff.

[2] J. B. Bury, *The Ancient Greek Historians* (1909), 231.

[3] B. W. Henderson, *The Life and Principate of the Emperor Nero* (1903), 9 f.; A. Rosenberg, *Einleitung und Quellenkunde zur r. Geschichte* (1921), 255 f.; J. S. Reid, *JRS* xi (1921),
193; E. E. Sikes, *CAH* xi (1936), 739; V. Scramuzza, *The Emperor Claudius* (1940), 20;
R. G. Collingwood, *The Idea of History* (1946), 38 f.; M. L. W. Laistner, *The Greater
Roman Historians* (1947), 131.

[4] Commenting on iii. 55 in his translation (1, 1904), G. G. Ramsay observes: 'this is the
solitary passage in which Tacitus acknowledges that Rome owed anything to that influx
of provincials into the city which came in with the empire', &c.

[5] H. Willrich, *Hermes* LXII (1927), 64: 'als Stockrömer hat Tacitus überhaupt wenig
Herz für die Provinzialen.'

[6] K. Wellesley, *Greece and Rome²* 1 (1954), 32.

[7] *Tacite* (1903), 184: 's'il avait fait un séjour plus long dans les provinces; s'il avait
consenti à les étudier de plus près', &c.

one scholar boldly alleges.[1] Now it cannot be proved that Tacitus saw service as a military tribune, though it is probable; and there is the 'quadriennium' of absence after his praetorship (*Agr.* 45. 4). Tacitus continues to be roundly denounced for ignorance about the realities of warfare.[2] Yet it can happen that a critic, finding fault with a Tacitean narration, himself in the same breath emits an error about warfare and geography.[3] One of those critics awards to Livy the first place among the Roman historians.[4]

The Roman senator answers to Polybius' definition of the πραγματικός (XII. 27. 10). Like Polybius, he had been close to great affairs, and he travelled. Tacitus is a guide to political life, i.e. in the first instance to life for senators under the Caesars. But the author of the *Agricola* was aware of all the aspects and implications of imperial policy.

The *Annales* betray serious defects. The exordium of the work presented a problem almost insoluble: the author, while compressing or postponing (at times in a masterly fashion), gets into difficulties, and also, by inserting annotation, overloads the structure (App. 37). The treatment accorded to Germanicus Caesar is over-generous on any score; and Tacitus was not able to do justice to Tiberius—paradoxically, for he went to the original sources.

The historian himself has not received justice. Five causes contribute. First, undue preoccupation with the style and literary qualities of the writer. Secondly, the neglect to take into account the items of a senator's career at home and abroad (Ch. VI). Next, the refusal to investigate the social milieu of a Roman historian (Ch. XLV). Then, the anachronistic approach and assessment. Tacitus should be judged by what he intended, and by what that age in the development of human thought permitted: history as written by the ancients dealt in facts, not ideas; it was concrete and personal; it used the device of speeches.[5] Finally, there are large gaps in the *Annales* as surviving. The peak and catastrophe of Seianus is not there.[6] Books VII–X will have furnished valuable provincial and foreign items (p. 449). Above all, XVII and XVIII (if the author survived to compose them) must have answered many questions about the state of the Roman Empire—and quelled most objections (p. 463).[7]

---

[1] W. Kroll, *Studien zum Verständnis der r. Literatur* (1924), 379.

[2] R. G. Collingwood, o.c. 39.

[3] e.g. M. L. W. Laistner, o.c. 130. See App. 69 (on Boudicca's rebellion).

[4] ib. 139.

[5] Observe the judicious remarks of Nipperdey on the nature of ancient historiography (*Opuscula* 1877), 411 ff. Collingwood (o.c. 38 ff.) is over-censorious.

[6] Tacitus is rebuked by A. Rosenberg (o.c. 257) for neglecting a remarkable fact about Seianus' election to the consulate (i.e. *ILS* 6044).

[7] E. Paratore finds the *Annales* inferior on this count to the much (and rightly) admired *Historiae* (*Tacito* (1951), 707). Naturally enough—for such is the subject-matter of the *Historiae* as extant.

H. THE DATE OF COMPOSITION

71. RUBRUM MARE

TACITUS alludes to an expansion of Rome's empire—'nunc rubrum ad mare patescit' (II. 61. 2). Does he mean the Persian Gulf or the Red Sea? Most scholars since Justus Lipsius assume the former, without effort or disquiet. The other view has had sporadic champions. They believe that the historian is referring to the annexation of the vassal kingdom of the Nabataean Arabs, carried out by the legate of Syria in 105 or 106 (p. 222).[1] Not likely—and so unlikely that it is not necessary to point out that the Roman province Arabia took in hardly any of the Nabataean littoral on the Red Sea.[2]

An opinion even less plausible has recently been put into circulation.[3] Not the Nabataean coast, it is contended. Tacitus has in mind a stretch of the western shore of the Red Sea, in the neighbourhood of Berenice (which is on the same parallel as Elephantine and Syene). This tract had been a 'military district' (so it can be designated) in charge of the *praefectus montis Berenicidis*. A change, however, occurred. The zone was 'incorporated in the province of Egypt.'[4] That was done (it is suggested) after the year 100, and by 115 at the latest. Hence a date for the first hexad of the *Annales*. It was completed (and also published) in the period 105–14.[5]

This new explanation has secured adherents.[6] Perhaps it is all a misconception. The context and colour of the Tacitean sentence seem to have been neglected.

Now 'rubrum mare', as all agree, has the general meaning of 'the Indian Ocean'. The Persian Gulf and the Red Sea are its two great inlets, each of which can bear the name.[7] But Tacitus is not thinking of either inlet as such. Rather, the eastern Ocean, the one end of the world, like Gades the other—'omnibus in terris quae sunt a Gadibus usque | Auroram et Gangen' (Juvenal X. 1 f.). To elucidate Tacitus, the language of poets, of orators, and of historians is relevant, the theme of Alexander, and the theme of world conquest.

[1] J. Asbach, *Römisches Kaisertum und Verfassung bis auf Traian* (1896), 153. Also R. Paribeni, *Optimus Princeps* II (1927), 14; C. Marchesi, *Tacito*[3] (1944), 78; E. Paratore, *Tacito* (1951), 623. Paratore adduces the milestones—'a finibus Syriae / usque ad mare Rubrum' (*ILS* 5834, &c.). Irrelevant for Tacitean style and usage.

[2] cf. A. Grohmann, P–W XVI, 1462.

[3] K. Meister, *Eranos* XLVI (1948), 94 ff., taking up the thesis of O. Clason, *De Taciti annalium aetate quaestiones geographicae ad mare Rubrum et Aegyptum maxime pertinentes* (Rostock, 1871).

[4] K. Meister, o.c. 115. The region in question (he argues) could not previously have been regarded as a part of the Roman Empire. Not an argument.   [5] o.c. 121.

[6] F. Altheim, *Die neue Rundschau* LXIV (1953), 192; P. Treves, *Il mito di Alessandro e la Roma d'Augusto* (1953), 167 f.; 186.

[7] Mela III. 72; Pliny, *NH* VI. 107, &c.

Virgil on Marcus Antonius (*Aen.* VIII. 686: 'litore rubro', cf. p. 470) would be enough to discount speculation about small tracts of the Red Sea coastland, whether Egyptian or Nabataean. Tacitus has been describing the monuments of ancient Egypt; he registers a Pharaoh's wide conquests in Asia—'regem Rhamsen Libya Aethiopia Medisque et Persis et Bactriano ac Scytha potitum', &c. (II. 60. 3); and he refers to the empires of the Romans and of the Parthians (ib. 4). Not a writer who indulges in bathos without deliberate intent.

Livy provides the clue for the understanding of 'urgentibus imperii fatis' (*Germ.* 33. 2, cf. p. 46). And Livy can help here too. The consul Acilius Glabrio, inciting the legions to battle against the army of Antiochus, orates grandiloquently on the fruits of victory—'quid deinde aberit quin ab Gadibus ad mare rubrum Oceano finis terminemus, qui orbem terrae amplexu finit?' (XXXVI. 17. 15). Perseus, the King of the Macedonians, appeals to the conquests of their ancestors —'nec ante vincere desierint quam rubro mari inclusis quod vincerent defuerit' (XLII. 52. 14). The historian himself, in epilogue on Macedonia, recalls Alexander's dominion 'Arabas hinc Indiamque, qua terrarum ultimos fines rubrum mare amplectitur' (XLV. 9. 3).

That is not all. The verb 'patescit' is emphatic, and implies a wide extent of territory. Thus the peoples of immense and barbarian Germany—'ceteras civitates in quas Germania patescit' (*Germ.* 30. 1). Or, in the Roman Empire, all the regions of Asia in a vast sweep that swore allegiance to Vespasian—'quantumque introrsus in Pontum et Armenios patescit' (*Hist.* II. 81. 2). And again, Livy on the growth of Rome's dominion abroad—'sex praetores illo anno primum creati crescentibus iam provinciis et latius patescente imperio' (XXXII. 27. 6). The reference to new Roman provinces is significant and valuable.

Finally (and briefly) the relevance of the sentence to the date of the *Annales*. It could not have been penned before Trajan overthrew the Parthian power in 116.[1] Is it an integral part of the narration, or a subsequent insertion? At first sight several passages in the first hexad give the impression that the Parthian Empire still exists as a world power. Thus the description of the Armenians— 'maximisque imperiis interiecti et saepius discordes sunt, adversus Romanos odio et in Parthum invidia' (II. 56. 1). Again, the vassal princes, 'accolis Hibero Albanoque et aliis regibus qui magnitudine nostra proteguntur adversum externa imperia' (IV. 5. 2). And, in the near context of II. 61. 2 (and also containing the word 'nunc'), the reference to the revenues of the Pharaohs—'haud minus magnifica quam nunc vi Parthorum aut potentia Romana iubentur' (II. 60. 4).

These passages are duly adduced by scholars who refuse to concede that the historian is referring to Trajan's conquests.[2] If their validity were admitted, it

---

[1] But it could have been retained after 117 (cf. p. 471).

[2] C. Marchesi, o.c. 78; R. Meister, o.c. 119 ff. Similarly H. Volkmann (*Gymnasium* LX (1953), 236 ff.), who disagrees with Meister about Egypt, and who, not able to make up his mind about the 'rubrum mare' of II. 61. 2, argues none the less that the first portion of the *Annales* was written before 114. Also (independently), K. Wellesley (*Rh. Mus.* XCVIII (1955), 135 ff.), with much erudition about the Red Sea coast of Egypt. He argues that Tacitus refers to the annexation of Arabia, that *Ann.* II was composed between 108 and 114 (o.c. 149).

could be argued that a portion at least of the first hexad had been completed before 116. Similarly those scholars who state that Tacitus completed the *Annales* in 116 or 117 must be making the assumption that the sentence about 'rubrum mare' is an insertion put in at the end, or towards the end.[1]

There is a danger of assigning too much weight to the passages about Parthia mentioned above (Tacitus was narrating the reign of Tiberius in the light of the conditions then obtaining). Without them it could still be claimed that the sentence about 'rubrum mare' is an insertion (possibly added when the author had completed I–III, or I–VI). Otherwise, if it is integral (and it stands at the conclusion of a digression that evokes world empires past and present), there will be no reason to suppose that the author had begun writing before 115. It follows that almost all the books of the *Annales* are Hadrianic.

72. TRAJAN AND ALEXANDER

THE fame of Alexander among the Romans is a notable theme, and by no means neglected in scholarly inquiry.[2] Alexander stands for martial glory and the conquest of the world (cf. the remarks on 'rubrum mare', p. 470 and App. 71). Of the Roman generals, Pompeius Magnus was open in his pretensions, exploiting his resemblance in bodily form to the Macedonian, and encouraged by friends or flatterers.[3] Julius Caesar by contrast occupies a modest place in the legend.[4] With Trajan there is more than ample compensation. Dio's narration of the Parthian War registers his longing for India, the sacrifice at Babylon, and the boastful dispatches to the Roman Senate (LXVIII. 29. 1; 30. 1).[5]

'The praises of Alexander, transmitted by a succession of poets and historians, had kindled a dangerous emulation in the mind of Trajan.' Thus the historian Gibbon. It may be so. Caution is prescribed. The enhanced importance that the eastern lands at this epoch assume in Roman imperial policy is a plain fact, with its own explanations. It owes nothing to stories about the Macedonian.[6] Nor did Trajan in his pride and obstinacy require that romantic incentive.

One of the traditional motives in history writing was the πόθος of Alexander.[7] Tacitus applies it to Germanicus. Thus the visit to the site of Varus' disaster— 'igitur cupido Caesarem invadit solvendi suprema militibus ducique' (I. 61. 1).

---

[1] e.g. K. Nipperdey (ed. 11, by G. Andresen, 1915), 19; J. Wight Duff, *A Literary History of Rome in the Silver Age* (1927), 562; 582; P. L. Strack, *Untersuchungen zur r. Reichsprägung des zweiten Jahrhunderts* II (1933), 55.

[2] W. Hoffmann, *Das literärische Porträt Alexanders des Großen im griechischen und römischen Altertum* (Diss. Leipzig, 1907); F. Weber, *Alexander der Große im Urteil der Griechen und Römer bis in die konstantinische Zeit* (Diss. Leipzig, 1909); P. Treves, *Il mito di Alessandro e la Roma d'Augusto* (1953); A. Heuss, *Antike und Abendland* IV (1954), 65 ff.

[3] Sallust, *Hist.* III. 88; Plutarch, *Pompeius* 2.

[4] Plutarch (*Caesar* 58), asserting vast designs of world conquest, has often been overvalued by the moderns.

[5] For this aspect of Trajan see W. Weber, *Untersuchungen zur Geschichte des Kaisers Hadrianus* (1907), 8 ff.; P. Treves, o.c. 159 ff.; A. Heuss, o.c. 89 ff.

[6] M. I. Henderson, *JRS* XXXIX (1949), 129.

[7] V. Ehrenberg, *Alexander and the Greeks* (1938), 52 ff.

Again, the tour in the East—'cupidine veteres locos et fama celebratos noscendi' (II. 54. 1). This looks significant. Another radiant and heroic figure had previously been singled out in that way, namely, Titus—'atque illum cupido incessit adeundi visendique templum Paphiae Veneris' (*Hist.* II. 2. 2). The force of those instances, however, will diminish considerably if they are supplemented by the 'cupido' which impelled Vespasian at Alexandria to consult the god Serapis or Julius Civilis the Batavian to make essay of naval warfare on the Rhine (*Hist.* IV. 82. 1; V. 23. 1).

The death of Germanicus evokes an elaborate and forced parallel with the Macedonian (II. 73, paraphrased above, p. 492). 'Erant qui . . .'. The commentators are left anonymous. Did Tacitus find the item in one of his sources, or did he invent it?[1]

The same region of earth witnessed each hero's end—'ob propinquitatem etiam locorum'. Antioch is a long way from Babylon—but Selinus, where Trajan breathed his last, is not much more than two hundred miles distant by sea from Seleucia, the port of Antioch. Readers of the *Annales* could hardly fail to be put in mind of Trajan. The sequel was also prefigured—the lavish and emotional description of scenes at Brundisium when a mourning wife brought the ashes back to Italy, and the melancholy pageantry of the long procession all the way from Brundisium to Rome (III. 1 f.).

There was also a sinister note. Some versions alleged that Alexander's end was accelerated by poison—'suorum insidiis externas inter gentis occidisse' (II. 73. 2, cf. Justin XII. 13. 10). Now Trajan, according to Dio (LXVIII. 33. 2), believed that he had been poisoned in Syria. It is necessary to add, however, that no extant source shows any trace of such a 'scelus uxoris' (cf. I. 5. 1, on Livia) imputed against Plotina.

Was Tacitus writing under the fresh impression of what happened in 117? It is not in itself impossible. That would imply a late date for the inception of the *Annales*—which again could be supported by sundry items in the historian's treatment of the accession of Tiberius (Ch. XXXVI).

On the other hand, the heavy emphasis on Alexander does not have to be explained by the hypothesis of Trajan's decease. The course of events can have made the historian's narration appear prophetic. More things than one in the early books of the *Annales* quickly acquired a sharp and contemporary relevance. The work became even more deadly than the author intended: 'volvenda dies, en, attulit ultro!'

73. THE YEAR OF THE PHOENIX

HADRIAN'S 'pietas' is perhaps a sufficient explanation of the phoenix on coins issued to commemorate 'divus Traianus' (p. 471 f.). None the less, the bird might have been reported recently in Egypt. The phoenix symbolizes change, renewal,

---

[1] It was assumed by W. Hoffmann (o.c. 50) that the passage is second-hand. That is not to be believed. See further P. Treves, o.c. 161; 166; 184 ff. That author, however (167 f.; 186), accepts K. Meister's views about *Ann.* I–VI—viz. that those books were composed and published by 114.

and perpetuation.[1] A phoenix had foreshadowed the death of Tiberius Caesar, so some believed (cf. Dio LVIII. 27. 1); and the specimen exhibited by Claudius in 47 was intended to illustrate the eight hundredth anniversary of Rome (Pliny, *NH* x. 7).

Anniversaries were regarded with fear until they were safely passed. Some had been signalized by calamities. Dio noted that 54 B.C. was the seven hundredth year from the founding of Rome (XL. 1. 1): there were disastrous floods, assigned to supernatural agency (XXXIX. 61. 1). Similarly, Orosius, putting the anniversary in the next year (so it appears, for he mentions the disaster of Crassus), records a conflagration the like of which had not been seen before (VI. 14. 5; cf. VII. 2. 11, citing Livy).

Various prophecies existed. There was the official repertory of the Sibylline Books; also alarming things in unauthorized circulation. In A.D. 15, when there were floods of the Tiber, Asinius Gallus proposed that the Books be consulted (*Ann.* I. 76. 1). Not perhaps in innocence. Dio has a strange story about the year 19 (LVII. 18. 3 ff.). The consul sounded a trumpet at dawn on the first day of office, causing universal consternation. Dio goes on to note a portent (the statue of Janus fell down); and he cites an oracle that threatened doom at the term of three times three centuries. Dio states that the period bore no relation to the era of Rome, but he proffers no further elucidation.[2] The oracle about the nine centuries crops up again at the Fire of Rome in 64: according to Dio it still terrified people (LXII. 18. 3). That disaster, as one learns from Tacitus (XV. 41. 2), could be linked to an earlier calamity: men observed that it began on the same day as the burning of Rome by the Gauls (July 19). Tacitus adds that others went so far in expertise as to calculate that the interval between the two events, reckoned in years, months, and days, produced the same three figures (i.e. 418 of each).[3]

It may not have been beyond the powers of ingenuity or malevolence to discover a portentous significance in the year 117, the year of Trajan's death. At first sight the era of the city is not promising. It will be recalled, however, that the earliest legends assume that Rome was founded not long after the Fall of Troy: Aeneas was the founder, his son, his grandson, or his great-grandson.[4] Three centuries of Kings of Alba Longa had not yet been invented. A verse of Ennius is of especial value—'septingenti sunt paulo plus aut minus anni' (cited by Varro, *Res rusticae* III. 1. 2). Who made the statement, and when? It is hard not to believe that Camillus is the speaker, adjuring the Romans not to abandon the city: in Livy's version of the oration Camillus appeals to Rome's duration, 365 years (V. 54. 5), that is, reckoning from the established Varronian era.[5] To Ennius (as to Naevius), Romulus is the grandson of Aeneas.[6] When did he put

---

[1] See J. Hubaux and M. Leroy, *Le Mythe du phénix dans les littératures grecque et latine* (Liège, 1939). The authors note Hadrian's coin (248), but do not indicate any special relevance of *Ann.* VI. 28.

[2] Dio could perhaps have known that the sound of a trumpet revealed the end of an Etruscan *saeculum*, as, vivid and terrifying, in 88 B.C. (Plutarch, *Sulla* 7).

[3] XV. 41. 2: 'alii eo usque cura progressi sunt', &c.

[4] Dionysius, *Ant. Rom.* I. 72 f.; Festus, p. 326 L.

[5] L. Holzapfel, *Römische Chronologie* (1885), 243.

[6] Virgil preserves a vestigial remnant—'quin et avo comitem sese Mavortius addet | Romulus' (*Aen.* VI. 777 f.).

the foundation? Perhaps about 1100 B.C.[1] One might take a further step. Ennius —or others—may have reckoned three generations, or a century, from the Fall of Troy (which Eratosthenes fixed at 1184 B.C.).[2]

If that were so, a remarkable consequence would follow. Twelve vultures was the omen seen by Romulus. In the last age of the Republic a persuasion emerged that Rome was destined to endure for twelve centuries: Vettius, an expert, revealed the matter to Varro.[3] One century from the Fall of Troy, and twelve more for Rome, would produce A.D. 117.

When the Jews rose against Nero, they had prophecies to encourage them. Failure would not quench faith. And there were fresh reasons for hope—Nero returning from Parthia to destroy Rome (as the Jewish Sibylline oracles proclaim). Great calamities would announce the end. Thus the eruption of Vesuvius is brought into connexion with the false Nero in the reign of Titus (*Or. Sib.* IV. 130 ff.). Trajan nearly perished in the earthquake at Antioch;[4] and Trajan incurred defeat in Mesopotamia. The Jews rose everywhere. There may even have been a false Nero in 116 or 117 (p. 518).

The phoenix portends a change in the history of the world. A later oracle puts Nero's return in the epoch of the phoenix,

> ἔνθεν ὅταν φοίνικος ἐπέλθῃ τέρμα χρόνοιο
> ἥξει ⟨ὁ⟩ πορθήσων λαῶν γένος, ἄκριτα φῦλα
> Ἑβραίων ἔθνος, κτλ.[5]

It goes on to mention the destruction of Rome and ends with the fatal number of Rome, 948 years (i.e. A.D. 195), derived from the numerical value of the letters of the word Ῥώμη. The text is not secure. There may be a lacuna after the first line;[6] and it is worth noting that the line preceding it refers to Hadrian. There is no warrant, however (despite Ἑβραίων ἔθνος), for attaching any part of this passage to the events of 116 and 117.

The year 117 belongs to a secular anniversary of the Fall of Troy (1184 B.C.)— and portentous for the new Troy, if Rome's foundation were put precisely one century later. It would be worth the inquiry, whether that calculation is relevant to any calamities at Rome, real or apprehended. In 83 B.C. the temple of Juppiter on the Capitol was destroyed by fire. Clearly most ominous for Rome and the rule of Rome (Appian, *BC* I. 83). The disaster recurred in the civil war of A.D. 69, and elated the Gauls—'finem adesse imperio' (*Hist.* IV. 54. 2). Tacitus confines the effects to the enemies of Rome, and goes on to rebuke the Druids for their 'vana superstitio'.

---

[1] O. Skutsch, *The Annales of Quintus Ennius* (Inaugural Lecture, London, 1953), 14.

[2] There is an inexplicable hiatus of a century in the calculation adopted by Virgil (*Aen.* I. 265 ff.)—three hundred and thirty three years from Aeneas' establishment in Latium to Romulus' founding of Rome.

[3] Censorinus, *De die natali* 17. 15.

[4] Dio LXVIII. 25. 5. Juvenal refers to a comet and to great floods in the East as well as an earthquake (VI. 409 ff., cf. App. 75).

[5] *Or. Sib.* VIII. 139 ff., with the emendation of A. Kurfess, *Würzburger Jahrbücher* III (1948), 194. Kurfess inserts ὁ, while τέρμα χρόνοιο for πενταχρόνοιο is due to Mendelssohn.

[6] That is assumed by J. Geffcken in his edition (1902).

A prophecy indicated the twentieth year from the conflagration of the Capitol in 83 B.C. as 'fatalem hunc annum esse ad interitum huius urbis atque imperi' (Cicero, *In Cat.* III. 9; Sallust, *Cat.* 47. 2). There is, however, no statement anywhere on record that brings 83 B.C. into relation with 1184—or 1084.

It can be noted that the margin of a year or two appears to be admitted (indeed welcomed) by the adepts of significant calculations, ancient or modern.[1] After 83 B.C. the next season of peril should fall in A.D. 17 or 18. Dio, recording the panic at Rome on the morning of January 1, A.D. 19, happens to adduce prophecies of doom, but can assign no precise relevance (LVII. 18. 3 ff.).

Next, 117. The phoenix on Hadrian's coin can stand for a crisis faced and surmounted, a renewal of the 'aeternitas' of Rome. A few years later (in 121) the birthday of Rome (the 'natalis urbis'), receives novel and startling emphasis on a coin, the exact year from the foundation being registered (DCCCLXXIIII).[2] It is tempting to bring this commemorative issue into relation with Hadrian's design (not alien to the 'Troiana origo') of the *Templum Romae et Veneris*.[3]

Cornelius Tacitus, one of the *quindecimviri*, knew the Sibylline Books and could not fail to be expert in numbers. His remarks about the ingenious computation that was made to link the burning of Rome to the Gallic catastrophe betrays no sign of deference or belief (*Ann.* XV. 41. 2). He may have known about millenary prophecies adhering to A.D. 117—and their exciting influence on the enemies of Rome, on Jews, and perhaps Christians. A Roman senator would not have liked them. But also (it can be contended), he was not only a patriot but a sceptic.

Tacitus sets the phoenix that appeared in the reign of Tiberius in startling relief as the first item in the chronicle of a Roman year, introduced by the names of Roman consuls (VI. 28, cf. p. 472). For variety, for mockery—and to demonstrate in a gentle and insidious fashion that prophecies and portents have no meaning.

74. JUVENAL'S BIRTH AND ORIGIN

THE various *Vitae* attached to the manuscripts of Juvenal are miserable productions. Inferences from the poems, or guesswork, they cannot safely be employed (cf. p. 499, on his alleged exile).

When was Juvenal born? Some estimates put the date around 55.[4] Others around 60.[5] Perhaps he was a little younger than that. Addressing Calvinus (who may, or may not, be a real person), Juvenal exclaims 'stupet haec qui iam post

---

[1] M. Grant, *Roman Anniversary Issues* (1950), 1 ff. That author can serve a double employ.

[2] H. Mattingly, *BMC, R. Emp.* III (1936), cxxxii; 422.

[3] See now J. Beaujeu, *La Religion romaine à l'apogée de l'empire* I (1955), 128 ff.

[4] J. Dürr, *Das Leben Juvenals* (Prog. Ulm, 1888), 9 f., who argues for that precise year; G. Highet, *TAPA* LXXIII (1937), 484.

[5] L. Friedländer (in his edition, 1895) I, 15; J. Wight Duff, *A Literary History of Rome in the Silver Age* (1927), 506; H. J. Rose, *A Handbook of Latin Literature* (1936), 406; G. Highet, *Juvenal the Satirist* (1954), 5, cf. 40. Observe, however, the extreme caution of F. Vollmer, P–W x, 1041 f.

terga reliquit | sexaginta annos Fonteio consule natus?' (XIII. 16 f.). Which Fonteius? Not the *ordinarius* of 59, but the Fonteius Capito of 67 (*PIR*², F 467), as Borghesi divined. It should be asked, for what writer or reader in Hadrian's day would that name convey precision and a meaning? The year 68 was another matter, the last of Nero, and commemorated by the name of an orator and poet, Silius Italicus (cf. Pliny, *Epp.* III. 7. 9 f.).

Juvenal may himself have reached sixty in 127. That year recurs a little later on. Juvenal describes a murderous quarrel between two villages in Egypt. He furnishes a date 'nuper consule Iunco' (XV. 27). This consul, L. Aemilius Juncus (*PIR*², A 355), held the *fasces* for the last three months of 127 as colleague of Sex. Julius Severus. Now it is one thing for official documents to date by *consules suffecti*. Why should a writer know or care? Granted that it was the date of the incident, the registering of a *suffectus* is still peculiar. Juncus is not a person of abnormal notoriety. Perhaps Juvenal may have known and cared—if his own sixtieth birthday fell between October and December of 127. There are no other consular dates in his poems.

Juvenal possessed an estate on the territory of Aquinum (III. 319); and the dedication set up by ']nius Iuvenalis' (*ILS* 2926) can reasonably be claimed for the poet, or for some member of his family. The person was commander of a cohort of Dalmatians (number missing), local magistrate, and 'flamen divi Vespasiani'. It is generally assumed that Juvenal was Italian 'ultima ab origine'. Confirmation is found in the poems, thus 'his constant hatred of foreigners and his love of old Italy'.[1] At the same time, a 'western-provincial outlook' can be discovered in this 'Italico'.[2] One begins to wonder.

The nomenclature 'D. Iunius Iuvenalis' might help.[3] Of the western provinces, Spain offers the highest proportion of Junii. Among immigrants from Spain to Italy one will note the Gaditane L. Junius Moderatus Columella, who owned farms at Ardea, Carseoli, Alba Longa, and Caere (*PIR*¹, J 511). The Spanish invasion left a whole colony at Tibur (p. 602). Juvenal had property there (x. 65). Not evidence, however; nor is his friendship with Martial.

The *cognomen* 'Iuvenalis' suggests either low class or foreign origin. In the *CIL* volumes covering Italy it is commonest in the tenth, with five examples, two of them being freedmen in towns not far from Aquinum (4980: Venafrum; 5785a: Cereatae, cf. 5686). It will be recalled that according to two of the *Vitae* Juvenal was the son or foster-son of a wealthy freedman. That would not in itself be incredible.

As for the western provinces, the significant evidence comes from Africa and Gaul. There are about ten examples in Africa (one a *praefectus cohortis*, *CIL* VIII, 4292: near Lambaesis); and three of the four instances in legionary *cognomina* throughout the world are in III Augusta at Lambaesis.[4] Narbonensis shows four persons called 'Iuvenalis', Tres Galliae (with the Germanies) six; observe also 'Iuvenalis e primoribus Tungrorum' (*Hist.* IV. 66. 3).

---

[1] G. Highet, *TAPA* LXVIII (1937), 484. Cf. his book (1954), 233; 255.

[2] E. Lepore, *Rivista storica italiana* LX (1948), 193 ff.

[3] Manuscripts give the *praenomen*, and it is implied in one of the *Vitae*.

[4] L. R. Dean, *A Study of the Cognomina of Soldiers in the Roman Legions* (Diss. Princeton, 1916), 210.

Two consuls bear the *cognomen*, a Julius in 81, and a Cassius under Antoninus Pius. Also relevant is Flavius Juvenalis, *praefectus praetorio* in 193 (*PIR*², F 300). There is a chance that Juvenal's family was immigrant, and alien ultimately.

75. JUVENAL AND TACITUS

THE five books of the Satires comprise sixteen poems (the last of them incomplete, and perhaps never finished). When did Juvenal write and publish? What are the limits and the intervals? The reference to the condemnation of the proconsul Marius Priscus (I. 49 f.), in 100, carries a temptation to put the publication of Book I (i.e. the first five poems) not long after that year. For example, by 105.[1] Second thoughts produce a date five years later.[2] Still perhaps a little too early. It will be observed that the reference to Marius Priscus may be literary rather than historical: that is, not to an event in the year 100, but to Pliny's Letters (*Epp*. II. 11 f.).

Citing a detail about the habits of the Emperor Otho, Juvenal implies that it would have been worth a mention from Tacitus— 'res memoranda novis annalibus atque recenti | historia (II. 102 f.).[3] It does not have to be believed, however, that Juvenal must be writing immediately after the appearance of the *Historiae* (or a portion of them). That designation of the *Historiae* would remain valid for some years, until rendered obsolete by lapse of time or another historical masterpiece.

So far Book I. In Book II the female rumour-mongerer reports a comet threatening the Armenian monarch or the Parthian, great floods in Mesopotamia, and an earthquake (VI. 407 ff.). Now a comet can be assigned to 115;[4] and, although no floods happen to be attested, there is the earthquake at Antioch in 115, in which Trajan narrowly escaped death (Dio LXVIII. 24 f.). Welcome—but not enough to tie Book II down to 116.[5] Those striking events would keep their freshness for several years; and a prudent writer might prefer not to relate rumours or catastrophes belonging to the reign of Hadrian.

The Satires, it is argued, were given to the world between c. 110 and c. 130.[6] None the less (and whatever be the composition date of certain among the earlier poems) there is no proof that Juvenal published anything earlier than 115, perhaps even 117.

With Book III (i.e. Satires VII–IX) the question becomes relevant to the *Annales* of Tacitus. Illustrious victims of Nero are evoked by 'Camerinos | et

---

[1] G. Highet, *TAPA* LXVIII (1937), 484 ('in the period 100–105, when the Marius Priscus affair was still topical'); cf. 485. Similarly P. Ercole, *Studi giovenaliani* (1935), 61.

[2] G. Highet, *Juvenal the Satirist* (1954), 5: 'in or near 110'. Vollmer, however, suggested not long before 115 (P–W x, 1042), L. Friedländer (o.c. 14) between 112 and 116.

[3] cf. J. Dürr, *Die zeitgeschichtlichen Beziehungen in den Satiren Juvenals* (Prog. Cannstatt, 1902), 9. To illustrate 'constantia' in II. 105 he cited *Hist*. II. 47. 3.

[4] As established by L. Friedländer, o.c. 8 f.

[5] As some appear to assume, e.g. Schanz–Hosius, *Gesch. der r. Lit.* II⁴ (1935), 572. The attempt of P. Ercole to put the poem not later than 111 (o.c. 76) can be dismissed.

[6] G. Highet, o.c. (1954), 16.

Bareas' (VII. 90 f.); and the *cognomen* 'Camerinus' recurs in VIII. 38. The consular Q. Sulpicius Camerinus (*PIR¹*, S 713) was an aristocrat of ancient lineage, but not (one supposes) likely to achieve lasting fame outside the history books. Barea Soranus has been immortalized by Tacitus (*Ann.* XVI. 21 ff.). Camerinus perished in 67 (Dio LXIII. 17. 2), and therefore does not figure in the *Annales* (as we have them).[1]

The eighth satire (on pedigree) contains a plethora of Neronian material, as has generally been recognized.[2] Some characters may suggest that Tacitus has been drawn upon, for example (Plautius) Lateranus.[3] Perhaps there is direct derivation in one incident, namely venal descendants of the *nobilitas* employed by Nero at public entertainments (VIII. 192 f., cf. *Ann.* XIV. 14. 3).[4] If that be admitted, it bears upon the dates of composition of both writers. The year 120 may be too early for the publication of Book III of the Satires. The third hexad of the *Annales* could (perhaps should) be later than that (cf. p. 473).

Traces of the *Annales* have never been systematically investigated. Indeed, so long as it was widely believed that Tacitus completed the work in 117 or 118, one of the incentives of scholarly inquiry was lacking. For present purposes it will be enough to adduce a single item (not, however, of any chronological significance). Exemplifying and deriding the vanity of human wishes, Juvenal takes for a leading text the ambitions of Seianus and his end. He introduces a minor character called Bruttidius (x. 83).[5] Tacitus gave especial prominence to Bruttedius Niger as a prosecutor, with an ominous hint of the ruin that awaits great oratorical talents when put to evil uses for rapid rewards (III. 66. 4, cf. p. 327). Bruttedius, it can hardly be doubted, was to recur in the context of Seianus, in Book V.

Juvenal wrote about the dead (I. 170 f.). Also the fictitious. Not but what a name here and there (accident or design) might evoke the living. Hispo (II. 50) is a disgusting fellow, and the feminine form of that *cognomen* (Hispulla) designates a fat woman (VI. 74), and an unchaste woman (XII. 11). A rare name: but observe Ti. Caepio Hispo (*PIR²*, E 83, cf. App. 25), and two ladies among the relatives of Pliny, Calpurnia Hispulla and Corellia Hispulla (*PIR²*, C 329; 1296).[6] Was Juvenal intentionally alluding to persons and groups in his own day?[7] Again, Gillo (I. 40), which occurs in the nomenclature of Q. Fulvius Gillo Bittius Proculus (*PIR²*, F 544), who married the mother of Pliny's second wife.[8] 'Gillo' is also very uncommon.

---

[1] The item is not strong enough to contribute towards a proof that Tacitus lived to complete the *Annales*.

[2] cf. J. Dürr, o.c. 21f. Dürr's treatise did not go beyond the ninth satire.

[3] VIII. 146 ff., cf. G. Highet, o.c. 273. Not that there are details to suggest more than that he took the name from Tacitus (*Ann.* XV. 49. 3, &c.). For the mysterious Rubellius Blandus (VIII. 39 ff.) see App. 1.

[4] As argued by J. E. B. Mayor in his commentary (II², 1878). The names (Cassius) Longinus and (Plautius) Lateranus (x. 16 f.) reflect events of 65 and 66—and might derive from Tacitus.

[5] For the rare *nomen* 'Bruttidius' or 'Bruttedius' see R. Syme, *JRS* XXXIX (1949), 10.

[6] R. Syme, o.c. 14 f.

[7] That is suggested by G. Highet, o.c. 291 f.

[8] G. Highet, o.c. 293. Fulvius Gillo was proconsul of Asia in 115/16, Caepio Hispo in 117/18; for the evidence, App. 23.

It is credible that Juvenal had no reason to cherish Pliny, his family, and certain of his friends.[1] (Not, indeed, that Pliny's failure to mention Juvenal in the letters proves anything about either.) Does it follow that the satirist was attacking a known Hispo and a known Gillo, men of consular rank, for precise and notorious enormities? Enough if he chose 'Hispo' and 'Gillo' because he fancied the names, and may have disliked the men—and the more safely if they were ostensibly blameless, or now deceased.

Juvenal's selection of names is a tricky question. It deserves a methodical investigation. Failing that, erroneous assumptions acquire currency. Two names cited in a recent study may suffice. It is not certain that Ponticus (VIII. 1) is a real person. Vain therefore the notion that he derives from the old aristocracy,[2] none of whom bore that *cognomen*. Nor is 'Creticus' (II. 67 f.) likely to wound persons alive, powerful, and proud.[3] The Metelli were extinct, long since. An elementary question should have been asked: how many families of the Republican *nobilitas* were extant in the reign of Hadrian? To conclude (and to repeat, cf. p. 499), Juvenal does not attack any person or category that commands influence in his own time.

76. C. SUETONIUS TRANQUILLUS

THE parent, Suetonius Laetus, was a military tribune in 69 (*Otho* 10. 1). The son, describing himself as 'adulescens' when a false Nero appeared twenty years after the death of that emperor (*Nero* 57. 2), cannot have been born later than 72: perhaps a few years earlier, but not many, for he is 'adulescentulus' in an anecdote that ought to refer to something later than 88 (*Dom.* 12. 2).

The earliest trace of an official career is the abortive military tribunate of 101 (Pliny, *Epp.* III. 8. 1). Then a long interval until the splendid employment 'ab epistulis' which he was compelled to vacate in 122 (*HA, Hadr.* 11. 3). It was tempting to make speculation.[4]

The fragments of an inscription recently discovered at Hippo Regius in Africa bring a welcome supplement.[5] Suetonius was made a member of the jury panels (the 'iudices selecti') by Trajan, and he held two minor sacerdotal offices. That hardly matters. He served Hadrian, however, 'a] studiis a byblio[thecis] [ab e]pistulis'. The secretary 'a studiis' was the Emperor's expert adviser on literary matters, and presumably had charge of his private library.[6] The next post (the public collections at Rome) could be combined with it.[7]

Suetonius' patron was Q. Septicius Clarus (the dedicant of Pliny's letters), who was appointed Guard Prefect along with Q. Marcius Turbo in 119 (*HA, Hadr.* 9. 4). It could be conjectured that Septicius, like other friends of Hadrian,

---

[1] G. Highet, o.c. 293 f.   [2] 113; 272.   [3] 293, cf. 63.

[4] cf. H. A. Sanders, *AJP* LXV (1944), 113 ff., who suggested that Suetonius might previously have been in charge of the libraries at Rome.

[5] Published by E. Marec and H. G. Pflaum, *CRAI* 1952, 79, whence *AE* 1953, 73.

[6] B. Kübler, P–W IV A, 397 f.

[7] As, a little later, by L. Julius Vestinus (*IG* XIV, 1085), and by L. Volusius Maecianus (*CIL* XIV, 5347 f.).

was already rising in the late years of Trajan—and might, for example, have acceded to the Guard from the *Annona*. His nephew, C. Erucius Clarus, after no conspicuous advance in public life, won laurels in the East, with a consulate in 117 (p. 242).

Can anything else be divined? Pliny from Bithynia wrote to Trajan, petitioning that Suetonius be accorded the 'ius trium liberorum'. He says 'et mores eius secutus et studia iam pridem, domine, in contubernium adsumpsi, tantoque maius diligere coepi quanto nunc propius inspexi' (*Epp.* x. 94. 1). The word 'nunc' is decisive, if that emendation of the manuscript 'hunc' be accepted.[1] The balance of the phrase seems to demand it. Further, for language, observe Pliny asking Pompeius Falco to confer a military tribunate on a friend—'accepisse te beneficium credes cum propius inspexeris hominem omnibus honoribus . . . parem' (VII. 22. 3). Was not Suetonius perhaps on the staff of Pliny in Bithynia?[2]

Next, his disgrace. According to the *Historia Augusta*, the Emperor dismissed Septicius, Suetonius, and many others, 'quod apud Sabinam uxorem in usu eius familiarius se tunc egerant quam reverentia domus aulicae postulabat' (*Hadr.* 11. 3). A long digression follows, expatiating upon Hadrian's suspicious nature. The whole passage is appended to Hadrian's visit to Britain (11. 2), and the factual narration resumes with the words 'compositis in Britannia rebus transgressus in Galliam' (12. 1). That is to say, it is attached to the year 122.[3]

The anecdote is not wholly satisfactory—and it is strange to find Hadrian, of all people, insistent on court etiquette. The sentence goes on to assert that he would have liked to get rid of Sabina also.

Assuming that the passage has been grafted on to Hadrian's journeys at the right place, there is something more to be said. Where did the misdemeanours of Suetonius occur? At Rome, such is the standard and unquestioned opinion, the Emperor being absent. Why not in Britain? An emperor journeying abroad might have his consort with him, and one of the two commanders of the Guard. Thus Trajan in 117. Also surely the head of the secretariat.

Authors do not always disclose any familiarity they may have with the Roman provinces. There is nothing about Britain, for example, in the *Strategemata* of Julius Frontinus (p. 68). Now Suetonius can report an interesting particular about the early career of Titus—'tribunus militum et in Germania et in Britannia meruit summa industriae nec minore modestiae fama, sicut apparet statuarum et imaginum eius multitudine ac titulis per utramque provinciam' (*Divus Titus* 4. 1). Suetonius is emphatic—'sicut apparet'. How did he know? Suetonius or his informant must have visited both Germania Inferior (where Titus served in 57 or 58)[4] and Britain. Hadrian and his retinue were in Gaul and Germany in 121 (*HA, Hadr.* 10. 1 f.), crossing to Britain the year after.

---

[1] H. Keil expelled the 'hunc' of the MSS.; but P. v. Winterfeld substituted 'nunc', and recent editors concur, thus R. Kukula (Teubner 1912), M. Schuster (1933 and 1952), and M. Durry (Budé, 1947). However, if one proposed 'tunc', the inference about Bithynia would lapse.

[2] The inference seems to have been missed by scholars.

[3] The obsolete date 121 persists in many manuals, and is reproduced by E. Marec and H. G. Pflaum (o.c. 84).

[4] As is deduced from his 'castrense contubernium' with Pliny (*NH, praef.* 3), in the last stage of that officer's service, cf. F. Münzer, *Bonner Jahrbücher* CIV (1899), 122 ff.

Suetonius in Britain: not a wholly fanciful surmise. How does it square with the composition of *De vita Caesarum*? A late writer has the firm statement that the work was dedicated to Septicius Clarus, at that time Prefect of the Guard (Lydus, *De mensibus* II. 6). Hence, apparently, the limits of a triennium, 119–22. Perhaps the work was ready in 119, having been written by Suetonius in the leisure of his earlier secretarial occupations.

If that were so, how explain the reference to the inscriptions in honour of Titus? It may be that the original design (and first publication) was confined to the six books, from Caesar the Dictator to Nero, while VII (Galba, Otho, Vitellius) and VIII (the Flavian emperors) are a later supplement (cf. p. 501).

A passage can be adduced in support. Titus in his last hours said that there was only one thing he had to repent of. Hence speculation. Perhaps adultery with Domitia Longina—'quidam opinantur consuetudinem recordatum quam cum fratris uxore habuerit; sed nullam habuisse persancte Domitia iurabat, haud negatura si qua omnino fuisset, immo gloriatura, quod illi promptissimum erat in omnibus probris' (*Divus Titus* 10. 2). The way in which Domitia is referred to (the tenses as well as the tone) would induce one to believe that she is no longer among the living.

When did Domitian's widow die? There are tiles with her name bearing the consular date 123 (*CIL* xv, 548 f.; 553). Also of 126 (554). It has therefore been assumed that she was still alive in 126.[1] There is nothing against a long survival of this lady. Other tiles with 'Severo et Arrian. cos.' (552) would take her into the period 129–32. In 140 a temple was completed at Gabiae in memory of Domitia Longina (*ILS* 272).

A final problem: the 'patria' of the imperial secretary. It may well be Hippo Regius, a *municipium* of Augustan date (*ILS* 5976a), even though there be only one 'Suetonius' on all the inscriptions of Africa, viz. C. Suetonius Januarius, an officer commanding a post near Theveste (*CIL* VIII, 17589): probably from Africa, to judge by his *cognomen*.[2]

Now the inscription has the office of *flamen* immediately after the name of Suetonius Tranquillus. The natural assumption is a local priesthood. There follows his enrolment 'int[er selectos]', after which comes 'pont. Volca[nal]i'— this at Rome, or perhaps in some town of Latium, notably Ostia, for there is no *pontifex Volcanalis* at Rome.[3] Nothing is known to preclude Hippo as the 'patria' of the scholar. Yet there might be some reason for the dedication at that town, unrevealed and unverifiable.[4]

An author, and a great general (Suetonius Paullinus), lend lustre to the *nomen* 'Suetonius'. It happens to be very rare, but with a local habitation in Italy. All the signs point to the region of Pisaurum, a citizen colony founded in 184 B.C. in the Ager Gallicus. Not only 'Suetonius', but 'Sueto' as a *gentilicium*. The evidence

---

[1] E. Groag, *PIR²*, D 181: 'in vivis etiam a. 126 XV 554.'

[2] The statistics for soldiers are instructive, cf. L. R. Dean, *A Study of the Cognomina of Soldiers in the Roman Legions* (Diss. Princeton, 1916), 202 ff.

[3] See L. R. Taylor, *The Cults of Ostia* (Bryn Mawr, 1912), 14 ff.

[4] Hadrian might have passed that way, going from Spain to the East in 123 (*HA, Hadr.* 12. 7). But, if the *HA* is correct, Suetonius was already in disgrace.

is powerful and convergent.[1] Further, a neglected hint: when Suetonius compiled the biography of the poet Accius he was able to adduce a local detail—'a quo et fundus Accianus iuxta Pisaurum dicitur'.[2] There is a faint chance that the scholar and the consular both derive 'moribunda ab sede Pisauri' (Catullus 81. 3).

77. SUETONIUS AND THE *ANNALES*

SUETONIUS never mentions the name of Cornelius Tacitus. Why? Because, so some argue, when Suetonius published the *Vitae* (presumably in 121), though he had read the earlier books—and even the last—Tacitus was still alive: the historian did not die until 121 or 122.[3] Or, another view, the *Annales* were not completed when Suetonius published (in 120).[4]

Those arguments are circular, the trail a false one. Suetonius (it could be assumed) knew Tacitus. He was not obliged to name him, dead or alive. Suetonius does not mention any of the annalistic historians whom the biographies (subsequent to that of Augustus) presuppose and employ.

What is left to go by? Suetonius must have read the *Historiae*. One looks for signs in the biographies of Galba, Otho, and Vitellius. In vain, unless it be the sharp discrepancy about an emperor's address to the Guard (*Otho* 6. 3, contrasted with the oration in *Hist.* I. 37 f.). Nor could the Flavian *Vitae* furnish the shadow of a clue. There is no point in asking whether Suetonius did not lift from Tacitus the names of the twelve consular victims (*Dom.* 10 f.) or exploit (ib. 16 f.) the historian's account of an assassination in the Palace.

The prospect of discovering traces of the *Annales* is therefore of the slightest. Suetonius firmly repulses the malicious reason for Augustus' choice of a successor (*Tib.* 21. 2 f., cf. App. 36). Perhaps a criticism of the consular historian. Similarly his statement that Augustus was still alive when Tiberius returned.[5] Not, indeed, that Tacitus invented the 'comparatio deterrima' between Augustus and Tiberius (I. 10. 7, cf. Dio LVI. 45. 3). However that may be, a reference could perhaps be admitted. It does not touch the relative chronology of the two writers at any vital point. There is no difficulty in supposing that Suetonius could have read Books I–III or Books I–VI—that is, if he was still writing his *Tiberius* as late as 119 or 120.[6]

The third hexad is another matter. Certainty would be precious. At first sight the *Nero* looks like a deliberate and almost perverse challenge, biography to the scorn of history. Hardly a trace of chronology, foreign affairs come off miserably (thus Britain and Armenia in 39. 1 and 40. 2), and he can narrate the fall of Nero without naming Nymphidius Sabinus or Verginius Rufus. Observe

---

[1] W. Schulze, *LE* 300.

[2] Suetonius (ed. Roth, 1890), p. 295.

[3] A. Macé, *Essai sur Suétone* (1900), 206 ff. That writer assumed that the first six books of the *Annales* appeared before 117, the last part between 117 and 120 (ib. 209).

[4] E. Groag, *Jahrbücher für Cl. Phil.*, Supp.-Band XXIII (1897), 768.

[5] Some take it as indubitable, e.g. W. Weber, *Princeps* I (1936), 12*: 'sicher Polemik gegen Tacitus ann. I 5.'

[6] Yet Suetonius might have begun a little earlier than that, finishing by 119 (cf. p. 780).

especially the treatment of the various Tacitean heroes, the foils to Nero. No mention of Domitius Corbulo or Suetonius Paullinus; and what he has to say about Seneca (7. 1; 35. 5; 52. 1) and Thrasea Paetus (37. 1) is curt and trivial.

That argument would not be conclusive. Something more is requisite. One item has not failed to excite attention. Tacitus refers to poems of Nero as not wholly his own composition, implying that he had inspected them—'quod species ipsa carminum docet, non impetu et instinctu et uno ore fluens' (XIV. 16. 1). Suetonius, however, appeals to manuscripts he had seen for a contrary view about Nero's authorship—'venere in manus meas pugillares libellique', &c. (52). Perhaps an expert's pride—documents against the stylistic criteria.[1]

Furthermore, some might be tempted to adduce a verbal resemblance. Tacitus registers a 'sidus cometes, sanguine inlustri semper Neroni expiatum' (XV. 47. 1). Suetonius has the notice of the same comet, with Balbillus the astrologer explaining to Nero 'solere reges talia ostenta caede aliqua illustri expiare' (36. 1). That would not help much.

Proof is lacking so far that Suetonius could refer to the third hexad of the *Annales*.[2] It was perhaps not yet accessible—or rather not yet even written. Juvenal may have used it for his eighth satire, but there is no reason for putting that poem as early as 120 (cf. App. 75). One can maintain that the Neronian books, whether as extant or according to the plan that terminated the reign with Book XVIII, were not completed much before the year 123 (cf. Ch. XXXV).

[1] Macé (o.c. 179) assumes criticism of Tacitus.

[2] That is, on the assumption that Suetonius was composing between 119 and 122—and especially if the date of publication falls closer to the earlier date. For a possibility that the last two books of *Vitae* (covering 69–96) are a continuation, and later than 122, cf. App. 76.

I. PROVINCIAL ROMANS

78. PROVINCIAL *NOMINA*

THE twenty names most common in the Spains and in Narbonensis, furnished by the Indexes of *CIL* II and XII, are as follows (neglecting imperatorial *gentilicia*, such as 'Julius', 'Flavius', &c.), round numbers in each case:

Spain		Narbonensis	
Valerius	400	Valerius	400
Cornelius	350	Cornelius	290
Fabius	300	Pompeius	220
Aemilius	180	Licinius	100
Licinius	180	Attius	90
Caecilius	150	Domitius	80
Sempronius	150	Aemilius	70
Pompeius	130	Cassius	70
Junius	130	Caecilius	60
Antonius	120	Antonius	60
Baebius	90	Coelius	60
Terentius	90	Annius	60
Annius	80	Titius	60
Calpurnius	70	Fabius	50
Porcius	70	Junius	50
Sulpicius	70	Marius	50
Domitius	70	Terentius	50
Fulvius	60	Vibius	50
Marcius	60	Atilius	40
Marius	60	Octavius	40

79. NARBONENSIAN ROMANS

THE statistics furnished in App. 78 are instructive. Most of the *gentilicia* recall men who held the *imperium* in the western lands before the Republic ended. Not that it has to be assumed that such names always go back to any direct grant of the franchise. Fashion and predilection operated among natives and men acquiring Latin rights. However, for three *gentilicia* common among the notables of the *provincia* there stands splendid attestation.[1] The Domitii had a *clientela* in Narbonensis (cf. *In Verrem* II. 1. 118); C. Valerius Flaccus, proconsul c. 82 B.C., gave the franchise to Caburus, chieftain of the Helvii (Caesar, *BG* I. 47. 4), parent

---

[1] R. Syme, *CQ* XXXII (1938), 41; *Rom. Rev.* (1939), 44; 79 f.

of Caesar's friend C. Valerius Troucillus; and Pompeius similarly rewarded the grandfather of the historian Trogus (Justin XLIII. 5. 11 f.).

The nomenclature of two early inscriptions from Nemausus brings confirmation—one magistrate called L. Domitius Axiounus, another (C. Marius Celsus) married to 'Pompeia Toutodivicis f.' (*ILS* 6976 f.).

Nor will 'Cornelius' be neglected, after 'Julius' and 'Valerius' the third most common *nomen* in the 'provincia'. Its early emergence is attested in a dual and convincing fashion. First, C. Cornelius Cn. f. Gallus (*ILS* 8995), poet and Prefect of Egypt, from Forum Julii (p. 587). Secondly, by inscriptions, notably that from Glanum (St. Remy): the name of a Cornelia, on a Celtic inscription in the Greek alphabet.[1]

The *gentilicia* 'Domitius', 'Valerius', and 'Pompeius' are strongly in evidence among the Narbonensian senators of the first century (App. 82). Native names could also be adapted to a Latin form or flexion (hence the *cognomen* 'Atticus',[2] the *nomen* 'Attius').[3] They are not at all frequent in persons of rank. Observe L. Duvius Avitus (*suff.* 56); Togonius Gallus (*Ann.* VI. 2. 2), who might be Transpadane; also L. Dunius Severus, attested by coins as proconsul of an eastern province under Claudius (*PIR*², D 207).

Immigrants from Italy brought with them peculiar local or regional names. Narbo yields a rich and varied harvest—'Appaeus', 'Lafrenus', 'Perperna', 'Tolumnius', 'Vifidius', 'Votienus', &c.[4] The Roman *coloniae*, however, make a miserable showing on the roll of senators (cf. p. 620).

80. THE NOMENCLATURE OF ROMAN SPAIN

IMMIGRATION into Spain under the Republic can be documented in various ways.[5] The nomenclature of senators adds a powerful argument reaching a long way back. L. Decidius Saxa (*tr. pl.* 44) is a Samnite, to be sure, a recent arrival;[6] but some of the Baetican families of the Empire appear to descend, not from Roman citizen soldiers or settlers, but from Italian allied troops, or from traders, illustrating the mosaic of races and languages that was Italy.

The prime example is the name 'Ulpius' (App. 81). Half a dozen further instances will here be adduced. The *nomen* 'Annaeus', with a non-Latin termination, is claimed by Schulze as Etruscan:[7] it is also—and preferably—to be taken as Illyrian.[8] Another Corduban family is the Dasumii.[9] Beyond any doubt or

---

[1] H. Rolland, *CRAI* 1955, 92.

[2] For Julii Attici, observe the high-ranking procurator (*CIL* XII, 1854: Vienna); the viticultor from whom Agricola's parent learned so much (Columella I. 1. 14)—and, no doubt, A. Atticus (*Agr.* 37. 6).

[3] cf. App. 78. Hence convincing evidence for an important personage, Sex. Attius Suburanus Aemilianus: his tribe is the 'Voltinia' (*AE* 1939, 60).

[4] O. Hirschfeld, *Kl. Schr.* (1913), 30 f. For similar reasons Carthago Nova invites (and repays) inspection.   [5] E. Gabba, *Athenaeum* XXXII (1954), 297 ff.

[6] R. Syme, *JRS* XXVII (1937), 127 ff.   [7] *LE* 346.

[8] *LE* 32, cf. H. Krahe, *Lexikon altillyrischer Personennamen* (1929), 6 f. The Paelignian form is 'Annaus' or 'Annavus'.

[9] L. Dasumius the testator makes provision for Corduba (*CIL* VI, 10229, l. 31): Dasumii at Corduba (II, 2273) and elsewhere in Baetica (1801; 1089; 1096; 5391 f.).

cavil that name comes from south-eastern Italy.[1] Hence a Dasumius must be assumed somewhere in the ancestry of the Annii Veri (of Uccubi in Baetica), to explain an alleged descent from Dasummus, a prince of the Messapians (*HA, Marcus* 1. 6). The Dillii (Vocula and Aponianus) also come from Corduba: Vocula is enrolled in its tribe, the 'Sergia' (*ILS* 983), while Aponianus is honoured there (*AE* 1932, 78). That *nomen* is preternaturally rare. The only other epigraphic attestation (apart from the two senators) is in Spain (*CIL* II, 287; Olisipo). Now it can be presumed that M. Aponius Saturninus (*suff. anno incerto*) was related to Dillius Aponianus, who served under him as legionary legate in 69 (*Hist.* III. 10. 1). A dozen Aponii occur on Spanish inscriptions; the knight L. Aponius, attested in 46 B.C. (Dio XLIII. 29. 3), may well be a resident of Baetica, like that Annius Scapula whom the author of the *Bell. Al.* describes as 'maximae dignitatis et gratiae provincialem hominem' (55. 2). Observe further that the item 'Aponius Italicus' is part of the full nomenclature of Hadrian's friend, Platorius Nepos, whose tribe, the 'Sergia', speaks for Italica or Corduba.[2] The *gentilicium* 'Platorius' is flagrantly Illyrian in origin—compare the native 'Plator'.[3]

Finally, there is a senator from Baetica with a pure Etruscan *nomen*, viz. M. Accenna Saturninus (*CIL* XIV, 3585: Tibur). Date not certain: M. Accenna Helvius Agrippa (II, 1262: nr. Hispalis) is presumably Antonine.

Tarraconensis is a very different part of the peninsula (and itself heterogeneous). There had been settlement along the littoral, and some of the senators betray an Italian origin. Thus the illustrious Pedanii, of Barcino.[4] The *nomen* is probably Etruscan.[5] Again, M. Raecius Taurus (*PIR*[1], R 9), from Tarraco (cf. *AE* 1932, 84, and other inscriptions). 'Raecius' is both Etruscan and Illyrian, so it appears.[6]

The selected *gentilicia* here registered cannot derive from grants of the franchise. No known Roman magistrates of the Republic bore those names. On the other hand, many of the numerous senators from both Spains with indistinctive *gentilicia* like 'Fabius', 'Junius', 'Licinius', &c., will be presumed native by origin ultimately. Furthermore, the roll of Spanish senators could with this clue permit conjectural supplements. Thus perhaps C. Licinius Mucianus (*suff.* c. 64) or Q. Junius Marullus (*suff.* 62).

81. TRAJAN'S ANTECEDENTS

CASSIUS DIO comes out with a startling allegation about the Emperor—Ἴβηρ ὁ Τραϊανός, ἀλλ᾽ οὐκ Ἰταλὸς οὐδ᾽ Ἰταλιώτης (LXVIII. 4. 1). Perhaps prejudice speaks

---

[1] Note Dasimii as local magistrates (IX, 415: Canusium; 689: Herdoniae). Illyrian, cf. H. Krahe, o.c. 35 f.

[2] Aquileia honours him as *patronus* (*ILS* 1052): not necessarily his home. Observe, for what it is worth, that there are no other Platorii on inscriptions of northern Italy, whereas Baetica can show one instance (II, 1861: Gades).

[3] H. Krahe, o.c. 92 ff.

[4] Compare L. Pedanius L. f. Secundus Julius Persicus (II, 4513), and libertine Pedanii there (II, 4529; 4549; 4550 = *ILS* 5486): cited by Groag, P–W XIX, 23 f. Add now *Hisp. Ant. Epigr.* 4/5 (1953/4), 555; 559; *Archivo esp. de Arq.* XXVIII (1955), 207 ff.

[5] *LE* 365.

[6] *LE* 217, cf. 44; H. Krahe, o.c. 97 f.

there, prejudice against the Roman of the West who was a pseudo-Alexander: the Greek from Bithynia is crudely hostile towards Seneca (p. 551). Also ignorance about nomenclature. Whatever racial admixture there may have been in the past, none of the notables of Baetica has a native *nomen* or *cognomen*.

The name 'Ulpius' belongs to one of the languages of ancient Italy, cognate with 'lupus', 'wolf', 'vuk', as Jacob Grimm divined long ago. Schulze thought the notion fanciful.[1] In fact, a strong case can be made out for Illyrian. Observe the place-names 'Ulcinium', 'Ulcirus', 'Ulcisia'.[2]

A late and scrappy abbreviator derives the Emperor from Tuder in Umbria— 'Ulpius Traianus ex urbe Tudertina' (Victor, *Epit.* 13. 1). The fellow may be right, at least for Tuder as the 'ultima origo' of the Ulpii.[3] For guidance persons called 'M. Ulpius' are no good. They may owe the name to Trajan, or to his parent. Examples of *praenomina* other than 'Marcus' are exceedingly rare anywhere—and are very valuable.[4] *CIL* XI has two, one of them at Tuder—'Ulpia T. f.' (4725).

That is not all. The *gentilicium* 'Traius' is also very rare.[5] Perhaps Illyrian.[6] *CIL* XI shows a solitary example. Precisely at Tuder (4686). Is not the peculiar name of that city Illyrian? Compare Iader and Rider in Dalmatia.

82. PROVINCIAL CONSULS, 37–68

THE following twelve names can be adduced of consuls from Spanish and Narbonensian families under Caligula, Claudius, and Nero: note also C. Bellicius Natalis of Vienna (*PIR*[2], B 101), *suffectus* in the last three months of 68, who was probably appointed by Galba.

> L. Annaeus Seneca (*suff.* 56). Corduba
> Cn. Domitius Afer (39). Nemausus. Jerome, *Chron.* p. 179 H.
> L. Duvius Avitus (56). Vasio. *ILS* 979, cf. *I.l. de Gaule* 206
> M. (Julius) Vestinus Atticus (*cos.* 65). Vienna. *ILS* 212, col. ii, ll. 10 ff.
> L. Junius Annaeus Gallio (c. 55). Corduba
> M. Manilius Vopiscus (?60). From Spain. Above, p. 602
> P. Marius Celsus (*cos.* 62). ? Nemausus. App. 32
> L. Pedanius Secundus (43). Barcino. App. 80
> Cn. Pedanius Salinator (60 or 61). Barcino
> Pompeius Paullinus (? c. 53). Arelate. Pliny, *NH* xxxiii. 143
> D. Valerius Asiaticus (35, *II ord.* 46). Vienna
> Valerius Asiaticus (between 39 and 45 inclusive). Vienna. *ILS* 212, col. ii, ll. 17 ff. Brother of the preceding.

[1] He calls it 'ein hübscher aber grammatisch kaum haltbar Einfall' (*LE* 234). It is unfortunate that he failed to register any of the local instances.

[2] J. Bonfante, *Latomus* III (1939), 79 ff. There might be an independent Germanic form also, see a list of native Ulpii from *CIL* XIII in *Bönner Jahrbücher* CL (1950), 190 f. 'Ulpius Lupio' (XIII, 8705) is in any case suggestive.

[3] Bormann scouted Victor—'nescio quo errore' (*CIL* XI, p. 679, on Tuder).

[4] Thus L. Ulpius L. l. Rusticus (II, 1158: Italica).

[5] Two Spanish Traii can be registered (II, 1065: Arva; 5389: Hispalis). Also an amphora stamp (6257[199]: Ilici).

[6] Schulze adduces only 'Traianus' (*LE* 580), but he documents 'Travius' (245).

At the same time, though nothing can be asserted, some of the following, because of their *gentilicia* (cf. App. 78), may well be provincial:

Q. Fabius Barbarus Antonius Macer (c. 64)
L. Julius Rufus (*cos.* 67)
Marius Cordus (under Claudius)
C. Pompeius Longinus Gallus (*cos.* 49)
Pompeius Pedo (between 39 and 45)
Pompeius Pennus (39 or 40)
M. Pompeius Silvanus (45)

Five other consuls are worth scrutinizing. M. Aponius Saturninus (*suff.* under Nero), the governor of Moesia in 68/69, may come from Baetica, like other Aponii. His kinsman C. Dillius Aponianus is Corduban (App. 80). That province might also be the home of M. Annius Afrinus (*suff.* c. 67).[1]

P. Memmius Regulus (*suff.* 31, with a son who became *ordinarius* in 63) is highly enigmatic. It has been taken as axiomatic (given the period) that this *novus homo* is Italian, perhaps of old Roman or Latin extraction.[2] Certain facts counsel a doubt. Regulus was *patronus* of the colony of Ruscino in Narbonensis, which nothing known in his career explains (*I.l. de Gaule* 633). Further, there was a Memmia Galla of the early imperial age, mother of the senator A. Cottius (*ILS* 8343: Rome).[3] The *nomen* 'Cottius' is native by origin: compare Cottia, the wife of Vestricius Spurinna. The fact only recently emergent that a Narbonensian was *suffectus* in 35 (Valerius Asiaticus) renders a predecessor in 31 not beyond belief (but so far not quite to be established). The historian Tacitus betrays an especial interest in Regulus. Observe the remarkable tribute, 'auctoritate constantia fama, in quantum praeumbrante imperatoris fastigio datur, clarus' (XIV. 47. 1). Was it all deserved? Regulus agreed to surrender Lollia Paullina to Caligula, escorted her to Rome, and presided over the betrothal (Dio LIX. 12. 1, cf. Suetonius, *Cal.* 25. 2). Perhaps his behaviour was extenuated in Book VII. The obituary adds an anecdote about Regulus, and a comment that can be questioned.[4]

Finally, it is a duty to ask where Domitius Corbulo came from (App. 83), where Licinius Sura (App. 85).

If Regulus, Corbulo, and Mucianus are among the new Romans from the provinces of the West, a startling light is cast on many aspects and episodes of Roman history. Without them, the record is remarkable enough. Annaeus Seneca, Domitius Afer, and Valerius Asiaticus are shown not to be isolated phenomena (like the two Cornelii Balbi of an earlier age). The second consulate of Valerius Asiaticus is portentous, it is true. But otherwise the list shows two *ordinarii*

[1] For Annii from Baetica, App. 86.
[2] E. Groag, P–W xv, 626: 'sicherlich italischer, wahrscheinlich altrömischer oder lateinischer Abstammung.'
[3] Groag (o.c. 635 f.) cited this evidence and referred to Memmii at Massilia (e.g. *ILS* 6761).
[4] App. 60. Not a good anecdote (cf. Groag, o.c. 635). Some, however, both credit and exploit it, e.g. R. S. Rogers, *TAPA* LXXXVI (1955), 194.

(62 and 65)—and there are two others (49 and 67) among the consuls whose *gentilicia* are indicative, but fall short of documentary proof about origins.

Narbonensis advances more quickly than Spain in this period—five consuls by 56. Of its cities, Vienna shows three consuls, Nemausus two, Vasio one, but the Roman *coloniae* only one (Arelate). The subsequent period confirms triumphantly the predominance of those cities, the old tribal capitals of Allobroges, Volcae, and Vocontii (p. 620).

83. DOMITIUS CORBULO

CORBULO'S mother was the much-married Vistilia, the lady of six husbands (*NH* VII. 39).[1] The historian gives most of a chapter (III. 31) to his father, the tiresome man who got himself appointed commissioner for roads in Italy. Dio mentions him, and says that he became consul in 39 (LIX. 15. 3 ff.). Not surprising, since Milonia Caesonia, the consort of Caligula, was one of the children of that Vistilia.

If Dio is right about the consulate of the road commissioner (accepted in *PIR*², D 141), the son must have been *suffectus* not long after, perhaps c. 43. Dio nowhere alludes to the existence of two Corbulos. There is a possibility that he has amalgamated them.

Referring to Corbulo, Mucianus, when encouraging Vespasian, observes 'splendidior origine quam nos sumus, fateor' (*Hist.* II. 76. 3). The statement could be justified by senatorial parentage (if Mucianus, like Vespasian, lacked it), even without the parent's consulate.[2]

There is no hint of Corbulo's origin anywhere. Possibly Narbonensian. If Cn. Domitius Afer (*suff.* 39), whose provenance only a late and casual notice attests, why not Cn. Domitius Corbulo? The only other consular Domitii in the early Principate are the Ahenobarbi: Corbulo might derive from their old *clientela* in Narbonensis (App. 79).

The *cognomen* is exceedingly rare.[3] It can be Celtic, as is suggested by *CIL* XII, 2414 (Augustum, in the Allobrogic territory); XIII, 5178 (Salodurum). It may, however, be Italian—it is often difficult (and prejudicial) to draw the line. These Domitii might come from Appennine Italy. They had property near Peltuinum in the land of the Vestini: observe *ILS* 9518, attesting a *collegium* 'heroi Corbulonis et Longinae'.[4]

Corbulo's daughter, Domitia Longina, became an empress. His wife is nowhere attested. Perhaps a lady of the illustrious house of the Cassii Longini (p. 560), perhaps not.

---

[1] C. Cichorius, *Römische Studien* (1922), 429 ff.

[2] cf. Dio LXII. 19. 2: τῷ γένει λαμπρός. That need not mean much. Dio extols the γένος of Thrasea Paetus (ib. 26. 1), the first consul of his family.

[3] Schulze (*LE* 314; 576) cites no instances.

[4] cf. *CIL* IX, 3418 f.; 3432; 3438; 3469 (*liberti* or slaves of Domitia Longina). The fragmentary and puzzling inscription 3426 might refer to Corbulo, not, as Groag suggested, to A. Larcius Priscus, *suff.* 110 (*Jahreshefte* XXIX (1935), Beiblatt 193).

84. THE ROLE OF CORBULO'S LEGATES

APPOINTED to Cappadocia–Galatia at the end of 54, Corbulo later held that command conjointly with the governorship of Syria for about two years (60–62, after the death of Ummidius Quadratus), vacated it to Caesennius Paetus, but quickly resumed it, and in 63 was put in charge of the armed forces of Syria as well, with a special mandate and enhanced powers: he kept the northern command until recalled and compelled to end his life in the winter of 66/67.[1]

Twelve years with the eastern armies offered an unrivalled opportunity for extending a general's *clientela* among troops and officers.[2] Syria had four legions: III Gallica, VI Ferrata, X Fretensis, XII Fulminata. Corbulo took two to Cappadocia (III and VI), and a third before long (X). The needs of the war brought three legions from the Danube, IV Scythica (56 or 57), V Macedonica (?61), and XV Apollinaris (63). Hence seven legions in the East from 63. In 67 Vespasian took three for Judaea (V, X, XV), four remaining with Licinius Mucianus in Syria: from the latter force III Gallica was transferred to Moesia shortly before the death of Nero.[3]

By 68 a number of the *legati* of the earlier years had gone on to other posts, and had reached the consulate;[4] and some went back in disgrace.[5] But some of the commanders of the six legions (Judaea and Syria) that proclaimed Vespasian in July 69 had presumably known the great Corbulo. Not all will have been fresh appointments in 67: observe that Aurelius Fulvus (now in Moesia with III Gallica) had been in Armenia in 64 (*ILS* 232: nr. Harput). In Judaea Sex. Vettulenus Cerialis commanded V Macedonica, M. Ulpius Traianus X Fretensis, while Vespasian's son, quaestorian in rank, had charge of XV Apollinaris (Josephus, *BJ* III. 65, &c.). As for the three legions of Syria in 69, only one legate can be verified, viz. Cn. Pompeius Collega, attested as acting-governor of Syria in 70 (*BJ* VII. 58), hence commander of IV Scythica, the legion stationed closest to Antioch.

Cerialis, Traianus, and Collega look like senior *praetorii*. Vespasian and Mucianus had been at variance. Titus reconciled them (*Hist.* II. 5. 2). Not perhaps the only agent. Traianus may have had a big part in the proclamation of Vespasian— who, it can be conjectured, took him in his company to Egypt.[6] The subversive influence of Aurelius Fulvus may be surmised in Moesia (p. 166). Egypt on the

---

[1] For the different stages see *PIR²*, D 142.

[2] The distribution of the legions is furnished by the narrative of the *Annales*. For the different items (not that any are in dispute) see E. Ritterling in P–W XII.

[3] *Hist.* II. 74. 1, cf. Suetonius, *Divus Vesp.* 6. 3: 'sub exitu Neronis.'

[4] viz. M. Vettius Bolanus (*suff.* 66), L. Verulanus Severus (c. 66), Marius Celsus (69). Perhaps also Cornelius Flaccus (cf. *PIR²*, C 1362).

[5] Calavius Sabinus and L. Funisulanus Vettonianus had shared in the capitulation of Caesennius Paetus. The latter did not reach the consulate till 78, it appears. The year of A. Caesennius Gallus is not attested. He had been legate of XII Fulminata, which was roughly handled by the Jews in 66 (Josephus, *BJ* II. 510, cf. v. 41; VII. 18). Caesennius is attested as legate of Cappadocia–Galatia, rather late, in 80 (*ILS* 263).

[6] The legate of X Fretensis in 70 is A. Larcius Lepidus (Josephus, *BJ* VI. 237, cf. *ILS* 987).

first day of July out-distanced Syria. The Prefect was Ti. Julius Alexander, who had held a high post on Corbulo's staff in 63 (*Ann.* xv. 28. 3).

The promotion and subsequent employment of the eastern *legati* is instructive. Five names testify:

> Marius Celsus (*suff.* 69). Syria, attested in 72/3 (*ILS* 8903), succeeding L. Caesennius Paetus (*PIR²*, C 173). He had been legate of XV Apollinaris in 63 (*Ann.* xv. 25. 3). See further App. 32
>
> M. Ulpius Traianus (? 70). Syria from 74, perhaps previously Cappadocia–Galatia (cf. p. 31)
>
> T. Aurelius Fulvus (? 70). Hispania Citerior (*AE* 1952, 121)
>
> Cn. Pompeius Collega (? c. 72). Cappadocia–Galatia, attested in the first half of 76 (*ILS* 8904), perhaps from 74
>
> Sex. Vettulenus Cerialis (? c. 73). Moesia, attested in February 78 (*CIL* xvi, 22)

Two other names can be brought into the Corbulonian context (one of them by conjecture). First, C. Rutilius Gallicus (*suff.* ?71). He had governed Galatia for nine years as legate subordinate to Corbulo, and was legate to the proconsul of Asia for two years, 68–70 or 69–71 (Statius *Silvae*, I. 4. 74 ff., cf. *ILS* 9499). He is attested as legate of Germania Inferior in May 78 (*CIL* xvi, 23). Secondly, Sex. Julius Frontinus (*suff.* ?73). That consular author, who was singularly reticent about contemporary warfare (Britain is absent), has notices of Corbulo (*Strat.* IV. I. 21; 28; 2. 3) and, in particular, an anecdote about Corbulo at Tigranocerta (II. 9. 5).[1] Frontinus might have begun as an equestrian officer. The leap in two years, from being *praetor urbanus* in 70 (*Hist.* IV. 39. 1) to the consulate is peculiar. Perhaps he came very late to the praetorship: perhaps adlected into the Senate by Galba (for others, p. 592). Frontinus can be assumed Narbonensian, cf. the senator Q. Valerius Lupercus Julius Frontinus (*CIL* xii, 1859 f.: Vienna).

Of the seven men here registered, four are provincial—perhaps a fifth, Cn. Pompeius Collega (to judge by his *gentilicium*). One of Corbulo's legates was not named by the author of the *Annales*, perhaps reserving him for a more powerful entry—C. Licinius Mucianus (*suff.* c. 64). Mucianus was able to report on the sources of the Euphrates (Pliny, *NH* v. 83), therefore with Corbulo in 58, and perhaps longer, passing thence to the governorship of Lycia–Pamphylia (*ILS* 8816: Oenoanda; *AE* 1915, 48: Attaleia). Speculation ought not to be evaded concerning the origin of Mucianus (App. 85), or of Corbulo (App. 83). Corbulo, whatever his origin, had acquired a powerful following among his *legati*—and sundry links with groups of reputable persons at the metropolis can be surmised. Clearly a menace to Nero.[2]

85. SURA AND MUCIANUS

L. Licinius Sura constructed a triumphal arch near Tarraco, on the road to Barcino, and a public building in Barcino itself (*CIL* ii, 4282; 4508). Even if his

---

[1] Valuable because some argue that *Strat.* IV is not by Frontinus.

[2] p. 560. Note also that Verulana Gratilla, perhaps the wife of Junius Rusticus (cf. *PIR¹*, V 289), will be related to Corbulo's legate L. Verulanus Severus.

parents resided in either or both of those cities, neither can with confidence be claimed as his legal 'patria'. They were enrolled in the 'Galeria', whereas Sura's tribe is the 'Sergia'.[1] The 'Sergia' is the tribe of some of the earlier foundations in Ulterior. In Citerior only Carthago Nova can be proved to have it.[2] It must be added that the evidence is fragmentary and disproportionate—certain of the towns in the Ebro valley yield a miserable pittance of inscriptions. For example: Osca six, Ilerda seven, Celsa nine.[3] The tribe of Osca might be the 'Sergia'.[4] That of Celsa (otherwise Colonia Julia Lepida) is not known.[5]

Each the maker of an emperor, the parallel between Sura and Mucianus cannot escape notice. The former may have been, like the latter, 'omnium quae diceret atque ageret arte quadam ostentator' (*Hist.* II. 80. 2).[6] There was something much worse, luxury and vice (p. 229).

Sura is a prominent figure in Rome under Domitian (Martial VI. 64. 13). No parent is known, no wife—and he leaves no descendants. At the most a possible relative can be adduced, Licinianus of Bilbilis (*PIR*[1], L 113), cf. Martial I. 49. 40: 'dum Sura laudatur tuus'.

Mucianus was dead by 77 (as may be deduced from Pliny, *NH* XXXII. 62). No family known, no heir.[7] What was the origin of the great *novus homo*? A casual fact could be exploited. His tribe was the 'Sergia'—for it was taken over by certain families in Lycia that owed the citizenship to his agency (*IGR* III, 493 ff.; 633) when he was governor there under Nero. The 'Sergia' can mean Appennine Italy. Also Spain. Licinii are common in Spain, but there are no Mucii on the inscriptions anywhere. However, a dedication at Tarraco has recently revealed the fact that a P. Mucius Scaevola was active in Spain in the last age of the Republic.[8]

86. M. ANNIUS VERUS

THE *Historia Augusta* (*Marcus* 1) furnishes valuable details, along with gross fiction (viz. the descent of a Roman emperor from Numa Pompilius), and a statement that needs to be supplemented by emendation (see App. 87, under P. Calvisius Tullus Ruso). The first senator in the family was 'Annius Verus praetorius ex Uccubitano municipio ex Hispania factus senator'. The great ancestor is the 'cos. ter.'. He was adlected into the patriciate in 73 or 74,

---

[1] cf. E. Groag, P-W XIII, 472.

[2] W. Kubitschek, *Imperium Romanum Tributim Discriptum* (1889), 191. An up-to-date account of the distribution of the 'Sergia' in Spain would be valuable.

[3] *CIL* II, 3002–7 (Osca); 3009–14 and 5848 (Ilerda); 3015–20 and 5849–51 (Celsa).

[4] cf. II, 3003.

[5] It is perhaps worth noting that coins of Celsa name the pair of *duumviri* L. Sura and L. Bucco (G. F. Hill, *Notes on the Ancient Coinage of Hispania Citerior* (1933), 83). They might, however, be Cornelii, not Licinii.

[6] As Groag suggests (o.c. 484).

[7] The A. Licinius Mucianus to whom conjointly with Gavius Priscus an emperor's rescript is addressed (*AE* 1936, 128: Pergamum) cannot help, for the rank of the persons and the date of the document have not been established (cf. *PIR*², G 107).

[8] *Hisp. Ant. Epigr.* 4/5 (1953/54), 40. The other side of the block has a dedication to Pompeius Magnus. The Scaevola may be the *pontifex* attested in 64 (Macrobius III. 13. 11).

presumably on assuming the *toga virilis*: compare his coeval L. Neratius Marcellus, *suffectus* in 95 (*ILS* 1032: Saepinum).

The year of his first consulate, held with (L.) Neratius Priscus for colleague and commemorated by a *senatus consultum* against castration (*Dig.* XLVIII. 8. 6), was long in dispute (cf. *PIR²*, A 695). Unnecessarily—and a recent fragment of the *Fasti Ostienses* (*AE* 1954, 220) certifies 97 (App. 10).

M. Annius Verus married Rupilia Faustina, daughter of the otherwise unattested consular Rupilius Bonus (App. 87). One son was M. Annius Libo, the consul of 128. Another, who married Domitia P. f. Lucilla, daughter of P. Calvisius Tullus Ruso (*cos.* 109), died when praetor. The son of that match (the future emperor) was born in 121 (*PIR²*, A 697).

The Annii Veri were connected in some way with the family of Hadrian (Dio LXIX. 21. 2). Conceivably through the Dasumii of Corduba—L. Dasumius the testator probably had 'Hadrianus' for *cognomen* (App. 87), and his son, P. Dasumius Rusticus, stands in prominence as Hadrian's colleague in 119 (p. 600). Observe also, however, M. Annius Afrinus (*PIR²*, A 630), *suffectus* c. 67 with (C. Paccius) Africanus. Hadrian's father was called P. Aelius Hadrianus Afer.

According to the *Historia Augusta*, the stock of the Emperor M. Aurelius derived not only from Numa Pompilius but 'item a rege Sallentino Malemnio, Dasummi filio, qui Lopias condidit' (*Marcus* 1. 6). Some suppose the Calvisii to have transmitted the strain, viz. P. Calvisius Ruso Julius Frontinus (*suff.* ?79) and his son, P. Calvisius Tullus Ruso (*cos.* 109), who married Domitia Cn. f. Lucilla (so Groag in *PIR²*, C 350). Nothing, however, connects these Calvisii with southeastern Italy (cf. App. 87). The alleged Messapian ancestry surely comes from the Dasumii. The elder Calvisius might have married a Dasumia; but there could be some other link.

Sundry other Annii might be worth registering. There is a man from Gades, the consul L. Cornelius Pusio Annius Messalla (*AE* 1915, 60: nr. Tibur), *suffectus* either under Vespasian or in 90 (see App. 94). Another inscription, found at the same spot, mentions a military tribune ']ius M. f. Faustus' (*Not. Scav.* 1914, 102 = *Inscr. It.* I, 1, 107): to be brought into relation (cf. Groag in *PIR²*, A 645) with the knight Annius Faustus, 'qui temporibus Neronis delationes factitaverat' (*Hist.* II. 10. 1). Add 'M. [. . . . . F]austus', *suffectus* in 121.

87. SOME ANTONINE ANCESTORS

1. P. Aelius Hadrianus Afer. *PIR²*, A 185. Trajan's cousin, married to Domitia Paullina of Gades. Died in 86, when of praetorian rank. Above, p. 603. From Italica

2. M. Annius Verus (*suff.* 97, *II ord.* 121, *III ord.* 126). *PIR²*, A 695. See App. 86. From Uccubi in Baetica

3. Arrius Antoninus (69, *II* ? 97). *PIR²*, A 1086. Husband of Boionia Procilla (B 142), whose *gentilicium* is patently Celtic in origin. Probably from Nemausus (App. 32)

4. T. Aurelius Fulvus (? 70, ? *II ord.* 85). *PIR²*, A 1510. Twice consul and *praefectus urbi* (*HA, Pius* 1. 2). For the problem of his second consulate, App. 8. Wife not attested. From Nemausus

5. T. Aurelius Fulvus (*cos.* 89). *PIR²*, A 1509. Married to Arria Fadilla, the daughter of Arrius Antoninus. Died not long after his consulship, for his son (born in 86) 'pueritiam egit cum avo paterno, mox cum materno' (*HA, Pius* 1. 9). The passage shows that the *praefectus urbi* survived his son, was conceivably in office in 97, but was dead by 100

6. P. Calvisius Ruso Julius Frontinus (? 79). *PIR²*, C 350. His wife c. 106 (cf. *AE* 1914, 267), was '[? Eggia] C. f. Am[?bibula]', so Groag suggests (not, however, registered in *PIR²*, E). Not necessarily his first, who might be a Dasumia. The alleged descent of a Roman emperor from a Messapian Dasummus (*HA, Marcus* 1. 6) should run through the Dasumii (cf. App. 86), and not (as Groag assumes) through the Calvisii. The provenance of these Calvisii is not attested.[1] Perhaps North Italian or provincial. Sex. Julius Frontinus (*suff.* ? 73) can be assumed a Narbonensian (App. 84)

7. P. Calvisius Tullus Ruso (*cos.* 109). *PIR²*, C 357. Married to Domitia Cn. f. Lucilla (D 182), adoptive daughter of Cn. Domitius Tullus (*suff.* c. 79). Not her first husband (as can be deduced from Pliny, *Epp.* VIII. 18. 2). The daughter, Domitia P. f. Lucilla (D 183), is the mother of the Emperor Marcus. The *Historia Augusta* not only makes a mistake about her name, calling her 'Domitia Calvilla', but asserts that Tullus was twice consul (of which there is no evidence). The passage (*HA, Marcus* 1. 3) could further be improved as follows: 'mater Domitia Lucilla Calvisi Tulli ⟨filia, avia materna Lucilla Domiti Tulli⟩ bis consulis filia.' The gain would be double: first, to abolish the second consulate of Calvisius Tullus and substitute that of Domitius Tullus (in 98, cf. App. 11), and, secondly, to allow the *HA* to supply the 'avia materna' of Marcus—for it goes on to name the 'avia paterna', viz. Rupilia Faustina[2]

8. L. Catilius Severus Julianus Claudius Reginus (110, *II ord.* 120). *PIR²*, C 558. Allegedly the 'proavus maternus' of Marcus (*HA, Marcus* 1. 4; 9). As Groag observes, 'prorsus incredibile' (*PIR²*, C 357)— for Catilius cannot be the parent of P. Calvisius Tullus (*cos.* 109). No satisfactory explanation can be put forward.[3] Parentage, kin, and local origin of Catilius are also unverifiable. Items of his nomenclature suggest the provincial—but not 'Catilius', or his tribe, which is the 'Claudia' (*ILS* 1041, supplemented by *AE* 1913, 229)

---

[1] They cannot be linked to any descendants of C. Calvisius Sabinus (*cos.* 39 B.C.): from Spoletium (*ILS* 925, honouring his 'pietas'), cf. R. Syme, *Rom. Rev.* (1939), 221.

[2] This conjecture was put forward in *JRS* XLIII (1953), 156.

[3] Groag felt no enthusiasm for his own hypothesis that a son of Catilius Severus might be the first husband of Domitia Cn. f. Lucilla (cf. *PIR²*, C 357; *Jahreshefte* XXIX (1935), Beiblatt 181 f.). He also suggested (C 558) that the πρόπαππος gratefully remembered by Marcus (*Ad se ipsum* 1. 4) was Rupilius Bonus. Now the boy Marcus certainly bore the name of Catilius Severus for a time (Dio LXIX. 21. 1, cf. *HA, Marcus* 1. 9), and Catilius was still alive in 138. If Catilius himself had been the first husband of Lucilla, or married her after the decease of Calvisius Tullus, he could function as a 'substitute grandfather'.

9. L. Ceionius Commodus (*cos.* 78). *PIR²*, C 603. Married to Appia Severa (*ILS* 1003 f.), whose father's tribe, the 'Voltinia', suggests Narbonensis. The Ceionii are said to derive 'ex Etruria' (*HA, Aelius* 2. 8; *Verus* 1. 9). Their *nomen*, which is rare (cf. *TLL*), is attested in *CIL* XI—once for Etruria, otherwise only for places in the Aemilia, among them Bononia (cf. *PIR²*, C 605). Now Bononia was an old Etruscan foundation (Pliny, *NH* III. 119)

10. L. Ceionius Commodus (*cos.* 106). *PIR²*, C 604. First husband of the woman who married C. Avidius Nigrinus (*suff.* 110), if Groag's arguments and stemma are correct (A 1408). The son (*cos.* 136), whom Hadrian adopted, had married a daughter of Nigrinus (*HA, Hadr.* 23. 10)

11. Dasumius the testator (? 93). *PIR²*, D 13. To be identified with L. Dasumius, a Trajanic proconsul of Asia (D 14), attested by *CIG* 2876; also with the proconsul Hadrianus, known from coins of Thyatira (as Groag suggests, *PIR²* D, Addenda, p. xi).[1] His consulate could go in 93, his proconsulate in 106/7 (App. 23). Wife not recorded; the son whom he adopted by his testament in the summer of 108 is clearly P. Dasumius Rusticus (*cos.* 119), a son of P. Tullius Varro (*ILS* 1002), a dear friend and presumably a close coeval. Dasumius, it can be conjectured, was related to Julius Servianus (cf. *CIL* VI, 10229, ll. 6 and 110). See also under P. Calvisius Ruso Julius Frontinus. From Corduba (App. 80)

12. Cn. Domitius Tullus (c. 79, ? *II* 98). *PIR²*, D 167. For his presumed second consulate see under P. Calvisius Tullus Ruso, also App. 11. The younger of the two brothers adopted by Cn. Domitius Afer of Nemausus; adoptive parent of his niece, Domitia Lucilla (D 182), daughter of Lucanus (D 152), who predeceased him by about fifteen years

13. P. Julius Lupus (? 98). *PIR²*, J 262. The 'consularis' who married Arria Fadilla, daughter of Arrius Antoninus, after the death of T. Aurelius Fulvus, the consul of 89 (*HA, Pius* 1. 5). His consulate is attested also by *ILS* 8430a. Perhaps at the end of 98 (App. 11). No other evidence

14. Ser. Julius Servianus (90) = L. Julius Ursus Servianus (*II ord.* 102, *III ord.* 134). Cf. App. 7. Husband of Domitia Paullina, Hadrian's sister (*HA, Hadr.* 2. 5 f.). Presumably not his first wife. See also under Dasumius

15. (?Cn.) Pedanius Fuscus Salinator (c. 84). *PIR¹*, P 143. His proconsulate of Asia, early Trajanic (*ILS* 8822, and coins cited in P–W XVII, 20 f.), dates the consulate approximately. Son of Cn. Pedanius Salinator (*suff.* 60 or 61). Wife not known. From Barcino in Tarraconensis (App. 80)

16. Cn. Pedanius Fuscus Salinator (*cos.* 118). *PIR¹*, P 144. Married Julia, the daughter of Servianus c. 107 (Pliny, *Epp.* VI. 26. 1)

17. L. Pompeius. The parent of Pompeia Plotina (only Victor gives her full name, *Epit.* 42. 41). Deduced from the *praenomen* of 'L. Pompeius Aug. lib. Fortunatus' (*ILS* 1912). Men called 'L. Pompeius' are not uncommon in Narbonensis, the most notable being Vopiscus from Vienna (*suff.* 69). Note further (p. 32, n. 1) L. Pompeius Vopiscus Catellius Celer (*suff.* ? 79). Plotina's town may be Nemausus (p. 604)

---

[1] For the coins (or rather perhaps a coin) see *JRS* XLIII (1953), 156.

18. Rupilius Bonus (*anno incerto*). *PIR¹*, R 150. Known only through 'Rupilia Faustina, Rupili Boni consularis filia' (*HA, Marcus* 1. 4), wife of M. Annius Verus (*suff.* 97). The period of his consulate cannot be divined. Wife and relationships conjectural.[1] Observe the inscription 'Libonis Rupili Frugi' on a lead pipe at Rome (*AE* 1940, 39), and the senator Libo Frugi, of consular rank in 101 (Pliny, *Epp.* III. 9. 33): there is an unattested Libo, *suffectus* in 118; and a son of Annius Verus has that *cognomen* (*cos.* 128). Local origin unverifiable[2]

19. L. Vibius C. f. Sabinus. (? 97). Not in *PIR¹*. His nomenclature, consular rank, and a priesthood are revealed by fragmentary inscriptions (*CIL* XI, 5383; 8020; Asisium). Husband of Matidia, daughter of the senator C. Salonius Matidius Patruinus (*PIR¹*, S 81), and of (Ulpia) Marciana, Trajan's sister. Father of Vibia Sabina, and of the younger Matidia. If Vibius Sabinus was consul in 97, he must have died soon after, as may be deduced from remarks of Hadrian in the funeral oration on Matidia, his widow (*CIL* XIV, 3579). Local origin is not certified. Matidii and Salonii are frequent on the inscriptions of Vicetia, e.g. *CIL* V, 3117 = *ILS* 968 (Salonia, mother of a senator); 3111 (a dedication to the younger Matidia)

20. M. Ulpius Traianus. (? 70). *PIR¹*, V 574. See p. 30 f. His unattested wife Marcia is deduced from the daughter (Ulpia) Marciana. For a lady called 'Ulpia M. f. Plotina' see p. 604. From Italica.

---

[1] It has recently been conjectured that Matidia, the niece of Trajan, was twice married, not only to L. Vibius Sabinus but to Rupilius Bonus (J. Carcopino, *Rev. ét. anc.* LI (1949), 317). Rupilia Faustina would thus be half-sister to Vibia Sabina; and Annius Verus, by marrying her, would acquire a link with the family circle of Hadrian.

[2] The daughter 'Faustina' might seem to echo the 'Bonus' of her parent. That *cognomen* is not elsewhere attested in any senator, or knight of consequence. Could it be 'Bo⟨io⟩n-⟨i⟩us', cf. Boionia Procilla, the wife of Arrius Antoninus? However, 'Faustina' could perhaps derive from the daughter of an Annius Faustus (cf. p. 792). Further (as E. Birley suggests), 'Bonus' in the *HA* might be the compiler's mistake for 'Frugi': cf. (above) Libo Frugi and Libo Rupilius Frugi.

J. TACITUS' ORIGIN AND FRIENDS

88. FABLES ABOUT TACITUS' DESCENDANTS

THE *Historia Augusta* asserts that the Emperor Claudius Tacitus claimed the historian for ancestor (*Tacitus* 10. 3). Most of this *Vita* is pure fiction.[1] Even the statement that Florianus, the next emperor, was a brother of Claudius must be rejected (cf. *PIR*², C 1036).

There was a cenotaph of the two brothers at Interamna, 'in solo proprio', with their statues, of marble, thirty feet high. The statues were struck by lightning and demolished, whereupon *haruspices* being consulted came out with a prophecy about a future ruler who, among other things, would impose a governor at Taprobane and send a Roman proconsul to Ireland (*Tacitus* 15. 1 f.). With that support and encouragement the municipal pride of Terni annexes the historian Tacitus.

Late and poor writers can transmit items of genuine erudition. For Victor, the lineage of Theodosius went back to Trajan (*Epit.* 48. 1). That is nonsense. But Victor, by stating that Trajan came 'ex urbe Tudertina' (13. 1), permits conjecture about the ultimate origin of Trajan's family (cf. App. 81). The *Historia Augusta* alleges that the Emperor Balbinus was descended from Cornelius Balbus. Absurd. But, by calling the latter 'Balbus Cornelius Theophanes' (*Maximus et Balbinus* 7. 3), it discloses a peculiar fact that could only have been known to a close student of Cicero—'adoptatum . . . Gaditanum a Mytilenaeo' (*Ad Att.* VII. 7. 6, cf. *Pro Balbo* 57). An erudite author. There is a faint chance (very faint) that this *scholasticus* was aware of something that connected the Roman historian with Interamna.

Another trail leads to Gaul, so it happens. According to Sidonius Apollinaris, Polemius (*praefectus Galliarum* c. 471) was descended from Tacitus (*Epp.* IV. 14. 1). Polemius was Gallic (cf. *Carm.* XIV. 22).[2] Let it also be observed that Leo of Narbo had for ancestor the eloquent Cornelius Fronto (*Epp.* VIII. 3. 3)— Fronto, who came from Cirta in Numidia. The genealogical claims of the Gallic aristocracy cannot always stand up to inspection. There had been a great breach of continuity in the third century.[3]

The historian's works, after long oblivion, were read in Gaul in the fourth and fifth centuries.[4]

---

[1] E. Hohl, *Klio* XI (1911) 177 ff.; 284 ff.; *Hermes* LV (1920), 300. The anecdote about the Emperor was unfortunately admitted by F. Haverfield (*JRS* VI (1916), 198).

[2] Of Italian origin, according to A. Loyen, *Sidoine et l'esprit précieux en Gaule aux derniers jours de l'empire* (1948), 85. Why? Apparently because he believes Sidonius, and because he assumes that Tacitus was an Italian.

[3] C. Jullian, *Histoire de la Gaule* VIII (1926), 128 ff.; K. F. Stroheker, *Der senatorische Adel im spätantiken Gallien* (1948), 10 f.   [4] F. Haverfield, o.c. 199.

89. OPINIONS ABOUT TACITUS' ORIGIN

A FACILE assumption takes Tacitus to be 'by birth a noble' and leaves it at that.[1] The more erudite (or the more inquiring) go further and discover evidence in support, nothing less than the historian's scornful treatment of the parvenu and the 'homo municipalis'. Not merely a Roman of Rome, but a scion of the patrician Cornelii.[2] And responsive to the glorious traditions of that ancient *gens*.[3] Eloquence is added to delusion—'vero Romano antico, più antico ancora del suo tempo, era Tacito di famiglia patrizia et di sentimento repubblicano'.[4]

Even if not certified as an authentic descendant of the primeval aristocracy, Tacitus can be claimed as a 'Stadtrömer'. Or better, a 'Stockrömer'.[5] Hence, to be sure, his notorious lack of sympathy with provincials.[6] And Juvenal, a 'municipalis eques', can be contrasted with the son of the metropolis.[7]

Insisting that Tacitus 'Romano fu di spirito e di grandezza', a scholar makes light of the procurator of Belgica, because, he says, the relationship cannot quite be proved.[8] Yet the milieu from which Tacitus issues is plain and clear, on any acquaintance (however superficial) with the equestrian and senatorial orders of imperial Rome.

What matters most is environment, education, and training. The region (Italy or the provinces of the West) is not important. Not but what it might present some interest to keen students of Latin letters and Roman history. But a number prefer to evade the problem, explicitly or by total silence.[9] The more surprising, since one of them spreads himself on the 'Rassenzugehörigkeit' of the Roman poets.[10]

'Italicus es an provincialis?' One school embraces the former alternative, most enthusiastically. The age of Nerva and Trajan witnessed a literary renaissance, with Italy (it is alleged) predominant once more, and 'Tacito è il genio di questo risveglio'.[11] Tacitus stands for the reaction against Spain in letters, against the 'Iberici'.[12] Wherefore, presumably, the historian can be dubbed an 'Italico giovenaliano'.[13] Unfortunate, if it were to turn out that the family of Juvenal came from the provinces (cf. App. 74).

---

[1] G. G. Ramsay in his translation of the *Annales* (I, 1904), xviii.

[2] R. Reitzenstein, *Neue Wege zur Antike* IV (1926), 7.

[3] J. Vogt, *Tacitus als Politiker* (Antrittsrede, Tübingen, 1924), 10, cf. 1: 'dessen Blut und Geist urtümlich römisch war.'

[4] E. Ciaceri, *Tacito* (1941), 47.   [5] E. Kornemann, *Tacitus* (Wiesbaden, 1947), 17.

[6] H. Willrich, *Hermes* LXII (1927), 64. By contrast, I. A. Richmond, *JRS* XXXIV (1944), 43: 'no literary Roman ever published more telling accounts of provincial grievances or shrewder estimates of provincial character.'

[7] G. Highet, *Juvenal the Satirist* (1954), 234.

[8] C. Marchesi, *Tacito*³ (1944), 9 f.

[9] Thus J. Wight Duff, *A Literary History of Rome in the Silver Age* (1927), 559 ff.; E. E. Sikes, *CAH* XI (1936), 737 ff.; F. Klingner, *Die Antike* VIII (1932), 151 ff. = R. *Geisteswelt* (1943), 310 ff.; H. Howald, *Vom Geist antiker Geschichtsschreibung* (1944), 193 ff.

[10] E. Bickel, *Lehrbuch der Geschichte der r. Literatur* (1937), 55 ff.

[11] G. Funaioli, *Studi di letteratura antica* II, ii (1947), 132.

[12] E. Paratore, *Maia* II (1949), 116.

[13] P. Treves, *Il mito di Alessandro e la Roma d'Augusto* (1953), 159. And, according to A. Garzetti (*Nerva* (1950), 121), Italian 'senza dubbio'.

If Italian, from which Italy, the old or the new? That ought to have been asked. Harm has been done by the uncritical acclamation of a Celtic strain in certain Latin writers (p. 617). Another false trail is the discovery of Gallicisms in the *Dialogus* of Tacitus.[1] But it is too early to argue that theories about a Celtic origin for the historian have been rendered obsolete.[2] That was the assertion of a writer whose competence in this matter can be gauged by his undisguised surprise that Trajan and Hadrian were diverse in character, 'although they both came from Spain'.[3]

The term 'Celtic' is both too wide and too narrow for Cornelius Tacitus. A careful study of the local distribution of his *cognomen* suggests a native origin, northern Italy or Narbonensis.[4] The results of that investigation become slowly perceptible.[5] Indeed, the Narbonensian hypothesis (plausible because of Agricola and Agricola's daughter) can now be regarded as reasonable, at least by a recent convert.[6] The full and proper argument has never been set down in writing.[7]

90. CURIATIUS MATERNUS

THE Gallic origin of Aper and Secundus creates prepossessions. Gallicisms have been opined in the language of the *Dialogus*.[8] Further, the third of the four interlocutors, Curiatius Maternus (senator, orator, and poet) is claimed a Gaul, and, lest that be thought a hasty notion, facts are adduced—twenty-eight instances of 'Maternus' on the inscriptions of Gaul.[9]

It might have been worth glancing at Spain, where the *cognomen* is more frequent, both relatively and absolutely—over sixty. The *gentilicium* is a better guide. It is very ancient in Rome.[10] Probably Etruscan.[11] Romans from Spain show Etruscan names (cf. App. 80). It would not, however, be quite fair to adduce the Curiatius who about the year 88 died paradoxically at salubrious Tibur (Martial IV. 60), that nest of Spaniards (p. 602).

A polyonymous senator, consul suffect in 114, is called 'L. Stertinius Quintilianus Acilius Strabo C. Curiatius Maternus Clodius Nummus' (*PIR²*, A 83). He bears the tribe 'Maecia', and, in so far as 'Clodius Nummus', is Neapolitan (*CIL* x, 1486). Acilii are found among the notables of Spain,[12] and there are ele-

---

[1] App. 90.

[2] E. Kornemann, o.c. 17; E. Koestermann, *Bursians Jahresberichte* CCLXXXII (1943), 189.

[3] E. Kornemann, *Weltgeschichte des Mittelmeerraumes* II (1949), 127.

[4] M. L. Gordon, *JRS* XXVI (1936), 145 ff.

[5] P. Wuilleumier, *Tacite, l'homme et l'œuvre* (1949), 8.

[6] E. Paratore, *Tacito* (1951), 51 f., cf. 726 (a change from his positive opinion only two years earlier).

[7] Parts of Ch. XLV of this work (composed in 1948) were the basis of a lecture delivered in London in June, 1951.

[8] A. Gudeman (ed. 2, Berlin, 1914), 59; 235; 327. He suggests 'substantia facultatum' (8. 6), 'statio' (17. 3), 'cortina' (19. 8).

[9] A. Gudeman, o.c. 66.   [10] F. Münzer, P–W IV, 1830 f.

[11] For Etruscan names in '-anius' and '-atius' see Schulze, *LE* 343 ff.

[12] *PIR²*, A 45; 74; 79; 87. Also Aciliani, F 27; P¹ 658.

ments suggesting Spain in the nomenclature of the man's adoptive son (C 1423), and his relatives (C 1450 f.).

There is something better—the mysterious consular M. Cornelius M. f. Gal. Nigrinus Curiatius Maternus, 'leg. Aug. pro pr. provinc. Moes., / provinc. Syriae' (CIL II, 6013, cf. 3783: Liria). It is most unfortunate that his date and period cannot be ascertained (cf. Groag in PIR², C 1407).[1] There are no other senatorial Curiatii under the Empire.[2]

In the year 91 Domitian put to death a man called Maternus—Μάτερνον δὲ σοφιστήν, ὅτι κατὰ τυράννων εἶπέ τι ἀσκῶν, ἀπέκτεινεν (Dio LXVII. 12. 5). Is this the poet Curiatius Maternus? Some assume it.[3] Others deny firmly,[4] and PIR², C 1604 dismisses by omission. It was a little late in the day for Curiatius Maternus to be practising the art of declamation. The man for whom a bad end was waiting (if a hint in the Dialogus be taken), is not the poet, but Eprius Marcellus (p. 111).

91. MARCUS APER AND JULIUS SECUNDUS

APER describes himself as 'homo novus et in civitate minime favorabili natus' (Dial. 7. 1). That would not exclude one of the minor places in Narbonensis, such as Carpentorate or Alba Helvorum. But Aper employs the phrase 'ne quid de Galli⟨i⟩s nostris loquar' (10. 2), which would speak rather for Tres Galliae. For the emendation, and for the meaning of 'Galliae', see above, p. 456. Aper's gentilicium might be 'Iulius', but it might be 'Flavius'. There was a Flavius Aper senator in 105 (Pliny, Epp. v. 13. 5),[5] also M. Flavius Aper (cos. 130);[6] but the item 'Iulius Aper' recurs in the portentous nomenclature of the grandson of Q. Pompeius Falco (suff. 108), the consul of 169 (ILS 1104).

Aper had been in Britain. He there met an old man who made no secret of the fact ('qui se fateretur') that he had fought in defence of the island against the invasion of Julius Caesar (17. 4). If the effort be of value to sharpen the dramatic propriety (and to extenuate insular vanity), it could be conjectured that Aper went to Britain with the army of Claudius Caesar in 43. The victory honours were lavish. Towards the lower end of the list, some equestrian officers may have been granted the latus clavus and admission to the senatorial career. Observe two

---

[1] Degrassi puts him in the late first or early second century (FC 120).

[2] And no Curiatii of consequence except Curiatius Cosanus, curator of Caere in 114 (ILS 5918a, cf. CIL XI, 4347: Ameria): not in PIR².

[3] Thus E. Norden, Die antike Kunstprosa I (1898), 324 (but retracting in his Nachträge (1909), 18 f.); R. Reitzenstein, Gött. Gel. Nachr. 1914, 231; E. Paratore, Tacito (1951), 193 f.

[4] A. Gudeman, o.c. 67; J. Stroux, Philologus LXXXVI (1931), 338.

[5] The MSS. vary between 'Flavius' and 'Fabius'. No Fabius Aper is attested.

[6] This man (PIR², F 208) or his son (209) inherited the brick factories of Flavia Seia (? Servilia) Isaurica (PIR¹, F 288), cf. A. Stein, P-W VI, 2737 f.; E. Groag in PIR², F 209. There was also a Plotia Servilia Isaurica (PIR¹, P 399). Observe that the item 'Servilius Vatia' (pseudaristocratic rather than authentic descent) occurs in the nomenclature of T. Julius Maximus of Nemausus (ILS 1016), consul suffect in 112.

instances of this type of promotion under Nero (*ILS* 978; 981). Under Claudius the Narbonensian M. Julius Romulus may have been thus promoted—the last line of his fragmentary inscription permits the supplement '[praef. fabr]um, trib. [mil]itu[m]' (*Not. Scav.* 1924, 346 = *AE*, 1924, 85: Velitrae). Similarly, L. Coiedius Candidus (*ILS* 927: Suasa) was perhaps honoured for a loyal attitude in Dalmatia in 42 when Arruntius Camillus made his abortive proclamation (cf. *PIR*², C 1257). Not perhaps a *laticlavius* but an equestrian tribune: he enters the vigintivirate with the least resplendent post (that of *IIIvir capitalis*), but is quaestor at once, in 44. As relevant to this subject it may be noted that Sex. Julius Frontinus (praetor in 70) may conceivably have started as an equestrian officer (App. 84).

Aper was certainly not an adlected senator: 'non eum diem laetiorem egi quo mihi latus clavus oblatus est' (7. 1). He may have held the quaestorship before the censorship of Claudius Caesar. That would be of interest if he is a Gaul of Tres Galliae, not a Narbonensian.

Julius Secundus is registered along with Julius Africanus on Quintilian's short list of the best orators he had heard (x. 1. 118 ff.; XII. 10. 11). Africanus, deemed the peer of Domitius Afer, is known to posterity as the author of the loyal address to Nero—'rogant te, Caesar, Galliae tuae ut felicitatem tuam fortiter feras' (VIII. 5. 15).

Secundus came of an eloquent family, as witness his uncle, Julius Florus, 'in eloquentia Galliarum, quoniam ibi demum exercuit eam, princeps' (x. 3. 13). He wrote a biography of Africanus (*Dial.* 14. 4). Secretary of an emperor, he was present at the seat of war (Plutarch, *Otho* 9).

Tacitus will have known descendants of Julius Africanus, such as the barrister, his grandson (Pliny, *Epp.* VII. 6. 11 ff.). Coming across an earlier Africanus, he could therefore furnish the note 'e Santonis, Gallica civitate' (*Ann.* VI. 7. 4). There is no evidence about Secundus' 'civitas'. Possibly the Bituriges. C. Julius Secundus, a praetor, left money for an aqueduct or public bath at Burdigala.[1]

92. TWO FRIENDS OF TACITUS

WRITING on behalf of the quaestor Asinius Bassus to Minicius Fundanus (*suff.* 107), Pliny adds the fact that his father, Asinius Rufus, a senator of praetorian rank, is a friend of Cornelius Tacitus (*Epp.* IV. 15. 1). What is the family, and whence deriving? Clearly not of the descendants of Pollio. A certain L. Asinius Rufus is attested as *legatus* in Africa under the proconsul Q. Pomponius Rufus in 109/10 (*IRT* 537). These people might come from Acholla in Africa (which is probably a *colonia* of Caesarian or Augustan date). Observe M. Asinius Sex. f. Hor. Rufinus Valerius Verus Sabinianus (*AE* 1954, 54), *suffectus* c. 184 and father of M. Asinius Sabinianus (*PIR*², A 1251). Asinius Rufus had married

[1] *CIL* XIII, 596 ('litteris bonis saeculi primi incipientis'). Not noted under *PIR*¹, J 363. A senator is attested in 55, Q. Julius Q. f. Qui. Secundus (*ILS* 6103). The tribe 'Quirina' could perhaps fit Tres Galliae—but the nomenclature cannot be called distinctive.

the daughter of a certain Saturius Firmus—perhaps the procurator 'C. Saturius ['
attested as governor of Raetia in 80, and perhaps Picentine, from Asculum.[1]

The family circumstances of Asinius Rufus (but no local affinities) are elabo-
rately explained to Minicius Fundanus. Where did Fundanus himself come
from? Hardly from Fundi.[2] Transpadane Italy is plausible. The *nomen* occurs
frequently there; and observe the aspirant to the senatorial career, M. Minicius
Annianus (*CIL* v, 6360: Laus Pompeia); Minicia L. f. Paetina, the wife of the
consular Rutilius Gallicus (6990 = *ILS* 1008: Augusta Taurinorum); Minicius
Macrinus of Brixia, 'equestris ordinis princeps' (*Epp.* I. 13. 5); Minicius Justus,
who married a Corellia (VII. 11. 4). The surmise now comes close to certainty.
An inscription reveals the tribe of Minicius Fundanus as the 'Papiria'.[3] Therefore Ticinum (in what can be regarded as the 'Pliny country').

What is said to Fundanus about Tacitus lacks warmth or colour. It seems
formal—'idem Cornelium Tacitum (scis quem virum) arta familiaritate complexus
est. proinde, si utrumque nostrum probas, de Rufo quoque necesse est idem
sentias' (IV. 15. 2). At the least, nothing to encourage any theory of a Transpadane
origin for Cornelius Tacitus.

The other reference to a third party also concerns, though indirectly, the same
Minicius Fundanus. Pliny earnestly requests his help for Julius Naso, a young
man embarking on the senatorial career, and furnishes full details (VI. 6). Naso's
father had been a man of great distinction, and devoted to oratorical studies. But
he had long been dead, and the son needed more help than the memory of his
father's glory could provide. Pliny himself had not enjoyed the friendship of
Naso's father—he was too young at the time.

Now the *nomen* 'Iulius' suggests an origin from Narbonensis or from Tres
Galliae. It is a material fact that not a single specimen of the numerous Transpadane senators in the early Empire is a Julius. It is appropriate that Pliny, in his
epistolary art at least, should assume that Julius Naso is a stranger to the Transpadane Minicius Fundanus. This Naso crops up again a little later in the correspondence. Tacitus has commended him to Pliny. Pliny protests in a brief note:
he knows the young man—'Nasonem mihi? quid si me ipsum? fero tamen et
ignosco. eundem enim commendassem tibi, si te Romae morante ipse afuissem'
(VI. 9. 1). Tacitus was absent from Rome (cf. IV. 13. 1). He was perhaps away for
some time, hence unaware that his Transpadane friend knew (or had meanwhile
come to know) the young Naso.[4]

Not many Narbonensians can be certified among the correspondents of Pliny.
Old Arrius Antoninus receives three letters (IV. 3; 18; V. 15), Valerius Paullinus,
a close friend, five (II. 2; IV. 16; V. 19; IX. 3; 37). The Ruso of IX. 19 should be, not

---

[1] Vollmer, *Inscr. Baiv. Rom.* 257b, cf. 196 (77/8). There was a family of Saturii Picentes
at Asculum (*CIL* IX, 5241, cf. XI, 1437).

[2] Groag admits Fundi as a possibility (P–W xv, 1820).

[3] 'C. Minicio L. filio Pap. / Fundano, VII / vir epulonum, trib. / leg. VII Fulminatae /
quaestori, tribuno / [pl]ebis, praetori, leg. / [leg. XV A]pollinaris / . . . .]
piae / . . . . ur. / . . .' Found at Šipovo, near Jajce in Bosnia, and published
by D. Sergejevski, *Glasnik zemaljskog Muzeja* XXXVIII (1926), 155. There is a lapicide's
error in l. 4, 'VII' for 'XII'.

[4] Pliny knows the family and laments the death of Naso's promising brother Avitus
(V. 21. 3 ff.).

Cremutius Ruso (VI. 23. 2), but P. Calvisius Ruso Julius Frontinus (*suff.* 79), or his son, the consul of 109 (for these people, see App. 87). Otherwise only some minor characters, such as perhaps Julius Valerianus (II. 15; V. 4; 13),[1] or Attius Clemens (I. 10; IV. 2).[2]

93. TACITUS ON TRANSPADANA

In 49 B.C. Caesar bestowed the full franchise on the Latin communities in Gallia Cisalpina north of the river Po (Dio XLI. 36. 3, cf. *CIL* I², 600: Ateste). But Gallia Cisalpina was still kept in the anomalous status of a province. In 42 after the Battle of Philippi the Triumvirs, invoking (and perhaps inventing) a design of the Dictator, agreed to abolish that province (Appian, *BC* V. 3. 12, cf. Dio XLVIII. 12. 5).

Tacitus in his version of the *Oratio Claudi Caesaris* has a statement most enigmatic. Tracing the growth of Rome's power through the incorporation of men and of peoples, the imperial orator, after a brief allusion to the remoter past, comes to the last age of the Republic, when men from Etruria, Lucania, and from all Italy were brought into the Senate; and finally, he says, the boundaries of Italy itself were extended to the Alps—'postremo ipsam ad Alpis promotam ut non modo singuli viritim sed terrae gentes in nomen nostrum coalescerent' (XI. 24. 2). The next sentence proceeds: 'tunc solida domi quies et adversus externa floruimus, cum Transpadani in civitatem recepti, cum specie deductarum per orbem terrae legionum additis provincialium validissimis fesso imperio subventum est' (ib. 3). Now the trouble begins. Does 'tunc' refer backwards or forwards? To what date and epoch is the unification of Italy assigned?[3]

The Principate of Caesar Augustus is unequivocally designated, namely the era of peace and order after the Civil Wars. Also, so it should seem, victories abroad, inevitably balancing peace at home. How, then, does the grant of Roman citizenship to the Transpadani come in? What the commentators offer is lame and confused.[4] And Tacitus himself is guilty of confusion, it can be argued.[5]

There is a double danger to be watched. First, the original of the speech: Claudius Caesar may have chosen to glide unobtrusively over the twenty years

---

[1] *CIL* XII, 2608 (Genava) records an important knight with this name (which is not very distinctive). However, his 'patria' appears to be the *colonia* Noviodunum, which lies just outside the frontier of Narbonensis.

[2] Compare *CIL* XIV, 2961 (Praeneste): '. . .]ttio Cn. f. Tro / [. . . . .]ti Viennensi / [praef.] fabr. bis', &c. 'Attius' is sixth in order of frequency among Narbonensian *nomina*.

[3] For 'tunc' looking forward to 'cum' the *Lexicon* of Gerber–Greef cites only this passage and *Hist.* V. 25. 3: 'tunc infensos Batavis deos cum obsiderentur legiones.' It is presupposed in the translation of G. G. Ramsay (II, 1909), 31: 'peace was assured at home, and affairs abroad were prospering, when the Transpadanes received the citizenship.'

[4] Thus Nipperdey (ed. 11, revised by G. Andresen, 1915) and Furneaux (II², 1907). G. G. Ramsay (o.c., note 3) grasped the main line of argument (i.e. peaceful change, not foreign or domestic pressure) but argued over-boldly that 'solida domi quies' is appropriate to 49 B.C.

[5] G. E. F. Chilver, *Cisalpine Gaul* (1941), 10: 'both Strabo and Tacitus confuse the enfranchisement with the Italianization.'

of tribulation from 49 to the end of the wars.[1] Secondly, on any interpretation of the passage, Tacitus may have created a problem for the reader by his concision and rapidity—stages in argument suppressed, and latent antithesis in his mind.

Perhaps Tacitus is not wholly at fault. The punctuation may be wrong. All modern texts link 'quies' and 'floruimus', putting a comma after 'floruimus' (as cited above). Now 'et' need not be a mere copula. It can have a dynamic function, carrying argument or narration a step forward. There is a good example in the preceding chapter—'multus ea super re variusque rumor. et studiis diversis apud principem certabatur adseverantium', &c. (23. 1 f.). Ought there not to be a pause before 'et' in the passage under debate? A semicolon would do. To make the contention clear, let it be a full stop, reading 'tunc solida domi quies. et adversus externa floruimus cum Transpadani in civitatem recepti, cum . . . subventum est.'

On this reading, of what nature is the orator's argument? Clearly that the unification of Italy is not due to compulsion—internal or external. And observe that, previously, he had suppressed all mention of the *Bellum Italicum* and the consequent enfranchisement of Italy up to the Po. He expounds a process of peaceful change. To it belongs Italy's extension as far as the Alps. That process is completed in a time of peace—'tunc solida domi quies'. Then, as suggested above, comes the beginning of a new sentence. The orator, proceeding with 'et', carries the argument forward a step—but backward in time.[2] The words 'adversus externa floruimus' describe the external condition of the Empire when the Transpadani received the franchise in 49. The link in meaning with what goes before is furnished by a suppressed antithesis. The orator means 'it was not a season of peace then, it is true (for the civil wars had begun), but Rome stood glorious and powerful as confronting the outer nations,[3] and the grant to the Transpadani was not caused by any foreign danger'.

The phrase 'adversus externa floruimus' also covers the military colonies referred to in the second of the two clauses introduced by 'cum' (for the Parthian incursion was only a brief episode in twenty years' history—they were quickly dispersed by Ventidius). One does not have to think mainly or solely of the Augustan colonies (down to 13 B.C.), though the argument can be understood to move forward and include them. The process begins earlier. There are the numerous colonies of the Caesarian and Triumviral period—and the latter period can be prolonged *de facto* down to 28 B.C., cf. *Ann.* III. 28. 2.[4]

The next sentence brings confirmation. The orator is still in the age of tribulation—'num paenitet Balbos ex Hispania nec minus insignis viros a Gallia Narbonensi transivisse?' The cardinal dates of the two Balbi are the quaestorship

---

[1] Claudius omitted Caesar's new senators from the *municipia*, cf. R. Syme, *BSR Papers* XIV (1938), 8.

[2] As later in the speech—'capti a Gallis sumus: sed et Tuscis obsides dedimus' (24. 5).

[3] Especially after the conquest of Gaul, cf., on 51 B.C., Sallust, *Hist.* I. 11: 'res Romana plurimum imperio valuit.'

[4] The continuity of this process, like the continuity between Triumvir and Princeps, is not always emphasized enough; and a Narbonensian senator would know that Forum Julii was a *colonia* of the Triumviral period. Observe further that the author brings out the admixture of natives.

of the younger in 44, the consulate of the elder (not hitherto a senator) in 40. And the excellent Narbonensians are those brought into the Senate by Caesar[1]— and some no doubt by the Triumvirs.[2]

So far so good. But, it will be said, if Tacitus is liberated from the reproach of confusion, he is still involved in error. He puts 'postremo ipsam ad Alpis promotam' after the end of the Civil Wars, when there was 'solida domi quies'. But the Cisalpine province had been abolished long ago, in 42. A material fact, and ever-present in the minds of commentators on Tacitus.

The Triumvirs' decision was not prompted by benevolence towards the Cisalpina. Their purpose was to remove the region from political and military competition.[3] It might fairly be contended that if provincial status and the subjection to military government was the principal grievance of the Romans in Cisalpina, they were not likely to find much alleviation or advantage under the dictatorial régime of the Triumvirs, when Italy itself was treated in no other fashion than if it had been a province. 'Non mos, non ius' (*Ann.* III. 28. 1). The full consummation of Italian unity might without impropriety be assigned to the return of civil government and normal conditions in 28 B.C. On this view, Tacitus has abbreviated history rather than falsified it.

Tacitus omitted (and discounted) the Triumvirs' act. Such may have been the doctrine followed by Claudius Caesar. The historian's procedure is comprehensible. Any gross error about the earlier history of northern Italy might be of interest as telling against the view that his family derives from Italia Transpadana.

94. SOME CORNELII

FOUR Cornelii deriving from the ancient patrician *gens* (blood, adoption, or deceit) find a place on the *Fasti* from Vespasian's reign to the accession of Hadrian. Namely, Dolabella Petronianus (*cos.* 86), the son of Galba's relative; Dolabella Metilianus Pompeius Marcellus (*cos.* 112); Scipio Salvidienus Orfitus (*suff.* before 87); Scipio Salvidienus Orfitus (*cos.* 110). See *PIR*[2], C 1351; 1350; 1445; 1446.

Nine other Cornelii reach the consulate. A heterogenous collection—and not at all responsive to inquiry about antecedents, family, and exploits.[4] By far the most important is the marshal of Trajan, A. Cornelius Palma Frontonianus (*cos.* 99, and again in 109), from Volsinii (cf. *PIR*[2], C 1412). Next Cn. Pinarius L. f. Cornelius Clemens (*suff.* c. 71), and his son Cn. Pinarius Cn. f. Cornelius Severus (*suff.* 112), whose honours (*ILS* 1043) show him a patrician (*PIR*[2],

---

[1] R. Syme, o.c. 15; *JRS* XXVII (1937), 131.

[2] The first admission of provincials to be registered by Dio is in 39 B.C. (XLVIII. 34. 4).

[3] cf. Dio XLVIII. 12. 5.

[4] Excluding 'Q. Co(r)nelius Fa[' (*CIL* IV, 4748, cf. *PIR*[2], C 1354 and 1362), who may be late Neronian, and 'Q. Co[', *suffectus* in 116, who might not be a Cornelius, and cannot be Q. Cornelius Senecio Annianus (*CIL* II, 1929), cf. R. Syme, *JRS* XLIII (1953), 151 f.

C 1341 and 1453 respectively). These people are enigmatic.[1] So is C. Cornelius Rarus Sextus Na[?so), *suffectus* in 93, proconsul of Africa, and a member of Tacitus' sacerdotal college (*IRT* 523),[2] whereas Cn. Cornelius Urbicus (*suff.* 113) is only a name.

For two Cornelii a northern origin could be surmised, for C. Cornelius Gallicanus (*suff.* 84) because of the *cognomen*, and for (L. ?) Cornelius Priscus (*suff.* ?104) because of a Brixian inscription that names a senator '[e]lius Q. f. Fab.[' along with his wife 'Secunda Prisc[i]' (*CIL* v, 4364, cf. 4363: not noted under *PIR²*, C 1420). Then the last two Cornelii, of a Gaditane family, viz. L. Cornelius Pusio, consul with Pegasus in an unknown year under Vespasian (Gaius. I, 31, &c.), and his son L. Cornelius Pusio (revealed as *suffectus* in 90 by the *Fasti Potentini*). The former is amalgamated by Groag (*PIR²*, C 1425) with the consul and proconsul L. Cornelius Pusio Annius Messalla of an inscription found near Tibur (*AE* 1915, 60)—who, however, might be the latter. A legate of a proconsul of Africa, M. Annius Messalla, has recently been disclosed at Lepcis (*IRT* 516).[3]

Finally, the Spaniard M. Cornelius Nigrinus Curiatius Maternus (*PIR²*, C 1407), deserves an entry somewhere. He governed two consular provinces. Unfortunately, he baffles dating (see App. 90).

So far, nothing relevant to the origin of Cornelius Tacitus. The *gentilicium* of the great jurist Pegasus happens to lack attestation. Nor, indeed, is the *cognomen* 'Pegasus' at all common.[4] Worth noting therefore is an inscription at Vasio in Narbonensis, *CIL* xII, 1297: 'Marti / ex voto / T. Cornelius Pegasus.' Another dedication to Mars is set up by a man called Tacitus (1301 = *ILS* 4841), on which see p. 622. The nomenclature 'T. Cornelius' happens to be very rare. It recurs with a senator's son T. Cornelius Anneus Fuscus in 170 (*CIL* VI, 1978 = *ILS* 5024), possibly, so Groag suggests (*PIR²*, C 1321), a descendant of Cornelius Fuscus. Vasio, however, could not be the 'patria' of Fuscus, which was a *colonia* (*Hist.* III. 86. 3), perhaps therefore Forum Julii (cf. App. 33).

According to the *Digest* (I. 2. 2. 53), Pegasus was appointed *praefectus urbi* by Vespasian. That might be wrong. The words of Juvenal suggest Domitian— 'Pegasus attonitae positus modo vilicus urbi' (IV. 76), cf. App. 66. The dramatic date of the satire is 83. At that time Fuscus (of senatorial stock) was Prefect of the Guard (ib. 111 f.): since when, there is no evidence. Pegasus (perhaps a Cornelius) and Cornelius Fuscus, high dignitaries in office and in command of patronage early in Domitian's reign, that is a fact of relevance to the fortunes of Cornelius Tacitus, himself (it should seem) deriving from a city of Narbonensis. Afranius Burrus, who came from Vasio (*ILS* 1321), may have helped his parent (p. 623).

---

[1] The former, legate of Germania Superior in 73/74, has the 'Papiria' for tribe (*ILS* 997: Hispellum, the tribe of which town, however, is the 'Lemonia').

[2] To be identified as the 'Ço̧ri̧[' of the *Fasti Potentini*, cf. R. Syme, o.c. 153.

[3] For Annii from towns in Baetica, see App. 86.

[4] W. Kunkel (*Herkunft u. soziale Stellung der r. Juristen* (1952), 133) adduces the following instances:—*CIL* III, 4150, col. i, 23 (Savaria); vIII, 128 (Capsa); xII, 1297 (Vasio). Add xII, 5686⁶⁸² (amphora stamp in the Vienne Museum)—but neglect vIII, 14184 f. (in the Christian cemetery at Carthage). There are no instances in the Italian volumes of *CIL*.

95. TACITUS' KNOWLEDGE OF NARBONENSIS

THE narration of the march of Fabius Valens through the Allobrogic and Vocontian territories is full and accurate (*Hist.* I. 65 f.). A good source could explain it (p. 171)—and, for that matter, the account of Caecina's dealings with the Helvetii near Aventicum is admirable, with local detail (Aquae Helveticae alluded to in periphrasis (67. 2), and the mountain Vocetius (68. 1)), and also the name of an eloquent native, Claudius Cossus (69).

There is something else, the feud between Lugdunum and Vienna, 'uno amne discretis conexum odium' (I. 65. 1). An ignorant or careless writer might not be aware that, whereas the Altar of Rome and Augustus was situated at the confluence of Rhodanus and Arar, the Roman *colonia* of Lugdunum (the modern Fourvières) was in fact on the right bank of the combined streams, Vienna being further down, on the left bank. Tacitus reproduces in vivid language, deliberately exaggerated, the anger of colonist against native—'irent ultores, exscinderent sedem Gallici belli. cuncta illic externa et hostilia. se coloniam Romanam et partem exercitus et prosperarum adversarumque rerum socios' (65. 2). The historian would know that if Vienna helped Vindex, it was not for Gaul against Rome (p. 463).

Odd facts might be instructive. Tacitus can add the detail that T. Vinius (*cos.* 69) had been governor of Narbonensis—and a good governor (I. 48. 4): not in Suetonius or Plutarch. Moreover, Valerius Paullinus, procurator of Narbonensis in 69, a citizen of Forum Julii (and presumed parent of the *suffectus* of 107): Tacitus knows that he had previously been a friend of Vespasian, and a tribune in the Praetorian Guard (III. 43. 1).

More significant perhaps is that which can be omitted from sheer familiarity. Registering the *suffecti* of 69, Tacitus notes that L. Pompeius Vopiscus' consulate was reckoned an honour to Vienna (I. 77. 2). Nothing, however, about the origins of Arrius Antoninus and Marius Celsus (probably both from Nemausus, cf. App. 32). That omission can have a plain reason, it is true—distaste for excessive annotation. But there is the unnamed *colonia* of Cornelius Fuscus (III. 86. 3), which, it can be argued, was Forum Julii (App. 33). Further, the author of the *Annales* has neglected to publish the notable fact that Sex. Afranius Burrus was a Narbonensian from Vasio (*ILS* 1321). That is encouraging (p. 623).

Certain senators from Narbonensis are depicted in a very sympathetic fashion, notably the great Valerius Asiaticus and M. Julius Vestinus Atticus (*cos.* 65). Both were victims of emperors inferior to them in courage and honour—and hence not safely to be invoked to commend a hypothesis.

The earliest Narbonensian senators and their descendants earn a remarkable tribute from the historian in his version of the Claudian oration (XI. 24. 3, adduced and exploited at the end of Ch. XLV). That tribute winds up one stage of the argument, and it would stand in high relief if modern editors (since 1607) had divided the oration at that point and ended a chapter there: XI. 24 is inconveniently long for a single chapter.

There is a negative clue—ignorance about northern Italy or a lack of special interest (Ch. XLV). The fact that Tacitus calls Verona a 'colonia' (*Hist.* III. 8. 1) has no significance (the language is not technical or juridical): but he falls into confusion about places and distances near Cremona (App. 30).

A Narbonensian senator might see the valley of the Po seldom or never. It was preferable to go to the 'provincia' by sea, taking ship at Cosa or Pisae. The mother of Agricola owned Italian property very close to his home: Albintimilium (*Agr.* 7. 2), at the extreme end of Liguria, is not more than seventy miles from Forum Julii. Tacitus (it will be presumed) inherited those estates. The property owned by the Ostorii Scapulae cannot have been far away—'apud finem Liguriae' (*Ann.* XVI. 15. 1). Tacitus shows some interest in that family (p. 303), which is Italian by origin.

ABBREVIATIONS

AE	*L'Année épigraphique*
AJP	*American Journal of Philology*
BGU	*Berliner griechische Urkunden*
BMC	*British Museum Catalogue*
BSR Papers	*Papers of the British School at Rome*
CAH	*Cambridge Ancient History*
CIG	*Corpus Inscriptionum Graecarum*
CIL	*Corpus Inscriptionum Latinarum*
CQ	*Classical Quarterly*
CR	*Classical Review*
CRAI	*Comptes rendus de l'Académie des Inscriptions et Belles-Lettres*
FC	*I Fasti Consolari* (ed. A. Degrassi, 1952)
FO	*Fasti Ostienses*
HRR	*Historicorum Romanorum Reliquiae* (ed. H. Peter, Vol. II, 1906)
IG	*Inscriptiones Graecae*
IGR	*Inscriptiones Graecae ad Res Romanas pertinentes*
ILS	*Inscriptiones Latinae Selectae* (ed. H. Dessau)
IRT	*The Inscriptions of Roman Tripolitania*
JRS	*Journal of Roman Studies*
LE	W. Schulze, *Zur Geschichte lateinischer Eigennamen*
MAMA	*Monumenta Asiae Minoris Antiqua*
OCD	*The Oxford Classical Dictionary*
OGIS	*Orientis Graecae Inscriptiones Selectae*
PIR	*Prosopographia Imperii Romani*
P–W	Pauly–Wissowa, *Real-Encyclopädie der Classischen Altertumswissenschaft*
S-B	*Sitzungsberichte*
SEG	*Supplementum Epigraphicum Graecum*
SIG	*Sylloge Inscriptionum Graecarum* (ed. H. Dittenberger)
TAPA	*Transactions of the American Philological Association*
TLL	*Thesaurus Linguae Latinae*

BIBLIOGRAPHY

WHAT follows is not a bibliography of the subject (or rather subjects) of the work, but a guide to writings cited in the footnotes. It registers periodical articles, transactions of academies and the like, items in *Festschriften* or collected papers, also several long or detailed reviews. Books are omitted, however. Similarly other separate publications (such as pamphlets and dissertations) to which date and place can furnish an adequate clue.

ADAMS, F., 'The Consular Brothers of Sejanus.' *AJP* LXXVI (1955), 70.

ALEXANDER, P. J. 'Letters and Speeches of the Emperor Hadrian.' *Harvard Studies* XLIX (1938), 141.

ALEXANDER, W. H. 'Julius Caesar in the Pages of Seneca the Philosopher.' *Transactions of the Royal Society of Canada*³, Section II, XXXV (1941), 15.

—— 'The Tacitean "non liquet" on Seneca.' *Univ. of Cal. Pub. in Class. Phil.* XIV, 8 (1952), 269.

—— 'The Communiqué to the Senate on Agrippina's Death.' *Class. Phil.* XLIX (1954), 94.

ALFIERI, N. 'I fasti consulares di Potentia (Regio V).' *Athenaeum* XXVI (1948), 110.

ALFÖLDI, A. 'Insignien und Tracht der römischen Kaiser.' *Röm. Mitt.* L (1935), 1.

ALLEN, W. 'The Death of Agrippa Postumus.' *TAPA* LXXVIII (1947), 131.

—— 'Sallust's Political Career.' *Studies in Philology* LI (1954), 1.

ALTHEIM, F. 'Tacitus.' *Die neue Rundschau* LXIV (1953), 175.

AMUNDSEN, L. 'Notes to the Preface of Livy.' *Symbolae Osloenses* XXV (1947), 31.

ANDERSON, J. G. C. 'Trajan on the Quinquennium Neronis.' *JRS* I (1911), 173.

—— Review of R. P. Robinson, *The Germania of Tacitus* (*Am. Phil. Ass.*, Phil. Monographs V). *JRS* XXVI (1936), 272.

ANDRESEN, G. Review of R. Reitzenstein, 'Bemerkungen zu den kleinen Schriften des Tacitus I–II' (*Gött. gel. Nachr.* 1914, 173 ff.). *Wochenschr. für cl. Phil.* 1915, 747.

—— 'Tacitus in Livius.' *Wochenschr. für cl. Phil.* 1916, 210; 401; 688; 758.

ASBACH, J. 'Quo anno Britanni Boudicca duce a Nerone defecerint.' *Analecta historica et epigraphica Latina* II (Bonn, 1878), 8.

BAEHRENS, W. A. 'Zur Praetur des jüngeren Plinius.' *Hermes* LVIII (1923), 109.

—— 'Noch einmal zur Praetur des jüngeren Plinius.' *Phil. Woch.* XLVII (1927), 171.

—— 'Sallust als Historiker, Politiker und Tendenzschriftsteller.' *Neue Wege zur Antike* IV (1926), 35.

BALSDON, J. P. V. D. Review of D. M. Pippidi, *Autour de Tibère.* *JRS* XXXVI (1946), 168.

—— 'Tacitus, *Annals* IV. 57.' *CR* LXI (1947), 44.

BARBIERI, G. 'Mario Massimo.' *Riv. di fil.* LXXXI (1953), 36 ff.; 262 ff.

—— 'Nuovi frammenti di Fasti Ostiensi.' *Studi Romani* I (1953), 365.

BARDON, H. 'Dialogue des orateurs et Institution oratoire.' *Rev. ét. lat.* XIX (1941), 113.

—— 'Recherches sur la formation de Tacite.' *Mélanges de la Faculté des Lettres de Poitiers* 1946, 195.

—— 'Tacite et le "Dialogue des Orateurs".' *Latomus* XII (1953), 166.

BARDON, H. 'De nouveau sur Tacite et le Dialogue des Orateurs: les critères grammaticaux et stylistiques.' *Latomus* XII (1953), 485.

BARWICK, K. 'Der Dialogus de oratoribus des Tacitus.' *Sächsische S-B, phil.-hist. Kl.* 1954, Heft 4.

BEGUIN, P. 'Le *Fatum* dans l'œuvre de Tacite.' *L'Antiquité classique* XX (1951), 315.

—— 'La Personnalité de l'historien dans l'œuvre de Tacite.' Ib. XXII (1953), 322.

—— 'Le Positivisme de Tacite dans sa notion de *fors*.' Ib. XXIV (1955), 352.

BÉRANGER, J. 'L'Hérédité du principat.' *Rev. ét. lat.* XVII (1939), 171.

BERVE, H. 'Sertorius.' *Hermes* LXIV (1929), 199.

BICKEL, E. 'Die politische und religiöse Bedeutung des Provinzialoberpriesters im römischen Westen.' *Bonner Jahrbücher* CXXXIII (1928), 1.

BIRAGHI, G. 'Il problema economico del regno di Nerva.' *La Parola del Passato* VI (1951), 257.

BIRLEY, E. 'Senators in the Emperors' Service.' *Proc. Brit. Ac.* XXXIX (1953), 197.

—— 'Britain under Nero: the Significance of Q. Veranius.' *Roman Britain and the Roman Army: Collected Papers* (1953), 1.

—— 'Britain and the Flavians: Agricola and his Predecessors.' Ib. 10.

—— 'Britain after Agricola, and the End of the Ninth Legion.' Ib. 20.

—— 'The Brigantian Problem, and the first Roman Contact with Scotland.' Ib. 31.

BÖMER, F. 'Naevius und Fabius Pictor.' *Symbolae Osloenses* XXIX (1952), 34.

BOER, W. DEN. 'Die gegenseitigen Verhältnisse der Personen im Dialogus de Oratoribus und die Anschauung des Tacitus.' *Mnemosyne* VIII³ (1939), 193.

BOGNER, H. 'Petronius bei Tacitus.' *Hermes* LXXVI (1941), 223.

BOISSIER, G. 'Les Prologues de Salluste.' *Journal des Savants* 1903, 59.

BONFANTE, J. 'Le Latin *Ulpius* et le nom osco-ombrien du loup.' *Latomus* III (1939), 79.

BRASSLOFF, S. 'Patriciat und Quaestur in der romischen Kaiserzeit.' *Hermes* XXXIX (1904), 618.

BRINK, C. O. 'Tacitus and the Visurgis.' *JRS* XLII (1952), 39.

—— 'Justus Lipsius and the Text of Tacitus.' Ib. XLI (1951), 32.

BRUÈRE, R. T. 'Tacitus and Pliny's *Panegyricus*.' *Class. Phil.* XLIX (1954), 161.

BÜCHNER, K. 'Tacitus und Plinius über Adoption des römischen Kaisers.' *Rh. Mus.* XCVIII (1955), 289.

—— 'Das Proömium zum Agricola des Tacitus.' *Wiener Studien* LXIX (1956), 321.

CALDER, W. M. 'Silius Italicus in Asia.' *CR* XLIX (1935), 216.

CALZA, G. 'Due nuovi frammenti di Fasti Ostiensi.' *Epigraphica* I (1939), 151.

CAPELLE, W. 'Zu Tacitus' Archäologien.' *Philologus* LXXXIV (1929), 201; 349; 464.

CARCOPINO, J. 'La Table Claudienne de Lyon.' *Journal des Savants* 1930, 69; 116.

—— 'La Table Claudienne de Lyon et l'impérialisme égalitaire.' *Points de vue sur l'impérialisme romain* (1934), 159.

—— 'Les Richesses des Daces et le redressement de l'empire romain sous Trajan.' *Dacia* I (1924), 28 = *Points de vue sur l'impérialisme romain* (1934), 73.

—— 'L'Hérédité dynastique chez les Antonins.' *Rev. ét. anc.* LI (1949), 262.

CHARLESWORTH, M. P. 'The Banishment of the Elder Agrippina.' *Class. Phil.* XVII (1922), 260.

—— 'The Tradition about Caligula.' *The Cambridge Historical Journal* IV (1933), 105.

—— 'Providentia and Aeternitas.' *Harvard Theological Review* XXIX (1936), 107.

—— 'The Virtues of a Roman Emperor: Propaganda and the Creation of Belief.' *Proc. Brit. Ac.* XXIII (1937), 105.

CHARLESWORTH, M. P. 'Nero: Some Aspects.' *JRS* XL (1950), 69.
CHARNEUX, P. 'M. Vettulenus Civica Barbarus.' *Bull. corr. hell.* LXXXI (1957), 121.
CHILTON, C. W. 'The Roman Law of Treason under the Early Principate.' *JRS* XLV (1955), 73.
CHILVER, G. E. F. 'Augustus and the Roman Constitution.' *Historia* I (1950), 408.
CIACERI, E. 'L'Imperatore Tiberio e i processi di lesa maestà.' *Processi politici e Relazioni internazionali* (1918), 249.
—— 'La Congiura Pisoniana contro Nerone.' Ib. 363.
—— 'Claudio e Nerone nelle *Storie* di Plinio.' Ib. 387.
CICHORIUS, C. 'Zur Familiengeschichte Seians.' *Hermes* XXXIX (1904), 461.
—— 'Die ägyptischen Erlasse des Germanicus.' *Römische Studien* (1922), 375.
—— 'Der Astrologe Thrasyllos und sein Haus.' Ib. 390.
—— 'Untersuchungen zu Pomponius Secundus.' Ib. 423.
COLIN, J. 'Sénateurs gaulois à Rome.' *Latomus* XIII (1954), 218.
—— 'Le Préfet du Prétoire Cornelius Fuscus: un enfant de Pompei.' Ib. XV (1956), 57.
COLUMBA, G. M. 'Il processo di Cremuzio Cordo.' *Atene e Roma* IV (1901), 361.
CONWAY, R. S. 'The Venetian Point of View in Roman History.' *New Studies of a Great Inheritance* (1921), 190.
COUSIN, J. 'Rhétorique et psychologie chez Tacite.' *Rev. ét. lat.* XXIX (1951), 228.
—— 'Suétone physiognomiste.' Ib. XXXI (1953), 234.
CROOK, J. A. 'Titus and Berenice.' *AJP* LXXII (1951), 162.
CUMONT, F. 'L'Éternité des empereurs romains.' *Revue d'histoire et de littérature religieuses* I (1896), 435.
CUNTZ, O. 'Zum Briefwechsel des Plinius mit Traian.' *Hermes* LXI (1926), 192.

DEGRASSI, A. 'Osservazioni su alcuni consoli suffetti dell' età di Augusto e Tiberio.' *Epigraphica* VIII (1946), 34.
—— 'Sui Fasti Consolari dell' Impero.' *Athenaeum* XXXIII (1955), 112.
DE LA VILLE DE MIRMONT, H. 'Afranius Burrhus.' *Rev. phil.* XXXIV (1910), 73.
DESSAU, H. 'Die Vorgänge bei der Thronbesteigung Hadrians.' *Festschrift für H. Kiepert* (1898), 85.
—— 'Die Herkunft der Offiziere und Beamten des römischen Kaiserreichs während der ersten zwei Jahrhunderte seines Bestehens.' *Hermes* XLV (1910), 1.
DE WITT, N. J. 'The Druids and Romanization.' *TAPA* LXIX (1938), 319.
DIENEL, R. 'Quintilian und der Rednerdialog des Tacitus.' *Wiener Studien* XXXVII (1915), 239.
DIRLMEIER, F. 'Die Germania des Tacitus. Versuch einer Deutung.' *Die alten Sprachen* II (1937), 37.
DOMASZEWSKI, A. v. 'Die Heimat des Cornelius Fuscus.' *Rh. Mus.* LX (1905), 158.
DREXLER, H. 'Bericht über Tacitus für die Jahre 1915–1927.' *Bursians Jahresberichte* CCXXIV (1929), 257.
DURRY, M. 'Le Bellum Suebicum de 97 et le Panégyrique de Pline.' *Mémorial d'un voyage d'études en Rhénanie* (1953), 197.

EHRENBERG, V. 'Pothos.' *Festschr. für M. Winternitz* (1933), 296 = *Alexander and the Greeks* (1938), 52.
EVANS, E. C. 'Descriptions of Personal Appearance in Roman History and Biography.' *Harvard Studies* XLVI (1935), 43.

FABIA, PH. 'Les Ouvrages de Tacite réussirent-ils auprès des contemporains?' *Rev. phil.* XIX (1895), 1.

—— 'Le Troisième Mariage de Néron.' Ib. 218.

—— 'Le Point finale des Annales de Tacite.' *Journal des Savants* 1901, 423; 563.

—— 'La Préface des *Histoires* de Tacite.' *Rev. ét. anc.* III (1901), 41.

—— 'Tacite.' *Journal des Savants* 1903, 452; 482.

—— 'L'Adhésion de l'Illyricum à la cause flavienne.' *Rev. ét. anc.* V (1903), 329.

—— 'L'Avènement officiel de Tibère. Examen du récit de Tacite (*Ann.* I, 11–13).' *Rev. phil.* XXXIII (1909), 28.

—— 'La Mère de Néron.' *Rev. phil.* XXXV (1911), 144.

—— 'Officiers gaulois dans les légions romaines au Ier siècle de notre ère.' *Rev. ét. anc.* XIV (1912), 285.

—— 'Dillius Vocula.' *Studi Romani* II (1914), 153.

—— 'L'Irréligion de Tacite.' *Journal des Savants* 1914, 250.

—— 'Les Histoires de Tacite.' Ib. 1922, 49.

—— 'La Carrière de Tacite.' Ib. 1926, 193.

—— 'A propos de la Table Claudienne.' *Rev. ét. anc.* XXXIII (1931), 117; 225.

—— 'Sur une page perdue et sur les livres XVI, XVII, XVIII des Annales de Tacite.' Ib. XXXIV (1932), 139.

—— 'La Concentration des Othoniens sur le Pô.' Ib. XLIII (1941), 192.

FAVEZ, CH. 'Les Opinions de Sénèque sur la femme.' *Rev. ét. lat.* XVI (1938), 335.

FEGER, R. 'Virtus bei Tacitus.' *Würzburger Jahrbücher* III (1948), 301.

FERRERO, L. 'La voce pubblica nel proemio degli Annali di Tacito.' *Riv. di fil.* LXXIV (1946), 50.

FINK, R. O., HOEY, A. S., and SNYDER, W. F. 'The *Feriale Duranum.*' *Yale Classical Studies* VII (1940), 7.

FISKE, G. C. 'The Politics of the Patrician Claudii.' *Harvard Studies* XIII (1902), 1.

FLETCHER, G. B. A. 'Notes on Tacitus.' *AJP* LXVI (1945), 13.

—— 'Some Certain or Possible Examples of Literary Reminiscence in Tacitus.' *CR* LIX (1945), 45.

FRAENKEL, E. 'Tacitus.' *Neue Jahrbücher* VIII (1932), 218.

FRÉZOULS, E. 'Inscription de Cyrrhus relative à Q. Marcius Turbo.' *Syria* XXX (1953), 247.

FRITZ, K. v. 'Aufbau und Absicht des Dialogus de Oratoribus.' *Rh. Mus.* LXXXI (1932), 275.

—— 'Sallust and the Attitude of the Roman Nobility at the Time of the Wars against Jugurtha.' *TAPA* LXXIV (1943), 134.

—— 'Tacitus, Agricola, Domitian, and the Problem of the Principate.' *Class. Phil.* LII (1957), 73.

FROT, J. 'Tacite est-il l'auteur du "Dialogue des orateurs"?' *Rev. ét. lat.* XXXIII (1955), 120.

FUCHS, H. 'Tacitus über die Christen.' *Vigiliae Christianae* IV (1950), 65.

FUKS, A. 'The Jewish Revolt in Egypt (A.D. 115–117) in the light of the papyri.' *Aegyptus* XXXIII (1953), 131.

GABBA, E. 'Le origini della Guerra Sociale e la vita politica romana dopo l'89 a. C.' *Athenaeum* XXXII (1954), 41; 293.

GAGÉ, J. 'La Victoria Augusti et les Auspices de Tibère.' *Rev. arch.* XXXII (1930), 1.

—— 'Hercule-Melqart, Alexandre et les Romains à Gadès.' *Rev. ét. anc.* XLII (1940), 425.

GAGÉ, J. 'Gadès, l'Inde et les navigations atlantiques dans l'antiquité.' *Rev. hist.* CCV (1951), 189.

GALLAVOTTI, C. 'Pensiero e fonti dottrinarie nel "Dialogo degli Oratori".' *Athenaeum* XIX (1931), 35.

GARZETTI, A. 'Nerviana.' *Aevum* XXVII (1953), 549.

—— 'Sul problema di Tacito e Tiberio.' *Riv. stor. it.* LXVII (1955), 70.

GEER, R. M. 'Second Thoughts on the Imperial Succession from Nerva to Commodus.' *TAPA* LXVII (1936), 47.

GELZER, M. 'Die Nobilität der Kaiserzeit.' *Hermes* L (1915), 395.

—— 'Zur neuen Germanicus-Inschrift.' *Festschrift für Rudolf Egger* I (Klagenfurt, 1952), 84.

GERCKE, A. 'Senecastudien, II.' *Jahrbücher für cl. Phil.*, Supp.-Band XXII (1896), 159.

GODOLPHIN, F. R. B. 'The Source of Plutarch's Thesis in the Lives of Galba and Otho.' *AJP* LVI (1935), 324.

GÖTZE, H. 'Ein neues Bildnis des Nerva.' *Mitt. des d. arch. Inst.* L (1948), 139.

GORDON, A. E. 'Quintus Veranius Consul A.D. 49.' *Univ. of Cal. Pub. in Class. Arch.* II, 5 (1952), 231.

GORDON, M. L. 'The Family of Virgil.' *JRS* XXIV (1934), 1.

—— 'The *Patria* of Tacitus.' *Ib.* XXVI (1936), 145.

GRANT, M. 'Constantiae Augusti.' *Num. Chron.*⁶ X (1950), 23.

GRENADE, P. 'Le Mythe de Pompée et les Pompéiens sous les Césars.' *Rev. ét. anc.* LII (1950), 28.

GRIES, K. 'Subconscious Repetition in Livy.' *Class. Phil.* XLVI (1951), 36.

GRIMAL, P. 'Deux figures de la *Correspondance* de Pline: le philosophe Euphratès et le rhéteur Isée.' *Latomus* XIV (1955), 370.

GROAG, E. 'Zur Kritik von Tacitus' Quellen in den Historien.' *Jahrbücher für cl. Phil.*, Supp.-Band XXIII (1897), 761.

—— 'Die Adoption Hadrians.' *Röm. Mitt.* XIV (1899), 269.

—— 'Prosopographische Beiträge V. Sergius Octavius Laenas.' *Jahreshefte* XXI/XXII (1924), Beiblatt 425.

—— Prosopographische Beiträge VI. Sex. Quinctilius Valerius Maximus.' *Ib.* 435.

—— 'Zur Ämterlaufbahn der nobiles in der Kaiserzeit.' *Strena Buliciana* (Zagreb, 1924), 253.

—— 'Zum Konsulat in der Kaiserzeit.' *Wiener Studien* XLVII (1929), 143.

—— 'Zu neuen Inschriften.' *Jahreshefte* XXIX (1935), Beiblatt, 177.

GROSSO, F. 'Tendenziosità dell' *Agricola*.' *In Memoriam Achillis Beltrami Miscellanea Philologica* (1954), 97.

—— 'Aspetti della politica orientale di Domiziano.' *Epigraphica* XVI (1954), 117.

GUEY, J. 'Le *Pomerium* de la Rome impériale.' *Mélanges de l'École française de Rome* LIV (1937), 165.

GÜNGERICH, R. 'Der Dialogus des Tacitus und Quintilians *Institutio Oratoria*.' *Class. Phil.* XLVI (1951), 159.

—— 'Tacitus' Dialogus und der Panegyricus des Plinius.' *Festschrift Bruno Snell* (1956), 145.

HAAS, H. 'Virtus Tacitea.' *Gymnasium* XLIX (1938), 163.

HAASE, H. 'Tacitea'. *Philologus* III (1848), 152.

HAMMER, S. 'Réflexions sur Tacite.' *Eos* XXXII (1929), 545.

HAMMOND, M. 'Corbulo and Nero's Eastern Policy.' *Harvard Studies* XLV (1934), 81.

HAMMOND, M. 'Pliny the Younger's Views on Government.' *Harvard Studies* XLIX (1938), 115.
—— 'A Statue of Trajan Reproduced on the "Anaglypha Trajani".' *Mem. Am. Ac. Rome* XXI (1953), 127.
HANSLIK, R. 'Der Prozess des Varenus Rufus.' *Wiener Studien* L (1932), 194.
—— 'Plinius der Jüngere. Bericht über das Schrifttum der Jahre 1933–1942.' *Bursians Jahresberichte* CCLXXXII (1943), 38.
HARDY, E. G. 'Tacitus as a Military Historian in the "Histories".' *Journ. Phil.* XXXI (1910), 123.
HARRER, G. A. 'Tacitus and Tiberius.' *AJP* XLI (1920), 57.
HARTE, R. H. 'The Praetorship of the Younger Pliny.' *JRS* XXV (1935), 51.
HATT, J. J. 'L'Incendie d'Argentorate en 96–97 ap. J.-C.' *CRAI* 1949, 132.
—— 'Le Passé romain de Strasbourg.' *Gallia* VII (1949), 161.
—— 'Les Résultats historiques des fouilles de Strasbourg.' *Historia* II (1953), 234.
HAVERFIELD, F. 'Four notes on Tacitus.' *JRS* II (1912), 195.
—— 'Tacitus during the later Roman Empire and the Middle Ages.' *Ib.* VI (1916), 196.
HEINZE, R. 'Urgentibus imperii fatis.' *Vom Geist des Römertums* (1938), 255.
HELM, R. 'Zwei Probleme des Taciteischen Dialogus.' *Neue Jahrbücher* XXI (1908), 474.
HENDERSON, M. I. Review of F. A. Lepper, *Trajan's Parthian War. JRS* XXXIX (1949), 121.
HERAEUS, W. 'Tacitus und Sallust.' *Archiv für lat. Lex.* XIV (1906), 273.
HERRMANN, L. 'Quintilien et le Dialogue des Orateurs.' *Latomus* XIV (1955), 349.
HEURGON, J. 'La Vocation étruscologique de l'empereur Claude.' *CRAI* 1953, 92.
—— 'Tarquitius Priscus et l'organisation du collège des haruspices sous l'empereur Claude.' *Latomus* XII (1953), 402.
HEUSS, A. 'Alexander der grosse und die politische Ideologie des Altertums.' *Antike und Abendland* IV (1954), 65.
HIGHET, G. 'The Life of Juvenal.' *TAPA* LXVIII (1937), 480.
HIRSCHFELD, O. 'Beiträge zur Geschichte der Narbonensischen Provinz.' *Westdeutsche Zeitschr.* VIII (1889), 1 = *Kl. Schr.* (1913), 19.
—— 'Das Neujahr des tribunizischen Kaiserjahres.' *Wiener Studien* III (1881), 97 = *Kl. Schr.* (1913), 438.
—— 'Zur annalistischen Anlage des Taciteischen Geschichtswerkes.' *Hermes* XXV (1890), 363 = *Kl. Schr.* (1913), 855.
HIRST, G. M. 'Note on the Date of Livy's Birth and on the Termination of his History.' *Collected Classical Papers* (1938), 12.
HOHL, E. 'Vopiscus und die Biographie des Kaisers Tacitus.' *Klio* XI (1911), 177; 284.
—— 'Tacitus und der jüngere Plinius.' *Rh. Mus.* LXVIII (1913), 461.
—— 'Über den Ursprung der Historia Augusta.' *Hermes* LV (1920), 296.
—— 'Wann hat Tiberius das Prinzipat übernommen?' *Ib.* LXVIII (1933), 106.
—— 'Primum facinus novi principatus.' *Ib.* LXX (1935), 350.
—— 'Zu den Testamenten des Augustus.' *Klio* XXX (1937), 323.
—— 'Der Prätorianeraufstand unter Otho.' *Ib.* XXXII (1939), 307.

INSTINSKY, H. U. 'Consensus universorum.' *Hermes* LXXV (1940), 265.
—— 'Kaiser und Ewigkeit.' *Ib.* LXXVII (1942), 313.
—— 'Salus generis humani.' *Hamburger Beiträge zur Numismatik* I (1947), 5.

JAX, K. 'In componendis synonymis quae ratio adhibita sit in Taciti *Germania* et *Agricola*.' *Studi in Onore di U. E. Paoli* (1956), 423.

JONES, A. H. M. 'The *Imperium* of Augustus.' *JRS* XLI (1951), 112.
—— 'The Elections under Augustus.' Ib. XLV (1955), 9.

KAPPELMACHER, A. 'Zur Abfassungszeit von Tacitus' *Dialogus de oratoribus.*' *Wiener Studien* L (1932), 121.
KEYSSNER, K. 'Betrachtungen zum Dialogus als Kunstwerk und Bekenntnis.' *Würzburger Studien* IX (1936), 94.
KLAFFENBACH, G. 'Die Ausgrabungen in Klaros.' *Das Altertum* I (1955), 214.
KLINGNER, F. 'Über die Einleitung der Historien Sallusts.' *Hermes* LXIII (1928), 165.
—— 'Tacitus.' *Die Antike* VIII (1932), 151 = *Römische Geisteswelt* (1943), 310.
—— 'Die Geschichte Kaiser Othos bei Tacitus.' *Sächsische S-B, phil.-hist. Kl.* XCII (1940), Heft 1.
—— 'Tacitus über Augustus und Tiberius.' *Bayerische S-B, phil.-hist. Kl.* 1953, Heft 7.
—— 'Beobachtungen über Sprache und Stil des Tacitus am Anfang des 13. Annalenbuches.' *Hermes* LXXXIII (1955), 187.
KNOCHE, U. 'Der römische Ruhmesgedanke.' *Philologus* LXXXIX (1934), 102.
—— 'Magnitudo Animi.' Ib. Supp. XXVII (1935), Heft 3.
KOESTERMANN, E. 'Der taciteische Dialogus und Ciceros Schrift De re publica.' *Hermes* LXV (1930), 396.
—— 'Statio Principis.' *Philologus* LXXXVII (1932), 358; 430.
—— Review of N. Eriksson, *Studien zu den Annalen des Tacitus. Gnomon* XI (1935), 319.
—— 'Tacitus. Bericht über das Schrifttum der Jahre 1931–38.' *Bursians Jahresberichte* CCLXXXII (1943), 78.
—— 'Der pannonisch-dalmatinische Krieg 6–9 n. Chr.' *Hermes* LXXXI (1953), 345.
—— 'Die Majestätsprozesse unter Tiberius.' *Historia* IV (1955), 72.
—— 'Der Sturz Sejans.' *Hermes* LXXXIII (1955), 350.
—— 'Das Charakterbild Galbas bei Tacitus.' *Navicula Chiloniensis*. Festschrift F. Jacoby (1956), 191.
—— 'Der Rückblick Tacitus Hist. I 4–11.' *Historia* V (1956), 213.
KORNEMANN, E. 'Die historische Schriftstellerei des C. Asinius Pollio.' *Jahrbücher für cl. Phil.*, Supp.-Band XXII (1896), 557.
—— 'Die unmittelbare Vorlage von Appians Emphylia.' *Klio* XVII (1921), 33.
—— 'Hadrian und der Donauraum.' *Gestalten und Reiche* (1943), 304.
—— 'Der Prinzipat des Tiberius und der "Genius Senatus".' *Bayerische S-B, phil.-hist. Kl.* 1947, Heft 1.
KRAAY, C. M. 'The Coinage of Vindex and Galba, A.D. 68, and the Continuity of the Augustan Principate.' *Num. Chron.*[6] IX (1949), 129.
KROLL, W. 'Die Sprache des Sallust.' *Glotta* XV (1927), 280.
—— 'Die Entwicklung der lateinischen Schriftsprache.' *Glotta* XXII (1934), 1.
KROYMANN, J. '*Fatum, fors, fortuna* und Verwandtes im Geschichtsdenken des Tacitus.' *Satura* (Festschrift O. Weinreich, 1952), 71.
KRUUSE, J. 'L'Originalité artistique de Martial.' *Classica et Medievalia* IV (1941), 248.
KÜBLER, B. Review of R. S. Rogers, *Criminal Trials and Criminal Legislation under Tiberius. Phil. Woch.* 1937, 380.
KURFESS, A. 'Phoenix quintus? (Or. Sib. viii, 139 f.).' *Würzburger Jahrbücher* III (1948), 194.

LAMBRECHTS, P. 'Trajan et le recrutement du sénat.' *L'Antiquité classique* V (1936), 105.

LÄMMLI, F. 'Sallusts Stellung zu Cato, Caesar, Cicero.' *Museum Helveticum* III (1946), 94.

LANDI, C. 'L'Autore del Dialogus de oratoribus.' *Athenaeum* XVII (1929), 489.

LAST, H. M. 'Sallust and Caesar in the "Bellum Catilinae".' *Mélanges de philologie, de littérature et d'histoire anciennes offerts à J. Marouzeau* (1948), 355.

—— 'Rome and the Druids: A Note.' *JRS* XXXIX (1949), 1.

—— Review of A. Magdelain, *Auctoritas Principis*. Ib. XL (1950), 119.

—— Review of G. Tibiletti, *Principe e magistrati repubblicani*. Ib. XLIV (1954), 119.

LECOCQ, R. 'Quelle date assigner à la première catastrophe de Campanie, 62 ou 63 p. C.?' *L'Antiquité classique* XVIII (1949), 85.

LEEMAN, A. D. 'Sallusts Prologe und seine Auffassung von der Historiographie.' *Mnemosyne*,⁴ VII (1954), 323; VIII (1955), 38.

LEO, F. 'Die staatsrechtlichen Excurse in Tacitus' Annalen.' *Göttingsche gelehrte Nachrichten* 1896, 191.

—— Review of A. Gudeman's edition of the *Dialogus*. *Göttingsche gelehrte Anzeigen* 1898, 169.

LEPORE, E. 'Un sintomo di coscienza occidentale all' apogeo dell' impero.' *Rivista storica italiana* LX (1948), 193.

LESCHI, L. 'Inscriptions latines de Lambèse et de Zana.' *Libyca* I (1953), 189.

LÖFSTEDT, E. 'Zum Stil des Tacitus.' *ΔΡΑΓΜΑ M. P. Nilsson . . . dedicatum* (Lund, 1939), 297.

—— 'On the Style of Tacitus.' *JRS* XXXVIII (1948), 1.

LONGDEN, R. P. 'Notes on the Parthian Campaigns of Trajan.' Ib. XXI (1931), 1.

LUNDSTRÖM, V. 'Nya Enniusfragment.' *Eranos* XV (1915), 1 ff.

—— 'Det första kapitlet i Tacitus' Germania.' Ib. XXV (1927), 249.

—— 'Kring Livius' liv och verk I.' Ib. XXVII (1929), 1.

LUTZ, C. E. 'Musonius Rufus, the Roman Socrates.' *Yale Classical Studies* X (1947), 3.

MACDONALD, G. 'Verbum non amplius addam.' *JRS* XXIX (1939), 5.

MANSEL, A. MÜFID. 'Fouilles de Sidé et de Pergé.' *Anadolu* II (1955), 58.

MAREC, E., and PFLAUM, H. G. 'Nouvelle inscription sur la carrière de Suétone, l'historien.' *CRAI* 1952, 76.

MARSH, F. B. 'Tacitus and Aristocratic Tradition.' *Class. Phil.* XXI (1926), 291.

MARTIN, J. 'Zur Quellenfrage in den Annalen und Historien.' *Würzburger Studien zur Altertumswissenschaft* IX (1936), 21.

MARTIN, R. H. '-ere and -erunt in Tacitus.' *CR* LX (1946), 17.

—— 'Variatio and the Development of Tacitus' Style.' *Eranos* LI (1953), 89.

—— 'Tacitus and the Death of Augustus.' *CQ* XLVIII (1955), 123.

MARX, F. A. 'Untersuchungen zur Komposition und zu den Quellen von Tacitus' Annalen.' *Hermes* LX (1925), 74.

—— 'Aufidius Bassus.' *Klio* XXIX (1936), 94.

—— 'Die Überlieferung der Germanenkriege besonders der augusteichen Zeit.' Ib. XXIX (1936), 202.

—— 'Tacitus und die Literatur der exitus illustrium virorum.' *Philologus* XCII (1937), 83.

MATTINGLY, H. 'The Restored Coins of Trajan.' *Num. Chron.*⁵ VI (1926), 232.

—— 'The Imperial *Vota*.' *Proc. Brit. Ac.* XXXVI (1950), 155.

MEISTER, K. 'Zur Datierung der Annalen des Tacitus und zur Geschichte der Provinz Ägypten.' *Eranos* XLVI (1948), 94.
—— 'Der Bericht des Tacitus über die Landung des Germanicus in der Emsmündung.' *Hermes* LXXXIII (1955), 92.
MEISTER, R. 'Die Tacitusinschrift von Mylasa.' *Jahreshefte* XXVII (1932), Beiblatt 233.
MENDELL, C. W. 'Literary Reminiscences in the Agricola.' *TAPA* LII (1921), 53.
—— 'Dramatic Construction in Tacitus' Annals.' *Yale Classical Studies* V (1935), 7.
MEREDITH, D. 'Inscriptions from the Berenice Road.' *Chronique d'Égypte* XXIX (1954), 281.
MERRILL, E. T. 'On the Date of Pliny's Prefecture of the Treasury of Saturn.' *AJP* XXIII (1902), 400.
MESK, J. 'Die Überbearbeitung des plinianischen Panegyricus auf Traian.' *Wiener Studien* XXXII (1910), 239.
—— 'Zur Quellenanalyse des plinianischen Panegyricus.' Ib. XXXIII (1911), 71.
MEYER, E. 'Apollonios von Tyana und philostratos.' *Hermes* LII (1917), 371 = *Kl. Schr.* II (1924), 133.
MILTNER, F. 'Der Tacitusbericht über Idistaviso.' *Rh. Mus.* XCV (1952), 343.
MOGENET, J. 'La Conjuration de Clemens.' *L'Antiquité classique* XXIII (1954), 321.
MOMIGLIANO, A. 'Corbulone e la politica romana verso i Parti.' *Atti del II Congresso Nazionale di Studi Romani* I (1931), 368.
—— 'Vitellio.' *Stud. it. fil. cl.*, N.S. IX (1931/2), 117.
—— 'Osservazioni sulle fonti per la storia di Caligola, Claudio, Nerone.' *Rendiconti della R. Accademia dei Lincei*[6] VIII (1932), 293.
—— 'La Personalità di Caligola.' *Annali della R. Scuola normale superiore di Pisa* II ser., I (1932), 205.
MOMMSEN, TH. 'Die Chronik des Cassiodorus Senator vom J. 519 n. Chr. II. Die Auszüge aus Aufidius Bassus.' *Abh. der sächsischen Gesellschaft der Wissenschaften* VIII (1861) 558 = *Ges. Schr.* VII (1909), 677.
—— 'Die patricischen Claudier.' *Römische Forschungen* I² (1864), 285.
—— 'Zur Lebensgeschichte des jüngeren Plinius.' *Hermes* III (1869), 31 = *Ges. Schr.* IV (1906), 366.
—— 'Edict des Kaisers Claudius über das römische Bürgerrecht der Anauner vom J. 46 n. Chr.' *Hermes* IV (1870), 99 = *Ges. Schr.* IV (1906), 290.
—— 'Cornelius Tacitus und Cluvius Rufus.' *Hermes* IV (1870), 295 = *Ges. Schr.* VII (1909), 224.
—— 'Die zwei Schlachten von Betriacum im Jahre 69 n. Chr.' *Hermes* V (1871), 161 = *Ges. Schr.* IV (1906), 354.
—— 'Der letzte Kampf der römischen Republik.' *Hermes* XIII (1878), 90 = *Ges. Schr.* IV (1906), 333.
—— 'Das Verhältniss des Tacitus zu den Acten des Senats.' *Ges. Schr.* VII (1909), 253.
MOORE, F. G. 'Annalistic Method as Related to the Book Divisions in Tacitus.' *TAPA* LIV (1923), 5.
MORRIS, J. 'The Consulate of the Elder Trajan.' *JRS* XLIII (1953), 79.
MOTTA, L. 'La tradizione sulla rivolta ebraica al tempo di Traiano.' *Aegyptus* XXXII (1952), 474.
MOTZO, B. R. 'I commentari di Agrippina madre di Nerone.' *Studi Cagliaritani* I (1927), 19.
—— 'Libri della guerra di Germania di Aufidio Basso.' Ib. 58.

MÜNZER, F. 'Die Quelle des Tacitus für die Germanenkriege.' *Bonner Jahrbücher* CIV (1899), 67.
—— 'Eine "echt taciteische" Wendung.' *Hermes* XXXIV (1899), 641.
—— 'Die Entstehung der Historien des Tacitus.' *Klio* I (1901), 300.
—— 'Aufidius und Plinius.' *Rh. Mus.* LXII (1907), 161.
—— 'Zu dem Nachruf des Tacitus auf Arminius.' *Hermes* XLVIII (1913), 617.

NESSELHAUF, H. 'Tacitus und Domitian.' *Hermes* LXXX (1952), 122.
—— Review of A. Degrassi, *I fasti consolari dell' Impero Romano*. *Gnomon* XXVI (1954), 265.
—— 'Die Adoption des römischen Kaisers.' *Hermes* LXXXIII (1955), 477.
NICCOLINI, G. 'La prima battaglia di Bedriaco e la foce dell' Adda.' *Rend. Acc. Lincei* XV (1906), 278 ff.
NIPPERDEY, K. 'Von der antiken Historiographie überhaupt und der römischen insbesondere.' *Opuscula* (1877), 411.
—— 'Variarum Observationum Antiquitatis Romanae, Caput I.' Ib. (1877), 511.
NISSEN, H. 'Die Historien des Plinius.' *Rh. Mus.* XXVI (1871), 497.
NORDEN, E. 'Josephus und Tacitus über Jesus Christus und eine messianische Prophetie.' *Neue Jahrbücher* XXXI (1913), 637.
—— 'Dreieck.' Ib. N.F. I (1925), 35.
NUTTING, H. C. 'The Use of *forem* in Tacitus.' *Univ. of Cal. Pub. in Class. Phil.* VII (1923), 209.

OERTEL, F. 'Zur politischen Haltung des jüngeren Plinius.' *Rh. Mus.* LXXXVIII (1939), 179.
OLIVER, J. H. 'The Augustan Pomerium.' *Memoirs of the American Academy in Rome* X (1932), 145.
—— 'The Descendants of Asinius Pollio.' *AJP* LXVIII (1947), 147.
—— 'The Divi of the Hadrianic Period.' *Harvard Theological Review* XLII (1949), 35.
—— 'The Ruling Power. A Study of the Roman Empire in the Second Century after Christ through the Roman Oration of Aelius Aristides.' *Transactions of the American Philosophical Society*, N.S. XLIII, 4 (1953), 871.
—— and PALMER, R. E. 'Text of the Tabula Hebana.' *AJP* LXXV (1954), 225.
OLIVER, R. P. 'The First Medicean MS. of Tacitus and the Titulature of Ancient Books.' *TAPA* LXXXII (1951), 232.
OPPERMANN, H. 'Q. Ennius und die Entwicklung des römischen Epos.' *Gymnasium* LXI (1954), 531.
OTTO, W. 'Die Nobilität der Kaiserzeit.' *Hermes* LI (1916), 73.
—— 'Zur Lebensgeschichte des jüngeren Plinius.' *Bayerische S-B, phil.-hist. Kl.* 1919, Abh. 10.
—— 'Zur Prätur des jüngeren Plinius.' Ib. 1923, Abh. 4.
—— 'Zur Praetur des jüngeren Plinius.' *Phil. Woch.* XLVI (1926), 732.
—— 'Schlusswort.' Ib. XLVII (1927), 511.
—— 'Zur Lebenszeit des P. Pomponius Secundus.' *Philologus* XC (1935), 483.

PAPPANO, A. E. 'Agrippa Postumus.' *Class. Phil.* XXXVI (1941), 30.
PARATORE, E. 'Tacito.' *Maia* II (1949), 93.
—— 'La figura di Agrippina minore in Tacito.' Ib. V (1952), 32.
PARETI, L. 'Per la storia degli Etruschi.' *Stud. Etruschi* V (1931), 147.

PASSERINI, A. 'Le due battaglie presso Betriacum.' *Studi di antichità classica offerti
. . . a Emanuele Ciaceri* (1940), 178.
—— 'Per la storia dell' imperatore Tiberio.' *Studi giuridici in memoria di P. Ciapes-
soni* (Pavia, 1947), 195.
PELHAM, H. F. 'Two Notes on the Reign of Claudius. (1) Claudius and the Chiefs
of the Aedui.' *CR* IX (1895), 441 = *Essays on Roman History* (1911), 152.
PELKA, W. 'Zu Aufidius Bassus.' *Rh. Mus.* LXI (1906), 620.
PERRET, J. 'La Formation du style de Tacite.' *Rev. ét. anc.* LVI (1954), 90.
PETER, H. 'Der Brief in der römischen Literatur.' *Sächsische S-B, phil.-hist. Kl.*
1901, Abh. 3.
PFLAUM, H. G. Review of A. Stein, *Die Präfekten von Ägypten in römischer Zeit.*
Latomus X (1951), 471.
PICARD, G.-CH. 'Un homme de confiance d'Hadrien: Le Consulaire Bruttius
Praesens.' *Revue africaine* XCIV (1950), 25.
—— and PFLAUM, H. G. 'Notes d'épigraphie latine. I. Les Vicissitudes de Bruttius
Praesens.' *Karthago* II (1951), 91.
PICHON, R. 'Les *Histoires* de Tacite.' *Journal des Savants* 1919, 183.
PIGANIOL, A. 'Le Codicille impérial du papyrus de Berlin 8334.' *CRAI* 1947, 376.
PIPPIDI, D. M. 'Tacite et Tibère.' *Ephemeris Dacoromana* VIII (1938), 233 = *Autour
de Tibère* (Bucureşti, 1944), 11.
—— 'L'Avènement officiel de Tibère en Égypte.' *Rev. hist. du Sud-Est européen*
XVIII (1941), 87 = *Autour de Tibère* (1944), 125.
PÖHLMANN, R. v. 'Die Weltanschauung des Tacitus.' *Bayerische S-B, phil.-hist. Kl.*
1910, Abh. 1.
PÖSCHL, V. 'Tacitus und der Untergang des römischen Reiches.' *Wiener Studien*
LXIX (1956), 310.
PRÉAUX, C. 'Une source nouvelle sur l'annexion de l'Arabie par Trajan: les papyrus
de Michigan 465 et 466.' *Phoibos* V (1950/1), 123.
PREMERSTEIN, A. v. 'Vom Werden und Wesen des Prinzipats.' *Bayerische Abh.,
phil.-hist. Kl.* 1937, Heft 15.
—— 'C. Iulius Quadratus Bassus Klient des jüngeren Plinius und General Trajans.'
Bayerische S-B, phil.-hist. Abt. 1934, Heft 3.
—— 'Das Attentat der Konsulare auf Hadrian im Jahre 118 n. Chr.' *Klio*, Beiheft
VIII (1908).
PRINGSHEIM, F. 'The Legal Policy and Reforms of Hadrian.' *JRS* XXIV (1934), 141.
PRINZ, O. 'Inclutus.' *Glotta* XXIX (1942), 138.
PRYCE, T. D., and BIRLEY, E. 'The Fate of Agricola's Northern Conquests.' *JRS*
XXVIII (1938), 141.

RAMBAUD, M. 'Les Prologues de Salluste et la démonstration morale dans son
œuvre.' *Rev. ét. lat.* XXIV (1946), 115.
—— 'L'Apologie de Pompée par Lucain au livre VII de la Pharsale.' *Rev. ét. lat.*
XXXIII (1955), 258.
REID, J. S. 'Tacitus as a Historian.' *JRS* XI (1921), 191.
REITZENSTEIN, R. 'Bemerkungen zu den kleinen Schriften des Tacitus I, II.'
Göttingsche gelehrte Nachrichten 1914, 173.
—— 'Tacitus und sein Werk.' *Neue Wege zur Antike* IV (1926), 3.
RICHMOND, I. A. 'Trajan's Army on Trajan's Column.' *Papers of the British School
at Rome* XIII (1935), 1.
—— 'Gnaeus Julius Agricola.' *JRS* XXXIV (1944), 34.
—— 'Hadrian's Wall, 1939–49.' *Ib.* XL (1950), 43.

RICHMOND, I. A. 'Queen Cartimandua.' *JRS* XLIV (1954), 43.
—— 'Roman Britain and Roman Military Antiquities.' *Proc. Brit. Ac.* XLI (1955), 297.
RITTER, F. 'Bemerkungen zu Tacitus.' *Rh. Mus.* XVII (1862), 99.
ROBATHAN, D. M. 'Domitian's "Midas-touch".' *TAPA* LXXIII (1942), 130.
ROBERT, L. 'Le Culte de Caligula à Milet et la province d'Asie.' *Hellenica* VII (1949), 206.
ROGERS, R. S. 'Lucius Arruntius.' *Class. Phil.* XXVI (1931), 31.
—— 'The Conspiracy of Agrippina.' *TAPA* LXII (1931), 141.
—— 'Ignorance of the Law in Tacitus and Dio.' Ib. LXIV (1933), 18.
—— 'A Tacitean Pattern in Narrating Treason-Trials.' Ib. LXXXIII (1952), 279.
—— 'Heirs and Rivals to Nero.' Ib. LXXXVI (1955), 190.
ROLLAND, H. 'Deux nouvelles inscriptions celtiques.' *CRAI* 1955, 91.
ROLOFF, K. H. 'Caerimonia.' *Glotta* XXXII (1952), 101.
ROSTOVTZEFF, M. 'Kaiser Traian und Dura.' *Klio* XXXI (1938), 285.
RYBERG, I. S. 'Tacitus' Art of Innuendo.' *TAPA* LXXIII (1942), 383.

SADÉE, E. 'Die Örtlichkeit der Schlacht bei Trier im Bataverkriege 70 n. Chr.' *Bonner Jahrbücher* CXXXII (1927), 165.
SANDERS, H. A. 'Suetonius in the Civil Service under Hadrian.' *AJP* LXV (1944), 113.
SCHLICHER, J. J. 'The Historical Infinitive II. Its Literary Elaboration.' *Class. Phil.* IX (1914), 374.
SCHMID, W. 'The Christian re-interpretation of the rescript of Hadrian.' *Maia* VII (1955), 7.
SCHULTEN, A. 'Martials spanische Gedichte.' *Neue Jahrbücher* XXXI (1913), 462.
SCHUMACHER, K. 'Beiträge zur Topographie und Geschichte der Rheinlande II.' *Mainzer Zeitschr.* VI (1911), 8.
SCHUR, W. 'Die Orientpolitik des Kaisers Nero.' *Klio*, Beiheft XV (1923).
—— 'Untersuchungen zur Geschichte der Kriege Corbulos.' Ib. XIX (1925), 75.
SCHUSTER, M. 'Tacitus und der jüngere Plinius.' *Wiener Studien* XLVI (1928), 234.
SCHWARTZ, E. 'Die Berichte über die catilinarische Verschwörung.' *Hermes* XXXII (1897), 554 = *Ges. Schr.* II (1956), 275.
SCHWARTZ, J. 'Pompeius Macer et la jeunesse d'Ovide.' *Rev. phil.* LXXVII (1951), 182.
SCOTT, K. 'The *Diritas* of Tiberius.' *AJP* LIII (1932), 139.
SEECK, O. 'Der Anfang von Tacitus Historien.' *Rh. Mus.* LVI (1901), 227.
—— 'Zur Quellenbenutzung des Tacitus.' *Festschrift für Otto Hirschfeld* (1903), 45 ff.
SESTON, W. 'Le *Clipeus virtutis* d'Arles.' *CRAI* 1954, 286.
SHERWIN-WHITE, A. N. 'Procurator Augusti.' *Papers of the British School at Rome* XV (1939), 11.
—— 'The Early Persecutions and Roman Law Again.' *Journal of Theological Studies*, N.S. III (1952), 199.
SKARD, E. 'Sallust als Politiker.' *Symbolae Osloenses* IX (1930), 69.
—— 'Sallust und seine Vorgänger.' Ib. Supp. XV (1956).
SKUTSCH, O. 'The Fall of the Capitol.' *JRS* XLIII (1953), 77.
SMALLWOOD, E. M. 'Domitian's Attitude toward Jews and Judaism.' *Class. Phil.* LI (1956), 1.
SOLTAU, W. 'Einige nachträgliche Einschaltungen bei Livius.' *Hermes* XXIX (1894), 611.
—— 'Der geschichtliche Wert der Reden bei den alten Historikern.' *Neue Jahrbücher* V (1902), 20.

STACEY, S. G. 'Die Entwicklung des livianischen Stiles.' *Archiv für lat. Lex.* X (1898), 17.

STECH, B. 'Senatores Romani qui fuerint inde a Vespasiano usque ad Traiani exitum.' *Klio*, Beiheft X (1912).

STEIN, A. 'Die Protokolle des römischen Senates und ihre Bedeutung als Geschichtsquelle für Tacitus.' *Jahresberichte der I. deutschen Staats-Realschule in Prag* XLIII (1904), 5.

—— 'Tacitus als Geschichtsquelle.' *Neue Jahrbücher* XXXV (1915), 361.

—— 'Zu dem kaiserlichen Ernennungsschreiben in P. Berol. 8334.' *Aegyptus* XX (1940), 51.

STEIN, E. 'Kleine Beiträge zur römischen Geschichte II. Zur Kontroverse über die römische Nobilität der Kaiserzeit.' *Hermes* LII (1917), 564.

STEVENS, C. E. 'The Will of Q. Veranius.' *CR* LXV (1951), 4.

STEVENSON, G. H. 'Ancient Historians and their Sources.' *Journ. Phil.* XXXV (1920), 204.

STEWART, Z. 'Sejanus, Gaetulicus and Seneca.' *AJP* LXXIV (1953), 70.

STOUT, S. E. 'The Coalescence of the Two Plinies.' *TAPA* LXXXVI (1955), 250.

STROUX, J. 'Eine Gerichtsreform des Kaisers Claudius (BGU 611).' *Bayerische S-B, phil.-hist. Kl.* 1929, Heft 8.

—— 'Vier Zeugnisse zur römischen Literaturgeschichte der Kaiserzeit.' *Philologus* LXXXVI (1931), 338.

SUTHERLAND, C. H. V. 'The State of the Imperial Treasury at the Death of Domitian.' *JRS* XXV (1935), 150.

—— 'Two "Virtues" of Tiberius: a Numismatic Contribution to the History of his Reign.' Ib. XXVIII (1938), 129.

SYME, R. 'Rhine and Danube Legions under Domitian.' *JRS* XVIII (1928), 41.

—— 'The Imperial Finances under Domitian, Nerva and Trajan.' Ib. XX (1930), 55.

—— 'M. Vinicius (*cos.* 19 B.C.).' *CQ* XXVII (1933), 142.

—— 'A Governor of Syria under Nerva.' *Philologus* XCI (1936), 238.

—— 'Notes sur la légion IIIᵉ Augusta.' *Rev. ét. anc.* XXXVIII (1936), 182.

—— 'The Colony of Cornelius Fuscus: An Episode in the *Bellum Neronis*.' *AJP* LVIII (1937), 7.

—— 'Who was Decidius Saxa?' *JRS* XXVII (1937), 127.

—— 'Caesar, the Senate and Italy.' *Papers of the British School at Rome* XIV (1938), 1.

—— 'The Origin of Cornelius Gallus.' *CQ* XXXII (1938), 39.

—— 'The First Garrison of Trajan's Dacia.' *Laureae Aquincenses* I (1938), 267.

—— Review of M. Durry, *Pline le Jeune: Panégyrique de Trajan. JRS* XXVIII (1938), 217.

—— 'Roman Senators from Dalmatia.' *Serta Hoffilleriana* (Zagreb, 1940), 225.

—— Review of A. Stein, *Die Reichsbeamten von Dazien. JRS* XXXVI (1946), 159.

—— 'Personal Names in *Annals* I–VI.' *JRS* XXXIX (1949), 6.

—— 'Tacfarinas, the Musulamii and Thubursicu.' *Studies in Roman Economic and Social History in Honour of Allan Chester Johnson* (1951), 113.

—— 'Tacitus on Gaul.' *Latomus* XII (1953), 25.

—— Review of A. Degrassi, *I Fasti Consolari dell' Impero Romano dal 30 avanti Christo al 613 dopo Christo. JRS* XLIII (1953), 148.

—— 'The Consuls of A.D. 97: Addendum.' Ib. XLIV (1954), 81.

—— Review of A. Stein, *Die Präfekten von Ägypten in römischer Zeit.* Ib. 116.

—— 'Marcus Lepidus, *capax imperii*.' Ib. XLV (1955), 22.

—— 'Seianus on the Aventine.' *Hermes* LXXXIV (1956), 527.

SYME, R. 'Some Pisones in Tacitus.' *JRS* XLVI (1956), 17.
—— 'Deux proconsulats d'Afrique.' *Rev. ét. anc.* LVIII (1956), 236.
—— 'C. Vibius Maximus, Prefect of Egypt.' *Historia* VI (1957), 480.
—— 'The Friend of Tacitus.' *JRS* XLVII (1957), 131.

TAYLOR, M. V. 'Roman Britain in 1954.' Ib. XLV (1955), 120.
TERZAGHI, N. 'Tre fonti secondarie del Panegirico di Plinio.' *Maia* II (1949), 121.
THEILER, W. 'Tacitus und die antike Schicksalslehre.' *Phyllobolia für Peter von der Mühll zum 60. Geburtstag* (1945), 35.
THIEL, J. H. 'Kaiser Tiberius. Ein Beitrag zum Verständnis seiner Persönlichkeit.' *Mnemosyne*³ II (1935), 245; III (1935/6), 177; IV (1936/7), 7.
TOD, M. N. 'The *Corrector* Maximus.' *Anatolian Studies Presented to William Hepburn Buckler* (1939), 333.
TOYNBEE, J. M. C. 'Some "Programme" Coin-Types of Antoninus Pius.' *CR* XXXIX (1925), 170.
—— 'Ruler-Apotheosis in Ancient Rome.' *Num. Chron.*⁶ VII (1947), 126.
TRAUB, H. W. 'Tacitus' use of *Ferocia*.' *TAPA* LXXXIV (1953), 250.
—— 'Agricola's Refusal of a Governorship (Tac. *Agr.* 42. 3).' *Class. Phil.* XLIX (1954), 255.
—— 'Pliny's Treatment of History in Epistolary Form.' *TAPA* LXXXVI (1955), 213.
TREU, M. 'Tacitus und der Anfang der Historien.' *Atti Acc. Peloritana, Classe di Lettere* XLVII (1947–50), 1.
—— 'M. Antonius Primus in der taciteischen Darstellung.' *Würzburger Jahrbücher* III (1948), 241.
—— 'Zur clementia Caesars.' *Museum Helveticum* V (1948), 197.
TURNER, E. G. 'Tiberius Julius Alexander.' *JRS* XLIV (1954), 54.

ULLMAN, B. L. 'History and Tragedy.' *TAPA* LXXIII (1942), 25.

VALMAGGI, L. 'L'imprecisione stilistica in Tacito.' *Riv. di fil.* XXXVI (1908), 372.
—— 'Sulla campagna flavio-vitelliana del 69.' *Klio* IX (1909), 252.
VITTINGHOFF, F. 'Zur Rede des Kaisers Claudius über die Aufnahme von "Galliern" in den römischen Senat.' *Hermes* LXXXII (1954), 348.
—— 'Römische Kolonisation und Bürgerrechtspolitik unter Caesar und Augustus.' *Ak. der Wiss. u. der Lit.*, Abh. 14 (Mainz, 1951).
VOGT, J. 'Tacitus und die Unparteilichkeit des Historikers.' *Würzburger Studien zur Altertumswissenschaft* IX (1936), 1.
VOLKMANN, H. 'Zur Datierung der Annalen des Tacitus.' *Gymnasium* LX (1953), 236.

WAGENVOORT, H. 'Obiter tacta.' I. *Mnemosyne* XLVII (1919), 359.
—— 'De Reguli in Taciti Dialogo Partibus.' Ib. LIV (1926), 416.
WALSH, P. G. 'Livy's Preface and the Distortion of History.' *AJP* LXXVI (1955), 369.
WALTON, C. S. 'Oriental Senators in the Service of Rome.' *JRS* XIX (1929), 38.
WALTZ, R. 'A propos d'Afranius Burrus.' *Rev. phil.* XXXIV (1910), 244.
—— 'Le "Rôle" de Secundus dans le *Dialogue des Orateurs*.' *Rev. phil.* LXI (1935), 296.
WEBER, W. '. . . nec nostri saeculi est.' *Festgabe für K. Müller* (Tübingen, 1922), 24.
WELLESLEY, K. 'Can you trust Tacitus?' *Greece and Rome*² I (1954), 13.
—— 'The date of composition of Tacitus, *annals* II.' *Rh. Mus.* XCVIII (1955), 135.

WELLESLEY, K. 'Three historical Puzzles in *Histories* 3.' *CQ* XLIX (1956), 207.

WENDLAND, P. 'Das Gewand der Eitelkeit.' *Hermes* LI (1916), 481.

WIJKSTRÖM, B. 'Clarorum virorum facta moresque.' *Apophoreta Gotoburgensia Vilelmo Lundström Oblata* (1936), 158.

WILCKEN, U. 'Plinius Reisen in Bithynien und Pontus.' *Hermes* XLIX (1914), 120.

WILLRICH, H. 'Augustus bei Tacitus.' Ib. LXII (1927), 54.

WINDIRCH, H. 'Die Orakel des Hystaspes.' *Verhandelingen der koninklijke Akademie van Wetenschappen, Afdeeling Letterkunde*, N.R. XXVIII, 3 (1929).

WISSOWA, G. 'Die germanische Urgeschichte in Tacitus' Germania.' *Neue Jahrbücher* XLVII (1921), 14.

WÖLFFLIN, E. 'Jahresberichte. Tacitus.' *Philologus* XXV (1867), 92; XXVI (1867), 92; XXVII (1868), 113 = *Ausgewählte Schriften* (1933), 22.

—— 'Die hexadische Composition des Tacitus.' *Hermes* XXI (1886), 157.

—— 'Die Nachahmung in der lateinischen Prosa.' *Archiv für lat. Lex.* XII (1900), 114.

—— 'Plinius und Cluvius Rufus.' Ib. 345.

—— 'Zur Komposition der Historien des Tacitus.' *Bayerische S-B, phil.-hist. Kl.* 1901, 3.

WOLFF, E. 'Das geschichtliche Verstehen in Tacitus' Germania.' *Hermes* LXIX (1934), 121.

WOODHEAD, A. G. 'Tacitus and Agricola.' *The Phoenix* II (1948), 45.

ZECHNER, I. 'Hat Tacitus seine politische Überzeugung geändert?' *Wiener Studien* LIV (1936), 100.

INDEX

Emperors and members of dynasties are registered by their conventional English names. Likewise classical authors. Senators have their rank appended, also *praenomen*. They are entered by *gentilicia*, but four exceptions have to be admitted (viz. Barea Soranus, Cornutus Tertullus, Piso Liciniaus, Thrasea Paetus), and several *polyonymi* are abbreviated. The bare entry of a city name generally means that the place is notable as the *origo* of a person or family.

The Index covers names in the footnotes as well as in the text. It has not, however, been practicable to draw up an inventory of the dense material in the ninety-five appendixes. Readers who wish to consult them will be guided by the list (p. 625 f.) and by the footnote references.

We are pleased to announce the
#1 HEALTH AND NUTRITION Company in
the entire world is expanding again! We specialize in
helping people LOOK BETTER & FEEL BETTER &
LIVE BETTER. We are committed to improving health
and preventing disease through the use of exclusive,
patented, and life-changing products. Currently seeking
help to expand into Taiwan, Korea, Japan, Israel,
Hong Kong, Mexico, South Africa and Venezuela.
Experience in languages, customs, or regions a
plus! Call for interview.

901-452-2158

Haterius Antoninus, Q. (*cos.* 53), 324.
Haterius Nepos, T., Prefect of Egypt, 246 n.
Hatra, Trajan at, 240, 495.
Heliopolis, oracle at, 470.
Helvetii, in Caesar's *BG*, 455; in 69, 170, 171.
Helvia, aunt of Seneca, 126 n., 536.
Helvia Procula, wife of Dillius Vocula, 175 n.
Helvidius Priscus (*suff. ann. inc.*), his consulate, 83; prosecuted and executed, 25, 76; avenged, 77, 120; his wife, 561 n.; daughter, 82 n.; friends and partisans, 92, 120.
Helvidius Priscus, C. (*pr.* 70), his youthful pursuits, 63 n.; under Nero, 544; in 69 and 70, 101, 187–8, 209; his feud with Eprius, 101, 109, 111, 187, 212; his fate, 212; partisans and relatives, 25, 76, 212 n., 559–61, 596–7; origin, 559;
his love of fame, 99 n., 554; as depicted by T., 189, 554.
Hercules, Trajan compared with, 57–58; of Gades, 58, 470–1.
Herennius Senecio, victim of Domitian, 25, 76, 82 n., 83, 177 n., 190 n., 298 n.
Hermunduri, 127 n.
Herod, king of Judaea, 507.
Hispania Citerior, *see* Tarraconensis.
Hispulla, wife of Corellius Rufus, 86 n., 326 n.
Historia Augusta, 59, 503.
HISTORIAE, first hint of, 98, 117; date of composition, 118–19; completion, 120; total of boks, 211, 362 n.; structure, 118, 213–14; missing books, 211–16; fragments, 215 n., 489; followed by Dio, 215 n.;
prologue, 145–6; point of departure, 145; Book I, 150–6; Book II, 156–67; Book V, 211; sources, 171–90; style, 197, 340–1, 350–2; narrative power, 193–4; imitation of Sallust, 196–9; of Livy, 200–1; parallels to *Panegyricus*, 207 n.; corrected in *Ann.*, 290; bias, 204–11;
contemporary relevance, 120, 129–31, 150, 156, 206–9, 229; reception at Rome, 201–2, 229.
Historians, Roman, 125, 130–1, 132–50, 178–81, 196–204, 222–7, 287–94, 312, 337–8, 358–9, 420–1, 433, 443–5, 474–5, 503, 520–2, 526–9, 540, 545–6, 566–9, 570–1.

History, beginnings at Rome, 132–3, 566; and poetry, 110, 142, 356–8, 362–3; different from oratory, 117, 202, 344; Cicero's views, 132–3; Pliny's, 117; Fronto's, 502–3; imperial, its character, 125, 145, 364–8, 398, 420, 435, 443–5, 499, 570–1; its end, 503.
HORACE, echoed by T., 357; on birth and rank, 570.
Hordeonius Flaccus (*suff. ann. inc.*), 172.
Horoscopes, 524–5, 561.
Hortensius Hortalus, M., grandson of the orator, his petition and oration, 325, 426, 572.
Hortensius Hortalus, Q. (*cos.* 69 B.C.), his ostentation, 102, 109 n.; his oration in 55 B.C., 324.
Human sacrifices, in Gaul, 457; at Rome, 458 n.
Humour, in T., 206, 349–50, 472, 476, 539.
Hypocrisy, official, 410, 411, 423, 427.

Icelus, freedman of Galba, 150.
Iceni, 394.
Idealization, of the Republic, 27, 571; of Marius, 40; Pompeius, 433–4; Cato, 557; Augustus, 373, 431; of rusticity, 39, 446; of Roman imperialism, 528–9; of natives, 126, 174, 530–1.
Idistaviso, battle at, 393.
Ignotus, historian of 69, 180–90, 199.
Ignotus, consular from Nemausus, 53 n., 604 n.
Ilium, Nero's oration on, 515.
Illyricum, insurrection of, 275, 369.
Imitation, literary, 198; of Cato, 121 n., 351, 356; of Sallust, 196–200, 353–6, 545; Livy, 200–1, 357; Virgil, 194 n., 357–8.
Imperialism, Roman, 496–7, 506, 527–31.
Imperium consulare, 409, 411 n.
Imperium proconsulare, 409, 410; granted to Germanicus, 411; to Seianus, 405; to Nero, 409 n.
Impietas, 415.
Incest, 301, 315, 543; alleged against Agrippina, 290, 376–7.
Inconcinnity, 135, 347.
Insubres, 86, 624.
Irony, in T., 206, 320, 349, 472, 494, 497, 515, 524, 539, 542, 623–4.
Isis, cult of, 65, 468.

INDEX OF PASSAGES IN TACITUS